"Traveling abroad is a progressive exercise in the discovery of our own ignorance."

- William Blake

HOW NOT TO TRAVEL

"Where are you going next? I won't go there!"

*The Peripatetic Professors' 44 Years' Sojourn:
Middle East and North Africa before the Arab–American Wars,
America, Europe, China, Macau*

Norman L. Lofland
*Ph.D. in Drama, Carnegie Mellon University
M.A. in Drama, University of Southern California
B.A. Double Major in Speech and Drama and in English
Literature, Wichita State University*

and

Betty J. Lofland
*M.A. in History, University of Bridgeport
B.A. in English, McPherson College*

GoToPublish LLC
1-888-337-1724
www.gotopublish.com
info@gotopublish.com

Contents

Finnegans Wake In Amsterdam
Invitation To Tehran, Taliesin West
Travel To Iran, Tunisia
Libya, Tripoli, And Leptus Magna
Egypt, Cairo, And Upper Egypt
Back To Cairo And Hotels
The Bazaar And Balloon Theatre
A Job Offer, Beirut
Arrival In Tehran, Meningitis (Again)
Persian Food, Tehran Transport
Rumbles of Revolution

Damavand Theatre,
Damavand Theatre: A Revised Plan
Damavand Theatre: Years Of Progress
Move To New Campus, Shah's Divans
Revolution, Caspian Sea, Gonbad-E-Kavus
Village Hospitality, Crowded Train
Crowded Taxi, Princess Ashraf's Palace
Travel To Turkey, Tabriz To Erzurum
Erzurum To Trabzon, Trabzon
Black Sea Cruise, Istanbul
On To The U.S., Kansas
A Changed Ranch, Return To Tehran
Isfahan, Persepolis, And Shiraz
Life In Tehran, Natasha's Baptism
Restaurants And A Fire

Shahreza Apartment, Shah House
The Texan, Dodge City Interlude
Darband, Tehran, Apartment No. 1
Darband, Tehran, Apartment No. 2
Campus Dramas, Iran-America Society
Damavand's Curriculum
Rudaki Hall, Culture And The Revolution

Colonel Muamar Khaddafi
Leaving Beirut, Bj's Journal
Miscellaneous Notes, Bj's Journal

Macau, Digression, Interjection, Tunisia

How Not to Travel

Who doesn't love a great adventure story?

A story of romance and danger, challenge and chance ... spur-of-the-moment decisions leading to a lifetime of engagement with the world, the exploring of strange and sometimes dangerous lands, exotic food and terrible food ... cold homes, cold water, and crummy beds; illness and hardship ... fascinating people, amazing friends, the world around the corner ... churches and preachers, choirs and concerts ... the promise of pay delayed by months ... books and baggage left hurriedly behind as the gunfire erupted; buying new sheets on most every continent ... and then, the students ... some who didn't want to learn, and those who did ... tragedy, hardship, and loss; moments of great delight, a chance to share some of humanity's greatest truths with hungry hearts and eager minds ... art, theater, architecture, books and libraries... to create and challenge, to restore and make new ... to live life to the fullest, and sometimes on the run ... as life unfolds for all of us, and especially those who choose the road less traveled, or, in this case, How Not to Travel, which is, in fact, the way to travel, not for all, but for some upon whom the hand of God takes a firm and dramatic hold.

As Norm writes: "In the spring of 1963, when my wife Betty Jean (BJ) and I accepted an offer to teach at Beirut College for Women in Lebanon, we had no idea where these two years would lead."

Which is to say, here's a first-rate adventure - two bright and engaging people who took a chance and lived a life beyond the boundaries. Forty-four years of overseas teaching and travel - the Middle East and North Africa, America, Europe, China, and Macau.

Here's a roadmap for any of us who would rather know how not to travel rather than to travel all the usual, well-worn paths of convention, comfort, and consistency. Here's a book for folks who would like to take some chances when those kinds of opportunities come our way. They never announce themselves beforehand; they arrive suddenly, and wait but a few moments for us to decide, and then they're gone; we're with them on the road, or on the curb waving goodbye.

Norman L. Lofland and Betty J. Lofland, what we might call ordinary people from ordinary origins ... they met and fell in love, and here's their love story ... loving one another, dearly, deeply, and loving the world that God gave to them, giving back to life everything they could, even as life gave to them an abundance of intellect, spirit, and faith.

Ordinary people who choose the unordinary road, though, at the time, who would have known?

Neither they nor anyone else could see the road ahead. But it took them to the far corners of the earth, to be with people of charm and craziness, to sample life in its fullest, to see the world, to know its promise, and its dangers, to visit markets and shops full of life's curios, and to navigate a thousand difficult moments.

This is a book to savor ... to read at leisure ... with a cup of coffee in hand, or a martini extra-dry. You will marvel at their experiences, and the skill with which they relate their journeys, their hopes and dreams, and their fears and frustrations, too, in letters to family and friends.

The Loflands have given many a gift to the world - their passion and compassion, their love of teaching, their respect for the student, even when such made it clear they weren't interested in learning, but only in getting a diploma.

Art, theater, music, literature, faith, and their beloved Karmann Ghias, of which they owned four, are the bulwarks of their journey.

If looking for a book of adventure, a book of wisdom and wonder, common sense and humor, delightfully presented in hundreds of letters and postcards, with a fine catalogue of snapshots taken along the way, and thoughtful commentary added after the fact, this book gets my highest recommendation.

One never knows what pathways will appear until one begins to take the one nearest at hand ...

- Rev. Dr. Tom Eggebeen
Lecturer, Writer, Pastor,
Interim Pastor Westminster Presbyterian Church
and other churches.
Reviewer of books for GOOD READS

One never knows what pathways will appear until one begins to take the one nearest at hand…

PREFACE

In the end it seems we two college professors have followed in the tracks (not precisely, nor knowingly) of walking (not literally, perhaps wandering, sometimes in the Middle East driving in our Karmann Ghia) the earth; it is somehow reminiscent of Aristotle's lecturing. We, with other professors, taught the ideas of classical as well as modern literature (including Aristotelian elements of drama), history, and ideas as incorporated in the curriculum of a baker's dozen universities for Norm, and another baker's dozen schools and universities for BJ, even though it wasn't very empirically practical and often downright dangerous: avoiding kidnapping or being shot. Certainly while exposing students to the practical designing and handling of theatre scenery, lighting, speech, public speaking and English grammar, composition, essay writing, typing (before computers), European and World History made up for the "pie in the sky" (to quote our adversaries), Aesthetics (such as Classic Greek plays, Shakespeare, Yeats, Joyce, and modern playwrights), we taught around much of the world. An international peripatetic experience, indeed.

In the spring of 1963, when my wife Betty Jean (BJ) and I accepted an offer to teach at Beirut College for Women in Lebanon, we had no idea where these two years would lead. Our experiences in Lebanon gave us a determination to return to overseas teaching. This desire took us (after finishing my Ph.D. and BJ's MA) to Iran, Beirut a second time, Tunisia, China, North Cyprus, and finally to Macau, China. This adds up to nearly four decades' teaching abroad, plus ten years' teaching in the U.S. These years have been rewarding, and we're satisfied that God led us to make the right choices. In the end, for seventeen years we continued to spend approximately six months of the year as volunteers with Macau's Anglican Choi Koh Schools, Dr. Michael Poon, principal, followed by Dr. Eric Chan, principal.

Left with wonderful — and sometimes not-so-wonderful — memories of those years' adventures, we have attempted to record some of the events. This account is mainly for family — especially for granddaughters Portia and Nina and their progeny; perhaps it will help them better understand who their grandparents were, and their mommy.

These memoirs have been written over a rather long (nineteen years) period of time, on several different computers, with various complications. The letters which have been added were not available until the manuscript was nearly complete. I have complained that BJ's editing — in her attempt at clarity — has in some places diminished my style. Since I at first used as a working title "How Not to Travel," I appreciate the influence of my wife Betty Jean, whom I call BJ. It was a brilliant way to travel much of the world.

Thank you, L.L. Alexandria, our teaching colleague, for typing and organizing the first draft from my casual dictating into a Walkman nineteen years ago in Macau, China [1999]. Little did we know that it would take so long for us to finish the "remembrances." Proust's approach is not ours; he also took a long time. Though this remembrance seems to jump around a bit, it does not become an attempt at transcending reality; the reality we experienced was enough of a TRIP!

These memoirs are dedicated to the memory of our dear friend and world traveler, Elma Esau, whose remarkable life helped initiate our travels, and who rode with us in our Karmann Ghia to Jerusalem and Palmyra, Syria.

I wish also to mention here two remarkable educators whose lives were dedicated to women's education in the Middle East: Dr. Frances Mecca Gray, president of Beirut College for Women, Beirut, Lebanon, and later of Damavand College, Tehran, Iran, and Dr. Mary Thompson, academic dean, Damavand College. Their wisdom and compassionate understanding of humanity were a source of inspiration and deeply influenced our lives and the lives of so many students and teachers in the Middle East, as well as the ex- pat teachers who learned to love and appreciate that world. How sad that world is gone.

Above all, our thanks to a loving and merciful Providence, who has watched over us throughout these years. Without this eternal presence, some of our adventures would have ended quite differently. We were fortunate and are grateful!

Norman L. Lofland and Betty Jean (BJ)
Macau, China, and Pasadena, California, 2017

First Thoughts after First Writing

Dear Helena Portia Ariane and Nina Francesca Allegra, our grandchildren, Grandmere and I thought you would like to know of a few interesting experiences your mother, Natasha, had as a child and young lady growing up all around the world. No, this is not really about Natasha, but is the story of her parents, your Grandmere and Grandpere, and about a whole lot of other people who knew your mommy when she was — like you — a charming, sensitive, bright, and wonderful child, who grew up and became the caring, loving mommy you know, who, along with your daddy, is also raising you around the world.

Enjoy the story of Mama Natasha's childhood. It is presented to you, Helena (whom I always want to call Ninotchka, as a twin name to Natasha) Portia Ariane and Nina Francesca Allegra, with the tenderest love from your Grandpere Norman and — maybe, if she puts her name on this substandard writing — your Grandmere BJ.

Grandpere Norman
Macau S.A.R., China
July 2000

FOREWORD

Our former teaching colleague and editor of our original book kindly cut 200 pages of our book to make it less expensive. She did a tremendous job, but I felt sad to lose all those letters from so many people who had contributed thoughts and comments, and were included in the first edition. So, after consulting with several persons who have read the book, we decided to keep the contents of the original book. Dear reader, feel free to read the parts you wish. As BJ often says, "Just hop around in the book; something will interest you." The letters often support a trip somewhere or comment on happenings, perhaps philosophizing. Skip them if you wish to get on with the happenings of BJ and myself.

Norm
Norman L. Lofland, Ph.D.
Carnegie Mellon University
Pasadena, 2022

CHAPTER 1

KANSAS to LEBANON (1960 – 1965)

Bethel College, Summer in Europe, The Birth of Natasha,
Beirut College for Women,
Summer in London, A Bad Experience,
Baghdad, Into Iran, Tehran, Esfahan, Shiraz,
Baghdad via Kassaroon, A Narrow Escape,
Baghdad YMCA, Back to Beirut

BETHEL COLLEGE

After finishing my M.A. coursework and thesis on James Joyce's dramatized *Finnegans Wake* in the graduate school at the University of Southern California, my wife BJ and I drove (in our first Karmann Ghia, a beautiful ivory 1956 VW sports car) from Los Angeles to Kansas to start teaching. Through the influence of Walter Jost, one of my fellow Ph.D. [Music] students at USC, I'd been offered a teaching job by Dr. Winfield Fretz, president of Bethel College, a small Mennonite liberal arts college in Newton, Kansas, just north of Wichita. I had sworn that I didn't want to go back to Kansas, where I had grown up ["How ya' gonna keep 'em down on the farm after they've seen LA?"], but I nevertheless accepted the job. BJ had taught at Newton High School prior to our marriage and subsequent sojourn at USC, and she liked the place. After two years in the U.S. Army, I had graduated from the University of Wichita, so I also knew the place. Before arriving on campus I was skeptical and discouraged, but it rapidly turned into a brilliant teaching experience with outstanding theatre productions of six productions a year from Classics to Moderns, and I loved teaching Public Speaking and Theatre Courses, and the students excelled. Indeed for forty years we have frequently compared Bethel with the rest of the world, and Bethel always won!

Bethel College had no theatre department at that time. We used the gymnasium as a theatre, which had an enormous stage with a 50-foot proscenium opening. During my three years at Bethel College, we did everything in terms of converting that gymnasium into a theatre, leading finally to a new theatre. It was a very exciting venture because we built from scratch everything for the theatre — even a cyclorama (huge sheets of fabric extending around the entire backstage) using the technique taught to me by film and stage designer John Blankenchip at USC. Our students sewed together one-hundred-foot-long strips of cotton fabric, and dyed the "cyc" on the winter grass with pails of blue, purple, and soft green dyes, working the cyc while wet, gradually unrolling the fabric, dying it from top to bottom. It was thirty feet tall. We also made scrims; one was bought from a New York theatre service company, and we made the other scrims from fabric bought at J.C. Penney's. During those three years, I designed sets galore, all beautifully lighted with the techniques learned from Bill White, lighting director at USC. We even had to build a lighting board and install about sixty spotlights on the front pipe-batten to cover that large stage, which were added to the four huge two-thousand-watt ellipsoidal spotlights attached to the gym ceiling. It was thrilling to discover twenty rheostat dimmers in a storage cabinet attached to the stage right wall. We attached them to an old library table, ran lines to a patchboard, which had electrical cables to a great number of Fresnels and ellipsoidal spotlights newly hung on a batten downstage and out in the house. I had learned from USC's lighting director, for that's how the university had lighted its huge, older Bovard Auditorium. Student technical director Ron Hatchet was the clever lighting engineer who put together the ideas I came up with; he was a great contributor to the Bethel Theatre. All this came about after we got permission to spend what we made from the shows we presented. First we spent $60.00, which was the year's budget, on the cyc. Then we bought spotlights from the income from Shaw's *Pygmalion*.

As I mentioned earlier, Bethel had no theatre department, and I was the sole person in charge of the productions in addition to teaching a full load, consisting of several theatre classes, public speaking, and debate. I designed and directed six shows a year including a yearly opera (cooperating with the excellent music department under the direction of Professors Dr. Walter Jost and Dr. Rupert Hohmann), a musical one year, and a Shakespeare play every year. I was constantly involved in productions and rehearsals. This was difficult because we had to squeeze it all in between course exams and mid- terms on the quarter system. The quarter system lasts a shorter period than the semester system; therefore, theatre productions had to be done very, very quickly. It was then that I became well entrenched in a three-week rehearsal period for each production. Three weeks for rehearsal and the same three weeks for building the sets, getting them lighted and on stage for opening night in a theatre that seated 3,000 people because it was a gymnasium. Never did we have 3,000 people ... yes, we did! For the annual Mennonite Folk Festival I would do a production dealing with Mennonite history (in addition to those already mentioned), and the house was packed for those events. The operas attracted anywhere from 500 to a thousand people. No wonder I never saw television, I was too busy — all over the world; that's why I watch *Gunsmoke* and *Bonanza* and *I Love Lucy* these days, forty to fifty years later. We were always too busy.

One day as I walked through the campus, I noticed a black limousine parked in front of one of the faculty apartments — formerly an army barrack. I later learned that the limousine had brought Pearl Buck to the campus to check on two Chinese orphans who, sponsored by Pearl Buck's agency, had been adopted by Professor Spaulding's family. This may have been a foreshadowing of our work in China thirty years later. Dr. Spaulding played Hamlet's father's ghost two years later on the outdoor steps of the castle-like Administration Building during the summer theatre workshop.

SUMMER IN EUROPE

It was during that period at Bethel that we met Elma Esau, a marvelous, interesting lady who has become a dear friend. Elma at that time ran the Menno Travel Service in Newton, one of an international network of travel offices. She had a wealth of travel experience, having worked with Mennonite relief and refugee services during and following World War II. She was on convoys delivering war relief supplies during the war; several ships went down under submarine attacks. "Every morning we would wake up, go out on deck, and count the ships to see how many were sunk in the night by German U-Boats," Elma confided to us. Recently, at age eighty, she translated from German, and privately published, letters written by her relatives of more than 100 years ago — written before, during, and after their emigration from Russia to the U.S. This sizeable volume makes a significant contribution to U.S. and Mennonite history.

Elma set up our first trip abroad; my first trip to Europe and BJ's second, since she had gone in 1955 with a Mennonite student travel/work group, scraping bricks in bombed Germany to rebuild a school after traveling Europe. This was 1961, and we had saved half of our income that year (BJ had again taught at her former Newton High School job), and we planned to spend the entire summer in Europe. We had a glorious time, sailing from New York on the Greek ship, *Queen Frederica*. But first, our short stay in New York was exciting. My brother Jim, who was living there at the time, took us to dinner at the Pierre Hotel, at which he had a penthouse apartment for a time. We had made arrangements to see another friend, Bob Balay, who was working in New York and years later was a librarian at Yale. When we drove up to the Lions at the New York Public Library in Jim's driver-rented limousine (another element of a short lived time of Jim's money, soon to be a lost adventurous scandal), Bob said, "I'm not getting into that thing!" But he did and off we went to pick up another friend from USC days, Jack Francis Brown, and the limousine dropped us off to see *Camelot* on Broadway with Richard Burton and Julie Andrews. Being the adventurous theatre buff, I left *Camelot* and went to see the last act of Ionesco's *Rhinoceros* at a theatre nearby. I was bored with the Middle Ages musical, anyway.

The next day we walked up the gangplank onto the *Queen Fred* to embark on what might have been its last trip to Europe, or maybe we thought it should be the last trip when five people died on the crossing: three old persons returning to Greece to retire, a middle aged man with a heart attack, and a child who hit his head on the swimming pool. "Never mind," said a shipmate, "on the last crossing seven died."

"Older travelers?" Since we were on a very low budget trip [we were proving to friends that one could do, as Frommer said, Europe on five dollars a day], we were in the lowest level of the ship, across from an old couple who never left their cabin, and I thought they might not make it to Athens. We had booked to Piraeus, Greece, but after five days crossing, when we arrived at Gibraltar, we asked the purser if we could get off. "Why?" he asked. "Do you not like the food?"

"No, no, the food is great fun — Greek meals daily; we want to start our trip in Spain and work towards Greece instead of the other way; another five days sailing the Mediterranean is sort of a waste of our time." He agreed, but we had to agree to no refund; that was okay. A Greek shipmate, who was bringing the refrigerator we saw strapped to the deck stairs to her family in Greece, told us she would have gotten a refund. I'm certain SHE would have! After cruising to Tangier, Morocco, and flying back to Gibraltar in a Piper Cub plane, we started using our Eurail Pass in Algeciras, Spain, which then let us go by first class train all over Europe, except Great Britain. We were joined on our train by a young man running away from his university (and his father after he crashed his dad's Daimler auto days before), coming to Spain to learn Spanish while living with a Spanish family. "Spanish is the coming language, isn't it?"

"Well, depending on where you are, perhaps ..."

Over the next ninety days we visited the whole of the Continent, arriving in Greece, seeing one of my professors from USC, John Blankenchip, at the Athens Festival. Riding up the length of Italy, visiting Roma, Vicenza, and Firenze, Venice, Italy; we decided that in later years we would do Ravenna; we did — marvelous mosaics!

A Bethel colleague had asked us to pick up a Volkswagen for him in Switzerland and put some miles on it so it could enter the U.S. at that time tax-free. After visiting Copenhagen (Tivoli is a gas!), we drove to Upper Jutland, Denmark, to see the father and sister of a dear friend, Borge Williamson, who told me he was in love with BJ before we were married; he was very annoyed when we married. Bob Bayley was also. Borge's father had visited us in Los Angeles and when he saw a huge sign mounted above the freeway which said "Slow Down and Live" he turned to me as I was driving our Karmann Ghia speedily in the fast lane and shouted, "Slow down and live!" and gestured to all the mad drivers on the freeway! That was 1960; he would be shocked to see the traffic mess in 2017. We had a wonderful dinner in Borge's father's house of Danish meatballs prepared by Borge's sister, made with ice water stirred in the chopped steak before cooking, and cream, added to the drippings from the frying-in-butter of the meatballs and brought "to just before the boil," served with boiled potatoes; the meal was invigorating!

We drove the car back to France doing the wonders of Paris and, saving the Loire Valley Chateaux for a later trip when we again had a car, crossed over to Dover, England. "Stay on the left; it's dangerous on the right," said the bobby as we left the port at night. En route to London we stopped at Canterbury Cathedral, after sleeping in our car because it felt dangerous driving at night on the left, and being welcomed as Swiss travelers (since we had Swiss plates on our VW Beatle/Bug) to come into a local British house for a wash-up! In London at the American embassy we were joined by long- time friend, Jack Brown. After doing London and lots of theatres, we drove through the Lake District, past Macbeth's Hermitage Castle, continuing to Scotland and the Edinburgh Festival. In Edinburgh we found rooms in the home of Mr. and Mrs. Hunter; hotels were overcrowded because of the festival. Mrs. Hunter, a pleasant, talkative woman, served us breakfast in her cozy parlor, and asked us to please have baths only every other night. I'm afraid, being the then-naïve Americans we were, we cheated and showered! One morning we were surprised to see Mr. Hunter knitting a sweater, which looked much like a Norwegian ski sweater. He said the pattern was actually Scottish, and he said that many Scottish men knit. He told the story of how a Spanish ship was wrecked off the Scottish coast, where the crew was forced to spend the winter. To pass the time, the sailors learned from the locals to knit sweaters. BJ says the Hunters left a stronger impression on her than the festival! But we did see several outstanding festival productions including John Osborne's *Luther*. [I would never have believed that seven years later I would be directing a production in the Edinburgh Festival Fringe.] The Scottish Tattoo at Edinburgh Castle was also memorable. We arrived back in Kansas with some money left over, which proved that you could, as Frommer said, "Do Europe on $5 a Day" in the early 1960s. Following Frommer's advice to stay in hotels that the local travelers used, for example, all through Germany we would stop at small Gasthov hotels located above little taverns. I would ask, "Haben zie ein zimmer mit heisen wasser?" If they shook their head or said "nein," I would pantomime holding a bucket of water and add, "In a bucket?" They would respond "yah, yah," and laugh, and welcome us to their frugal but comfy hotel.

THE BIRTH OF NATASHA

Before our summer in Europe, BJ had resigned from her teaching job at Newton High School to work as resident director of Haury Hall, the girls' dormitory, and assistant to the Dean of Women, who turned out to be a real pain. But with this job came an apartment in the girls' dorm, which was a real blessing when baby Natasha arrived in November. She was born at Newton's Bethel Deaconess Hospital right when I was in the middle of rehearsals for *The Marriage of Figaro*. Music director of this opera, Walter and Mary Ann Jost's son Scott, was delivered in the same week of the production. Between rehearsals and classes, my trips to the hospital were limited. In those days new mothers were kept for five days. The hospital did allow fathers in the delivery room, which was a rather unusual practice at the time. So I, in a small way, shared this life-altering experience. BJ's office was just across the hall from the apartment, so she could easily look after Natasha while on the job. One big advantage to this dorm job was the availability of babysitters. The thing BJ hated most was chasing the boys out of the public areas at closing time, so I often took over that duty, sometimes with surprises, usually involving my theatre guys or the football team, including chasing them out after a panty raid. I learned later that I had missed a guy hiding under a bed; the rest escaped out the fire exit. They were laughing the next day at rehearsal, but no one bragged about it. Oh, the theatre guys kept up with the fads! Perhaps because they were often the football team as well as the theatre participants. I used to say that the athletic coaches and I had the same challenge: to please the audiences, to help establish the image of the college. All over the world we compared the present university with Bethel — except for Beirut and Damavand College, Tehran, most of the universities were not up to Bethel standards.

During our third year at Bethel, Elma was transferred to the Beirut, Lebanon, Menno Travel Office. We were leaving Bethel because I had been a replacement for someone who was doing his Ph.D. and he was coming back. Elma wrote and said, "You've been wanting to teach abroad. Why don't you try the universities here?" So we did.

BEIRUT COLLEGE FOR WOMEN

We wrote to the American University of Beirut and Beirut College for Women. Both university-level schools had been started by the Presbyterian Church in the late 1800s, and both of them were/are excellent schools. The men's university grew larger than the women's college, which is understandable in the Middle East. Beirut College for Women was a very special place because it was one of the few women-only university-level schools in the Middle East, where conservative families were willing to send their daughters.

I received contract offers from the American University (AUB) to teach English, and from Beirut College for Women (BCW) to teach in my field: theatre and speech. Needless to say, I grabbed the theatre and speech job, BJ taught freshman and sophomore English and literature at BCW, and we moved to Beirut. We cruised to Europe on the Holland America Line's *Rotterdam*, drove our one-year-old Karmann Ghia convertible to Venice, where we boarded a ship to Alexandria, Egypt. Lack of funds prevented our taking the overland tour to Cairo.

We arrived in Beirut with insufficient money to cover import duties for our baggage and car. Fortunately, the college's business manager, who met our ship, came to our rescue. Our financial shortfall was due to the fact that our travel agent [not Elma Esau] tried to save money, but didn't. Instead of sending our shipment directly to Beirut, he had arranged for it to be transported to Europe on our ship, then overland to Venice, where we had to pay extra charges for a customs official to accompany the shipment between countries before it would be loaded on the Mediterranean ship we took to Beirut. This was 1963, way before the European Union's borderless customs.

We had a marvelous two years' experience, although I must admit that after the first year I went to see the president, Dr. Frances Gray, who has since then always been a close friend of ours. (In her 80s she led tours around Europe to the art museums where the great paintings of the Renaissance are exhibited.) I told Frances I wanted to leave since I didn't like doing only one or two plays a year, because that's all that the girls were allowed to do. (Oh, those theatre people, always wanting to be on stage!) They were busy with their academic affairs, and Frances wasn't about to let anything infringe upon that. I said I wasn't particularly wanting to stay there, and she said, "I'm not going to let you leave. You're going to stay here. I will not let you ruin your career, breaking your contract, simply by deciding that you are unhappy and are leaving." It recently occurred to me that she must have thought I was a spoiled young man. Goodness! How wrong she surely was!

We have always been thankful that we completed that contract. Our two years at BCW strongly influenced the direction of our teaching careers. The school's liberal arts curriculum, founded on Christian values, emphasized the Classics, from the Greeks to Shakespeare to Michelangelo to Sartre, and more. BCW exemplified literature and the arts as a source of truth. A dear friend and former colleague, Lucy Sullivan, once said that BCW, under Dr. Gray's presidency, was undoubtedly the school's Golden Age, although none of us realized it at the time. One usually doesn't. After Frances left BCW it became more and more a business and engineering co-ed university: Beirut University College (BUC), and a few years ago Lebanese

American University (LAU). It developed an outstanding Theatre-Communications Department, which later we shall write about.

Thank heavens Frances insisted we stay at BCW! Frances's source of truth through the Bible, Art, Literature, and the rest of the Humanities, has been our constant guide through nearly forty years of teaching, literally, around the world. Actually, our three years at Bethel College, North Newton, Kansas, was the first place we experienced this Humanities-approach to teaching, and the Beirut universities (both the American University of Beirut — originally for men, later co-ed — and Beirut College for Women) exemplified how this concept can be taught and shared on an international basis. Several years later, when Frances teamed up with Dr. Mary Thompson and Lucy Sullivan in Tehran, Iran, we all continued that crusade of the Humanities. But, that comes later.

SUMMER IN LONDON

Along with the decision to stay for another year, BJ and I decided to spend the summer in Europe, in London. I arranged, through the British Council, to take a course in contemporary British literature, so off we went to the University of London. We drove up from Beirut through Turkey, all the way to London by way of Bulgaria, then-Yugoslavia, and across Europe. We were robbed in Ankara, Turkey. The thieves cut the top of our VW Karmann Ghia convertible that we had brought with us from the U.S. and stole everything that was in the car. We had our year-and-a-half-old baby, Natasha, with us, and had taken her things inside the hotel, but had left the suitcases with our things hidden inside the car. We were so tired of driving, and the trip had only just begun!

This robbery left us in no mood to explore Istanbul, but on our return trip we did take in a number of the sights, especially enjoying the Sultan's Seraglio, where I watched a production of Mozart's opera in that setting, and the huge bazaar. We agreed then that we'd someday return to Istanbul to teach. This wish never materialized, but we have visited this most interesting city several times, certainly later on when we taught in Turkish Cyprus.

I was left with no clothes after this robbery except for the trousers and shirt that I was wearing, and BJ with little more. Later, in Germany, we replaced several items. The new German trousers fit wonderfully — wonderfully snug. Before leaving Germany, the trouser seams had to be repaired because they had broken open; BJ's 80-year-old Tante Elizabeth had her friend, Mrs. Luther, restitch them on her treadle sewing machine; I don't remember if it said Singer. (Mrs. Luther's husband was not only a descendant of Martin Luther, but one of Hitler's S.S. men, who died in prison after the war.) Tante Elizabeth, actually a cousin not an aunt, was a Christian missionary to Germany after World War II, which she found a tremendous challenge since so many Germans were "in denial" of the horrors of the war. We exchanged stories over coffee and kuchen in a charming coffeehouse; my army stories left her laughing and wondering "how the Allies had won the war when they had soldiers like me," and her accounts of Germans practicing spiritualism during that post-war period intrigued us.

Before leaving Beirut, we had contacted the Mennonite Center in London, hoping that they would have space to house us for our two months in London. They didn't, but suggested a family in Wembley Park who were willing to rent us "an apartment," which was part of their house, and which we immediately grabbed. The apartment wasn't quite what we expected, but the Kwan family was delightful — friendly and generous. Our quarters consisted of a bed-sitting room plus an alcove with hot plate for cooking and small table with two chairs. We were invited to put food in the Kwan's refrigerator, and we shared their bathroom. And this arrangement worked out amazingly well! Natasha loved being in the garden, watching the Kwan's three children play. At that time she was in a plaster cast from chest to ankles with a dislocated hip socket, crawling some, but not very mobile. Being in London we could take Natasha to the Royal Orthopedic Hospital where our Beirut specialist, Dr. Boulos, was trained and where they checked her hip and repaired her cast; she wore casts for a year and grew a hip socket, which has held up all her life. Mrs. Kwan, Wally, offered several times to babysit Natasha so we could go out together. I daily hopped the Northern Line on the Underground to attend excellent classes at the University of London with outstanding professors, authors, artists, musicians lecturing on substantive ideas and how they are conceived and developed into the art we could observe and have an empathic response to. A marvelous summer!

Wally was German, the daughter of a Mennonite pastor, and had been a member of Hitler's Youth Corps; she had fascinating experiences to share. She had met her husband, Hoki, a Chinese from Hong Kong, on a ship en route to the U.S. where she spent a year with an American family, in a Mennonite Central Committee-sponsored program for European youth. They later married and lived in England where Hoki worked as an engineer.

BJ learned a lot from Wally, especially about cooking. She learned how to make a number of Chinese dishes, and one of the Kwan's favorite supper dishes: Spam fried with lemon juice and brown sugar! Yummm! We still have this occasionally. Wally introduced it to us as the "American dinner."

During that summer of 1964 in London, we had great exposure to the theatre, because London during the 1960s had, as always, brilliant theatre; but at that time the additional attraction was the fact that it was so cheap. If you really wanted super cheap entertainment, you could sit in the second or third gallery for something like a sixpence. We always had good seats and sometimes caught several shows in one day if tickets were available. However, I often went alone since one or the other of us stayed home with the baby, although Wally did babysit occasionally.

That summer, and many summers thereafter, I kept running into my former USC theatre design professor, John Blankenchip, in one or another of the theatres. He would smile and say, "Hello, Norm." We usually were in the same row. He asked me to direct the Mary Manning dramatization of Joyce's *Finnegans Wake* for the Edinburgh Festival in 1968. Again, in 1969, I directed it for the Holland Festival. Great shows! The two completely differing in style of production. More of that in the Holland Festival section.

A BAD EXPERIENCE

One of the problems during that summer was that one day I became quite ill, and noticed that there was some indication that I might have a parasite. I looked around for a doctor. I didn't go to the doctor who lived next door to our house with his clinic. I had the feeling that I should go someplace a little farther away. I walked a few blocks, went around the corner, and there sitting upon a hill was the home office of a medical doctor. I rang the bell, and a lady answered the door. I came in, and she indicated that I should wait for the doctor.

The doctor came in, and the first thing that he said to me was, "Sprechen sie Deutch?"

The only Deutch I knew was, "Haben sie ein zimmer mit heisen wasser?" It didn't help much. Years later "Sprechen sie Deutch" saved me!

He struggled through with English as I described the symptoms, and showed him my little sample of a symptom. He said, "Ahhh … das ist ein …" He called it something in German, and it turned out to be a parasite which, for lack of a better word, was a long worm. He ran back and checked his book to make sure that he had the right prescription, and he came out and wrote it down on a prescription pad and said, "You must take this. First you take these little tablets, and then, later, you take the second, which will be a liquid."

I thanked him, paid him, and went to the first pharmacy in the area. The guy looked up at me over his half-rimmed glasses and said, "Worms, 'eh?"

"Yeah, do you just have the prescription?"

"No, we don't have that here. We don't use it anymore."

"What do you mean you don't use it anymore? Give me what you use!" "No, you've got to take what the doctor told you to take."

"Well, where can I get it?"

"You might try Marble Arch Pharmacy."

So I hurried to the Bakerloo Line tube station and rode from Wembley to Marble Arch and the pharmacy. I went in and they said, "We haven't had a call for this in years." Then they sent me off to someplace else. I went there, and while I was waiting the pharmacist came out and said, "Sit down." She laughed and said, "George back there is heating it up to get it out of the glass vial. It will be a moment or two."

So I waited, and they came out with a vial about four inches long, half an inch wide, of something which can only be described as looking like axle grease. The woman gave it to me along with a couple of tablets, which were to evacuate the colon, and I said, "Are you sure this will work?"

She said, "It has for years." I rode the underground home, took the tablets, and after progressing along the right procedure, having cleaned out and evacuated the colon, I took the fatal vial of green-looking axle grease. I thought that I was playing Hamlet, or perhaps I was again playing Romeo, and was taking the terrible poison at the end of the play. As I swallowed, I thought, "It does feel like poison going down my throat and into my stomach." I could feel it running through me, and I sort of fainted onto my bed, and woke up hours later with a mad dash to the communal bathroom. Fortunately, our friendly neighbors, with whom we stayed, were not around. After cleaning myself out, I called to BJ and said, "BJ, you've got to come and look at this."

I held up in the air, by way of the stool brush which always comes with European toilets, at least six or eight long tapeworms. I could remember the German doctor saying, "You must get the head or it will come back!" There were six or seven, perhaps eight, heads hanging there, each attached to a seven-foot-long body. I flushed them all away, went back to bed, and tried to forget the whole thing.

I learned at that point that it is not unusual to get tapeworms when living in Lebanon because they sometimes serve raw meat, which is like "steak tar- tar," and the meat is not inspected as thoroughly as in the West. This raw meat dish is called raw kibbe. Cooked, it's a great delicacy. Raw, it's an even greater delicacy, so they say. For me, I hope that I never eat it again.

Perhaps I had contracted the tapeworms when traveling with Yussef, my technical assistant in the theatre, a Lebanese. He enjoyed showing me all of Lebanon, telling me where to go, as I drove our convertible. He took me into the Shouf, a mountainous area, to meet his family, and I spent the night there. They served the delicacy, raw kibbe, which, as an honored guest, I must eat. Coming down the mountain into Beirut I had a mad dash to get home before I exploded!

After we returned to Lebanon from London, I had the same experience the next year again with Yussef. Again I became ill with the same problem. I went to a Lebanese doctor and told him my experience in London the previous year. He said, "Ah, yes …" He had also once taken that medication, "but we no longer use it; now there are special tablets that you take which simply explode the parasites." And that's what he gave me this time.

While we were in Beirut, in between doing theatre productions, teaching full academic loads, and in addition to driving from Beirut to London by way of Turkey and back, we made numerous shorter excursions by car. Frances Gray, the president of Beirut College for Women, said that every time the door was closed for more than three days, the Loflands must be off driving someplace — if not into Syria or Jordan, at least into the mountains of Lebanon or along the beach. In fact, driving along the beach was almost a daily occurrence, for the view of the coast was magnificent. We would stop to eat at some small café on the beach; when feeling we had a little money, we dined at one of the restaurants at the Grotto de Pigeons or another luxury eatery on the Corniche, which curved round the sea, with snow-covered mountains looking down upon us. It was not uncommon to ski during the morning and swim after lunch; we seldom did either, but we loved to absorb the beauty. The mountains held lovely destinations, and we often, on a Saturday, packed a picnic lunch and the many necessities for baby Natasha into the car, lowered the top, and headed into the mountains. The beach was a problem because sand got inside the cast. Yaffa, our excellent Druze helper, loved these excursions, and often rode along.

BAGHDAD

Having spent nearly two years in Lebanon, we were due in the summer to go back to the States where I was to do a doctorate at Carnegie Mellon University — then Carnegie Institute of Technology. BJ and I were determined to see more of the Middle East during our

Easter holiday. Miss Irani, the art teacher, had recently taken a group of our students to Iran and had shown slides of gorgeous Persian architecture. Those slides convinced us that our Easter trip would be to Iran. David, a student from the American University of Beirut, came along to help drive. We went through Syria to Damascus, over to Amman, then picked up the TAP Line, the Trans-Arabian Pipeline, which follows the road across the desert to Baghdad. We sometimes had to find petrol/gasoline in curious places such as in a barrel in a shed in the backyard of some house out in the country somewhere along the road, even off the road. I would have to ask, "Petrol?" and point to the car; "Inshallah, petrol?" Filling stations were rare except in cities.

When you go to Baghdad across the desert (we are all a bit familiar with that from the Gulf Wars), it isn't just sand, especially along the TAP Line. There is a paved road that is full of chuck-holes in the springtime, so our car was constantly hitting chuck-holes, although I was dodging them every time we went across any area where they could be dodged. There is also black volcanic rock all along the road for miles and miles. One wonders how the camels walk over it because it is sharp, flint-like, volcanic rock.

We drove past the various stops that are along the way because once you get into the desert, as in the old caravansary days, there are perhaps only three or four designated places where you can stop. Each of these had a motel, guest houses they called them. They are pretty awful, pretty basic. One of these is at the border between Syria and Iraq.

Coming into Iraq, on that trip in the spring of 1965, I had become quite ill; the first of the illnesses that were to haunt me/us for the next thirty, and more, years. David was driving. David and BJ went into the passport border control with the carnet and with the passports to get them stamped. The carnet is the passport for the automobile, issued by the Royal Auto Club in London. The fight to get across the border is pretty strenuous. It's not like coming from Hong Kong into Macau. It's much more adventurous. You have to slap your passport down, and almost beg them to look at it and stamp it. We didn't realize it then, but somehow the carnet had not been stamped properly.

We drove on into Iraq; our papers, we thought, duly approved. We came into Baghdad and stayed at the Young Men's Christian Association, the YMCA Hostel. It has since been turned into an officers' club for the Iraqi army. Since the recent wars I have no idea if it's still standing. Then it had been the British Officers' Club, turned into the YMCA Hostel.

We drove up, checked in, spent the night, and wandered around Baghdad. We were disappointed to learn that the National Museum was closed for remodeling but were fascinated by the central bazaar. It was there that we first observed carpet merchants turning new carpets into antiques by laying them in the street for the passing vehicles to drive over!

The next day we drove along the Euphrates, then headed up toward what, we thought, was the right direction to the Iran border, only to discover, when arriving in Kirkuk, that we had taken the wrong road. Kirkuk is an oil center. Perhaps it's pumping again, now that the United Nations is allowing them to pump more oil, but in those days Kirkuk was a vast oil center. And it was heavily guarded. As we approached, military troops and police stopped us and asked, "What are you doing here?" We kept saying, "Tehran! Tehran!" They said something that we didn't understand. Our Arabic was no more than how to go forward, left, right, and how to buy things for the kitchen. And we knew no Farsi, the Persian language; that attempt came years later.

We kept going. Finally, someone who spoke English stopped us, in the city of Kirkuk, and said, "Look, the road is closed. You cannot go any farther. You must turn around and go back to Baghdad. When you go back to Baghdad, the road will be blocked with a log across the road, and they will stop you there, and you will have to spend the night outside in the desert, and it would be much better for you to spend the night in my hotel." He smiled his toothy, tea-stained grin.

We were not very comfortable with that idea, and there was still some light in the sky, so we thought, "Why not head on back?" So we turned around and went back, driving on the highway, and, sure enough, eventually there was a log across the road, and the person who stopped us demanded that we get out of the car and that we stay there.

We said, "No, we just want to go to Baghdad." And for some reason they moved the log, and we continued back to Baghdad.

When we arrived in the outskirts of Baghdad, we found a pharmacy. We had learned that pharmacists usually know English. We asked, "Where is the road to Tehran?"

They laughed and said, "You must not go on the road you came. You must go on a different road." So we took the different road, heading this time toward the border of Iran.

As we approached the border it was dark. The border was definitely closed. The little man at the border gate spoke rather good English and said, "You have to come back tomorrow to see the passport person to get permission to go across into Iran." This person would not be there until the morning.

He further said, "Now, never mind, I've made reservations for you in the hotel, which is local and very close. You'll find it." He told us to drive back into the town and to continue until we see a light. The light will be red, and that's the hotel. The red-lighted hotel. "Upstairs is the accommodation, and I have reserved it for you."

We drove back, naïvely accepting that we would get there, be the guests for the evening, and go on tomorrow.

Once there, I stopped the car. The gates were closed. David and BJ opened the huge gates and I drove the car in, locked it, and left it. At the top of the stairs, sitting at a very old telephone switchboard, was an obese pasha, dressed in a very dirty galabia, and he asked, "What do you want, Buster?"

I said, "We have reservations for the three of us for tonight."

He said, "Yes? Well, what do you want? There's the big room that costs you twenty-five cents a bed, or there's the little room, and that will cost you fifty cents a bed."

"How many beds are in the little room?"

"Oh, about four or five, but you can have the whole room for fifty cents each." (Of course the prices were quoted in dinars.)

So we paid the $2.50 and took the whole room. BJ didn't bother to undress, saying the beds must have been slept in by a month of motorcyclists. She simply wrapped a scarf around her head and lay down on top of the soiled sheets. David changed into his pajamas, as I changed into my pajamas, and crawled in for the night, little inhibited by the condition of the bedding. We all had our separate beds, with two left over.

BJ did not sleep a wink. She was not rested the next day, but then no one was. After having gone to the lavatory to wash and do the other necessary things, we agreed that these accommodations were at the lowest end of Middle Eastern fare, which was pretty bad. We got out of that hotel as quickly as we could, and went back to the border.

INTO IRAN

The man had not arrived, but he came shortly, dressed in a black suit, white shirt, and tie, looking very much in control of the whole situation; as though he owned the world, which I guess he did, right there. The little man who had sent us to the hotel the night before was there, looking rather apologetic. The man who was in charge would not even talk to us. We waited and waited and waited. Finally, he looked at our passports, and then looked at the carnet and said, "No. You cannot go. You must go back to Baghdad."

We repeatedly asked, "Why? Why? We are in your country. Why?"

"You do not have the stamp on the carnet." It had been missed when we came across the border into Iraq. He just shouted at us, saying, "No, you must go back to Baghdad."

We kept saying, "No, we are staying here. You call Baghdad! Telephone!"

I stood over the top of him, all six feet four inches of me, and I pointed at the telephone shouting, "Telephone! Telephone! Telephone!" Perhaps I didn't shout. Perhaps it was just a stern kind of demand. He sat there and did nothing. All of a sudden BJ, who had been walking around in her then no- longer-white skirt and dark sweater, whirled around in front of him, slammed her hand down on the desk and said, "Why do you allow tourists into your country if you treat us like this?" Then she started crying. I'd seldom seen BJ cry and was taken by surprise.

The black suited Iraqi gentleman, who was not very gentle, looked at her firmly, looked at us, stood up, and said to David and me, "Come." We went behind a screen. He stamped our passports and shouted, "Go!"

We went out to our car and jumped in, BJ in the back on the jump-seat as usual, David and I in the front, and I drove out. Back there, at that border, at the same time that we were waiting to go across, there was an Iraqi lady, or perhaps Iranian. She was dressed in a black chador. In those days we were not used to them since not everyone wore black chadors. From head to toe she was covered in this black, sheet-like garment similar to the white sheet worn by members of the Ku Klux Klan in the southern part of the United States. While we were standing there saying to this man, "Telephone Baghdad. Let us go," this lady was kneeling, caressing his arm, and saying, "Yallah. Yallah." "Hurry. Let us go." He simply ignored her.

As we were driving across the border into Iran, it looked wonderful. We were so happy because Iran just looked beautiful in those days with a border gate, not like the wretched places we had just seen in Iraq. Here was lovely countryside. We drove across, and they nicely stamped our passport. Just as we were getting back into our car to drive on, along came this same lady, dressed in the black chador, driving a yellow, 1957 Chevrolet. She drove up to the border and made it across, just as we had. She looked so happy, possibly because of BJ's "protest." Hopefully, it got her through as well as us. At least, it's a nice idea.

Natasha was not along on this trip. She was two-and-a-half years old, and was in Beirut with friends. We exchanged babysitting at that time. When our friends went to Egypt, we kept their children. When we went on this maddening trip to Tehran, Natasha was with Kermit and Sharon Yoder, who managed the Beirut Menno Travel Office after Elma Esau was transferred to the Akron, Pennsylvania, headquarters.

We crossed the border and found that Iran looked wonderful after Iraq. It was still desert-like, but there were mountains. We drove through the mountains, heading toward Tehran. There were many sights to see en route, but we didn't stop. We kept going because we knew we had only a short time. We arrived in Tehran, met our friend Aziz, talked with him some, visited the mosques, the bazaars, and did all of the things in Tehran that I'll mention when I tell about living in Tehran years later.

TEHRAN

In Tehran, when our friend Aziz was driving us around with his driver at the wheel, I kept asking him questions which I, in my naïveté at that time, didn't realize were political in nature. Questions about the Shah, about the government, about the economy. After all, Aziz had a Ph.D. in Economics and Public Administration from USC where we lived next door to him, as well as another Ph.D. in Accounting. He was sitting in the front seat with the driver, and BJ and I were in the back. All of a sudden he turned around to me, laughed, and said, "Tell me, Norman, did you come to Iran to see me or to have me put in jail?" Of course, it was because his driver was along, and nobody trusted anybody. Savak, the secret service, was very strong in those days, just as that which replaced Savak is as strong, if not stronger, these days.

ESFAHAN

After visiting numerous tourist sites, never dreaming we'd in the future live there for six years, we left Tehran, driving south to Esfahan. We stayed at a wonderful, old, interesting hotel, right across the street from the great Friday Mosque. We became enchanted with the tile work of the Esfahani mosques, with the architecture, with the beauty of those magnificent religious structures. We are still moved by mosques, interestingly, just as we are moved by magnificently-designed-to-the-glory-of-God churches.

We went to the public field in Esfahan, where earlier leaders, the Shahs, had played polo, a game they had learned from India, or perhaps they taught the Indians. We looked up at the balcony where the Shah used to sit with his court overlooking the playing fields of the polo grounds. Polo was no longer played there, not in the twentieth century.

Around the outer edges of that great open field, surrounded by buildings and mosques, were workshops: coppersmiths, tinsmiths, potters, workers in cloisonné and block print; artisans who made fittings for horses and camels — enchanting Middle Eastern, Persian artifacts. Artifacts appealing especially to western tourists. We have collected our share (perhaps more than our share) of these lovely souvenirs, which were in storage for twenty- eight years. When we got them out of storage, it was like Christmas. Each item evoked memories which would otherwise have been forgotten.

SHIRAZ

From Esfahan we drove on to Shiraz, farther south. En route to Shiraz, I noticed that something seemed rather wrong with the car. That was nothing new to us. The car was only two years old, but on that trip it had deteriorated rapidly. All of a sudden there was a kind of knocking sound in the engine. We managed to arrive in Shiraz and proceeded to look for the house that belonged to a friend of our friend Aziz. He had given us the address. We kept showing it to people. The address was written in Persian, in Farsi. We finally drove up to the house, and someone came to the gate. I showed them the letter from Aziz bidding our hosts, Aziz's friends, to welcome us to their home. The gates opened, and in Farsi they said, "Befar myeed." "You are most welcome to our house."

I drove the car through the gates. The house was lit with soft lights that glittered from the garden. There was a shimmering in the pool. Pillars, perhaps six of them, led up to the second floor with trees everywhere. It all looked as though we had entered the Antebellum South of the United States. It was as though we had somehow moved from Islam to Natchez, Mississippi, on the Mississippi River, for this was a house exactly like the southern plantations, those few that were spared in Sherman's march to the sea at the end of our Civil War. This house in Shiraz, in Persia, reminded me very much of those southern United States homes.

We walked through the pillars, across a huge porch, up to the front door. The door opened. We were invited in. From the moment we walked inside, it no longer seemed like *Gone with the Wind*. It was no longer the enchanting kind of set that could come out of Hollywood. It was very down to earth. The first thing one saw upon entering was a refrigerator at the bottom of the staircase leading to the second floor. Half-way up the grand, high staircase, guarding the landing, stood a large stuffed brown bear, which in earlier days must have been quite menacing, but now tamed by the ravages of time.

We were invited to have tea. We were taken up the stairs, turned to the right, and passing through double doors, entered an enormous room, all silver and white. It was a little bit shabby, but still grand in a sort of run-down way. Bentwood chairs lined the long walls, and the bentwood chairs were painted silver. This was the ballroom. The ballroom that certainly is not being used now, and, undisturbed, was not being used then when we visited in 1965.

We sat in that ballroom with two of our hosts — two ladies — sipping tea, sweet, mint tea, out of small glasses, Persian cups, with little saucers and tiny spoons, and a cube of sugar. You're supposed to put the sugar between your four front teeth, and then suck the tea through the sugar. It's rather thrilling. Unfortunately, it was thrilling for people for too many years, and it decayed their teeth, because you could notice the rotten teeth every so often, and you knew that they had been sucking and sipping tea in the Persian manner.

While we were there in the ballroom, sipping our tea, not through our teeth, BJ asked if they had a bathroom. The ladies laughed and said, "Tomorrow we will take you to the bathroom." BJ then realized that "bathroom" is not the same in Iran as it is in America, because in America the bathroom, of course, is a euphemism for the toilet. BJ said, "No, no. A toilet." They immediately took her to the room which served that function.

Ever since then, unlike myself, BJ has been very uninhibited about asking for the toilet, especially overseas. If you ask for the toilet in America, it may sound crude.

(Recently, in Los Angeles, an East European immigrant desperately asked a check-out person of a large store, "WC?" The clerk said, "What's he want?" "A bathroom or a men's restroom," I said. "Oh …")

The next day, sure enough, the ladies took BJ to a bathroom, to a bath house. She reported that she was given some green powder that was shampoo as well as soap. A massage came with the price of the bath. Traces of the green powder finally disappeared after several more shampoos without the green powder.

David and I took the car to a repairman. As we drove into the garage, the repairman, who obviously knew what he was doing from the very beginning, said, "Cylinders one and three are going out. You have to have a valve job."

We said, "Okay, how much will it cost?"

He quoted the price in dinars, which we calculated as being US$21. We had between us only US$21. We said, "Okay, go ahead and fix it." We then asked, "Where is the American Express?" I had my American Express card with me, and I thought that I could surely get some money with that; cash a check or something. He told us where the travel office was in downtown Shiraz.

We found it, went in, and cashed a check for US$100. Remember, this was 1965 in Persia, and Persia at that point was very inexpensive. Hence, we had US$100 in Persian dinars. The first thing we did, because we already had enough money to pay for the car, was to go to the bazaar in Shiraz. A bazaar anywhere in the Middle East is enchanting. We heard the coppersmiths pounding on the copper, turning it into tables, into jugs, into vases, into pots and pans, into artwork. Smiling children and teenagers hammered away with their lively chisels and their pikey things that they could punch and grind, making great marks and creating intricate designs. Small boys smiled the biggest, grandest smiles, because they were so happy to be seen doing their work that they were so proud of. Oh, so much more fun than being in school! Hammering. Pounding. It sounded like something out of T.S. Eliot with this pounding of musical sounds coming forth. Perhaps more like James Joyce. Or Gertrude Stein. "Still fall the bombs …"

Wandering through the bazaar, we inevitably were attracted to the carpets. We were captivated as the wily merchants unrolled them, flipped them over, and pointed out their beauty and quality. Wherever we went, there always seemed to be somebody who could speak English to us, enough of some kind of English to entice us to buy something. And that's how we spent part of our hundred dollars — to buy a carpet. Not a very big or expensive one. We had only a hundred dollars, and the carpet had to fit into our small car along with us. We bought a Baluchi carpet. I wonder where that carpet is now. Probably lost. We've lost more than one carpet.

The next day we returned to the mechanic. The car was repaired, and we paid the man his US$21 in dinars. He was very happy, and so were we.

BAGHDAD VIA KASSAROON

Our next destination was Kassaroon. We had asked in the American Express office if the road to Kassaroon was okay. That lying man said, "Yes. We send tours there all the time." (I noticed the workers in the office looking at each other …) Kassaroon was marked on the map, and there was a road marked on the map, and there was also a road shown from Kassaroon to Abadan, the oil center in southwestern Persia, so we hurriedly left Shiraz that evening, driving toward Kassaroon. It looked shorter on the map to get back to Iraq and Baghdad; well, it was … !?

We decided to go in the evening, thinking it was advantageous to get farther down the road, and it didn't look very far on the map; and, naïve drivers that we were, we believed that map. As we drove along, we saw tanks moving past us, and some soldiers, and people on foot in the growing darkness. The only lights were our headlights. All of a sudden someone stopped us and said, "They closed this road because the Shah doesn't trust the tribes. The tribes are in revolt and they like to move and cause trouble. That's why the army's out."

We thought, "Well, we've heard that before!"

We had heard it in Kirkuk, Iraq, just a few days before, where the road had been closed and that man had said, "Why don't you go back and stay in my hotel?" So we thought, "Oh, it's probably okay. We'll go ahead." BJ had shifted all of our money into her girdle. Women wore girdles in those days, although she certainly did not need one. We decided later that perhaps the girdle was not the safest place to store money, but at any rate, that's where it was at the moment.

We drove slowly on, and sure enough, before long, across the road was a log, and standing in front of the log, at the end of it, was a soldier, perhaps two soldiers. I said, "Yallah, Kassaroon. Kassaroon. Inshallah." "Let us go to Kassaroon. Hurry. God willing we'll get there."

They looked at us, and then looked at each other. The must have thought, "Who are these stupid, impossible people?" They probably concluded, "Well, they're Americans. It doesn't matter." They laughed, rolled back the log, and we continued to drive. The sun was down; we continued to drive. The road was full of potholes; we continued to drive. The road became muddy; we continued to drive. When it was completely, absolutely dark, so that we couldn't see anything, we continued to drive, barely seeing the road. Because by then the headlights were pointing down, for there had been so much jolting and bumping. The headlights were lighting only the dirt road immediately in front of us. The beams were aimed a very short distance. This road had to be among the worst in the world; my father's ranch roads were 100 times better. After what seemed interminable veering and jouncing, a few lights suddenly appeared ahead. It was Kassaroon!

Kassaroon. A "city?" A village! With a one-hundred-meter-long tarmac street lined by buildings on both sides. One of the buildings was a hotel, and downstairs was a fruit stand with a few groceries. We stopped the car. We bought some food. We asked if there were beds. They took us in. We spent the night. We washed in a filthy communal sink located in the central courtyard; the outdoor toilet facility was only a hole in the ground. It was all quite strange. Although outdoors, there was plumbing. But unfortunately, the water didn't run. You carried the water from a little outdoor faucet over a sink. Perhaps, however, it was better than the Iraqi border hotel. Here, David had his room, and we had ours, and they were quite tidy with clean beds.

Kassaroon. This was the place where that fellow in American Express had said, "We send tours there all the time."

Kassaroon. It was marked on the map as halfway to Abadan. Abadan was where the oil refineries were, and where we would go tomorrow.

The next day we drove on, and there was no tarmac now. It was all dirt road; just a track across the desert. We drove and drove. Fortunately, it was not a purely sand desert. There was some vegetation so we could follow the track, and then there was tarmac, and then there were some cars on a highway, and then we had our second blowout.

We had five flats on this trip, including three blowouts. We had had a flat just before and had changed it, so now we were without a spare tire. Thank God we had gotten to this "highway."

Now the tire had blown, so of course we stopped the car. David and BJ stayed with the car, and I hitchhiked into Abadan. I found a place that sold tires and took a service taxi back. A service (pronounced "sirveece") taxi is a taxi (usually an old Mercedes Benz) that fills up with people, as many as it will hold, and then it will go, and it will continue to pick up people en route. They picked me up. I brought back the tire, paid the service taxi, told him "merci," because in Farsi "merci" is "thank you," just as in French. We put the tire on, and we drove into Abadan.

In Abadan we looked for a way to get across the border into wherever. We were lost where we were, but we were heading toward Iraq. Officially, we could not figure out how to go through the border there. We finally found a dirt road because we kept asking, "Iraq? Iraq? Baghdad? Baghdad?" They would point in some direction, and we would go in that direction. Across the sandy desert we drove and drove, coming to a sort of oasis, and stopping at the only sign of people. It was a police station and the border crossing as well. We took our passports and our papers inside, and they stamped them all. Since it was the police, it was also the jail, and here were several men dressed in their galabias, dirty galabias, hanging onto the bars, smiling enormous smiles. Some with jagged teeth, Persian-tea-deteriorated teeth, but with great smiles, waving at us, saying something we couldn't understand, possibly, "Where are you from?"

I remember how the person at the passport control scrutinized our passports. He pointed to the first page and said, "Read this to me." So I turned it right side up and read to him, "The Secretary of the United States of America asks that you welcome this person into your country," or whatever it was that it said. These were old passports, not recent ones. He seemed content. He seemed to think that that was okay. He looked at the pictures, looked at me, looked at BJ, looked at David, and finally stamped them on an empty page, and even stamped the carnet, so we actually entered Iraq officially. We thanked him and waved good-bye to those poor, dirty prisoners. We wished we had time to visit another friend from USC days who lived in Kuwait, we had seen a sign earlier that said Kuwait, but we were running out of time. Beirut, hopefully, calls!

Crossing into Iraq, and passing through a border town, I noticed tires hanging in front of a store. We continued into the desert when another blowout happened. With the blowout the car swerved and stopped. I sighed. We changed the tire, drove back into town, and found the place with tires for sale. They didn't have one to fit our car but sent us to the town center near the plaza, or open square, the bazaar area. A neatly dressed man came over to me and said, "I speak English. I used to live in Beirut. What's your name?" "My name is Norman. I need a new tire."

He said, "Ah, yes. Norman. That's a good name. I teach Shakespeare. Do you know Shakespeare?"

He kept talking to me and I kept saying, "Look, I need a new tire. Where can I find one?"

He said, "I ask." He spent about thirty seconds asking, came back and said, "This man says he has a tire for you. I want to talk to you in English. Help me to practice my English."

"Yes, of course." He kept talking and talking, and I asked, "How much does this man want for this new tire that will fit my car?"

He said, "It won't really fit your car. It's too big, but it's the only tire that will fit your Karmann Ghia." It was a tire for a Chevrolet because this was a Chevrolet dealer. "It's the only tire in town that will fit the rim."

"Fine. How much does he want?" "He wants US$36 in dinars."

"Tell him I cannot possibly pay that much. It must be less." I had exactly US$36 in dinars. That was all that was left.

He said, "No. The man says he will not take less. You must pay him US$36."

"Tell him I don't have enough money, because I won't have money to buy petrol, to buy food, anything. I have to get to Beirut. I cannot pay him $36."

He spent two seconds telling him that, and said, "No, no. The man says you must pay $36." Now it was getting dark. I finally broke down and paid him the money, and he put the new tire on the car. The tire that was just taken off could now be used as a spare. We'd bought three new tires on this mad trip. As we were starting to leave, my translator continued to talk to me in English and he asked, "How can I go back to Beirut?"

"Yes, yes, you can come back to Beirut. By all means, look me up." Never saying, of course, where I lived.

A NARROW ESCAPE

We climbed into the car, thankful for the new tire, but at the same time rather depressed at the thought of our empty purse. Why had we bought that stupid carpet in Shiraz? Our exciting purchase had become a memory of regret! We found our way to a highway. I remember seeing a sign which read, "Kuwait go that direction." "Gulf go that direction." "Iraq, Baghdad, go this direction." By now we had almost run out of time for our spring and Easter holiday and were eager to get back to Beirut. The road to Baghdad was a brand new, blacktop highway built by Americans with American money, and it was dark, very dark. I was tired of driving so David offered to drive. BJ was still in the back, in the little jump-seat, and I was now beside David in the front passenger seat. BJ suddenly said, "David, I think 85 miles per hour is too fast."

I said, "Yes, David. Pull it back."

He lifted his foot off the accelerator. Just at that moment I saw something red flash by me that looked like a stop sign, but it was written in Arabic. Through the headlights I saw a man standing there holding a rifle. I think he had a whistle. All of a sudden the road ended, and we went over the embankment.

"David, turn to the left," I shouted.

Fortunately, the car stopped, and we sank into the soft sand of the desert, perhaps twelve feet below the highway. Our lights went out. Just as the car stopped the engine stopped. We slowly climbed out of the car. I walked straight ahead, fifteen feet, and there was a river, or perhaps it was a marsh, because we were in the Arab marsh lands of the Tigris and Euphrates delta. I walked to the left a little farther, another twenty feet, and there was water. I walked to the right, ten feet, and there was water. There was only one place that David could have gone, and that was to the left, for we had rapidly driven over the side of the road, straight down, at an angle. As he turned to the left the engine stopped and our car stopped. Since we were in a convertible, had we rolled, it would have been rather difficult to get out, either on the desert embankment or in the marsh water, impossible with three of us in a small Karmann Ghia sports car! I still love the car.

Running down the embankment from the highway came a policeman, the soldier we had sped past. He said to me, with the rifle held across his chest, "I blow whistle. Why you no stop?"

I patted him on the shoulder and said, "Malishi." "Never mind." Another man, who had been driving a new wine-colored Mercedes, along with a third gentleman joined our little group. He ran to the back of the car. The VW has the engine in the rear. He opened the lid and reconnected the battery, which had become disconnected from the engine. This is what made the engine stop, apparently, if we look for a mechanical reason. I prefer to call it a miracle. I believe God wanted to keep us alive for a while longer, foolish as we were. I keep remembering a friend of many years reminding me of the scripture "Those who honor Me, I will honor."

Our well-wisher had reconnected the engine to the battery. I thanked him and thanked the soldier, "Shukran. Shukran." The three of us got back into the car, slowly drove up the embankment and onto the highway. The highway didn't end where we had left it, but made a ninety-degree turn. Apparently, there was a stop sign back there to warn us, but of course we couldn't read the Arabic. We didn't even see it. David had been driving much too fast. So then I took over. Shattered as we were, I drove about thirty miles per hour.

We were followed by that wine-colored Mercedes Benz. I was beginning to get suspicious and uncomfortable. We saw a little chai house, a tea house, pulled off the highway, went in, and ordered sweet tea. It always helps in shock. We sat there drinking, and the Mercedes Benz stopped also. We were rather annoyed by that. We wanted to be rid of him because we didn't know what he had in mind. When we finished, I called for the check, to pay for it, and the chai boy said something about its having been paid and pointed toward the

Mercedes Benz man. I said "Shukran," shook his hand, and we went back to our car, relieved that his intentions were friendly ones.

BAGHDAD YMCA

By then I was feeling better, so I drove about 45 miles per hour, 50 miles per hour perhaps, on toward Baghdad. Eventually, nearing the city, we came to a huge, new roundabout. It indicated many routes, and I had no idea which to take. We had been in Baghdad before, but when leaving it for Iran we had taken a different route. As we now entered the roundabout, the Mercedes pulled in front of us and stopped. I stopped. He ran back to me and asked, "Where you want to go?"

I said, "To the YMCA."

"What's that?"

"The Young Men's Christian Association Hotel."

He said, "I find out." He asked around and then he said, "Come."

We followed him, and he drove us right to the gate. I thanked him. I felt I wanted to offer him some money, but he said, "No, no, no." And he left. We said, "Masallami." "God go with you."

I rang the bell at two in the morning, and the doorkeeper appeared. He showed us to our old bedroom where we had stayed before, and David went to the hostel to go to bed. We all collapsed.

There we were, back in Baghdad.

The next day I found out where the Volkswagen agency was, because it was time for the automobile to have a checkup. Things had to be adjusted and changed, so I took it in for its mileage service and left it, knowing that I didn't have any money. I went back to the YMCA. Earlier I had left word that I wanted to see the manager, and by then he was there. He sat behind his desk, and I sat in front of his desk and told him about our mad trip. He laughed and said, "Ah, yes. People come from Beirut thinking that it's not very far; they can make it in a short time." He said that the maps are very misleading. "Let's see how much you need."

He called the front desk of the YMCA and figured how much that bill was. I had already asked the VW agent if I could give him a check out of an America bank, and he had said, "No, no, no, no. We cannot do that." So there I was sitting in the YMCA director's office while he called the VW service station to ask how much the bill would be.

He said, "Now, you'll have to drive the TAP Line, that's the Trans-Arabian Pipeline route, and you'll need to stop at Romula. You'll spend a night there, and you might have to spend another night at the next place. You'll probably have to spend a night in Amman. So that's three more nights. You'll need food. You'll need this much money." He opened the drawer of his desk, pulled out a batch of Iraqi dinars, and handed them to me. A large pile of them. I was overwhelmed.

I said, "May I give you a check on my American bank or something?"

He said, "No." He handed me his card and wrote on the back of it a number. "When you get back to Beirut, just go to the British Bank of the Middle East and deposit into this account a comparable amount of money in Lebanese pounds."

"Thank you very much."

When we got back to Beirut, I deposited that amount of money into his account at the British Bank, which was where we had our account anyway. So we settled the transfer. Of course, that was the way he was getting his money out of Iraq, by helping others. He was a Good Samaritan, but he was also rewarded for it. As were we, for which we were most grateful.

BACK TO BEIRUT

After getting the car out of the VW place, after having a delicious meal, after looking around a bit in Baghdad, after observing the crossed swords over the city's main highway and the closed archeological museum, we drove away from the city, along the TAP Line, heading toward Amman, Jordan, through the desert, through the volcanic ash area, the same that we'd passed through before, but this time the potholes had been filled. This was two weeks later. The spring thaw had ended, and the road had been repaired; it was smooth so we made good time, and we didn't have to spend the night en route. We managed to go through customs clearance easily. We stayed in Amman that night. The next day we drove on to Beirut.

When we arrived at our friends' house, Kermit and Sharon Yoder, and saw Natasha, we were overwhelmed with joy. Absolute joy because she was all right. And we were all right, praise God! For there had been times on this trip when we were almost not all right.

CHAPTER 2

BEIRUT (1963 – 1965)

Antigone, The Glass Menagerie, A Chapel Program,
The House of Bernarda Alba,
Life in Beirut, Day Trips, Damascus, BJ's Recollections, Jerash, Petra,
Palmyra and Krak de Chevalier, Jerusalem,
Tom Coran and Rich Johnson,
Meningitis (The First Time), Carnegie Mellon University

ANTIGONE

During our first year at Beirut College for Women, 1963, we did a theatre production of two versions of *Antigone*. The first one by Sophocles, the second by Jean Anouilh; both to be performed the same evening. Opening night was November 22, 1963. We opened the evening's performance with the Sophocles version. The setting, being impressionistic in its design, had a huge configuration of a Greek temple suspended above two sizeable, round platforms, and Greek scrim columns, dropped from the temple area, surrounded the acting space on the upstage level. Abstract, but solid, stairs led to the upper round platform, which was roughly five feet tall. That came to a lower platform, which was perhaps three feet tall. Both round, abstract stairs came off in angled directions to keep the configuration in a circle. A sky cyclorama, again sewed and dyed by our students, surrounded the entire set. The Sophocles play was done in Greek costuming, very stentorian acting, but very well performed, played with large gestures and strong lines. The whole presentation was powerful as if in a Greek theatre.

Antigone is the young niece of King Creon, who stands up against her uncle's edict and is loyal to her religious beliefs as established by the ancient Greeks. Antigone believes that the body of her brother, Eteocles, who was slain in a battle against her uncle's troops, should be buried according to the Greek rites, not treated as an enemy. She speaks out that Eteocles must be buried. In fact, she attempts to bury him, even though Creon has decreed that anybody who does this will be killed, guilty of treason, for his nephew, Eteocles, has fought against him.

Antigone and Ismene are daughters of Oedipus, who eventually realizes his redeeming features after having killed his father and married his mother; he puts out his eyes after his wife/mother has killed herself. True to her beliefs, Antigone does what nobody else would do, and buries her brother so that his spirit will be free to go to the heaven of the Greeks; otherwise, his spirit will have to roam the earth, forever unburied. As a result, Antigone is sentenced by her Uncle Creon to death. Antigone's love, Haemon, who is Creon's son, argues with his father that she be given the right to live. Creon refuses. Haemon, determined at all costs to support Antigone, chooses to go with Antigone into her death. She is to be walled up in a cave. Haemon joins her, making his death even more violent, killing himself by sword as he clings to Antigone, who has hanged herself with the woven linen of her dress. When Creon watches this, he is most distraught that this tragedy has come upon his head. He finally has understanding that he has done the wrong thing, and with that comes tragic enlightenment and ultimately catharsis for those in the theatre.

After that tragic play ended on the night of November 22, 1963, the curtain closed, and the stage was quickly prepared for the modern play. The Greek columns were removed but the platforms remained; a small table and some chairs were placed, and it became a unit set depicting anywhere, any possibilities. Then the curtain opened on the Jean Anouilh production of *Antigone*.

There were a number of American actors in this production. Just after the Jean Anouilh play began, the stage manager, backstage, telephoned me in the booth overlooking the balcony and the proscenium arch theatre. She said that Yussef had just returned from Hamra, Beirut's main shopping street, and he said that as he was walking past a restaurant bar, he heard the news that President Kennedy had just been shot in Dallas, Texas. Beirut is eight hours ahead of Dallas. The crew wanted to know whether or not to close the play.

I said, "Ask the cast what they want to do."

The cast, all of them, said, "We want to continue. As our tribute; as our statement to Kennedy."

As the performance continued, the spoken lines were incredibly significant and moving. The Anouilh play, a French modern version of the Sophocles play, was written during WWII and speaks about the German Nazis' invasion and control of France, the occupation of Paris in particular. Antigone herself symbolizes the French people, particularly the French Resistance, who fight against Hitler's occupying army. Creon represents Hitler. This show ran for many months in Paris, and everybody in France knew what it stood for, but the Germans never did, or so they said at that time. At least they were slow in catching on, because it ran for a long time. For Anouilh to successfully clear the German censors while expressing France's refusing to surrender to Germany's offer of "happiness" is a major achievement. But, it is a universal problem: Moral Law vs State Law.

Listening to this account of an individual's willingness and strength to fight against an evil power, and watching it while knowing that Kennedy was very likely dying, was incredible. Creon moving slowly on stage with his page — a small boy — says to the page, "Would you kill me with your toy pistol?" The news filtered through the auditorium. The American Ambassador, who was attending the play, was called out, and someone from the French embassy was called out. Everyone sensed that something was wrong. The audience, little by little, learned the tragic news. The production, strangely enough, lost its original momentum and gradually became more thoughtful than in rehearsal, where it had played in a clipped, powerful way. It now moved into a somber, thoughtful manner; not a dirge, but a mood that reflected the loss of a person, who stood for something great, and was dying.

By the time the play ended, the news had come that Kennedy was dead. Walking through the audience afterward, I saw many people crying, from the impact of the play (perhaps a little), but mostly from the loss of a great leader, John F. Kennedy. Indeed, at that time much of the world considered Kennedy a great leader, for he had stood up to the Russians during the Cuban crisis. He showed himself to be a man of strength. None of the negative rumors were floating around; they came later. He was still an idealized hero, almost a leader on a white horse, to whom we looked up, and who the world admired. And there in Beirut people were shattered by his death.

I later spoke with my brother Jim, who had been flying between the Middle East, New York, and Europe, and he said that he had talked with somebody who had just come back from Beirut. He said that they were weeping more for Kennedy in Beirut than they were in Washington, DC, which may well have been true.

THE GLASS MENAGERIE

Another production that first year was *The Glass Menagerie* by Tennessee Williams. It was rather strange the way *The Glass Menagerie* happened. There were four actors, three from BCW, one of whom was a teacher, and one from AUB, who wanted to do it as an extra activity. The school's emphasis was on academics and extra activities were frowned upon. At that point there was no major in Theatre, Communications, Television and Film as there now is (and all of which are still based upon theatre and humanities). But since *The Glass Menagerie* wouldn't involve a large number of students, we decided to go ahead and do it.

We four, or rather five including me, rehearsed for three weeks, and opened the production. An interesting, rather simple setting was used, with a platform upstage for the dining area, and scrim "portieres" hanging, with one or two unit pieces that established the St. Louis seedy apartment. The production was very well done and was most warmly received.

An interesting and rather embarrassing incident happened the night that we closed that production. We had to strike the set (clearing the stage and putting everything away) as I always required, just as in a professional situation. This was unheard of; usually in the past the hired servant, Yussef — an excellent helper-carpenter who worked with me

— cleared the set while the rest went off to party. We'd been invited to an after-theatre dinner party hosted by our student who worked on the show, Nafisa Sheikh, the daughter of the CEO of Pakistani International Airlines. But I didn't realize it was given for me. I had warned her that we would be late and to please go ahead with the party, and we would catch up when we got there. Nafisa held dinner until we arrived, which must have been quite late indeed, because dinners in the Mid-East are late anyway. There is generally an hour of drinking sweet sodas, sometimes wine if you prefer, and then dinner is served at 9:00 or 9:30 at the latest.

This time it was 10:00 or later, and the hostess was very nervous. She sent her driver over to pick us up. Rich Johnson, a fellow teacher and an actor in the play, and my wife BJ and I, jumped into the car, which took us to her house. Dr. Gray, the president of Beirut College for Women and later of Damavand College, Tehran, was there, among others, all waiting for dinner. She said to me, in her most ironic, Southern way, "Norman, it seems you're more important than the president."

I laughed and said something like, "I'm sorry, but very glad that it worked out."

This was in the springtime of 1964. The dinner proceeded, and it was a lovely party. A week or two later, the hostess's father was on an inaugural flight when it crashed into the Egyptian desert, and he was killed. I remember that the daughter, Nafisa Sheikh, wept bitterly and withdrew from school. We were sorry for she was a very nice student and was missed by all.

The Glass Menagerie had a usual weekend run, a split run covering two weekends. Within two days after it opened, a local ex-pat reporter, a marvelous woman who had lived in Beirut most of her life, wrote in the *Beirut Daily Star* a review of the play which was, to me, upsetting. Not as a review, but as a pre-review. Perhaps she thought that she was doing us a favor. The headline read: "American Director Presents American Play at American College." The article went ahead to discuss *The Glass Menagerie.*

Frances Gray, the president of BCW, was away when this article came out in the newspaper. She had been in the States for some weeks raising money for the college. The college had been established almost 100 years before by the Presbyterian Church Mission Board in New York, on Riverside Drive, and it was established to offer girls in the Middle East university-level education. It was the only women's college in the Middle East at that time, and we taught many girls from all over the Middle East. Upon her return, Dr. Gray read the newspaper and that headline inflamed her so much that she called me in a few days later and said, "Norman, the American flag has not waved from the gates of BCW for many years, and I'm not going to let you put it back."

I was very angry. "Frances, I had nothing to do with that article."

"Yes, but you went ahead and did the play, and I told you not to do so many productions because the girls are to concentrate on their classes."

"The girls weren't doing it. It was only we five people. All of us were Americans. And not students."

"Yes, that's another point. It was all Americans. It was not done by the Lebanese girls." The students/girls were signed up for a theatre production class that lasts a year. Other courses covered theatre history and literature, so I needed to train them in theatre production and that is best done on stage doing some kind of dramatic production in addition to scene study acting.

I said, "Okay, Frances. Thank you very much." And I left her office.

I think that that was one of the contributing factors that made me want to leave after the first year, and she told me, "I'm not going to let you ruin your career by leaving at the end of the first year. You are going to stay on and complete this contract."

A CHAPEL PROGRAM

Interestingly, there was an opportunity for me to get a little bit even with Frances, whom I adored (even though we argued at times) for she had style, sparkle, charm, and guts to run a women's University College in the male- controlled Middle East! Each year the faculty entertained the students at one of the chapel programs. This time a script had been written by a committee of teachers, I guess, which was a rather boring script dealing with the activities at BCW and the various things that the girls did. The teachers were going to act out these activities in pantomime. The chapel program was to be headed by Dr. Frances Gray. She read the script, approved of it, called me in, and said, "It's okay, Norman. The content is very good."

Then Frances made a big mistake in one way, but in another way it was a great decision. She said, "Norman, I don't want to read this. You read it. You would read it much better than I. Your voice is better, and the girls would enjoy seeing a man up there reading it and telling all of these things. You just go ahead and present it."

"But Frances, it's written for you! 'Presenting Dr. Gray,' it says, 'who will narrate the activities of the girls at BCW.'"

"Yes, yes, but please, dear, you go ahead and do it."

I said I would do it, not wanting in the least to get involved in this. First of all, it was not my style, and secondly it was deadly dull. I went backstage and told Edna Stuar, the tennis coach, what Frances had said. The tennis coach (whom I have described for years as looking and acting exactly like Mammy Yokum in the cartoon strip "Li'l Abner") jumped up in the air, kicked her heels together — and she was about eighty years old — and said, "Hot dog! You read it!" And off she went saying, "Come with me. Let's find something for you to wear." [The first time we met Edna, we mentioned the book *I Married an Arab*, and she immediately said, "I wish I had!" Her former husband was European, we understood.]

We went into the wardrobe section, pulled open the cupboards, and she started pulling things out. "Here, put on this gallabiyah." It was a full length, all white Arab robe with some gold glitter. It fit me nicely, for in those days I was very thin. "Put on this hat." It was a huge straw hat with a big, round brim, which covered my entire head and most of my shoulders, and it had a red bow on top and a flower. "Great! Hot dog!" Then she grabbed some lipstick, and started painting my lips and cheeks. She accented my eyes with brown pencil, and then the chapel program began.

The students had already come in, and the announcements were made by the Dean of Students, Daad Jabara, and then she, who was in on the deal, said, "And now I present Dr. Frances Gray."

Frances was sitting in the balcony, and some of the students knew that she was in the balcony, but those who didn't gently applauded as out through the side curtains stepped myself; six feet, four inches tall, thin as a rail, with an enormous hat, standing there looking up, lipstick glowing in the spotlights, and eyelashes fluttering, because that's what Frances Gray often did when she became nervous. The 500 students just yelled, screaming with applause and laughter. Frances, I am sure, was sitting up there grinding her teeth in agony wondering, "What have I done now?"

I began to read. The script was there, but I didn't read it in a straight, dull way. I talked about the students who were actively engaged in painting, and the curtain opened and we saw Rich Johnson, a new teacher (concerned by his macho image, originally from Walnut Creek, California, at that time from Columbia after Yale) who taught mathematics, dressed in Bermuda shorts with a huge paintbrush and an easel, painting, smiling away, looking over at me absolutely horrified and angry, saying, "What on earth are you doing, Norman?" He went through his routine, doing the activities of a BCW girl swirling her paint brush onto his large abstract painting. Great job! (Later, he would hardly speak to me until he finally laughed at the joke.) The curtain closed, and the narration continued. I don't think they could have gotten him to do a ballet movement routine!

The narration continued all the way through, and I played it in an American Southern drawl (which I could do rather well at that point) of Frances Gray, and throwing in a few little "dears" and "heres" as it went along.

I made it through the whole chapel program as they went through their music and their routines. Everything was very exciting for that Chapel Program, I must admit, and at the end I put my hands up, waved good-bye to them, and thanked them all for the wonderful years, and off I went.

Frances wouldn't talk with me for a number of days. Finally, when we met at a dinner party, I said, "Frances, it wasn't my idea. Edna was the one who put me up to it and said I had to do it that way."

She said, "All I can say is, you have a lousy Southern accent."

We both laughed, and I suggested she might have coached me. I suppose that we mentally hugged, and decided that we were friends forever. Which we were.

In a way that got me a little bit even with the stormy situation over *The Glass Menagerie*. Frances had decided that I had to stay there and teach, and I decided that if I had to stay there and teach then I might as well enjoy it, and so I did, up to a point; BJ and our year-old daughter Natasha loved the campus and the school. Later, so did I!

THE HOUSE OF BERNARDA ALBA

The second year I wanted to do a production of Federico Garcia Lorca's *Blood Wedding*, but instead we did *The House of Bernarda Alba*. We talked about *Blood Wedding*, but it required too many characters. The men for these productions were brought up (or rather they ran up eagerly, so intense was their desire to see the girls) from the American University of Beirut. We usually had abundant actors, as it was a popular theatre, indeed. And drama wasn't part of the curriculum at AUB. But we couldn't find enough people, both on campus and at AUB, to do this play, because the script called for so many men. *The House of Bernarda Alba* had an all-women cast.

At first the students were against this play with all women, because they said that a main point of doing these dramas was to involve men. The year before, we had done a production of the French farce, *The Doctor in Spite of Himself*, by Moliere. We did that with an all-girl cast, and also did three one- act plays with only girls. (No wonder Frances was angry with me, saying that I was doing too many productions, but I had a theatre class, and felt that they needed to keep busy and involved.) Even the Dean of Students questioned the only-girls cast saying, "Are you trying to put us back fifty years?" She referred to the earlier time when men were hardly allowed on campus. I said that if the girls wanted to see the boys, and if the boys came up to see them, fine. But they shouldn't be involved with both chasing the boys and being in the productions. We were becoming a professionally-oriented theatre troupe, and I think one of the reasons why a professional training center was developed after I left, in which years later I again taught and directed productions.

We did finally decide upon Lorca's *The House of Bernarda Alba*, written by the Spanish playwright just before he died in 1936. Lorca was a part of the Spanish resistance against the Fascists. For this he was killed, and his grave was never found. In addition to his very successful poetic dramas, Lorca wrote puppet shows and poetry rich in symbols and poetic devices. The time he spent in New York resulted in a number of poems about that city.

The House of Bernarda Alba is the third part of a trilogy including *Yerma* and *Blood Wedding*. Bernarda is the mother, a widow, who in mourning has closed all the house shutters and forbidden most coming and going. She has five daughters, all unmarried. Because the oldest daughter, Martirio, is not yet married, the younger ones cannot marry. Martirio has a fiancé who comes to see her frequently, a kind of arranged marriage situation. His name is Pepe Romano, whom we never see; he is only talked about in true dramatic discovery form. Pepe courts Martirio, makes his required visits, and leaves; but then later on, unknown to the rest of the house, Pepe returns to secretly meet Adela, the family's youngest daughter. These trysts are usually in the horse stable, which is attached to the house. This is important because the horse is a strong, often-used male symbol in Spanish literature. Today we would call Adela and Pepe's relationship simply an affair; casual affairs were definitely taboo in 1936 Spanish culture. Chaperones were common practice, very different from the kind of freedom found in western culture and depicted in movies and television around the world.

As the action progresses, a feeling of impending tragedy becomes increasingly heavy until near the play's end, Adela's and Pepe's affair is discovered. Bernarda accuses Adela of not only ruining the marriage possibilities of her older sister but also besmirching the honor of the entire family. Adela, so full of vitality, and eager for freedom and love, realizes the seriousness and hopelessness of her situation and kills herself. The play ends on a powerful note, with Bernarda, in an attempt to protect the family honor, announcing to the world, "And my daughter died a virgin!"

The play actually has two endings. In the published one, which we used, Adela hangs herself in the stable. The second ending, unpublished but in the vernacular, has Adela enter the stable to be trampled to death by a stallion. Both endings, but especially the second, are permeated with the symbol of the horse, a Spanish (also Middle Eastern) symbol of male strength and virility. Here, the stallion is represented by Pepe, who, by his passion, has destroyed Adela. In Lorca's *Blood Wedding* the word goes, "My horse, he drinks by the stream in the dry arroyo (in the dry desert riverbed)."

The setting for this production was a number of shutters that extended, not from floor to ceiling, but from perhaps five feet above the floor all of the way up to the top of the stage area. Hanging with them was fabric: heavy, black, very wide-woven, almost like lace, but not delicate. Instead, it was bold- patterned, huge, open-weave squares which were pulled together into tassels, enormous tassels hanging up there with an open-weave trellis-like shutter concept that was developed behind it. Lighting from the back spilled onto and through this whole set. Hanging in front of the entire set was a black scrim, made by us, made of lace, Spanish lace bought in the Beirut souk, which covered the entire 30-foot proscenium opening, from the stage to the borders. Behind all of this was the stark white wall of Lorca's house, which belonged to Bernarda Alba. Lorca asked for a white-walled house with black accents. He had it in this production.

The show opens with the soft music of guitars, and finally the striking of a clock. We see only black lace floor to ceiling, and then the servant comes out. She sweeps the floor, she wakes the household up, the lights become brighter, the play begins. As the action gets stronger, people start moving in behind the black scrim, and slowly the scrim is taken out. The play progresses.

Early on we notice that all of the women suffer frustrations; frustrations from the father's death; the mother now has full responsibility for her daughters; she must find them suitable husbands, and most important, she must protect them from the outside world. She clusters them closer to her, in terms of stage blocking, in terms of movement. I put the mother in the center, and it was as though the daughters were held by a huge spider web that reached out and pulled those girls toward her into the center of this configuration. As this concept developed, of keeping these girls within the house, imprisoned within the mother's control, the black scrim returned, covering the front of the stage. If lit from behind, a scrim is transparent; and if lit from the front, it appears to be solid. In this case the scrim is lace, solid lace, and we can look through it and see the family caught in the web, symbolic of their predicament. We feel the mother's power as she holds her daughters together within the confines of the house. The concept of the webbing takes over, pulling the family together, pulling especially against the will of the youngest, Adela, who is so determined to be free, to throw off the constraints of society, not caring that her lover is her sister's fiancé.

Lorca's script certainly meets the requirements of Greek tragedy as established by Sophocles, and written of by Aristotle; a concept I'd often lectured that good theatre should do.

The play was very well received, with many in the audience quite overwhelmed with its powerful impact. And most agreed that its statement was relevant to the time and place. The students said, "We like doing this play because it makes our statement; it speaks about us and our position." Indeed Lorca's Spanish women and women of the Middle East have much in common. Centuries ago, the teachings and customs of Islam, many pertaining to women, moved from the Middle East across North Africa and into Spain; and some of these customs were still practiced in the 1960s, even in 2017, often leading to death. A professor friend says it's a culture thing: Christians as well as Moslems; the same situation in India, I've heard from an Indian student. The importance of a bride's virginity, arranged marriages, and the importance of producing a male heir were the realities of life for many of our students. For the first time I learned from students the importance of blood on the sheets of the marriage bed; so important that if there was anticipated a doubt, the women would have sewn in a small bladder of chicken blood to insure there would be proper evidence the next morning! Oh, what one learns in a girls' school, especially in the Middle East!

One afternoon when we were rehearsing *Bernarda Alba*, one of the girls came running in from the Middle East's Champs-Élysées,

Hamra Street, West Beirut's main shopping area, very upset. "I have just witnessed a man kill a woman on the street." We were all stunned. She repeated, "Just now I saw a man kill a woman, probably his wife or sister. I was in a taxi, and this man was in the taxi ahead of me. He jumped out of the car, chased after the woman, pulled out a knife, stabbed, and killed her." I was very moved by her story, although I'd heard of similar happenings before. This was most likely a "family honor killing."

Middle Eastern families place an extreme value upon their honor. If a wife is even suspected of being unfaithful, or a single woman leaves home to live alone, the family's honor has been besmirched and can be cleansed only by shed blood. It is the duty of the male head of the family to cleanse that honor by murdering the offender. This practice is a theme of *The House of Bernarda Alba* as well as Lorca's *Blood Wedding* and *Yerma* (which means "barren").

Another example came up in speech class one day; the story of a student who visited her aunt in the Bekaa Valley, near Baalbek, with its wonderful Roman ruins. One day when in her aunt's house, she all of a sudden heard screams in the street. She ran to the window, looked out, and saw several men dragging a girl through the door of a nearby garage, or perhaps a stable, she wasn't sure. She kept hearing screams, more screams, many more screams, until all screams stopped. She went for her aunt, and said, "Auntie, what is happening?"

Her aunt replied, "They have just restored the honor of their family. You see, the daughter of our neighbor married a Syrian boy, went to Syria with him, but later ran away. She ran away from her husband. She ran home. She obviously thought, or at least hoped, that she would be secure there, but the family's honor had to be avenged. She left her husband, which made her an adulteress. Therefore she had to be killed."

A man just then came out of the barn next door, and he nailed the girl's severed hand to the door of the house. The story later came out that the father, head of the house, couldn't bring himself to kill his daughter, so the cleansing had to be done by her cousin, who was next in line. The father could only cut off the girl's hand, which he did before she died, we assumed, because of all the screams. Her death avenged the family honor.

These honor murders have continued in the Middle East, even until today, according to newspaper accounts. An article, appearing shortly before the death of Jordan's King Hussein, told of Queen Noor's unsuccessful efforts to end this practice. A large number of women, who have soiled their families' honor, are living in Jordan's prisons solely for protection from their families.

Lorca's dominant theme of the importance of a bride's virginity comes straight from Spain's culture. After all, the Spanish celebrate the blood that is shed on the sheet of the bridal bed, which must be put out in front of the door on the wedding night. The husband's honor depends upon the proof that the marriage has been consummated. Our students told numerous stories (straight out of the harem) of how some brides have to be sewed up, repaired, so the blooded sheet can be set outside the door. Some stories involve inserting a bag of chicken's blood. All this to save the bride's life. Some of these speeches were graphic indeed!

This theme is summed up in *The House of Bernarda Alba* when Bernarda exclaims, "My daughter died a virgin!" Virginity is also important in *Blood Wedding*. *Yerma* deals with the need to have children. The lady, yearning for but unable to have children, goes to a sorceress, and the sorceress says, "I guarantee that you will have a child." She then arranges for her son to sleep with the woman, who conceives. That is how this theme is handled in several of the Lorca dramas.

Years later, when in North Africa, BJ and I were teaching in a university in Tunisia, in Sousse, down the coast from Tunis. Tunis had an annual drama and music festival, held at Carthage, the extensive Roman ruins just outside the city. Dr. Evelyne Accad, a former student, who had been in my production of *The House of Bernarda Alba* in Lebanon, contacted me. She, a Fulbright Professor at the University of Tunis, was in Tunis with friends who wanted me to direct a production of *The House of Bernarda Alba* for this festival. I strongly considered doing it, but unfortunately my university schedule was such that I couldn't have made the rehearsals. Several former Beirut theatre students, now working in Paris theatre and radio, were eager to come to Tunis to act in and stage this play, and were quite peeved when it didn't happen. I, too, was disappointed, but the performance was exactly during the time of final examinations, and I couldn't have made it. I should have done it; perhaps Dr. Accad or her colleagues would have been able to handle rehearsals. I'm sorry we didn't consider that. The university indicated that if I, a new professor in Tunisia, didn't properly prepare the students for the exams and did not monitor/invigilate the exams, I would not have fulfilled my contract. Tunisia operates on the French system, but I imagine a Matre de Conference — which was my rank (the same as Professor in the U.S. university system) — would have had a lecturer or even an administrator do the monitoring of the exams. Of course I/we had just gotten away from the bombing and kidnapping in Beirut, and that factor was an important influence on my decision.

Dr. Evelyne Accad, at that time, 1985, a professor of Comparative Literature and French at the University of Illinois in Champaign, was the contact. My student in 1965 at Beirut College for Women, Evelyne, had now caught up with me. We were now both professors. It's interesting that we practically grew up together in the world of universities, although in different parts of the world. The Lorca play's statement of women's position in the world, particularly in the Islamic world, was a subject that especially interested both of us at that time. In Lebanon, the play had made a strong impact, and we believe had a positive influence. We felt that Tunis was an appropriate setting for the play. Evelyne was/is very active in making known these women's issues: writing articles, books, even a novel about the circumcision of women in Africa and the Middle East. She has had at least one Fulbright grant for the purpose of researching the situation of women in the Middle East. Now Professor Emeritus of French Literature, University of Illinois, Dr. Accad continues her quest at the Sorbonne, Paris, and at the Lebanese American University, formerly Beirut College for Women and Beirut University College, Beirut, Lebanon. She and her sister, Professor [LAU] Jacqueline Hajjar, hold international forums in Paris and Beirut on the subject of Women (very much Lorca's women) in the Middle East and Africa.

LIFE IN BEIRUT

Many interesting people passed through Beirut; people whom one would never run into in most out-of-the-way places, except that they came on special assignments such as American State Department tours. One such tour brought the famous actor-couple, Mr. and Mrs. Frederick March, who performed magnificent short scenes from American dramas. Another memorable State Department-sponsored program was by a musical dance troupe from Brigham Young University in Utah. After their brilliant, exhausting-looking performance I asked one of the performers what they were going to do now, and he said, "Oh, we're going to go out dancing, and we will dance all night." In the Church of the Latter Day Saints, I suppose that "dancing in the spirit" is comparable to dancing all night. 1965 presented an interesting State Department performer, a fine poet, Sam Hazo, from Pittsburgh, Pennsylvania, who visited Beirut reading his excellent poems. He told me he thought a fun film reflecting the life of Beirut would be just shooting people and places in Beirut while riding in a service taxi, listening to the music of Egyptian singer Uum Kaltum huskily, powerfully singing her Arabic songs reflecting life, love, and hopeful happiness. Having ridden those service taxis in the Middle East and North Africa, I can agree with his colorful proposal. These taxis cannot stop, the rider hops on and off while traffic moves, the driver constantly honking to attract riders. In Tehran, Iran, the traffic is so heavy, I would turn my feet sideways to avoid being run over. Those taxis did not have specific routes; the rider shouts his destination and if the driver is going somewhere near it, he will take you — maybe!

DAY TRIPS

We made a number of trips away from the city of Beirut. Usually on a Saturday, we'd pack a picnic lunch and the many necessities required by one- year-old Natasha (happy in her cast from armpits to ankles) into our Karmann Ghia convertible and head for the grandeur of the Lebanon Mountains that overlook Beirut. Those mountains were magnificently high, overshadowing the city of Beirut, which thrusts into the Mediterranean. The Lebanese were pleased to remind one that here you could ski in the morning, and in the afternoon swim in the Mediterranean; we didn't! We visited many mountain villages, tidy and lovely with their sturdy stone buildings with arches and domes. Lebanese handicrafts — pottery and glass, straw baskets and mats, metalwork, etc. — were lovely and usually practical. In good weather, there was scarcely a weekend that we didn't make an excursion to some interesting spot.

I remember once seeing a farm woman making "mountain bread." We stopped the car and approached to observe the process, and she appeared to be pleased with our interest. This very thin bread is like an enormous pancake, but it's not made like a pancake. The dough is stretched over a round pillow, making it very thin and round. The thin sheet is then placed on top of a disc-like oven. The disc, like a dome, is turned upside down, with a fire of twigs and wood, or perhaps charcoal, underneath it, and the heat from the fire warms the disc, baking the bread. Interesting to watch. Delicious to eat. We offered the woman one Lebanese pound (about 33 cents) for which she gave us several loaves. Thin, wonderful bread called mountain bread or lavash. Now one can buy it everywhere, it seems.

This tiny country had many interesting destinations for our day trips. The amazing Roman ruins at Baalbek and Anjar next to the Ante Lebanon Mountains en route to Damascus. North of Beirut are the famous ancient Cedars, the mountain village that had been home to Khalil Gibran, wonderful Maronite Christian Monasteries and Orthodox Churches. South of Beirut (north of Israel) a charming crusader castle rests on the water at Sidon and another one in the city of Tripoli. There is also Beaufort, the crusader castle strategically located on a hill near the border with Israel and guarded by the military. Conspicuous were signs forbidding photography. Beaufort was bombed by Israel in 1982 when Israel invaded Lebanon. But from 1963-65, when we first lived In Lebanon, all was at peace after a short war in 1956, during which President Eisenhower sent in the U.S. Marines to line the beaches of Beirut, stopping, momentarily, the nonsense that has oftentimes nearly destroyed the Middle East.

Longer journeys which we made during those two years include Palmyra, the Krak de Chevalier Castle, said to be the largest crusader castle, and Damascus, all in Syria; and Amman, Petra, Jerash, and Jerusalem in Jordan, not to mention our drives to Tehran and London, which I've written about in chapter one. Sadly, much of this has been destroyed in the Syrian War.

Haram!

DAMASCUS

Damascus was only a two-to-three-hour drive, and we went there a number of times. Passport control on the Syrian side was always a time-consuming hassle, each time offering new adventures. While the huge covered bazaar was for us the main attraction, Damascus had numerous tourist sites: an excellent historical museum, the great Omayyad mosque, Saladin's tomb, the Street Called Straight, the house of Ananias, where St. Paul took refuge after his sensational conversion just outside one of the city gates, and the very window where Paul was supposedly lowered in a basket to avoid arrest; also a number of lovely old palaces and a large glass-blowing factory with gift shop. In spite of our low salaries at that time, Damascus hotels were inexpensive, and we always returned to Beirut with a number of exotic purchases from the bazaar: a large copper tray with folding stand, collapsible mosaic game table, small Druze chest, brass Arab coffee pots, embroidered tablecloths, etc. What does one do with these things now fifty years later? Probably the refugees from Syria waiting in the deserts of Jordan, Lebanon, and Turkey could use them, but the thousands who are walking/boating/swimming and dying to get to Europe could not! Sad.

During our second sojourn in Beirut, in the early '80s, we traveled to Damascus much less frequently because of the dangerous Lebanon Civil War situation. In 1981 we found ourselves there, but not by choice. During the Easter holiday several of the BUC faculty flew to Amman, Jordan, and while there the Beirut airport was closed for security reasons. Our stay in Amman was quite pleasant, first at the Philadelphia Hotel, very near the magnificent Roman amphitheatre. BJ joined Judy and Dr. Neil Foland, and their daughter Cassie, who had hired a car and driver to go to Aqaba and Wadi Rum, of T.E.

Lawrence fame, and where the film *Lawrence of Arabia* was shot. This side- trip turned out to be very entertaining, with housing difficulties, causing them to spend a night at a construction site at the invitation of one of the overly- friendly workers. In those days the Arab men were very friendly — in a usually wholesome way. They never did figure out whose beds they slept in. It was nearly time for classes to begin, and Beirut's airport was still closed.

We, along with the Folands and Dawn and Dr. David Nottingham, had by now moved to less expensive quarters at some school dormitory. There was talk of hiring taxis to take us back to Beirut, but I said no, it was too dangerous; I'd not budge until the airport opened. And it began to look as though I'd be in Amman alone, since BJ said she was joining the others in taxis. By now Sara Bailey had joined our group; she was returning home to Beirut from the U.S. and rerouted to Amman because of Beirut's closed airport. Sara had lots of luggage — books for her father, Dr. Ken Bailey, clergyman and writer, well-known among theologians (in whose home nineteen years later we lived for a year while Ken and family were on leave during the kidnappings of the Civil War).

So one afternoon David and Neil went off to arrange for two taxis to pick us all up the next morning, for I, too, had now succumbed to the return overland. The first two taxis — the Folands and Sara in one, and Nottinghams and the two of us in the other — took us to Damascus, which trip was no less hair-raising than I'd known it would be, and the worst was to come, through the mountains after Damascus. We lodged in Damascus at a French convent, a place we'd stayed at before. Dawn's knowledge of French eased the situation.

The next morning one of the nuns arranged for two taxis to take us on the final leg of our journey. By mid-day, we had made it across the Syrian border, managed through Syrian and Lebanese customs, and reached the approximate half-way mark, Stura, a town famous for its wine industry. By this time we all felt in need of something to calm our nerves, especially with the "most exciting" mountain roads still to come. So we asked the driver to stop at a roadside store where I purchased a half-gallon of Stura's best. This helped make the remainder of the trip much less stressful, almost jolly, especially for David, who was sitting in the front seat! Since service taxis are notoriously speedy drivers, overtaking cars in very inopportune places on both flat roads and worse on the mountain switch-back roads, David shouted back to me, "Norm, now I know why you gave me the comfortable front seat. This driver is terrifying!" But, safe!

BJ'S RECOLLECTIONS

I made another trip to Damascus when the Beirut Airport was closed. This was in the spring of 1984, and Natasha was graduating from Scripps College, a part of the Claremont Colleges [based on the Oxford, England, concept of university structure] at Claremont, California. There was no way that Norman could get away from classes, but fortunately Haigazian College, where I was teaching, had re-arranged the schedule because of the war situation, so that I just happened to have completed my assignments by the end of April. So we agreed that I should go to Natasha's graduation and arranged to fly out of Damascus, going there by service taxi the day before the flight. I'd hoped to stay at the French convent, but it was full, so I went next to the Semiramis, where we'd stayed in the past. It was also full — full of Iranian women who had lost husbands and sons in the Iran-Iraq war. These women's pilgrimages to Damascus were a form of compensation the Iranian government offered them. I finally found a room in a small hotel very near the bazaar.

Having a late lunch in a restaurant near my hotel, I asked the waiter where I could buy a particular kind of cookie that Damascus was famous for. He didn't know but asked three persons at another table, and this resulted in my conversation with them, two brothers and their sister. Their family name was Tslas. One of the men was a businessman from Homs; the other a pilot in the air force; the woman was a doctor at the women's hospital in Damascus. They insisted on taking me to a store that sold the famous cookies. One thing led to another, and although I'm always reluctant to let myself in for this type of situation, I accepted their invitation for tea with them at the nearby home of the pilot. They spoke excellent English and seemed to be interested in almost everything. They showed me a large attractive book about the plants of Syria; it had full-page color illustrations and had been written and photographed by their uncle, also with the name Tslas, and who was the Syrian Minister of Defense, no less.

When I suggested that it was time for me to go, the businessman asked if there was someplace, perhaps a tourist site, that I'd like to see. I'd been wanting to visit the tomb of Saladin, the Moslem hero of the Crusades, and Arab counterpart of Richard the Lion Heart, and knew it was someplace in the bazaar. He said that would be easy to visit, so off we went — the businessman, his sister, and myself. Quite a few tourists were viewing the tomb, which was typically Islamic, a sarcophagus draped with green fabric, with Koranic inscriptions, surrounded with tall, metal grillwork. It was not a spacious setting, but rather crowded between a hodge-podge of bazaar shops. I took several photos and prepared to say good-bye to my hosts, when the businessman ushered me into a small shop selling women's garments. After some Arabic conversation, the merchant showed us several lovely cotton floor-length gowns, which immediately took my eye. My host suggested that I choose one, that it was a gift. I was hesitant, but knew better than to refuse, so I graciously accepted. But then came my mistake. I was thinking, what a nice gift one of these gowns would make for my sister Kathleen and for my friend Lyla, with whom I'd be staying in California. I knew I'd not find this shop again, even if I had time, which I didn't. It was now or never. So after accepting my host's gift, I explained that I'd like to buy two as presents for my friends in America. And true to Arab hospitality, he insisted on paying for those as well. I should have known! How embarrassed I was and still am when I remember.

I had just returned to my small, basic hotel room when there was a knock on the door, which I cautiously opened. There stood the young man I recognized as the pleasant, nice-appearing desk clerk. "Hello. Is there a problem?"

"You're an American." He'd of course seen my passport, "And maybe can help me."

"How?" I asked.

"This hotel job is part-time. My real job is at a grain elevator, and I want very much to get a college degree in agriculture. Do you know of a university in America that might accept me?" Well, I thought, his English wasn't too bad ... and I did know of one; Kansas State University at Manhattan, which I mentioned. Next came, "Could you please write me a recommendation?" My word, I didn't even know this guy's name! But after answering a few questions, he brought me some hotel stationery and I wrote a few facts about his situation and my impressions based on his appearance, use of English, and his demeanor at his hotel job. I remember writing positively, without lying, at least not much! Considering some of the university students I'd had, he seemed to me a better-than-average risk!

And I now wonder how things have gone with him. Is he still in Syria, now during the Arab Spring uprisings? Did he manage to get a degree in agriculture? And what about the Tslas family? What is happening to them as the uprising in Syria continues [written September 2, 2011]. How terrible the Syrian Civil War is and the Isis conflict as well as the whole Middle East madness conflict today in January 2016. What about tomorrow!?

JERASH

Jerash, Jordan, the site of extensive Roman ruins (second century A.D.), reached the peak of its prosperity during the early Christian era. Bertha Spafford Vester in *Our Jerusalem* tells of visiting Jerash in 1914 and mentions that it is located not far from the River Jabbok, which Jacob of the Old Testament crossed as he returned from the land of Haran with his entourage of wives, children, and animals. Mrs. Vester's description of Jerash's fabulous monuments includes the impressive Triumphal Arch, the Forum with its colonnade of 56 Ionic columns still standing, the Temple (Beit et Tei) with columns with Corinthian capitals, the Basilica, as well as the huge theatre where mock sea battles had been fought in Roman times.

When we visited Jerash, in the spring of 1965, considerably more restoration had been done since the Vester visit mentioned above. Sitting in the marvelous amphitheatre, we enjoyed our lunch of boiled eggs and peanut butter sandwiches, observed by several young and curious Arab males. One of them was eager to show us something

— we weren't sure what, for his English was limited, and our Arabic worse — but we followed him to the "moving" or "swaying pillar." At first we were skeptical, but when the young man placed a flat pebble in the crack between the pillar and its stone base, the near-edge of the pebble moved slowly up and down, with the back-and-forth movement of the huge marble pillar! Amazing! Seeing is believing, and our young guide happily pocketed his small reward for sharing with us this unique phenomenon. In recent times the Jordanians have staged annual arts festivals in these fabulous ruins.

PETRA

In the spring of 1965, a long weekend encouraged us to make the trip to Petra, the ancient rose-rock city in Jordan. We were still a bit tired from our Iran odyssey at Easter, but needed to do Petra now if ever, since we planned to return to the U.S. shortly after classes ended in June. This meant driving through Syria, by way of Damascus, and then into Jordan. In Amman, where we spent the first night, our car was robbed — someone had cut into the canvas roof. But unfortunately for the thieves, the only thing in the car was a bright pink box of disposable diapers, which we had unwisely left in full view.

Petra, a city surrounded by towering hills of rust-to-pink-colored sandstone, was first established in the sixth century B.C. by Nabatean Arabs. Throughout the centuries various groups, including Byzantines and Romans, left their mark upon the place. After Crusaders built a small fort there in the twelfth century, Petra was lost to the outside world until the nineteenth century when it was rediscovered by Swiss explorer and archaeologist, Johan Burckhardt.

One entered Petra by way of a narrow passageway called the Sik (pronounced "Seek"). Our car was left in a parking area near this entrance, and BJ mounted a rented horse, with Natasha riding a small donkey. I walked, with one hand on Natasha's cast; it would have been serious if she had fallen off. Our minimal baggage (we were better at this in those days) was attached to the animals. A friendly little man named Musa (Moses) held the donkey's bridle and walked, leading the way; we followed. The Sik became quite narrow in places and eventually, perhaps a couple miles, the beautiful treasury building came into view. It was carved into the rock wall, as were many much less impressive buildings, which came into view as we entered a very large open area, Wadi Musa, or Valley of Moses. Especially impressive were the Roman theatre, the temple, and the monastery which was located atop a steep hill. There was so much to explore — so many buildings carved into the surrounding rock hills; but actually, one interior was pretty much like the next — big cavernous rooms, some were inhabited by Bedouin, and their flocks roamed freely about the whole area.

An interesting story about Petra was told to us by Betty Blackstone, with whom BJ once worked at a private school in Palm Springs, California. Betty's father-in-law, W.E. Blackstone, Christian philanthropist and owner of the Blackstone hotels, having visited the Holy Land, decided upon the following project. He believed that, according to the Bible, during the world's end-time, when the Antichrist would control Jerusalem, Jews would flee for their lives to Petra. Blackstone purchased a large number of Bibles and had them placed in niches carved into the stone walls of the buildings in Petra and plastered over. The idea was that the refugees would discover and read the Word of God, and thereby find salvation through Jesus Christ. But unfortunately, over the years, at least some of the Bibles were discovered by illiterate Bedouin who found many practical, if inappropriate, uses for the paper pages of the Bibles.

Our lodging choices in Petra were two. We could spend the night in either a tent or a cave. There was only one small building, which housed the archaeological team. We chose a cave, which was quite comfortable despite the intermittent distraction of several lizards (geckos?) darting across the whitewashed walls. Two camp-style single beds, a chair, and small table made up the furnishings. We had brought Natasha's fold-up travel bed. Best of all, there was electricity; a bare electric light bulb in the center of the ceiling. A good description of Petra and the cave-dwellings is given in Agatha Christie's novel and play, *Appointment With Death*, produced at the Piccadilly Theatre, London, on March 31, 1945, with Mary Clare playing Mrs. Boynton to her death.

PALMYRA AND KRAK DE CHEVALIER

It was a sunny winter day when we set out for Palmyra in the Syrian Desert. We had invited our good friend, Elma Esau, who managed the Beirut Menno Travel office, to join us for this trip. She and I were in the front, and BJ and Natasha shared the small back seat of our Karmann Ghia. As we commenced our journey along Beirut's seaside, a shipwreck caught our attention; a good- sized ship had foundered on the beach, not far from the famous Pigeon Rocks, a casualty of the previous night's storm.

Our route took us northward through Lebanon's city of Tripoli and across the border into Syria, then northeast to Homs, and straight east through miles and miles of dry, dusty desert, to what remains of the oasis Palmyra, city of palms. Tadmor in Arabic. But en route we took time to visit Krak de Chevalier, which is the largest crusader castle and sits on the crest of an elongated hill. As we drove through the village at the foot of the hill, Elma pointed out that the presence of pigs in the Middle East always means that the village is Christian, since pork is forbidden to Moslems. At the castle's entrance an elderly man emerged from the guard house/ticket office. He was to be our guide, and for the next half-hour he pointed out the castle's major points of interest. Of special interest were the nearly intact chapel and the extensive latrine, positioned high above the running mountain stream below. The Krak is an excellent example of medieval military architecture, and we thanked our guide for enthusiastically sharing his knowledge. As we continued toward our destination, we agreed that this diversion had been time well spent. In the Syrian Civil War the Krak was bombed, we understand; we hope that the damage was minimal.

Palmyra was the famous commercial center at the crossroads of ancient trade routes connecting the Holy Land, Egypt, Iraq, Syria, Lebanon, Jordan, and the Silk Road, which carried that precious fabric from China to the Mediterranean. This rich outpost was ruled in the third century B.C. by the remarkable and indomitable Queen Zenobia, who was a brilliant linguist and encouraged learning at her court. She rebelled against the powerful Romans, finally faced defeat in 274 B.C., and was paraded, in chains, through the streets of Rome. Palmyra was now reduced to extensive ruins, some very impressive, scattered over a vast area, which suggested to us the size of the ancient city.

Following the road past scattered rocks, we stopped the car in front of the only intact building in sight, a one-story, weathered concrete structure bearing the sign "Palmyra Hotel," more of a hostel or guest house, where we would be staying. After securing our room for the night, we took Natasha's collapsible stroller from the car, placed her in it (the sides were cut out so her legs, which were secured by her plaster cast, stuck straight out to the left and right in order to grow her hip socket), and started off on foot to see the nearby sights before the sun set — it was already dusk and very chilly.

A half-hour later we returned to the hotel to find it lighted by several gas lanterns, and supper, a kind of meat and vegetable stew with rice, was being served in the bleak, bare dining room. Two other travelers, probably Syrian, were at another table already eating. We were hungry and found the food quite tasty. I enjoyed a local beer while Elma and BJ had bottles of Sunalco, the Syrian not-too-bad version of Coca Cola. (Most Arab countries didn't have Coca Cola because of their embargo against companies doing business with Israel.)

As we left the dining room, Mohammad, the local tourist guide, was waiting for us in the lobby area. He was in western-style clothes except for his headdress, a red and white kafiya. He was offering to be our guide for the following day. After telling us a few interesting stories about Palmyra, and the important things to see — his English was quite good — he opened a small cloth bag that he carried. It was full of small, polished, semi-precious stones, some worked into geometric shapes. Elma and BJ each were to choose one, which they were pleased to do. BJ still has hers. It's shiny green, with ten or twelve facets, and as big as a medium-sized cherry. With these gifts given, it was time for a bit of haggling, and Mohammad and I soon agreed upon a fee for his services on the following day. He would pick us up in his well-worn van at 9:00 a.m. So, carrying a lantern provided by the manager, we went off to our cold, sparsely furnished room. There were four cot-like beds for the three of us, and the extra was handy to hold our luggage.

Natasha felt at home in her little travel bed. I went to ask for extra blankets and then disappeared long enough for the ladies to get into bed. As I recall, most of my clothes stayed on, that cold night, and it took forever to warm up enough to fall asleep.

After a breakfast of Arabic bread, honey, yogurt, and boiled eggs, we were ready when Mohammad arrived to drive us from one ruin to another. It was hard to tell what had been destroyed by the Romans and what was simply the result of time's ravages. Rows of columns lined a cobblestone road through a majestic triumphal arch. What had been a magnificent temple was now occupied by Bedouin. We explored the amphitheatre, baths and cemeteries. We thought the tower tombs especially interesting. We decided to explore the seventeenth century Arab castle on a nearby hill later in the day, after Mohammad's tour ended, which we did. In the castle ruins BJ found a black, patterned spindle whorl — damaged, but a nice memento. When it was time for lunch, Mohammad drove us to a very ethnic restaurant in a nearby village. The food was good. We noticed that Mohammad kept looking at his watch. When we'd barely finished eating, he said, "We must go now," and ushered us back into the van. We quickly drove to the edge of the village, to a small landing strip beside a small mud-brick building. After the van screeched to a halt, we could see and hear a small plane approaching. Mohammad threw his kafiya over the steering wheel, donned a black and white pilot's cap, which came from the back of the van, and ran into the small building. He emerged with two flags with which he expertly signaled the plane to a stop. After he and the pilot exchanged packets (mail perhaps?) and salutes, the landing routine was repeated for the take-off.

A guided tour isn't complete without visiting a souvenir shop; this one was a carpet shop belonging to Mohammad's brother, who was delighted to see us. He immediately sent a small loitering boy off to bring three glasses of Arab tea, which is strong with mint and sugar — delicious and notorious for getting one in the mood to buy! I parted with approximately $20 for a geometric-patterned carpet, mainly red; its quality was mediocre, but it was interesting, and a wonderful souvenir. The rug was practical for me that night, for the nights in the desert were very cold, and there was no heat in our room (which is true all over the Middle East outside the wealthy hotels). I slept under the rug, something I have often done. Years later in China I have wished for a rug to sleep under rather than the terribly heavy, local cotton-filled quilt. Even that is better than being cold! The locals stay in bed, if they can, to keep warm.

Mohammad had now fulfilled his commitment to us and drove us back to our hotel where we told him goodbye. Many years later, Elma still wonders what happened with Mohammad's wife who, he told us, had been twelve months' pregnant and still no baby!

It is sad that in 2015 a newly established ISIS army growing out of the Iraqi army, trying to recreate the Caliphate, attacked Palmyra, destroying the temple and some of the pillars. In 2016 it was discovered they were digging up graves, finding artifacts to be smuggled into Europe and sold for huge profits to finance the ISIS army. A catastrophe! The killing and displacement of the hundreds of thousands is, of course, worse, but the purloiners of history are a great loss for future scholars and persons desiring to seek the wisdom and lives of past civilizations. After driving out the ISIS army, it returned in late 2016 to destroy more of lovely Palmyra.

JERUSALEM

In 1964 at Christmastime, BJ, Natasha, and I drove from Beirut to Jerusalem. We visited several tourist attractions, including the pilgrimage to Bethlehem's Church of the Nativity, built on the spot where many believe Christ was born. On Christmas Eve we attended the midnight service at the Anglican St. George's Cathedral. The Mennonites, fifteen to twenty mostly Americans and Canadians, invited us for Christmas dinner at the home of the family who headed their work with Palestinians. We had such a good time — delicious familiar food and warm fellowship — almost like being at home. And Natasha was so pleased to get a present — a small handmade cloth doll. One of the more popular Mennonite projects was the embroidery work. The Palestinian women made beautiful cross-stitch tablecloths, runners, and panels to be inserted in garments. These embroidery products sold well back home in the U.S. and Canada.

We heard about a religious service to be held on Christmas night at Shepherd's Field just outside Bethlehem. Since it was quite cold and wet, BJ decided to remain with Natasha at the YMCA, where we were staying. So I went alone, driving into the countryside toward Bethlehem, joining other vehicles and what seemed to be hundreds of people on foot headed in the same direction. Our destination was a rather large cave in a gently hilly field. Indeed, after experiencing the place, it was not hard to believe that angels had visited shepherds near this very place, and the shepherds, following the angels' advice, sought the new-born Christ Child in Bethlehem.

As I drove along, I almost ran into, literally, a student from Beirut, whom we knew fairly well, Tom Coran. Tom was also headed for the Shepherd's Field cave. He was dressed in a burnoose cloak as it was raining. When I recognized him, I stopped the car and said, "Jump in, Tom," and he rode with me through a pasture to the cave. We crowded into the cave, which was brightly lighted with gasoline lanterns, so commonly used throughout the Middle East, with some people standing outside. We heard the Christmas story read in several languages and then joined in the singing of carols. The heavenly message, our thoughts, and the surroundings took us back two thousand years to that miraculous night that changed everything. As the crowd dispersed, the freezing chill and our tired feet brought us back to uncomfortable reality. So Tom and I found our car and drove slowly back to Jerusalem.

The first time Christmas carols were sung at the Shepherd's Field near Bethlehem was Christmas Eve, 1925, and was a result of the American Colony, Jerusalem. "There was a full moon, and the weather, which is often wet and cold at Christmastime, was pleasant." Mrs. Vester wrote that as she was walking down the hill leading from the School of Handicrafts and Dressmaking, established by the American Colony, she met a woman carrying a bundle of rags. The woman was held up by a man and an elderly woman. Mrs. Vester peeked into the rags and saw a baby only a few days old. They were trying to get to the hospital and had ridden a donkey for six hours, only to find the hospital closed for a feast day. Mrs. Vester wrote, "I was greatly touched. I thought as I stood beside the mother and child that I was rushing off to sing carols in the shepherds' fields to commemorate the birth of a babe who was born in a stable and placed in a manger because there was no room in the inn, and here before me stood a rustic Madonna and babe, and, metaphorically speaking, no room for them in the inn." She discovered that the hospital was closed to outpatients, because many of the British nurses were joining the party to sing carols. Mrs. Vester arranged for someone else to lead the singing, and she got the mother and baby into the hospital. The mother died that night while others sang of the joy at Jesus' birth. The next day the father stood at the Vester's front gate, asking if Mrs. Vester would take the four-day-old child, for he would die if the father took him home. The baby was named Noel, and with that baby Mrs. Vester started what became the Anna Spafford Baby Home. Baby Noel grew into a handsome young trooper in the Trans-Jordanian Frontier Force (Bertha Spafford Vester, *Our Jerusalem*).

This account of the celebration of the birth of Christ is interestingly contrasted by the telling of the celebration of Christmas in Bethlehem in a journal written in 1895 by Marion Harland. The crowd of worshipers and spectators stood for hours, waiting for the Bishop to finish lunch and the progressive changing of the Bishop's robes several times from black to purple, the sliding of purple gloves over fingers pointing out straight, which ended up crossing his chest in perhaps a foreshadowing of the position of death/burial. The service sensationally progressed through choir and stentoric "Gloria" organ music, arriving to the penultimate moment when a small window was uncurtained, and the worshippers sighed as a lullaby wafted its motherly tones while a baby doll was revealed in the open window. To Harland and company it was an anti-climax, but not so to the devout in that incense-laden Church of the Nativity in 1895. Marion Harland shared her wonderful account of travel in the Holy Land, published by the Historical Publishing House, Philadelphia, 1895, and entitled *Under the Flag of the Orient*.

TOM CORAN AND RICH JOHNSON

Tom was a gregarious, intellectually curious young man, whose studies at the University of Beirut were sponsored by his hometown Rotary Club in Dodge City, Kansas. Perhaps it was this last fact that first drew us to Tom, for we also were from western Kansas. Tom was interested in theatre and had taken the role of the fireman in our production of Ionesco's *The Bald Soprano*. As we were driving from Beirut to Jerusalem, on the Christmas trip described above, on the outskirts of Damascus, we quite by accident saw Tom and two friends in a field near the road. They were with a camel and, strangely enough, the camel was white. Tom laughed and said, "Well, we fed the camel all our left-over tuna fish sandwiches."They had brought a huge plastic bag of tuna sandwiches with them and had fed most of them to the camel. He added that they'd also poured beer down his throat, and all of a sudden the camel surprised them by falling over.

I asked, "Whose camel is it?"

"It belongs to the man who lives over there. We've been practicing our Arabic with him." And Tom pointed to a distant Bedouin tent.

Richard Johnson was an American friend and colleague who taught math at BCW. He was athletic and adventurous and had traveled to Beirut from Europe by motorcycle, but he had to leave the motorcycle at the Lebanon- Syrian border because of customs difficulties. Richard helped out with the theatre program in many ways and played one of the parts in *The Glass Menagerie*.

At the end of the school year, Richard hitchhiked from Beirut to India. Our friend Tom also hitchhiked, not with Richard, but alone. Riding over land, riding in trucks, sometimes taking a bus or two when available, you could do it in those days. Later on, when we lived in Iran, a number of students, or pseudo-students, made that trip, also by bus. At that time it was called the Hash Trail because of the hashish that was coming through, overland, from Afghanistan.

Tom was hitchhiking around India. Richard was also hiking around India. Separately. At the end of their travels, in the autumn when it was time to come back, Tom discovered that he had rather a large trunk, a chest, that he was carrying. He had bought it in an Indian bazaar. One day as he was walking around in an Indian bazaar in his sandals (he was a very interesting young man), he saw Richard. Richard said he had given up hitchhiking, had decided that he'd had enough of it, and so he was flying back to Beirut. Tom asked Richard, "Please, would you take this trunk for me?"

Richard didn't really know Tom very well but, amazingly, he refused to take the trunk. I've always wondered why. Perhaps it would have made him overweight. This was before the days when passengers were warned not to check-in baggage for other people for fear of drugs. Tom didn't have much money, so he had to hitchhike back to Beirut carrying his trunk. He arrived very late for classes, and he had gangrene in both feet; they said very likely from wearing sandals throughout India. At any rate, he spent the first several weeks of the university term in the infirmary recovering from his walking trip to India.

Richard told me that he had gone to Kashmir to visit the houseboats so well described by M.M. Kaye in her book *Death in Kashmir* or in the TV series *The Jewel in the Crown*. One night after a party with new friends on a houseboat, Richard found himself swimming in the lake where the houseboats are moored. It was full of water reeds and grass. His legs and feet became caught in the grass, which wrapped around his legs, pulling him down, down into the water. Richard is a strong man, tall like me, but much stronger. He finally relaxed as he thought he was drowning, and the grass let go of his legs, and he floated to the top. He said in his panic he actually thought he had met his end. He was a nicer guy after that, I think, but I still don't know why he refused to take Tom's trunk.

MENINGITIS (THE FIRST TIME)

After we had made that rather mad trip to Tehran and back, we had another weekend holiday, perhaps a week later, and BJ and I decided to make a last trip to Jerusalem. We had been to Jerusalem before, but felt we'd not seen enough and wanted another visit before returning to the States after our two-year commitment in Beirut was over. In those days Jerusalem was a part of Jordan. We had to go through Damascus, over to Amman, and then come into Jerusalem on the West Bank. This was in 1965, before the war two years later when Israel occupied that land. This final Jerusalem trip went smoothly, in beautiful weather. We again stayed at the YMCA and visited a number of the holy places we'd missed on our earlier trip at Christmastime.

Less than a week after this trip, I fell ill. It was near the end of the school year and a very busy time in any academic vocation. This school year was particularly traumatic for me because it was our last year in Beirut, and we wanted to do so much and remember so much, but I was unable to do much of anything because I had come down with something that we were not able to diagnose very quickly. I had severe headaches and was terribly ill in my abdomen. I went to my doctor, but he was not there. He was in New York at a conference. His substitute was there, and his substitute said, "Well, you drive over to this medical clinic, and they will draw blood, and make the white corpuscle count; then we will decide what to do. Very likely you have appendicitis, and then I'll take you to the hospital and let them operate."

So I drove through Beirut traffic, which was absolute chaos in those days as well as now. I finally made it to the clinic and struggled in. They drew blood. I drove back to my doctor's clinic, and the substitute doctor said, "Ah, yes, the clinic has called and the white corpuscle count is so-and-so, and therefore you have appendicitis, and we must go to the hospital."

I said, "Okay, shall I drive to the hospital?"

He said, "No, no, no. You cannot drive. You are a sick man." I had only just driven for an hour through heavy Beirut traffic, bumper to bumper the whole way, and now he says I cannot drive because I am a sick man.

He said, "I will take you to the hospital. You will leave your car here. Somebody can get it."

So we went to the hospital. They didn't check me into the American University Hospital as it was full; they were building the new, huge AUB hospital. They checked me into a private hospital that used AUB hospital physicians. AUB was, at that time, probably the finest American-trained hospital in the Middle East. I was under the care of their doctors.

By that time I had passed out. When I woke up a doctor, along with another doctor, was standing at the foot of my bed. I recognized one of them. I heard them say, "No, it is definitely not appendicitis. I think it is …" Then, oblivion again.

When I awoke, I was lying on my side, and I saw another doctor whom I recognized as our daughter's pediatrician, the brother of the first doctor I had wanted to see and who was in New York at that time. The doctor I knew was giving me a spinal tap, and I said, "But doctor, don't you have to push the needle in farther for an adult than for a child?"

He said, "Yes, a little bit. Just now you will feel a kicking of your leg." I did, and I passed out again. He withdrew the fluid for that particular test and grew the culture, which proved I had meningitis, which they suspected. There I was with meningitis, which I had apparently picked up on the trip to Tehran, and they started giving me injections of penicillin and another kind of antibiotic. As I recall, I took 85 shots. I was just so sick of the nurses coming in and giving me injections. One nurse was particularly bad about it, and she used to almost cry when she gave a bad injection because the needle would bounce out of the hip.

I was in the hospital for several weeks, and during that time the president of Beirut College for Women was told by several people that Norm Lofland was just not getting well quickly enough, and he should change doctors. Being concerned, she contacted my doctor. I had excellent specialists from AUB. My doctor said, "You are doing fine. You are being taken care of and will be okay. Don't worry about it. If you want to change doctors, certainly you can. But I want no more harassment from all of these people who keep telephoning to say that I'm not doing the right thing, and I'm not doing enough. You are progressing correctly and normally."

I said, "No, no, doctor, please don't worry about that. It's quite all right, I'm sure." And I stayed there, under his care, and slowly, little by little, became well enough to leave the hospital. Students came to our house for the final exam and to show their projects in Stage Design and Theatre. I listened to some of the final speeches in Public Speaking, and some duties were taken over by BJ and other teachers.

Somehow we got through the final semester that year. One student, a strikingly beautiful girl from Tehran, brought her design project after class when I was recovering from the Finals Evaluation session. I was at home, lying down on our very basic bed; she was ushered in by Yaffa, who took care of our daughter Natasha, and she lay down beside me, explaining her project, smiling, saying how much she enjoyed the class and asked what her grade was.

"For this design class, probably a C," I said. "Oh!" she groaned.

"But your acting grade is an A. You were excellent in *The House of Bernarda Alba!*"

"Oh!" she smiled (I felt she wanted to kiss me) and left. I saw her years later in Tehran and, after the Iranian Revolution, in Los Angeles when she asked me to drive her husband home in the Hollywood Hills after we all had escaped the Revolution.

CARNEGIE MELLON UNIVERSITY

It was a very traumatic experience because right after having meningitis the first time (I had it again seven years later) we returned to the United States, for I had received a letter from Carnegie Institute of Technology, now Carnegie Mellon University in Pittsburgh, Pennsylvania. They had not only accepted me into the Ph.D. program in Drama but had also given me a fellowship, made possible by the Heinz Food Company. That letter had been waiting for me when we returned from that rather horrendous trip into Tehran. I was quite overcome by this, although Jean Rosenthal — who lighted practically everything on Broadway from *Oklahoma!* to whatever was playing when she passed away in 1969 — had recommended that I apply to CIT "because it is the best!"

In the same mailbox was a contract to teach, also in Pittsburgh, at Duquesne University. One of the persons who had come on a State Department tour to Beirut, and with whom I had spoken a great deal, was a poet, Sam Hazo. This poet was Dean of Arts and Sciences at Duquesne University in Pittsburgh, and he had sent the contract. Both offers arriving at the same time convinced us that God wanted us to go to Pittsburgh and do my doctorate. He had even provided a full-time teaching job, which I must admit was difficult to do along with classes, but it worked out very well, in spite of the fact that I could barely walk when we arrived in the States that summer. Meningitis is a killer and can have awful after effects; I was lucky my speech cleared up! BJ also had a teaching job at a high school in Wilkinsburg, which she gave up the second year in order to take graduate courses in African Studies at Duquesne University.

So we spent the next two years in Pittsburgh. I was one of five persons admitted into the Ph.D. program. Later I learned, because BJ was working in the College of Fine Arts office, that I was one of the unusually lucky persons who was selected out of 200 applicants for Carnegie's drama doctoral program. Those applicants had to be involved professionally in the field of drama. Many of them were professionally involved in the New York theatre, a few in the educational area, but all very involved in theatre as such. I was lucky, indeed.

It's interesting that in that program I was the only one who finished within the time allocated, which was two years; two years beyond the Masters, plus years and years of experience. They gave me my diploma at the commencement ceremony. The fellow next to me also received a diploma folder, but with no diploma inside because he had to rewrite his thesis. He figured that he would have it in the summer. I suppose that they wanted two persons to stand up to receive their doctorates.

A third person received his doctorate the next year. The fourth person returned to Canada and gave up on his degree. The fifth person died. He had been a colleague when we taught together at Duquesne University, but he never finished his doctorate. Following the ceremony, we invited friends to our apartment to celebrate with sangria and hors d'oeuvres. We were happy that two members of my family had come from Kansas to share this day with us: my stepmother, Alice, and my brother, Mark. Two memorable things happened on that day of June 6, 1967. First, Israel went to war and took the now-occupied Palestine from Jordan. One of my major professors looked at all the stuff we had brought from Lebanon and the Mid-East and declared,

"Norman, protect all of these things for after today it all will be gone!" He would have been horrified had he known what happened to his home town of Damascus and Aleppo, Syria, almost fifty years later!

The other thing that happened the same time as my commencement Robing and Hooding ceremony was the announcement that Carnegie Institute of Technology was joining The Mellon Institute of Science to become Carnegie Mellon University, with what then was mentioned as the biggest endowment of any university in the U.S. I suppose Harvard questioned that.

The whole Pittsburgh experience was an interesting and rewarding one, and we felt that it grew out of our having been in Beirut with its unique opportunities and experiences. At any rate, Carnegie had offered me an amazing opportunity, made possible by a fellowship from the Heinz Food Company, and I have been most grateful for it. Every time I see the Heinz ketchup on a restaurant table, I silently give thanks for food as well as the Ph.D.

One of the problems with doing the doctorate, just after having meningitis, was that it was extremely tiring; I could hardly walk, and my motor control was affected. Sometimes my speech, and that's my professional area, was slightly impaired with almost a stutter. Sometimes this still happens when I am tired, but usually not.

Interestingly, that was not the last time I had meningitis. I had it again when we first arrived in Tehran, after completing the doctorate, after teaching in Connecticut for three years and in California for two years. We returned to the Middle East, to Tehran, to again work with Frances Gray, the same president we had worked for at Beirut College for Women. She must have forgiven my Southern accent, which we have since laughed about.

The second meningitis again left me exhausted, with a motor control problem. Tehran is a very difficult city to get around, in terms of transportation, but we did it from 1972 until the Shah left and Khomeini came at the end of 1978, and until our contract ended in 1979.

CORRESPONDANCE (1963 – 1965)

Written from the *Rotterdam* of the Holland America Line Tuesday, August 20, 1963

Dear Mom and Dad,

Our voyage is over half finished, and I've not written a single letter. We've been sleeping a great deal — think the motion of the boat makes one drowsy. This ship certainly is a nice one; there are so many lounges, etc., that nothing ever seems crowded as it did on the *Queen Frederica*, which we took last trip. The entire crew is Dutch. The food is good — the menu has so much to choose from, it's hard not to eat too much. This noon we had an Indonesian dish — a kind of fried rice with chicken, apple, and banana slices deep fried in a batter. Delicious!

There are six other people at our table: a professor and wife from Indiana Univ. who are going to England and Holland to make a study on religion in the public schools; a couple from Chicago going to Germany to visit her parents; a nurse who's going to her soldier husband in Germany, and one of the ship's officers. We feed Tasha in the cabin and then she's nearly always been asleep when we leave to eat. The cabin steward's chair is right beside our door, and he has given her a bottle a couple times when she's awakened. He has a daughter about a year old. We take her out on deck a little while each day, although there's not been much sun lately — too far north I guess. There's been a lot of mist and it's quite chilly.

Your letters were awaiting us at the boat. Kathleen and Melvin sent us a beautiful flower and fruit arrangement. We appreciated the cool weather while driving to N.Y. Think I told you that we spent one nite with Lorraine Galle in Topeka and another with Gary and Mary Yoder in Goshen, Indiana. We stopped frequently either to change or feed Tasha, drink coffee, buy gas, etc. It all took longer than we wanted, but we did enjoy it.

Our only day in N.Y. was spent buying baby food, depositing our baggage at the pier, and leaving our car at another place to be shipped. That evening Jim [Norm's brother] took us to a swanky place for dinner. We did have a good time. He was very nice — down to earth — no putting on airs. The restaurant was decorated like a castle in the time of Henry IV — suits of armor standing around, etc. There was a drawbridge at the entrance. I had Rock Cornish Hen with wild rice — delicious.

Bob Balay took us to the boat Friday morning; we left from pier 40, which is brand new and very nice. We've discovered that we can get disposable diapers and baby food on ship. There are several other babies on board — one very small one.

Tasha has been very good — eats more than usual. She loves to eat in restaurants. Right now she's playing on the floor. I spread the Pendleton robe on the carpet and put the large pillow behind her in case she falls backward. But she sits up well in her saddle splint.

We have a room reserved at the Mennonite House in Amsterdam. We hope to visit Marwood Dyck and family — he runs the travel office there. We also plan to look up the Dutch couple who lived in Welty when we did in N. Newton. [Piet and Tieneke de Graaf of Driebergen, Netherlands, who helped Norm get our VW Karmann Ghia car released when Norm forgot to take the Bill of Lading along when he went to pick up the car from Dutch customs. He felt stupid for his naïveté but very grateful to Piet!]

Friday, August 23, 1963

The ship docks at Southampton, England, in the morning; LaHavre, France, in the afternoon; and Rotterdam Saturday morning. We plan to take a train to Amsterdam, where we'll wait for our car to arrive. Our itinerary is rather indefinite — from Amsterdam we want to go to Paris, Chartres, and the Loire Valley, where so many chateaux are located. Then through southern Germany. Would like to get to Vienna if time permits — then to Italy. Write to us at Munich, Germany, so it arrives there no later than Sept. 5, and Florence, Italy, Sept. 13. We sail from Venice, Italy, Sept. 15. Send to us c/o American Express.

Amsterdam, Netherlands
Sunday, September 8, 1963

Dear Mom and Dad,

We're enjoying Amsterdam. We're staying at the Mennonite Center and it's working out well. Our car came today, so now we're free to go. Plan to leave Friday morning. The people who run the Center have been good to us; they've babysat Tasha a couple times. We have a nice crib for Tasha and she's been very good. [We dined at the "world's thinnest restaurant": three floors high and only about ten feet wide, but longer than wide.]

We ate out last nite with Marwood Dycks at a Swiss restaurant; we cooked small pieces of steak on skewers in little kettles of hot fat — heated with alcohol burners. It's called Swiss meat fondue. [Unknown in America in 1963, I guess.] Tonite when we were uptown we saw hundreds of people in a protest march about the segregation problem in the U.S.

Pete & Tenika De Graff (Dutch students at Bethel) had us over for supper one nite. He now works at the YMCA here. Sunday we went to the big Mennonite church, and in the evening a little Dutch man took us and several others on a three-hour walking tour of the old part of town. It was very interesting; he knew so much of the history.

Norman went to Rotterdam by train to get the car this afternoon. The diapers stored in it were still there, so that's good.

Lots of love, Betty,
Norman, and Tasha

Beirut, Lebanon
Monday, September 23, 1963

Well, we are finally here, but far from settled. Our ship, which we didn't enjoy very much — our cabin was such a tiny hole — were spoiled by our Atlantic crossing on the *Rotterdam* — arrived here at 6 a.m. yesterday. Dr. Odell, acting president of BCW (Pres. Gray is on leave) and his wife; the Dean, Miss Orme; the Business Mgr. (who is a member of the Church of God) and a maintenance man with pickup truck to haul our things were all there to meet us; so we were well-taken care of.

We are temporarily living in the infirmary and having meals in the school cafeteria. We'll look for an apartment this afternoon. The O'Dells had us over for supper last nite. Haven't seen much of Beirut yet, but the BCW campus is beautiful, with so many kinds of trees. Most of the buildings are of stone. Norman isn't so discouraged with the stage as he thought he might be. We hear there are many apartments available, although expensive. It seems that wealthy people invest in apt. buildings, not caring whether or not they rent.

The car came thru customs with little difficulty, and it now looks as if we can keep it here eleven months without paying the expected $400.

Elma Esau is traveling in Turkey at the moment; we're eager to see her. Marianne Fisher, from Menno Travel is coming to see us this evening.

Beirut, Lebanon
Tuesday, November 12, 1963

Dear Mom and Dad,

I just got home from classes, and have to go again tonite — to a book review. It's a book I'm to teach before long, and the students will hear this review, so I have to keep up with them! The girl across the hall will babysit. Her father teaches pharmacy at AUB, and they lived in Seattle for several years.

Yes, our building has an elevator. In our kitchen there's a sort of pantry cupboard with shelves at one end from floor to ceiling; it's about a yard wide— and one like it in the dining room (no drawers). Our bedroom has a fair- sized closet. I think we have better storage facilities than the average apt. here.

Well, the Baptist preacher was just here again (every time I write) to invite us to their house for coffee and cake tonite, but we can't possibly go. They're nice people. Norman was there (at church) Sunday. We've been taking turns lately, because it's difficult to take Tasha with the cast ... she's doing fine. At the rate she's eating, she'll likely grow out of the cast before the three months are up. She patty-cakes really well now and is just learning to wave goodbye. [She wore three different casts for a year. The casts forced pressure from the femur onto the socket so a new socket would grow. The casts rotated the leg bone so the socket would develop correctly. Dr. Boulos, trained at the Royal

Orthopedic Hospital, London, did an excellent job on a very wrongly treated medical problem! Thank God we came to Lebanon and Elma Esau knew about Dr. Boulos; Natasha would have limped her whole life, unless surgery could later correct the abnormality.]

We finally got the x-rays from the Bethel Clinic, and they show no improvement in the hip. We didn't get to see the last x-ray before we left. Why on earth did the doctor there assure us that it was improving? They're to x-ray again in three weeks, and we hope something starts to happen.

Love, Betty

Beirut, Lebanon
Wednesday, November 27, 1963

Dear Lyla and Bill,

Now that we have overcome some of the first phase of the shock of last weekend's despicable act in Dallas, we can start thinking again of things that surround us ... Friday night at 10:05 p.m. just after the opening curtain of the Anouilh version of *Antigone* (this would have been 2:05 NY time) the news reached the cast backstage and was phoned up to me in the over-the-balcony booth. The entire cast was stunned, but kept the show going. The U.S. ambassador was called out of the audience, back to the embassy. Only a handful of people knew the news — but rumors were circulating. After a few moments, the cast began to realize the irony, the apropos factors within the Anouilh play, and all of a sudden the drama became more than simply a good evening in the theatre, it became a catharsis — and overwhelmingly important for that moment.

After the show some of us trailing backstage found a cast bewildered — silent — not interested in the ovations of an appreciative audience. Fantastic the way all of this blended with the tragedy at home. It seems so far away. How strongly we would like to be home — at this time, and at many more moments in the future, I suspect: Christmas, for example.

Would you again save for us the church programs from Hollywood Presbyterian? [They included summaries of Lindquist's sermons.] We enjoyed them last year very much. Read from them nightly — for about two months.

Still haven't told you about the service taxis, the local transportation method. These large Mercedes Benz cars follow a designated route, honking at every pedestrian to locate passengers. By law, these taxis are not allowed to stop except at the end of their route, downtown next to the souk, so often times one must jump in while it is moving. Great fun.

Traffic in Beirut is impossible. Would love to see these service drivers in L.A. There are almost no traffic lights (city of 600,000 people) and all but one or two streets are one-way. These one-way streets change <u>every block</u> — they all pour onto a thoroughfare, which goes through for about ten blocks, then changes. There are about four or five of these thoroughfares. Mad — the one getting to the corner first and honks loudest gets the right-of-way. Great sport. Our horn is not working properly. Did we tell you that we brought over our Karmann convertible? It's great fun. BJ hasn't yet tried to drive in this city.

At Christmas I am going to Egypt for about twelve days. It bothers me to be away from BJ and Tasha for that long, but guess they will be alright. Plan to go with a tour — a rarity for us — through Cairo, Nile Valley, and the to- be-flooded valley in Southern Egypt. BJ may go next year. She wanted to go on either this or to Jerusalem, but Tasha is a bit of a problem. Must stop — have a class.

Later. Beirut is highly cosmopolitan. You can find anything — and anyone. There is a rather large American section. Oh, no, they don't live together, but the American community sort of migrates together for almost any function. You see many of the same people at plays, church, school, etc.

On the other hand, Beirut is not at all American or Western. One goes to the "sukh" to shop. What mad fun that is. This is the market place. Everything can be found. Tiny shops, each one having some specialty. One goes from shop to shop, bargaining ... Little old-looking men (they may be young, but look old) to carry your purchases. In fact, they will carry a refrigerator on their backs all the way to your home — in Beirut. Seriously, you see these little old men walking down the streets carrying chests of drawers, refrigerators, or loads of lumber or metal — for distances of a couple of miles or more. All for five pounds or less — about $1.50. And the costumes — not everyone wears the western dress. Many wear the local costume. Perhaps we should send Bill a pair of the pants — huge balloon seats, tiny legs, and all this drooping balloon bottom and front going together at the waist in gathers. The back of these things actually go to about two feet above the ground. You'd look dashing, Bill. I'm sure Mr. Guy [in Beverly Hills] would like to stock them.

It is noisy here. This place is loaded with peasants, a few donkeys, no camels yet, cows, dogs, men pushing carts loaded with all the things found in the kitchenware section of Woolworth's or the vegetable section of the local market or tablecloths, oilcloth, chestnuts — wonderful to eat while walking along the beach — or fruit, fish, or who knows what. Shine boys are everywhere — almost. Each of these vendors yells, sings, rings bells, blows horns, etc., to gain one's attention. Since everyone — except the landowners — live in tall apartment buildings, the vendors have to make lots of noise to reach the ears of those of us who live on the fifth-and-up floors.

As I am writing, BJ is buying flowers from a fat vending lady who carries her flowers in a flat basket on her head, and stops by the apt. each Wed. Used to stop by also each Sat., but that became too many flowers.

To add to the noise, there are schools everywhere — and noisy playgrounds. Kids yelling all the time, either outside of the ball field (kick the ball with their feet) or in the classroom where they teach by the very vocal rote method: teacher says one thing, the students repeat this — over and over and over.

Beirut, Lebanon
November 28, 1963

Hi Lyla and Bill,

At the moment Tasha and I are sitting out on the terrace, enjoying the sunshine. The climate here is much like that of L.A. I do hate for the rainy season to begin. Tasha has been in a plaster cast now for over a month, with a minimum of five months to go. The brace she'd been wearing was not correcting it — the orthopedist we go to here has an excellent reputation; he was very surprised that a brace was recommended for a complete dislocation. He uses braces too, for some cases. Makes me angry that the doctors at home didn't do this in the first place — and she'd be okay by now. She's really quite heavy to carry around [forty-five pounds with her cast], and should be learning to walk before long —

was a year old yesterday. Actually, she doesn't seem to mind the cast too much, and is quite mobile in spite of it. The worst part is the odor — she's to wear the first one for three months, and then a second one for three months. I'm expecting a third one, although the dr. hasn't suggested it.

We're enjoying our apartment, although don't have much furniture — just the necessities: two beds [pushed together], a stove, refrig. (which we had to buy new), a low round rattan table and six stools (used), a rickety kitchen table with 2 Mexican type straw-seat chairs, and a couple wood-straw type chairs for the living room. Only one bedroom, but use living room for Tasha's room, and dining room for our living room. Kitchen is very small — long and narrow, with a pantry-type floor-to-ceiling cupboard at one end, and high marble shelf along each side wall for storage. Two bathrooms — actually only one with ½ tub with shower and lavatory; other room has awful, European-type stool, with pull-chain and lavatory. [We learned how lucky we were when we used the more common squat-hole-in-the-floor toilets in the Mid-East and Asia!] Cooking here is all done with bottle gas, and water heated that way too — hate it! Keep running out and buying bottles — nuisance. Running a household here is about three times as much work as at home. I hate it!

Shopping for groceries is an ordeal, and they're terribly expensive — almost everything except fresh fruits and veg. is imported. We have no central heating — still must buy a stove — also bottle gas, and the fumes are rather bad! We have two very nice balconies, one all along the front of apt, and another sort of terrace about 12' x 14' in the back; we're on the 5th floor, and have barely a glimpse of the sea. Our view of the mountains is hidden by tall buildings. We're about five blocks from the sea.

Beirut, Lebanon
Friday, November 29, 1963

Dear Mom and Dad,

I'm teaching ten semester hours of English — two classes of freshmen and one of sophomores. Can't say that I especially enjoy it, except for the fact that it does force me to read a few novels, etc. The freshmen classes are at high school level. [By the time they graduated they were reading Great Books of literature and philosophy, since they were all Humanities majors, as well as Fine Arts. Science, other than general science, was taught at AUB; this was the understood agreement with AUB. AUB had little Fine Arts at that time.]

We hope that Norman can go to Egypt during Christmas vacation — I feel I must stay with Tasha — will take my turn next year.

The American faculty had a Thanksgiving dinner last nite — but classes proceeded as usual yesterday — no holiday. Have a woman who comes in to clean, do laundry, and babysit on Tuesdays, Thursdays, and Saturdays. She cleans well, and seems to get along well with Tasha. I had a regular broom and mop, but the first day she requested ones without handles. She is Druze and speaks only Arabic.

Lebanon has no compulsory education laws, and we understand that the few govt. schools are pretty bad. But there are all kinds of private schools — German, French, American and British as well as Lebanese. But so many of their children don't go to school — many girls are housemaids at the age of six. Our neighbors have one who looks about ten years old; it's not unusual for her to be up at 5 a.m. doing the laundry (by hand) and she's nearly always up working in the kitchen 'til 10 p.m. These people grow old early. Most of the middle class Lebanese housewives almost never lift a finger in the house. And these maids work for three to six Lebanese pounds a day. We pay ours six ($2).

Beirut, Lebanon
Wednesday, December 18, 1963

Hello Lyla and Bill,

We will both be going to Egypt for a week's tour. I at first planned to stay home with Tasha. Then several things developed: they badly needed a chaperone for the BCW tour, and a friend who's an R.N. offered to keep Tasha for us. It means a free trip for me, and I couldn't resist, although I do hate to leave Tasha. We leave this Sunday and return the following one — flying both ways. This chaperone deal could be a fiasco — these girls are really quite silly and childish; however, they are to have quite a lot of freedom to come and go pretty much as they please, providing they're in small groups. We'll stay in a Cairo hotel and make bus trips from there to pyramids, Alexandria, and I'm not sure where else. Norman and another fellow plan to leave the group in about the middle, go to Luxor and maybe on to Abu Simbel and rejoin the group in time to return to Beirut. We'll stay in a fourth class hotel, which could be awful.

Tasha is doing okay — the x-ray shows that the hip socket is now barely beginning to form, so it will probably take a long time. She's been so good — so very little trouble. The only problem is that she always wakes up a couple times during the night. I think she gets tired of her position and has to crawl around a bit now and then.

We visited Baalbek a couple weeks ago. It's the site of the principal Roman ruins of Lebanon, and really marvelous. It is far more impressive than we'd expected — comparable to the Acropolis in Athens. Baalbek is about 50 miles from Beirut. One drives through mountains and then into a valley where quite a few Bedouins wander about. We saw some of their tents, and several caravans with camels, burros, sheep, etc. Exciting for us. We are enjoying this place a great deal — if only it were not such a financial fiasco. Ah, well, we rather expected it. We've big dreams to drive to London for the summer. N. wants to attend London U's summer session. This likely won't materialize, unless we're very lucky.

Love, Betty

Beirut, Lebanon
Thursday, January 2, 1964

Dear Mom and Dad,

I don't know where the time has gone since we returned from Egypt. I did send a card from Cairo. We had a good time in spite of all the disorganization. The girls behaved pretty well, so chaperoning was no great problem. We stayed at the same hotel in Cairo the whole time (the Omayyad), which wasn't very nice, but not bad, and right in the center of the city. Went to Alexandria one day — all the way through the desert. There we saw two palaces of ex-king Farouk and an old castle fortress on the sea.

Cairo is a huge, modern city which appears more western than Beirut, although the people are more eastern. Enjoyed an hour's boat ride on the Nile. Probably the most exciting event was the visit to the pyramids, just at the edge of Cairo — with the Sphinx nearby.

Rural Egypt has changed little for a number of centuries. Farmers live in little mud huts, plow with water buffalo and wooden plows. We saw them harvesting grain by hand with flails. Many camels are used for transportation. The poor are supposedly much better off since Nasser; they seem quite happy with him; it's the rich who have "suffered." Many managed to invest in other countries, and then got out, many of them coming to Beirut.

Norman and Richard Johnson (math teacher) left our group on Christmas nite and took a train to Luxor where so many of the ancient tombs and temples are. They returned to Cairo Sunday in time to fly back to Beirut with the rest of us.

The most impressive thing in the Cairo Museum was the room housing the King Tut treasures. His mummy was in a coffin of solid gold, very ornately decorated; this first coffin was placed in a second wooden one gilt; the second within a third, and the third within a fourth. All these four looked alike except for size. These four coffins were held by four gilt boxes, each successively larger. The early Egyptian tombs were filled with all kinds of objects which they believed they'd need in the next world — everything from food to boats.

Thanks for the Christmas gifts; we had to pay only 66 cents customs for the package. Tasha likes her kitten and the put-together toy — so far all she does is take-apart.

Our maid, whom we liked very much, quit just before vacation. Through our neighbor we now have another who started today, and who we think will be as good as the other one. She wants to work six days a week for LL110, which is approx. $37 per month. Considering what our other maid coming three days a week, plus our Wed. afternoon babysitter, this is very little more. Will have her come late and leave early on the days I'm at home — Mon. Wed. and Fri. Her name is Yaffa, and she's nice appearing and pleasant. Tasha seems to like her so far. She's only fifteen, but looks older and is married. Has worked for another American family and speaks quite a bit of English. She did a good job today, and says she can cook, but don't think we'll have her do that.

Thanks for the peppernuts. We had New Year's cookies at Elma's yesterday.

Love, Betty

Beirut, Lebanon
Tuesday, January 14, 1964

Dear Mom and Dad,

Just the reading for my classes keeps me hopping — eight novels, plus the papers … next semester I'll again teach ten hours, but one class is a repeat, so less preparation. Four new novels to read for one class.

We're now gradually switching Tasha from soy milk to Carnation. Ever since she caught a cold, she's refused the bottle; drinks some from a cup. Her appetite is good. The doctor plans to change her cast to a different position at the end of this month. She'll not be hospitalized this time. She has learned to get into a sitting position, and looks so pleased with herself.

We're happy with Yaffa, the new maid. She comes at 10 a.m. on M W and F; and at 8 a.m. on T Th and Sat. She does the laundry every day — by hand and hangs it on the balcony; some people do have washers and even dryers. So far I've not seen a rubbing board in Lebanon. She washes all floors (tile) once a week, bathroom and kitchen every day; irons, washes windows, cleans cupboards, etc. She even restrung some beads for me and wants to knit sweaters or embroider things in her spare time, so I'm going to buy yarn for Tasha a sweater. We'll see how that goes.

Our apartment is beginning to look better, with curtains up — but not hemmed and a two-piece buffet-like affair lent by the school. We painted it and use it for books, etc., in the living room. We brought two cheap but nice looking rugs from Egypt: a 6' x 9' rust and beige tweed and a 5' x 7' striped. We did enjoy the Egypt trip. The girls gave very little trouble although they sure are a noisy, spoiled bunch. But it was a good deal for me, since I paid nothing for the trip. Now we hope we can get to Jordan and Jerusalem during Easter vacation, but not sure how we'll work it since it will be our turn to take care of Houk's kids. (A teacher friend and family who alternates babysitting with us on trips.) Think I'll go to their house while N and Tasha stay here the first week. We don't want her around other kids because of communicable diseases. Our doctor says a measles epidemic is starting, so we're again taking turns going to church, keeping her away from other kids. Once she's out of the cast, it won't matter so much.

We're having quite a time keeping our four gas stoves supplied with bottles of gas (two heating stoves, kitchen stove, and hot water heater.) We're using fourteen bottles per month which comes to $33 which is a lot for this small apt. and our bedroom never gets heat. They say winter lasts only three months; even now it's quite warm during the day — I wore a wool suit today — no coat.

Saturday afternoon Norman and I drove to Byblos, which is about an hour's drive. Byblos is considered by some to be the oldest city in the world and has very interesting ruins. It's right on the sea and has a crusader castle.

We hope our next little trip will be to Sidon.

We were very surprised to get a package of peppernuts from Mrs. Harrison Unruh and Emelia Bartel [BJ's mother Ruth Baerg's cousins] along with a letter from each of them!

Beirut, Lebanon
Monday, January 20, 1964

Dear Mom and Dad,

shampoo and set costs about 90 cents, including a 10% tip. Construction workers are paid the equivalent of $1 per day. I don't understand how they live. They don't have refrigerators or much furniture of any kind and seldom eat meat. Our maid has no refrig. Or stove — cooks on a little charcoal broiler. To get to work she walks an hour each way. She's knitting a blue sweater for Tasha, and I'm knitting (learning from her) a red one.

Norman went tonite to hear the Lebanese symphony orchestra. It gives regular concerts on BCW's campus. At the moment he's in the kitchen heating the milk. We buy fresh milk, which is supposedly pasteurized, but it's best to reheat it. Last Fri. nite we hired a babysitter and went to the operetta, *The Mikado*, at BCW. We've not taken Tasha out at all since New Year's Day. She's almost over her cold. It's quite important that she doesn't have a cold when they put the new cast on her because of giving her anesthesia.

The maid brought us some Syrian bread, which is interesting — round and at least 2½ feet across, and very thin. Is baked in outdoor ovens and very tasty. Our neighborhood grocer has both Arabic (flat round loaves about 8 in. in diameter) and French bread.

Beirut, Lebanon
Friday, January 31, 1964

Dear Mom and Dad,

There are no classes tomorrow — students are preparing for exams — so we're planning a little trip. We want to go to Anjar and Niha where there are Roman ruins, by a scenic route. Will leave about 9 a.m., take our lunch, and return by 4 p.m. N just now left to see if Rich Johnson wants to go with us. Next Saturday Elma Esau is going with us to Tyre and Sidon. She's been there several times and will give us a guided tour.

We have a vacation from Feb. 11 thru the 20th. I think we'll be at home most of that time. We'd like to go to Damascus one day and come back the next; that is if we can arrange for Yaffa (and her sister) to stay here with Tasha. Our friends across the hall have volunteered to supervise things here if we go. I feel that this would be much better than dragging Tasha to Houks again. She's much better off here in familiar surroundings, and accustomed to Yaffa. We're grateful for a helper who's so good with Tasha — and one who speaks English.

Yaffa volunteered to go downtown to the big market to buy fruit and vegetables, so I decided to try it. She came back with 2# apples, 2# potatoes, 2# bananas, 2# oranges, 4 tomatoes, 4 lemons, ½# shelled walnuts, 1 bunch of lettuce, 1 large cauliflower, 2# sugar, and parsley and mint for approximately

$1.80. The reason so many things are 2# is that things here are sold by the kilo, a little more than two pounds.

Beirut, Lebanon
Friday, February 14, 1964

Dear Mom and Dad,

Happy Valentine's Day! Today is the big Moslem holiday — something like Christmas. It's the feast day that marks the end of the month of Ramadan during which they fast during daylight hours. About an hour before sunrise a man comes around beating on a drum and shouting to wake everyone up so that they can eat breakfast before the sun comes up. At the month's end the drummer comes around to collect his pay for having awakened everyone.

Tasha is doing well in her new cast; was unhappy with it at first because it's more restrictive. We're disappointed to learn that she'll have to have a third cast through the summer, which makes us more eager to get to Europe and cooler weather. The next cast will turn the right leg in more, to rotate the leg. This wouldn't be taking so long if the Newton doctors had put a cast on in the first place.

We had a good overnite trip to Damascus this week. We left Beirut at about 9 a.m. and arrived there around 12:30. It's usually considered a three hour drive, although only 60 miles. Checking in at the border takes time, and there are two ranges of low mountains to cross. As soon as we arrived, we found a hotel and then went to the bazaar or market, which is huge. We wandered thru it all afternoon. It goes for blocks and blocks, winding about, and is mostly covered with a high, curved tin roof. We bought little, but the best buys were in brass, mosaic work, and brocade fabric — some of the most beautiful fabric I've ever seen, selling for from $1 to $8 per meter. We didn't buy any. We did buy an Arab outfit which included a black robe with white gown to wear underneath, a white headpiece with fancy gold band to hold it on — all for $5!

Mixed in with the shops are the tiny factories where they make most of the things they sell. Almost everything is done by hand. It was especially interesting to watch them bake the huge, flat, thin, round loaves of Syrian bread. Instead of an oven, they had something like a rounded grill and spread thin dough on it for only about a minute. Sort of like frying pancakes three feet in diameter. We also saw them doing metalwork: coffeepots, pans, etc., in little cave-like places along the street. The ceilings were so low the workers couldn't stand up.

Everything looked so ancient — very narrow, winding streets with many cave-like passageways. The buildings all joined together so that one couldn't tell where one ended and the next began. The streets were jammed with people, donkeys, carts; and on the wider streets, cars and busses. They use lots of donkeys. It rained much of the afternoon, so it was good that most of the bazaar is covered. We had supper at a restaurant near the hotel that served both Syrian and European food — cheap and good. Syria is supposed to be a poor country, and does look it, but seems to have fewer beggars than Lebanon.

The next morning we set out to find the "Street Called Straight." This street runs through the bazaar, and we followed it to an old Roman arch which used to be the east gate of Damascus. I bought a little something for you in a little shop on this street, just next to the arch; will mail it before long. Didn't see the house of Ananias, which is now a Catholic chapel. We spent the rest of the morning in the museum, a beautiful modern building with far more to see than we had time for. Right after lunch we started back to Beirut. Everything went well here at home. The maid stayed overnite with Tasha, and her husband came for the nite. The neighbor, Mrs. Abou Char, came in periodically to see how things were going.

I want to briefly tell you about our trip to Sidon and Tyre last Saturday with Elma. We left here at 8:30 a.m. and got back at 5 p.m. The drive is right along the seacoast and very interesting. Spent most of the morning wandering about in Sidon, which feels very ancient. Went through the crusader castle, and then on to Tyre. The modern city isn't much, but the excavations are tremendous. Seven different civilizations existed there: first the Phoenicians, then Egyptians, Greeks, Romans, Byzantines, Crusaders, and last, the Arabs. From Tyre one can see the mountains of Israel, including Mt. Tabor. Also saw Mt. Hermon, which is in Lebanon. Tyre juts out into the Mediterranean, and the view is beautiful. We hope to get back there sometime.

We're invited to Elma and Marion's for supper; Mary, the neighbor girl, will babysit Tasha. You asked about Tasha's talking; all she says is Mama and Dada — just jabbers a lot. I'm considering cutting bangs for her. Have been tying a bunch of hair to the side with a ribbon, which works pretty well. We're also considering coming home this fall, but some disadvantages as well as advantages. Write more of that later.

Beirut, Lebanon
Wednesday, February 26, 1964

It usually rains a time or two every day, with sunshine between showers.

Weather's getting warmer — don't usually need both stoves now.

We're busier than ever now. N. is starting on another play, as well as helping with a one-act play which is student-directed for the alumni association. I'm teaching another class this semester — so now I have two Freshman English and two of Sophomore. It doesn't change my schedule much; I'm still at home on Mon. and Fri. and Wed. a.m. and Sat. p.m.

It's so nice not to have housework to do, too. We always come home to a clean house. This afternoon when I got home,

Yaffa had given Tasha her bath, which I usually do. I don't know why she did it today, but I was glad she had, because I had a headache and appreciated the break. She is so good with Tasha that I do hope we can keep her. She is to have her baby in late May or June, and this could present problems. She plans to send a substitute for one month and then come back bringing the baby along — that's the practice here. Norman doesn't like the idea of a bawling baby in the house, but neither do we like the idea of getting a different maid. She knows that we hope to be gone for the summer months, but says that even if she has to take another job while we're gone, she wants to work for us again next fall. These maids are very eager to work for Americans. Most Lebanese work them to death, it seems, and gripe at them, never satisfied with their work. And we Americans are so happy to have a maid that we do our best to keep them happy.

Yaffa and her husband seem to be extremely poor. He works in a grocery store for little more than she earns, and they pay nearly half their combined salaries to her brother (head of the family) for letting them get married. She pays this amount (110 Syrian pounds, or $33) out of her 110LL ($36.60) when she didn't want to marry him in the first place. That leaves her about

$3.33 for herself each month. They live in one room for about $18 per month rent. Have no stove or refrigerator. Cook on a little charcoal burner and sleep on mats on the floor. So her husband says she can't go to the hospital to have her baby — it costs too much — about $28. This is as a fourth class patient, and includes several visits to the doctor beforehand. So we decided to pay it for her. Many of the Arab women, instead of paying the $28 at the hospital, stay at home and hire a midwife for 15LL ($5); the midwife remains for ten days to do housework, laundry, etc. Can you imagine doing all that for $5?

Sunday we had the Abou Chars over for supper — they're our next-door neighbors who have done so much for us; he teaches in the Pharmacy Dept. at the American University. And they spent two years in Seattle, Wash., recently. Their daughter is the one who babysits for us occasionally. Very nice people.

We still attend the Baptist Church, but take turns most of the time — measles and mumps are quite bad now. Tasha is doing fine. She's happy about everything except going to bed at nite — this just started about a week ago. I guess it's a phase. In another week or two her formula will be entirely cows' milk, so that's an accomplishment. And she's now eating an egg yolk each day. Next we start on the whites.

I made some chocolate syrup, which is good, and much cheaper than Hershey's. Norman's been wanting me to make some marshmallows — can you imagine? So he can make some Rice Krispie candy. Well, I'm glad I found some at an English market yesterday — they're from the U.S. — fifty cents for a package. We've already eaten half of them.

Beirut, Lebanon
Thursday, March 12, 1964

It's raining again, and has been rather windy today. It's not very cold, but chilly enough to have the stove going tonite. I had four classes today, which left me quite tired. N has to go over to the stage a little later to build scenery. The auditorium is in use until about nine o'clock. His play, *Glass Menagerie* comes off next week, so he's pretty busy now.

We had steak, potatoes, and artichokes for supper. Bought the steak at an Australian store — a package of eleven small frozen club steaks weighing a bit more than two pounds for about $1.33. They're good, so think I'll go back for more. Most of the meat here comes from Denmark. You wouldn't believe the sugar they manufacture here — so coarse — I'm sure that's what spoiled the last two cakes I've baked. From now on I'll buy American sugar for baking. There's also a problem with the salt — it's not iodized, and the salt companies have promoted a law against importing salt. As a result, there are many cases of goiter here.

We took Tasha to the doctor yesterday for a checkup. She's doing fine but hates to go to the dr. — starts bawling the minute we enter the building. He does nothing but look at her, but she doesn't like it. In about six weeks he'll remove part of the cast from her left leg. She loves to crawl on the floor, but it's rather hard on the cast, and our tile floors are too cold for much of that until the weather's warmer. She wants to feed herself now, and I don't have to tell you what a mess that is. [Her casts go from ankles to armpits completely surrounding her torso.]

I just finished making a dress for Yaffa — made it from a costume, and it looked so good I was tempted to keep it for a house dress, but didn't.

Last Friday Norman went with Rev. Kirkendall to the Baptist Theological Seminary in the mountains near here. Rev. K. teaches a class there and wanted N to lecture on public speaking. This is done thru an interpreter, since they speak Arabic. He's to go back another time. Says it's a beautiful place. The Baptists seem to be quite active in Lebanon. They have a school, elementary and secondary, in Beirut.

Beirut,
Lebanon March 1964

Dear Mom and Dad,

I went to church this morning, and then we both went to the University Christian Center tonite for a lecture on the cities of St. Paul. We saw slides of Tarsus, Ephesus, Perga, and other cities which Paul visited. Very interesting. Then afterward, at one of the AUB professor's house, we saw slides of Europe and the Middle East selected to coordinate with Beethoven's *Unfinished Symphony* which we enjoyed. Elma was with us.

N is relieved that *Glass Menagerie* is over. After the last nite of the play, we were invited to a student's home for a dinner party. Here, a typical dinner invitation says 8 or 8:30 p.m. and you're expected to arrive at 9 or 9:30. Then at 10:30 or later the meal is served. This student is from Pakistan, and her father is with Pakistani Intn'l Airline. There were around 30 guests, and the buffet-style meal was delicious: broiled chicken, meat balls in a hot spicy sauce, curried beef, shish kabab, rice with almonds, several green salads, and a vanilla pudding with sliced apples and bananas in it for dessert. We arrived at around 11 and left at 12:30. [We had told Nafisa Sheikh, my student and our hostess for the dinner, that we would be late, and to go ahead with dinner as we had to strike the set of the play. She waited; it became very late indeed.]

Monday: Today is Arab League Day, so no classes. It's nice and sunny, so we'll take Tasha for a drive into the mountains. Just read in the paper that Nixon is to be in Beirut part of today. He's to visit the American University and the Lebanese President. They're having a big reception for him at the Pepsi Cola Co. [Coca Cola is forbidden in the Middle East because of its connection with Israel.]

This week comes our turn to take care of Houk's kids while they go to Jordan. I'm not looking forward to that. The boy's about 2½ and the girl nearly five. I plan to sleep at their apartment and will probably bring them here for much of the day. After they return, we'll have about four days, and would like to drive to Jerusalem. We'll see. A peddler was just now at the door selling kerosene. They come around with all kinds of things.

Jerusalem, Jordan Sunday,
April 5, 1964

Dear Lyla, Bill, and Tate,
This is Jerusalem! Wonderful city — for tourists. Loads of shrines, churches, dedicated to Christ's fourteen stations

of the cross, birth, etc. — not to mention the Moslem tombs of Abraham, Isaac, Sarah, etc. Ah, the confusion of religion. Really has been wonderful making the journey but am filled to the saturation point.

The MCC [Mennonite Central Committee, actively doing relief work with needy people around the world] group here is pretty great. Feel at home with them after Bethel. Will show one around BCW next week. Today at the YMCA church service Dr. Kendall of Hollywood Methodist spoke. Had a great sermon — his whole tour group of about fifty poured into the small room half-way through the service. Little old rich ladies from Pasadena. Afterward he came up to us — after making the rounds — and introduced himself, handed his card, and went sweeping away. A far cry from Dr. Lindquist!

Tasha is doing well. Won't be out of her cast until Sept. She's into her second cast now and goes into third in June. We hope to get to England for the summer. Won't make it if we keep spending money in the Middle East. Still looking for something for you. Wonderful brass and copper ware in Damascus.

Norm

Elma Esau, MTS [Menno Travel Service] agent in Beirut, came with us and has been an excellent guide. We'll go home tomorrow by way of the Dead Sea and Jericho. These Arabs are really impossible. I hope we can get out of here for the summer. I'm teaching full time (12 semester hrs.) this semester. Don't like it, but need the money so.

Love, Betty

Isfahan, Iran
Wednesday, April 15, 1964 (postcard)

Dear Lyla and Bill,

   Iran is quite wonderful, but never again by car. So many miles of nothing. Isfahan with its blue-tiled mosques and exciting bazaar should have far more than ½ day plus one nite. We haven't enough time! Tomorrow we'll attempt to see the "shaking minaret" and then on to Shiraz. Remember Aziz Nabavi, our neighbor in L.A.? We saw him yesterday in Tehran.

Love, B and N

Beirut, Lebanon 1964

Dear Lyla and Bill,

   Today was election day for Beirut, and everything still seems to be under control. They told everyone to stay at home except those going out to vote — afraid of outbreaks, riots, etc., and they didn't want to have to call in the U.S. Marines again to restore law and order as at the last election six years ago. You should see the thousands upon thousands of election posters plastered all over Beirut — plus the usual type; there are many actual photographs and more awful paintings. They all look so masculine and successful behind their big black moustaches. One has to put up quite a lot of money just to run for an office, and it's common knowledge that these politicians pay for their votes. [Almost twenty years later during another election, a man at the gate of a large palace (house) tried to usher BJ into the house as she passed by. We learned later that the servant thought she had voted for the candidate living in the house and was paying her off. Probably helped the economy.] The people (voters) look forward to elections as times to make some money. At least three candidates' homes have been bombed and one candidate's car shot at. Which reminds me, is the race problem as bad at home as we've been reading? Mainly in *Time Magazine.*

Love, Betty

Beirut, Lebanon
Tuesday, May 5, 1964

Dear Mom and Dad,

I bought Tasha a couple more dresses — warm ones for England. One is a red heavy cotton smock with long sleeves, and the other a heavy Dacron and wool, drip dry in gray with red trim. Her three new summer dresses are basically blue. Tasha now points at things and says "thee;" we hope she means "see."

We have another holiday tomorrow and plan to go to Beaufort Castle. It's located near Tyre and supposed to be interesting, and from it one can look over into Israel. Elma and Marion plan to go with us; hope we're not too crowded. We had another holiday last Friday and Norman and I drove into the mountains to Beit Eddine, which has an old Arab Palace from which Lebanon was ruled at one time. The mountains are beautiful and look much like the Rockies in places.

Well, the election is over without any catastrophes. For two nites after the Beirut election day, we had difficulty sleeping — so much noise, fireworks, etc. The winners had paid around $100 per vote. It's really terrible. Then after they're in office they make all this money back through crooked deals, etc.

Beirut, Lebanon
Sunday, June 21, 1964

I must tell you about our experiences of the last two days. Remember to never go to Syria unless you simply fly into Damascus and out again. Believe me, Lebanon is Paradise in comparison to Syria. We left Beirut for London yesterday at about 11:30 a.m. and planned to spend the nite in Syria since we got a late start, and visas are cheaper if you stay overnite. Most people don't stop until arriving in Turkey (which I'm not sure will be much improvement). What a hot, rough ride to Latakia, a port town.

The tourist office there suggested two hotels, which Norman looked at. The first room rented for the equivalent of $1.60 for both of us (we carry a travel bed for Tasha). He said they promised to change the filthy bedding. (They explained that motorcycle men had slept there the previous nite.) The second hotel rented a room for $2.30 — including three beds, although we didn't use one. The bedding looked quite clean, so we took it. Hot showers were extra; so when N. went to shower, they said it would be awhile before the water would be hot — they heated it with kindling! So he had a cold shower, and I had a cold sponge bath! [How Syria improved itself until it had a civil war in 2011 and destroyed all their new high-rise buildings!]

We had dinner in a next-door restaurant, which was "sort of clean," with five or six guineas (something like chickens) wandering among the tables, looking like they expected bits of food. N. ordered beefsteak and I, shish kabab. They immediately cut the meat from a carcass hanging in the front window and cooked it in the open oven at the back. The food wasn't bad, but we nearly did ourselves in with our "purex-disinfected" water. We got mixed up and put two drops into each glass instead of two drops per quart! We asked what they served for breakfast, and they said hummus (a paste-like dip made from chick peas, oil, and spices) and foul (beans).

Well, as it turned out, we didn't worry about breakfast — left in too big a hurry. Early this morning, Tasha fell off a bed and cut her chin. I won't go into details — it was due to my carelessness. It looked like a bad cut — probably needed stitches, and there we were in that awful hole of a town — a good five hours of hot, bumpy driving (part of the roads aren't bad) from Beirut. Perhaps it was silly to drive clear back; perhaps it was stupid to take her to a doctor who didn't use sterile instruments. Well, we did drive back. Took her to the American Univ. Hospital emergency room; they called a plastic surgeon, and he stitched it up. (Twelve stiches!) He said we did the right thing in bringing her back. If not properly treated, could develop a serious infection, bad scar, etc. He's going to check it tomorrow, and then possibly we'll start out again early Tues. morning.

Oh, yes, just after we crossed the border into Syria, the car kept stopping — great! We'd just had it all inspected. To make a long story short, an "electrical specialist" in a small town put a new ignition in, for which he charged too much, discovering that we were Americans. But amazingly, the car works fine now. Norman is convinced he put in a tractor ignition, but so long as it works, fine …

Love, Betty

PS: Our London address for the time being is c/o Menno Travel Service. We'll arrive there July 6 and stay until Aug. 21. Then, hopefully to Scandinavia and back to Beirut. We've decided that once up by car is enough. (Will tell you later about being robbed in Ankara — lost nearly all our clothes!)

Norm

London, England
Friday, July 17, 1964

Mom and Dad,

The postal workers are on strike here, and almost no mail is coming in or going out. The Kwan family, with whom we're living, is leaving this afternoon for a week in Germany, so will send this letter with them to be mailed from Germany.

We are fine. Tasha especially likes it here — she wants to be out in the yard all the time, so that takes a lot of my time. The kids entertain her some and she's crazy about Topsey, the dog. I usually move the playpen outside. I'm to look after

Topsey and water the plants while they're gone. Shouldn't be too bad; the dog's quite well-behaved.

Norman is already a little tired of the 15 min. walk to the subway, and then 45 min. train ride to his class every day. I went to meet him Monday afternoon, and we went shopping. I found a couple skirts and sweaters which were on sale.

We went to church with the Kwans Sunday at the Mennonite Center. It's mainly a group of Americans — small group. Some friends from Beirut are traveling thru England, and Monday evening we all saw a play together.

We're very fortunate to have a reliable babysitter, but it would be nice to live closer in. This house has very pretty front and back yards with lots of flowers — mainly roses and hydrangeas, with hedges enclosing the whole place. The house is old, but nice.

What is happening in the U.S.? Is Goldwater as bad as so many people here, in Germany, and throughout the Middle East think? He and the Republicans are getting terrible publicity abroad. They believe that he's another Hitler or Mussolini. We're afraid the Republicans have made a serious mistake. What do you think? One of Elizabeth Wiebe's nephews, who's majoring in history, has carefully studied Goldwater's writings and says they sound very much like Hitler's *Mein Kampf.* Do the people really know what he is, or are they so eager for a change that they are behind any fanatic that will bring it? I sure hope things aren't as bad as we hear.

I'm learning to cook a few Chinese dishes; since Mr. Kwan's Chinese, they eat quite a lot of it. There's a small shopping center about two blocks from here, which is convenient. But shopping here is worse than in Beirut except that food is cheaper. They need supermarkets — there are very few.

Vienna, Austria
Monday, September 7, 1964

Dear Mom and Dad,

We're enjoying Vienna, although find it rather expensive. It's a lovely city and very much changed since I was here nine years ago. We're staying in a very old but nice hotel. Building is supposed to be 400 years old, and used as a hotel for 200 years. It's about a block from St. Stephan's Cathedral, and near the main shopping area.

It rained lightly most of today. This morning we went to see Schönbrunn Palace. The gardens are beautiful. Tonite N went to the opera. I don't mind at all staying with Tasha — much rather than go to the opera alone.

We arrived in Neustadt Thursday early evening, and again had a nice time there. They seem to be fine. Elizabeth would like to visit the Holy Land while we're in Beirut, but it's doubtful that she will. We left there Sat. late morning and drove to Munich, then on to Vienna Sunday (yesterday). We plan to leave here tomorrow morning and get as far as possible into Yugoslavia. The road thru Yugo. is excellent, and they have fairly nice motels along the highway. We had hoped to avoid Bulgaria because of the bad roads, but that would mean going thru Greece. We think crossing the Greek-Turkish border might be difficult right now, so will probably go thru Bulgaria again. If so we'll likely stay in Sofia again — it's a nice city — we had a good hotel there last time. We should be in Beirut approx. one week from today.

It's really too bad we couldn't be there for your anniversary. Didn't realize it was your 40th until we got Kathleen's letter. Were afraid the card wouldn't arrive in time, so sent the cable, which should have arrived on Saturday. Your letter and the package with girdle and pants were waiting for us in Neustadt. Thanks! Norman just returned from the opera and says he had to stand the whole time because he couldn't see sitting, but loved the production.

Lots of love, Betty,
N, and T

Beirut, Lebanon
Sunday, September 13, 1964

Dear Mom and Dad,

[W]e drove pretty long and hard every day. We arrived here tonite at about 7 p.m. Left Tarsus at 7 a.m. We stayed at the American School in Tarsus. The principal and his wife invited us to have supper with them last nite, and it sure tasted good! We'd been eating so much from cans we had with us. [Going, we stopped in Antioch, Turkey, just over the border from Syria.]

We're glad the drive back is over. The distance is about the same as that across the U.S., but seems farther because of the roads, and the trucks, wagons, livestock, people, etc., on the roads. Turkey is especially difficult, and quite a bit of the road was torn up. Most roads in Yugoslavia are good, and we spent two nites there in a very nice hotel in Maribor, and a rather awful motel on the freeway; however, the beds were clean. It was filled with mostly German tourists who were really complaining about the place. All the lights went out twice for about ten minutes. At the Bulgaria-Turkey border we stayed in a nice motel. We're not fond of Bulgaria, and their roads aren't good — mostly brick roads and very bumpy. We did almost no sightseeing this time — just drove. Had excellent weather although the last two days have been quite hot. Tasha travels very well; has her travel bed to sleep in each nite, the mattress of which she travels on during the day. [She was secured with a seat belt on the jump-seat behind our two seats.]

Zenobia Hotel Palmyra, Syria
Saturday, November 21, 1964

Dear Mom and Dad,

Monday is a Lebanese national holiday, and no classes, so we're taking advantage of it at Palmyra, Syria. Elma came with us, and we left Beirut at 8 this morning, and arrived here at 2:30 this afternoon. Was raining when we left home, but is quite nice, although chilly here. This is really a marvelous place — thirteen miles of ruins — some in good condition. A beautiful crusader castle stands on a high hill. We didn't have time to see much today— more tomorrow. Then back to Beirut on Monday.

This hotel — the only one here — is small and nothing fancy, but okay. But I do wish there were some hot water! The hotel has only one double room, so Norman is sleeping in one of the lounges on a bed which they'll set up. I hope there are plenty of covers on the beds, for it's getting pretty cold outside. Put Tasha to bed at about six o'clock — before we ate supper. She seemed to enjoy the drive. Brought her travel bed and stroller.

Palmyra is in the middle of the Syrian Desert — about one hundred miles from a town of any size. It is said that Palmyra, then called Tadmor, was started by Solomon.

We had an unfortunate incident at BCW last week; one of the girls was shot by her boyfriend. The story is that her parents (Christian) refused to let her marry him (Moslem). It seems that this type murder is not uncommon in this area. The girls were all quite upset about it.

The American faculty is again having a Thanksgiving dinner at school, although we have to teach that day.

A bearded Arab just came around with a bunch of "antique" jewelry. We didn't buy, but did agree to let him guide us around tomorrow. As he left, he gave me a polished stone which I was interested in for my chain bracelet. Eleven people just arrived, so now they're putting up a third bed in our room.

[This bearded man also met the one airplane that flies into Palmyra, as we discovered the next day.]

Love,
Betty

Beirut, Lebanon
New Year's Day 1965

Dear Mom and Dad,

We had a wonderful trip to Jerusalem. Our classes ended on Tues., Dec. 22, so we left Beirut about 9:30 a.m. Wed. The weather was good the whole time. The only sizeable town on the way was Damascus; we packed our lunch and stopped only for gas. Got to Jerusalem at 5:30, just as it was getting dark. Had reservations at the YMCA, and our room was very comfortable — private bath and central heat. Thurs. morning a student who lives near Jerusalem showed us around a bit — museum and part of the old city, which is all enclosed by a wall. Late that afternoon Norman went to the Shepherd's Field service held in a cave near Bethlehem. They had a worship service and then served roast mutton sandwiches. He said it was quite nice. I didn't go because I thought Tasha was coming down with a cold, which disappeared by the next day. On Christmas morning we ran into an American friend [Tom Coran, Dodge City, Kansas] who goes to school in Beirut [AUB], and we all drove up to the Mt. of Olives and enjoyed the marvelous view of Jerusalem. Then we went to a service at a Lutheran church inside the old city. I spent most of the time outside with Tasha.

We had Christmas dinner at the MCC house, invited by the Herb Schwartzes. All the MCC [working with the refugees] people were there, and they served a huge, delicious meal — turkey, chicken, dressing, etc., ending with pumpkin and mince meat pies. We all brought gifts for a grab bag, and

Tasha got three packages, including a couple of small dolls, a couple of books, and candy. We were very surprised by it all.

After leaving there, we went for tea to a student's home in a village near Jerusalem. Three other BCW teachers and we had decided to have supper together that evening at a new hotel on the Mt. of Olives. So that was too much food for one day. On Saturday we walked around in the old city, pushing Tasha in the stroller. It was a bit difficult sometimes because of the many steps up and down, but she really enjoyed all the children, donkeys, etc. On Sunday we drove to Amman, which is just a dirty city except for a huge Roman amphitheatre in the center of town. Amman used to be the Biblical Philadelphia and is now the capital of Jordan. [Amman has since become a thriving city — now (2016) perhaps overrun by the Syrian refugee problem and the wars around Jordan. Hopefully this war won't come to Jordan.]

Then we drove on to Damascus, where we were to meet a friend [Dr. Aida Tomeh] from Beirut and who teaches at BCW; she was in Damascus to shop. We stayed at a small hotel run by her aunt. It was cheap, but not the best. No hot water in our room, and a small oil-burning stove, which wasn't too bad. The aunt, who ran the hotel, babysat with Tasha Mon. afternoon while we shopped in the bazaar. With part of the money you gave us, we bought a small Druze chest — walnut with carving on the front; it's similar to a cedar chest, but opens from the front instead of the top. We also bought a book, *Shorter Atlas of the Classical World*. Thank you very much! We also stayed Mon. nite in Damascus, and drove back to Beirut Tues. morning. Spent a quiet New Year's Eve and New Year's Day at home.

Beirut, Lebanon
May 1965

Dear Mom and Dad,

Tasha is sitting here beside me on the sofa, going thru the box of stamps we've collected. It's one of her favorite pastimes. She's learning to brush her teeth now, and you can imagine what that's like. It's more playing in the water than brushing, and she'd do it five or six times a day if we'd let her. We were going to go to the horse races with Elma, the Yoders, and two others, but Norman feels he's too busy helping with a variety show on campus, so I'll not go to the races either. I'll help Yaffa babysit the Yoder's baby.

Beirut, Lebanon
Tuesday, June 29, 1965

Dear Mom and Dad,

Norman is beginning to feel better — still tires easily, but I think he'll be ready to fly by at least the 10th of July. The doctor says he's okay — just needs to exercise more. So we've been walking some. [This, after recovering from meningitis.]

Tasha went to the beach with Hajjars today. She really likes to play with their kids. Tomorrow we plan to go to the beach with another couple from school. It's been very hot during the day but cools off at night.

Dr. Gray, ex-president of BCW, leaves Beirut tomorrow and a large group are going to the airport to see her off. I'll not go, but N. may if he feels up to it.

We have nearly everything packed now. We'll likely be here at least until July 8, and in Amsterdam until July 13, so you could write to us there.

CHAPTER 3

PITTSBURGH (1965 – 1967)

We arranged to return to the United States by way of Amsterdam and Dublin, Ireland, so that I could visit several spots connected with James Joyce. An airlines strike made it possible for us to enjoy a long, beautiful drive across Ireland, from one airport to another. We flew directly to Kansas to visit family. Then BJ flew to Pittsburgh to begin her teaching job at Wilkinsburg High School, while two-and-a-half-year-old Natasha and I drove the Volkswagen Squareback (which I had picked up from the port at Houston, Texas) from Kansas to Pittsburgh, with Natasha crying much of the way. That drive from Kansas to Pittsburgh was not a pleasant one.

We had sent from Beirut a sizeable shipment of household items — wicker table and stools, safari chairs, mosaic game table, Iraqi tapestries, pottery, and baskets. This arrived in a large wooden crate, which stood outside our apartment building until I was able to turn part of it into a dining table on which I wrote my Ph.D. dissertation. The furniture at our Carnegie Tech apartment was minimal.

Among the many exciting experiences at Carnegie was the Christmas pageant I directed two Christmases for the Anglican-Episcopal Cathedral. A beautiful theatrical staging of the Christmas story presented in the stained glass English — I think — Gothic church with a carved rood screen in which we placed six, lovely, female angels with spreading wings, who, on cue, as Mary rode her burro led by Joseph, swooped their winged arms toward Mary. The audience gasped in joy as the winged angel Gabriel mimed the horns blasting from the glorious pipe organ and the rood-screened angels swooped over the Mother of Jesus. The production was deliciously lighted by Bill

Matthews, Carnegie graduate and tech man for the Seattle Opera Company. The rood screen was reminiscent of those carved by Riemenschneider in Germany.

I taught full time, Speech and Theatre Production for which I produced Beckett's *Waiting for Godot*, Albee's *Sandbox*, Archibald MacLeish's *J.B.*, and other theatre experiences. They were a busy two years with Ph.D. classes and writing a dissertation and typing the final copy myself on a neighbor's IBM.

Unhappy with her teaching job, BJ, during the second Pittsburgh year, took graduate courses in the School of African Affairs at Duquesne University, where I taught full time both years. However, after one semester, because of financial problems (Duquesne University — at the request of my department chairman — chose not to continue her tuition waiver as a faculty wife), she took a part-time job in the Carnegie Fine Arts Department. Natasha spent two happy years in Pittsburgh. She was accepted at an excellent government- operated day-care center (they needed white kids to get the place integrated), which was an experience that she loved. At the end of the second year, I graduated with a Ph.D. and had signed a contract to begin teaching in September at the University of Bridgeport, Connecticut.

CORRESPONDANCE (1965 – 1967)

Pittsburgh, Pennsylvania
Monday, September 6, 1965

Dear Lyla, Bill, and family,

Strangely, I'm finding Pittsburgh more difficult to adjust to than Beirut was! At the moment I hate it, but things will improve.

I dislike my job, not because I'm teaching new subjects … but because the administration treats the faculty like children. For instance, no coffee machine for faculty because they're not paying us to drink coffee; no pay for sick leave without signed document from a doctor; must have permission from the Supt., no less, to leave school before 4 p.m. (classes end at

3:30); teachers supervise lunch rooms, after school detentions, etc. I keep comparing with L.A. and even Newton and am furious. I also have 1½ hrs. study hall supervision each day besides my five regular classes (2 of world geog. (not bad), 2 of sales (bad), and one of typing (ok).) The amount of paperwork is disgusting. My school is in Wilkinsburg, about a 20-25 min. drive thru rather bad traffic. [In winter the snow was so heavy even the trolley had difficulty getting her to school and driving was treacherous!]

Our apt., which will be quite nice once we get our things into it, is very near Carnegie Tech, where Norm's classes are. (At the moment their football team is noisily doing warm-ups in the field directly across the street.) We have two bedrooms and pay $150 per month, which is more than we can afford.

Norman and Tasha aren't here yet — but are now on their way. The ship on which the car came to Houston was late, so N. had to wait for it. We had purchased air tickets from Beirut to Houston, so were able to convert my Houston part to Pittsburgh, so I could fly here in time for my meetings and classes.

The one recommended full-day nursery school in the area has been closed for vacation — opens tomorrow, so I'll call but opinion is that it's full-up. It's community chest-subsidized and charges $18 per week. Somehow this seems high, but of course I don't really know what to expect.

Yes, Norman had spinal meningitis in May. In the hospital only eight days, but could do nothing but rest for about three more weeks. We were beginning to wonder whether he'd make it home before fall, when all of a sudden he began to improve. What a relief that was. Because of this, our trip home was very limited. We stopped only in Amsterdam and Dublin (his interest in James Joyce). [Norm's Master's Degree in Drama included an interpretation and production on stage of a dramatized Joyce's *Finnegans Wake*.]

It's great that you're planning on Europe in the spring. By all means, don't let the travel agent make your hotel reservations. $26 per nite is atrocious for Spain, or any other place … Get Frommer's *Europe on $5 a Day* and write directly to hotels, once you get your itinerary planned. Spain is becoming more expensive, but I'd say $6 or $7 per nite should be top price. We paid, as I recall, $3 or $3.50 for a nice double in Madrid. You will love The Prado, the art museum in Madrid. It's small but excellent! Concerning clothes to take: For Lyla, I suggest a wool suit, another skirt, several drip-dry blouses, cardigan sweater, a dressy dress, and a lighter weight dress (possibly drip- dry) for Italy where it will be warmer; two pair of walking shoes — one a bit dressy. For Bill, a suit, couple pair of trousers, sport jacket, cardigan sweater, several drip-dry shirts. The lighter you travel the happier you'll be. And you may want to buy things en route. [What wonderful experiences we had in 1961; beautiful hotels in Spain in converted monasteries and other splendidly tiled and carved architecture for those amazing prices!]

Yes, seeing Rome is a must; besides the Sistine Chapel, see the Vatican Museum and the statue of Moses by Michelangelo, which is in a church called St. Peter in Chains. It's marvelous. And you must see Florence; this is one place we're so mad we've not gone back to. It's tremendous! All the art there is unbelievable. It's #1 on our "return-to" list. There are some lovely old hotels right on the Arno River for $5 or $6 per nite per double. Florence has scads of antique/junk shops. We didn't know much about these when we were there. Be sure to visit the museum called The Academy, which has so many of Michelangelo's originals, including "David." The Cathedral is lovely, and the original of the famous "The Annunciation" is in Florence.

And do try to reserve one day to take a train or bus to Sienna, a marvelous medieval town famous for its cathedral and city hall. It's really worthwhile.

Love, Betty

PS: I forgot to mention that you'll want to take a light-weight raincoat.

Pittsburgh, Pennsylvania
Friday, December 23, 1966

Dear Lyla and Bill,

Can you imagine, I have seven research papers and a seminar report due before semester's end, plus the three papers I've already turned in, plus five book reports. Since the English Master's entailed much more than a year's work, I'm taking courses (at Duquesne Univ.) toward a Master's in African Affairs — more or less for "fun"?! It's actually quite dull and disappointing— could be fascinating, but have several lousy professors — boring — several with such heavy accents it's impossible to understand much of what they say. I'm taking History of West Africa, Educational Problems in East Africa — both taught by Brits; Politics of African Nationalism, by a Yugoslav; Cultural Anthropology and Social Organization, both by a Czech priest who's impossibly dull and says that "Africa has no history;" and last but far from least, Arabic taught by a Spaniard whose thick accent (Spanish) kept me so in the dark for several months that I've never caught up. At least I like to blame it on that. It's horribly difficult — we're "learning" to read, write, and speak it!

I'm seriously considering going back to teaching in a high school for the second semester — much as I hate it. I'm not interested in pursuing this African bit since I've discovered that the African literature course won't be offered.

Norman hates his job (Duquesne theatre dept.), as we expected; I won't attempt to describe the idiot he has to work with. We knew he was an idiot before signing the contract, but thought it so important to remain in the area until the degree is complete. Now they pile so much work on Norman he hasn't time to write his dissertation. Next semester he'll do more class work (teaching) and less directing, so we think he'll have more time to write.

Love, Betty

Pittsburgh, Pennsylvania
Saturday, March 25, 1967

Dear Lyla, Bill, Tate and Todd and Courtney,

Am sick to death of the weather; we've had snow daily until today, and today it's like L.A. in the winter. We've written sixty letters for jobs, chiefly to California, New York; now we're desperate, and I wrote K.U. I'm going to write Hays State next! In desperation I wrote this passionate letter, pouring out my frustrations, to Dr. Butler (he was so nice to me in Chicago at Christmas) wanting a job at SC — or anywhere he could suggest! He wrote back this straightforward letter: Norman, you must publish! (And added, and I don't think you're ready for that yet!) The B! [Dr. Butler, Chairman of SC Theatre, was happy with my Master's thesis production; so happy that he chose to use the written thesis for future thesis productions at USC Theatre, so I was told by faculty members of the SC Theatre. When SC asked me to direct the Passages from Finnegans Wake at the Edinburgh Festival in 1968, the thesis was used by the crew, and it looked well-worn, indeed!]

So my Ph.D. dissertation is going to be sent out to every publisher in the country, section by section, until every chapter is turned down by everyone — even the lowliest! (And we might then know who is the best, and the worst!) [I never bothered to send any of it to anybody, although it was recommended by the head of Carnegie's Department of Theatre that "this dissertation should be published; I see nothing wrong with it." This from the former editor of The Tulane Drama Review.]

Dissertation! Am about one-third finished with it. Have only been writing for about a month now. Must finish off this section on Waiting for Godot (am now dealing with the sexual allegory in it! I need to include something on sex to get the degree, thanks to my advisor!) and start on King Lear and then House of Bernarda Alba. Something in all this must be of value! Somewhere! Maybe I'll have to go back to the ME to be recognized! The Ph.D. ought to be handed to me in June, 1967! Thank God it's finished! I hope. Now I want to get started on a cinema study. Hence Southern California, aside from the climate, friends (whom we miss terribly!), and salary!

BJ is no longer in the African Affairs program at Duquesne University where I teach (only until June; I resigned!), but is now working half-time at Carnegie Tech in the Painting and Sculpting Department of the College of Fine Arts. She loves it and is tempted to pursue a Doctor of Arts degree in Fine Arts — but won't, because we won't be here long enough. She left the African Affairs study because she could get no literature, art, or drama of the African tribes. She got all "A"s in her classes. Wild time getting all eleven papers written. That's really why she left it, I think. I think she should try to publish the one on African drama (under my name, preferably, so I can get a job! Or else get good enough at it so she gets a job, so I can just write and direct for some non-paying venture — ah, such a romanticist!)

I am still teaching at the girls' finishing [modeling] school. Taught an acting class today. Such madness!

I'm run down, so I'll sign off. Write.

Love to you all,
Norm

PS: We'll likely be in Kansas most of the summer. N's dad is going back into oil and activity is picking up at the ranch. I dread summer, although N. looks forward to it — he never sees as far ahead as I do. It looks like we'll not find a job in Calif. — it seems that Reagan's budget cut limited jobs considerably.

Love, Betty

CHAPTER 4

CONNECTICUT to CALIFORNIA TO IRAN (1967 – 1972)

University of Bridgeport and College of the Desert, *Finnegans* Wake,
Invitation to Tehran, Taliesin West, Travel to Iran, Tunisia,
Libya, Tripoli, and Leptus Magna, Egypt, Cairo, and Upper Egypt,
Back to Cairo and Hotels, The Bazaar and Balloon Theatre,
A Job Offer, Beirut, Arrival in Tehran, Meningitis (Again), Persian
Food, Tehran Transport,
Rumbles of Revolution

UNIVERSITY OF BRIDGEPORT
AND COLLEGE OF THE DESERT

In 1967, after having been in Beirut and at Carnegie Institute of Technology (now Carnegie Mellon University) in Pittsburgh, Pennsylvania (1965-67), we moved to Bridgeport, Connecticut, where I taught for three years at the University of Bridgeport. During this time, in addition to teaching a full load in the Department of Speech and Theatre, the burden of chairmanship of the fifteen faculty departments fell onto me. And during this time at the University of Bridgeport, BJ earned her Master's Degree in Middle East History. Then in the autumn of 1970 we moved to Palm Springs, California, and there, while teaching theatre and speech at College of the Desert, I established and directed the Palm Springs Festival of Drama, along with Henry Bacher, the wife of Hollywood film director, Bill Bacher. Thanks to

Dr. Roy Hudson, my former professor and Chairman of the Department, I was invited to direct Die Fledermaus for Lily Pons and the Palm Springs Opera Guild, using the orchestra and singers from the Los Angeles Civic Light Opera Company, now the Los Angeles Opera. Sets were designed and executed by New York designer Jane Putnam, who did excellent costumes and enormous drops for my sets for Finnegans Wake in Holland.

FINNEGANS WAKE IN EDINBURGH

I had first produced and directed it as a Master's thesis production at the University of Southern California in 1960. Curiously, the thesis I had written, strongly guided by Professor James A. Butler, became the model for all of the thesis productions that followed. No doubt that was why Dr. Butler had given me such a hard time in the writing. Professors John Blankenchip and Bill White were the guiding lights in the actual mounting of the production. They were so pleased with its success at the USC theatre that they asked me to come to the Edinburgh Festival of Music and Drama, Edinburgh, Scotland, and direct it again for their California Theatre Fringe production in 1968. During that Edinburgh summer season we did fifteen shows in five weeks, and built a theatre inside a girls' school at the same time. It was a marvelous venture that made Edinburgh-Festival-Fringe history. Hans DeWitte, head of the Holland Music and Drama Festival, was in Edinburgh and saw the productions, including Finnegans Wake. I met Hans, and we kept in touch.

FINNEGANS WAKE IN BRIDGEPORT

The next year, 1969, I decided to do Finnegans Wake again, this time at Bridgeport. This thought was further encouraged by Rita Hassen, a Broadway theatre producer who was teaching an advanced acting class at the University of Bridgeport. She and her husband, Ira Blue, a New York lawyer specializing in theatre production business, thought the possibilities were ripe to take the show to Amsterdam for the Holland Festival of Music and Drama. Hans had told me that if I put it together again to contact him so that he could do the leg work in getting it cleared by the Holland Festival committee.

The production in the campus little theatre was exquisite. Rather more surrealistic than the productions at either the Edinburgh Festival or the USC theatre, which had been more Irish and realistic. We decided that the music of the Joyce language was Irish enough, and that elucidation was impossible. We decided that a bit of guidance through imagery might be gained by letting the music of Joyce's words help speak the visual images we wanted to communicate to our audience. In Holland we did not have actor John Ritter, an excellent comic actor who subsequently was headlined on TV in Three's Company, who played in the California Edinburgh production, to add comic elements that Joyce may have approved of. We did, however, have the expert design of Jane Rowe Putnam, not yet married to John Putnam, the art director of Mad Magazine in New York. John was a fine artist, and a sensitive film and stage buff, as well as a satirist in the Mad genre. He and I later worked on a stage production of Theda Barra films. Unfortunately, I went off to Iran before we could get it pulled together. John also photographed excellent material for a production of the life of American Shakespearian actor Edwin Booth; more of that later.

Jane agreed to design the costumes for Finnegans Wake at Bridgeport. She joined us in our Milford, Connecticut, house with its lovely view of Long Island Sound. Jane took a daytime job at a department store and designed the costumes at night. From this Bayview Beach house, Natasha attended Calf Pen Meadow School, while BJ and I commuted to the university where I taught full time, and BJ pursued a Master's Degree in history, which had 54 hours of course work in it, since she was required to do an undergraduate major in history as well; her undergraduate major had been English Literature.

Jane's costumes were magnificent, for a very unusual Joyce's Finnegans Wake. She took as a point of departure the dream cycle, which is what the show is all about, and placed H.C. Earwicker, drunk, in a coffin, as the Mary Manning script conceived it, but this coffin had wheels, and Jane painted on it the Eye of Horace from the tombs of ancient Egypt. Joyce wrote of eternity. Jane made visual, eternal symbols, which subtly spoke to the audience.

During rehearsal, we asked the girls what was the most restricting thing a woman had to put up with; they said a girdle or corset. Remember that this was 1969. Since Warner's girdle factory was located in Bridgeport, not far from the campus theatre, we asked for, and got, a huge sheet of Warner's elasticized girdle fabric. Jane sewed the fabric into rather narrow, vertical, hem-like strips, too narrow for some of the bodies, five feet tall and one foot wide. Some of them were less than a foot wide. There were perhaps eight girls, 18 to 22 years old, who had to fit into these full length corsets, which were all connected. Several of the girls were not thin. After we persuaded the girls to wear this brilliantly-conceived costume piece, Jane slit holes in the fabric between the girls, so when they pulled away from each other, and moved in a small-step manner, they created a distinct look of protoplasm, or perhaps ectoplasm, connective tissue of the placenta as the birth process emerged. The girls each had one arm inside the corset, the other outside. The movement would have done Martha Graham proud.

One night, Jane, who had studied dance in New York, got up onto the ramp and started moving. The students copied her movements.

I said, "Okay, Jane. Where did you study?" "Martha Graham," she replied.

Other unique creations emerged. For Anna Livia Plurabelle, a body suit in clear, see-through plastic, with huge breast configurations in plastic colored flowers, was conceived. A headgear made of tubes, and wires, and transistors, all coming out of broken TV sets, and now coming out of Anna Livia's head like a Medusa-Minerva-Medea wig. We joked that Anna Livia Plurabelle should go either nude or in a body stocking.

Jane had done costumes for a production in the Village in New York of see-through costumes for a production which had been closed by censors of some kind (police probably) because of nudity! They asked Jane to cover the male actor so he could still show his nudity slightly hidden. A challenge! I was asked by Jane to try on the short pants, which were tailor-perfect in their fit! Without showing her or my wife, I assured her the pants were effective! I heard that the actor stood for a while outside the door of the theatre; no one seemed to notice. The show didn't run very long, I think!

We settled for a body-like, closely knit jumpsuit that worked very well, making Joyce's last soliloquy for Anna Livia Plurabelle almost as sensational as Molly Bloom's soliloquy at the end of Joyce's Ulysses.

FINNEGANS WAKE IN AMSTERDAM

These few touches took us through the production at the university, after which Sally Thompson's husband, Ivor, a New York copper industry man, surprised me and gained my lasting gratitude by contributing $10,000 toward taking the production to the festival in Amsterdam. I had a tentative invitation from Hans DeWitte, and was gaining an official invitation, and was begging the university to come up with more money, for we had a large cast, and these students could not afford the air fare and hotel. The university's chancellor, Dr. James Halsey, and his wife Julia, contacted KLM, got reduced air tickets at student prices, and paid for them; and KLM secured rooms at a student hotel in the heart of Amsterdam for the three weeks that we were there. Sally (a beautiful redhead who played a washerwoman), Rita, and Anna Livia Plurabelle stayed in the nicer hotel across the street.

During the first two weeks in Amsterdam, Jane, a couple of students, a young man who wanted to take the trip on his own and paid for his ticket, and I worked daily on the additional set design. I told the heart-broken but finally cooperative student designer that his execution of the design had been great for the student theatre, but that this one had to look like New York, and that Jane, whom I finally persuaded to come to Amsterdam, would design drops for the set, which we had not had in Bridgeport.

The thought in the minds of Rita Hassen, her husband Ira Blue, and Sally was that we would probably take the show immediately into New York to be placed in one of Ira's potentially available theatres, probably the Cherry Lane Theatre. Rita said, "We'll bill it 'Direct from the Holland Festival.'" But that was to come later, if it was to come at all.

The original student-designed set had used a single, broad backdrop of Mylar, which reflected the audience as in Cabaret. Using the sheet of Mylar, Jane created a huge face of Ramses II, as reflected in the ancient Egyptian temple of Karnak, at Luxor, Egypt. She cut out the face and removed the eyes, nose, eyebrows, and parts of the ears. These she glued onto a big sheet of clear plastic, so we had two drops; a positive and a negative face of Ramses. Sometimes we would use one, and then add the cut-out parts, or remove the full face, leaving the outline parts. The eyes were filled with blue cinemoid gels and red filled the lips.

"Hells bells, my water's gone b-b-black on me; the dud d-d-dirty devil," says one of the washerwomen, during the scene when they gossip about the affairs of Anna Livia Plurabelle and her lovers.

Beautiful redhead Sally Thompson, later a theatre producer in Connecticut, replies, "It was put in the newses wot he did."

For this long discussion of the eternal libido drive of human kind, Jane created a swirling metamorphosis of the creation of life from the centrum of the egg configuration into a gestalt, rather like a comet, piercing the heavens of life's creation. All of this was painted on an enormous sheet of clear plastic, so it acted like a scrim. When the light came from the back, the image developed outlining these two women, magnificently sexual in their peasant skirts, blouses, and shawls; one black-haired, one red-haired. As the lights developed on them, they glowed with the power of life.

At the end of this scene on the banks of the Liffy River, with a long ramp thrust into the center of the theatre, one washerwoman became a red-haired tree and the other became a black-haired stone as the chorus of the river made the sounds of the ducks and river running past Adam and Eve. Joyce's "Riverrun past Eve and Adam ..." is softly chanted as the backdrop is lighted from behind and fades to a blackout. A marvelous scene and a brilliant design. Thank you, Jane.

The ramp, which was longer and more pitched in Amsterdam than in Connecticut, was almost like a ski-slope. The coffin which rode on it carried a 6'2" man, H.C. Earwicker, and was preceded by Anna Livia Plurabelle, and controlled by Sean and Shem. The scene transforms from the Irish public house, with Potboy and others in the tavern, sending H.C. Earwicker on his way into his eternal life after death. All of the dreams came rolling abstractly out of Earwicker's memories, including the girls in the floor-to-chin Warner girdles, and side strips of clear plastic flew in from above the stage to reflect the light as the Ramses-face-backdrops, used at selected moments, came to life.

Finnegans Wake, in the Holland Festival of Music and Drama, was an enormous success with the Dutch people. This was partly due to its overwhelmingly positive reception by Amsterdam's James Joyce Society. This literary group was so appreciative and promoted our production in an amazing way. As he watched its being featured on Dutch TV, Shem asked, "Are we that good?"

"Of course, or we would not have made it to the Holland Festival, and I would not have proposed it to the Director of the Holland Festival of Music and Drama."

The students never realized how powerful the show was.

During try-outs for the show's casting, I had carried around the department's heavy tape recorder — this was before cassettes — and during the breaks between classes I recorded the whole play, since I was the only person available who could read the Joyce text. Then they listened to it as they prepared to read the audition scenes. I left the tape running in the theatre while I went to get some coffee, and a student who joined me commented, "Dr. Lofland, hearing you read Finnegans Wake is like going on a trip." Drugs, I gathered, rather than a physical journey.

The Holland Festival is held from the end of June through the first two weeks of July. Most of our troupe had commitments for the remainder of the summer and returned home. But one of the main actors, Sean [Bob Fiveson, later a Hollywood film director Robert Fiveson], stayed on in Amsterdam, having fallen in love with a Dutch girl. I had a teaching contract in Canada at Conrad Grabel College, University of Waterloo, which was running a summer workshop in cooperation with the Canadian Shakespeare Festival of Ontario. Unfortunately, this commitment kept me from pursuing the possibility of a New York opening of the "direct from the Holland Festival" production. And other factors would also have made that difficult. Too bad, for it could have been fantastic; I'm convinced our production was more than good enough; it was professional, indeed.

At any rate, Sally Thompson, the red-headed washer woman, years later called me in Tehran, asking me to direct a Broadway musical just being written in London about Sir Francis Drake and his ship, the Golden Hind. But that's another story …

INVITATION TO TEHRAN

We were invited in 1972 to return to the Middle East by the former president from Beirut College for Women, Frances Gray, who had been transferred to Tehran by the New York office, the Presbyterian Missions Board, to head a finishing school for women. She was actually to diplomatically close down the school, but instead, she turned it into a four-year university-level college. Neither the New York Board nor the Tehranis themselves, at first, encouraged her in this project. This was in the early 1970s and the late 1960s; the time of the Shah, a time when Tehran was becoming a cultural center. Tehran had a symphony orchestra, a ballet troupe, and an opera company that was comparable to most opera companies in Europe, with directors, scene designers, and major stars coming from Europe to sing in it. I occasionally worked with the opera company chorus, which was especially interesting because of its international makeup. Rudaki Hall, the opera house, had more equipment in it than any theatre I know of, outside of the Metropolitan Opera and some European theatres. Tehran's opera company did, indeed, produce marvelous productions in this magnificently fixed theatre, which technically was superb, using three revolving stage areas, elevators, wagons, and about one hundred counter-weighted lines for sets, drops, all of which were creatively used by designer Theo Lau. For Mozart's Magic Flute, Theo created many drops in small, vertical sections about the stage with Persian Miniature paintings establishing doors, boxes with singers in them, filling a full stage when they were all in place, flying out when the music changed dynamics, another coming in upstage or down as the music spoke the beauties of Mozart's genius. Breathtakingly delicate!

In the spring of 1972, Frances Gray came to California. She was looking for teachers, and she was looking for money to build the new campus in Tehran. We had kept in touch over the years. BJ, Natasha, and I drove into

Los Angeles to meet with Frances at the Biltmore Hotel. Frances looked, just as she did, marvelous; a wonderful woman, filled with tremendous enthusiasm for education of women in the Middle East, where few were being educated. (Now, during the post-revolutionary period, women's education is down from what it was prior to the revolution in Tehran.) Frances invited us to come and teach, and of course, we agreed. We knew what Frances emphasized in her curriculum: Humanities, Literature, Arts, the sociology of living including challenging the mind to live fuller and better, just as we had worked with her in Beirut.

At first Frances thought that we should not come until perhaps after a year because they were building a new campus at that time. It was just being designed, and the program, although it was going, was not a full-fledged curriculum. She thought that I wouldn't be very happy because there wasn't a theatre. Little did she know how tired I was of theatre at that point. I had done many, many shows, and was very happy to teach something else.

I said, "Frances, if they're going to build a new theatre, I ought to be there when they're building it to make sure it's built as a workable theatre."

Finally, she said, "Okay, Norman, you can come. If you will teach, not theatre, but Shakespeare ..."

"Certainly."

"Contemporary English Literature ..." "Certainly." That is another field of mine. "If you will teach Public Speaking ..." "Certainly."

"Oral Interpretation ..." All my areas.

I said, "By all means, I certainly will." BJ would teach history, perhaps some English, and perhaps some typewriting (for these were pre-computer- for-everyone days). Frances assured Natasha that Iran had many imported foods — even Corn Flakes — and we happily accepted her offer, for we were eager to return to the Middle East.

In the late summer of 1972, we sold our house in Palm Springs, at least we thought we sold it, and loaded our things into a Ryder truck to drive to my father's Kansas ranch to store them. We were planning to go to Damavand

College, known as Daneshkade Damavand, Tehran, Iran, a university college for women.

TALIESIN WEST

I had been asking all along to see the plans for the theatre, and Frances sent them to me. It was simply a lecture hall, and there were so many problems with converting it into a usable theatre that I finally asked, "Could I meet with the architect before coming to Tehran?" I requested this, assuming that the architect's work was being done in the States. I wasn't even completely sure who was doing it.

I heard nothing from Frances until the day before we left. Then a cable came from Tehran saying, "Norman, go to Taliesin West, Scottsdale, Arizona, and meet with the Frank Lloyd Wright architect, William Wesley Peters, to discuss the new lecture hall."

I was delighted, especially to know that we were going to Taliesin West! I had certainly heard of and read about the Frank Lloyd Wright group of architects, and about William Wesley Peters. I knew that Peters was an excellent architect. He had assumed the helm of Taliesin West, and of Taliesin East, which was in Wisconsin.

We packed our household goods, having sold some things, and drove east with Tom Aitchison, a former student who was now an actor and a theatre technician. Tom drove the rental truck, because I certainly didn't want to drive it, and BJ and Natasha, age ten, followed in our Karmann Ghia. We were taking everything to my father's 3,200 acre ranch in Kansas where it could be stored in the meat packing plant. With that we left California, one of our many departures from that state over the years.

We drove to Scottsdale, Arizona, which is next door to Phoenix. We left our Ryder Truck at the Holiday Inn the next morning, and Tom and I drove the Karmann to Taliesin West, the creative center of the Frank Lloyd Wright associated architects.

We must have been exceedingly early that morning because when we arrived Wes Peters was still eating breakfast. Later in the morning he became quite warm and hospitable, but at the beginning he was rather cool. The first thing he said to me was, "Who are you? And what are you and Frances planning behind my back?"

Apparently some things had developed that he wasn't very happy with. I had no idea what had gone on. I laughed, somewhat nervously, because I had pushed and begged and cajoled Frances Gray to let me talk to the architect, and I finally had a chance. I said to Wes Peters, "I'm simply a university professor who's going to teach theatre at Damavand College. I've worked for Frances before, in Beirut, and she asked my wife and me to come back to teach at her college."

"You're not a theatre architect?"

"No, not at all. I know a bit about technical theatre, because I work in it all the time."

"You're not somebody hired by Frances as a theatre consultant who is trying to do something behind my back?"

"No, not at all. Nothing like that."

He laughed and said, "Ah, good. Well, let's talk." And we talked.

As we talked I remembered that Wes Peters was married to Svetlana Stalin, and I remembered the stories that I'd heard about Frances setting up this new Damavand College. Frances had met Svetlana at a Christian spiritual retreat for women in the early 1970s, or perhaps the late 1960s, and they had become close friends. Frances told Svetlana that she was the president of Damavand College, which was a former girls' finishing school, which now was being turned into a university college for women. As they talked, Svetlana said, "Ah, if you're building a new campus, you must have my husband do the designs for this new campus."

"Who's your husband?"

"Why, he's William Wesley Peters, the top architect for the Frank Lloyd Wright associated architects."

Frances, of course, was delighted. As always, she followed whatever lead came in order to turn her vision into reality.

That's how Wes Peters started to do the designs, because a local Tehrani architect had been doing them initially. I had seen those earlier designs, and they were simply boxes; cubes that said nothing. The designs by Wes Peters were brilliant concepts based upon the ancient Persian caravanserai. The camel caravans would cover the desert in one-day journeys from one caravansary, or inn, to the next. The caravanserai were large, bare buildings facing a central court, with a gate at the front, and often domes. The madrassas, which are schools, look very much like lower level Esfahani mosques, in terms of design. The dome that came across the top of what ultimately became the theatre and the library was straight out of the domes of Esfahan, though wider and not quite as tall as most in Esfahan.

It's interesting how this university college for women came into being because Frances, as college president and attempting to develop support, accepted invitations to embassy parties and government dinners, places where people in the government and the business world came together. She met people who were influential during the days of the Shah, who could help and guide her; guide her toward money to build it; guide her toward influence to get the permission to operate the school; guide her, ultimately, in this case, to designing the campus.

One interesting account that I remember is a story of Frances at a dinner party. At this party was Farah, the Shahbanu, the Empress of Iran, the wife of the Shah. Farah, always magnificently beautiful to look at, was standing in the room. Frances got up her nerve, approached the empress and said, "Your Highness, how would you like a junior college for Iranian women?"

When Frances tells the story she says, "My faith wasn't very strong just then."

The empress looked her straight in the eye and said, "We would not like a junior college for women. We would like a fully accredited, qualified, university college for women."

Frances said, "You shall have it!"

That's how it started. And that's all she had: a faith that believed that, because she was told this by the wife of the Shah of Iran, with God's help she could gain enough support to get it done. Frances is a marvelously faithful Christian woman.

When Frances retired from Tehran in 1975, she moved to San Francisco, California, to teach an arts course in a university and to lead educational tours to view paintings and other works of art throughout the world. Before she left Iran, a huge dinner was held for her. I was the Master of Ceremonies. Among the many things that went on, wonderful tales were told of moments that were accredited to her. One of the stories was told by the Dean, Mary Thompson. Mary had come from her work in Cairo and Alexandria to teach at Damavand and to be the Dean. Mary told the story that when Frances finished college she had to make a decision. She had to decide whether to be a missionary or a cocktail waitress. Fortunately, she chose the right one. She became a missionary whose influence spread throughout the Middle East, enabling women to become not only successful wives and mothers, but thinking, productive individuals who contributed in a positive way to society. This is the same Frances who had invited us to come back to the Middle East, to come to Tehran, and to teach at Damavand College. Wes Peters had asked me what I was going to do there. He said, "Well, if you're going to teach, that's great, because then there will be a theatre program developing which has relevancy; something to hang onto."

I replied, "Yes, that's what I hope to help with."

We started talking about the lecture hall which had been designed. A very fine lecture hall, but it was a lecture hall. The campus was being built into the side of a mountain, clear up at the north end of Tehran. The magnificent Elburz Mountains shoot up 14,000 feet into the sky, with Mount Damavand in the distance, 19,000 feet high, which could be seen on clear days. It was after that mountain that the school was named Damavand College.

Since the campus was being built into the side of the mountain, the lecture hall slanted down the slope of the mountain, so that you had the seats on the mountain side, and the lectern at the base of the mountain. All of this was underneath a six-story building which housed the library with a magnificent domed roof over it. Now the size of this building was half the size of a football field, so there was an amazing amount of space. Wes Peters said, "Why should we destroy a good lecture hall to build a bad theatre? Let's turn it around, and turn it into a theatre which can be used as a lecture hall."

Which, of course, was the only logical thing to do.

By turning it around, we realized that we were going to have to cut into the mountain, and displace a lot of dirt, which wouldn't be necessary had we not decided to turn it around. Now the seats are coming around, and are slanted up away from the rise of the mountain. The stage is being built into the mountain, and going up, above the mountain. That didn't seem to be a huge problem. The concept was wonderful. I used to draw it everywhere, because for years I was simply ecstatic about this idea. We were in Tehran from 1972 until 1979, with a year and a half away, during the time when my father was dying of cancer, so I was constantly promoting this whole project. The revolution, of course, killed it all, but for now, at least, the theatre was being built.

The concept of the theatre rather resembled an outline drawing of a cow's head, at least that's what it looked like to me when I drew it, with the rounded jaw that comes down being the rounded seating area, very much like a Roman or a Greek theatre, and the ears of the cow being the staircases that went upstairs. Within this shape of the theatre, Wes Peters and associates designed the cavea, that is the seating area, the stage itself, and rather extensive dressing rooms and scene design shops, all of which caused a great deal of trouble for me later on.

TRAVEL TO IRAN

We left Taliesin West and continued to Kansas to store our things at the ranch and say goodbye to our families. Tom flew back to Los Angeles and Palm Springs, joining us later in London for the remainder of the journey.

On this trip we left London, went to Amsterdam, on to Milan, took a commuter plane from Milan to Rome, which was sometimes rather discomforting, over to Florence, to Tunisia, to Libya, to Cairo, to Beirut, and finally to Tehran.

TUNISIA

As we waited to board the Tunis Air flight from Rome to Tunis, the enormous doors of Rome's Leonardo de Vinci airport opened.

Each one of us squeezed through a small space, about one foot wide, and I noticed that all the passengers were running toward the aircraft. I thought that this was very odd. All of a sudden, everybody was jammed onto the staircase of the Boeing 727 aircraft, and the Tunisian men had lifted Tom above their heads and were carrying him up the stairs. We were quite amazed at this. We couldn't figure out why, but later we thought that possibly the reason was that he was wearing shorts, similar to those worn by soccer players; and men simply didn't wear shorts in North Africa in those days. This was just before tourism became big in Tunisia. This fashion was still quite new, and they were no doubt surprised [delighted to make fun of him] at seeing him.

At any rate, we went on to Tunisia, the breadbasket of the Roman Empire. In Tunis, we wanted to go out to Carthage, and people kept saying, "No, there's nothing there. There's nothing to see." Unfortunately the Bardo, the magnificent mosaic museum, was closed that day. But years later when we returned to Tunisia to live, we discovered a great deal to see at Carthage, and made a number of visits to the Bardo, a highlight of the museum world.

LIBYA, TRIPOLI, AND LEPTUS MAGNA

We flew from Tunis to Libya to see Leptus Magna. Leptus Magna is a magnificent Roman ruin site on the Libyan Desert, which is spectacular and rarely visited nowadays. Actually, we were nearly the only tourists on that day in 1972, shortly after Colonel Khaddafi's take-over; and our arrival at the Tripoli airport in 1972 was very different from my arrival at that city's airport ten years later, when I was one of a group invited by the Colonel. When we got out of the plane in '72 we didn't realize that the airport was miles and miles away from Tripoli. It was the old airport which the British Royal Air Force used during the war. We carried our bags which, of course, were too many. There are always too many bags that we are carrying, because we're always going from one job to another, and we have to have certain things for teaching. There was a local bus going into Tripoli that was very full. People were hanging on the outside. We said that we would wait for the next bus.

They kept saying, "Yallah. Yallah." "Hurry up. Come on."

We said, "No, we'll wait for the next bus." Little did we realize that there was no "next bus." There wasn't another flight, so why would there be another bus? At dusk a car came and took us the long distance into Tripoli. On the outskirts of the city was a large shanty-town, which we learned was a Palestinian refugee camp. It was getting dark when the taxi let us out in the town center. After several inquiries we finally found a hotel and then, with more difficulty, we found a restaurant. After dinner we looked around while walking along the rather charming but run-down-looking seafront. The palm trees lining the corniche gave it a tropical air. Our impression was that Libya was far from prosperous; things looked stagnant and in need of repair. No tourists were visible. Our main purpose in coming here, because we only had one day, was to go to Leptus Magna.

The next morning we went by taxi to Leptus Magna. It was a long drive and took most of the morning. We were able to wander around the ruins for a couple of hours. Tom took lots of excellent pictures, and then we drove back to Tripoli. The ruins are closer to Benghazi than they are to Tripoli, but perhaps there weren't any flights into Benghazi at that time. We did see the magnificent ruins, with a Roman theatre, which had a cavea of the seating area in excellent condition. Perhaps they had just restored it. The scena, the back wall of the stage, was made up of Roman columns. Through those columns you could see the Mediterranean. A magnificent backdrop for any play that they may have done, for there was the sea beyond, as well as the loggia, the stage area on which the actors performed.

Leptus Magna had silted in, which caused the demise of the Roman city because the port could no longer be used. This disaster was caused by men; it was not a natural phenomenon. Then the desert moved in. We were the only people on that long Mediterranean beach. We did manage to get a Coke or Pepsi on the beach in front of the Roman theatre. Ten years later in Libya, I was served only pear juice.

EGYPT, CAIRO, AND UPPER EGYPT

From Tripoli we went on to Cairo. Cairo, that enchanting, intimidating city which we years later saw in the film The English Patient, which stirs you and makes you think, "Ah, it's Lawrence Durell writing again." He wrote, however, about Alexandria in The Alexandria Quartet, four magnificent books which, we learned later when we lived in Kyrenia, North Cyprus, were written in Bellapaise, above the Mediterranean Sea, in North Cyprus.

Cairo makes us so aware of the history of ancient Egypt. There is the magic of such places as the Islamic Museum. Natasha was with us on this trip; she was age ten. The three of us were wandering through the Islamic Museum when we were approached by a journalist who asked Natasha if she would pose for a photo, sitting on something to do with Islam, for a newspaper article she was writing entitled "Women in Islam." The lady journalist said that Natasha's hairstyle, long braids, were just what she needed for her article; and of course she posed for the picture. We never saw that article. It would have been nice if the lady had sent us a copy.

We stopped for a rest in Groppie's Café-Pastry-Chocolate Shop, a not-so- little café-restaurant which in 1972 was quite elegant, but when we returned in 1997 it was no longer elegant. In 1972 it was the meeting place of hopeful lovers. They could hold hands in the booths and talk quietly. Now all of that has been taken over by the five-star hotels, of which Cairo has a number. In 1972 I recall only Shepheard Hotel and the Cairo Hilton, where we went for tea a couple of times, although, needless to say, we did not stay there. We stayed at the more affordable, and far more interesting, Minerva House, now torn down, and to which I refer later.

We took the overnight train to Upper Egypt, following the Nile with the clackity-clack of the train's wheels, clicking our way into ancient Egypt. I'm always a romantic for trains. Indeed, in 1994, when we took the Trans- Siberian railway all the way from Shanghai, China, to Paris, France, halfway around the world, then too it was the hypnotic wheel-click that charmed me. That monotonous melody kept us company as we traveled up the Nile to ancient Egypt. This was the setting for Agatha Christie's Death on the Nile, which was superbly captured in both the book and on film. We stared through the train's windows at the timeless terrain and watched the feluccas floating on the water, just as they had floated a few thousand years earlier.

When we arrived in Luxor we saw the magnificent Luxor Temple with the red granite obelisks. One of the obelisks had gone to Paris to the Place de Concorde, as have others to London and New York. The obelisk in Rome is from the Sudan, farther up the Nile, and is being returned to Sudan. Within the temple are enormous pillars reaching to the sky. Each pillar has a circumference of 35½ feet, and is perhaps 120 feet tall; that's a twelve-story building. They diminish man as he stands beside them. In 1838 and 1839, the lithographer David Roberts created brilliant drawings of ancient Luxor, Egypt. He caught the magic of these pillars, the ones as tall as a twelve-story building. Frescoes, carved figures and patterns, mainly hieroglyphs, cover the columns. David Roberts worked colors into the patterns, which still give a substance to the images that were originally created by those ancient Egyptians, to tell the story of life, and death, and eternity.

That's what we had come to see.

Many journeys have been made there by many people, but this ancient center of the pharaohs holds its wonder. I had been there before, but continued to be captivated.

Today's visitors to Luxor Temple can see the walkway at the entrance lined with carved stone lions. Those weren't visible when David Roberts made his magnificent drawings in the nineteenth century, because they hadn't been uncovered. As you wander around these ruins filled with columns, the imprint of Ramses is on every wall, on every pillar, and in Queen Nefertiti's chamber, which the guide shows the men, but not the women, due to the fertility symbols. Ramses looked very fertile, indeed.

On an earlier trip to the Luxor Temple, in 1963, with a colleague, the guide took us into a chamber of stone columns with King Ramses on every wall and column; each picture placed two or three meters apart. Every other Ramses had a meter-long phallus. Richard, my colleague, said, "Norm, if these guys were built like that, no wonder they thought they were gods."

Perhaps there's some truth in that!

In 2016 I learned via a visitor to Luxor that the "Fundamentalists," in their passion to clean up Egypt, chiseled out all these enormous phalluses. That must frustrate the guides who made considerable "bakshish" on those images! The traveler indicated that there were almost no tourists there when he was visiting Egypt, that it was emptier than it was when we visited it in earlier times. That is sad, for tourism was very big, indeed. When can it come back to the Middle East? Syria, Iraq, Libya — and maybe Tunisia since they were attacked on the Sousse beach, where we used to live — are gone. Terribly, many of the historical artifacts are destroyed, stolen, or defaced! After a century or more of museums collecting archeological wonders, the wonders in situ in the soil of these locations are being destroyed. Second only to the thousands of deaths being inflicted therein, the destruction of history is reprehensible!

On a visit to the tombs in the Valley of the Kings, and a visit to the Valley of the Queens, we imagined the objects in the Cairo museum placed in their original locations, the sand tombs, for the tombs were now empty. All of the mummies, and King Tutankhamen's layered coffin, which are displayed in the Cairo Museum, came to life as we trudged through the sand; the buried tombs of the ancient Pharaohs.

When we were in Luxor, we went out into the desert to see the two huge seated statues, the Colossi of Memnon, which are images of Amen Hotep III. These statues have watched the daily rising of the sun for 3,000 years. A tourist there asked Tom, "Please, would you take a picture of me running around these statues?"

"Sure."

Tom laughs when he remembers it and says, "I rotated the camera so that it went round and round and round." It must have been a funny filmic surprise for that guy when he developed the 8mm film and watched it.

BACK TO CAIRO AND HOTELS

We went on to Aswan, looked around, but did not go down to Abu Simbel. Then we returned to Cairo by train. Fortunately, we love trains, as did Agatha Christie before, as she put it, those "boring airplanes" came into fashion which took away the romance of the great seagoing luxury ships, and many interesting, but not luxurious, ships. Air travel also took away most of the trains. The Orient Express has come back, but it is horribly expensive.

Fortunately, today in the early twenty-first century, a few of the beautiful, old, interesting hotels are still around in Cairo, and a couple more in Luxor and Aswan, as described by Dr. Elizabeth Peters in her delightful accounts of early twentieth century and late nineteenth century Egypt involving the ancient findings from archeological digs that Peters' characters are involved in. After all, Peters has a Ph.D. in Egyptology from the University of Chicago School of Oriental Studies; it's great that she uses her knowledge in writing excellent novels! The interesting Barons Hotel at which Agatha Christie lived while her husband Max did his archeological work in Aleppo is gone, I suppose, from the bombing in the recent Syrian Civil War. Agatha, as well as we, loved the rocking chairs on the terrace that overlooked persons walking in Aleppo. No doubt the little exquisite museum to which Max Malloran contributed so much is also gone, as well as thousands of homes, restaurants, souks — some of which we have visited. Too many sad horrors lately. Is it another Crusade-era, reflecting more religious misguidance?

When returning to Cairo, we stayed at the very interesting Mina House, next to the pyramids. We had already, on a previous trip, ridden the camels, and climbed as far as we wanted on the Cheops Pyramid. This trip we simply relaxed and enjoyed the Mina House, except for the fact that Tom was dreadfully ill and had to be near the plumbing facilities at all locations where we were staying. He had an especially bad experience while trying to change money in the lobby area and standing behind a line of German tourists. His vision became blurred, with colors and faint images moving in slow motion. With his money finally changed, he was so weak that he had to crawl up the stairs to his room. This kind of experience has happened to me so often that we rarely mention it anymore. It is simply the expected, almost daily, fate of one who travels in this part of the world and some of us are more susceptible than others! A friend who, years ago in Beirut, ran a food service business at a university cafeteria said, "Norm, the State Department should have the U.S. Health Service introduce a few germs into U.S. culture so people don't get sick when they travel abroad."

The Mina House is a magnificent hotel, and architecturally most interesting. It was used for the interior shots in the Agatha Christie film Death on the Nile; the dancing in the arabesque salon and the people descending the long staircase. This wonderful structure has been renovated since then, and unfortunately been turned into Southern California, pseudo- Oriental, pseudo-Egyptian architecture. It was marvelous the way the desert came clear up to the steps of the Mina House, with the pyramids right there, within several hundred feet. We were awakened early in the morning by complaining donkeys and camels and the shouting camel-men. Looking out the windows, we saw the animal sheds several yards from the hotel and the pyramids just beyond. Now (when we visited in 1997) the Mina House had been enclosed by a green hedge-fence with a gate opening into the hotel. Grass was everywhere, where there once was sand. It had become like a Palm Springs golf course in the heart of the desert — rather silly and most inappropriate — a very "1920s Hollywood" design.

Before the Luxor excursion we had stayed at the Minerva House, recommended by a dear friend, a New York designer who had designed a number of sets for several shows that I had directed and produced in Beirut, Connecticut, Amsterdam, and Palm Springs, California. In fact, she designed Finnegans Wake for the Holland Festival; brilliant surrealistic settings. Her name is Jane Putnam; originally Jane Rowe. She married an Egyptian and became Jane el Hawary. That was when she was my student at BCW; her husband taught then at the Egyptian University, Beirut. Years later, after her husband divorced her in the Egyptian/Moslem way, she married John Putnam, the art designer for Mad Magazine. Our first choice of hotel was the Omayyad, old and interesting, where we and the Beirut students had stayed in 1963, but the Omayyad had long since been torn down. So in 1972 we took Jane's advice and checked into the Minerva House. It was an old, interesting, but rather flea-bitten hotel, right in the heart of downtown Cairo, the exciting part of the city. We could run all around, eat at various restaurants, and see many places of interest. It was a convenient and exciting location. In addition, it was quite cheap, and we were on a tight budget. The Tehran college had provided our air tickets, but all other travel expenses came out of our own pockets. One disadvantage of the Minerva House was the mosquitoes. Tom's room was especially vulnerable. He described for us how he'd wrapped the bed sheets around his bed to keep them off, but to no avail. My experience with insects was soon to come.

One day while staying at the Minerva House, we went across the street for lunch, not very far from the hotel, fortunately. We were enjoying our lunch when all of a sudden the seat of my pants felt as though it was on fire; absolutely burning; inflamed! I jumped up from the rush-bottom, or perhaps reed-bottom, chair, looked down at it, and I couldn't see anything except some tiny, tiny black dots that looked like fly specs. I pulled some money out of my pocket and said, "Pay the bill."

I ran from the restaurant, ran to the hotel, ran up the stairs, ran into the communal shower which we shared, stripped off my clothes, jumped into the shower, and ran cold water on my backside, trying to relieve the burning pain from bites all over my legs and buttocks. I was simply burning up. In a few minutes, BJ, Tom, and Natasha arrived, not knowing what was wrong. I showed them, perhaps not ten-year-old Natasha, my backside, covered with tiny blisters from insect bites; from little, crawling, almost microscopic insects that live in the seats of those cane chairs. I've been afraid to sit on cane chairs ever after.

When we returned to Cairo in 1997, we searched that whole area to find the Minerva House, and the local-type eating places that surrounded it. We found a couple pensions catering to backpackers and students. No sign of the old, interesting hotels that used to be there. Downtown Cairo had been renovated with five-star hotels and modern office buildings madly, rapidly being put up. On this visit we finally located a cheap hotel on the fourteenth floor of an office building overlooking the main square (actually a circle) of Cairo. Everything in the square had been knocked to the ground to make way for a new underground walkway, new streets, and an additional metro line. The land had been cleared all the way to the Cairo Hilton and the National Museum complex. Everything between us and those landmarks was barren, creating the larger Tahrir Square of the recent Arab Spring. In 1997 all the interesting old buildings we enjoyed when we stayed at the Minerva House were gone. After riding the creaking elevator to the fourteenth floor, the expansive view from the hotel's balcony tempted us to rent the room at less than half the price of our room at the Carolina Hotel. But the camp-like atmosphere of the place and its hippie-type clientele sent us back to the amenities of the Carolina.

In 1972 while we were waiting for a plane at the Cairo airport, Tom was deeply impressed by a beautiful Arab girl. She was stunning. Her eyes — so strong — captivated him and suggested, "This is a forbidden encounter." Tom says those eyes still haunt him, almost thirty years later.

One day in Cairo, when Tom and I were en route to a museum, our cab stopped, the driver jumped out and started shouting and beating another driver. Tom kept saying, "Let's get out." I sat, as though dazed. He finally grabbed me, threw some Egyptian money on the seat, and pulled me from the car, an old Mercedes. He told me recently, "I've always wondered why you waited so long to climb out of that taxi." Oh, Tom! We've had many such experiences; it's par for the course of travel — of a certain kind.

THE BAZAAR AND BALLOON THEATRE

One of Cairo's most popular tourist spots is Khan El Khalili, that overwhelming bazaar in the heart of old Cairo. The minarets, which rise between the high walls, have for centuries called people to prayer. The walls are layers of brown, taupe, off-white, and red. This busy labyrinthine shopping center continues to provide the locals' daily needs while attracting throngs of tourists. When we were there in 1963, again in 1972, and again in 1996, few changes were visible; Khan El Khalili held the same exotic sights, and probably smells and sounds, as are portrayed in the drawings of nineteenth century English traveler and artist, David Roberts.

Khan El Khalili's stunning, oriental-style structures with wooden spooled shutters on overhanging balconies are typically North African, and so successfully portrayed in the films The English Patient and

Casablanca. These balconies almost cry out the venders' wares: brilliant dresses and fabrics draped from the shop openings, giant bottles of jasmine and ambergris in the perfume shops, and burlap bags of innumerable spices in the spice bazaar. As in the ancient days of the Middle East, whether in North Africa or farther into the Middle East of Syria, Turkey, or Iran, donkeys are the burden-bearers. The loaded beasts push persons aside as they thread their ways, sometimes almost rushing, through the crowded alleyways filled with people, filled with wares, filled with scents and memories of the Middle East. In the '60s a popular place of entertainment was the Balloon Theatre. It was an old tent theatre on the bank of the Nile, which featured a variety of performers: singers including the famous Um Kalthun, an orchestra, and even acrobats riding bicycles on a high wire over the audience. When we saw it in 1963 it was great fun, with all of the razzmatazz of a circus in the theatre, without the animals. Exciting things happened over our heads. I didn't find the Balloon Theatre the last time we were there. If it's gone, then that's sad.

So much is gone now of that wonderful city.

A JOB OFFER

In Cairo in 1972, en route to Iran, I met the president of the American University in Cairo. His secretary sent me to his apartment, and he was just ready to go out and play tennis. I noticed that one leg had a support stocking on it, but thought nothing of it. We talked. He was a congenial fellow with an athletic build, was kind, and a great conversationalist. He offered BJ and me jobs if we would stay in Cairo. How we both wanted to stay, for the American University is a very attractive campus with an excellent reputation. But we were committed to go to Tehran. We had signed contracts with Frances and Damavand College. (I have to admit that if our shipment of personal things hadn't already been en route to Iran, making this decision would have been much more difficult.)

"Ah, what a pity. I wish you could stay, because we're trying to develop a theatre program on the campus." I agreed how much I would have liked to accept his offer, and how I hoped to take him up on it sometime in the future. A few months later, I learned that he had died from leukemia, so I had missed my chance to teach there and to work with a very charismatic guy. The same thing had happened to me when Dr. Sam Hazo, Dean of Arts, Duquesne University, offered me a job in Pittsburgh, Pennsylvania, only to be gone from it when I arrived! So, it's good that we stayed with Dr. Frances Gray — we knew her and supported her work of educating the women of the Middle East, just as we had done at Beirut College for Women. It would be good to watch the building of the new Frank Lloyd Wright Taliesin West-designed Damavand College campus. The theatre would be outstanding for any theatre company and training program! Little did we know ...

BEIRUT

So we departed from Cairo, flying next to Beirut. In Beirut, we found an inexpensive hotel on the Hamra shopping street, not one of the lovely hotels we had dreamed of staying in when we lived there, but an inexpensive hotel mid-way up the hill between the American University of Beirut and Beirut College for Women, where we had taught from 1963-1965. We walked up to the BCW campus to see some old friends.

Daad Najm, who had been Dean of Students and then became Registrar, asked, "What are you doing here?" She knew that we had not applied to come back.

"We're on our way to Tehran."

She immediately replied, "Gray! You're going to work for Frances Gray." Daad and Frances were great friends, and she had worked for Frances also.

As we talked with old friends in Beirut, they wondered why we weren't returning. 1972 was a good time to be in Beirut. It was just before the war, which broke out a few months later. On this stopover we saw many friends from times past and enjoyed their hospitality with wonderful Lebanese food and much reminiscing. We reluctantly departed from Beirut on the last leg of our journey.

ARRIVAL IN TEHRAN

We flew Pan-Am from Beirut to Tehran. Wonderful Pan-Am before it was pulled apart by Lockerbie and Libya. Interestingly, our ticket went on to Delhi, India, but we never could use it. We arrived in Tehran in September 1972. The college had found us a hotel in the mid-city. All new teachers were staying in the hotel until housing could be found. We enjoyed meeting the new people, and BJ enjoyed the hotel's swimming pool. Tehran was said to be second only to Hollywood for swimming pools in those days. We enjoyed, for the first day or so, our carrot jam breakfast, but we got over that rather quickly.

Tom enjoyed his nightly talks with Bulgarian air pilots who taught him the luxury of tea-drinking in the Middle Eastern world, only in this case it included a Bulgarian addition of brandy with the glasses of tea. This, of course, was possible under the Shah, but would be most difficult now, and most unnecessary.

We searched for an apartment we could afford. I had taken a $9,000 cut in salary to come to Tehran from my Palm Springs job. Fortunately, BJ could also teach, and that made her happy. It also helped our income.

Tehran is a huge, sprawling metropolis on the side of the Elburz Mountains. The city limits go from an altitude of 3,500 feet to 5,500 feet, right up the side of the mountain. We first lived in the Shahreza area; that's the mid-city area fairly close to the old city's bazaar and close to the Armenian section of town where one could get wonderful selections of pork, forbidden elsewhere, and wine. We were not far from Ray's Pizza, where lots of ex-pat people, as well as young Tehranis, ate. Other, more luxurious (and less luxurious) restaurants and coffee-tea houses were within walking distance from our apartment. The American and British embassies were nearby, and taxis could take us anywhere in the city; if we were lucky enough to get a taxi.

MENINGITIS (AGAIN)

We were very happy in Tehran. The first week that we were in our spacious apartment in the Shahreza area, Natasha became ill. I called Lucy Sullivan, a dear friend and colleague who had also taught with us in Beirut at BCW. Hers was the only telephone number that I had.

"Lucy, Natasha's ill. Do you know a doctor I can take her to?"

Lucy gave me Dr. Surouri's telephone number. I called him, and he told me to bring her to the clinic. I carried her down the stairs. We lived on the sixth floor of the building, with no elevator. BJ, Tom, and I took her to the doctor by taxi. We arrived, the doctor was examining her, when all of a sudden, much to our embarrassment, she threw up, adding an awful green to the doctor's lovely carpet. Very embarrassed, I remember thinking, "Well, the colors seem to be compatible."

It was pistachios. She'd not had them before and had eaten an entire kilo. We didn't even know that she was eating them. She was reading, which she loved to do, while snacking. They, of course, had made her very ill.

We arrived back home. Since she was still feeling bad, I carried her back up the six flights of stairs. The next day and evening I was feeling very ill with a severe headache. An aching stiffness went down my neck into my back. I knew the symptoms because I had been through this before. I had had meningitis during our last months in Beirut. I called Dr. Surouri again and described the symptoms. He was at home then, in the northern part of the city.

He asked, "Can you get to the hospital?" "Where is it?"

"It's right next to my clinic. I will meet you there."

Tom went with me in a telephone taxi. We managed to get to the Jam Hospital. I arrived, and I remember being horribly weak. I sat there waiting for the doctor, because he had to come through heavy traffic. Tehran traffic was incredibly bad. While waiting for him, after being terribly ill, I passed out. When I awakened, I was lying on a table, saw the doctor's kind face, and said, "Ah, you're here."

"Yes."

"Please, just give me the medication. Please don't bother to do a spinal tap; there is not time. Just give me the antibiotics."

"That's what we're going to do, because it looks like it's exactly the same thing."

I passed out again. They put me in a hospital bed, and when I woke up there was a drip in my arm. At least I wasn't taking 85 injections in the hips as I had done in Beirut when I had meningitis before, just a mere seven years earlier, when I was so terribly, desperately ill. Again I was so ill. The doctor told me later, and Tom confirmed this, that when he arrived at the hospital I was delirious, was reciting Shakespeare. I was relieved to know that I'd repeated the magnificent works of the greatest writer in the English language. I could have done far worse! Those were our first weeks in Tehran.

PERSIAN FOOD

We became familiar with the food of Persia. Our favorite dish is fessinjun, which is made with beef, lamb, or chicken. I've learned recently that the very wealthy people use duck meat. The meat is simmered in crushed walnuts and pomegranate juice, making a rich sauce. It has a most unusual flavor and is served over rice. Fessinjun, with a green salad (although in Iran it would probably be a cooked vegetable) makes a marvelous, rather exotic meal.

The first time that we had it was at the University of Southern California, Los Angeles, when I was in graduate school. While I was working on my Master's Degree, BJ and I lived next door to a young Persian couple, Aziz and Assi Nabavi. Aziz was, interestingly, working on his second Ph.D. He already had one from Iran in accounting. This Ph.D. was in public administration. Assi studied music and, judging from her piano playing, was having a hard time of it. One day they invited us for a fessinjun dinner. He said, "I apologize, because I didn't have the actual ingredients. I didn't have any pomegranate juice, so instead I used lemon." We, of course, didn't know the difference. Later, in Tehran, fessinjun made with pomegranate juice was equally delicious.

Polo-shirin is another popular Persian dish. This is chicken baked in sweet rice, raisins, sometimes almonds, thinly-sliced orange peel, and dates. Delicious. Iran's national dish is chello kebab, a long skewer of meat chunks served with yogurt, raw egg, raw onion, and sumac over rice. Sometimes the meat is long enough to fold over to fit the platter. Sabze, which means "greens" — fresh greens of any kind, including radishes and green onions — along with goat cheese and lavash bread is often served as an appetizer in restaurants. When BJ serves it, she simply goes to the fresh greens section of the market, anywhere in the world, and picks out all of the interesting leaves. I don't even know which leaves to take. She washes them thoroughly, dries them, and arranges them on a large platter with feta cheese and barbari or lavash bread. I suppose that it could be eaten with pita bread if you have nothing else, but it needs to be something that can be wrapped around the sabze. You take a piece of the bread, perhaps two inches by two inches, and place on it the strips of greens, green onions, green parsley, green everything, add some feta cheese, and roll it up and eat it, rather like a small sandwich. It is not only delicious but healthful.

Then there's "bottom-of-the-pan," uniquely Persian. A pan of rice is boiled over a very low flame. The fire is covered with a metal pancake-like utensil, which has holes in it. These holes allow the heat to slowly rise. A chunk of butter is added, and the rice cooks until barely burned. The rice on the bottom becomes very crisp, and thus gets its name, "bottom-of-the-pan." After the fluffy rice is served, the crisp rice pieces remain at the bottom of the pan. Sometimes pita bread is placed on the very bottom and becomes fried to a crisp. Either way, it's delicious.

TEHRAN TRANSPORT

When we needed a taxi, we stood at the side of the street and shouted our destination. That's why in the first week of Farsi (Persian) lessons, we were taught taxi vocabulary so that we could at least get around in Tehran. If the taxi driver was going where you wanted to go, you could share the taxi with everybody else. It was a good, economical system, because you seldom had only one person riding in one taxi. It was five people, plus the driver, usually. These were called service taxis. Sometimes the taxi driver had to take devious routes. You never knew where you were actually going until you finally ended up where you were heading. But the driver knew, and he made it work, and you arrived there.

There's a wonderful story about one of the teachers, after several years there, who was going to the northern part of the city to a new area. She had the address, and for this trip she called a telephone taxi. You telephoned for that taxi, he came for you, and it was a one-person-in-one-taxi situation. They were driving around Northern Tehran in the Tajrish area, and they could not find the address. The taxi driver finally said to her, "Madam, you should know better than to take a taxi to someplace where you have never been before!"

She, unlike most of us, was quite fluent in Farsi, and responded, "That's what you're supposed to do."

It was a very workable system. When taxis became scarce, and they often were scarce, especially toward the end of our stay in Tehran — toward the end of the Shah's stay also — young Peykan owners turned their cars into taxis. "Peykan" means arrow; it drives straight as an arrow. The Peykan car was an English Hilman built in Tehran. In the last years of our time in Tehran, I had my own system of measuring the economic and general situation of that city by riding with these young drivers. When we first came to Tehran, in 1972, everything was "wonderful," and nearly everybody thought that "all went well." The young Peykan drivers would caress the steering wheel or the dashboard of the car and say, "This is my Peykan. Hamdallah. Very good." They would stroke the car and say how wonderful it was to own, but they were buying it on the credit system. The longer a driver paid for it, the more he hated the car.

RUMBLES OF REVOLUTION

In the autumn of 1978, we had come back to Tehran from being on leave in 1977, and I noticed that the attitude of these young Peykan drivers had changed considerably. No longer was it this "wonderful Peykan." Now it was this "damned Peykan." One driver said, "I have to drive every day, all day long, just to get enough money to make the monthly payments." Is it any wonder that when the revolution finally came, the first thing they did was burn down the banks?

I was speaking with a banker friend of mine in the States when this was happening. We had come back to the States for a short visit. I told him this story, and he said, "Can you think of a better way to retire a loan than to burn down the bank?"

"No, indeed."

He said, "You know, several times a year the bank examiners come to us and they say, 'Do you have everything properly secured against fire? Do you have all of your accounts on computer discs?' We always say, 'Yes. We're working on it.'"

"Yes, it is difficult to conceive of such a thing happening. By the way, would you renew my loan, please?"

My banker laughed and said, "Yes, of course."

CHAPTER 5

IRAN (1972 – 1978)

Damavand Theatre, Move to New Campus, Shah's Divans,
Revolution, Caspian Sea,
Gonbad-e-Kavus, Village Hospitality, Crowded Train, Crowded
Taxi, Princess Ashraf's Palace, Travel to Turkey, Tabriz to Erzurum,
Erzurum to Trabzon, Trabzon, Black Sea Cruise, Istanbul,
On to the U.S., Kansas, A Changed Ranch,
Return to Tehran, Isfahan, Persepolis, and Shiraz, Life in Tehran,
Natasha's Baptism, Restaurants and a Fire

DAMAVAND THEATRE

Desperately ill with meningitis, I stayed in the hospital for perhaps
three weeks. My classes had been taken over by a colleague. The college
president, Frances Gray, called me at the hospital and said, "Norman,
when are you getting out of the hospital?"

"I think, Frances, today."

"Fine. You'll come immediately to my office."

"Frances, I can't even walk. How can I come to your office?"

"Never mind. I will send Ibrahim, the driver. He will pick you up
and bring you directly here. You can lie down on the sofa in my office.
Just come. Come now." And she hung up.

Ibrahim came and helped me down the stairs. I sat in the car
and rode to Frances's office on the campus where we were admitted
through the gates. I struggled into her office, and she said, "Sit down
on that sofa. Lie down.

Anything. This is Nazam Amari. He's the Frank Lloyd Wright
architect in Tehran. He is the one who designed our new campus,

and he has been talking to me about this new theatre complex. I won't have it. You'll have to give it up. You and Wes Peters have put together this huge theatre structure. I will not raise the money for it. It will cost another million and a half dollars, and I am not going to raise the money for it. I simply will not!" She went storming out of her office.

I turned to Nazam and said, "Hello, Nazam. Nice to meet you. Really, what has Wes Peters done?"

"Well, Norm, he has excavated half of the mountain, and that's what's costing so much money."

"What for?"

"For dressing rooms, and for construction rooms, and for a little theatre." "Oh, Nazam, we don't really need any of those things, just the bare minimum. Can't we have just the theatre and some space for dressing rooms and for sets?"

"Yes, we can do that, but we must stick with the existing pillars, because if we have to move those, we will have to go to an entirely new design, otherwise the poured concrete and Esfahani blue tiled roof will collapse. In the floors above the theatre are the two storied library and other facilities and a huge domed roof."

"Fine, Nazam. Where are the pillars?"

He started to draw the theatre. Remember the shape of a cow's head looking directly down onto the head? Inside the rounded part (the jaw of the cow) is the seating area. In Greek theatres, it's the theatron; in Roman theatres, the cavea. In the middle of the stage area are two pillars. These go all the way to the top of the five floors. These two pillars are at the back wall of the stage. Downstage, to the front of the stage, are two more pillars, one on either side, exactly where the proscenium arch would be, 46 feet apart.

"Fine, Nazam. Draw it up, and let's do it."

DAMAVAND THEATRE: A REVISED PLAN

In a few weeks he returned with a revised design. I said, "Marvelous. Wonderful."

He had put in a proscenium stage, the opening, and the seating, rounded Roman style, and then the back wall where the two pillars were. At the front of the stage, it was 46 feet from one pillar to the other pillar; along the back wall were two pillars in the center. "Nazam, we have the two pillars here in the center. Tell me, can we have a fly gallery above the theatre?"

"No, Norm. Above is the library, which is extremely heavy. Plus, on top of that is a poured concrete roof, with blue Esfahani clay tiles two inches thick."

I went after him for weeks trying to get a fly gallery.

"No, Norm. If we put the fly gallery in, the roof will cave in." This was, after all, a domed, poured concrete roof, covering half of a football field in size, on top of which was two inches of tile on top of a tar base to seal it.

I finally became convinced that we could not have a fly gallery. We were having to squeeze this stage into a smaller-than-desired space because of the existing pillars, but the mainstage could become a large thrust stage in the concept of the Tyrone Guthrie Theatre design in Minneapolis, Minnesota, and the Canadian Shakespeare Theatre, Stratford, Ontario. Since there was almost no wing space on the sides to accommodate wagons and shifting scenery, I made a suggestion.

"Let's design a doughnut revolve."

Nazam asked, "Norm, what is a 'doughnut revolve'?" He had a glimmer of glee in his eyes as he put the question; he's a delightful fellow.

"With the two pillars that are in the back wall, let's make the center of the stage permanent, still."

"Ah ... then the doughnut becomes the revolving stage." "Right! We'll have a 45-foot revolving stage."

"Ah, brilliant! It will feed right in through the existing pillars."

"Let's have sliding, soundproof doors that go along the back wall. Then we can close those doors and with the stage in the front, we can perform to the audience of 508 seats; we'll have a firm back wall, if we want it. Then we can open those doors, and on the other side there will be an open space for a studio theatre. Nothing permanent."

Nazam had originally simply run a hallway behind the back wall with rooms off to the side.

"Don't put anything in it; keep it all open. Then we can use it for scene construction. Or we can use it for a theatre. We can put in module pieces or step-units to build up any kind of a theatre arrangement we want. That side can be used as an experimental theatre. The flexible seating of this smaller theatre can then be thrust, or theatre-in-the-round, even another smaller proscenium theatre if desired." This was a good-sized space. As I have mentioned, it covered half a football field. It will be a most creatively usable performance space.

"It can even be opened from both sides and used for graduation ceremonies or large meetings," added Frances, when we later convinced her of the plan's value, at no extra cost!

Nazam said, "You have one thing to consider, though. Upstairs are the entrance doors to the theatre."

One would enter the theatre through the two sides of the cow's head, through the ears, which were the stairwells. One came through those doors, went around the back of the theatre, and down aisles on either side. For a long time we wanted continental seating, with no aisles at all, which was in vogue then, for I was greatly influenced by Jean Rosenthal, Broadway lighting designer for every major show from Oklahoma! to whatever was playing when she died in 1969, and with whom I joined in designing a similar sized theatre in 1963, but one that was not nearly as creatively flexible as this Damavand design. Jean would have loved the concept. We decided to put in step units to make certain aisles within the theatre, however, because it was such a small, intimate house anyway. From those entrances, through the ears of the cow on either side, we needed to get from one side of the theatre to the other during the intermission.

"Right. Let's put a crossover at the back, and we can turn it into a gallery. We can hang paintings in the crossover space." Nazam thought that the crossover would be an excellent way to connect those two areas. "That's good."

"Nazam, since we have no door to enter directly from the outside into the backstage area because it's underground; we need to have a door at this far upstage end. With the crossover, however, the door would be quite small, and it would be difficult to get units through it. Perhaps we can make it work."

The door wasn't small at all. It was a good ten feet high and eight feet across.

"On the outside of the theatre, up on the crossover level, let's clear a space." This was the design concept that Wes Peters had in mind originally, which upset Frances so much, because he had designed an enormous 2,000 seat theatre extending up the side of the mountain. "Let's go ahead and also put that theatre on the mountainside. We'll terrace it, and put the seating up the side of the mountain looking down upon this area on the ground, which will be a stage area. It will be marvelous for outdoor performances."

"Yes! We'll terrace it, and put in plants, so that when it's not in use, it appears to be green plantings on the hillside."

And so it was done. The terracing went into the plan. All of the door areas went in. The building's construction began. We ordered a Steinway concert grand piano; fortunately, the Steinway was never delivered.

DAMAVAND THEATRE: YEARS OF PROGRESS

To begin with, all of the architectural areas were there; everything that Taliesin West had designed. The sliding doors were there. They were enormously heavy, but they were on sliding arrangements that would work all right. One of the problems was the air conditioning. In order to cut the cost, certain things such as air conditioning were to be locally designed. Why there was air conditioning I do not know because at the base of the mountains it was always quite cool. It's just at the edge of the city, at the 5,500 foot level, and was never hot, as I recall. Always a bit cool. Tehran had no central heat, except perhaps in the Shah's palace. In the winter time, the snow crept down the mountainside to just above the campus so heat needed to be considered. Those 14,000 foot mountains, with 19,000 foot Mount Damavand in the distance, were covered with snow. A magnificent sight.

Every summer the three of us went back to the U.S. ranch to see my parents and to see BJ's parents; our families lived within twelve miles of each other. I usually taught summer school, to occupy half of the summer, and we'd spend the other half in the States. We had decent vacations at that college — the whole summer. Unlike China, where we had one month. Unlike Macau, where we had forty-two days for the entire year, and recently only twenty-two days. There we had three months' vacation. Every time we returned to Tehran, the first thing that I'd do was to step into the theatre. Progressively, over the years, something would be knocked out of the theatre. At first I thought, "This is looking good. The stage is level, although it has to have a wooden floor put on it, and it still needs the revolve." Then I reminded Nazam, "Don't make the stage too high because you're going to have all sorts of vertical things that come in."

The next year when I came back there was a huge trough that had been cut down the middle of the stage, from downstage to upstage, just right of center stage. I asked, "What is that?"

"The return air ducts. They were not planned for. They have to be installed."

I looked up above, and I noticed that there were flat, metal sheets, air ducts, which were coming from the studio stage, through the doors, onto the main stage.

I said, "There are doors there. They have to close. You can't run these ducts from the back to the front of the stage like that. There will be hanging battens that have to go up and down." Even though there wasn't a fly space, there had to be something. "Plus, there are traveler curtains that have to go around the back. Plus, there is a cyclorama that has to fit in there. The air ducts can't be left there."

The air ducts were there for a year until it was finally realized that they had to be removed. They were then going to bring them in from the sides.

I said, "Why have them at all? Leave them out. Put them in the seating area. That should be enough."

I realized that with hot spotlights one might need the air ducts on stage, but there simply was not enough space. They finally were removed. And as I mentioned, it was cool at this elevation of 5,500 feet. I hope they put heat in the seating area at least. Most of the heat in Tehran was in the form of kerosene (naft) heaters, either stoves or "Alladines," which are small, upright, kerosene heaters with a rounded wick inside a green metal vertical pipe housing over a flat tank of kerosene. It probably still is in private homes, but the wealthier homes and office towers would have commercial heat/air conditioning.

Apartment buildings then had central heat and air conditioning, but not the older interesting homes with "Persian Gardens" inside walls. We lived in one and it did not have central heat. Nor did some of the beautiful homes of our students, who would invite us to their homes, the same, almost, as the poorer students and workers, with naft being delivered to the door.

The doors came in to the theatre. We put in extra outside entrances. It wasn't feasible to think of only the one entrance on either side of the stage, at the cow's ears, so we put two more entrances down on the cow's jaw, on either side. This allowed people to enter from the main part of the campus. The campus always reminded me of a long train with lots of carriages, which were the individual buildings, which went all the way around the front of this oblong, rounded theatre-library, creating a caravanserai-like semi-circle.

MOVE TO NEW CAMPUS

The college finally moved into the campus. It wasn't ready, but we had been downtown in the old campus, which was very tiny, and now we had well over 1,000 students, and it simply wasn't big enough. Dr. Frances Gray had retired, and the new president, Dr. Ray Heisey, decided that the only way to get it finished was to move into that new campus.

We all said, "Don't do it. That's insanity." Because it was nowhere near ready, but he was determined that we were going to do it, and we did it. It was sheer chaos for the first few months; almost for the first year. No heat. The heat was not even installed, because that was also locally contracted in order to save on cost. There had been no water for a long time. Water finally came up to the campus when they were building it. Frances Gray had managed to get the water by a direct appeal to the Shah.

SHAH'S DIVANS

Every so often the Shah held what was called a "divan." At this divan he received everybody of importance, and a few of us who were not important. Any guest who had the nerve could approach him and ask him for anything. If they had the nerve. I went twice. As president of a college, Frances was invited to all divans for educators. She represented the school and could take one or two guests, so she took each of us teachers on a rotating basis.

We arrived at his palace, not the Niavaran Palace in northern Tehran near the campus, but his father's palace, the old Golestan Palace of the Qajar rulers, opposite the entrance to the Tehran bazaar. During the divan, he met with the ministers first. Then we all lined up around an enormous Persian rug. We knew where to stand; our feet were to touch the edge of the pattern of the rug. Then the door opened, and the Shah came out, dressed in his full regalia, medals and all. The Prime Minister was with him and a scribe with tablet and quill pen. They moved around and greeted each one there.

The time I was with her, Frances said to him, "Your Highness, you've been most generous. You've given us the land on which to build a new university- college campus, but we have a big problem. Although the building is being built, and it's going up very nicely, the problem is that we have no water, and we are unable to get anybody to send us a pipe of water. We have to haul it in for the workers, and we cannot start classes until there is water. We'll appreciate so much your help in this matter."

The Shah turned to the Prime Minister and said, "See that this is done," as the scribe recorded the command with his quill pen, attached to a ballpoint.

Within a short time there was, indeed, water; a pipe had been extended from the city main up to the campus. Thank heavens because the next autumn, after Frances retired, the new president decided that we were going to move into the campus. There wasn't much water, hardly enough to make the toilets operate, but little by little the amount increased, and things became much better.

REVOLUTION

By the time the revolution came, in 1978, the theatre was in no better condition than it had been three years earlier when Frances retired. It was amazing. It was not in good condition mainly because there was now a trough running down the middle of the stage. We called it the "jube," and the jube was not fixed by the time the revolution came. The engineer who was supposed to be overseeing this was obviously taking all of the money, or as much as he could skim off. He must have known something that the rest of us didn't know. In fact, most of Iran seemed to know something that the rest of us didn't know. When the revolution was imminent, one Sunday at church the First Secretary from the U.S. embassy asked me, "Norm, what's happening on that theatre?"

"It's still not finished. I'm beginning to feel absolutely ridiculous about it." The U.S. government had given a lot of AID (American International Development) money, every year for a number of years, to finish the campus and mainly to finish the theatre.

"Well, Norm, I will recommend that, one more time, this year, AID furnish additional money for the theatre." It was quite a sizeable amount of money, several hundred thousand dollars. But he added, "This is the last. I will not recommend any more."

"I think you're absolutely right. I'm not sure what's going on, but it's certainly not getting finished."

Irony of ironies. When the revolution finally came, the theatre was still not finished. Everything fell apart in Iran, and all foreigners were getting out. When we returned to the States, I rang up the school's then-president, Dr. Carolyn Spotta. She had just taken over when President Ray Heisey left after three years. Being new, she didn't know what she was doing about certain things, but she certainly was in control of one thing. She was from Washington, DC, and she knew enough people in Washington to go after the AID money, which had been financing what I referred to as "my theatre." I guess it was, in effect, my theatre.

She said to them, "Of course, you do not send that money to Tehran." The money had been frozen. "Now we have no money at all to pay the salaries of all of the teachers who have been stranded. Please, could you possibly advance us the AID money designated for the building of the theatre, and let us use it to pay salaries instead?" The officials in charge agreed.

Thank heavens she was able to do that because there were perhaps fifty American Damavand teachers who had been forced to leave Iran in the middle of the school year, who were now jobless. That's the one time that BJ and I went to the unemployment agency to see if we could qualify for unemployment insurance income, but of course we couldn't. Our situation was rather unique. Although Damavand College was run by an American organization [the Presbyterian Church Mission, Riverside Church, New York City] and did pay into U.S. Social Security for American teachers and TIAA Retirement [thanks to Frances], the college had not paid into the unemployment fund. Indeed, why would they for missionaries, I guess they thought.

We were grateful to Carolyn Spotta and the State Department for helping us survive this difficult time. The AID theatre money paid the American teachers' salaries for the rest of that year.

CASPIAN SEA

The years in Iran were challenging but rewarding and often exciting. Iran's a large country with many interesting places to visit. The trips we made within the country were always interesting and sometimes hazardous. One eventful trip was to the Caspian Sea, that inland sea of fresh water where the sturgeon are filled with caviar, which, via Iran or Russia, makes its way to the tea tables of cocktail parties all over the world.

We, along with Damavand colleague Margaret Moore, went north to Bandar Pahlavi by overnight train, which crosses the mountains between Tehran and the Caspian Sea. Then we traveled by taxi to Gorgon, where we stayed at a hotel.

One evening in Gorgon, as we walked down the street, a man pinched eleven-year-old Natasha's bottom. (Iranian men seemed to delight in doing this to western women, possibly because they didn't wear the chador.) She was tired of that happening, and so ran after him and pounded him on his back. He was surprised. He stopped, turned around, laughed with his friends, and walked away.

GONBAD-E-KAVUS

One day we went by taxi to Gonbad-e-Kavus, famous for its unusual tomb, a high, cylindrical stone tower — about six stories high – that originally held a glass coffin suspended from the pointed roof. The roof had an opening that allowed the sunlight to enter for the enjoyment of the occupant. It was one of the most eccentric things we'd ever seen, but there it was.

Gonbad-e-Kavus had little shops, mainly food, surrounding the main square. We walked around, found small things to eat, and BJ bought several old, metal, Russian army buttons from a junky little antique shop. At the Bandar Pahlavi railroad station she found a stunning ring that she wore for years. However, I haven't seen that ring for a while. It's probably been lost or stolen.

VILLAGE HOSPITALITY

Another day Margaret joined us in taking a small local bus to a neighboring town known for its colorful market that sold everything from gorgeous Russian wool shawls to horses and donkeys. The bus trip began and ended (plus each crossing of the frequent bridges) with the passengers invoking Allah in unison for road safety. An expedient practice! We all arrived safely. While walking on a village street, an Iranian young man approached us; he was so effervescent and excited about our visiting his town that he insisted that the four of us go to his house with him for tea. He was a student and showed us his English book, English for Special Purposes: Engineering. So, a bit reluctant, but at the same time curious, we agreed. His mother and sister welcomed us to seats on floor cushions. Bed rolls were piled along one wall, and colorful carpets gave the room a cheerful ambience. After sipping several cups of tea, along with a Persian sweet, and long since running out of things to talk about — especially with our limited knowledge of each other's language — we finally said, "We're sorry, but we have to go and catch our bus back to Gorgon."

He said, "No, no, no. You must stay. You must stay and go with me tonight to the wedding of my friend. His family will be honored if you will come."

"No, we must run to catch our bus," as I pulled my hand from his grasp. After much arguing and arm-pulling, we finally managed to get away. This is so typical of an almost aggressive, Middle Eastern hospitality.

CROWDED TRAIN

When we arrived in Bandar Pahlavi to catch our return train, we had already bought an entire compartment of the train for the journey back to Tehran. The trains were based upon the European equivalent, with separate compartments in each train car, about six feet by eight feet. Our compartment had eight seats, four on either side. There were only four of us. No porters. Margaret Moore, Natasha, BJ, and I had bought all eight seats. It was terribly "ugly American," but we were so tired of being cramped in small spaces, and we thought we'd just take these seats and stretch out. So we did. Many others had done the same thing. They hung chadors across the windows because all of these compartments had glass windows and doors.

The people who were outside in the hallway could, unfortunately, look in. It did make me feel guilty, but I must admit that as the train moved on for hours and hours that night, and we tried and tried to sleep, I felt less and less guilty. Many people crowded the corridors, but they hadn't paid as much as we had. When any of us had to leave the compartment for the WC, it was a mess, with more determined passengers trying to force their way in, but in spite of all, it was a great trip. No doubt this kind of behavior, more extravagantly performed by wealthy Iranians, encouraged the revolution.

Sometime later, BJ and Natasha joined a weekend trip to the Caspian, sponsored by Tehran American Community Church. This outing, a mother- daughter retreat, traveled by an ancient blue bus which, after detours and road blocks, crept its way through the rolling tea fields to finally reach its destination.

CROWDED TAXI

Tom, who had come with us to Tehran, had traveled to the Caspian Sea earlier, just before he returned to Palm Springs. He rode up in a small school bus with other teachers from the American Community School and from Damavand College. Their mini bus broke down, and so they all had to cram into a taxi. Now the taxi was a Mercedes, which is quite large, but nevertheless won't hold as many people as a mini bus. This was a mini school bus that the American Community School hired out to people on the weekends, and of course this was a weekend. Tom likes to tell the story of riding back in this taxi and holding Carol, who was the music teacher at Damavand College, on his lap. Tom is quite short, perhaps five foot five, and well built, but finally it turned out that he sat on Carol's lap, because Carol is considerably larger than Tom; not fat, merely taller.

PRINCESS ASHRAF'S PALACE

An interesting day trip I made was with the Frank Lloyd Wright architect, Wes Peters, to see the palace of Princess Ashraf, the Shah's sister. Natasha was for some reason not in school that day, so went also. The palace, which had been recently completed, was designed by the Wright architects. It was quite magnificent and had the same basic dome configuration that the Frank Lloyd Wright people had designed for Damavand College. An enormous dome covered the whole palace; in the case of Damavand, it extended over the whole library-theatre complex. The palace had much that was impressive, but the room I remember best is the library. Ashraf is a Christian, a fact that was hushed up in Tehran because, of course, Iran is Moslem. She wanted a chapel in her new palace, so Wes Peters gave her one that was designed to look like a library and which served also as a chapel. Natasha best remembers the solarium in which numerous bird cages of live parrots were suspended from the ceiling to mingle with the giant potted plants.

During our time in Tehran, we dreamed of taking the train from Tehran to Moscow. A friend of ours, Daphne Athos, who's a novelist and a professor at the University of North Carolina, was in Tehran on a Fulbright fellowship and took this train one winter. She described it as just like the Dr. Zhivago film. She looked out at the fields of snow, the mountains of snow, as she traveled up through Azerbaijan and on to Moscow. We were fascinated by her description of the changing of wheels at the Russian border to a different gauge and a different size of the railroad track. This was to prevent invasion, so they said. We learned what she meant 24 years later when we traveled to and through Russia by the Trans-Siberian railroad. Starting from Hong Kong by boat to Shanghai, we passed through Beijing, through Mongolia — where we had to wait for two days for the railway track, which was washed out, to be rebuilt by 200 Mongolians — so that we could go on to Moscow to St. Petersburg to Warsaw, Poland, and finally to Paris.

TRAVEL TO TURKEY

During our first summer in Tehran, in 1973, we decided to go to Istanbul, Turkey. Friends of ours, Henry and Gloria Riemenschneider, had told us that we should take the train. We had learned recently that the train trip was really very interesting. The train goes to Lake Van in Eastern Turkey, is floated all the way across Lake Van, and then continues on to Istanbul. That sounded interesting. We rode trains everywhere if we could, except in these past years, when we've had tens of thousands, and it seems like millions, of miles of airplane travel.

We then talked with some people about taking a ship along the coast of the Black Sea. Even more than trains, we loved ships. We had crossed the Atlantic Ocean by ship several times. We especially enjoyed our voyage on the Rotterdam from New York to Rotterdam; it was magnificent. We've always wanted to repeat it, but no longer are there trans-Atlantic ships. So we decided on the route including the ship along the Black Sea, which was several days' journey.

TABRIZ TO ERZURUM

In order to reach the ship, we had to get to the port city of Trabzon in Turkey. Trabzon is next to the Russian border of the Black Sea, so we took a flight from Tehran to Tabriz because it was faster. Then we waited for a bus. The bus was supposed to come at 11:00 in the morning. It came six hours later, which meant that everything down the line on the schedule was six hours late. The bus came to Tabriz along what was then called the Hash Trail across Asia. This trail went to India and back. The bus, an appropriately ramshackle affair, was loaded with hippies from the Woodstock land of India, grimy and bedraggled, who were mostly sick, as was I, for I was still recovering from meningitis.

Our bus stopped at the Turkish border where we had a stunning view of Mt. Ararat of Noah's ark fame. We got off to have our passports stamped. Some officials opened the outside baggage compartments to check the contents. Dust rose as one officer removed the cover of a large birdcage to reveal a sizeable, once-colorful parrot, which let out no words, only several subdued squawks; he was possibly dumbfounded by life's sudden turn of events The bird was claimed by one of the more emaciated travelers, who looked dangerously close to losing his worn-out britches that exposed much of his bare bottom. The officers appeared satisfied with his answers to their questions. They replaced the parrot's covering and closed the baggage compartments. All climbed aboard and were off again.

We rode through the evening, into the night, and the bus never stopped for food. Passengers screamed as we passed restaurant after restaurant, "Stop! Stop! Let us have some food. Let's eat here. Stop! What's wrong with this restaurant?"

The bus driver shouted, "No, no. Another very nice place come soon."

It was way after dark when we found this coal-oil-lighted hole-in-the-wall. The hungry passengers crowded into the small, semi-dark restaurant. Natasha and I stayed on the bus while BJ went inside for food. Thank God for BJ throughout these mad years of travel! I was in a pre-diabetic, low blood sugar situation since having meningitis. There wasn't much choice, and the fried eggs seemed the safest.

It soon became clear that there wouldn't be enough eggs to go around, and BJ found herself in the shadowy kitchen with ten or twelve irritable passengers surrounding the cook stove, all attempting to grab the eggs as fast as they were fried. She eventually returned to the bus with four eggs between thick pieces of bread. But the fracas didn't end in the restaurant. As the last passengers boarded, a row broke out between some passengers and several restaurant employees who followed them onto the bus, yelling something about money. It seems that some hadn't paid for their food. After much arguing, the problem was finally settled, the driver revved up the engine, and we were off again.

After hours of mountainous roads, scary because of the driver's nodding and jerking awake, we finally arrived in Erzurum well after midnight. Now Erzurum was where we were supposed to spend the night. We were to find our own hotel. The bus stopped in the square. We were told to get out and go find a hotel. All of us looked at each other. We claimed our bags and headed off in some direction to find a hotel room. "Do you have a room?"

"No room. Finished. Hallas." Hallas is Arabic, but they use it in Turkey also, meaning "finished." Finally, some young men who looked like students came up to us and asked, "You want hotel? Come with us."

About twenty of us followed them.

We climbed some stairs and entered a room that resembled a lobby, but it wasn't a real hotel. Our guides said, "You sleep here on floor; costs fifty cents" (equivalent). All twenty-some of us; most of the bus. Some spread their bedrolls. We had no bedrolls. We just had ourselves and a medium-size suitcase. So we sat there, and people started to go to sleep. Then there were two, possibly three, guys sitting on a table in front of the door. We noticed that they had locked the door, which we thought rather strange. We looked at each other. BJ became very concerned. We had been robbed three times in the Middle East. We decided not to stay. We took Natasha, went up to the desk, and said we wanted to leave.

"Why? You no happy here?" "No happy here."

"You go police?" "No go police." "You want out?" "Yes, we want out."

"You want money back?"

"No, you can keep the money." It wasn't very much. "Just let us out." "You no go police?"

"We no go police."

So they finally opened the door, and as we left, we looked at all those people asleep there, and we wondered, "Are they planning to rob them or what?"

We went down the stairs to find the front gate locked. But a man came downstairs to ask, "You no go police?"

"No, we no go police."

He opened the gate, and we went out with our bags. He slammed the gate shut and locked it. There we were, at about three in the morning, relieved, but wondering, "Well, where do we go now?"

We walked across the street a little way and came to a large, lighted window, blue painted walls, and a terrace that was being swept by what looked like a bellhop. We asked him, "Is there a room for rent here?"

"Ask the desk. Maybe."

We went to the desk, which was unoccupied, and rang a bell. A disheveled fellow emerged from a nearby doorway.

"Yes," he replied to our question and to our elation.

He quoted a price to which we agreed, and led us up the stairs to a clean-looking room with a bath, a shower, and one bed — a double. It didn't matter; we were so exhausted that we fell asleep immediately, three peas in a pod.

ERZURUM TO TRABZON

BJ went out early in the morning to find a dolmus, which means "stuffed", but in this case was a mini bus. Practically everything one eats in Turkey is stuffed. There is stuffed eggplant, stuffed squash, stuffed green leaves. They are usually stuffed with rice, meat, cinnamon, and spices. Dolmus are delicious until you have eaten them for several days. The word "dolmus" is pronounced "dol moosh." The mini buses are aptly called dolmus for the many passengers that can be stuffed inside.

BJ reserved seats on the dolmus leaving for Trabzon at noon. While looking for the dolmus, she saw people from the day before who had been on the bus and at the "hotel"; they had survived the night okay. She returned and got me out of bed. I'm a late sleeper since I usually can't sleep early. We hurried from our hotel to find some breakfast before boarding the dolmus. BJ and Natasha sat together in the back, and I sat immediately in front of them, next to a Turkish gentleman. The dolmus was stuffed with all male passengers, and two sat on stools in the aisle, a practice we later observed on the crowded busses in China. Everyone wore western-style wool caps, which were part of Ataturk's modernization policy. Several of these men spoke a little English and told us that they were all on their way to Germany where they had jobs.

Our dolmus pulled away from Erzurum's bus terminal and made its way to the city's outskirts. Erzurum is located on a plateau, surrounded by high mountains that extend all the way to the Black Sea. These tree-covered mountains reminded us of Switzerland. In winter they're covered with snow. Now they were beautiful with flowers, green, magnificent mountains. We U- turned back and forth through one hairpin curve after another, all the way across those mountains. The road's many potholes gave constant jolts and bumps. BJ and Natasha soon discovered that there were no springs beneath their seats. My seat was little better. We bounced and bumped around the hairpin curves until nearly six o'clock in the evening, when we descended to the lovely Black Sea port of Trabzon. Fabled Trabzon with its exotic mosques and minarets. At the bus station we shook hands and bid our fellow travelers goodbye. Then our search for a hotel room began.

TRABZON

We walked and walked around the town center, asking at every hotel. No hotel rooms. None at all. We learned why: this was the weekend when the university exams were held, and students from all over Turkey were converging on Trabzon to take the entrance exam. So every hotel room was occupied. Finally, one hotel told us, "Look, we have one room that is reserved, but the student has not yet arrived. If that student does not arrive by 9:00, we'll let you have it."

We had between two and three hours to wait. Although we were exhausted, we walked along the sea and saw a few sights, including our ship waiting in the harbor. We had a good dinner at a seaside restaurant, came back to the hotel, and sure enough, the student had not arrived, and we were allowed to have the room. How lucky for us! We shoved the twin beds together. Never mind the crack in the middle. We gratefully passed the night, thanking God.

Early the next morning, we happily awoke to bright sunshine and found that our room had a grand view of a lovely seascape. But we had little time to enjoy it for we needed to purchase tickets for the voyage to Istanbul. Fortunately, the ticket office was nearby and we had our tickets in no time, with four hours to spare before sailing time, which is what we'd hoped for. We'd read about a third century church with outstanding murals from that early period. It was located in the countryside, a few miles from Trabzon, so we needed a taxi, which was quite easy to arrange. We were not disappointed. The church's setting was lovely, and although damaged by time, the murals remained beautiful. Although it appeared abandoned, the church had not become a mosque as so many had!

BLACK SEA CRUISE

The taxi got us back to Trabzon in ample time to catch the boat. Friends had advised us to buy only first class tickets, which were actually quite inexpensive. So there we were, in our walnut-paneled first class stateroom, anticipating a luxurious three-day cruise to Istanbul. It may not have been luxury by some standards, but for us it was a magnificent reward for our long, exhausting trip through Iran and Turkey. As we stood at the rails of this lovely white ship, staring at the blue-black waves, we felt so lucky to be enjoying this cruise.

I went below to look around, saw the engine room, talked with the first mate, talked with the captain, talked with the various crew members and some of the passengers before finding a place to relax on the deck. The ship's food was quite good, and we shared our dining table with two teachers from Natasha's school, Tehran Community School. One was Mrs. Stewart, who would be her math teacher the following year.

Our ship followed the Turkish coastline, stopping at a number of cities along the way; at Samsun, for example, we picked up tobacco, and at Sinope, cotton. This was a combined freighter, passenger ship, and car ferry, which made its voyage very interesting. It unloaded cars at certain places. It loaded tobacco and unloaded cotton. Everywhere we stopped business was transacted, and the dock was a hive of activity.

ISTANBUL

Eventually we sailed through the Bosphorus beneath the old Ottoman palace, the Palace of the Sultans, on the side of the hills overlooking the Bosphorus as we passed between the continents of Asia and Europe. This was just when they were building the first bridge across the Bosphorus in 1973. Ferries were still crossing between the European and Asian sides. Perhaps we even saw the palace door through which the sacks of bodies were moved to be thrown into the Bosphorus. This is how the Ottomans disposed of people who got in their way. So many mysterious tales have come from The Arabian Nights of Turkish delight and from ancient Istanbul, then Constantinople, until Ataturk changed the name as Turkey became a republic. Before Constantinople it had been Byzantium.

Our ship docked, and we found ourselves in this ancient, historical city, rich with priceless churches and domed mosques whose minarets five times daily call the faithful to prayer. The religious architecture, constantly pointing toward heaven, reminds the faithful that God, here known as Allah, patiently awaits their prayers.

We explored the city. Although we'd visited Istanbul earlier, when living in Beirut, there were many things we'd not seen, and most were worth many visits. First to Santa Sophia, the sixth century church, designed by Armenian architects, famous for its wide dome covering a vast expanse with no supporting columns. The ring of arched windows, which horizontally intersect the dome, give the illusion of its floating in mid-air. It did collapse once and had to be rebuilt. Now it's a museum. After Turkey's conquest by Islam in 1453, this magnificent Christian edifice was converted into a mosque. Four minarets were added to the exterior, and the exquisite mosaics inside, including the Christ Pantocrator in the dome, were covered with plaster/whitewash. Some of the mosaics are still visible in nooks and crannies. We found the huge green plaques with Koranic calligraphy, added at the dome's base, aesthetically ugly and detracting. When we were there in 1997 and

1998, they had a huge scaffolding going up to the center of the dome, and we thought that maybe they were going to clean off the mosaics. We heard later, in Athens, that no, they were not. They were covering them over even more, so that none of the dome's Christian symbols could be made out. On the other hand, Byzantine motifs remain visible around the corners and in little archways. In Greece, now, it is said by some that Santa Sophia is being turned into a mosque, not to be used just as a museum. I don't know. But considering Turkish-Greek relations, one wonders. I should check with a friend who lives in Istanbul.

We walked from Santa Sophia to the Blue Mosque named for its brilliant blue and green tile. As we approached, the amplified call to prayer broke through the street noise. "There is no god but God. There is no god but Allah, and Mohammed is his prophet!" After buying our tickets in the vast courtyard, we entered and added our shoes to many already on the shelves. Later, in 1996, BJ bought a lovely wool knit cap from an old man who sat in this courtyard, knitting with four pair of needles. The following year we did not find him there.

Hundreds of worshippers knelt on colorful Turkish and Persian carpets that covered the thousands of square feet beneath the dome. We non-worshippers were allowed to move around the perimeter of the enormous room to view the architecture and amazing tile work with its Islamic decorations: calligraphy, plants, and geometric patterns. Islam forbids human or animal figures. Here, as in every mosque, two centers of attention were the mihrab, which indicated the direction of Mecca, and the minbar or pulpit, from which the holy word was preached each Friday.

We were told that one church we must see was Kariye Camii (St. Savior in Chora). "Chora" meaning countryside. The most important Byzantine church. Its mosaic murals and frescos, from the fourteenth century, are considered the finest examples of Byzantine art in the world. Since this church, now a museum, was quite far from the center of town, we hired a taxi and had some difficulty finding the right place. But this gem of a church was well worth our effort. The mosaics illustrate the lives of Christ and the Virgin Mary. One memorable scene shows a resurrection: Christ is pulling Adam and Eve from their tombs. Our guide book explained that the reason they remain in such good condition is thanks to the whitewash spread on them during the centuries of Ottoman rule when the church was a mosque. Familiar stories were here depicted with exquisite beauty, and we were saturated with all that we were seeing. Before heading back to our hotel, we relaxed with cold drinks at an old Ottoman house turned into a teahouse.

As we visited many places in Istanbul, just as we did 25, 27, and 29 years later, we recognized how wonderful the place was and longed to teach there. But the closest we have come to that is a year in Turkish Cyprus. Fortunately, none of these "historical statements in stone" collapsed in the 1999 earthquake that killed 18,000 people in its terrible fury.

Hotels in Istanbul can be a problem. On this 1973 trip, we first checked into a hotel recommended by friends, who I hope had better luck with it than we did. After the first night Natasha awoke with a rather severe rash. We were pretty sure that it was from bedbugs, so we checked out of that hotel and crossed the Bosphorus to a better part of town. First to the U.S. consulate, where they gave directions to the American hospital. A doctor there prescribed helpful medication. Then we took a hotel room near the American consulate and also near one of our very favorite hotels, the Pera

Palace. The Pera Palace is the hotel featured in Stambol Train by Graham Greene; his characters, after arriving in Istanbul, are transferred to the Pera Palace. Agatha Christie wrote while staying in that hotel, which was actually built to accommodate travelers from the Orient Express train. The hotel has wonderful, Ottoman-looking, old Turkish architecture on the inside. A few years later, we enjoyed the dining room and the old, solid bathroom and bedroom luxury of the Pera Palace. On this trip in 1973, however, we stayed just across the street, a block away, in a less expensive hotel, but with good, clean beds and sometimes dined at the Pera Palace. Lovely memories.

ON TO THE U.S.

After we'd been there for perhaps a week, I began to wonder, "What are we going to do here for a whole summer, sitting in Istanbul?"

Now I could do it easily; then I was far too nervous and depressed. Our money was going to run out, and I somehow wanted to go home. My father was diabetic, and I had been diagnosed as being pre-diabetic, and I had just had meningitis. It was a terrible, terrible kind of illness that just went on and on, and I couldn't seem to get control of it. I wanted to go home to be with my father, who I thought would give me some kind of spiritual, if not physical, encouragement, for he was a very spiritual man. While we were always close, we were also somehow distant. Perhaps all sons and fathers are that way, but I still had to be near him — every summer.

I asked around at travel offices and all of the tickets were terribly expensive. I finally found someone who said, "Yes, we have a flight. The fare is this much to New York. It's on Czechoslovakian Air."

As I calculated the cost, I realized that I didn't have enough money. After changing my money, there wouldn't be enough to pay for the tickets.

"Look, buddy, see those taxis down on the street?" He pointed to a Mercedes parked below us. "You go to one of those taxis, you open the door, and you step inside, and say to him that you want to change your money. He will change it for you, and he will give you double or triple the exchange rate." It was a huge amount of money for dollars. Of course, it was the black market.

"Really? If that's true, I can afford the tickets." "Yes, really. You can afford to buy the tickets."

In my naïve way I dashed down there, approached the first taxi I saw, tapped on his window and asked, "Could you change money?"

"Sure. Whatcha' got? Climb in."

So I got into the Mercedes service car, which was his office. I don't remember how much money I had, but it couldn't have been much because we weren't paid a huge amount of money at Damavand College. I had taken an $8,000 cut in salary when I signed the contract with Frances. He said, "Look, I'll give you this much." He pulled out this enormous roll of Turkish money, and he started peeling off money, money, money. All of a sudden I had an enormous stack of bills.

I said, "Are you sure?" Because it was enough to buy the air tickets and have a little extra.

"Sure!"

"Okay, here are the dollars." I immediately went to buy our tickets home. This flight went from Istanbul to Prague. We had managed to get

Czechoslovakian visas, and we were hoping to go into the town to see it, but for some reason they would not let us get off the plane. The plane went immediately on to New York, and so we asked, "Can we stop when we come back?"

They said, "Yes, of course." They always say, "Yes, of course."

So we flew on to New York, and it seemed like an eternally long flight, although it wasn't. It was an Illusion jet, one of the best that Russia built, which was very much like a Boeing 707. The service on this Illusion jet was quite good, except that they had nothing to drink except beer and non-freshly- squeezed orange juice drink. So, while I don't like beer very much, I drank beer and orange drink, and BJ and Natasha had the orange drink until they couldn't stand it anymore.

KANSAS

We arrived in New York and found a flight to Wichita, Kansas. Somebody drove us to the ranch, 220 miles west. We spent the rest of the summer with my father, stepmother, and with my three brothers who were there. My youngest brother had died two years before. BJ spent much of the time in town — Liberal, Kansas — with her parents.

It was always a very moving time for me to go back to the ranch, especially when it was busy. In earlier days, it had been very busy, indeed. During the summers there used to be sixteen of us working on the ranch; moving irrigation pipes, moving cattle, farming. There were hundreds of cattle, and my brother had 28 Appaloosa horses. There was less activity in later years.

A CHANGED RANCH

This was the summer of 1973, and my brother Mark had died quite tragically near the ranch in the spring of 1971. He was sixteen years old, the youngest of six boys. He was driving home from high school, and he started to cross a main road, which had a rather high hill. He stopped at the corner, we presume, because he had always stopped, looked, and then took off. His car was not the brand new "0-to-60-miles-per-hour-in-60-seconds" type of car that is being built nowadays. His car was perhaps a bit slow, but over the hill came two guys in a jeep who had been out hunting. They had been drinking, or so their blood tests indicated later, and they were driving very fast. They hit Mark's car from the side. They hit it so hard that his car was pushed 100 feet into the field off the road, and Mark's neck was broken instantly. That had happened two years before.

I remember that day when my brother, Gurney, called and said, "Mark ... Mark is dead."

I asked, "Are you sure?" "Yes. His neck was broken."

I was in the middle of directing Panteglaze by Michele de Ghelderode. *Panteglaze* is an innocent person who goes through life totally unaware that he has influences that are amazing: sometimes for good, sometimes for revolution. His quiet naïveté says so much about the innocence of mankind, and Mark was certainly innocent; would he have been a Panteglaze? Immediately BJ, Natasha, and I caught a plane from Palm Springs, California, where I was teaching, to Amarillo, Texas, where my brother Jim picked us up and drove us the 200 miles to the ranch.

A terribly devastating experience. Not only because of Mark's death but because, somehow, that was the death of the ranch as well. It was February, the ranch was cold, the trees were without leaves, and wintertime had turned into the image of death. Since graduating from high school, I'd not been at the ranch in winter, except sometimes at Christmas, with much holiday cheer. I came back only in summers. The rest of the time I was at a university somewhere. Every time I came in the summer the ranch was full of life, and energy, and excitement, and the greenery of growing things, and enormously tall trees that surrounded the house. Now, with the death of Mark, those live trees were dead. Somehow, it was absolutely devastating.

After the funeral, we went back to Palm Springs, and I had another play to direct, *Edwin Booth* by Milton Geiger. It is a play about the life of the American actor Edwin Booth and was filled with many Shakespearean scenes and the assassination of President Lincoln by Edwin's brother. It was an active life that pulled me out of the deep depression brought on by the death of my sixteen-year-old brother whom we all loved.

Now, two years later, I was back at the ranch, but it didn't seem alive, even though it was summer. Something else had died when Mark died. Things didn't seem to be as energetic as they had been for twenty years ever since Dad had discovered oil, and became quite well-to-do, built the 3,200 acre ranch, and leased oil lands of 32,000 acres. So it was very strange for me to come back from Turkey, and from Iran, and not to see the excitement. We did spend some time in California, though, visiting friends in Los Angeles and Palm Springs.

RETURN TO TEHRAN

When preparing to return to Tehran, we booked our flight in Wichita. I had already booked reservations on Pan-Am from New York to Tehran. That was in the computer. In Wichita we checked in our bags, and they went to New York and on to Tehran by Pan-Am. That was before the days when the luggage had to be paralleled with the tickets through the computer. We flew to Chicago, where we changed planes and checked some more luggage through to Tehran because we were so loaded. We were always carrying things back that we needed, at least thought we needed. We had winter coats, we had clothes, we had books, everything. BJ had taken her white, fake fur coat with her, because I remember somebody saying as we got on the flight, "Ah, somebody's going where it's cold." We were! Tehran was like an enormous ski slope when the snow came below the usually above-the-city snow line. The new Damavand College campus was being built on the snow line.

In New York, we arrived at the Pan-Am building. I went up to the ticket counter and said, "We have reservations on your flight to Tehran." I had booked the reservations in California by telephone.

"Yes, show me your ticket."

I showed him our tickets. He smiled and said, "You know, these tickets have to be endorsed over to Pan-Am by Czech Air."

"Oh, how do I do that?"

"You see that lady standing over there, looking at tickets?" Czech Air flew into the Pan-Am terminal.

"Yes."

"You go over there and ask her to endorse these over to Pan-Am. If she agrees, you can ride on Pan-Am to Tehran. Otherwise, you will have to take Czech Air."

Naïvely, I said, "Okay, very good." How easily one's naïve confidence tumbles when one travels all over the world.

After looking at our tickets, the Czech Air employee said something like, "Gott in Himmel! What are you trying to do? Of course you can … not … take Pan-Am. You must take Czech Air."

"But they'll do it if you'll sign it."

"Well, I won't sign it." I learned later that she wouldn't sign it because Czech Air was undercutting all other airlines, in terms of the prices. You couldn't go with this kind of a cut-rate deal onto a full-fledged, in this case, Pan-Am flight.

"Where can we change the route? I don't want to go all the way to Warsaw. Can we cut through to Istanbul and on to Tehran?"

"You can go to Amsterdam, and in Amsterdam pick up Lufthansa to Istanbul."

"Well, okay, that will be all right. You're sure we can change planes in Amsterdam?"

"Yes, of course." They always say, "Yes, of course."

So we flew to Amsterdam, with more beer and orange juice, and very little food.

Once in Amsterdam, I asked, "Where can we get the Lufthansa flight on to Istanbul?"

The man replied, "Oh, no, you can't. You have to ride this all the way to Prague."

"I was told in New York that I could." "No, that was a mistake."

So we flew on to Prague. By then the flight was late; it was getting very late. When we arrived in Prague, the connecting flight to Istanbul had already gone.

"Never mind, we will put you on another route to get you to Istanbul." "How?"

"We'll put you on the Czech flight to Zurich."

We rode the Czech flight to Switzerland. It was a Tuplov, with two seats on one side and one on the other. A Tuplov is more like a fighter plane: small, very fast, very up and down, and very swift around the corners. Natasha started looking ill, and she needed the assistance of the little paper bag in the back of the seat in front of her. We were very frustrated, only to arrive in Switzerland to discover that the flight on to Istanbul, that we were trying to catch, had gone. But they put us on Swiss Air to Istanbul. When we reached Istanbul, we picked up the original Lufthansa flight that we were trying to take out of Amsterdam, which had had some connections, and we took that flight on to Tehran by merely walking a short distance on the tarmac where the planes were parked, waiting for takeoff. Our trip had taken 24 hours, which at that time we thought was a long time. Now that we have flown, many times, all of the way from America to China, and on over to Macau, 24 hours doesn't seem bad. That's what it takes to fly Los Angeles to Hong Kong, take the airport bus to the jetfoil, and the jetfoil to Macau, plus a taxi on to the university campus where we taught for six years. So, 24 hours became standard procedure. At that earlier time, however, we thought it excessive. Fortunately, one can now fly directly to Macau via several airlines, with one stop in Taiwan, Bangkok, or Kuala Lumpur. It still takes 20-24 hours, but is much easier for us than going via Hong Kong. However, many people do go via Hong Kong, and someone helps with luggage onto the jetfoil boats.

ISFAHAN, PERSEPOLIS, AND SHIRAZ

Many of Iran's interesting sites could be reached only by bus, and while some of our friends took advantage of the local busses, we were hesitant because of the unbelievable number of fatal bus accidents.

There were even reports that bus stations collected the names of "closest of kin" before passengers boarded! We limited ourselves to destinations reached by train or plane. One summer we managed to tack on to our return tickets both Isfahan and Shiraz. That was when one could still buy mileage tickets.

Lovely Isfahan with its fabulous mosques and no less fabled Shiraz were much the same as when we'd visited them on our overland trip ten years earlier. But there's always more to see, especially in Isfahan with its countless mosques, madressehs, and palaces. One charming site is the Portico of the Forty Pillars. Actually, there are only twenty octagonal, wooden pillars, but with their shimmering reflections in the opposite pool, they total forty. How typical of the Persian romantic imagination!

Our main purpose in returning to Shiraz was to visit Persepolis. We hired a taxi to drive us the fifty miles north of the city, to ancient Persepolis, ruins of the luxurious palaces and residences built by Darius I approximately 500 B.C., and continued by his son Xerxes. Although Persepolis was an important ceremonial center during Achaemenian times, it never became the main capital because of its remote location. We arrived at around 4:00 p.m. and wandered over the vast area of monumental stairways, walls, and gates with their bas relief carving of winged bulls with human heads, much like those found in Assyrian architecture.

The column capitals, many now on the ground, were especially striking. The capitals had both a bull's head and a horse's head, each facing away from the other, balanced on top of very tall, thin pillars. Quite interesting to compare with their ancient Egyptian competitors, whose pillars are much thicker. Both are expressive of their "Shah 'n Shah" or "King of Kings" status. Ramses carved his message into some very thick pillars; Cyrus placed horses and bulls as if they were the top of his head!

A small museum set up in one of the ancient reception rooms displayed a number of choice objects as well as some items from Islamic times. We felt rushed to see as much as possible before the gates closed at sunset. Leaving, we felt saturated, although there was much we'd not seen. Mary Renault wrote *Persian Boy*, a revealing (quite literally sometimes) account of Alexander the Great taking and burning Persepolis. Seeing these architectural ruins it saddens one that Alexander destroyed the great palaces!

We especially enjoyed Shiraz's huge, covered bazaar where we watched artisans at work on copper pots and trays, ceramic tableware, filigreed silver jewelry, block-print table cloths, and wool carpets. We bought more than we should have, gifts for family and friends, and souvenirs to make us remember these precious sights and sounds.

One trip within Iran that I did alone was to Shiraz for the Shiraz Drama Festival. It was most interesting with plays from all over Asia. Japan had probably the most unusual production, with actors on stilts. Its setting was also interesting, in the open-air at an old, abandoned Shiraz palace.

Another time, I traveled to Isfahan by the new train, which gave a sensation of floating across the desert sand dunes. Wonderful Isfahan. Magnificent as always. I had first seen Isfahan ten years earlier when we drove there from Beirut. Thank heavens the Iran-Iraq war did not destroy this exquisite sixteenth century architecture. The main purpose of this trip was to see a very new, but old Persian-style building, a church hall. It had been designed by a British architect friend, who had been brought in originally to design a new bazaar for the city of Mashad. The charming church hall, which belonged to Isfahan's Anglican congregation, with its arches and caravansary-like design, did suggest an earlier period of Persia. Indeed, it was a more traditional design than our caravansary-like Damavand College created by the Frank Lloyd Wright Taliesin West.

It was during this time in Isfahan that the Bishop of Jerusalem and Middle East, Bishop Deghani, who served on the Damavand board, and I first discussed the possibility of his son, Bahram, teaching at Damavand College. Bahram was then finishing his studies at Oxford and had decided to return to Iran, an unfortunate decision, which eventually led to his premature death at the hands of Khomeini's Red Guard.

LIFE IN TEHRAN

While teaching at Damavand College, in addition to the academic-related activities, we had busy social lives. There was always something to go to. Iran is a gregarious society. A number of our students came from very wealthy families. They often held marvelous, extravagant dinner parties, with everything from small orchestras to belly-dancers (too often they always seemed to gravitate to me), with enormous tables spread with every kind of Persian food. Fessinjun, Polo-shirin (chicken with sweet rice), shish-kebabs, pomegranate juice, and a variety of soft drinks, wine, if the household was not Moslem, which it usually was. Even if it were Moslem, alcoholic drinks were often offered to non-Moslems. Beautifully decorated palatial homes, with enchanting, sculptured gardens, charming with humming birds and birds in cages. The gardens are all walled in. Someone once pointed out that Persian rugs are modeled after the gardens. Throughout history gardens have been especially important in the lives of Persians, because they live in the dry desert, with water fed throughout the cities through jubes (small open channels). The water originates in the distant mountains, and moves through a series of qanats (pronounced "kaanots"), rather like deep, connected-by-tunnels cisterns, across great areas of desert. This qanat water system is ancient. It goes back hundreds of years and covers many miles. From the air, qanats look like a giant has hopped along the desert on a pogo stick.

Until the campus moved to the northern part of the city and transportation became very difficult, we attended many of the cultural events at Rudaki Hall. Iran at that time had not only an excellent symphony orchestra but an outstanding opera company with a brilliant German designer, Theo Lau, plus a very acceptable ballet troupe. These three groups of performers included quite a number of foreigners, mainly eastern Europeans.

Another important part of our lives was Chapel. The church we attended was located in the southern part of the city on the old, original, mission compound; at least a hundred years old. Worship services took place in the old Presbyterian mission church referred to as the Chapel; Sunday mornings in Farsi (Persian) and in English at 4:00 p.m. The

Presbyterian Church had this huge mission compound in the heart of Tehran. The large school for boys had been closed for some time, and many of the buildings now stood empty. But the grounds were still beautiful, even though not very well cared for.

BJ played the Chapel organ for congregational singing. It was an old, push- pedal organ, a reed organ. She would pump up the organ, play the wonderful hymns, and we sang them. Since it played so loudly I was very happy to sing, for while my voice is not always on pitch, it is always loud, and the organ's bass notes covered my basso gusto.

We were a small group at the Chapel, mainly teachers, and very close-knit. Most of them taught at the American Community School, Iran Zamin School, or Damavand College. The discussion/study sessions after the service were memorable. Bob Pryor, whose main job was handling the much larger American Community Church, also preached for the Chapel. His sermons were excellent, partly because he always tried to relate the Biblical message to Iranian culture and history, and our "present circumstances."

There was another sizeable English-language church, the Tehran Bible Church, which several of our faculty attended, but the American Community Church located in the far north of the city was where most of the Americans lived. Reverend Pryor had been pastor there for years. He and his wife, Mary Lou, had earlier been missionaries in Tabriz, Iran. When the revolution came, his family left, but he stayed on, trying to protect the church. Finally, it was partially destroyed; even the hymnals were ripped and burned. Bob tells of being held prisoner for a time in his church office and eventually being released by his loyal Iranian custodian. From Iran the Pryors moved to Santa Barbara, California, and now live in Ventnor, New Jersey. Marvelous Christians who understood Persian people as well as their flock. He was an ambassador for communication between Western and Eastern thought and religion. BJ studied Church History under Rev. Bob Pryor.

After Chapel we often went for perushkies, delicious Russian meat-filled pastries, and chai, tea, at a little Russian tea house on Naderi Street. The Chapel was on Qavam Sultaneh, a small, tree-lined street in the south of the city and just below Naderi Street, which was in the Armenian Christian section of Tehran.

[In 2017 a fire broke out — was set, we heard — in a high-rise building near the Chapel compound area, killing a number of people. The news releases showed clouds of smoke rising in the building. Having been involved in building the theatre on the Damavand College campus, it occurs to me that the procedure of building the floors of a high-rise might be instrumental in the deaths from this fire. Each floor is built by the arch known as the Roman Arch in which bricks are placed in the steel girding of the floor and next to it another brick arched together and held by grout with a keystone in the middle of the arch. These arches are filling the complete space between girders, until they make up the complete floors. Once I knew that was the way the floors were built, I would automatically step from the low place to the next low place for that was where the steel beams were located. On top of this brick arched floor, tar/pitch was spread so that no water could get to the bricks so they would stay dry. Bodjies, servants, would wash the floors after tiles made of ceramic with glaze were put on top of the tar. Now, when that building burned from a fire starting on the lower floor, the heat rose, the tar melted, caught on fire, the bricks crumbled, and fell, and the people upstairs could not get out of the building since all floors and stairs are made of brick in the above mentioned procedure, and the fire moved steadily up. This is, of course, only a theory. If I could I would like to discuss it with my colleague Nazam Ameri who was the brilliant Frank Lloyd Wright Taliesin West architect in Tehran. Our work together is discussed elsewhere, regarding the designing of the theatre.]

Only in this part of town could we buy pork meat and wine, both forbidden in Moslem shops. Interestingly enough, in the late part of our time in Iran, we learned that in the northwestern part of Iran, in the Azerbaijan area, which is an Armenian section, there was the world's largest distillery for wines. Established by the French, they reportedly produced a great deal of it but started only in the last few years before the revolution. These wineries were destroyed during the revolution, so we understood. Iranian wines were very good!

NATASHA'S BAPTISM

Natasha was baptized on the mission compound, where the Chapel was located, in the mission water reservoir, which sometimes served as the mission swimming pool. Reverend Bob Pryor baptized her. BJ comes from the Anabaptist-Mennonite tradition, and I come from the background of Quaker, Methodist-through-Church-of-God-through-Presbyterian tradition. For the many years when we have been in Los Angeles, Hollywood Presbyterian has been our church. Over the years we had discussed baptism with Natasha. She had not been baptized when a baby. She wanted to be immersed as a young teenager, which is the Anabaptist tradition: baptism is by personal decision. Bob was happy to immerse her since he occasionally did immersions, although his parishioners were usually sprinkled when infants. So one spring Sunday, after the Chapel service, the congregation gathered around the water reservoir to witness Natasha's baptism. Some had never before seen an immersion. Afterward we went to the social hall to celebrate with refreshments. Recently, when discussing her daughter's baptism, Natasha said she had been quite afraid when she was immersed. It was a rather large reservoir, and she feared she might drown, even though when a child in Palm Springs, California, she won a swimming contest.

RESTAURANTS AND A FIRE

Tehran had excellent restaurants, and many served western food. The outdoor garden restaurants, which often had pleasant, live music, were especially popular during the summer, and we loved to go to them. Although we didn't have much extra money, we usually ate out once or twice a week. We found cooking meals rather a problem in Iran; good, tender meat was almost non- existent and much of the fresh produce looked as though it had rolled off the truck more than once. The weekly major shopping trip was always an ordeal and getting the stuff home was a big effort. In between trips to Iran Super, we'd rely on the hole-in-the-wall neighborhood stores that were stocked with mainly tomato paste and cooking oil. Eggs were usually available, but not always fresh. One of our colleagues used to carry a small pan of water to the store, to test the eggs, refusing the ones that floated. She'd learned that technique in Afghanistan. Another friend called them garbage stores.

Two of our favorite garden restaurants were the Paprika, which was very much like the name suggests, very Eastern European, and the Naderi Hotel's huge outdoor area with fountain and often a small orchestra. A restaurant, just off Naderi Street, offered delicious Korean food and had a few other Korean items for sale. We once bought a gallon of soy sauce, which was hard to find in the grocery stores, as were many foreign items, and Natasha bought a native Korean dress there. That was fun. Another Korean restaurant featured bar-b-que, which was cooked at the table on a pyramid-like utensil. The pyramid had rings around it and holes in it; the meat, marinated in a sauce, was placed on this pyramid, and a hot, peppery sauce was poured over it every so often. The pyramid was designed so that the sauce was caught where the meat was held, and it was all cooked by the gas flame underneath it. A bottle of gas was brought to our table, and we sat there and cooked it, ignoring the noisy, basic, undecorated surroundings. The food was wonderfully delicious.

One evening we were enjoying dinner in a restaurant on Avenue Roosevelt, not far from our first apartment. It served western and Persian food and also had a pizzeria upstairs. BJ, Natasha, and I had just come in from a very cold, snowy, winter's evening. This is at the 3,500 foot level in the city. Natasha had brought her book and was reading it. She often took a book to restaurants and social functions where there would be no children. All of a sudden, into the dining room poured smoke, billowing down the stairs from above. One of the waiters came running in, shouting something, probably "fire." I told Natasha to grab her coat.

Black smoke was everywhere. I took hold of Natasha's hand, and by then it was pitch black. We could see very little and heard the roaring of the fire upstairs. We had to follow the wall, BJ going first, feeling her way to the door. I stumbled on something; it was someone lying flat. Someone had fallen. I held onto Natasha, pulling her along, and we reached a door that wouldn't open. All of the doors swing in; they don't open out, and that made it more difficult. People kept pushing against the door, and we kept pulling the door to get it open. We finally got through this inner door, and I remembered that you turned right to go through the front door. Continuing to pull Natasha along, we found our way out. BJ was already out, standing in her Iranian pusteen (sheepskin, fur-lined coat) and illuminated by the yellow flames. I yelled, "BJ, go across the street! Run!"

Plate glass windows were bursting and shattering straight in front of where she stood, but she was so worried that we weren't getting out. "Go! Run!"

We jumped the jube and dashed across the street where traffic had stopped. We looked back; the flames reached the top of the building, and people were stranded on the roof. We heard later that some had jumped down, to be caught in firmly-held Persian rugs grabbed from neighbors' floors. Then I noticed that Natasha didn't have her coat. It was still inside the restaurant, but she was holding her book.

"Natasha, why didn't you bring your coat?"

"Daddy, I couldn't carry both my coat and the book," she held out the book, "and this is a library book!"

Years later, as I reread this today, I am struck by remembering Dr. Zhivago's brother searching for Zhivago and Lara's daughter; the man she was with let go of her hand. She cried, "And I was lost!" Thank God we weren't "lost."

CHAPTER 6

IRAN 2 (1972 – 1979)

Shahreza Apartment, Shah House, The Texan, Dodge City Interlude,
Darband, Tehran, Apartment No. 1,
Darband, Tehran, Apartment No. 2,
Campus Dramas, Iran-America Society, Damavand's Curriculum,
Rudaki Hall, Culture and the Revolution

SHAHREZA APARTMENT

We lived in four different places in both the central and northern parts of Tehran. Our first apartment was at Shahreza Avenue and Roosevelt. I'm sure they have now changed the names of those streets. It was in the heart of the city, at a 3,500 foot elevation, and just south of the American embassy. We were on the sixth floor, with no elevator, although it was a new building. Quite a nice building, really.

The apartment had a very spacious living room separated from the dining area by a floor-to-ceiling, open-shelves divider, which provided a roomy, open feeling. The kitchen had space for a small table and chairs, and there were three sizeable bedrooms and one and one-half baths. The plumbing was rather primitive, but western: no Persian version (often described as a hole in the floor) toilet. The floors were tile, and no matter how much they were washed, never seemed clean; they always looked dusty. The college provided basic furnishings, which left much empty space in these big rooms. However, the very large oval dining table and chairs did nicely fill the dining area.

We needed the third bedroom for Tom Aitchison, friend and former student from California, who had come to Iran with us, mainly for the adventure. But during the several months there, he helped in Damavand's theatre program and taught English at the Iran America Society. Around Christmastime Tom packed up and returned to southern California, leaving our extra bedroom unoccupied, but not for long.

Noah Lindsay, an American teacher at Iran Zamin, an international high school, approached us about renting the room. We were not interested, preferring to keep the room for a study and occasional guests, and our bathroom situation wasn't conducive to the addition of another person. But Noah persisted, pointing out how he would be happy to babysit Natasha at least once a week. It was the babysitting offer that convinced us to let Noah move in — babysitting that never materialized. He was almost never at home, always out with his friends. Noah said he wasn't interested in lectures about Persian culture but only in the people. He did babysit once, asking us to please be home by nine o'clock because he had something planned. Noah was from Lake City, Florida, and when he was duly impressed by something Iranian, his favorite comment was, "They've never seen anything like this in Lake City!" On occasion we still find this comment appropriate.

Noah returned to Florida, and we had the apartment to ourselves for the second year. It was in this Shahreza apartment that both Natasha and I were ill. Shortly after moving in, I was hospitalized for three weeks again with meningitis, and Natasha had a severe case of what was called Tehran tummy, and what most foreigners experienced from time to time. My illness left me very weak and put more responsibility on BJ. Just cleaning this large apartment was a big job, and we were pleased when Miss Doolittle, retired missionary and former head of Damavand College when it was still a girls' finishing school, offered us her maid, Fatimah, to clean once a week. That made all the difference in the world. We were dismayed at how little Fatimah earned, but Miss Doolittle strongly advised us not to give her more, as Americans tended to do, because it would spoil her; she would then expect her Iranian employers to also pay more. This frustrating attitude was prevalent all over the Mid-East as well as the Far East.

SHAH HOUSE

After two years, we moved a mile to the south, from the Shahreza apartment to a house just off Shah Avenue, still in the heart of the city. We were there for two and a half years. It was a wonderful, old, three-floored house; the third floor actually being the roof. There was a skylight on that floor with a spiral staircase going up, up, up to the glass sky-lighted third floor area with a glass door to the roof garden. The back garden to the house had a wall around it with seventeen pine trees around the perimeter and 64 small shelves for potted plants on the walls. There was also a swimming pool, which in the wintertime was used as a basketball court. The terrace porch had a ping-pong table. Our friends, Dr. and Mrs. George Brasswell, George and Joann, had lived there before us. George was a philosophy professor at Tehran University. He was very active in searching out information on mosques and life around the mosques, and I am convinced that he must have known something sinister was happening since he was constantly talking with people who knew things in the mosques, and, of course, it was in the mosques that the revolution started. Returning to Wake Forest University, George has written several books on Islam and politics in Iran.

When George and Joann lived there, we had seen the house a number of times, and I thought, "Wow, couldn't this be magnificent!" It was painted blue and green at that point. I was determined to rent that house. When the Brasswells moved out they arranged for me to meet their landlady. She was very wealthy and very skeptical about my idea of having the whole house interior painted white. She said, "White? It will be like a hospital!"

"No, no. It will be absolutely magnificent with Persian rugs. You will be thrilled with it."

And she was. After it was painted, she came to see it, and said, "Oh, it is like a gem; like a diamond that glows."

There were so many windows. The whole back of the house, which overlooked the garden, was solid glass; letting in worlds of sunlight. You were keenly aware of the brightness of the place. Even in winter it seemed bright, and warm, and sunny, and charming.

We put our Persian carpets all around and hung Persian Kilims as a partial divider between the sitting and the dining areas. We had banquette-type sofas built and placed along the walls. They were the height of a chair and slightly longer than I am; they were 6'6" long and the width of a deep chair. On these sofas were fitted mattresses covered with a wonderful brick-red and-a- contrasting-color striped fabric that blended well with the Persian carpets. Persian saddle-bags were stuffed and filled and placed against the walls. It was very much like a Persian ottoman, a Persian sitting area that went all the way around the walls.

The house was absolutely radiant with glass windows looking out over the swimming pool, which sparkled from the sunlight and shimmered in the moonlight. The bedrooms upstairs had the same view, for there were windows on the back of the entire house. The view of the garden was lovely, and on summer nights we were aware of the soft scent of jasmine. The house was especially charming by moonlight. From upstairs, however, we could actually see, over the garden wall, the parking lot of the National Iranian Oil Company.

In the winter, guys would walk up and down the kuchies, the little streets where people lived, shouting, "B-a-r-f!" It meant, "We will clear your roof of snow!" Heavy snowfalls were constant in Tehran because it is on the side of a mountain, like Denver, and heavy snow came. When the airport roof fell in, we heard it on National Iranian Radio Television. We took this as a sign to remove the snow from the roof of our home, so BJ, Tasha, and I took buckets and a broom — we didn't have a shovel — and whatever we could find to clear the two feet of snow on the flat-topped roof. As we finished, some boys walked through the mist in the little street behind our home, shouting, "B-a-r- f!" We sighed, saying, "Why didn't you come sooner?"

It was a lovely, big house. It needed a houseboy to care for it. For a while, two guys from the college came once a week and cleaned the house, but they didn't want to wash the clothes in the bathtub as the maids would do. They said, "Please, Dr., that's women's work!"

So I filled the tub, added some Tide detergent, and started washing the clothes. Finally one of the guys, Ali, said, "Okay, yes, we do it. Just don't tell anyone!"

In some ways the house was inconvenient; there was no built-in heating. We used huge stoves that were piped and ventilated, and a couple of the boys who worked at the college came in occasionally to clean out the flues for the smoke stacks. To heat the house, kerosene, called "naft," was burned in three huge stoves and several small stoves. They had to be filled every night by us, for we had no servants, although we did have a servant for the first few weeks, I must admit. This house with four bedrooms and two baths clearly needed at least one servant to help take care of it.

The Nafty Man, sometimes called the Nasty Man by others, although ours was a good guy, came daily to fill the storage tank, out of which we ran our heating oil. Sometimes when he came I was gone, quite often meeting theatre and film people. When I was not there to fill the stoves, BJ filled them. At least once when I came home, naft was running all over the floor of the naft room next to the kitchen and out into the hall and stairway. The filling can had run over, and my BJ was happily playing the piano out of sight of the naft barrel. She had forgotten that the tap was turned on. It rather smelled up the house. Fortunately, no one smoked!

We had a houseboy for a few weeks in the beginning. He came with the house and had been the houseboy for George and Joann Brasswell. He was named Gohlem Shah, after the Shah, and it meant "the servant of the Shah." Once he spilled naft on a carpet, and we never could get it out. He left, fortunately, soon after we moved in. He was quite a waste. He didn't really want to do anything. I don't know how George and Joann put up with him for all those years. He was a young Christian, and I think that they took pity on him since he was very much in the minority. It was illegal to convert from Islam to Christianity. Perhaps he could have become Zoroastrian, since that's a Persian religion. I don't know. Actually, Zoroastrianism was not one of the state-approved religions.

We had a number of parties in that house. Under the Shah the wine and the soft drinks flowed freely. Even though we were not paid much, we had quite a few parties. I took a US$9,000 cut in pay to go to Damavand College in Tehran after leaving my Palm Springs/Palm Desert job. Fortunately, BJ could also teach to add to my US$7,000 salary, and so we were able to survive and really do quite well. We didn't save any money, but we lived a kind of wonderfully exciting life in Tehran.

THE TEXAN

In our third year in Tehran, after being ill for two and a half years following meningitis, I came home from the college campus on the very late school bus one night, in the cold of December with light to heavy snow on the ground; that is, light snow down the mountain at 3,500 feet and heavy snow up the mountain at 5,500 feet, which is where the new campus is located. When I arrived home, BJ was buttoning up Natasha's pusteen, a sheepskin-lined leather coat, the one replacing the lost-in-the-fire coat that had saved the library book. BJ also had on her pusteen, orange plaid scarf, and matching beret.

"Where are you going?" I asked.

"To Bob and Jimmy Old's. You know, I told you about their having these inspirational, sort of evangelical meetings at their house."

"Yes, may I go?"

"Of course! I thought you probably didn't want to. You usually don't much like that kind of thing." So I went along with BJ and Natasha.

About forty people were there that night. One man with a very Texan drawl led the singing, which included a trio of guitarists and singers, and Bible readings and testimonials. I had been very ill for two and a half years by then, first with meningitis and then with a pre-diabetic hypoglycemic reaction. I was on a very strict diet; all protein, almost no carbohydrates. I could eat two slices of bread, or thirty grams of carbohydrates, per day; no more, or my blood sugar would shoot sky-high and then drop to the bottom of the chart so that I would be almost comatose as I tried desperately to function as a normal human being. This happened at the age of forty. Constantly I was trying to get my blood sugar leveled. That's why, when we were in Istanbul, I felt that I had to see my father because he was heavily diabetic and, while on daily doses of insulin, he was able to do a heavy day's work and live an almost normal life, and I could not.

At Bob and Jimmy Old's house that night, both husband, Bob, and wife, Jimmy, were deeply in prayer, as was everybody, including myself. The Texas stranger, who was no stranger in the spiritual sense, asked, "Anyone here tonight want to get healed? Anyone sick and tired of being sick and want God to heal you here tonight? Now? Just come right up here, and we'll do some praying, and you'll get healed. God will do it."

All of this was familiar to me. I had been around many of these types over the years; everything from camp meetings to evangelistic services. Although I preferred a different kind of religious service — a bit more formal — I somehow felt drawn to what this man had to say. I was sick of being sick. I looked at BJ, and she looked at me; beautiful BJ. She smiled an encouraging "yes." I stood up, all six feet almost four inches of me, and made my way to the front of the room where two electric guitars and the speaker were. A few more people came; I don't remember who. We formed a ring. Perhaps Bob and his wife Jimmy came up also to pray. The Texas man started praying for us, and as he came past me he put his hand on my shoulder, a firm hold, and he prayed, and I silently prayed, and the strangest burning sensation happened in my abdomen, like it was on fire. I never again had trouble with my blood sugar. It healed. It has registered normal ever since, unlike before the experience, when it showed a definitely low blood sugar graph, shooting way up and then way down. From the 1974 prayer it stayed well until probably 2012 when there again have been diabetic problems, but not large diabetic symptoms. I am usually okay, but sometimes when I eat a little more than a small amount of sweets the blood sugar becomes elevated.

After the service, when I was feeling quite good but hadn't told anyone about the sensation I had felt, I asked the Texas man if he could have lunch with me the next day. I used to have lunch in those days, now I tend to have brunch, I'm afraid.

"Why, sure. Where will we meet?" I told him of a small, very nice restaurant we often went to on Qavam Sultaneh.

I arrived a little early, for I have found over the years that evangelicals are very often early for meetings. He wasn't there, so I took a booth; a very luxurious white leather booth. The waiters knew me, and I told them that there would be a man looking for me. Soon I heard this loud Texas voice saying, "I don't know his name, but he's tall, and we're to meet here at this restaurant."

I stood up, and he came over and shook hands saying, "What is your name?"

"Norm."

"Well, howdy."

We talked a bit, and he gave me his name, which I can't recall now. As we ate a delicious filet mignon steak with mushroom sauce, a lovely meal, we talked. I don't know why I'm writing about this, for I have told almost no one, following, I think, Christ's guidance when he healed people and said, "Go and tell no one." But they usually did, didn't they?

My Texas friend, as he cut his steak, said, "Have you been filled with the Holy Spirit?"

I coughed and said, "Well, I suppose so." After all, I had grown up at Church of God camp meetings, as well as having been baptized and attending the Methodist Church as a child. I had received all of the Church of God baptism, sanctification, and experiences they talked about before I went to college. In later years, we attended Hollywood Presbyterian Church services, and Anglican services still later in Macau, on the south coast of China. With a Ph.D., perhaps I thought I had grown away from that sawdust trail and those altar calls at the camp meetings of my young days.

This Texas friend asked me again, "Yeah, but have you had the 'in-filling' of the Holy Spirit?"

"Well, maybe not."

"Well, where do you live?" "Not far."

"Well, let's eat, and you're gonna get it."

I was apprehensive; very dubious that I wanted this experience. Some of the people I knew, who had boasted of it, were rather questionable sorts, and some I didn't much care for, but I was willing.

We walked the few blocks to our house. It was Christmastime, and we lived in the Shah Street house with the three floors and the spiral staircase. We walked through the glass hallway doors into the living room with the ten- foot-high Christmas tree and the twelve-foot ceilings. Colorful Persian rugs, both hanging and lying on the floor, led the eye to the garden beyond the glass walls.

The Texas man looked around, "Nice place you have here."

Wasting no time, he put his arm on my shoulders and prayed, "Lord, brother Norm comes to you asking you to forgive him of any wrongdoing and to fill him with your Holy Spirit as you have promised in your Holy Word."

Then he looked at me and said, "Now, Norm, just open your mouth, and let God's blessing come out. There now, go on. You've got it. The Lord is with you. Let him speak through you. Make a sound."

"Gaaa … Gaaa …" And then came some amazing sounds that I had never before made.

My Texas friend said, "There. That sounds like some kind of American Indian talk. Well, the Lord knows what it says, even though we don't just now."

I was then hopping around, jumping up and down, for I was filled with the happiest joy I had ever felt. It was not unlike the joy from sex, only happier even than that. I kept singing the music that came out of my mouth. Perhaps that is partly what Christ meant when he said, "Care not what goes into the mouth, but take care what comes out."

This was thrilling, and the same feeling, though less intense, comes each time I experience this singing in the spirit … always alone.

Not long after the meeting in their home, the Olds, who had heard me read scriptures at the Sultanadabad Community Church, which catered mostly to American ex-pats in northern Tehran, came for a visit one day. Bob said, "Norm, I think the Lord wants you to record the Bible on tape." I gasped.

"Which part," I asked.

"The whole Bible," Jimmy replied. I said, "Well, maybe the New Testament. Perhaps we should start with the gospels."

And we did.

We met every Saturday morning. For me that was a real sacrifice, for I am a late-to-bed, later-to-get-up kind of person. It's good that we did it quickly, for Bob was soon to be sent back to the U.S., being retired from his National Iranian Oil Company job. And, unknown to me, there had been an unexpected happening at my family's ranch. My father was diagnosed with terminal cancer and also with a temporary psychological instability. The recorded gospels were transferred to cassette tapes to make them more portable. Listening to them kept Dad spiritually stable, or so it seemed to me when I was with him during that summer. He nearly always carried the tape player and one of the cassettes throughout the summer.

Bob and Jimmy Old established a spiritual conference center in Telephone, Texas, a real town, Bob's home. They played the tapes frequently at the retreat. Prof. Lucy Sullivan, a colleague and a friend of ours from Beirut and Tehran teaching years, attended Old's spiritual retreat and said, "Those tapes help put people in the mood for prayerful discussions." I'm glad they were helpful. They certainly helped my father.

After being home at the ranch that summer, we flew back on Swiss Air to Tehran. I taught late summer school at Damavand College, and then we taught the first semester. In January, 1976, my brother, Gene, called and asked if I would please come home to be with Dad because he had only three months to live. Dr. Frances Gray had retired, so I asked the new president of Damavand College, Dr. Ray Heisey, and was granted a one-and-a-half year's leave of absence. We packed up our house in case we could not come back; in case I had to stay at the ranch for some reason. After all, it was 3,200 acres, and there were 36 oil wells around the area that Dad had interest in via the 32,000 acres of leased oil land, a daunting feeling of responsibility. From the will that I knew about, I knew that I was one of the trustees. We turned our wonderful house over to a fellow faculty member, and we left Tehran, wondering if we would be back; hoping that we would.

DODGE CITY INTERLUDE

During the year and a half in Kansas, I luckily found a job at St. Mary of the Plains College in Dodge City. Dad had passed away the week before that school year began, but there was no way to return early to Iran, for our jobs there were filled. So we settled into Dodge City for the year, buying (thanks to a GI Bill loan, for no money came from my father) a rather old but attractive two-story house with a large, inviting front porch, right on top of historic Boot Hill. Our year there was interesting and quite pleasant in spite of a most hurtful and damaging situation with my family over late changes in Dad's will. These changes entirely cut out my three brothers and me — sons from the first marriage — in favor of my half-brother and my stepmother. Unfortunately, this family rift has never been repaired, although we're all on speaking terms, however minimal. My stepmother died a few years ago, aged just short of 93; her sister, my mother, died at age 93, nine years earlier. Dad and mother were born in the same year; he died age 68.

Dodge City was no doubt the friendliest place we've lived. We knew all our neighbors, although the Baptist preacher next door wasn't always very cordial, and before leaving had a party for them in our back yard, showing slides of places we'd lived and traveled, and serving ice cream and cake.

We also had a big yard sale before leaving Dodge City. BJ's sister, Kathleen, and family lived in nearby Copeland and brought a pickup truck filled with items for the sale. It was Kathleen's idea to run an ad on the radio, and the sale was well attended. I decided to sell one of our Persian Kilims, which brought enough for the three of us to enjoy a five-day cruise of the Greek Islands on our way back to Iran.

Teaching at St. Mary was okay, too. This was our second experience at a Catholic school, and we felt much more comfortable there than at Duquesne University in Pittsburgh, Pennsylvania, where I taught while doing my Ph.D. at Carnegie and BJ studied African Affairs. Maybe this was partly because St. Mary was smaller. Luckily, they needed BJ to teach two freshman English classes the first semester and then, during the last several months, to supplement our income as well as have something to do, she took a part-time job at Woolworth's.

The high points of my work there were productions of the musical Godspell and fifth century B.C. Greek playwright Euripides' Trojan Women and Milton Geiger's Edwin Booth. St. Mary had an active theatre program, and productions were well attended and reviewed by the local paper. The reporter for the Dodge City Globe was very appreciative and supportive of our theatre efforts. She'd lost a son in the Vietnam War and was especially moved by our production depicting the tragic events after the Trojan War in Trojan Women, when wives of the slain soldiers were sold into slavery. Her response to the events of the drama was, "War never changes!"

The sounds of Dodge City are among our favorite memories. Our house was near the town center and several blocks from the fire station, so every time the trucks went out we heard their sirens. Each day at twelve noon the First Presbyterian Church's carillon chimed forth with a different familiar hymn, the message that "all's right with the world." At around 6:00 p.m. shots rang out from the rebuilt Front Street as a historic gunfight was reenacted for the tourists; a reminder of the days when Dodge City was part of the Wild West, with Bill Hickok and Doc Holliday, and TV's Matt Dillon, Marshal. Now, being back in TV Land Los Angeles, I often watch Gunsmoke.

Then, breaking the silence of the night, at 1:55 a.m., came a distant shrill cry, gradually increasing in volume, as the California-bound Santa Fe Chief passed through town. Unlike some prairie stations where the Chief stopped only if necessary, for passengers, it stopped daily at Dodge City. An hour or so later the silence was again pierced, this time by the Chicago-bound train. What comfort the railroad must have been for the early settlers; what comfort to know they were not completely isolated in the middle of a vast Kansas or Nebraska prairie but connected to the outside world. A horse or stagecoach was no longer the only means of escape; there were the Missouri-Pacific trains, the Rock Island Railroad and the Santa Fe, which later became Amtrak. Today in Newton, Kansas, the Amtrak California Chief trains are scheduled to meet at almost the same time: 2:45 a.m. going west to Los Angeles and 2:59 a.m. going east to Chicago, and are mostly on time. How wonderful the sound of the train's mournful cry as it travels through the night, calling, almost seducing me to travel all those years ago when I was a mere boy! One rarely loses one's love of travel: seeing … hearing … tasting … touching … loving it always.

DARBAND, TEHRAN, APARTMENT NO. 1

In late summer of 1977 we returned to Iran. Our first task was finding a place to live not too far from the new campus on the northern edge of Tehran. Earlier, living in the center of the city, we'd found it increasingly difficult to get to the new campus, for Tehran's traffic had become extremely difficult to cope with. Both taxis and busses were impossible. More than once, when headed for some event, day or night, we'd given up and returned home. When first in Iran, we could easily phone for a taxi to pick us up, but even that had become hopeless.

After much searching, we found a two-bedroom ground-floor apartment in Darband, the northernmost part of the city. It was several blocks north of, and up a steep hill from, Tajrish Square and market. Busses all stopped at the Square, and the hill was quite difficult to climb, especially carrying books and groceries, and especially in the frequent ice and snow. The apartment had a very spacious living-dining room, with a large bay window overlooking a lovely garden filled with roses. The kitchen was typically Persian, basic and small, although there was space for a washing machine. Typical Iranian kitchens didn't have proper cupboards, only open shelves. Three of our four Iranian kitchens were typical. The inconvenient location of the single bathroom was a real disadvantage; getting to it required passing through one of the two bedrooms. The landlady, who was confined to a wheelchair, lived upstairs, and although she was very friendly, she was also quite aggressive, and we never felt comfortable with her but rather intimidated. This was especially true for twelve-year-old Natasha who, when returning home from school one afternoon, heard the landlady calling for help. Natasha went upstairs, found her lying on the floor, and barely managed to help her back into her wheelchair. Fortunately Natasha arrived when she did; the landlady's husband did not come for a while.

Across the large, beautifully cared for by the husband rose garden from the main house was a one-room guest house that came with our apartment. For several months this small but pleasant cottage was used by Steve and Lucy, a young couple who had come from the U.S. to work with the youth at the American Community Church. When they decided to house-sit for a family on leave from Iran, we let it to Randall Brown, a former Damavand colleague who had returned to teach the second semester. His fellow science teachers, with a few accessories, turned it into colorful, cozy quarters, but Randall never seemed very happy there. He missed his family and had hoped to stay with an American family, the Fribergs. It's too bad this little house wasn't empty when a teaching acquaintance from California passed through Tehran, hoping to find lodging for a few weeks to do research. All the hotels were full, even the little ones we knew that had interesting kitchens like the German Hotel. I said yes, since he was willing to sleep on our sofa; BJ said no, because of the bathroom situation, and he didn't stay. Unfortunately, this disagreement became a bone of contention. I think BJ did not realize I knew him quite well; he was a theologian and philosophy professor. One of the few times I've been surprised and disappointed by her decision. I must have not given her enough background on him. All of a sudden he was at the airport telephoning me, ready to leave, and I begged him to come and stay with us. He said no, it was all too difficult to work out; he was tired, having traveled around the world on a research project. Probably he felt he was imposing. He was, but that was okay. The garden house was occupied by Dr. Brown, and that would have interested both persons. Communal living is often frustrating, and we've done a lot of it. But, I am sorry about that particular situation.

DARBAND, TEHRAN, APARTMENT NO. 2

When Dr. Mary Thompson retired as Academic Dean of the College and returned to the U.S., we jumped at the chance to rent her vacated apartment, which was also in Darband but more spacious and more conveniently located. The large terrace would be lovely for parties. Our landlady now was Akhtar Azadagan, Damavand College's Dean of Students. Akhtar was also the school's liaison with SAVAK, the Shah's secret police. This position put her in jeopardy when the revolution came. She and her family lived on the ground floor of the two-story building, and we were upstairs. We were so pleased to be in this pleasant apartment; little did we know that we would have only a few months to enjoy it. The approaching revolution shut the college down in early December, and the school asked all foreign teachers to leave the country temporarily. So we managed — with difficulty because many were scrambling to get out of Iran — to get tickets on

Royal Jordanian Air. We left Iran in December of 1979, very near the leaving of the Shah and family, not to return. Fortunately months later Akhtar managed to sell our piano and somehow got enough money together to ship to us our Persian Kilim rugs and other things, some not worth shipping but all so very much appreciated. We continue to love our rugs! Books, lecture notes, etc., all lost, of course.

CAMPUS DRAMAS

On the original, downtown Damavand campus, the facilities for putting on plays were limited, but we managed to put together a number of charming and quite impressive productions. Christmas was always a big event. The girls loved to sing Christmas carols and every noon, during the month of December, they gathered in the large meeting room for carol singing. One Christmastime, for our program, we borrowed from the art history classes slides of paintings of Western Christian art, of both the Christmas story and the Easter story, and projected them while the choir sang traditional carols and songs reminiscent of Bach. We ended with a speaking chorus from my speech class doing How the Grinch Stole Christmas with slides, taken by a missionary friend of ours, Sherman Fung, of the book's illustrations. The students narrated the various parts, told the story, played the roles, and closed with something akin to Dickens' "Happy Christmas to all."

Another Christmas we did The Second Shepherd's Play from the Chester cycle, with the help of Mina, the school's London-trained technical director. Again, paintings were projected, paintings of Western Christian art, as the shepherds visited the Christ child, in an interesting platform setting with multi-ramps and with large, stylized leaves "floating" above the acting and seating areas.

We also did productions in the garden during the summer. This was the Persian garden at the old downtown campus. We set up folding chairs and used kerosene pressure lanterns that Akhtar Azadagan, Dean of Students, always rented from a restaurant supplier. These made a very white, flowing light, and were used in Tehran for garden parties and outdoor restaurants. They create atmospheric theatre

NORMAN L. LOFLAND AND BETTY J. LOFLAND

lighting when one has no spotlights! And they were charming in the campus garden.

We used these lanterns for the production of Moliere's The Doctor in Spite of Himself, and also used quite a number of Persian carpets; some were brought from our apartment and others borrowed. We hung the kilims (one — which we still have — is fourteen feet long) from the twenty-foot high walls with weights (bricks; all of Tehran is built of bricks) holding them at the top. These colorful carpets made a lovely backdrop for the French comedy. This production became more interesting with the insertion of verses by the Persian poet Molavi, who wrote during the same time as Moliere. Molavi's poetry was read in Farsi by one of the more talented students, and the parallels between Moliere the Parisian and Molavi the Persian are quite remarkable.

All productions at Damavand were in English, but we tried to work in, where possible, Persian language and culture. For Ionesco's The Bald Soprano we also experimented with the use of some Farsi. At periodic moments the actors froze while Persian translations of selected short passages were spoken. This intermingling of the two cultures gave an entirely new dimension to the production.

IRAN-AMERICA SOCIETY

A large proportion of our cultural activities were provided by the Iran- America Society (IAS) and the USIS (United States Information Service). They sponsored three theatres and five galleries. Phil Pillsbury, a friend of ours, was the director of this American Cultural Center. We kept in touch for years, but then Phil went to the State Department's War College, and I lost track of him after his stint in Buenos Aries. In Tehran we often saw each other. Phil ran a wonderful ship at the Iran-America Society, which included three theatres and five galleries. There was the main stage theatre with sliding back doors that opened up the whole back of the stage. This opened to an outdoor theatre, which was built in a half-arena style and was used for concerts in the summer and sometimes for other events. Then there was a smaller theatre, which had been a storehouse but now converted into an experimental theatre.

Of the five galleries, two were opened while we were in Tehran. The largest gallery was in the main building. There always seemed to be exhibition openings at the IAS. One time it was Native American paintings and artwork, with some Remington paintings and Russell sculptures. This was a stunning exhibition. Another time it was an exhibition of African art, actually Phil's own private collection, for he had spent time in Africa before this and was a collector of African art. He had had it sent from the U.S. for the Tehran exhibition. These American centers, like IAS, are expected to present American thematic material, and Washington frowned on this exhibit's lack of "Americanism," but it was very well received locally, and Phil felt justified in combining African and African-American themes.

There were always one or two theatre productions in progress. I was asked to direct for them Tennessee Williams' A Streetcar Named Desire, but I was ill at the time, so another director did a very good production of it in the experimental theatre. I did direct for the IAS a collage of scenes called Great Women in the Theatre, selections from the History of Theatre, with an all- woman cast from Damavand College. I'd always wanted to do a production of Riders to the Sea; that powerful, one-act play by the Irish playwright Synge, with a women's chorus, the women of the sea, the wives and mothers of the men who go down to the sea to die in those ships. Iranian culture inspired me to do it with the women's chorus dressed in black chadors and face masks from the Persian Gulf area. This was before the revolution, and I was cautioned against it. Rightly so, as it turned out.

One season the Iran-America Society sponsored a most exciting production of Aristophanes' The Clouds. Banipah Babilla, as Socrates, was lowered from the fly gallery in a huge laundry basket, and The Clouds' chorus, comprised of some men and women dressed in wedding dresses from the bazaar, was seen through the opened back wall of the theatre, to the outdoor theatre, way beyond. It was interesting, indeed.

The IAS also showed a constant succession of films. The Civilization series by Kenneth Clark, depicting the history of Western Civilization through paintings and architecture, was shown weekly at the Iran-America Society. This was before you could get these on video, to show in the classroom, as we did in China and in Macau. We took our students to the IAS to see this series, projected in the theatre. Also shown there was the America series by Alistair Cooke, a really magnificent presentation of the history of the United States. I only wish that Alistair Cooke had done one more, bringing it from the Cold War to today. Then we saw Bronowski's The Ascent of Man, which is a complicated, scientific, philosophical history of the world. It was almost too scientific for our students, but nevertheless we took them to see it. These were all in English, with no Farsi subtitles. For the last eight years we have used these series in China and Macau, sometimes with Chinese subtitles, but usually without.

DAMAVAND'S CURRICULUM

After teaching for years in Alexandria, Egypt, Dr. Mary C. Thompson joined Dr. Frances M. Gray and a faculty of American, European, and Iranian teachers at Damavand College. They taught in their fields in English, introducing the students to ideas through literature, philosophy, and other arts. This was a different curriculum from those of national or state universities where we have taught in the Middle East, North Africa, and the Orient. These universities instruct mainly toward jobs, not values and ideas that strengthen character and make one adaptable and trainable for jobs.

Dorothy Adibi is a prime example of the educational possibilities of this curriculum based on the arts, on literature, on philosophy, on ideas in the search for truth, and she was willing to do it as an adult after working for years. Dorothy arrived on our old downtown Damavand College campus during registration for second semester on a day when three feet of snow covered the city at our 3,500 foot level; much more snow was at the 5,500 foot level. Dorothy "floated" into my office in a floor length mink coat. Later, I learned that one of our students who worked at the American embassy had seen Dorothy at an embassy party the night before and told her, "Dorothy, you're wasting your life. It's time you got it together. I'll call for you in the morning and take you to Damavand College, where you can at least take one course and start thinking again."

She arrived after lunch — I know, because that's when I would have arrived — looking a bit confused by all this academia. I had watched Dorothy on-stage at the Iran-America Society playing a number of roles; she is a professionally qualified actress. After we talked a few minutes, and I expressed how I hoped she would be in my Acting-Theatre class, and Public Speaking (I wanted her to inspire the students), and Twentieth Century Literature, and Shakespeare classes, she said, "Well, maybe one to start with. I've read a lot of books, but I haven't done a course in university for some years. I've been working at the British embassy in various parts of the world, and married an Iranian businessman here, and, well, I don't think I can do all this academic work."

I assured her that often the best students are older students. Just then, the adult student who had brought her to me appeared at the door and said, "Come on, Dorothy. Dean Thompson wants to see you."

Not for nothing was Mary Thompson trained in psychology, and she could charm students whether in Egypt, Persia, or Europe-America. Less than an hour later, Dorothy arrived back at my desk, since I was a part of the registration procedure that day. Looking a bit alarmed, but nonetheless determined, she had been signed up by Dean Thompson for a full sixteen credit course load of mostly literature; skipping freshman subjects that she had had at a university in England years before. We later received her transcript and could properly award her credit for those courses she already had.

Dorothy turned out to be absolutely brilliant! She was immediately put into classes with the "irregulars;" the students who had already been studying at Damavand for a few semesters and whose English was so good they could handle the advanced courses. Oh, it was a challenging class. They had Drama with me, where they covered scene study, acting, scenic design, and English voice and diction. They also studied literature: Shakespeare and Twentieth Century English Literature with me; Milton and Thomas Mann with Lucy Sullivan; Advanced Writing with Margaret Moore; European History with my wife, BJ. All students had to take English Literature because it was the only major approved by the Ministry of Education, so there were several sections but only one irregular. A major was fifty credit hours. We had several minors; a minor was thirty credit hours, like an American major in a Liberal Arts College. Anthropologist Margaret Meade's daughter, Kathryn Bateson, taught them Sociology. It went on and on — the opportunities students had at Damavand College with excellent, dedicated teachers.

The graduate program — which was co-ed — came into offer just before the revolution. By then, the college had been taken over by the government (it was inevitable), so a few changes happened. We were paid more money, and Frances didn't have to raise all the funds from private sources. She wanted to retire anyway, to teach art and philosophy in Berkeley, California, which she has done for 25 years since! Other changes included adding another major in Sociology and minors in Fine Arts, with a graduate M.A. to be offered in Communication, using the National Radio and Television studios nearby. This was before computers took over the Speech-Theatre-Communications major.

Then the revolution came.

Three years before that happened, Dorothy Adibi graduated Magna Cum Laude and had performed the grandmother's recognition scene from Anastasia for Frances' retirement banquet. Dorothy's thoughts had solidified, truth as expressed through literature and the arts, and she was able to express her thoughts clearly, challenging us all as she did it.

I never again saw her floor-length mink coat.

Dorothy is only one example; many of our graduates were so well-trained, so capable. It must have been devastating for these educated women to watch the revolution destroy their freedom and position in society. In September, 2016, the BBC Radio presented a program on Iran, which indicated that most of the graduate students in Iranian universities were girls. The girls interviewed also said something about "now we have women doctors and judges and other professionals." As I heard them say that, I wondered what had not been told to the youth. All that was true in the years we were there, except for the graduate studies. There were not so many, apparently, for that is why Damavand was established; to serve those women of Persia.

Of course, there were those who weren't concerned about the future of Iran's women or anyone else. About two months after leaving Iran, and giving up on going back, BJ and I were at a party in Bel Aire, California, given by a wealthy, former Damavand student, who had immigrated to the U.S. during the revolution. I was on the dance floor in this very posh house, dancing opposite to one of our former students, who wore the latest: a red silk dress, a Dior, no doubt, high heels, and the heavy makeup of an Iranian society woman. While waving my arms and hips around the room, I said, "The last time I saw you, you were marching around the circle of the new Damavand campus, wearing a black head-to-floor chador and shouting, 'Kill the Shah! Kill the Americans!' What happened? Why are you here?"

"We didn't like it!"

RUDAKI HALL

Besides our campus activities and those at the Iran-America Society, many cultural events went on in Tehran. There was state-supported Rudaki Hall, which housed the opera company, the symphony orchestra, and the ballet company. Rudaki had an outstanding opera theatre. The theatre was not huge, but not small, and appeared to be a copy of the Vienna Opera House on a smaller scale. It was not as big in terms of seating, and perhaps the stage was not as large, although the stage was enormous, but there were many tiers of boxes around the theatre as well as the main floor orchestra seating. The royal box was directly opposite the stage, as in European theatres.

I've always said that there was more equipment on that opera house stage than in any theatre I knew of outside of New York. Probably the New York Metropolitan Opera House has as much, perhaps more. Rudaki had lifts in various areas of the stage and had three revolves that were center stage and stage right and stage left. You could use them simultaneously or individually, and I seem to recall a large revolve as well. The most exciting thing was an elevator that came up center stage, just a little upstage of the main acting area, and it could lift an entire set; box sets came up on it. There was a wagon that moved from stage left which could hold an entire set. For Wagner's The Flying

Dutchman, the ship rode in on a huge wagon which covered the entire acting area; an enormous wagon, the biggest one I've ever seen. There were wagons that could be pushed from upstage, because there was as much space behind the cyclorama, which was very far upstage, as on the main stage. There were hundreds of lines that came in from the fly gallery. I worked some with the Tehran Opera Company, with the chorus primarily, giving them acting and movement lessons, so I was in the theatre several times backstage, as well as many times in the front hall.

It was always thrilling to notice how cleverly they used the scene design. The Tehran Opera Company had Theo Lau, a German scene designer, who came every year that we were there, and I don't know how many years before. His designs were absolutely marvelous, but I'm sure his work in Iran ended, along with most things cultural — Persian as well as Western — with the coming of the Islamic revolution. This German designer used very effectively all of the equipment on that stage. A memorable moment was his concept for Wagner's The Flying Dutchman. That full scale sailing ship, mysteriously floating in and out from stage left, to the ominous Wagnerian strains was an experience to be remembered.

A production of Mozart's The Magic Flute had many amazingly designed and painted Persian miniature paintings flying in from the overhead fly gallery. I think Mozart, had he seen it, would have been absolutely delighted. Sometimes these paintings would descend in sections. The fly gallery resembled an open frame as the painting descended, and then behind it appeared another open frame of another Persian miniature. Perhaps the edges were only the miniature. Sometimes the main miniature was enlarged into an enormous painting and came in on a drop from the fly gallery. They must have used sixty lines just to drop in those paintings. It was fortunate that I could stay on and catch the entire production of The Magic Flute, because Natasha became ill in the middle of the performance, and BJ had to rush her home.

In addition to the regular performance of operas, there were the ballets. When we first arrived in Tehran, the ballet company was somewhat weak but had become quite strong by the time the Iranian

Revolution swept away all of this Western culture. They were such a strong ballet company, in fact, that they culminated in doing Carl Orf's maddeningly beautiful music of Carmina Burana, just before the Iranian Revolution. The choreographer had earlier choreographed the show in New York, which had shocked many people. The husband of one of those dancers whom I knew, he lived for a time in our garden house, had told me that in New York they had performed nude. Everybody had heard about it, and everybody was coming to see what they dared to do. We knew that they certainly would not dare to do that in Tehran at any time, and certainly not during the Iranian Revolution. The costume designer did have the least amount of clothing on them that they could possibly get away with. It was a great production, really magnificently done, but it closed the Rudaki Hall. Nothing was performed after that.

In addition to the opera and ballet orchestras, there was a symphony orchestra, and each orchestra was a separate entity, excellent, and with a number of musicians from Eastern Europe. Interestingly, the symphony conductor had been trained in New York by Leonard Bernstein — one of his protégés.

During the spring of 1975 the telephone in our Shah Avenue home rang. It was wonderful, delightful, red-headed and strong-willed Sally Thompson calling from Westport, Connecticut, just outside of New York City. This phone call brought back many memories.

Sally had been my student at the University of Bridgeport, Connecticut, in the Department of Speech and Theatre Arts, which I chaired. Sally had played one of the washer women in our production of James Joyce's Finnegans Wake, as originally adapted by Mary Manning for the Harvard Theatre. She sparkled as that washerwoman in our production in the Holland Festival of Music and Drama in 1969. Sally was now raising funds for a new musical, and asked me if I would direct it. But that's another story …

CULTURE AND THE REVOLUTION

Iran's Islamic Revolution brought grave difficulties for two acquaintances who worked with a small theatre company located not far from our house, and which I occasionally visited. I knew the director, Arby Ovanessian, quite well, mainly through his mother, Lucy, who was a fellow teacher at Damavand. Arby was an Iranian Armenian Christian, trained in Paris, where I hope he returned to when theatre became a risky occupation in Iran. Especially impressive and politically provocative was his production involving the movement of chadored women. The chador is the head-to-floor flowing veil, usually black, which lent itself so beautifully to the undulating movement of this production. The dialogue was in Farsi, so although I had no idea what was said, the haunting visuals inspired my desire to do Synge's Riders to the Sea, with the women's chorus in black chadors and Persian Gulf masks.

Banipah Babilla was an actor with this theatre group, and he occasionally directed. I mentioned him earlier as playing Socrates in the IAS production of The Clouds and being lowered from the fly gallery in a basket. But it was an exhibition of Banipah's paintings that got him into serious trouble with the revolution. Some fundamentalists became very angry because all his paintings in this particular exhibition were of Banipah Babilla in the nude, and apparently he had made himself look very masculine, indeed. I never saw the paintings, so I don't know. He was in so much trouble that he was tried in court. His defense was primarily that the Shahbanu, the Shah's wife, had bought one of these paintings to be placed in Tehran's Gallery of Modern Paintings. This gallery, which opened shortly before the revolution, is a copy, in terms of architectural style, of the Guggenheim Museum in New York, designed by Frank Lloyd Wright, where all the paintings are exhibited on a slanting ramp that curves round and round, up the height of the building. Banipah said, "Surely my painting cannot be that bad if the Shahbanu (the Queen) approved it for the gallery." That didn't help in terms of his defense, since the revolution was largely against the Shah's westernization policy, including the arts. Banipah, however, did get a reprieve, and managed to escape to Europe the next day. In June, 2016, a reporter for the BBC, I think, did a story on the "hidden Museum of Modern Art," which had just been revealed as containing a substantial collection of sculpture and paintings by Picasso, Modigliani, Rouault, Degas, Van Gogh, Manet, Monet, and others which I cannot remember from our visit (before Banipah Babilla's personal exhibition). The report said that all of the art works have been locked up, stored, and will be exhibited one art piece at a time until further notice. I seem to remember that visitors have to have permission to see the exhibited art pieces. I wonder where they hang the one painting, on the ramp going down to lower floors — as the Guggenheim goes up in New York — or just placed on a wall in the vast area at the bottom of the ramp? I also wonder if Nabil Ameri of the Frank Lloyd Wright Taliesin Associated Architects designed the museum, since it is inspired by the Wright Guggenheim. It was certainly designed and built before the revolution. We saw it.

After we left Tehran, during the revolution, (we left just before the Shah left), some powerful music was composed, reflecting the soul of the revolution and what led up to it. We heard it in London at the home of one of our former students, Dorothy Adibi. Listening to it, I so wanted to stage a musical-opera of the pre-revolution, revolution, and post-revolution based on that score. Someone had smuggled the tape out of Iran and had given it to her in London. I loved it. The drama of it, the rhythm, the images, the horror, and the sense of success were the material of great theatre. In my naïve understanding of the Middle East, even after living in it for then a decade, I would not have anticipated the attack attitude that probably would ensue had we staged such a production; it has become evident in these 2016 years of ISIS.

Interestingly, the ballet company troupe from Rudaki Hall was on the same flight as we, to escape to Jordan and to Athens when the demonstrations became intense during the revolution. We went out with small suitcases because we were instructed to come back in a month, and we naïvely believed that we could come back. Foolish thoughts, but the American embassy kept saying, "Nothing is wrong. Everything is fine. It will be okay. Everything is going well. No problems." And yet we heard nightly shooting and shouting.

We flew to Athens by way of Amman, Jordan, on almost the last flight out because they closed the airport at midnight that night. Another friend managed to get on another flight out just before they closed it. At the Tehran airport I looked around and recognized members of the ballet troupe, who were primarily from New York, and some from Europe. They were pushing their luggage, floating it over our heads, literally, to the baggage clerks behind the counter as hundreds and hundreds of people jammed together, jostling their way to the check-in counters, trying to get out before the airport shut down. The departure lounge was a crowded mess, with dirty Styrofoam food and drink containers everywhere.

Natasha, at the end of our stay in Tehran, had a pixie haircut, losing about three feet of hair, and wore a baseball cap, partly for the safety of looking more like a boy. She was devastated when she learned that we could not return. She had many good friends in Iran; also, she lost her extensive LP record collection. This was long before CDs. Even now, Natasha says that she searches for them in used record shops, Goodwill, and Salvation Army thrift stores when she is in the States, which is not often since she's married to a State Department diplomatic person and moves around the world every few years.

Why, we're often asked, was Iran so wonderful? Although it was, in many ways, the most difficult place we've lived, Iran was also one of the most interesting and rewarding. Persian culture — the history, music, archaeology, food — is extremely rich and fascinating to the westerner. And one is easily drawn by the friendliness and generosity of the Iranian people. We knew so many Persians. It helped to work with quite a few Persian teachers and staff at the college, and of course, nearly all our students were Iranian. We were often invited into Iranian homes, sometimes for very luxurious parties.

Some of the best food we've ever had was Persian, yet undoubtedly some of the worst we've cooked was in Iran. I'm sure that if we'd had a good servant to shop and cook Persian-style, our meals at home would have been much better. Shopping for food was hard. Few things were imported, so there was little to choose from on the store shelves, and it was usually difficult getting it from store to home since transportation was so impossible. We'll never understand why the fresh produce was so bad — often smashed, covered with mud, and dumped into boxes. A colleague referred to the grocery stores as garbage stores. This was so different from the beautiful, attractively displayed fruit and vegetables we'd seen earlier in Lebanon and later in China. Tunisian food shopping fell somewhere in between!

And shopping for clothes in Iran was almost out of the question, since most Iranians are smaller than we were. So we brought our clothing from the States. However, Tehran had excellent tailors. I had a beautifully cut and fitted double-breasted black gabardine suit tailored there. The coat looked wonderful for years, and I wore it on occasion. The bell-bottom trousers were not worn as long.

Damavand College, with its sound liberal arts curriculum and good administration, was undoubtedly the main thing that made our six years, spread over seven, in Iran so rewarding. Also, the Persians' generous hospitality; warm, intellectually-stimulating fellowship at the Chapel; good, interesting friends among the foreign community; excellent cultural events and travel opportunities all helped make the very challenging Iran years some of the best of our lives.

CORRESPONDANCE (1977 – 1978)

London, England
Monday, August 1, 1977 (postcard)

Shows are great! Shaw's Candida w/ Deborah Kerr; musical mystery Something's Afoot; 18th century Wild Oats; Shakespeare movie The Slipper and the Rose with Richard Chamberlain (good!) Br. Museum is wonderful. Really wish you were here! Even though London is terribly crowded (and hot). Not much fun to get around! Hotels awful! North Ireland was great fun; also Oxford. On to Venice Friday, Ravenna, Vicenza, Athens to Islands, Istanbul, Tehran, Esfahan, Shiraz, Tehran.

Love, Norm, BJ, Tasha

Tehran, Iran
Thursday, September 15, 1977

Dear Elma:

Tehran is as crazy as ever! Awful finding an apt: $600 a month minimum; can you believe that those kinds of rent would exist? Penthouse in NY! Fortunately, we are a bit subsidized, so our $900 apt. costs $300 less. Too bad! Everything is a fortune here now!

Tasha has hated school up until now, but is adjusting I think. At least she came home all excited and laughing and happy instead of crying! Taking Geometry, Spanish II, French I (She's had four years of French already!), Science, English, Chorus, PE, Social Studies (not History, which is what she wanted).

We are living for the next two weeks at Miss Doolittle's and Miss Norallah's house, 78 and 80 respectively, and missionaries to Persia for fifty years! They are in the States and London respectively. Kinda fun; we've known them for years. Miss Doolittle ran the school (then a high school) before Frances Gray took over. She disliked Gray!

PIA was an awful flight; all the others were super! Esp. Sabena! PIA was so packed — like a pilgrimage to Mecca — all these people with bundles. And was at the first of the London slow-down, so was five hours late, so we missed on to Esfahan; went into town and out at 5:30 on Standby (awful getting them to take us, so full.) Good trip, though. Wonderful cruise; Ephesus great! As well as Patmos and other islands.

Love, Norm, BJ, and T.

Tehran, Iran
Wednesday, March 22, 1978

Dear Lyla and Bill,

How are you? Well, we trust. We are in the middle of Now Ruz (Persian New Year) holiday of 2 weeks plus a couple days, and it is so restful that it is an enormous bore. I thought we would go to India, but BJ set her foot down and indicated that she had nursed me through these Mid-East hospital experiences and was not interested in doing it again, and that I should stay home. Besides, she and Tasha didn't much want to go. Thought of going to Athens and Rhodes, but were just there. Would love to go to Laguna!! Or LA!!

I'm in the middle of Steinbeck's Grapes of Wrath. He told it all — almost all. Interesting, and brilliantly written. Oh, look in bookshops for Bridge of Turquoise by Roloff Beney. Great photos of Iran! Makes one want to visit — but am tired of living here. Any jobs at Ambassador College? Write.

Love, Norm

Hi,

Our vacation is nearly over, and it has really been very pleasant. The weather has been sunny, so have spent time outside. The garden is quite lovely — flowering shrubs and trees have begun to bloom, although most of the trees are still budding. It's considerably warmer downtown where the altitude is much lower. Tasha was baptized yesterday downtown at the old mission compound. It was done outdoors and was a lovely occasion — it's a lovely place, full of trees, surrounded by a wall in the heart of the city. In fact we're thinking of possibly moving to the compound next year — into the apartment of one of the missionary families who are going to the States on a year's leave. There is much unrest here — considerable rioting — smashing of bank windows. Seems to be mainly anti-West, and anti-women's rights; appears to be a result of the Shah's relenting some on human rights, thanks to Jimmy Carter. People are suddenly much more open in their anti-govt. feelings. A number of Xian churches have been receiving bomb threats. Hope to see you this summer.

Love, Betty

London, England Monday, August 14, 1978

Dear Lyla and Bill,

We're packing up things, getting ready to return to Tehran. What a job! We came light, knowing we'd want to buy a few things. Finally bought two more suitcases and shipped some books thru the mail. We've really enjoyed London, although it's been quite rainy. We're looking forward to Tehran sunshine. However, the news from there doesn't sound very encouraging. Hope it settles down. We'll leave here tomorrow, be in Amsterdam a couple days, and then on to Iran. I hope you got our letter inviting you to come to London — would have been fun. We've seen some really good theatre here, and some not so good. C. Fry's The Lady's Not for Burning and Shaw's St. Joan and Man of Destiny were excellent. A Midsummer Night's Dream in Regent's Park was exceptionally good, too.

My niece, Kathy, was here for several days before going on to the continent. We took her to Stratford to the Shakespeare places and to Warwick Castle. About the middle of July Tasha and I went to Kansas to see my folks; we were there only ten days — rather a hectic trip. My parents really looked good — Dad had been ill last winter. He still works a few hours a week at a lumber-hardware store.

The house we're staying in has two dachshunds, two aquariums, and garden to look after. The dogs have been quite a nuisance, getting into everything and chewing things up. But it actually has worked out very well. Oh yes, we've also seen Tom Stoppard's new play Every Good Boy Deserves Favor. Remember seeing his Travesties with us at the Music Center? This latest one involves a full orchestra with music composed by Andre Previn. Interesting! Hope you're having a good summer.

Love, B and N

Tehran, Iran
Wednesday, September 27, 1978

Dear Lyla and Bill,

Thank you for the invitation for Christmas! We would love to come, but have only five days off for that holiday. Why don't you come here? Do it!

Martial law isn't bad to live under after all the mess before it came in. Now that the curfew is midnight, it's okay; when it was 9 o'clock and then 10 o'clock, it was a bit frightening to get home because there was a very strong chance that one could be shot while hurrying home after hours; they stop you and if you don't hear them, you've had it!! And they are real bullets!

Tehran is a bit like L.A. — 5,000,000 population spread all over, with limited freeways. And the taxi driver has to get to his home after taking you home, which means one must start off two hours ahead of time (sometimes) so he can get back. I was panicky a couple times!!

Tasha is in a different school this year. It was just too dangerous on her old campus. Pretty funny, because now BJ is on that school board, and Tasha goes to the one other school in town which is their "opponent" in everything, The Tehran American School. Not sure she likes it! London was great.

Love to you all, N, B, and T

Athens, Greece
Monday, December 18, 1978

Dear Lyla and Bill,

We're in Athens for several weeks. Decided we had to get away from Tehran for a while (actually, the college advised all foreign teachers to leave the country temporarily). All colleges and universities in Iran have been shut down for almost two months. Tasha's school ended its semester two weeks early, so we came to Greece ten days ago. We and several other teachers rented a house on the island of Hydra; but when two who went ahead of us reported back, we all decided the island house was a bad deal — too cold and 400 steps to climb up to the house, with all the shops at the bottom. So we decided to stay in Athens. Are in a small inexpensive hotel, The Cleo, near the main (Syntagma) square. The sidewalk cafés are in full swing — most of the days have been sunny and warm, but chilly in the shade. Yesterday we went to the service at the American church, which was very nice. The church itself is small, seating approx. 250; the front wall is solid stained glass with scenes from the life of Christ. The pipe organ was especially impressive — excellent organist. We plan to return to Tehran early in January. Have discovered that we can go to Cairo en route to Tehran for almost no extra cost, so are tempted to go for a week or so. Coming here, on Royal Jordanian Airline, we had an overnite stop in Amman, Jordan, which was interesting. If we don't go to Cairo, I'd like to stop off in Amman and go to Damascus for a day or two.

We're wondering what to expect when we get back to Tehran; things were getting pretty bad when we left. Every nite at curfew time mobs of people marched in the streets chanting anti-govt. slogans, tossing a few Molotov cocktails into American houses, etc. They say that very few of these attempts at burning private homes have been successful: evidence of the Iranians' technological expertise! Power failures occurred nearly every nite, and sometimes also during the day. We were beginning to feel some of the anti- American sentiment. Getting out of the airport on Dec. 9 was a terrible experience — everyone trying to get out before the 11th, the big Moslem holy day. The college is feebly hoping to re-open in January, but we have our doubts. But we'll probably stay on so long as we're paid.

Thanks for the Christmas invitation; hope you got our reply. Have a merry Christmas.

Betty, Norman, and Tasha

[We could not return to Tehran; the revolution consumed the whole country as the Shah was overthrown and our college was terminated. We returned to Los Angeles via New York on Royal Air Maroc via Casablanca, Morocco. As we waited for our plane at JFK New York, I phoned our former Dean of Damavand College.

She told me, "They want you in Beirut, Norm."

"Mary, we've lost everything in Tehran, and they are bombing the sense out of Beirut. It would seem now is not the time to go there."

"Never mind, Norm. In six months you will be in Beirut."

And I was, with BJ and Tasha following after Natasha graduated from Hoover High in Glendale, California, in January of 1980.]

CHAPTER 7

BEIRUT (1979 – 1985)

Colonel Muamar Khaddafi, Leaving Beirut, BJ's Journal

COLONEL MUAMAR KHADDAFI

We did, indeed, return to the Middle East. Adventures, as always, were in store for us.

In 1983 when BJ and I returned to teach at Beirut University College, the old Beirut College for Women campus, a number of university professors were invited by the Libyan embassy to visit Tripoli for an educational workshop. People from AUB, American University of Beirut, BUC, and Lebanese University all went to Libya via Rome. We stopped in Rome, seeing Rome's splendor in the middle of the night, with St. Peter's circle of Corinthian pillars welcoming the night visitor where thousands of people fill it by day. Excited by the visit to Rome, and the potential experience in Tripoli, we flew on to North Africa — to meet with Muamar Khaddafi, we were told.

Every night we were all grouped together to study Khaddafi's "Green Book;" his philosophy of government and social intercourse. Nightly, his ideas became more confusing to my Western-trained mind, although his ideas seemed to stem from ancient Greek, as well as Arabic, philosophers. Since the entire discussion, nightly, was in Arabic, my two American friends and I had difficulty understanding Muamar's ideas, although his deputies gave us English translations of the Green Book. I can only say that Khaddafi's Green Book is not nearly as interesting, nor as shocking, as Khomeini's Iranian Green Book of his ideas to live by. We seemed to wander around the world learning to live by someone's little book of ideas; when we lived and taught in China, we were exposed to Mao's little Red Book, although those days of following his ideas had been replaced by Deng Xiaoping's "one country, two systems" idea of capitalism.

As we waited for the time we would meet with the "Big Man," Khaddafi, we stared at — the others discussed — the Green Book. During the day, we visited a new textile factory and other industries. The noise level in the textile factory was unbearable. One day, we were taken to a large store and told that we could have anything we wanted. Several persons chose things, I did not. Later, my wife said I should have chosen something ... but what?

For four days we stayed in their one four-star hotel, being served lavish (for the desert) meals of lamb, in various culinary forms, couscous, vegetables, melons, and an aperitif of pear juice. Every time we met for "drinks," we were served chilled, thick, heavily sugared pear juice. Following the Green Book philosophy, everything served had to be locally produced, even though Libya is a major oil producer.

The fifth day we were in Libya, we were told to pack up and were taken to the Tripoli airport, which was a much more modern one than the airport at which we landed in 1972, where we waited all day for a bus. We were flown on Air Libya to Benghazi and taken to a resort hotel in the Benghazi harbor. They had brought several cruise ships, ferry types, and had docked them in the harbor. We were guests in these luxury floating hotels. After being assigned our rooms, we were allowed to enjoy the various areas of the ship — particularly the bar, with pear juice. At the end of the day, we were told that tomorrow — "inshallah" (meaning "God willing") — we would all meet Colonel Khaddafi. We thought, "Yeah, right." We had been told that every day. I had daily asked, as I had asked before leaving Beirut, if we would be going to Leptus Magna. Now that we were in Benghazi, and therefore closer to Leptus Magna, maybe we could go there.

"Yes, yes. Maybe. If we have time. Inshallah!" The usual response in the Middle East and North Africa, which means "no."

The next day, at about 5:00 p.m., we were told to change our clothes and get ready to meet the Colonel. The one American girl was in the shower, having just washed her hair. She dashed out, with wet hair, and had only seconds to put on something. She settled for wearing a bib overall made of striped, mattress-ticking cloth, and a T-shirt. Before leaving Beirut, when I called a friend at the American embassy to tell them I was going to Tripoli (it was not recommended that Americans go there), he said, "Wear your best clothes. You'll be on TV."

When we were in the room at the presidential residence — not at one of Khaddafi's tents in the desert — we waited for him to enter. I had been asked a few hours earlier if I would please address him on behalf of the Americans there. Three of us were from the U.S., although there were a number of Lebanese who had American passports. I said that I would, and then met with the other two, plus a Lebanese friend who had U.S. citizenship as well as Lebanese citizenship. We wondered what I could say, since America and Libya were not close political friends. I thought through the request, and when Khaddafi entered the reception room, the time came.

Khaddafi was preceded by what the general consensus of the men decided were the most striking bodyguards we had ever seen; absolutely stunning young ladies. (Rumor said they were from Israel, but that seems unlikely.) Dressed in tailored, khaki combat uniforms, berets, boots, and carrying AK- 47s or Kalashnikovs, they entered ahead, beside, and behind Muamar Khaddafi.

As Khaddafi shook my hand, as he moved past each of us, there was the strongest and strangest electrical current that ran through me. We looked at each other as though we had known each other for years, and I felt as if I understood him. His charisma was tremendously engaging.

As soon as we sat down, Khaddafi spoke in Arabic and English. I missed what he said, but several persons said, "Norman. Norman. He said that he was glad that America had someone here at this pre-conference meeting and added that he welcomed all of us."

I was then asked to address him, responding to his welcome. Standing — not in my best clothes, but well-dressed — I greeted him. "Your Excellency, Colonel Khaddafi, our brother (I had no idea why I used this term of address, but later learned he liked it, and that he liked to be called "our brother"), on behalf of us American visitors, I would like to thank you for your invitation to visit your country. Your hospitality, the hotels, and food have been generous and comfortable.

As we have become acquainted with your ideas in the Green Book, it seems to me that the world, and particularly the United States, has the wrong opinion of Muamar Khaddafi. The United States should learn to know the real Colonel Khaddafi, because the image the world has of Muamar Khaddafi is not the one we have gotten to know during this week- long visit to your country. Somehow, it is important that there be a bridge to span the chasm, the separation, between Washington and the real Colonel Khaddafi. If there is any way you could build that bridge, we feel it would be very beneficial to a new world of tomorrow."

Or something to that effect.

And I sat down to excited applause. [That was 1983, before Reagan bombed Tripoli in the late 80s.] From that point on, the meeting was all in Arabic. Late that night, the Libyan Ambassador came to me and said, "The Colonel wants to see you tonight or tomorrow night." He is a night person as I am. No one came for me that night.

The next day everybody packed up, got onto the bus, and they were taken to the Benghazi airport to return, via Rome, to Beirut. The Ambassador said to me, "He has asked to see you. Will you please stay for another day?"

I thought, "Well, BJ and Tasha are not back yet from their trip to Italy." Natasha was studying in Paris, and the reason I came on this trip was because I would have a free stopover anywhere in Europe. I said, "Yes, I'll stay one more night, but I must be in Paris the next day."

He said, "Okay." They always say "okay."

I walked the others out to the bus that was taking them to the airport. As they left, someone shouted, "He'll build you a new university! Remember to hire us when you get your new university."

Others said, "You'll be sorry! You'll never get out of Libya. It's a good thing you admired his new University of Benghazi." We had looked at the campus, and particularly the library, the day before. It was almost bereft of books. The bus left ... I stood there on the dock, waved, and another person I had seen around was standing there. As we went to the entrance of the ship-hotel, the policeman there asked us for our identity badge. We had none, for we were a special delegation of what we learned was a huge conference of educators coming from all over the world: Asian, African, European, South American, but I saw no other North Americans. After they gave me a new identity card with my picture, I talked some with a British professor, and others, who were admiring the Khaddafi ideas. They had diligently studied the Green Book on their own. It was all rather interesting, indeed.

I waited near the bar — where I told the Lebanese Ambassador's First Secretary I would be — or in my room, awaiting my summons from the Colonel. Perhaps this meeting would be in a desert tent with Persian rugs! I waited in vain, fell asleep, awoke the next day, and went to find my host. I found the First Secretary, told him I had to go to Paris, that I had waited as instructed, but that no one had come for me. Now I had to go to Paris, as his boss promised.

"No, no, you must stay here and wait for Colonel Khaddafi to call you for an audience."

I said, "Wait a minute, my friend ... !" I was no longer friendly, and he knew it, as I told him in no uncertain terms that I was leaving, and he had better get me to the airport and on to Paris, today. (I kept hearing in my mind, "You'll never get out of Libya!")

For some reason he said, "Just a minute." He went to a telephone, called someone, and in Arabic no doubt told him that this American was not happy. Then he said, "Come!"

I said, "Where to?" He said, "Airport."

I said, "Let me get my little bag!"

I dashed to my room. My bag was already packed, so I grabbed it and ran to the exit. The guy jumped into an old, black car, dusty from the desert, as did I, drove very fast to the airport, no seat belts, and I ran for the plane. The steps had to be pushed back to the door. There was no security check. I ran up, sat near the front, they pulled the steps back, and we took off. I looked around and there were older people, and a few younger people, with vegetables and chickens to take to market. It was the milk run from Benghazi to Tripoli. We had noticed the changes in the lifestyle from 1972, when we were previously in Libya. The people no longer lived in black tents made of sheep's wool and skin; they now lived in high-rise buildings. We were told by friends living in Libya that the tribal race was having difficulties adjusting to the new way of life. One problem was that the shepherds had difficulty getting their flocks of sheep and cattle into the elevators to take them home at night. This, for a time, caused great disturbances to the lifestyle of the people. No doubt, they sorted out these problems, just as they sorted out how to get food to the two major cities across the desert and across the gulf between Benghazi and Tripoli. Libya used air travel to expedite solutions to their desert needs.

As the door of the aircraft opened, the steward let me out first, and as I went down the steps, there was the Libyan Ambassador to Lebanon coming toward me. He said, "Did you meet with the Colonel?"

"No," I said, and told him what happened.

He exclaimed, "But why not? It was all set up! He wanted you to become an ambassador from him to Reagan … !"

I said, "Well, perhaps I'm not quite the guy to do that, but if I could help, I would gladly do so." I laughed to myself.

He then took me into town for dining (no wine, just pear juice), and told me that all flights had already gone to Europe, but that tomorrow he would get me on a flight to Rome and then on to Paris. I said that was okay. What else could I say?

Another night in Tripoli. I saw the square where the People's Revolution was led by Khaddafi, and other sights, being led by the ambassador himself.

Now in 2016 as we watch Libya and so many of the Middle Eastern countries wake up to the fact that the Arab spring did not grow into the "free democratic society" that they thought would develop, becoming instead a battleground killing the population over control of the society, destroying the cities, housing, and hopes for all, leading to mass migrations to Europe, if possible. The next day I did, indeed, catch the flight to Paris, changing planes in Rome, to go to Orly International. BJ had journeyed to Paris from Florence, Italy, with Natasha, and had already flown back to Beirut. I had missed her. We were to go back together, but she had classes to get to, as did I, so she had returned to Beirut as scheduled. I had only a short visit with Natasha, then back to Beirut.

The next day, my friend Gordon Gurley, the librarian, who also had gone to Tripoli, and I were called to the office of the BUC Administrator, Fawzi Hajjar, a friend of mine from the BCW years. Both Fawzi and the president acted like they did not know us. The police were there from customs and immigration and asked if we had journeyed to Libya. We both said, "Yes."

"And why are there no Libyan stamps in your passport?"

We said that we didn't know why, but that we had a group visa which covered all of us on the trip. A customs policeman said, "Yes, well, may we please have your passports? You can have them back when you leave Lebanon."

So we gave them up. That was Easter time. We often asked for, but never got, our passports back. It seems that Lebanon broke diplomatic relations with Libya during Easter, during our trip to Libya. Libya had not bothered to tell any of us. (It might have interrupted our studying the Green Book.) We also learned later that several Lebanese professors were asked by customs as they came in, "Where have you come from? There's no consecutive stamp in your passport."

One professor replied, "We came from the sky."

During the next few months, I was repeatedly telephoned by someone whom I did not know, but who told me we had met in Tripoli. I kept trying to get rid of him, a Dr. Somebody from Lebanese University, but he kept saying that he and I could make a lot of money from Khaddafi by my talking to Washington about relations between Tripoli and the U.S. I kept telling him that I was not the one to do this. I called the U.S. embassy, and they told me to keep listening to him. I told him that I would be glad to help if I could, but I don't know how to do such a thing. During all of this, the Libyan Ambassador to Lebanon was assassinated in the Lebanese Bekaa Valley; by whom, nobody knew at the time. The calls stopped.

Finally, the summer break came, and it was time to travel. We had no passports. The customs and immigration offices still said, "If you wish to leave Lebanon, you can." But it was understood that we could not come back. The Lebanese professors were given back their I.D. papers, but Gordon and I were not. In fact, we had requested new work permits and residence cards. Before, they were always automatically given to us when we went to get them from customs. This time, the head guy was in his brass-laden Lebanese military uniform, and he said that Gordon and I could not have our new papers, nor our U.S. passports, until we were ready to leave Lebanon. All of this was happening while bombs and shells and shooting were going on all around us. Indeed, one day when shells were hitting the campus, and one hit the roof of the library, Gordon risked his life running to the library to save the books in case of a fire. Everybody said he was foolish for that. It was sort of like ten-year-old Natasha, who saved the library book in Tehran but lost her coat, years before during a fire in a restaurant. It would seem that we would all have been ready to go back to America and forget about teaching and helping Beirut students.

At last, Gordon had had enough of all of this, and he telephoned his father- in-law in Washington, who was on the White House Middle Eastern desk, and told him the situation. His father-in-law sent, via diplomatic pouch, a letter from the White House requesting that the Lebanese government do all it could to expedite the return of the passports and relevant papers to Gordon and his friend — me! We went back to customs and the same guy, now in a blue blazer with colorful breast patches, met us saying, "Oh, Mr. Gordon, why haven't you come out to this office and taken your passport and new work permit? It has been waiting for you."

Gordon said something like, "Oh, I wonder where it was when I came out here every week for the past many months?"

The officer told him to go get the passport, and I said, "Sir, I am the friend the State Department wrote from the White House to include. May I please have my passport?"

"Oh, my God," he explicated. "Go with Mr. Gordon and get yours." We waited several more hours but got the passports.

LEAVING BEIRUT

Natasha graduated in May, 1983, with a degree in Art History from Scripps College, a part of the Claremont Colleges University in Claremont, California. Claremont prides itself on being set up like Oxford, England, with the four associated colleges: Scripps, Pomona, Pitzer, and Claremont McKenna College. Students of one can take courses for credit in any of the colleges. It works well, and it is economical, I should imagine, for the colleges need not copy each other in bricks and mortar as well as faculty. Natasha liked it. After graduation she taught English for a year at the American University of Beirut, and then she went to Paris to study at the Sorbonne. BJ had gone to the graduation ceremony. I couldn't go because of my lack of papers, and I was committed to teach summer school. I also had to move from our BUC apartment since I had been offered, and had accepted, a full professorship at Lebanese University, the east side campus. I took the job, at the same salary as BUC, and without the pressure of doing theatre, which at BUC amounted to a show almost every two weeks, including student productions and major theatre productions, plus a full load of teaching. It had become too stressful, so I went into teaching only British and American English Literature. It was marvelous! I discovered that one does much less physical labor when teaching literature than when teaching theatre with productions, and I kept doing only literature for the next eighteen years.

Unfortunately, the second year at Lebanese University the Lebanese pound dropped from three to the U.S. dollar to five to the U.S. dollar. Since I was paid in Lebanese pounds, I lost a great deal of my income. At BUC, half of the income was in U.S. dollars. Had we stayed there, I would not have lost very much. After that it dropped most alarmingly.

While in Beirut, after leaving Beirut University College, we lived in several missionaries' apartments who were away on leave. For a time we lived in Ben Weir's apartment but had to move when he and his wife came back from home leave. Two weeks after we moved from their apartment, Ben was kidnapped by Hezbollah from in front of his house. They said they were after an American university professor who lived in that apartment. Ben was not a university professor; he was the head of Presbyterian Missions.

Previously, on a return flight to Beirut from Budapest, I had sat near an active socialist AUB student who had told me on the flight that they were planning lots of bombing for Beirut for this fall. I said to him, "Don't you think we, down in Beirut, have had enough of the bombing and shelling? Can't you stop doing it?"

He became rather cold but was still conversant. We then shared the last taxi from the airport, and he insisted on dropping me off first, at Ben Weir's apartment, which was where we lived at that time, and then he went on to AUB, which was where he lived. When Ben was kidnapped I remembered the flight from Budapest and felt terrible; no one else thought there was a connection. Perhaps they simply tried to comfort me.

For a time, at the end of our exhausting but rewarding venture in Beirut, we lived in Dennis Hilgendorf's apartment. Dennis, a Lutheran Minister, had established the CRC, Contact and Resource Center, in Beirut to help paraplegics, 150,000 victims of the civil war, to discover they could take care of themselves in their own domestic living areas and lead productive lives. The CRC continues to operate in Beirut and can be contacted through Lutheran Missions.

It was there, in Dennis Hilgendorf's apartment, that I spent my remaining weeks in Beirut crawling around on the floor, trying to avoid being seen through the picture window — covered by only an open-weave "glass curtain" — by the militias that stopped across the street at a petrol station to fill up their machine-gun-laden jeeps with gasoline. I stayed close to the floor, remaining out of sight, for fear of being kidnapped, because they were kidnapping so many Americans. Terry Anderson and others, along with Ben Weir, had already been kidnapped. BJ was teaching English Literature and English language at the Armenian College, Haigazian College, in West Beirut. BJ said I had to get out.

A former student of mine, Dr. Evelyne Accad, had gone to teach at the University of Tunis in Tunisia and had asked the University of Tunis if they would consider me for a professorial post. She finally telephoned, by way of her sister, Fawzi Hajjar's wife, and said that I had a job in Tunis, and for me to get there and ask for it. My transportation from our apartment to the airport was arranged by two students; one the son of a member of Lebanese Parliament (who a few years ago was assassinated, I was sorry to learn). The car stopped not far from West Beirut. My students got out saying, "The driver works for my father as a driver and the other one is father's bodyguard. You will be safe with them. We have to get out here or we will be kidnapped. Take care." And off we rapidly went, stopping a few miles along the road when a gunman was at a roadblock. The driver did a "bootlegger's turn" and we went another direction past Palestinian camps and hurried along. I was driven to the airport by two gunmen who had been firing on a

Palestinian camp, Chatilla; the same Palestinian camp where earlier, in 1982, Lebanese Christians had massacred many Palestinians. These two gunmen took me to the airport. I tried to pay them a little money, but they laughed and said, "No." They told my former students, who had arranged my escape to the airport, that I had offered them money to keep from being kidnapped. I laughed, later, when I heard that. I had only been offering taxi fare.

I flew out to Cyprus, and eventually found my way to Tunis, by way of Athens. Beirut was an earlier trial ground for today's civil war in Aleppo, Syria. It had all become too much, so we moved to Tunisia. Thank God and Evelyne!

BJ'S JOURNAL

Written During the Israeli Invasion of Lebanon June 10 – July 6, 1982

Thursday, June 10, 1982

Awakened at 5 a.m. to the sound of heavy gunfire in the distance — probably anti-aircraft guns in the airport area where Israeli troops are reportedly attacking, as they have been all night. Between the volleys, the neighborhood rooster can be heard. I wonder why there are no morning mosque calls — perhaps I just didn't hear them. At 6 I got up, went to the kitchen for a cup of coffee, and looked into the street from the balcony. Already there was a sizeable group gathered at the bakery.

Since the invasion began last Sunday (June 6), the bakeries have been mobbed with customers. Many of them are obviously not the usual neighborhood folk, but must be the refugees that we're told are pouring into Beirut from Sidon, Damour, and other places in the South. Regular customers appear to have priority, as hot loaves of hot bread are passed over heads, and money is passed back. Although angry voices occasionally erupt, it is amazing how patiently they wait. By noon everyone was gone, and the bakery locked up, which is normal.

Several buildings under construction near the campus have been occupied by refugees, and at about 9 a.m. Jackie Hajjar called to say that armed men were at the upper gate, trying to persuade the university administrators to allow refugees into the campus buildings. Jackie was calling for people to pray for the administration. She said, "We've been through this before, and once the refugees are in, there's no way of getting them out." I asked her about the leaflets, which we'd seen fluttering from the sky as a plane flew overhead. She had heard that they carried an Arabic message which advised the Syrians to leave Beirut.

Several times this week cars and trucks with loud speakers have come through the streets, collecting food and clothing for the refugees. The response appeared good: many people carried out food, especially powdered milk, and bundles of clothes were tossed from balconies. Today, however, no one came around. Things felt tense. People in the street were carrying bags of groceries, containers of water — many buildings are without water. But by afternoon many shops were closed and the streets deserted, except for a few fast-moving vehicles including an occasional ambulance. There was an almost constant sound of planes overhead, with occasional volleys of anti- aircraft fire.

All afternoon we worked at packing — one small bag each for possible evacuation — and filled the black trunk with things we valued: carpets, several pictures, pieces of brass, plus a couple bags of clothing. Natasha packing some things for the U.S. and some for Paris.

At about 2 p.m. a huge explosion, which sounded like a shell, hit nearby. We all grabbed blankets and the bomb shelter bags we'd prepared earlier. Each contained a small amount of food, a flashlight, books, etc. But as it developed, we didn't go to the shelter this time.

In the evening we took a walk around the campus and discovered that the refugees had indeed moved into Nikel and Sage Halls. The chairs and desks were all piled outside, and people seemed to be settling in for the nite — arranging mattresses, etc. There was a large Red Cross flag attached to the gate. The lounge of the girls' dorm has been converted into a first aid station, manned by some of the students.

Clarke Bloom called late afternoon to say that he, Jackie, and the Nottinghams are thinking of going to Jounieh (East Beirut) in the morning in hopes of taking a boat to Cyprus. But we hear that no boats have gone for several days — the Israelis have stopped them. Blooms were scheduled to fly to the U.S. on Saturday, but the airport's closed.

Friday, June 11

Just talked with Jackie Bloom on phone, and they've decided they're better off here; the Green Line crossing is said to be "hairy" — and not sure of boats after arriving. It seems that the Israelis want no boats leaving. However, I later talked with Evelyn Richards, who reports that they plan to drive to Jounieh before dark, possibly stay at the Rabbia school and wait for a boat or things to clear up here. It's been terribly noisy around the Richards' house — near the beach where many anti-aircraft guns are located.

Israelis reportedly fought all nite again around the airport. Awakened at 4:30 a.m. to loud shooting. Got up and wrote a letter home in case someone decided to try to go via Jounieh. Went across the street to Abu Abed's store, and shelves are full. Bought a few fresh vegetables. Shortly after I returned home, there was a minor shoot-out at the bakery. (I think they were actually only shooting into the air.) Several, including Fuad Rifka, have sent their families to their villages, and these men have since been eating on the campus most of the time. The refugees are now trying to take over the gym.

At 10:30 three huge crashes, which sounded like shells, frightened us from our chairs to close our shelter bags. Jackie Hajjar and children (David and Lynne), who live on the top (and most dangerous) floor, joined us in our safer apartment. The children immediately became involved in a card game, and Jackie wrote a letter to her sister. After an hour or so, Najla Dabaghi stopped by for a few minutes. Then a young fellow came around to tell everyone to go to the bomb shelter. Someone asked, "Why?" thinking that perhaps some particular incident had occurred. He replied, "This is war!" So the Pirris, who lived across the hall, decided to go. Jackie asked me, "Do you want to go?" "Not especially, do you?" "No." So we agreed to wait awhile, and it turned out that didn't go down that time. Tasha decided to bake some bread, so I mixed up some nutbread to get double use of the oven. Gas bottles are bound to be scarce.

At around 11 a.m. a ceasefire between Syria and Israel was announced, to begin in one hour; the Palestinians were still discussing it. During that hour, the Israelis madly shelled four or five places, killing several hundred people!

After a lunch of tostadas we all took a nap. At about 4 p.m. the Richards came over to get away from all the big guns in their neighborhood. They had supper with us and are going to sleep on the living room floor. We hear that seventy-five more refugee families have moved into the campus. There are now approximately three hundred of them.

Saturday, June 12

Up again at 5 a.m. Israelis bombarded all nite, but at a distance. At 11 last nite planes circled and circled. As they left, we opened the shades to look out, and the whole sky toward the airport was lighted up. Perhaps incendiary bombs had been dropped. Larry Richards went off to a meeting for Americans at the American University. He learned that some "Go-Home- Americans" notes were placed in mailboxes at AUB.

At mid-morning the Nottinghams and Janet Hyde-Clarke left by military police car for the East Side, hoping to get a boat out — with tons of luggage. They plan to stay with Selim (employee of BUC who lives in East Beirut) in the meantime. Interesting how upset was Duwayne (photography teacher) — the moocher who hasn't yet done one favor for anyone — because Nottinghams had told very few people that they were leaving. It is a bit annoying that they were so secretive about it. But I can understand, considering that Duwayne might want to join them!

It seems that the ceasefire is only between Israel and Syria. Israel and Palestinians have been fighting all day, hitting the airport area and Maazra. They've killed at least one thousand people in Sidon. The Richards were with us for supper. Evelyn brought kibbe and hummus from her freezer and squash, which I fried. Then we all went to the Blooms, on the upper campus, for cake. Everyone appeared to be exhausted. We saw the students painting a large red cross on the parking lot near the upper gate and also on the roof of one of the buildings — hoping to keep the campus from being bombed from the air. En route home, we learned of a new ceasefire between Israelis and Palestinians. This brought a few hours of quiet.

Sunday, June 13

We had a very nice church service with 40-45 people. The Arabic church also had their service on campus, with very few attending. Around noon the ceasefire broke down, and we again heard shooting. In the afternoon I went upstairs to see Jackie. She was washing piles of dishes. Besides Daoveed, the children's friend who lives with them, the Dean and Fuad Rifka, who have both sent their families to their villages, have been eating with the Hajjars most of the time. The refugees are now trying to take over the gym.

Monday, June 14

As I was sitting and listening to the 7 a.m. news, the doorbell rang and it was Mimi. She'd come from her village, Bishmizzine, with the village service bus to get some of her things from her apartment. She said there was room in the bus for us if we wanted to go to her village with her. Her family had room for us to stay with them. So after waking Norman, we decided to go. Fortunately, the bus was a few minutes late, and we managed to be ready. Norman even got some transportation money from Fawzi.

Things were quiet as we drove through Beirut. The Syrians were very nice about letting us through their check points. But when we entered Phalangist (pro-Israeli Christian militia) territory, they went through some of the bags with a fine-tooth comb and made nasty comments about the Americans. "Why are you taking these Americans with you? Let their govt. take care of them." To prevent refugees staying in their area, they now keep people's identity cards and return them at the opposite border. This means a wait; however, we waited no more than 45 minutes. We were told some had waited six hours. We (13 of us) were really jammed into the micro-bus with luggage everywhere and piled on top. Looked like a bunch of refugees, which some of us actually were.

While waiting at the checkpoint for IDs, Mimi and Natasha walked to Hala Nassar's house to tell them to come to the checkpoint for a suitcase we were delivering to them from Riyad in Beirut. In the meantime, the IDs came, and we in the bus went on without them, the driver saying that they'd follow in a car — we assumed Nassar's car.

But Natasha didn't have any ID with her (Mimi had a work permit.) So Mimi hitched rides in two different cars from the checkpoint, catching up with us one village before Bishmizzine. After lunch Mimi and Norm returned to Helwe with Nassar's suitcase and picked up Natasha. I, feeling ill, slept. The Nassar grandmother fed Natasha, as well as the others there, horrid leftovers for lunch, and Natasha was sick for a couple of days.

Tuesday, June 15

I left my journal in Beirut, so now must start another.

We drove today to Byblos to try to make a call to the folks, but the international lines weren't working. So we drove on to Jounieh and had a lovely seafood dinner overlooking the sea. Mimi, Tasha, and I had small fish of some kind, and Norman had shrimp. A nice restaurant called Chez Sami; bill: 260 LL ($54). We shopped at the Jounieh supermarket, which we had much trouble locating. It's a huge mkt. With nearly everything you'd find in

U.S. stores. Then we had a terrible time finding the autostrada to get back to the village, but finally did. We met some Nigerians who left Ras Beirut last Thursday and were hoping to take a boat on Tuesday (today). We also learned from them that the Fayyads are unable to leave Lebanon because Israel is allowing no Lebanese to leave, and that excludes him.

Leila, Mimi's sister, plans to take the village bus to Beirut tomorrow to get some of her things and come back on Thursday. The news tonite says that the Israelis have given the Syrians 48 hours to leave Beirut.

Wednesday, June 16

Leila's mother had a bad dream and didn't let her go to Beirut today. It seems that Israelis and Syrians have been fighting in several places. We're talking about going to the beach this afternoon. Went to Helwe and learned that the Richards had stopped by to see Hala Nassar; they had left Beirut on Monday, the same day we left, and were staying at the Rabbia School. Supposed to leave this afternoon on a French boat for Cyprus. So we decided to go to Jounieh to try to see them. After much hassle in heavy traffic, we never found them.

However, the pier area was packed with Egyptians trying to get on boats — they were there with apparently all their household goods, under tents improvised from blankets and whatever was available. Dozens of black umbrellas served as sunshades. Many shiny new electric fans were also in use.

Note: When we returned to Jounieh one week later to catch our boat, the pier was still packed with Egyptians — whether the same ones, we don't know.

Thursday, June 17

Leila went to Beirut and brought back Natasha's large suitcase. Says that things there are quiet. I went with Mimi to Tripoli in the morning. She wanted to have her car's carburetor cleaned. While it was being worked on, we walked to Samir's (Mimi's brother-in-law) mother's house. The house is an old four or five story building with two apts per floor. However, her apt. takes the entire floor; it's huge, with high ceilings. Samir's mother, Mrs. Obeid, around sixty, stylish and attractive but harried looking, with short brown hair which hadn't been recently done. We were surprised to see Monir (Samir's brother) there. He's a med student at AUB.

They ushered us into the salon, which was at the front of the building — large with many windows in the curved wall. The draperies and carpets had been removed for the summer, according to the Lebanese custom. The perimeter was lined with very "aupessant" furniture. Small end-tables stood twice the height of the other furniture. For plants?? We had just been served glasses of a sweet, cold drink, when one of Monir's classmates from AUB arrived. They both had been living at the NEST dormitory until Wednesday, when an Al Fateh group led by Arafat's brother had turned the NEST into a hospital. Afraid of being held captive if it were discovered that they were doctors, they immediately came home to Tripoli. Dr. Fletcher asked the Sudanese students to take them as far as Jounieh and to tell the Phalangists that they were monks trying to get out.

As we talked, Samir's cousin Farideh, who lives with the family, came in and introduced herself as an American citizen. Farideh is slight, probably less than five feet tall, weighing around eighty lbs. Her long hair, light brown, was ornately styled with a wide headband. Her dress, of a Damascus brocade with green floral pattern, was floor length with long sleeves, wide lapels, belted at the waist, and trimmed with black grosgrain ribbon. She wore makeup and rather ornate jewelry — a choker made of clusters of black and pearl beads, earrings, several large rings, and a bracelet made of two interlocking silver hearts. Small green fuzzy slippers completed her costume.

Truly a vision from another time! She sat delicately, listening attentively, saying little. But she did tell me that she had attended the American Girls' School in Tripoli.

Later, Mimi told me that Farideh, now 79 years old, had been quite young when her mother died; she never got along with her stepmother. After high school she worked in her uncle's (Samir's father's) office — he was a doctor. Later, she lived with her uncle's family, serving more or less as a nanny for the children, and has been there ever since. She has been given by some the nickname "The Vase," because of her decorative quality.

After leaving Samir's family, we walked back to pick up the car. It was ready except for reassembling several parts in our presence. They had cleaned the carburetor for 50 LL ($10). The normal price was 100 LL, but special price for George's friend. George is Mimi's future brother-in-law. As we drove to the end of the block and turned around, the engine died once. So Mimi stopped to complain to the mechanic, who replied, "If it stopped, it was your fault." And sure enough, the car worked fine after that!

We drove to George's house (apt.), which is quite nice, in an old, rather interesting building with shutters, beautiful tile floors, high ceilings. Furniture is typically Lebanese. There is much discussion of whether or not Zaffar, Mimi's fiancé, would come on the 24th as planned. George is to go to Saudi Arabia the 25th via Damascus. Mimi is tempted to go to Damas with him, and then go on to the U.S. since she must go regarding her Green Card status. However, if Zaffar is coming, she wants to wait for him; they'd planned to go together.

George said the news reported that a freighter leaving Tripoli the night before had had an explosion four miles out of port. It was reported that of the 250 people aboard, only fifty survived. We were upset because yesterday Hala had told us that Ziad had taken his friend Nadeem to Tripoli to catch a boat for Cyprus. He was on his way to California to serve as a camp counselor in an international YMCA camp. Next, we heard that 25 were killed and 25 missing. George said that one Tripoli man sold a piece of land to send two of his sons out of the country, and both were killed on that boat. No one knows exactly what happened. Some say the bomb was planted; it did go off near the captain's cabin. Others say it was a rocket fired from the Palestinian camp in Tripoli — but a direct hit from four miles?? Others say it was a shell from an Israeli gunboat. We know that Israeli gunboats are checking closely all boats leaving from Jounieh. Israel has ordered no Lebanese to leave the country. But it seems that "illegal" boats are leaving Tripoli, which is in Syrian territory.

We returned to Bishmizzine around 1 p.m. and Mimi went to Tripoli again to bring Monir to check her father. He also took a look at Natasha, who's had an upset stomach, and checked most of our blood pressures, pronounced us all okay. Mimi and Norm drove Monir back to Tripoli.

Friday, June 18
Mimi took the "bus" to Beirut. Leila and her mother cleaned house and did laundry, so I helped where I could. Mimi returned shortly after noon and reported that things were "okay" in Ras Beirut. She's worried, however, that her apartment will be occupied by refugees, since it's empty. Wants to go back on Monday.

Saturday, June 19
Went to the beach at Chekka, but it was so crowded that we decided to go to Hala's at Helwe. Everyone there was all upset about Nadeem's boat blowing up — he's missing. The beach area at Helwe is really neat, although it's mainly large rocks with natural steps down to the water. It's a natural cove, almost surrounded by high rocks. The water is cold, perhaps because it doesn't get direct sunshine many hours. Thirty-five to forty people were sunning or playing card games under the two sun-shades. Hala and children live with Riyad's parents, whose house is an old stone one-story with very simple, but comfortable furnishings. One

goes from front door straight through the sitting area (with bedrooms and kitchen on either side) to a patio. We returned to Bishmizzine, all very depressed about Nadeem.

Sunday, June 20

Mimi took us to Belmont (Balamund), about 15-20 miles away. It is the site of a beautiful crusader castle, which later became a monastery. Now there is a huge French elementary and high school, plus a theological school. One of the theology students, Abraham, showed us around. His English was quite good — the theology school is conducted in English. Strange?? He plans to go to Boston to study this summer. The church is gorgeous with its simple stone walls and very ornate iconostasis, with wooden beamed ceiling. (This is the church where Laura and Samir were married.) The smaller chapel was similar, with beautiful icons. A young priest asked us not to cross our legs in the church (which we happened to be doing at that moment), so we learned something new! Later, as we were looking around the courtyard, Abraham offered us each a piece of bread that was left over from the service. Interesting! [An interesting element to this crossing of legs happened twenty years later in Istanbul in an Armenian Cathedral, when BJ was asked to uncross her legs when she visited the Cathedral listening to its music. It is easy to forget some customs.]

The theology school is very modern and huge — but has only around forty students. The excitement of the day was when Natasha and Mimi saw a large snake near the stairs we climbed to get back to the car. What a commotion! There was also a series of Roman arches left standing near the entrance to the area.

When we returned home, Sunday dinner was being prepared, and what a lovely meal it was. The dining room table was set. Leila had charbroiled several chickens, and stuffed grape leaves, squash, tossed salad, and fresh fruit were also served. Mimi and I went to pick up her uncle, Mr. Milki's brother, who has never married (there's another single brother in the village.) What interesting old houses this village has. I took a few photos.

After dinner we heard much horn-honking and were told that it was the groom's entourage. There was to be a wedding that afternoon.

Leila asked if we'd like to go, so we got into the car and arrived at the church in time to see the bride in white traditional gown enter the church on her father's arm, followed by a large crowd. Many others, including the groom, were at the church waiting. We stood at the back of the church, listening to the sing-song chanting of the scriptures while the bride and groom stood, completely surrounded by smiling well-wishers. Some people also sat in the pews. There were few decorations — a few ribbons on the pews, a couple small floral bouquets taped to the walls added to the already ornate Greek Orthodox sanctuary. There was much picture-taking, and much coming and going in the congregation. Many electric lights — electric candelabra, etc., took the place of candles.

We decided these weddings were much simpler to plan than the ones we knew. It was an informal, festive affair, which lasted about forty-five minutes. It was followed by a reception in the church hall.

In the early evening I went with Leila to buy some fresh hummus (chick peas). They grow on bushy branches in pods and taste much like green peas. There's an art to eating them: one cracks them and removes the pea with one bite. Leila was skilled and could go through a pile of those branches in no time.

I also went several times with Leila to a green-house to buy cucumbers, which have become momentarily scarce. On the fourth trip, we finally got two kilos and some tomatoes. Yesterday Leila took the car to a service place to be cleaned up — they steam-cleaned the engine, washed inside and out, and charged 13 LL ($2.60).

Leila told me the following story. There is an old woman in the village, eighty-some years old, who, though a Moslem, has been a caretaker of an old, no-longer-used church. She keeps the keys. After many years of this, only this year she requested to be baptized a Christian.

Monday, June 21

At 3:30 BBC radio announced that British citizens who wish to evacuate are to telephone Cyprus Airways at 333887 & 6. Evacuation will take place June 24.

Mimi and I decided to take the village "bus" to West Beirut. We left at 4:30 a.m., and after many digressions to pick up and drop off (eleven with driver), we arrived at BUC a bit after seven. Very few cars were coming into West Beirut — more were leaving. The lower gate was locked, but soon we roused the gateman, who reported all-nite shelling in airport area.

I was working in the apartment when at about 9:30 a rocket hit a building about three blocks from campus — Near the Commodore Hotel. I think no one was killed, just injuries.

Had lunch with Hajjars; the Dean was also there. The cafeteria is cooking for the twenty-some dorm girls, and usually sends some food to the Hajjars. Today it was hamburger patties and fries.

The refugees have now been on the campus approximately two weeks, and three babies have been born. The students who supervise the refugees have been gathering money to buy food for them, but they complain about the food, and don't like the Beirut bread! Every three days each refugee is given 100 Lebanese pounds by their party (Fateh). It seems that these people are not from the South but from the camps near the airport. One mother and her daughter returned to their home to wash their hair because they don't like the BUC water. Neither do we! And supposedly one family moved to a hotel.

Tuesday, June 22

There was heavy shelling all nite. Jackie says it was the worst since she returned from the U.S. Mimi and I slept thru it. This a.m. the village driver didn't come for us, so another day in Beirut. Intermittent shooting throughout the day. Lunch again with Hajjars: chicken with greens — delicious.

In the afternoon Jackie and I went to see Nadia Nachmann, who lives just above the campus. Patrick was there; he's been reading Chekhov plays and a Kafka book. We all berated both the Palestinians and Israelis and decided that they deserve each other.

There is another ceasefire, and it's very quiet tonite. It was announced on the radio that a British ship is coming to pick up their people who want to leave.

Wednesday, June 23

The village driver arrived at 6 a.m., yelled to Mimi from the street that he'd pick us up at 7. When I took the apartment keys to Jackie, she said the Israeli news the previous nite announced that the American embassy was moving to Cyprus. Fawzi thinks that she and the children should leave, but they don't want to. She who only yesterday asked why we didn't return to West Beirut, now says, "It's good that you're going back to the East side."

From passengers on the bus we learned that Americans and others would be picked up by an American ship on Thursday. So Mimi talked the driver into going past Jounieh city hall to check it out with John Reed, who works at the U.S. embassy. He said we had to come back to fill in papers in the afternoon. So we went on to Bishmizzine and had a delicious lunch: rice with tiny worm-like brown macaroni, greens cooked with onions and spices, and peas with pieces of beef, and some other kind of meat and onion.

Then we headed back to Jounieh and signed up for the boat. We rather preferred to go to Damascus to catch a flight, but were told that Americans were being turned back from the border.

We stopped by Helwe to see Hala Nassar, but no one was home except the grandmother, who told us that Nadeem's body had been found — so the end of all hope. We returned to Bishmizzine once again, rather depressed about that, and about leaving. John Reed said this was the only boat to be provided for the Americans. So, not wanting to continue staying with Mimi's family indefinitely, with the chance of summer school slight, it seemed that we should leave. Were told to take only one suitcase per person. This meant repacking, so spent the evening doing that. We're taking the largest bags, leaving three small ones, which would eventually be returned to our apartment.

Thursday, June 24

Had a terrible time getting our luggage into Mimi's car, with neighbors all watching and advising. She was concerned that the baggage would bring questions from the Syrian checkpoints. But nobody said anything — just waved us through.

At Jounieh city hall we were told to go the Wakim Center where buses would take us to the boat. After waiting from 10 a.m. to 11, in the hot sun, an IC (school) type bus took us to the pier where we unloaded luggage and joined the line to board a small boat which would take us to a larger one. The entire front end of this boat lowered to make a ramp, which made boarding easier. We were exhausted and burned up from the sun, so were grateful to the sailors who helped with our luggage. As we moved away from land, through swimmers and past crowded beaches, several speed boats circled us, passengers waving. Our departure was strangely festive in spite of the serious situation.

Something rather irritating occurred while we were waiting on the beach. A taxi pulled up, and the four passengers who emerged were missionary friends from church, the Vidanos, with no less than eleven suitcases! Irritating, and embarrassing to say the least! Something else that was surprising. While waiting, we saw from a distance Hazel Syngen getting into a small boat; she gave the V-for-victory sign. And we thought she'd left Lebanon over a year ago!

When we arrived at the USS Nashville, our small boat [a military landing craft used in landing troops such as at the WWII Normandy Invasion] entered the open end of the large one [a destroyer]. We first had to be processed, which took until after 7 p.m. We stood in lines — and stood in lines, which seemed to take forever. The sailors were extremely friendly and helpful. Handed out Popsicles and ice cream bars. We were assigned to marines in groups of approximately ten. Baileys and we were assigned to a marine named Bob from Marietta, Ohio.

While the men processed the passports, I asked a fellow where a women's toilet was. He said, "I'll escort you there." So Mickey, Tasha, Sarah, and I followed him. We walked through the door marked "Women Only," and discovered only urinals, showers, and sinks. We looked at each other in dismay, considered using the showers, but no paper. Looked outside; sailor gone. Finally he returned and Mickey asked him for toilets, and he took us to another "Women Only" next door with all the necessities.

We were given royal treatment. The marines gave us their beds with clean sheets, towels, soap, showers, etc., and appeared so pleased to do it. This was all free to us. Thank you, America!

Dinner was served on deck: roast pork, hot dogs, mashed potatoes, pork and beans salad, coffee, and cookies. After eating, we were entertained by watching a helicopter landing.

We felt especially lucky after hearing, later, about the British evacuation. Their ship, Royal Princess, provided no food, and they had to sleep on the open deck.

Friday, June 25

Arrived in Larnaca, Cyprus, between 4 and 5 p.m. Breakfast in Captain's dining room: crisp bacon, scrambled eggs, grits, toast, and coffee. In the crew's dining room they had fried potatoes and several other things. Cypriots came aboard to check passports, which took forever. The smaller boat made three trips to shore — 50 people, and then all the rest, including us. They took us then by bus to a hotel just outside Larnaca, where we made a hotel reservation at Fairway Apts. in Larnaca. The owner of the apts drove us to them, so that's good. The apt. is quite nice, at 15 Cypriot pounds per day —$31-32. A bit of a walk from the center of town and the beach. Ate dinner at a small taverna right across the street.

Saturday, June 26

Exhausted and slept in. Checked on air tickets at one travel office, but they seemed to know little. Today is my birthday; this whole situation takes the cake!

Sunday, June 27

Since there are no tours on Sunday or Monday, we hired a taxi which took us to Nicosia, thru the Troodos Mountains to Limassol. Nicosia appeared evacuated — the old Turkish area was quite interesting. Saw several interesting churches, but museums were closed. Ate at an outdoor place in the mountains and had excellent trout. Beautiful scenery, with lots of pines, etc. Limassol is considerably more developed than Larnaca — more hotels along the beach, but everything seems so strung out. We saw en route a number of interesting churches. Especially nice was a small one just outside Larnaca on a hill — obviously abandoned. Beautiful pine tree nearby, and another small building nearby — house for the priest?

Monday, June 28

The check-cashing and airlines ticket hassle has begun. Cyprus Air and British Air control things, and everything's done by the book. Impossible to arrange anything with stops except for exorbitant prices, and we want to go to Malaga, to stay at a friend's apartment there, and then to London before the U.S. Can't cash check from BUC. Bank here telexed N.Y. bank.

Tuesday, June 29

More travel offices. No answer to telex. Met Afif Malek, our Beirut travel agent. He too left Beirut without a ticket. He joined our dinner table for coffee, and next to him was George, an Air France employee, also from Beirut. George said his boat was stopped four times by the Israelis, so he took a taxi to Damascus where the only flight he could get was on Aeroflot, with almost no one aboard. They told several stories. At Sidon vast underground ammunition storage places have been found; men have been digging them in the dark for 5-6 years, not seeing light. They've long hair and beards. At least one was blinded when brought out.

Palestinians, needing blood for wounded, with the help of Swedish nurses, were taking all the blood from people in a Christian village. Incidentally, Norwegian nurses report that Israelis are maltreating Palestinian prisoners.

Thursday, July 1

More of the same. But finally today, we did go to the beach — rather dirty sand, but warm water and not very crowded. We are enjoying the food here — Souvlaki sandwiches, moussaka — not so good as in Greece — good curried chicken, and village salads (feta cheese). Called to wish Dad a happy 80th birthday, but he wasn't home. Talked to Mom.

Friday, July 2

Now it looks as if we may take a boat to Brindisi, Italy. If we can just figure out how to handle all this luggage.

Saturday, July 3

Went to beach again today — nice. Tonite Norm went to a restaurant hang- out that Billy, taxi driver, introduced him to. Seems to have enjoyed it. It's called "Jimmy's Place." Tasha and I walked in search of a Presbyterian church shown on our map. Couldn't find it, but saw an interesting one, deserted looking, called St. Helena's Church, with sign in Greek. Also directly across from the American Academy, a 3-story dilapidated house overrun with weeds, which later learned from Michael (little friendly man who runs this hotel) is used for a chapel by the Am. Academy when it's in session. Michael says he attended the Am. Academy; it's the best school in area. The huge Larnaca high school has impressive modern architecture with lots of glass; he says it's a commercial school, whatever that means.

Sunday, July 4

Happy Fourth of July! This hotel has a rather pleasant breakfast room — light and cheerful. Usually rather warm, though, by the time we eat. They serve from 7-10:30, and even later! This morning an electric fan moved the breeze, and fresh flowers were on most tables. Breakfast consists of a tall glass of Orange Crush with ice, toast, a plate with cheese, cucumber (peeled), tomato slices, sometimes egg slices, tea or coffee, butter and jelly. Quite nicely served, although sometimes there's loud rock music playing. Once it was classical!

Although Michael says the service at the nearby Catholic Church is in French, I've decided to go — perhaps he's wrong: the sign giving service times is in English. Well, the interior of the church is quite ugly and modern; about 70-80 people, plus a few nuns. All liturgy in Latin, with exception of English scripture read by a nun — taken from St. Paul, but difficult to understand. When communion began, I left; as I crossed the street, a taxi let out a rather tall priest in a brown robe. I approached him, thinking perhaps he'd come to give the sermon. But no, he'd just completed a full service at another church, with choir and all. Said he was from Poland. The priest at this church I just left never preaches, he said. How dull. He had a pleasant, genuine spirit, and wished me Bon Voyage after I told him I was leaving tomorrow. I must now see about re-packing. If we take trains from Italy to Spain, we've far too much luggage. Perhaps we can ship a bag — at least check a couple at stations when we stop over.

Monday, July 5

We've definitely decided to take a boat to Piraeus (Athens) where we'll try to cash our check. Norman phoned Hotel Cleo for reservations. Billy (cab driver) drove us to Limassol to catch boat, The Virginia. (8 Cypriot pounds + 2 pounds for an hour's wait while we bought tickets and paid hotel bill.) Hotel charged 10% service charge, which was not mentioned earlier. The boat is okay — not great. Is Greek. Seems as though the backpackers have taken over. Mostly deck passengers, and entire ship has that atmosphere. Most people are eating in the self-service area; the dining room looks almost the same — is separated by a scant divider and is much more expensive although offers no choice, unlike self-service where choices are the same ones all the time.

Vesa's (one of Natasha's former boyfriends) parents are on this boat. They came from W. Beirut this a.m. by the Sea Victory, which they say was a mess — crowded and with many sick people. They'll drive on to Finland from Brindisi, Italy. Our cabin is quite all right, with no one in the 4th bunk. Has a terrible shower!

Tuesday, July 6

As of a week ago, this war has cost the Israelis $3 billion. We're to arrive at Heraklion, Crete, at 3 p.m. and will have several hours there. This ship appears to be far from full. Last nite they played horrible music in the main lounge and turned on the disco lights, but no one danced. The lounge for the deck passengers was full of TV viewers, watching the World Cup. Met a couple from California. He's made some films, and now they're taking a year or two off to yacht around the world. Were on her father's yacht from Haifa to Cyprus, but had a problem with her father, so are now going to Athens to try to rent or join another yacht. Also talked with a French woman who's lived in

Israel three years. Her husband is a reporter for a German paper. She says Israeli inflation is 150% per year, and Israelis, especially soldiers, are sick of the Lebanon war. Compulsory military service is 3 years for men (age 18-21) +one month per year 'til age 65; and two years for women. The Israelis don't like Egyptians. I said, "We've always liked them — they're very friendly people." She replied, "That's the problem. But the Israelis really like the Lebanese, and like all the inexpensive merchandise in their stores."

The Warellas (Vesa's parents) report that Don, the freelance photographer who carries sound equipment for NBC, was captured by Israelis at Damour, treated badly, and later showed up in Rome, then in Jounieh really looking bad. Haven't heard exactly what happened. Another bit of information: as of a week ago, this war has cost the Israelis $3 billion.

[Later] We explored the harbor area of Heraklion, and in Rhodes we had plenty of time to venture farther and visit the huge, wonderful castle built by the Knights Hospitaller during the crusades.

MISCELLANEOUS NOTES

On Sunday, October 31, we observed that there are 275 villages in Lebanon; 83 have been hit by the war, and World Vision is helping reconstruct three of them.

How Bishmizzine got its name: The village is known for growing quince, which requires a special climate. One night a man from another village was caught by the land guard. Guard: "Bish!" (Oh, my goodness!) "What are you doing here?" Man: "They're sour and chokey (not juicy)."

Another story villagers tell: Bishmizzine is known as a village of education. A group of people went to meet the governor (appointed by the Turks) of the area. He asked his lieutenant to introduce the group. Lieutenant: "I'm pleased to introduce the people of Bishmizzine, a village with very high standards."

Many villagers make their own soap, with the main ingredient of olive oil, with lye. Mimi's parents, Afif and Katherine Milki, have lived in their large stone house, with its red tile roof, since their marriage, approximately forty years ago. They're both fluent in Arabic and English. He attended the Tripoli School for Boys, with one year at International College in Beirut. She also attended an American English school and taught in the village school, mainly English and French. He is a farmer, with a small acreage of wheat, large olive orchards, as well as all kinds of fruit trees. He also owns several properties in Tripoli. The family is quite wealthy, although this isn't evident in their lifestyle.

The Milki's comfortable, L-shaped, stone home has two levels; the upper one being the family's living area and the ground level consisting of a garage and apartment rented to a school teacher and family for 100 LL per month. An outdoor stairway joins the two levels. The main feature of the upper floor is the large terrace, where most family life occurs, when weather permits. Running parallel to the terrace is the long living room. Across the hall from this spacious room are two bedrooms (the parents' and Mimi's, which she gave to us, moving to the living room) plus a bath. The corner bedroom, with its balcony, joins the two arms of the "L," and is shared by Leila and the eighty-year-old aunt; the dining room, small bath, kitchen, with a balcony at the end, comprise the other arm of the "L." Gardens are on either side of the driveway, which leads to the public road.

When Tom Friedman asked me, on the beach of Beirut the day we were evacuated out of Lebanon to Cyprus, "What did you lose in the Iranian Revolution?" I stupidly merely said something about the university teaching position and all else of our living there. He looked rather disappointed, for there was no story in that response. I should have said what we really lost: the opportunity to educate women of Iran with western thought and in my field of theatre arts and speech-communication. Our speech emphasis (36 credits) was within the English major of 56 credits. Our campus, just finished and opened, was designed by the Frank Lloyd Wright Taliesin West and holds a fully-equipped theatre I was to use. That's what we lost!

BJ'S JOURNAL

Written During the Evacuation to Cyprus February 11 – 26, 1984

This was our second evacuation from Beirut. The first had been during the Israeli invasion of 1982. That time, Mimi Milki, a colleague at BUC, invited us to her village, Bishmizzine, where we spent ten days with Mimi's family before evacuating on the USS Nashville. The second evacuation, in 1984, followed escalated activity by the various militias that had shut down normal life including the universities. Along with many others, we had taken refuge from the bombing in the Near East School of Theology. Norman encouraged me to join the evacuation to Cyprus, but said he'd not leave until collecting the salary owed him. He remembered how difficult it had been to cash the check last time in Cyprus.

Saturday, February 11

Baileys gave me a ride from NEST to the Corniche near the embassy, where evacuation was taking place. A few mortar shells had earlier fallen into water nearby and exploded — also, one woman barely injured by a stray shell or perhaps a sniper?? One AUB architecture student had brought her final project — huge drawings — to be graded by two of her professors who were evacuating. The drawings were spread out on the British ambassador's Rolls Royce, and both profs signed them. She was very pleased — supposed to graduate at end of this semester.

We were helicoptered to the Fort Snelling (ship) in groups of 12, fed a huge lunch and dinner, and were assigned to bunks. Was exhausted and in bed by 8 pm; up at 7 for breakfast (huge) but not taken into port at Larnaca 'til noon. They handed out peanut butter and jelly sandwiches — the crew were extremely hospitable. Also evacuating: Ramez Malouf and editor of Daily Star, the Turners, Hendersons, Marianne Hourabi and family, Ruth Schmucker. Several of the new people at BUC, the Bykers, I discovered were going to be staying at Raja Hajjar's condo in Paphos. So I asked if I could join them — I would sleep on sofa, floor, whatever — and they agreed — not heartily, I felt. But it worked out okay — we went by rented car to Paphos, had a good dinner near condo, and when unpacking trunk of car discovered we had two small suitcases not belonging to us.

Monday, February 13

We drove from Paphos to Nicosia — pretty scenery — which took three hours. Returned suitcases to the U.S. embassy. I telephoned Dale and Sue Rice, missionaries whom I knew from when they lived in Beirut. They very generously invited the Bykers and me to spend the nite with them, which we did.

Tuesday, February 14

The Bykers and I visited the archeological museum which is great.

Bykers returned to Paphos. I rested in the afternoon. Sue fixed a lovely Valentine dinner. Then I babysat baby Sara while they went out. I telephoned Kathleen. She said that Dennis' cousin had heard my ABC radio interview I'd given during the evacuation.

Wednesday, February 15

Went with Sue and Sara to a huge supermarket. Bought some things to make Mexican food. I fixed enchiladas for dinner. It rained in the afternoon, so stayed in and rested. Sue wanted to go see Annie in the evening and asked me to join her.

Thursday, February 16

I babysat while Sue went to American Women's Club meeting. I made noodle soup from chicken broth. Good. In afternoon I walked to USIS, but it was closed so went on to the old city within the wall. Very interesting. Mailed letter to Tasha and cards to Lyla and folks. Discovered "new" shopping area where old interesting buildings are being turned into small shops — mainly for tourists; very nice. Had tea in a non-tourist tea place. Started to rain, so ate a cake (dry); after 1½ hours (nearly 6 p.m.) it barely sprinkled so tied on rain bonnet and walked home. I babysat while Dale and Sue went to a banquet at the Hilton. I called NEST, but Norman has moved back to house!? Talked with Lucy. Ron Castillo (nurse from Hamlin Hospital) called and wants me to go with him to Paphos tomorrow in his rented car.

I'm not quite ready, but will join him since it's a ride. I made a pot of potato soup tonite.

Friday, February 17

Went by taxi to Popular Bank — World Vision is on the 7th floor. Bruce, friend who works for World Vision, went with me to the bank, and I managed to cash Norman's bank draft — got $500 of traveler's checks; charged fee of approx. $10. Then Ron and I set out for Paphos in his little car. Stopped for lunch at archaeological site of Curium, at Episcopi; interesting mosaics of Achilles and Odysseus and ruins of Apollo temple, etc. Beautiful view overlooking the sea. Ate kabab lunch outside. Arrived at Paphos at 5 p.m. Bykers were not at home, so we went to see the Tombs of the Kings — most interesting. Bykers still not back, so had coffee at seaside, watching the sunset. Bykers were then back, but they have to leave the apt. in the morning since Peter Crooks' family moves in tomorrow; they're coming for a Christian Intervarsity Convention. Bykers have discovered where the DeJunges live, so Ron offered to take me there. (I knew the DeJunges from when they lived in Beirut and attended Community Church.) After some difficulty, we found the DeJunge house, which is beautiful. They've turned a stone ruin into a lovely home. Sjoeke was glad to see me, and welcomed Ron to also spend the nite. He will return to Larnaca in the morning. Sjoeke's husband is away, as he is much of the time — he works for the U.N. — in charge of feeding the Palestinian refugees.

Saturday, February 18

Sjoeke took the children skiing at Troodos. I spent most of the day sitting in the patio in the sun. They got back at about 7 p.m., and we had a rice and chicken dish plus a delicious green salad for dinner.

Sunday, February 19

In the afternoon we drove to the village of Khoulou to see the place which the Lockwoods have bought; very interesting old village. Their house has one room upstairs and one down. Could be nice … The drive was beautiful — many fruit trees in bloom. Stopped by the Bykers in Paphos, but they were gone. Went to a pub to phone the

Rices; Norman had called them saying that Haigazian is to start again on the 27th. Had supper at the village restaurant.

Monday, February 20
Sjoeke and I went to Paphos to see the Roman mosaics — really outstanding. Then we took Galen Byker to look at a little old house that's for sale in a little village four miles from Paphos. The old shopping area of Paphos is very interesting. We bought a few things to make potato soup, which we had for supper, with a salad. Have been eating lunches outside — it's warm and sunny.

Tuesday, February 21
The Bykers came late a.m. Sjoeke took them to see several houses in Peyia. While they were here, the Giesens and Cooks (AUB professors who also evacuated) arrived — nine people altogether. We all had coffee on patio. After Willem and Roelick got home from school, we met Bykers at a beach restaurant and had delicious squid.

Wednesday, February 22
Sjoeke went with G. Byker to realtor to discuss purchasing a house — three room cottage + repairs, bathroom, etc., (in Konje) for around 14,000 Cypriot pounds. Sjoeke's house has 15,000 C.P. invested in it. I explored the old shopping area of Paphos — interesting. Bought pair of sneakers and sox.

Thursday, February 23
Sjoeke and I sat in the sun — did laundry, etc. After the kids returned from school, we all went for a drive to the forest — beautiful grove of pine trees above Peyia. Beautiful view — looked down on goat and sheep corral.

Friday, February 24
I phoned Jackie Hajjar; she thinks it's okay to return to Beirut — Haigazian is still starting on the 27th!? We went to Bykers. Ann and two kids were there. Went for a drive to "the house" and saw Stone's

house which is under renovation. Ate at LeEtoille and spent the nite with Bykers in Paphos.

Saturday, February 25
Bykers went somewhere, so I had the house to myself. Went to the beach and stopped at a store to buy the ingredients for pea soup. I then cooked a pot of soup for our supper. Bykers seemed to appreciate it.

Sunday, February 26
Sat in the sun. Had lunch at the Paphos Beach Hotel — a special Sunday brunch. Good food, with much variety — quite a lot of fish — caviar, etc. Sjoeke and kids and her Danish friends were there. Called Sue Rice and then Kathleen. I plan to take service to Larnaca tomorrow and then the boat to Beirut. A Danish friend of Sjoeke also plans to go, so we will travel together. This friend works for some Scandinavian adoption agency that arranges adoptions of Lebanese orphans.

CORRESPONDANCE (1980 – 1985)

Beirut, Lebanon
Saturday, June 28, 1980

Dear Lyla and Bill,
    We just got back from having dinner at a restaurant on the Corniche, or beach. We ate outside, just over the water — very nice, and food okay, not great. Tasha and I had broiled chicken, and Norman, steak. It's about a 5-10 minute walk from our apartment, and there are quite a few restaurants, tea houses, etc., along the sea. It's really very festive. It's quite amazing, I think, that some of the restaurants remain open all nite; it's the area where the Israeli gunboats occasionally appear and are shot at, but never hit! However, we've not heard of their coming for several weeks now.
    I've had a nice week with no classes. I'll have one section of Freshman English I and one of Freshman Eng. II. Have to go only on Mon., Wed., and Fri. Have a ride over with a

fellow who will also teach there. But coming back I'll have to hire a taxi. I don't look forward to the ride, but am grateful for the classes. With nothing to do, this place could get terribly boring. And crossing over to the Christian sector has been no problem so far. Only once did the guards stop us, and that was to lecture the driver for honking his horn, which is ridiculous considering the constant horn-honking in Beirut. [BJ taught at AUB in East Beirut.]

Norman's classes are now underway, and he has one of speech and one of Freshman English I, which he didn't want to teach, but they needed someone, so he agreed to do it. We finally convinced Tasha to take a class to avoid boredom, so she's taking speech. Actually, she's keeping quite busy.

Fourth of July evening the Americans on campus are having a cook-out on the 4th floor terrace of one of the buildings on campus. There are exactly twelve of us, and what an assortment! We're convinced that one fellow is a spy. He teaches journalism and is in charge of the yearbook, which hasn't yet appeared — they're just now trying to decide what kind of paper to print it on. And no newspaper appeared all year.

Tasha finally got a letter with information from Scripps. She's supposed to be there for orientation on Aug. 29, which will be a bit difficult for us since Norm teaches until the 30th. But we'll work it out somehow.

Then registration for freshmen is on the following Sunday morning from 9- 12:30; isn't that a bit strange? As of now our plan is that Tasha and I will go to London around Aug. 15; then N. will join us around Aug. 25 and continue to L.A. with Tasha. Am afraid it will be rather hectic. Sure hope she'll like it there. Scripps is on the 4-1-4 system, so she'll have a month for Christmas vacation, which is good.

We've been eating lots of peaches, which are delicious. All got sick from the strawberries and cherries, so are now eating only peeled fruit. Have been hearing quite a lot of shooting and bombs mainly at nite. They say the action picks up in July and August. A couple weeks ago a bar near the beach was bombed, and two persons were killed, and around 35 injured; ten cars burned and buildings without glass.

Love to all,
Betty and Norman

Beirut, Lebanon Monday, July 21, 1980

Dear Elma,

I've decided that it's time that I write you a letter. Tasha and I have now been here six months and are really enjoying most of it. Our trip was fine. Lake was okay, although I guess at that season we should have done the cheapest plan. We had a good time in London, although I'm not as fond of it as formerly. As you know, for one thing, it's getting too expensive. But the British Museum was still free! Perhaps you're aware also of how terribly particular British Airways is on luggage weight. We got by without overweight charges only because we managed to sneak more hand luggage through than we should have.

Shortly after arriving here, BUC said "no" they couldn't hire me to teach at the main campus, but would I be interested in teaching at the Louazi Satellite Campus, over in the Christian sector, very near Jounieh. I had learned that nobody wants to go there to teach because of the 45 min.-1 hr. commute (traffic problems) and having to pass through all the checkpoints. I was also expected to pay for my taxi, which has to be private (services don't go across the border) and costs $25 per round trip. Well, for several reasons, I decided to take the job. Although it's been exhausting, and I feel exploited in paying out all that transportation money (then they also loaded me with so many students), it's been interesting, and I've liked doing it. Fortunately, it's arranged so I go only three days a week — really don't think I could survive every day. But my classes have to be concentrated into the three days, so it means a heavy schedule when I do go.

I come home exhausted. Then I have lots of papers on the at-home days. The campus there is a French Catholic High School (and elementary) of which BUC uses a portion. I've had to miss only one day because of the political situation and have had no trouble going back and forth. (Was aware of shooting only once.)

The day I missed was nearly two weeks ago when the Phalangist party "finished off" the smaller Chaoun followers. Now they say the Phalangists are in complete control of the Christian sector, and there are many who believe the Phalangists will before long move in and take the Western sector. You've likely heard that the PLO has moved its offices from Beirut (at least it was supposed to have happened last weekend). Some say this is due to the strength of the Phalangists. One hears so many conflicting things. It's been extremely quiet the past several weeks — before that we were hearing quite a lot of shooting and explosions, especially at nite. But day time life goes on pretty much as usual. There are more street venders than ever and the shops – boutiques, etc. — are loaded with merchandise. Business is said to be good. Quite a lot of building is going on also. It's an amazing place. Beaches are loaded, although the sea is filthy with sewage! Many private beaches have been built — very exclusive, some for members only; others allow guests at 15 pounds per person. AUB beach is available at 10 pounds per person.

People are staying out later at nite now. Things do seem to be better at the moment. However, within one week (about 2 weeks ago) two BUC students were shot; one of them was a trouble-maker, involved in one of the political parties; the other was completely innocent — just happened to be riding by in a car, at the end of Hamra just below the college.

I'll likely teach at the same job in the fall — at least so far I've not managed to find anything satisfactory closer to home. They've told me that next semester I'll have several classes of Cultural Studies, which is a combination of literature and history — I think mainly the former. They teach almost no history here. Now I have all English.

Norman and I are both teaching summer school — each with two classes, and it's about to do us in. Tasha has received an aid-grant from Scripps College (Claremont, Calif.) and plans to be there next year. It's worth $6,200 and covers most of the year's cost except for transportation, etc. She has enjoyed many things here. She was very frustrated at first about all the aggressive men, but has learned pretty much to cope with them.

We met a mutual friend some time ago — Margaret Purchase. She's a good friend of Larry and Evelyn Richards, who have lived in the M.E. for years. You may know them, too. Margaret is teaching English presently at a town in the mountains, Hamana, I believe. Do you happen to know the Hilgendorfs? They came either shortly before, or about the time you left. He runs a counseling/drug-abuse center and is part-time pastor of Community Church.

How are things there? Are you for Reagan? Carter? Neither? Am wondering if you'll go to Kansas this summer. Sounds as if the heat there is terrible. Tasha and I plan to leave here Aug. 15, probably on SAS with an overnite in Copenhagen. Then want to have a couple days in Paris before going on to London, where Norm will meet us at end of August. He's trying to decide whether to accompany her to Calif. or to accept friend's offer to help get her settled into college. Her school begins Aug. 29, and Norm and my vacations come in Sept., so there's no time for a family vacation.

Do let us hear from you. What trips have you made lately?

Tasha says I must tell you about the rather bitter little cakes which were passed around in the cafeteria on the day that a memorial service was held for the two students recently killed. Interesting custom.

Take care of yourself. Will you be anywhere in Europe during Sept.?

We're not sure where we'll (Norm and I) go — maybe Vienna or Venice.

With love,
Betty, Norm, and Tasha

Beirut, Lebanon
Saturday, August 23, 1980

Dear Elma,

Am sitting in Casino/Restaurant NASR on Rouchi, looking at a magnificent sea that is slowly turning from green/blue to silver/reddish black — enchanting. Pigeon Rock is ablaze in color ...

Now look back inside the restaurant; it is empty. A few more people will come later, perhaps, but nothing as it was in those "grand days before the war." Rouchi is a mess. The Yeldizar is okay and quite full of patrons. The Gondole is empty with broken windows and looks semi-sacked! All along the Corniche from LaGrotte de Pigeons (which is closed!) to as far beyond the Shell building as the location of the once-downtown Bab-e-driss suk — a couple miles long shanty town of shops sprung up overnite and operating just like it did downtown. Oh, how I love this place — and how I cry for it; "Don't cry for me Beirut ..." But how the people do, when they don't laugh it off with sarcasm.

Some students stopped by today and talked of the fighting in Tripoli; seems helicopters are today attacking the Tripoli castle. It seems still to be a stronghold of a faction fighting against the local government, just as during the Crusades. Will history never cease to repeat itself?

And in the South: Beaufort Castle has been bombed to its cellars, and the Israelis hope the tunnels beneath have been shelled into oblivion — not to mention the Palestinians who inhabit those tunnels.

Hamra sighs for the old days, although most shops are open and many new ones open weekly. All of them are full of goods; expensive goods, as you would know! The latest from

Paris, London, New York, LA (but nothing from Lancaster County)! It seems much is shipped in via Junea port, and if it is not confiscated before it gets to Ras Beirut, it is sold either in shops or on the street. One of my students last spring bought a truck loaded with TVs, recorders, videos, etc., and en route from Junea port it was stolen — truck and all. He lost LL150,000. He should have studied harder and played in business less. Actually, he ran a travel agency with a friend. He has since left and gone to Nigeria to work.

BJ and I think you should come live here and set up a travel office. You could do well; as BJ says, "These people come in and out of here like flies." Every time the fighting breaks out, they leave; when it's over, they come back! Guaranteed round trip tickets! Often!!

It's dark. BJ and Tasha are in London. (See, there are one/two/three tickets you could have sold — if you cut it enough!) Tasha goes on to L.A. on Wednesday and out to Scripps College for the school year. Hope she likes it as much as we would have. Excuse me ... dinner! Delicious. Rather nice not having people here, by the way! Only several tables are occupied — and those only have one or two persons. Rather a strange change from before the war! "Before the war" and "the other side" are familiar phrases which say why anything is wrong today. The war, the ghastly war! Somehow I always think of you sailing those convoys, watching for submarines.

BJ and I meet in Athens next Monday for several weeks while Beirut decides whether or not to blow itself up again. Many here think it will wait until the U.S. elections are over. Not sure how Carter or Reagan (could it really be he??) would solve the mess. Eisenhower tried in 1958. It's more complicated now. How are you? Well, I hope. Write sometime.

Love,

Norm, BJ, & Tasha

PS: I do JB on November 8th. Did you see it at Bethel?

PPS: So far three political party members have come around during dinner, selling their propaganda magazines. Interesting! Raising money. If the stores don't buy, they bomb them.

Beirut, Lebanon
Thursday, October 9, 1980

Dear Lyla and Bill,

How are things there? Is Reagan really going to be the next President? Good grief! What a mess the world is in. This Iraqi-Iranian thing could really spread. Poor Lebanon always gets repercussions. Last nite Beirut had three bombings: Iran Air office, Alia office (Jordan's pro-Iraq stand), and Swiss Ambassador's residence — don't know why, except several ambassadors here have been attacked in various ways.

Our classes are now in session. Unfortunately, I'm still commuting to the Christian (East) sector. There are several others, who go there from here, but our schedules don't allow us to pool cars; but I've been able to get the same driver I used last year — at least he's dependable, if expensive. Besides English classes, I now have a class of Cultural Studies, which includes things like the Book of Job (Selections from New Test. also come later), Homer's Odyssey, Selections from Plato, St. Augustine, the Koran and an Islamic philosopher, and two plays, Oedipus Rex and Hamlet. Should be fun. In my English class where the research paper is taught, I'm having them read Shaw's Candida, Arms and the Man, and Hemingway's A Farewell to Arms. The student load, however, is too heavy.

Norman is having many problems casting JB. Found an excellent British fellow to play Nickles (Satan) who just today called to say he feels a nervous breakdown coming on. We know he's had one before. I'll be glad when this play's over — it's supposed to be the only one he has to direct this year, although he's agreed to do one for the British-American theatre group.

Norman talked with Tasha today; says she sounded happy and likes her classes. Says she's going to quit going to L.A. so much and stay home more. I'm wondering how often she's gone.

We enjoyed Greece, although this time we did little besides relax. The week on Paros Island relieved the monotony some. Was good to get back to Beirut, but found our apt. in an awful mess. Among other things, water heater had leaked, and bathroom all moldy and nasty.

With love,
B and N

Beirut, Lebanon
Thursday, January 15, 1981

Tasha's vacation has gone far too fast. But it has been good to have her here. Although she's not completely content at Scripps, I think she's quite content to return. This place is so chaotic — the students are on strike again, and in danger of losing the first semester. They're angry about the raise in tuition for next year. They think inflation shouldn't affect them. They've again occupied the administration building, and it all becomes complex with the involvement of political parties. However, classes on my campus go on. The fascist-oriented Phalangist party, which rules the Christian sector, forbids such nonsense as student strikes, I'm told. Frankly, I'd welcome a few days off!

We had a lovely trip to Damascus during the week between Christmas and New Year. One nite only, but wish it could have been longer. The gigantic bazaar is as fantastic as ever. Of course, prices are higher, but still lots of exciting things to buy. We bought only a few small pieces of copper and glass. The small glass-blowers factory was most interesting. Visited the museum (excellent) as well as the old Azem Palace and the mosque (both 8th c.), which is huge and fascinating. It contains a shrine containing the bones of John the Baptist. Guess it's possible since there was a church on the site before the mosque was built. We stayed at the Convent of the Church of St. Paul's Window, which I don't recommend as a hotel, except that it is just off the Street Called Straight and very near the Bazaar. It's supposedly at the spot where Paul was lowered over the wall in a basket. We also saw the house of Ananias, where a church now stands.

Thank you for the very nice towels. They're luxurious indeed up against the campus-provided ones. Also, thanks for looking after Tasha, and making her feel at home.

With love,
Betty and Norman

Amman, Jordan
Friday, April 24, 1981 (Madaba Mosaic Map postcard)

Dear Elma,

Came to Jordan for R and R. Beirut is too much! Supposed to go back to Beirut tomorrow (here a week) if airport opens! Guess bombardment has been going on — the rest has been good, but rather apprehensive about returning. BJ went to Petra, Aqaba, and Wadi Rum with friends. I decided to say in Amman and do some things with the "Art Crowd." Philadelphia Hotel is being redone. Son of owner has leased it from his father and is redoing it. Some talk of tearing it down for a freeway!

Have been invited to Nigeria next year. May go if I have a leave from BUC.

Love,
Norm and BJ

Beirut, Lebanon
Saturday, August 15, 1981

Tasha and I leave tomorrow for Paris. Hope we enjoy it — keep hearing how nasty the French are to foreigners who don't speak French! Things here have been generally good, except for the big attack by the Israelis. They managed to knock out an oil refinery, which resulted in a gas shortage. I missed a couple days of school — to say nothing of all the people killed. But I understand the PLO office and headquarters — the target — operated without interruption.

Norman finishes teaching Sept. 3, and we'll meet in London on Sept. 7.

Then after 3 or 4 days we'll be in Milan and Venice until around Sept. 28.

Betty, N, and T

PS: Hi … Don't know whether we'll take the job in Nigeria in spring. I finally turned it down for this fall semester. I just want a nice long restaurant tour with you two, riding in luxury on the freeways, chauffeured by Bill.

Miss you very much.
Love, Norm

Paris, France
August 1981 (postcard)

Yesterday we visited this small chateau where Josephine and Napoleon lived for a time. This room, like a tent, is where he made all his decisions. It has quite a few furnishings and artifacts – paintings, etc. Interesting, but involved lots of walking since we went by public transport. Today's a French holiday, Assumption. Tasha's going to say goodbye to her Lebanese friend, Zela, who has a grad. assistantship at KU. Then we're going to eat at Pizza Hut. It's been quite hot here.

Love,
Betty, N, and T

Paris, France
Thursday, August 20, 1981 (postcard)

Tasha will arrive Sunday, August 30, on Air France #003 at
7:35 p.m. Since flights are often late, customs, etc., take time.
Perhaps you should meet her a little later. Paris is beautiful
but exhausting — so much to see. We especially liked the
Cluny Museum and the wonderful unicorn tapestries. We're
finding the French people much nicer than expected!

London, England
Monday, September 7, 1981 (postcard)

Dear Elma,
Norm and I are on a train between London and Belfast,
enjoying the scenery. We were in London a week. Tasha and
I spent the previous two weeks in Paris. Had a good time
although housing (friend's apt.) wasn't ideal.
We'll be with friends in Ireland for a few days. Then on
to Milan and Beirut. My campus managed to finish spring
semester in July and August, so it was good that I went back
to Beirut. Tasha's back in California.

Love,
Betty and N

Beirut, Lebanon
Saturday, November 28, 1981

Our church had a combined Thanksgiving service with the
Baptists, but we weren't able to go. We had classes as usual,
but did have a nice Thanksgiving dinner with friends here
on the campus — about 25-30 people. Somehow the food
just wasn't that good. We're wondering if Tasha was with you
for Thanksgiving — did learn that she got only the one day
off. So had planned to call her since it was also her birthday.
It sounds as though she's enjoying Scripps more this year.

Wonder if she'll change her mind about coming here for the second semester.

Fortunately the political scene has been unbelievably quiet — we keep expecting something to blow up. Hope the PLO-Syrian disagreement over the Saudi Peace Plan doesn't cause trouble.

Perhaps Tasha has told you that I've changed jobs — am now teaching two courses at the American Univ. East Campus (half the distance to go compared to previous job) and two courses at Haigazian College, which is a 20 min. walk from our apartment. Is much better for me. Next semester I'll teach only at Haigazian. It's an Armenian college, but only 1/3 of the students are Armenians. I'm finding it most interesting.

Hope Tate is still enjoying his work with the graphics company. Sounds interesting. It's great that he's taking the art classes. Norman is busy directing Anouilh's Thieves' Carnival. One of his acting classes is doing it as a class project, so he's having to train them from scratch.

Looks like we'll be right here for Christmas; may go someplace not too far.

Mid-winter isn't a very nice time to travel to most places.

Bill, may we please impose on your kindness? Will you please select something from your shop and mail it to my folks? I realize their taste is rather mundane, but anything you think is nice for them will be great. Enclosed is a check for $50.

Thanks!

Beirut, Lebanon
Saturday, November 28, 1981 (postcard)

Dear Elma,

Enjoyed your card from China. How are things working out in Kansas? Have you built a house? Things here have been amazingly calm so far this fall; keep wondering when something will erupt. Hope the PLO and Syria don't come to blows over the Saudi peace plan. According to the BBC, some PLO deserter has made several attempts on Arafat's life — instigated by Assad. Assad's after a Greater Syria, including Lebanon and Jordan, and doesn't want an independent Palestine. But perhaps this has been in the news there, too.

Tasha plans to come for Christmas and stay on for the second semester. Then next year she's to do a Jr.-year-abroad program in Paris — with art history courses at the Louvre. She and I did have a good time in Paris in August. I think our good experience encouraged her to do her Jr. year in France. I've changed jobs. Am no longer at BUC's Eastside campus. Now teach two courses at AUB's East Campus (1/2 as far as BUC's) and two courses at Haigazian College. Next semester I'll be only at Haigazian. No more commuting if I can help it. Have recently been crossing through the port — it's the fastest, but lots of military checkpoints.

Norm is busy directing Anouilh's Thieves' Carnival, which comes off in two weeks. The Kennedy Center is closing in the near future. They got rid of most of their books, etc.; are moving some things to the embassy. Sure hope the British Council manages to hang on.

With love,
Betty and Norm

Beirut, Lebanon
Thursday, April 1, 1982

Except for occasional bombs, things have been exceptionally quiet here; big problems predicted for April. We hope they wait until after Easter. We plan to go to Budapest with a tour sponsored by the Physical Ed. Dept. We'll leave the 9th and return the 15th. No, we don't hear much about the recession in the U.S., although some American friends recently talked of a general drop in real estate prices — that now is the time to buy.

My brother-in-law, Melvin, died about a month ago; he was 53 — had a heart attack. His parents are still living there in Copeland and not at all well, so this leaves a lot of responsibility on Kathleen, since they have no other children now. Roger, Kathleen's son, had just moved to Dallas a couple months ago.

Tasha is doing okay. She's been going out some with a Finnish fellow whose parents are reporters here. We're hoping this doesn't go on too long, for he smokes up the house and drinks all the beer out of the fridge! But he is cute! I'm enjoying my lighter teaching load this semester — only three classes and have Tues. and Thurs. free.

BJ

Budapest, Hungary
Thursday, April 15, 1982 (postcard)

Budapest is marvelous! We're loving the newest western hotel — Intercontinental Forum. Here with basketball and soccer teams. After the opera La Bohème, will see Chicago and maybe Lohengren. Discos all night with very western shows almost what Hollywood offered pre-X! Wonderful restaurants, museums, and architecture. Marvelous Haydn Mass in 13th c. church.

N, B, and T

Beirut, Lebanon
Sunday, June 13, 1982

Hi,

We are okay. Thank God to be alive … not sure when we'll be back to Calif. Trying to avoid coming again as refugees! Do you need a housesitter in August or September? So far the telephones sometimes work. Will probably get to Europe sometime in summer and on to L.A., maybe, if we come at all. May go to Nigeria — everything is up in the air. Not sure what we'll do. But all are safe. Expecting fighting to break out in the streets. We have 300 refugees living in campus classrooms. Expect more later. An aid station, with red crosses on roofs and parking lot; hoping the Israeli aircraft don't bomb it, I guess.

Love to you all,
Norm

Estepona, Spain
Sunday, July 25, 1982 (postcard)

Dear Elma,

The Alhambra is still fabulous to visit. Tasha and I took a bus there from our little rented house in Estepona. We left Beirut with American evacuation to Cyprus, then to Athens and on to Malaga and here. Having money problems — can't cash BUC check. Hope to fly to U.S. Saturday. Norm is to help Jane (Creston, Iowa) with a TV project. Don't know what about the fall; Beirut sounds impossible. Perhaps Nigeria. Will be in Newton sometime in Aug. Will give you a call. Hope all is well with you.

Love,
Betty, N, and T

Los Angeles, California
Thursday, October 7, 1982 (postcard)

Dear Elma,

Our New York office called to say that classes begin Oct. 25 — we're due there the 14th. So we're en route to Chicago on Republic via Denver and Memphis. Then from Chicago to Paris to be with Tasha for a few days. She had a wonderful three weeks in Nante, Brittany, swimming, sailing, hunting, etc. Hope you had a good time on your reunion trip.

Love,
Betty and Norm

Saturday, October 23, 1982 (postcard)

We are pretty well settled into our apt. again — which took some doing since so many different people had lived in it — was a mess! There's lots of destruction, but fortunately not in our area. The govt. has demolished lots of buildings illegally built during the last 10 yrs. — causing many problems — terrible housing shortage, especially in the South. Student registration is nearly as high as it was last year, although quite a few people have not yet returned. So far as we have learned, all our friends and acquaintances are ok. The army appears to be in control; everything is unbelievably quiet, and no guns visible except on legit. soldiers. The French are out in big numbers in our part of town. The multi-national soldiers are using our college gym for basketball games. Thank you for a really good time. No food in Paris surpassed that at LaMonde!

Beirut, Lebanon
Sunday, December 5, 1982

Norman's busy directing Major Barbara by Shaw. Interesting for here, now. About armaments manufacturing, etc. Opens the 15th. Fifty U.S. marines are supposed to come to each of five performances. [Not sure that they showed up.] Things in Beirut are pretty good now except for an occasional bomb. A 40 kilo bomb went off a few days ago on the edge of the campus where I teach — it was an attempt to kill the leader of the Druze. It made a shambles of the interior of the administration building, which houses the library. A number of people were injured, mainly from glass and shrapnel. One student was killed, plus a number of passers-by. The target, Walid Jumblatt, escaped, slightly injured. It's felt here that the fighting outside Beirut — between Christian and Druze factions — won't stop until the departure of the Israelis, who are inciting both sides. A stable, peaceful Lebanon is not in their interests. A lot of people are temporarily in Lebanon now — from organizations such as Save the Children, World Food Organization, AID, World Vision, etc. We hear very little of what's happening in the south, except that the Israelis are digging in for a long stay.

Beirut, Lebanon
Saturday, December 25, 1982

Dear Elma,

Beirut is quite festive this year, with lots of Christmas decorations. Hamra is beautiful with many lights strung across it. If only the rest of Lebanon were doing as well. We went to an excellent Christmas concert by the Orpheus Choir — perhaps you remember it; Afif Bulos started it years ago; since he died last spring, they had a guest conductor, a professor from Haigazian College this time. Haigazian also had a nice Christmas concert at the Armenian Church nearby. Perhaps you heard about the big explosion here. It seems that the Myrdom House Restaurant was Jumblatt's favorite restaurant. I was teaching a class at the time; the noise, of course, was ear-splitting and glass flew across the room. Fortunately, no one in the main classroom bldg. was injured, although every room lost windows. The worst injuries were in the Mugar Bldg. and Adv. Bldg. and Library (almost directly across the street from Myrdom House.) The Sursock Museum has reopened — has been closed since civil war began. Hope to get to the opening exhibition. [BJ's hearing was affected, perhaps by the bomb.]

People are complaining that we need rain. But it is fortunate for the many without houses in the south. It's amazing how little we hear about what's going on in the south of Lebanon. There are lots of short-term people here now from the U.N., Save the Children, World Vision, etc. — all involved in the rebuilding process. From what we hear, there's ample provisions, but it's a matter of distribution. The Beirut market is being flooded with Israeli goods (mainly fresh fruit and vegetables) but it's difficult to know what's Israeli and what's Lebanese. It seems that the Israelis are cleverly cutting their prices and Lebanese wholesalers are going for it. I asked the merchant across the street how much of his stuff was coming from Israel (he probably doesn't really know), and he showed me a box of Johnny Walker whiskey, and, sure enough, the writing on the side of the box was Hebrew.

Tasha is here for the holidays and having a good time. Is off to Brumana for crepes tonite with a group of young people. Was invited to a BUC Christmas party in Jounieh which she seemed to enjoy and is going to a concert at the Casino with one of the Marines who's attached to the embassy. We don't see much of the American marines who are with the peacekeeping forces. The French and Italians are very visible, but the Americans are kept pretty much out of sight, which is probably wise. They have participated in several basketball tournaments here on the BUC campus. Nearly all that we've seen are Black.

Back to Tasha; she's enjoying her stay in Paris and learning quite a lot of French. Isn't terribly happy with her classes — feels she's not learning as much as she should — doesn't like the French system.

This letter will go out with Dennis Hilgendorf, who goes to the U.S. in a couple days. Hello to Victor. We hope you had a good Christmas and that 1983 will be a good year for you.

As ever,
Betty, Norm, and Tasha

Florence, Italy
Tuesday, April 5, 1983 (postcard)

Dear Lyla and Bill,

I'm enjoying my holiday and hope that Norman is enjoying his. He went off to Libya with a group of professors on a study/consultancy trip at the Libyan govt's expense. I met Tasha in Rome; then we met Kathleen and Georgia in

Florence. It's been cold and wet here, but the galleries are fantastic. Thursday we'll all go by train to Venice; then Tasha and I on to Paris by train. Norman is to meet us there for several days, then back to Beirut. Hope all is well there.

Betty and Tasha

Florence, Italy
Wednesday, April 6, 1983

Dear Elma,

Tasha and I are doing Italy while Norm is off to Libya with a group of professors on a study/consultancy tour. I met Tasha in Rome; then we went by train to Siena and Florence, where my sister and niece have joined us. Tomorrow we'll all go to Venice and then T and I go on to Paris, where Norm will meet us for a few days before back to Beirut. Cold and wet here — ready for Beirut sunshine.

Love,
Betty and Tasha

Beirut, Lebanon
Thursday, July 14, 1983

Dear Lyla and Bill,

School finally ended here, and summer school has been in session for a week. Norman is teaching, but I'm taking a break. Am having a problem with one of my ears and have to keep running to the hospital for tests, x-rays, etc. Fortunately it's a 10-15 minute walk. We'll move to a different place at the end of this month, so that will be time-consuming — sorting and packing.

Tasha seems to be having a good time going to the beach, partying, etc. So far she's not had much time for studying. She's taking a physical science course in order to get her science requirement out of the way. Is also doing an individual study on Islamic Art.

Things in Beirut appear to be normal, although the multinational forces are highly visible — especially the French and Italians. Just now I see two French soldiers, well-armed, coming up the street, evidently on routine patrol. More often, they're in jeeps.

Our friends, the Burkholders (MCC people), have now completed their Arabic studies and have moved to Nabatiya, a town near the Israeli border. They're doing agricultural work with Lebanese farmers, plus work with Palestinians. We enjoyed them a lot and miss them.

Tasha and I plan to fly from Beirut Aug. 22, arriving in NY the 23rd, after an overnite in London. T will go directly to L.A., but I may go to Conn. for a couple days and visit a friend in NY for a couple more. Then to Texas to Kathleen's, to the folks in Garden City via Wichita, etc. Then to L.A. around Sept. 10 or 12. I have a TWA special ticket which allows 16 stops anywhere in the U.S.

Betty

Beirut, Lebanon
Sunday, July 24, 1983 (postcard)

Dear Elma,

Thanks for your June 7 letter. Yes, we got your Christmas letter also. We're fine — enjoying having Tasha with us again. She's taking Intro to Physical Science and writing papers on Islamic art for an individual study. Norm is teaching summer school. I'm not, but keep busy. It's hot here now, and the situation doesn't look good at the moment. Lots of fighting in the mountains, with occasional shells into Beirut, not to mention car bombs, etc. We really enjoyed the MCC people. Bob and Jill Burkholder and 2 boys, who lived in our building while studying Arabic. They've now moved south to Nabatiya. We're supposed to visit them next weekend, but the conditions may prevent it — the road to Sidon was closed today. Tasha and I plan to come to the U.S. at end of August.

Probably come to Newton first or second week of Sept. and want to see you if possible.

Love,
BJ, N, & T

Los Angeles, California
Sunday, October 16, 1983 (postcard)

Dear Elma,

Just want you to know that I think I am finally leaving the U.S. Plan to fly from L.A. tomorrow a.m. and on from NY in the evening. Meet Norman in London and then on to Beirut after a few days. Have seen quite a lot of Tasha
— she's here with us this weekend. We had an early 21st birthday dinner for her last nite. I really did enjoy my time with you — thanks for inviting me to lunch. Hi to Victor. God bless both of you.

With love,
Betty

Beirut, Lebanon
Saturday, December 10, 1983

[In September, we moved to Ben Weir's apartment, and Norman was teaching at Lebanese University.]

Dear Lyla and Bill,

Your letter of Nov. 7 arrived yesterday. Airport's closed, but it seems that they use these "lulls" to catch up on sorting the back mail. The inefficiency here is unbelievable. Lebanon in general is in a terrible state. But West Beirut has been okay. Some of my students who live in East Beirut complain about sleeping in bomb shelters. Many people here are quite disappointed about the U.S.-Israel alliance Reagan recently announced. The alliance isn't surprising, but to advertise it so blatantly is annoying. Many here feel that "taking sides" automatically disqualifies the U.S. from participating as part of the peace- keeping force. I agree — and why should we be here doing Israel's dirty work?? I'm sure the Israelis are laughing up their sleeves, the way they've sucked the U.S. into this mess. Yes, the Grenada invasion was rather much — seems to have been successful — therefore right. My classes are going fine — really am enjoying the cultural history. This coming week I'll use some of the music I taped from the Brand Library. Have missed several days of school because of general strikes. It's ridiculous — when something bad happens — an assassination, etc., and they don't know what to do about it, they call a strike, and everything shuts down.

We had eleven people in for dinner Thursday evening. The maid had cooked the two main dishes — chicken and stuffed tomatoes, peppers, and squash — so it wasn't too bad. I don't teach on Thursdays. We still have an 8 p.m. curfew, so everything has to be early. I just stacked the dishes for the maid. I've found it quite easy to have two or three people in at a time for dinner, since the maid seems to want to cook something every time she comes – M, W, and F.

We're wondering whether Tasha will come for Christmas if the airport doesn't open. Many people are coming and going thru Cyprus, but I don't know if she'll be willing to do that. It's rather a nuisance. We'll try to call her.

Betty

Beirut, Lebanon
Saturday, January 7, 1984

This holiday sure has gone fast — of course, I've not had much vacation — just two long weekends for the Western and Armenian Christmases. Fortunately, Norman had ten days off. We did manage to do a little entertaining. Last Sunday had a few friends for lunch. I hate having guests on Sunday, but it was the only time that suited everyone. Then Thurs. from 4-8 p.m. (curfew time) we had forty-some people for a buffet-type thing. Utilized the maid by serving her meatballs and rice, tabbouleh salad, and baba ghanouj. I added several salads and cakes, plus wine and spiced tea. I'll bring the rum cake recipe next time I come — think you'll like it.

Tasha and I went to a concert of Armenian religious music at a large church near my college, Haigazian College. It was given by two church choirs combined and the music was quite magnificent — had a very Eastern, plaintive quality. The director wore a black, strange-looking hooded robe. All in all, it was an atmospheric performance.

Recently at school the students sponsored an Armenian meal in the cafeteria – really good! Then they performed some Armenian folk dances and songs. One of the better things they've done.

The political scene here doesn't look good. I do hope the U.S. is smart enough to get the marines out, as the Europeans are doing, but we'll probably be left "holding the bag." Power cuts have been more frequent, but we're lucky compared to most areas of town. Water is our problem at the moment. One party in the building has an unpaid bill, and since all water for the bldg. goes into a communal tank on roof, everyone's water is now cut off and the tank is now empty as of today. Not sure how long one can put up with this.

The skirt which you gave Tasha looks good on her, and she's enjoying it.

Love,
Betty

Nicosia, Cyprus
Tuesday, February 14, 1984

Hi,

I left Beirut with the American evacuation on Sat., arriving in Larnaca Sun. p.m. Am presently with friends, Dale and Sue Rice, who are with Navigators here in Nicosia. Norman stayed — is determined to collect the money his school owes him. He's staying at the Near East School of Theology, which is as good as one can do. I'll wait here a week or two. The Am. University has announced 2nd semester classes to start March 5, but I doubt that it happens. Weather is lovely. Hope all is well there.

Love, Betty

Paphos, Cyprus
Tuesday, February 21, 1984

I've been wandering in the old part of Paphos while the friend I'm staying with is busy trying to sell a house. Lots of Beirutis have places here for retreats when Lebanon blows up. It looks now as if I'll return to Beirut next week if things remain quiet there. Professors are supposedly returning to schools, and opening dates are announced. Sounds a bit crazy to me, but we'll see.

Love, Betty

Bain Militaire, Ras Beirut, Lebanon Sunday, May 20, 1984, at 10:30 p.m.

Ramadan starts first of June. (Watch moon!) All beaches have men and women on alternate days during R. Even Summerland! I can hear Tasha scream.

Dear BJ & Tasha:

I love you! And I've had it! Please return to L.A. sometime about first of August; I think I am coming to Calif. I can't stand it here — or Europe — for months on end. We can then return to London for a whole two weeks or something in September. I think you, BJ, have to be here by Sept 10th. I think I don't have to be back until December for classes, but will come in Oct., no doubt.

I move from Seman's next week, either Friday or Sat. Kens are leaving on Thursday. I'll send this out with them, so can be posted in Cyprus or Europe. [We later moved into Dr. Kenneth Bailey's apt.]

Later: 12:30 p.m. Tanks on back (?) Great film title! No, I'd like a month in London with you in August or Sept. Maybe I could go to L.A. when you come to Beirut. No! Or Italy! Venice!

[page 2] I'm sorry I couldn't be at your graduation, Tasha — after all, you came to my Ph.D. commencement. I would have enjoyed it very much. But, I would not have wanted to come back to Beirut, so it's as well I finish here now and then go for a longer time.

Does Alberta need a housesitter in Palm Springs? Del Rey? I just want to be with you. Guess I can spend a month in London but — what do you want? Wish it weren't so long a time! I hate being alone so much. It was okay until this weekend — now I can't stand it! Will be ok tomorrow as I trudge across to the mudhof — at least I'll do something! Had dinner at Ken Bailey's last Tuesday — and will again this Tuesday, to know how [page 3] to take care of stuff. Guess they forgot something last week and asked me to come again this week. They go on Thursday. (Sorry Tasha, I'm repeating myself!)

Kay and Barbara had a party last night — usual crowd — plus few more. Yussef did the shish kababs. I had stopped by Geraldine's and Yussef's yesterday afternoon — Yussef not there, but Geraldine and Barbara (not Kay's Barbara) were there; so I was as usual my hilarious entertaining self. (Yes, Barbara was most entertained!) Barb appreciated me — she was depressed. She's due – baby — June, and wanted to know if one child is ok— she said she couldn't stand to go through all this again — I assured her Tasha excelled — perhaps because [page 4] she is an only child. Not to worry.

How are Lyla and Bill and all? Give them my love. I made myself a margarita tonight — left over from Thursday when I had Evelyne and Gordon in for dinner — and thought I'd rather be driving to Los Arcos and drinking margaritas with you and Lyla and Bill!! I think I can get away as early as July 20th, maybe! And I want to go!!

I have 2-3 or 4 more weeks between classes and exams; maybe I'll go to Cyprus for a week. Must ask Harut if I am still to come to Aleppo. Since I haven't heard anything, I suspect not!

[page 5] I'll telex KSB some money in June — when I get paid — could you send the enclosed check to Menno Mutual Aid after June 15 — it's not due until July 5th. Note the date on the check; don't send it until after June 10th!! Should you send a check to Delzeit, 4th Street, Dodge City? Maybe Tasha paid it, but I don't think you had enough after paying tuition. What happened to Financial Aid? Am very mad at Mrs. Amerin! What can I say?

Hope Scripps adjusted it — but wonder …

[Near East School of Theology students visit.] Today as I sat on the balcony I stood up — and say … "who," I thought — oh — "Lazarus come forth." I shouted, "Lazarus" — and when I got to the gate, the bitch downstairs [page 6] had sent some relative (who was having lunch) to the door demanding, "Who are you? What do you want?" She looked terrified — three black men!! They were Sudanese from NEST. I said, "They are visiting me, I'll take care of it. And Keefik, Madam (bitch!)" She glared at me with hate — I'll be happy to leave this place. Lazarus and the other two said hello, and that they missed you! I told the guys at NEST I was leaving — so they had to take care of Seman's apt. Ken told me Wanis Seman has now been made Dean (and acting President) — and he is to return. But, Wanis's brother is telling him not to return to Beirut. Hilarious!! He has the whole NEST. Also Katcheek resigned as bus. mgr. [I moved from Seman's to Bailey's apt.

— with the help of students with a little truck.]

[page 7] Gordon had invited Harriet Jacobsen also on Thursday, so I invited Dr. Khalil — neither of them came — after saying they would — so I ate some of the food (tuna, artichoke hearts, purple spiced eggs. Jamili's [house

maid] chicken and potatoes, g. beans with mushroom and sherry, margaritas before on balcony, white wine — French (undecipherable — having frozen it). G. and Evelyne asked me to go with them to Krak de Chevalier; then I noticed the problems — lots, and I had promised Kieley to teach Friday at NEST — and I knew Gordon didn't want me to go — and I didn't much! So I didn't go.

Just called Jackie — couldn't get the switchboard to answer — they didn't get out of Lebanon! And they were stopped at a Syrian checkpoint and Gordon was held up at gunpoint (Kalashnikov at his head!!) by Syrians and they searched him and car thoroughly! Took tennis shoes from back of car! No money!!

[page 8] Then Jackie said the university was closed — a school was hit last week — so all schools are shut down — so I called Henry Milki — yes, it's closed for probably all week — and a taxi is supposed to pick me up at 10:30

a.m. Mon Dieu!! This place will be too much before long! And Milki asked if Ken would want to teach literature full time. I told him I'd ask. Henry is to see about my pay — if it has arrived — it hasn't been, but now should be on the computer. "Well, it will be a big amount," he said. So, I called Ken. He's as usual — he is being inundated with teaching requests — Church of God is starting a college on the East side — want him to teach a course. (And L.U. wants him to teach Biblical Literature; he doesn't want full time.) And Kamel Kostendi wants him to do the Prodigal Son in Arabic on video and sell it.

[page 9] So Ken is high — he lectures at Cambridge in June — and maybe Oxford — and Pittsburgh and Wichita. So — Eastminster Presby Church in Wichita, Kansas! Wonderful!!?? As he puts it, not much money in all these proposals, but at least he is now a "more major" writer in his field. Of course, the Church of God won't pay him much, and he can't afford to take a two day a week full-time teaching position — I think he's nutty!! Even with my mess

of getting over and back. Oh well — maybe his videos will sell — but sounds a bit too much like Iowa! He wants to show me how to use his electronic "memory" typewriter. It even corrects mistakes.

[page 10] Well, I doubt I'll like it very much — but maybe!! Leigh Douglas — next door — he's almost ready to leave — but not quite — wonder if he will decide to leave by January — maybe we could move back here to his house. Was talking with him and the editor of *Daily Star* last night after Kay and Barbara's party — couldn't stand charades, so I left! Alan Darby is the editor now; the fat Lebanese editor left when you went to Cyprus. We met him (Alan) at Ramez's party. Nice guy. Anyway, Leigh feels uncomfortable now — hasn't before — listed for AUB next year, but hasn't signed contract. [Leigh was later murdered.]

[page 11] Painted a couple paintings Thursday night and Friday night. One very like the big one, but probably better — interesting faces. One small sort of architecture — inside of Church of Nativity — perhaps good. One typical face — I'll re-do it probably. Did another tonight, Monday, Karnak? Yanni. Anyway, it passed the night. Wish I could have done one today — awful day! Thought of Hollywood Presbyterian — The only exciting moment was with the Sudanese! (Lazarus) A huge ship; now stops here at Baine Militaire — a large Greek cruise ship type. Three decks — one smoke stack. Afif says it comes three days a week — and the speed boat the other days. Saw Vesa — with "Hanna" but is Lucy at NEST — in captain's cabin at lunch yesterday. Yes, his mother's due Sept. and father went to [page 12] Cyprus yesterday on the Baine Militaire speedboat. Seems everyone gets seasick on it. Maybe can go to Cyprus on the cruise boat. Nuts, no classes all week? I could have taught your classes. DAMN!!

Be sure you call me at Ken's — any night; I'm sure I'll be in — unless you can't get through — his phone doesn't work well. TASHA — Imad Hallack is furious — I talked with him last night — he leaves for Cyprus and Europe tomorrow.

I want the guys to move me again, so I called him; maybe Thursday. Anyway, he says he has written you three letters, three months ago, and hasn't heard from you. He says, "Tell her to deign herself to write me in Cyprus … she has my address." Good luck. He's not Walid so … what did he write? How much? I feel so Arab! Don't agree to anything!

[page 13] Would it be okay for me to go to L.A.? In July? Last of July? When are the Olympics? Don't want to miss missing them! Now that the Russians are not coming, it may be less busy. No — I won't go to L.A. No — I'll go anywhere — I just want to be with you and get out of here … The tanks are going by again. They are so often now; about six of them at a time — yesterday the troops walked them down the street, going the wrong way.

No school tomorrow? What shall I do? I must write a novel! Am still walking the Green Line; a taxi working the line wanted to take me across tomorrow. LL40 to campus! He's supposed to know fast way. Maybe a novel in the "advanced experimental style" would help do away with my frustrations. But, I wouldn't dare submit it for publication. Maybe if it were bad enough it would get published. No, I doubt I could write it.

[page 14] Only think it! Ken will be angry when he has to haul this letter. Jackie wanted to know if I know of someone; am surprised Carol hadn't told her already!

TASHA — Write "Ali," Nadine's friend — he's nicer than Imad, no better looking — maybe he'll improve in N.Y. but has lots of advantages. I must write him a note. Guess I should check mail. I could go to Haigazian, but hate to go out "promenading." Maybe a service taxi will take me. I should have asked Clare and Victor to meet me for lunch today. I would have liked that. Wonder if Cairo TV will have a decent movie tonight? It's coming in quite well. [page 15] Did I tell you everyone has resigned from NEST — even Katcheek, Bus. Mgr. And he told "Lola Bell;" then she said, "You must give us notice and not go right away." He said, "If

NEST gives me any trouble over this I'll leave and never set foot here again; otherwise, I leave today and come each day for 1½ hours to answer questions" and left. He has doubled his salary — don't know where. This was at dinner at Ken's. Sara asked twice where, and he didn't answer. Guess I won't know — yet! He's a bit taken up with himself — wonder how he'll do teaching at Church of God College. Videos of his preaching-teaching.

Just watered the plants. It's now 12:00 midnight — I like to do it at night — hate all the audience on the balconies. The cats now sleep on top of the books. Top shelf. They go up the rug rolled up in corner, and they throw down the books. Ingrid will have fun.

[page 16] They also climb up the side by the door, but when they climb up there when I was dishing up their food by the door, I kicked out the box, so they can't do it quite as quickly. I really hate them anymore! Gladly not keep one for Tasha.

Tasha, are you coming next year? You can have Sara's room — awfully dull, but you can hang something, I guess. Cairo has soccer — and now the Koran — while BBC has church service. Tasha, maybe you could work at embassy; it's near — No — forget it!

I think I can pack in about two hours. I must remember to teach Kieley's class on Friday. Glad I didn't go with Gordon and Eve. Awful! Terrible roads. She went to sign books (hers) for Levant. The guy with a beard led them — too fast. They got lost in the Syrian camp twice. Gordon told me he is now spooked! I'm fine — I feel better. It's great that I can't get out much, I think. Carol Weir moved into Kieley's apt., said they'll leave when Ben is released; apparently he's ok. [Ben Weir was kidnapped after we had moved from their apartment, and they had moved back.]

Give my love to Lyla and Bill. I'd like to go for a drive with them. But I'd like a month in London. Let's do that. CALL ME!!

Love,
Norm

[page 17] Later — 12:35 a.m. I've just been looking at *A World History of Art* by Gina Pischel — it's excellent! Painting, sculpture, architecture, decorative arts. Do you have the other book ordered? This may be better for you: cultural approach — not history exactly, but has much from ancient Egypt, Greece through modern — wonderful paintings and architecture; (even TWA NY airport JFK bldg.) $17.95. Pub: Simon & Schuster, N.Y. 1975 ed. Simaan has good books. You should borrow this one next year from Ingrid.

12:55 a.m. Thanks. Last night there was a lot of the sound of bang, whoosh— explosion. I was afraid they might retaliate, but they didn't. Jackie said the word is that Israeli ships were at sea and they (AMAL, 6th brigade — army, Druze?) were trying to hit the ships! Today the Israelis hit the Iranian camps in E. Bekaa! Gordon said the other day he wanted to go to Baalbek. I declined! Wonder if he'll still go after this weekend with the Syrians. Guess Evelyne was quite afraid — Gordon? The Braggart Warrior!

[page 18] 1:05 a.m. Bomb just went off somewhere — what a place! I just saw a picture of mosaic of dome of Baptistry, Florence. Did you get into it last year? Detail shows the mouth of hell — devouring upper part of man and snakes eating people out of hell's ears! Ah, art! I hear the military radio at Bain Militaire.

1:20 a.m. Going through this art book really makes me want to go to Europe — so, probably I won't go to L.A. Maybe you could travel with me to somewhere in Europe — or I could work my way up — just hate doing it alone all the time. Wonder if anyone wants to travel! Lazarus?

Mont St. Michel looks wonderful; I see where you stood for your picture— there are cars in this picture — won't they get flooded when the tide comes in? Must have fun telling them to "move it." Have been reading the text. Good, but maybe a bit difficult — not as bad as Am. Govt. Why not use what's-his-name from the films? With the tooth! No — it's not bad.

[page 19] 2:05 a.m. Maybe I'll go to Morocco.

Monday, 9:30 p.m. Just talked with Samar Basalli — he sends greetings! He and his girl stopped traffic two weeks ago to ask about you, Tasha. He has (now) midterm exams — finals 28th of June. He says the guys will come by with the truck between Thursday and Sat. to move me to Mohammad's building (Ken Bailey's apt. bldg.) — another former student. (Ken says his parents just hope he passes — you know how it is!) Gordon called earlier. It seems he was quite scared — Evelyne was almost panicky. He says he's not taking E. to Bekaa; he thinks now he is even "spooked" — has finally found out what this place is really like. He says: W. Beirut is a mecca of stability. Tripoli is now completely without any alcohol — it has become a Sunni stronghold — not Shia — and filled with "Moslem Brotherhood" — (not the type from ORU) that Frangia territory is another country completely, even worse than the Phalange in terms of control. Interesting!! Both he and Evelyne are frustrated now because her Fulbright extension has come through. G asked me if BJ would really tell Betsy ... I told him he was too "pushy" before she left and she might, [page 20] but maybe you ought not to tell her. I don't know what Evelyne meant the other night when she told me when we were alone for two minutes (I told G. to go do the dishes), "I love him so much, but I don't want to hurt him ..." I asked if he reminded her of Jay at all. "Yes ..." Then Gordon came back; he couldn't get any water out of the faucet ... so I never knew what she wanted to tell me. But am I glad I didn't go with them!

I'll take this to Ken's tomorrow. He almost won't go out of the house now — I don't blame him. Wish they'd open the Corniche so could take a taxi all the way. Guess I'll try a service to AUH medical area and walk down the steps. Need to drop off a book order from LU to Lebanese Bookstore, but I've been there three times and it is closed! I finally gave up on *Man and Superman*. Can't get books. So I gave the students my copy of Major Barbara with my video of show and told them to watch and read it and evaluate Shaw. Tasha won't approve! Will still try for *Man and Superman* tomorrow. I miss you and love you. Where shall we meet? I'll fly back on Maalev so I can use my Hungarian savings. Ich Liebe Dich. I'm posing as a German instead of American on the streets.

Love, Norm

PS: I have searched everywhere for an airmail envelope — where are they?? [page 21] Tuesday, 2:45 p.m. Just talked with Wilma to see if any news

should be sent to you. 1) She sends her love. 2) Do we want Ralph's apt? No.

3) Geraldine may teach course summer sch. 4) BJ could teach S.S. but no. 5) Art appreciation will be offered and BJ is to teach it — if there are students, which there will be. 6) Wilma is going to check with the board at the elementary school (or high school) next door to Haigazian to see if they can hire Tasha to teach there this fall. It probably would be English, but could be French; probably no art history in high school, but the last word sounds like you could teach H.S. (Ralph and "Melikian" say "hi" — or is it "shalikian?") Wilma says that BJ can help Tasha with the English, and I said Tasha could help BJ with the art appreciation course. Wilma says go ahead and buy the slides you want, books, etc. That they are going to offer the course.

[page 22] I assured Wilma that Tasha is very good in class — has handled classes before and that she does it well. So, Tasha, you may have the opportunity, if you want it. Wilma says this would be better than the Peace Corps. You can see the Africans at Haigazian. Gordon stopped by — he's asleep on sofa now — tired — depressed. He now weighs 145 lbs. — the least since he was 14 years old. Dr. Nachman (Patrick's father) and I sent him to Dr. Abu Haidar. Gordon

is now on my diet — can have a little whiskey if necessary, or vodka — no other alcohol (hard for him!) and just basic food. He had a scrambled egg — no, ham and cheese omelet for lunch — and tea! No coffee … He's taking me to see Ken Bailey this afternoon. Sounds like they did have a bad time up north. Syrians shouting at Evelyne, "Are you married to him? Why are you with an American?" And they went through a war zone twice where they were actually fighting! Kept getting on wrong road and hitting a cul de sac, backing up into the shooting area! Nuts! I don't want a car! While one went through all their luggage, holding gun at G's head. [page 23] And Evelyne is renewing her Fulbright for Beirut. Aren't we all nuts! Betsy called twice in two days – "she wants him home to take care of her and let her run his life," quoting Gordon. So — we'll see. I love you. Eager to see you, but am determined to get out of this place for a while. Hope we don't have many more stoppages of classes at L.U. so I can go! Am happy to leave the cats! Wish I could bag them all and send them via a militia to the "Dean's" house and office!

Love,
Norm

[And that was the way it was for people separated by distance, war, and jobs; long before Skype, cell phones, and e-mail. Sometimes we had cables. Beirut landlines often did not work since the telephone central or district exchanges often were shelled to stop communication on the part of the enemy. Especially when it was a civil war, such actions removed the possibility of talking with family and friends.]

Garden City, Kansas
Tuesday, June 5, 1984

Dear Lyla and Bill,

Thanks for calling with the message from Norman. As you know, Dad is in the hospital in intensive care. He has had a number of seizures when his heart stops beating, and they use shock treatment to start it again. But he seems to be holding his own as they try different medications. He's amazingly alert and relaxed; doesn't miss a thing.

Betty

Garden City, Kansas
Tuesday, June 26, 1984

Dear Lyla and Bill,

Things are working out quite well — much better than I expected. We always thought Dad did too much for Mom, and she became too dependent upon him, but she's really taken hold and doing more for herself than in a long time. She gets around fairly well with her walker. She went to the Bible study this morning and then to the dining room for lunch. Sometimes I go with her to lunch, but more often I don't, partly so she'll get used to doing things alone. I've been at Georgia's some for overnites. Georgia and Dennis live 25 miles south and she works two or three days in Garden at a travel office. Tasha has stayed with her most of the time, and this has saved the situation for Tasha. Georgia has a huge flower and veg. garden and lots of animals, so Tasha has enjoyed helping her with those. And Georgia has been helping her with driving, so I hope she passes the driving test tomorrow.

Last evening Kathleen and Tasha came into town to take Mom and me to the Hilton Inn for dinner, since it was my birthday. It was quite pleasant, but food was mediocre. Then we stopped by the new frozen yogurt shop — quite nice. Garden City has grown so much since I was here in the old days. One pleasant discovery was the original Myers ice cream shop with its soda fountain and sandwiches. Looks just like it did when I was in grade school. Tasha loves it, too — just like in Happy Days. It's been operating for sixty years.

Sunday evening Tasha and I went to see the Community Theatre production of Death of a Salesman — not very good.

Lasted over three hours, and afterward we were soaked in a downpour of rain and hail.

Well, Tasha did pass her driving test today — took it at Sublette. Now we plan to drive Mom's car to Wichita-Newton for 5 or 6 days; then to Arlington to see Kathleen for a week or so. I think it would be interesting to stop by Teddy's place (Norm's brother) in Chickasha, OK, and Voralee's in Tulsa, but Tasha isn't very enthusiastic. I think, however, that if they're at home and at all welcoming, we'll do it — just a day at each place. The main idea in taking the car is to give Tasha practice in driving. Mom will sell the car since she doesn't drive anymore. An older lady from the Mennonite church has agreed to come in for a couple hours, six days a week, to help Mom with her shower, start the evening meal, etc.

Thanks for calling on Monday, and tell Todd that I appreciate his thinking to tell Norman that Dad died — the two telexes I sent hadn't got there.

Betty

PS: In case Norman calls again, please tell him that the Oberammergau side trip is off. I couldn't get the tickets.

Arlington, Texas
Thursday, July 19, 1984

Dear Lyla,

You have been in my thoughts and prayers the last several days; I trust that your operation went well. I'm sitting in a marvelous canvas swing enjoying a lovely view of Possum Kingdom Lake, with only the sound of birds and the lawn sprinkler. We've come to Kathleen's lake cottage about 90 miles from Dallas. People here are upset because the waterline is very low. Interestingly they're blaming the Sierra Club, who supposedly got a bill pushed thru the Texas legislature which calls for the draining of lake water into the small streams so the canoeists can operate.

We have enjoyed the art museums here. The new one in Dallas is a huge, impressive building, with mostly ethnic (Polynesian, S. American, etc.) and modern art. The Kimball Museum in Ft. Worth has an outstanding collection of all kinds of paintings and a marvelous special exhibit of Matisse. Right in the heart of downtown Ft. Worth (all the old buildings are being refurbished) is a gem of a small gallery of fifty Remington and Russell paintings.

This stationery must look familiar to you. My cousins, Lucille, Inez, and I went to Hillsboro one day to visit all the old spots. Started with coffee and ended with the German buffet, both at the Barnstormer restaurant in Goessel. We also drove on to Ramona, where my family lived for several impressionable years. We did have a good time that day. I stopped by to see Bill's mother one afternoon, and she seemed to be doing very well.

With love,
Betty

London, England
Thursday, August 2, 1984 (postcard)

Dear Elma,

We're finally together in London. Have rented a flat for a month. Plan to leave for Beirut around Sept. 10. Saw Merry Wives of Windsor last nite in Regent's Park; tonite will see Bashville, a musical about G.B. Shaw and/or his works. London is warmer than I've known it. Norm enjoyed doing the Oberammergau play with you. Take care.

Love,
Betty

London, England
Thursday, August 30, 1984 (postcard of Brighton Pavilion)

Dear Elma,

Have you seen this? Interesting, but looks better in books — perhaps because it's being worked on. Train trip was nice — good to see the countryside and the sea. We have nearly two more weeks here, then to Beirut, and it doesn't sound at all good there. We're trying to do a few different things this time in London — Bethnal Green Museum; today Tasha and I go to Chelsea to see where the Pre-Raphaelites lived.

Love,
Betty, N, and T

London, England
Sunday, September 2, 1984

Dear Lyla and Bill,

We have one more week here, and too many things on our "to do" list. Last Sunday we attended the a.m. service at Westminster Abbey. Today we plan to go to 6:30 vespers there, on our way back from Kew Gardens. Just discovered that boats go from near the Abbey to Hampton Ct. Palace, Kew Gardens, Greenwich, etc., so we hope to go by boat.

Yesterday Norman and Tasha saw the stage production of West Side Story. I chose not to go. I watched Song Without End (Franz Liszt story) on TV — marvelous! Can you believe there are only four TV channels here, and one of those has been on strike for a week — but we do find lots of good things to watch. Last nite there was an old Bette Davis film plus Patton. We saw part of each. They have fewer commercials and at less-frequent intervals.

Before Norman arrived in London, Tasha and I happened into a Chinese restaurant that served Peking Duck, so we ordered ½ duck. Not served quite so elegantly as I recalled —

one platter of crispy and one of soft meat, etc. — this place just mixed it up on the platter. But it was served with the thin "pancakes" or doilies, sauce (molasses?), green onions, and another vegetable I didn't recognize. It was delicious.

Friday Tasha and I went to the National Portrait Gallery and spent most of our time in the 20th century section. The most crowded area was that of cinema and stage. It closed at 5 p.m., so we then went next door to the National Gallery of paintings, which is open 'til 6. We bought the "Quick Tour Brochure" and saw a few things, but hope to go back. Norman joined us there, and afterward, we happened to see a Pizza Hut, which has recently arrived here and seems to be taking the place by storm. So we had pizza that evening — good.

With love,
Betty, Norman, and Tasha

Beirut, Lebanon
Saturday, September 29, 1984

Dear Lyla and Bill,

Our friend, Carol Weir, whose husband, Ben, was kidnapped, was here for lunch last week. She plans to stick around, hoping he'll be released. She teaches a couple classes at the Near East School of Theology. Our friends, the Haddads, took us to the Officers' Club at Military Beach; Victor's a retired col. We've been there with them several times — it's quite pleasant — good Lebanese food. The Haddad children swam, Victor fished, and the rest of us sat in the sun. For the past week we've had six hours of electricity per day — one day from 6 a.m. to 12 noon, and the next from 12 noon to 6 p.m., etc. Main power station's been bombed again.

We're enjoying our new apt. Has a big balcony all across the front, with a magnificent view of the sea. We're on the fourth floor, and luckily, no buildings to block the view. There's still quite a lot of boating, swimming, and water skiing. A wide sidewalk runs along the seashore for several miles (the corniche) and many people come there for outings. By evening there are many joggers, and people walking and buying things from the many vendors selling all kinds of things, from roasting ears and cotton candy to tee shirts and tennis shoes. Some things are sold from push carts, but some are arranged on the sidewalk. Most of the drinks are sold from small motor vans which park along the curb. Most of these set up small folding chairs and tables to attract customers. It's all very colorful, especially in the evening when the gas lights come on. The street lights are seldom turned on.

Our neighborhood is protected by the Druze; they operate out of a nearby coffee house, where they occasionally set up a checkpoint. There are also quite a few Moslems in the neighborhood, and we hear lots of Koranic chanting over loud speakers. This all started last week with the funeral of a young man who was killed in the U.S. embassy bombing. It will probably continue through next Saturday, the Moslem holy day, Ashura. At the moment there are around 150 men seated in a nearby open area listening to live Koranic chants with drum. The women in this society do have some lucky breaks!

With love,
Betty, N, and T

Beirut, Lebanon
Friday, November 9, 1984

Beirut is back to its old self! The port, about four blocks away, is being heavily shelled; we hear the bombs now! Last nite either Phalange or Israeli gunboats were shooting from the sea, with much returned fire. Our apartment faces the water, and the whole front is glass; so we gingerly walk from one room to another, trying not to say behind a wall. Too bad they didn't design these buildings for war; ours has a central hallway that runs all the way through from the sea-front living room to the bedrooms. We're on the fourth floor. In front of us is a small harbor with an old, wonderful house facing the fishing boats. Charming! I tried to rent one of these houses — one with a triple- arched floor-to-ceiling glass door-window opening onto the balcony; maybe later. For this year we'll be in this apartment. Our friends are staying in Pennsylvania until September.

Life here has been great until this week (probably the Israeli-Lebanon talks have sparked off this latest fighting). BJ and I went to see Sophie's Choice last week. Judging from the previews of forthcoming movies (we must have seen every soft porn shot Hollywood has filmed for the past year or so), Khomeini has been a failure in Beirut. BJ was the only woman in the theatre, which seats perhaps 300; thirty men were scattered around. Hanna K. comes next week. Don't know how the twenty-five or so theatres showing English movies keep their doors open. Videos have replaced all of them. Too unsafe to go out much ... although the restaurants in the next street are full.

Tasha is teaching at AUB in the University Orientation Program, teaching Intensive English. She has hilarious tales to tell! Every day she threatens to quit, but the fact they are paying her almost $1,000 a month keeps her at it. She is also taking a course in computer language, COBOL, and another in Business Management. She has almost given up on helping BJ in her art history course. Too bad, but it comes when she is teaching at AUB.

Love,
Norm

Beirut, Lebanon
Tuesday, December 18, 1984

Dear Lyla, Bill, Tate, Todd, Courtney,

Merry Christmas! We are sitting in the kitchen writing cards by the light of three candles and two coal oil lamps, trying to keep warm by the heat of the stove. Ah, what fun when electricity is on only six or so hours a day — and not always at the same continuous time. I carry a flashlight in my pocket ... I dashed over to "the other side" last Tuesday (I go only two afternoons a week) to teach my three hours of classes. We arrived on campus, and no one was there. I told the driver to wait, ran upstairs to check on whether there were classes, was told to "go home!" As my driver drove down the mountain to Beirut, he asked a student, whom we picked up, what this area is called; then he exclaimed, "This is the middle of the military firing zone which the Druze is always shelling." Today we had classes, although some shells came in as well as out. Always an adventure here! Tomorrow I go for seven hours.

Norm

Three weeks ago, Kathleen called to tell us that Mother was in the hospital— had fallen and broken her hip; she had been doing so well — writing regularly.

Things aren't quite as Christmassy in West Beirut as they sometimes have been, but some trees are being sold, lots of poinsettias and Christmassy things in shop windows. It looks like we'll be at home for the holidays — have a duck in the freezer that we're thinking of turning into Peking Duck. If it turns out okay, shall we try it next summer?? We have enjoyed a lot the two Italian restaurants nearby — just a block away.

I spent much of the afternoon putting some slides together for a Christmas program of Christian classical art with music — Handel's Messiah at the college (Haigazian) tomorrow — to be shown during the lunch hour. Then the students are having a party on Friday. Tasha's going to be Santa Claus — we're trying to think up some appropriate gifts to hand out. The church is doing less than usual — advent services, etc. — this year. Fewer people than usual, too.

Have a wonderful Christmas,
Betty

Beirut, Lebanon
Wednesday, January 2, 1985

Dear Elma,

Hope you had a good Christmas. Ours was a bit humdrum, but what we needed — especially as Tasha and I were quite exhausted. She's teaching pre-college English at AUB — hated it at first, but beginning to like it better. The school year's been quite good so far — only two days missed because of strikes. My art class has kept me terribly busy — every class involves looking at slides, so I'm constantly digging out information, which I love doing. I'm learning a great deal! The course is being offered again next semester. I hope sufficient students register for it. I'm also to teach an English cultural history course, which will be fun, but lots of work. It's a required course for English majors.

Perhaps you remember that this year we're living in Ain Mraisse — very near the bottom of the "Steps." Not far from the AUB Medical Gate. Our view of the sea is quite marvelous.

Santa brought Norm binoculars, which we all enjoy — watching passing ships, which are numerous, and the vendors, etc., along the Corniche. We've had quite good weather — lots of rainy days — fortunately because the apt. is drafty and cold — no central heat. We continue to have lots of power cuts. Do you remember the Spaghetteria restaurant overlooking the sea? It's between the bombed American embassy and Holiday Inn. Well, Smiths have put in another Italian restaurant nearby, the Rigaletto, right next to the Spaghetteria. The Rigaletto is in an old, very interesting house. Both restaurants serve really good food and are one short block from our apt. So we eat at one or the other occasionally. One doesn't feel safe going around much at nite, so it's handy to have these restaurants nearby.

We went to a lovely Christmas concert given by what's left of the Orpheus Choir and AUB students. Assembly

Hall (Chapel) was packed. We ate Christmas dinner at the Rigaletto, and then went to a party at a friend's house, near the lighthouse. We watched a video of Lion in Winter with Katherine Hepburn and Peter O'Toole — excellent! Video machines are very popular here, although the movie theatres still operate — to generally small audiences. From the looks of the sex movies playing, Hamra hasn't been much influenced by Khomeini. Every now and then one hears of a bar being bombed, and recently restaurant robberies have been rather prevalent.

The relatives of kidnapped persons have organized and have kept the Green Line crossing points closed for nearly a week. Today's news says West Side militia men have taken over crossings and are charging pedestrians 100 pounds and cars 500 pounds to get across. So it goes … Norman was supposed to have classes today, but couldn't go. My classes begin after the Armenian Christmas on Jan. 8. Hello to Victor and to Elma and Lloyd.

With love,
Betty, Norman, and Tasha

PS: Hi, Elma. Loved being with you at Oberammergau! Fun! All day of it! BJ and T gave great accounts of being with you. Beirut is still interesting — sort of, "yanni" — I spoke to Mi Lad this fall at MCC. He's staying in Beirut — can't go home much at all. South is cut off! Maybe it will open up and the "Cionists" (as the local Sunni radio calls them) will go.

Love,
Norm

Beirut, Lebanon
Sunday, March 17, 1985

Dear Lyla & Bill,

BJ and Tasha keep thinking I should leave. I don't want to leave them behind, and don't want to go at all!! So I stay here and try not to get kidnapped … it's difficult to maintain sanity staying in this apartment most of the time. Fortunately, the weather is again warm — house still cold and sea is beautiful. Such a bore! This week I couldn't go to the East Side because the U.S. embassy told Americans to stay low — for me that means "Don't cross the Green Line!" And the next day the whole East Side fell apart... a part of the Christian forces separated from the other and the war clouds are in the air. So, good that I did not get stuck over there. I would not have had my U.S. passport nor my Leb. ID card because both of them say "Nationality, U.S." So, I carry my "Canadian" ID. Can't travel on that! Such a mess!

Syria is moving into the Christian area. In 1978 they shelled the area heavily — this caused them (Xians) to shell West Beirut — and the cycle goes on — war is not a solution! I'm more of a pacifist than ever — just not enough of one to be kidnapped — I hope! Three have been taken in the last three days! What is this?!

Because the Lebanese pound has gone in three months from 5.5 to the U.S. dollar to 20 to the $, which means my salary has gone from $2,000 a month to $500 a month; and BJ's is less — almost — than the Sri Lanka maids who are paid in dollars!! Wonder when I'll get up my nerve and call my stepmother, who doesn't believe in watching the news — only gives to "700 Club" and "Trinity." They make her day! Lucretia Borgia watching Marie Antoinette!!

We've written a number of places, but you know how those jobs go — I've written them from your house in the past! Let's go back to Newport for Mexican food in glorious art deco setting. Take care of yourselves. Miss you.

Love,
Norm, BJ, & Tasha

PS: I'm thankful that more electricity is now available. Until last week the power was off more than on! The power station keeps getting shelled.

Beirut, Lebanon
Tuesday, April 2, 1985

Dear Lyla and Bill,

Happy Easter! Things here are bad, although except for kidnappings, Beirut has been quite calm, with the trouble concentrated in the South — and it's terrible there. Sunday at church an Australian young lady who lives in a village near Sidon and works with Palestinians in one of the camps — is with some missionary group — gave a most depressing report of looting and violence. Now that the Israelis are going, those Christian militiamen whom they supported and used, the SLA, feel deserted and threatened and are getting everything they can by robbing, etc., because their source of support is leaving. Also, Palestinian fighters are returning to the camps. So, many villages are being deserted — which is what the Israelis say they want — a buffer zone empty of people. We hear that one of the Mennonite couples (Americans) have left, but the Canadians with three children are still there — but their village is still under Israeli occupation.

Norman has temporarily moved to the East Side of Beirut — is at the Baptist Seminary in a mountain village fairly near his job. Isn't terribly happy with the arrangement, but it's too risky — esp. for foreigners — esp. Americans to cross back and forth. Now he's wanting to come home for Easter, and probably will. Things go on fairly normally at my school, except for frequent strikes; last week, one afternoon off because of high cost of living; today no school because of kidnapping of some Armenian political figures. I got lots of work done.

You'd love the small palace my art class visited recently — not far from the college. The building, about 100 years old, is a copy of an Italian one, and it's loaded with antique art — Greek, Roman, Phoenician, Byzantine, Islamic, Egyptian. The interior so tastefully done. Amazing how so many patterns and styles can blend into a harmonious whole

— tile, mosaics, carpets, etc., mainly in earth tones. Lovely gardens with statuary, mainly Roman and Egyptian.

Last Saturday I went with several students to an Armenian version of Cinderella, which they acted in. It was quite well done, but most interesting was the Soviet Cultural Center, where it was held. Unfortunately, everything —library, etc. — was closed except the theatre. They seem to have a lot of activities there.

Tasha is substitute teaching this week — third grade at the International School. Finds the young British male teachers more exciting than the students! Not sure of what summer will hold. Concentrating on finishing school year and are trying for jobs elsewhere.

Love,
Betty

Beirut, Lebanon
Thursday, April 11, 1985

Happy Easter ... we celebrate it twice here — both Western and Eastern — and not much in either case at our church. Miss Hollywood Pres. The Western Maronite Church canceled its Palm Sunday parade for fear of rumors of shelling. I have been living/staying on the East Side for the past two weeks — at the Baptist Seminary — no wine ... alone ... a bore! Couldn't go over for two weeks before that; too much risk of kidnapping. Will go back next week unless rumors of a battle happen. With the drop in the Lebanese pound, probably won't make it to California this summer. I'm ready to rent Bill's office and sleep on the desk. Sure glad I went home last year. Thank you for having us.

Norm

Beirut, Lebanon
Tuesday, July 2, 1985 (postcard)

Dear Lyla and Bill,

Just a note to let you know that we're planning to be in Sousse, Tunisia, for at least a year. Perhaps Norm has written you. Don't forward any more mail to Beirut or anywhere for a while. Tasha and I plan to fly to Athens July 4 to meet Norm. We hope to be on Paros Island for rest of July and Aug. Our address in Greece is at the Hotel Cleo.

Norman Lofland, Theatre Arts professor at Bethel College.

Arlo Kasper as Prof. Higgins and Rosalind Enns as Eliza Doolittle in Norman's 1961 production at Bethel College of George Bernard Shaw's Pygmalion. Enns later became a professor and Dean of Students at University of Vermont.

Norman directed Romanoff and Juliet,
Peter Ustinov's comic satire of the Cold War,
in 1962 at Bethel College.

Rosalind Enns performed in a 1963 production of Mozart's The Marriage of Figaro,
designed by Norman for the Music Department at Bethel College.

Norman directed Romeo and Juliet in 1963 at Bethel College, starring
Bruce Gray as Romeo and Carol Voth as Juliet.

In later years, Bruce Gray, Romeo, was active in Dutch theatre
and film in Amsterdam, Netherlands.

The burial of Ophelia in Norman's 1963 production of Hamlet, starring Arlo Kasper as the lead character.

In 1963, at Bethel College, Norman staged a production of Samuel Beckett's Waiting for Godot. From Left: Estragon played by Jim Stucky; Vladimir played by Bruce Gray; Lucky played by Lauren Friesen; Pozzo played by Ron Hatchett.

In 1962, Norman directed Julius Caesar on steps in the theatre that were built with choir risers going up to a platform at the back of the newly rewired stage. A covering made it look like a step pyramid. It was brilliant for the scene of the Roman senators killing Caesar on the steps, shoving him back and forth, side to side, as each conspirator knifed Caesar culminating in his legendary words, "Et tu Brutus?" It would have been easier to stage this production on the steps of the Administration Building, except for the snow covering the area at the time.

Hamlet injured in a duel with Laertes. Norman directed this production of Hamlet, which was presented outdoors on the steps of the castle-like Administration Building at Bethel College.

Ron Hatchett, Pozzo, rewired the stage of the gymnasium theatre, making it a very flexible theatre in terms of lighting.

Lauren Friesen (left) became Professor Emeritus of Theatre at the University of Michigan – Flint.

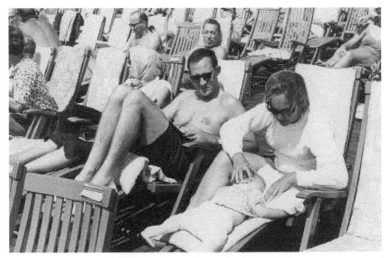

Norman and BJ enjoyed the sun at sea in the mid-Atlantic. Fellow passengers on the Holland America Line's Rotterdam were curious about nine-month- old Natasha's splint, which was later replaced by a plaster cast from chest to ankles.
Although in the cast for a year, it completely cured her dislocated hip socket.

BJ (left) and Yaffa, the young Druze maid who helped care for Natasha, each holding her own baby. The plaster cast, one of three that baby Natasha wore for a year, is barely visible at the bottom of the photo.

Yussef, Norman's devoted technical theatre assistant at Beruit College
for Women from 1963-1965 and at Beirut University College
/Lebanese American University from 1979-1984.

Norman's production of Finnegans Wake, which originated at the
University of Bridgeport, was performed in 1969 in Amsterdam for
the Holland Festival of Music and Drama. Angelo Zuccolo played
H.C. Earwicker and later became a professor of drama at
the State University of New York.

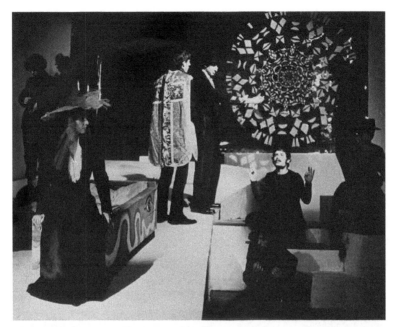

Marshall Kaufman, a senior, designed the original sets for Finnegans Wake, which amounted to a runway and an uncut, Mylar backdrop measuring fifteen by twenty feet.

Robert Fiveson, as Shaun in Finnegans Wake, became a renowned documentary filmmaker. Set designer Jane Putnam turned the original Mylar backdrop into brilliant large masks depicting history, since James Joyce included the universals of history in his story.

Anna Livia Plurabelle was played by Nina Derman, Norman's student who became a very successful actress in the New England theatre world.

In Finnegans Wake, women gossip on the banks of the Liffey River, the River of Life. The character played by Lenore Bifield (left) ultimately becomes a rock and the character played by Sally Thompson (right) becomes a tree. Thompson's husband financed much of the trip to the Holland Festival of Music and Drama. Thompson became a theatre producer and invited Norman to direct a musical in London when he was teaching in Tehran, Iran.

Norman in 1970 while teaching at the University of Bridgeport in Connecticut.

Norman was invited to direct Die Fledermaus for the Palm Springs Opera Guild, using the orchestra and singers from the Los Angeles Civic Light Opera Company, now LA Opera, with sets designed by Jane Putnam, wife of John Putnam, art director of Mad Magazine. Norman would not allow the scenery to be put up until Jane was paid for her work. As a result, the final nails were hammered into the set as the overture played for the opening performance. Tom Aitchison, who worked so diligently on all the productions and was a musician himself, pounded the hammer in time with the kettle drums' luscious heightening of the Strauss overture.

Construction of Frank Lloyd Wright's Taliesin West's design of Damavand College in Tehran began in 1973 and was based on the caravansaries located throughout Asia and the Middle East. The caravansary design went around the campus, with the theatre, which was the length of half a football field, located in the center of the complex, just under the library.

Two tremendously influential educators of women in the Middle East, Dr. Mary Thompson, Academic Dean of Damavand College (left), and Dr. Frances Gray, President of Damavand College and Beirut College for Women, heading a faculty meeting.

Norman directed Jean Anouilh's Eurydice, titled Legend of Lovers in America, at Beirut University College / Lebanese American University in 1979.

Actors Ziad Abuabsi, who became a professor in Beirut, and Nadine Camel Toueg, who worked with Radio France and taught yoga in Paris while her photojournalist husband, Alfred, and photojournalist son, Raphael, covered world events. So many fine students.

Lina Abyad played the title role in Eurydice. She became an associate professor at Lebanese American University, formerly Beirut University College, and taught theatre, dance, and directed plays in Beirut.

Norman directed a wonderful production of Archibald MacLeish's J.B., a play in verse, in 1980 at Beirut University College / Lebanese American University. The scenery showed a traveling circus filled with the trials of the Bible's Job and was set in today's sophisticated banking world. The Job story was significant to both Moslem and Christian factors in the civil war.Norman loved this play so much that he directed and designed it four times.

BJ in 1980 with students from Beirut University College, Louazi Campus. To teach there, BJ had to daily cross the Green Line restricted fighting area, since she and Norman lived in West Beirut. The next year BJ taught at Haigazian University. She continued teaching there until leaving Beirut in the summer of 1985.

Dr. David and Dawn Nottingham, colleagues and friends from Beirut. After working in the States and for the BBC in London, David retired and joined Norman as a colleague in Beirut and Macau in Television Communication.

Natasha Lofland overlooking a Greek Orthodox Church on Paros Island. After studying in Paris and teaching at the American University of Beirut, Natasha enjoyed Greece with Norman and BJ. They were all taking a break from the ongoing fighting in Beirut.

BJ and Natasha at the Marché des Fleurs on the Ile de la Cité near Notre Dame in Paris.

Natasha and Norman in front of the Notre Dame Cathedral in Paris in the early 1980s.

BJ and Natasha in front of the Notre Dame Cathedral in Paris.

Natasha and Norman in front of the Arc de Triomphe in Paris.

BJ wearing a necklace made of yellow amber beads. Norman purchased the necklace in 1963 from a sheik in Beirut. The heavier, amber beads came originally from a souk, a marketplace in North Africa, and brought to Amsterdam where BJ bought them in 1969.

Outside the Beirut University College / Lebanese American University theatre door after a bomb detonated in 1982. This was one of the two fully equipped theatres on campus. The actors had just left the stage before the bomb went off. One person was injured, but no one was killed. Although the stone wall held, substantial harm was done to the interior. That incident, along with another bomb that exploded while she was teaching at Haigazian University, permanently damaged BJ's hearing.

Norman on the Beirut University College / Lebanese American University campus in 1983.

In 1984, Norman presented George Bernard Shaw's anti-war play
Major Barbara at Beirut University College / Lebanese American University
during the height of the Lebanese Civil War.

Major Barbara was Norman's 61st production.

Norman's study in Tunisia. In the background is Natasha's Short-Arm Man painting, which she created in Athens when the family was chased out of Tehran during the 1979 Iranian Revolution.

When living overseas in 1985, Norman was often mistaken for John Wayne. As he ordered food at a restaurant in Tunis, the cashier looked at the poster of John Wayne hanging on the wall opposite the cash box and asked Norman, "Is that you?" Although Norman had a healthy sense of humor about this frequent comparison, at this point in his life he was stranded, was out of money, was trying to get to a job interview, and had just left Beirut to avoid being kidnapped.

Natasha (left) and BJ in the living room of the apartment in Guangzhou, China, where Norman and BJ lived while teaching at South China Normal University 1988-1989. Natasha also taught there during the second semester after studying for several years in Paris at Sorbonne University. The next year Norman and BJ taught at Jinan University, also in Guangzhou, China.

Norman (left) and Shawn, a graduate student at South China Normal University, traveling to Foshan to see the paper-cutting and creative ceramic factories. The paper factories made wonderful creations with exquisite, delicate, filigreed designs. One of the ceramic artists created a doll head of Norman. "Actually, I think she just put a large nose on an existing head and laughed delightedly!" Charming, lovely day.

Norman and BJ with the University of Macau English Communications students at the 1995 graduation dinner at the Dom Pedro Theatre Restaurant. In the back row, to BJ's right, are colleagues Don and Beth Baker. Also in the back row on the far right of the photo is L.L. Alexandria.

At the University of Macau's graduation dinner in 1996 with (from left) Don Baker, student Man Chiu, Norman, BJ, and L.L. Alexandria. Man did become a professor of English Communications at University of Macau after earning his Ph.D. at Hong Kong University. This was just the opposite of what Dr.David Nottingham had predicted for Man, but what Man wanted.

L.L. Alexandria presented BJ and Norman Lofland the gift of a silk rug at their retirement party from the University of Macau in 1996.

Norman in Paris in 1996.

Norman and BJ in Budapest, across the river from the Hungarian Parliament Building. After retiring from the University of Macau, they traveled through Paris, Athens, Istanbul, and Cairo.

A very cold Norman, in 1998 in North Cyprus, visited Richard the Lionheart's Saint Hilarion Crusader Castle. BJ, an historian, loved North Cyprus because of its many historical locations, including Salamis, the ancient Roman city where Barnabas and Paul brought Christianity.

Norman in front of his portrait created by Jane Putnam in 1963-1964. Putnam was a New York artist and scenic designer for Norman's theatre productions in Connecticut, Beirut, Amsterdam's Holland Festival of Music and Drama, and Palm Springs Opera.

Jane Putnam painted this portrait of BJ in 1963-1964. Now settled in Albuquerque, New Mexico, Jane is the widow of John Putnam, art director of Mad Magazine.

BJ in one of the four Karmann Ghias they owned. In the summer of 1964, Norman and BJ drove a convertible like this from Beirut to London and back for classes at the University of London. The following spring break at Easter, they drove from Beirut to Tehran and back on a rather hazardous journey.

BJ leaving for a fundraising dinner party benefiting Monte Vista Grove Homes, a retirement home for Presbyterian clergy. She is on the Board of the House of Rest, another Presbyterian home for missionaries on leave, which was established in 1923 by Mary Gamble of Procter and Gamble. Both homes are in Pasadena.

Norman and BJ together at home in Pasadena, California, surrounded by the items collected over a lifetime of travel throughout the world.

Norman and BJ Lofland en route to China and Macau after university teaching for sixteen years in the Middle East and North Africa.
Photo Credit: The Newton Kansan

BJ and Father Tcheira at historic table in Temple (Kum Iam)
where first US trade agreement was signed.

Dr. and Mrs. Norman Lofland at reception given by the
Embassy of Nigeria in Beirut with the Consul of Nigeria,
Mr. Adelojob Idowa, Norman's student.

Norm and BJ (Betty) Lofland on leave from Macau.

Dr. Frances Gray, retired president of Beirut College for Women, Beirut, Lebanon, and Damavand. College, Teheran, Iran, residing at home in San Francisco, after years of her teaching Art Appreciation and guiding tours of European museums.

President Bourguiba riding in his open Mercedes on the Rue Bourguiba Main Street of Sousse, Tunisia, tourist area on the sea. This picture was taken from Lofland's front balcony, and this was the last public drive for the president, who established the independence of Tunisia from France. The sea is behind the people at the top of the picture.

BJ and Ugur, our friend who drove us around some of North Cyprus. They are in the Icon Museum, Girne, North Cyprus (Kyrenia, Greek Cyprus). After the 1974 invasion of Cyprus by Turkey to stop the fighting between the Greeks and the Turks ("Ethnic Cleansing" some called the fighting), the Icons were taken out of churches when the churches were turned into Mosques, or abandoned to become something else. Fortunately, many Icons were saved and put into the museums or Orthodox Churches still operating. Perhaps they one day will return to the churches!

Over the 44 years abroad we often retreated to this Bartel home for rest and restoration.
Thank you, the Bill and Lyla Bartel family.

Norm and BJ Lofland in their home surrounded by memories.
Norm is 89 and BJ (Betty) is 91.

In Paris, from left to right, Norm Lofland, Lyla Bartel,
Natasha Lofland, BJ Lofland, Bill Bartel

CHAPTER 8

TUNISIA (1985 – 1988)

Macau, Tunisia, Onward to Athens, In Sousse,
Teaching in Kairouan, Digressions and Interjections

MACAU

I am writing on July 7, 2001, sitting in the study of our Macau (formerly Portuguese) apartment in the Barra area near the Ama temple overlooking the inner harbor. Significantly, the Ama Temple (called "MaKou'") is here to protect the people who sail the sea to save them from danger. The study has windows on two sides, a Persian Qashqai rug, paintings by our friend Bao Ze Wei, raffia bookshelves, a raffia easy chair with beautifully worked straw tables, and Chinese blue and white figured lamps. A twenty-eight-year-old Chinese student of mine, studying English with me, who works at the Bank of China, expressed pleasure when he saw it, saying, "It is the most beautiful room I have ever seen. When I have a house of my own, I am going to do a room just like this."

A cozy room for a day that has been filled with typhoon rains and winds. We just saw hundreds of ships, fishing boats, sampans, and larger freighters sail hurriedly into Macau's inner harbor to be safe from the typhoon, which is rotating and moving across the South China Sea as it nears land. As we wait for the typhoon to slam into China, placing us in Macau and Hong Kong in the middle of the typhoon, I, on the tenth floor overlooking the city and harbor and China, find that it has been interesting to remember how we got here. Somehow in my earlier recollections, I covered going from Tunisia to

China, but perhaps I've not told how we went from Beirut to Tunis that summer of 1985.

The kidnappings in Beirut had been bad and BJ and Tasha insisted I go out of Beirut to Cyprus and over to Tunis because a teaching job at the University of Tunis was awaiting my arrival for an interview. Two men took me to the airport. One was the driver for my student, Walid, and the other was a bodyguard for Walid's dad, a Member of Parliament in Lebanon. (Many years later Walid's father was assassinated.) They drove me past the shelled out Palestinian camps. My students had just informed me that I was in good hands on this trip for these guys were the ones shelling the Palestinian camps. At this information I groaned, for I had a number of students from those camps.

After arriving in Cyprus at Larnaca airport, I found a ship sailing from Larnaca to Athens. At first I tried to locate a ship from Larnaca or Limassol to Tunis, or at least to Egypt, and then, hopefully, I could get another ship to Tunis. But all the travel agents said there were none going that route, so I sailed to Piraeus, in Athens, and then found a travel agent who decided that I could go from Naples to Tunis, after arriving by train from Brindisi to Naples, having sailed to Brindisi from Patras, after a train trip from Athens to Patras.

DIGRESSION

Fortunately, earlier, BJ, Natasha, and I had stayed for six weeks at a rather wonderful little hotel named the Hotel Cleo, run by Bill and Cleo (no relationship to each other), a partnership that lasted many years during the heyday of youthful travel, the late '60s, '70s, '80s, when college youth were following the hash trail that started in Athens and ended in Pakistan, and back. (For an account of that kind of travel, see in these memoirs the section about going from Tehran to Istanbul by bus; grueling!) Many of the backpackers were staying at Cleo's House, an old, stately home just above Syntagma Square and just around the corner from the larger, but still small (with an elevator) Hotel Cleo. Cleo's House had geraniums in all the windows and a lovely rooftop garden where, under a trellised shade, Cleo served breakfast. Those of us in the hotel didn't get breakfast.

In the winter of 1978-79, when we were encouraged to leave Iran during the Iranian Revolution, we lived in the one-suite room in the Cleo Hotel for many weeks. Natasha had a single annex room next to our bedroom, and both rooms had French windows that opened out onto an enormous terrace. We felt so lucky! Looking down on an open-air restaurant with a happy man who sang Greek songs to his own guitar music. Lovely! We stayed there seven weeks through Christmas, when Natasha painted a large picture of a man — who looked like the F. Scott Fitzgerald Gatsby character of the "era of wonderful nonsense" in The Great Gatsby. Years later, when I found it again after moving it to North Africa and hanging it on the wall over my desk, he was referred to as the "short-arm man" because one arm looked shorter than the other, and also because the name reminded me of the day I was inducted into the U.S. Army, and I looked about as lost as he looked. Natasha also did a painting of a lollipop, as if on a children's book cover; a painting I would love to hang in our granddaughter's room, if only we still had it. Charming Christmas presents!

We loved being there for the winter weeks clear into February, if we hadn't been so cold. This was 1979 when the price of heating oil had become expensive and small budget hotels could not afford to heat the rooms very much; some not at all. Bill would heat up the furnace in the morning and again at night, and in between times we and all the other winter tourists in Athens would leave our rooms and hope for a sunny day to heat up our chilled bones, for Athens is like the Middle East and East Asia around Guangzhou, China, Hong Kong, and Macau with poured concrete rooms that stay about 45° F, or perhaps 15° C, and no heat!

We stayed on in Athens because the Iran Ministry of Education told us to; of course, when Khomeini took over the government we suspected we could not go back, but we were still under contract through 1979, and we hadn't been paid for months. At first it was interesting awaiting the outcome of the revolution when there were more people in Athens. Wondering what we could do. Wondering how to get our things out of Tehran. Several people went back to Tehran as the revolution raged on, but they were mainly people who had worked for companies that could get their things out, or who had access to someone who worked for one of those companies who could ship their things with them; we couldn't. Finally, when our money ran out, we had to return to the U.S. After borrowing money from our family, in February of 1979, we found the cheapest fares on Royal Air Maroc and flew off to New York, with a charming stop-off in Casablanca (not at all like Rick's Café Bar with Ingrid Bergman and Humphrey Bogart).

Now again in 1985 I was sleeping in one of the tiny but wonderful rooms with a private shower, toilet, but no terrace, at minimal cost. Indeed, I needed it to be minimal. Bill realized, after we had stayed with him nearly every year for six years, that I again had no money this trip, so he moved me to the roof, with a semi-private outdoor shower — oh, how I hate cold showers even in the hottest summers (and 1985 was a hot summer) — and a private toilet, at very low cost.

How great Bill always was to us. About five years ago we again went to one of our favorite cities and found that the Athens we knew so well through the '60s, '70s, '80s, and the late '90s had turned into a not-very-lovely place to visit. The Hotel Cleo was gone; oh, the building was there but Bill and Cleo had been ousted by the owner who wanted to sell it. Bill and Cleo couldn't afford to buy the hotel; they had rented it for almost twenty years. So the owner threw all the beds and furniture (owned by Bill and Cleo) out onto the street and sold the hotel to someone, who upgraded it and turned it into a five-star hotel; small, splendid — remember the two terraces on top that we stayed in for six years?

That year, 1996, we wandered around the town we had known so well and decided to ask, at a small hotel directly across from the Cathedral, one of the guests sitting outside on the steps if he thought the owner would rent us a room at a lower cost since we were staying for a month. Hotel costs in Athens had risen significantly, and we were traveling for a year. The guest said, "Well, Niki, the owner, won't, but you should talk to the night guy. Maybe he'll help." He said to come back after 6:00 p.m. We wandered around, asking at other hotels, but no one had a good deal to offer. (One converted house-hotel had rooms that were awful, and they were not inexpensive!) Even Brown's

Hostel, where youth slept on the roof after all the dormitories were full, was gone.

The great era of staying in Athens on the cheap of the last thirty years was over; tourism was down also. And that wonderful Syntagma Square with landscaped trees and cafés and restaurants where white-coated and tuxedoed waiters rushed across the traffic-heavy streets that circle the great square in front of the Palace — which now houses the Greek Parliament — all that elegance in front of The Hotel Grande Britannia was over. In the '90s, McDonald's and other fast food (Greek fast food also) had moved in, replacing those mirrored cafés with Kenny Rogers and Dolly Parton's Broasted Chicken. Well, the budget tourist could now afford to eat on Syntagma Square, and, oh, how I hated the change in the '90s, even though the coffee no longer cost as much as a McDonald's meal. During the years when we had no money, we would sip our coffees and teas and the moment seemed refined. No more! There are paper wrappings blowing all over Syntagma Square, making it seem more like that other more common, but very interesting and very oriental, Omonia Square where the cheaper hotels and restaurants are located, not the formerly elegant Syntagma with Paris shoppes, grande hotels, Parliament, and business and banks from the best and biggest companies. Perhaps in 2004 Athens will feel it has the Olympic Spirit, but it won't have the dignity it once had.

When we returned to the small hotel across from the Cathedral, the guest was again sitting on the stoop and said, "This is the night man." Bill came down the stairs. We looked at each other like ghosts greeting one another. We shouted, hugged each other, and kissed both cheeks, as we had many times and years before. We stayed in this hotel for over a month in 1996, as we had in the Cleo in 1978-79 during the heady days of the Iranian Revolution, again thanks to Bill, but with very little reduction!

I mentioned earlier that in 1985, when I was trying to get to Tunis for a job, Gregorio, the Trans Alpino Tourism travel agent in Athens, a great guy, "decided" that I "could" go to Italy by boat and overland by train to Naples and another ship to Palermo and on to Tunis. I say "decided" because when I finally got back from this trip, I was so exhausted that I said to him that this was not the easiest way to go (nor was it very cheap). He was from Chicago and understood Americans, so he answered, "I didn't say it was the easiest, and I wouldn't have sent most travelers who were not young backpackers on this overland trip, but you seemed to know what you were doing, so I decided that you could handle it." I thanked him, assured him that indeed I handled it very well — never telling him what I went through — but decided that maybe he could come up with some other way to handle this kind of trip. (Later Gregorio proved himself a friend, indeed, when he moved my whole family to Tunisia.)

When I embarked on this trip in1985 I didn't know that I had heart trouble, although since I had a lot of trouble climbing up the hill on the Beirut campus and on up the stairs to the top floor classes in one of the buildings — a vertical distance from our apartment of ten stories — I should have known. In Greece riding the train was lovely; I read all day from Athens to Patras, bought the ticket for Brindisi in Patras (if Gregorio hadn't already issued it, or at least I had to check in at the ticket office in Patras), walked the long distance to get to the passenger liner. They said there was no transportation for passengers. At least in Greece they still have ships to carry passengers to wonderful places. The distance, carrying my bag (although it was the smallest, it had no wheels; this was before wheels were placed on luggage), the heat, perhaps I hadn't eaten enough, all of a sudden exhaustion hit me when I got onto the ship. I had not slept the night before because I had to be up very early to catch the train. (I have long suffered from bad sleeping habits, and life in constantly bombed Beirut didn't improve those sleeping habits; the stress of the constant battle affected my heart, also.) The purser assigned me to my room, quite nice, but somehow I did not feel well, and I remembered what a friend said to me when on a similar trip to North Africa (Libya, where we met Khaddafi): "Take a sip of brandy (there was none available in Libya). It will help stimulate you and get your circulation going. We used to give it to my Great Aunt Matilda all the time for her heart. She lived to ninety." So, I slowly went to the bar on board and asked for a brandy.

"Courvoisier, sir?"

"Fine."

"Sir, are you sure you're okay? You don't look very good." I returned to my cabin, fell onto the bed. A truck driver had come in, and he took one look at me — for I was most exhausted and my color was grey — and left. Sometime later he returned, and I woke up long enough to see him carry out his bag, a blue duffel, said he had another cabin so I could sleep alone and not be bothered. I did! I awoke when the ship docked in Brindisi. I tottered down the gangway to the dock after clearing customs on board, took a taxi to the train station, learned the train to Naples left soon, and I bought my ticket and boarded when it was scheduled, after eating a breakfast of a croissant and coffee (I still drank coffee in those days), since I couldn't find a more substantial English Breakfast. I sat in first class until the conductor informed me that I had a second class ticket, which wasn't much different than the first class compartments. It made one wonder why the British made so much of it in their earlier novels traveling the Continent. Perhaps trains were better or more interesting in the nineteenth and early twentieth centuries. I would have loved using them then.

Our train rushed north through Bari to Barletta where we changed to westbound tracks through the Apennines Mountains to Naples. Glorious Naples! "See Naples and be fulfilled with life," said the poet, as he recommended going out to visit the ancient cities of the Romans destroyed by earthquake and, some say, sin. But I would wait for the beauties of Pompeii and even Sorrento until the return trip, or maybe BJ and I could come over sometime from Tunis and visit Pompeii. Instead I sailed out of the Bay of Naples, rode out of the inlet of the Tyrrhenian Sea, and crossed that almost enclosed sea, bordered by Corsica and Sardinia and the west of Italy, in a cruise ship of the Tyrrhenian Lines from Naples to Palermo, Sicily. "I'll see Palermo on the way back," I thought. Oh, how much is missed when one doesn't do it at the moment!

We had faced the same problem in 1963 when our travel agent badly instructed us to transport our baggage across Europe, when we were moving to Beirut, Lebanon, to teach at our first overseas university job. Upon arrival in Venice to catch our ship to Beirut, all our money was taken by Customs for the transporting of our baggage from the Holland-America Line ship, the Rotterdam, to the Egyptian ship in Venice, which we were taking to Beirut. Customs in Rotterdam had sealed the baggage and sent an armed guard across Europe from Holland to Northern Italy along with the small amount of things we were moving to Beirut. The value of those things was less than the cost of the trans-European guarded move! When we were sailing from Venice to Beirut via Alexandria, we so wanted to get off in Alexandria and ride the train to Port Said and re-embark on the ship to Beirut, but had no extra money to do so. Always, there was the concern about money. Now in 1985 I had only a few hundred dollars for this trip to Tunis and, since I had not been paid for months, that money came from BJ, who had hidden it from her salary teaching English and history at the Armenian Haigazian College. I thought, "Now I have less dollars than the original few, and I have to get that job in Tunis!" So, of course, I went on. Anyway the ticket was paid to Tunis; a stop would have cost a bit more.

It was glorious sailing across the Tyrrhenian and Mediterranean; they were so blue. The Black Sea in Turkey is noted for its color, like blue-black ink, but these seas are a glorious sea blue, almost a royal blue. When we arrived in the Gulf of Tunis, the customs officer asked me where I would be in Tunis. I said, "The embassy."

I have no idea why I said the embassy rather than a hotel. He said, "Sir, will you really be at the U.S. embassy?"

I couldn't back down now, so I said, "Yes." He believed me; probably my tall build and professorial look encouraged him to believe me, since I had said I would be visiting the University of Tunis.

I walked onto the quay in Tunis wondering what adventure this trip would bring. My former student, long-time friend Dr. Evelyne Accad, who set up the interview for this job at the University of Tunis, was shortly leaving Tunis, after her Fulbright year at the university, returning to her permanent job as a Professor of Comparative Literature at the University of Illinois. The only person I knew in Tunis was Costas Passalis, the consul at the Greek consulate, and a phone call told me he was out of town, in Germany buying a new car and driving it back to Tunis. I learned all this after convincing his secretary that I was a friend of Costas. I checked into a hotel — I think probably the same hotel that in 1972 BJ, Tasha, and Tom, our student from California who wanted the experience of traveling the world — and I stayed in: the Hotel Carlton on Ave. Bourghiba. It was right downtown, just across from the Hotel Afrique, the most posh hotel and tallest building in Africa at the time; possibly so popular because it is right in the heart of the city's adventurous life. It wasn't nearly as much fun alone in Tunis as with my family and Thomas. In later years when we lived in Tunisia, we would often stay at the old French, once-elegant, now run-down Hotel Majestic, with wonderful old big bathrooms and old, but once elegant bedrooms. Not then; I didn't even know about the Majestic, where the French administrators of the colonial power once stayed and enjoyed the veranda, surrounded by potted trees, now all gone.

INTERJECTION

I must interject at this point — as I have all along — that now in 2001 we have just recently returned from a trip to Tunis, again staying at the Majestic Hotel, and it is about to be sold and redone, keeping its historic-classical Arabic style. It was built in 1911, with French curved balconies and fourteen- foot ceilings with high transoms to guide the air through the hotel. There was no refrigeration air conditioning in 1911. The rooms had separate sitting rooms adjacent to the sleeping areas, with sometimes separate W.C. areas next to the huge bathrooms, with oversized tubs and showers. We loved staying in this hotel this August 2001 trip to Tunis. We stayed in five different rooms, trying the huge rooms and a smaller room — perhaps the chauffeur or maids stayed in this size? — depending on what was available. We had gone out to visit our friend, Anne Murray, with whom we had taught, now living in the La Goulette-Carthage area on the sea. We came back from her house and took another room at the Majestic. Then we sailed from Tunis to Trapani, Sicily, and on to Palermo to finally look at the magnificent mosaic- covered walls of churches that told the Bible stories in brilliant gold- leafed mosaic visuals, for that was a way of relating the stories of the Old and New Testaments to an illiterate populace. It is still overwhelmingly powerful to study these images today. From Sicily we returned to Tunis by boat and again returned to the Majestic Hotel. We wanted to take the ship on to Naples but were running out of time and had yet to visit Sousse, Tunisia.

In 1985 I felt both lonely and a bit panicky for I had to land this job. I had a family to support again, and again — like every husband and father — this father was a bit depressed because everything was again about to be lost in Beirut as was lost in Tehran in 1979.

University professors should stay out of wars and revolutions; so much is lost in research notes, papers for publication or for personal research, as well as books. We've left books all over the world. How we wish we had here in Macau the books on literature, drama, English writing techniques, history, etc., that were finally left in the rooftop storage in North Africa, and left before in Tehran, along with rugs, records, costume designs of an excellent costumier who came to Tehran when we were excitedly putting together a challenging university major in theatre and communication. They would support the new library at the Macau Anglican Choi Kou Schools that BJ has spent a year furnishing with books. We have literally carried suitcases of books bought in Manila — where they have excellent books for sale at wonderfully respectable prices — when the library purchaser has a small budget, and most of it being paid for out of the buyer's (our) pocket, to be reimbursed later. There have been book bags of books shipped through the U.S. postal service holding encyclopedias we bought for the school and shipped that have never arrived. Surface mail was not always as reliable as the very expensive air mail was.

Thirteen years ago we left two suitcases of books at a university in China — we had brought them from Paris, after bringing them from California — to help the English Language Department at South China Normal University in Guangzhou. We left them with students and teachers and the library because they had almost nothing in their library. We felt sorry for them then; now with China's entry into the WTO and planning to spend 35 billion English pounds on the 2008 Olympics, we think maybe the books could have been given to the Anglican schools, or some other needy school library, instead of "newly-capitalistic" China. Ah well, the students we gave them to will probably never gain much out of the wealth of the nouveau riche

China. Maybe my best student, now-teacher, Tom Chung enjoyed D.H. Lawrence's Women in Love. He wanted it, so perhaps the books were not wasted. I had taught Women in Love in North Africa and threw it into a suitcase (I didn't know it was then banned in China — I was surprised it was not banned in North Africa) as we went to Paris waiting to go to China. There were also the books we gave to James, who during the last days of classes brought several flower paintings he had done as gifts for BJ and me. James was the son of a farming peasant, who had to return to the farming community and become their English teacher. He didn't want to go there; it was so awful, and it still is. The last time we saw James he rode his bicycle several hours to Jinan University, Guangzhou, to see us for a few minutes, said he hated every moment of his existence. I pray life is better for the poor in China, but it is only better for those in business, and that's why every teacher-training student wanted to go into business, because the teacher only earned less than $75 a month, and James had to feed his entire family and even help farm the hopeless land. Even boxes of books shipped back to Los Angeles when we left our last university post at the University of Macau, and now sitting in our Pasadena attic waiting for us to put up shelves to hold them, would have been good for this Macau Anglican School's library. But, when I offered them six years ago, they said no, as there wasn't a decent library room to house them. Wish they were in this new secondary school's library, or the third school's library that is now being built next to the university in Macau, which with the theatre I'm helping design will probably house a fine arts program.

TUNISIA

Ah, but — as so often in this narration — I have gotten ahead of the story. Let's go back to Tunis, Tunisia, North Africa, and talk about the lonely professor looking for a job.

The next day I donned my gray trousers, striped white shirt, tie and blazer, and taxied to the University of Tunis to meet with the Chairman of the English Department, Dr. Hedi Sioud. An impressive guy, almost as tall as I, carried on a good conversation in English with me, was passionate about Hamlet (to my detriment later). We enjoyed each other's company very much. I had been told that I had to have at least three recommendations, which I thought had been included with the C.V. sent ahead by our friend Dr. Evelyne Accad from the University of Illinois, who was doing research for her new book and several articles on women in the Middle East and North Africa. They were not in the packet with the C.V. Luckily I had copies with me. (If you are going to travel this way, always carry copies of your Curriculum Vitae with you.) Dr. Hedi was impressed and immediately offered me a job — Maitre de Conference — with the probability of a teaching position for BJ when she arrived. I was ecstatic! Dr. Hedi said that the teaching position would be at the Sousse campus. I had been told that was so and traveled down the coast the next day to look at it. The location was wonderful! It was on the sea with miles of beaches, loaded with swimmers of many persuasions. I was quite shocked by the topless bathing, for we had spent many years in the Middle East and never found that sort of "Greek beaches" freedom. Almost totally nude skin on the sand was not shown even in Beirut then, and certainly not in Tehran, for all the stories told about the "immorality of the Shah's kingdom."

When I visited the Ecole Normale Superiore (the teacher training campus in Sousse, where we were to teach) with a curriculum modeled on the Paris school, I was a bit horrified by the architecture, as well as the goats that were eating and mowing the grass that was up to their udders in the inner campus. After the wonderful campuses we had been recently teaching at — although they were often shot-up and potentially shelled and bombed in Beirut — the Sousse campus did not seem inspiring. Anyway, the Doyen of the Ecole Normale Superiore was impressed (almost threatened, I learned later) by our credentials, and welcomed us to Sousse. While visiting the beach in Sousse, Dr. Hedi wanted me to journey over to Kairouan to view the newest campus of the University of Tunis, which he had been virtually the designer (probably architect, if he could have done it), curriculum deviser, and soon to be Doyen of the Kairouan University campus, and he desperately wanted us to be on his faculty, but the Tunis Ministry of Education said, "No, Hedi, you can't take all the new good teachers in the system." Thank God they said that. I journeyed back to Tunis, checked into another cheaper hotel, for my money was running out. I couldn't find the other hundred dollar bill I thought I had. I went again to the Greek consulate, but my friend Costas was still not back from Europe. He was having trouble getting to the same ferry that I had taken over to Tunis from Palermo in time for the sailing, and would have to wait several days before he could get the next sailing, which he missed also for some reason, the secretary later told me. (All this I related to Costas

months later, as he was sorry that he wasn't there to help me.)

I was in a Tunis fast food sandwich restaurant (quite good as it was not couscous, which I had already grown tired of) and the cashier, whom I had seen several times there, looked at the poster of John Wayne hanging on the wall opposite the cash box and said in Arabic, looking from me to the picture on the poster, "Is that you?" I laughing said "yes," for then I looked very much like John Wayne and had been asked about it when overseas; never in the States, of course, for they knew better. But the answer to his question made him happy, especially when I showed him my passport and picture, which looked amazingly like the good old Duke. The cashier nodded, smiled, and said, "Hamdallah! Good!"

I carried my lunch into the dining area, sat at a tallish table, very much like a bar table with bar stools, and ate. By then I was getting desperate for a free place to sleep, and I asked the young man across from me, who had told me he was a student from Morocco, if he knew of an extra bed not being used that I could borrow for a few nights until the ferry sailed after the weekend. He hesitated, then said, "Yes, I know of one. Come with me." Needless to say, I checked out of my hotel and moved into the room with the extra bed in the student housing of the University of Tunis. It turned out to be the single bunk bed in the room with him, which had no mosquito net, but did have a thick quilt, the kind that later in China I would know as a "Ming Toi." I was so happy! Until two days later when he asked if I could change his Tunisian dinars into some kind of hard currency. I said that I was in the same boat, that I really did not have much hard currency. This was before ATM machines and the convenience of plastic money. Besides, our stateside bank account at that time was empty, and they wouldn't have given us a Visa card to use, although I had had American Express and Diners Club Cards for years. Our money was almost totally gone, since the Lebanese Lira had devalued most of its worth and for two years we had been paid only in Lebanese Lira. I had almost no money. He couldn't believe it. "You're American. Where's your money? Go get some."

"I can't do it." He looked at my wallet, and I offered him the only hard currency I had: 20,000 Italian Lira, $10.00, I think, at least that is what it is today. I wasn't sure I had much more, but gave it to him for the room.

The next night there was a party. The Moroccan guys had their girlfriends in and ate lots of couscous, drank bottles of Tunisian Monag wine and beer, and started dancing rather feverishly. Somehow it reminded me of Greek vase paintings! A couple medical students got up off the floor to leave, and I decided that was a good time to join them outside the apartment, which was near the one I stayed in. I noticed my roommate was home, not at the party, and earlier I had gathered that he was pretty much the outsider, not a very friendly guy — but I was very grateful to him for the almost-free bed. I went to bed. I was happy that he always left on a light through the night as I sleep better with a nightlight, especially when I can't sleep very well because of pending problems. It did attract mosquitoes, but I'd rather have that than no light; at least I could keep an eye open for whatever would happen. Nothing did, but I kept an eye open much of the time.

The next day the med students took me in their car to the car ferry in the port, and as we went there, one of them (they were brothers, I think, or at least good friends) said, "Norm, when you come back, we have another apartment for you and your wife and daughter to sleep in for a few days until you go on to Sousse."

I thanked them both for all they had done for me and said, "Yes, we shall use the apartment." He gave me the telephone number at his parents' home — he was leaving the student hostel as it was too noisy — and I shook hands with both and went to the Tyrrhenian Sea Lines ticket window and bought a ticket only to Palermo, for I didn't have enough money to get to Naples, the route I had come before.

I sat up all night during the overnight trip in the "airplane seats" to Palermo. These seats are the most uncomfortable airplane seats, even worse than the seats in the economy class of a long 17-hour flight on a packed Boeing 747-400. The seats did not lean back, or maybe mine was broken, and one of the guys crawled out of the seat and tried to lie on the floor in between our feet and the seats in front of us. Awful! Yet many European travelers do these boat trips in these seats. The next day I talked to one of the guys onboard. He had spent the summer in Sicily and loved it. He spoke ecstatically of all the sights he had visited, and I envied him. I simply didn't have the nerve to ask if he would lend me some money. At the train station, he told me he was going to Syracuse, and I said I was going to Messina; that was all the money I had. We rode together, talking. I got off at Messina, and he went on east and south.

I carried my little, but too heavy, suitcase along the train tracks, because the stationmaster (or someone who spoke English) said I had to go across the bridge. So I walked, where he told me, along the tracks. When I came to a place where the trains curved left, there was no sidewalk area, only the tracks. I looked both ways, started along the curved wall, which followed the tracks, and a high-speed train came along. I pressed myself against the wall with my suitcase and prayed — as I had constantly on this trip, particularly in Tunis when I had no money. Somehow the space was enough for me to clear the train. My shirt got a little dirty, but I was okay. I still don't know, physically, how I was okay. I only know that God had again carried me through the possibility of crossing the Styx, and it wasn't yet my time to meet Charbydis.

DIGRESSION

On July 25, 2001, as we again watched boats and ships hurry into the Macau harbor before another typhoon hit our area, I telephoned our travel agent to cancel a trip to Palermo, Sicily, via ship to Tunis, to again visit North Africa. It seemed sad to have stopped that trip. Not completely sure it was the right thing to have done, but we were on our way to Singapore to see our daughter Natasha, Paul, and our granddaughter Helena Portia Ariane, for whom these memoirs were first written.

On July 31, 2001, we were supposed to fly to Singapore, but we again tried to get to Tunis first. It seemed inadvisable for us to do the same trip that I had done in 1985, although BJ and I wanted to go from Rome via night train to Palermo, and via ship to Tunis, returning to Sicily to visit Syracuse and other delights. Now, since we had to go later, it may have taken too long getting there for us to see our good friend from our Tunisian university teaching days, Anne Murray. Also there was a volcano erupting in Sicily. The airport was closed, so the train traffic would be heavy, and I didn't want to again walk through the tunnel while a high-speed train passed by. Anyway, we were trying to get to Tunis. Perhaps Anjo, our travel agent who had booked us on many trips for ten years, would succeed in getting us into Paris on Singapore Air from Singapore, and on an Air France flight to Tunis, with the return flight to Rome, so we could wander around Italy someplace before returning to Singapore and Macau in mid-September.

So, I reminisce well into the night about getting from Tunis back to Athens where I was to meet BJ and Natasha who were coming out of Beirut in 1985.

ONWARD TO ATHENS

I seem to remember that the station master told me that it was shorter to go through the tunnel to catch the eastbound train to Brindisi. Since I didn't want a long walk after the exhausting night ferry trip in the airplane seats, I went through the tunnel. "Our workers do it all the time," he had said. Apparently then I had enough money to take a slow train to Brindisi to catch the Greek ship back to Patras. The whole trip is gone from my memory, probably because I was so wondering how I was to get on the ship. When I arrived at dusk at the port of Brindisi, broke and concerned, I had to have something to eat. I went into a small store to look for something cheap. As I searched my wallet for the fiftieth time while drinking a Coke, I again pulled out everything in the wallet and laid all the cards, pieces of paper with people's addresses on them (BJ and Natasha have long complained about the addresses in my wallet; so cumbersome, they think), and opened a folded piece of paper that was very flat, and there was the one hundred dollar bill I thought I had but could not find. Thank Heavens I had not found it in the student's room in Tunis, or I might not have had it that night in Brindisi when I had to buy a ticket to Greece. I almost joined the Hallelujah Chorus that praises God openly with stentoric wonderment. I just did it quietly, "Thank You, Holy Father and Son Jesus!"

As I stepped into the kiosk office selling tickets just next to the table where I had discovered my treasure, I sighed as I bought a ticket for passage on the Greek ferry in the "Airplane Seats" section — the cheapest available. But, I was so happy to be onboard that ship that was about to leave Brindisi! The conversation was quite interesting on this part of the trip. I met a few people, a youngish communications teacher with whom I kept in touch for some time, and other backpackers that were typical of that route. Sometimes I've met quite fascinating travelers. On occasion there have been opportunities to visit them and have interesting conversations.

Years earlier when I was traveling up Italy to meet BJ and Natasha in London, Steve was one of those interesting persons. A social worker in Zurich, he was traveling home from Greece with his girlfriend when I first met him. I stayed with them one night, and he made arrangements for my flight from Zurich to London and arranged for me to stay with a friend of his, Lotti Nelson, in Zurich one night before catching the flight at 5:30 a.m. It was a great help. One summer a few years later, when BJ, Natasha, and I were staying in Lotti Nelson's home in Kusnacht am Zee just outside Zurich, Steve was traveling around Switzerland teaching youth to be clowns. He was fun to watch playing a clown, helping young people to overcome their inhibitions by becoming clowns — all a part of therapy. We've kept in touch with Lotti for years. She came to visit us in Sousse, Tunisia, and now spends her winters in Latin America rather than Zurich, Switzerland. In 2002, I learned that Lotti had to be flown back from Guatemala for cancer treatment, but she was doing well, she assured me via e-mail, "for someone in her 80s."

That summer, 1985, after another night of no sleep in the fixed-position airplane seat, we disembarked in Greece. The train, which was terribly slow, was not due for several hours, but a taxi driver offered his services. I managed to talk several ladies and the other teacher into taking the taxi; it cost no more and arrived hours earlier than the train. Driving along the sea over the Corinth Canal, along the route of the Marathon, I offered a running commentary to these tourists about what little I knew of Greece, which was mainly about classical Greek plays. When we drove into Athens, I was gloriously happy and had the taxi drop me off at the Cleo Hotel. Bill never looked so good! He immediately put me back up on the roof, and I was most contented.

Until the next day when I went to the public telephone service center where I could attempt to call BJ in Beirut. During the civil war in Beirut, which lasted for fifteen years, bombs constantly interrupted the telephone service as shells hit the telephone exchanges, the wiring, cables, and equipment, so it almost never worked. From outside the country it was almost impossible to connect with the party dialed. The equipment simply did not work. For years! (When we visited Beirut in 1998, mobile phones had replaced many fixed phones, and the regular phone system seemed to be working.) In Athens in 1985, I would stand in the telephone booth at the telephone center and dial all the numbers on a rotary telephone. I would do this for hours during the time when I thought they would be home. BJ was still teaching at the Armenian Haigazian College in the English Department. She was so happy teaching at that school, even in the midst of bombardment, which usually missed the university campuses. In spite of the agreement among the embattled armies, the campuses sometimes were hit. The president of the American University of Beirut was killed on campus, and one of the main buildings on that campus was totally bombed out. It was later rebuilt stone by stone in exact replacement, using the original plans. BJ was in two bombing incidents. One was on the Beirut University College campus where we lived and taught. Someone tried to do great injury to performers during rehearsal of a Gilbert and Sullivan musical production; not my production, but it was directed, conducted, and acted by Dr. Afif Boulos. The noise hit BJ, who was sitting at a desk with her left ear facing the theatre next to an open window not far from the theatre whose two side doors were blown out by the blast. Not long after, BJ was teaching a class at Haigazian College and had just turned to the blackboard with her left ear toward the street when another bomb went off very close to the glass-fronted building. The blast blew in the plate-glass window and everybody crawled around trying to get out. The bomb was intended to hit the Druze faction leader, Walid Jumblatt, who was dining at the German Hotel next door to the college. The two bombs cost BJ her hearing on the left side. Another time when BJ was teaching there and Natasha had a class there, they were crawling around the hall trying to keep from being shot, as two militias spent hours machine-gunning each other. Natasha was also teaching English at the American University of Beirut. I had most recently been teaching at Lebanese University, having left Beirut University College where I was a Professor of Theatre and Communications. At Lebanese University, I was a professor of English Literature, and loved the freedom of not being every night in rehearsal and building sets, but instead teaching Shakespeare (a course I was not allowed to teach at Beirut University College, but which was run into the ground by the professor who taught it to three or four students; my classes always had twenty to forty students!), novel, drama, literature, poetry — all my fields and such fun to share with eager students on the East Side of Beirut, who were going to be teachers of English, as well as graduate students. It meant that since we lived in West Beirut, that I had to cross the "Green Line" to get to classes, but only two days a week. Even though I started staying on the East Side and not often returning to West Beirut, I often was almost kidnapped or shot. There were simply too many close shaves with the militias. Finally, after being unable to cross over to the East Side because the Green Line was closed due to shelling and snipers on high-rise buildings shooting anything that went across the Green Line, BJ said I had to get out.

Now, I was in the telephone center trying daily, nightly to call BJ and Natasha. After days of this, weeks it seemed to BJ because I could not get through from Athens, I finally heard someone answer, "Hello?"

"BJ, I've been trying for days to call you. I've got a job in Tunisia!" She was happy with that but was having trouble getting our stuff shipped to Tunisia and getting out of Beirut. Finally, both BJ and Natasha got tickets on a flight to Athens for several weeks later. Just then a TWA flight was hi- jacked to Beirut with bad elements happening on the Beirut tarmac, with the hi-jackers killed or in custody. BJ and Tasha went out of Beirut with the TWA plane on the tarmac. Fortunately, the passengers survived and were released.

While waiting for BJ and Natasha to arrive, I looked for an apartment in Athens that we could live in for three months. I met someone who had advertised an apartment near the Hilton Hotel — not an area we would want; we preferred to be near Syntagma Square, since we knew it best. Then when I was walking around one evening, just near our Hotel Cleo, I saw an orange "For Rent" sign. I rang the bell, and a man and his wife answered and said, yes, this apartment is for rent, and they would be very happy if I would take it because they were moving to another apartment. He was a reporter for an Athens newspaper and needed a larger space. It was a nice, neat little apartment, with one small bedroom, mattress on the floor and nothing else in the room, which had been thinly partitioned off from the living room. There was a kitchen with a bathtub in it — with a curtain separating the tub from the cooking area, very reminiscent of an apartment BJ and I once considered renting in the Village in New York City — and a W.C. with a flower, I think, painted on the inside of the bowl, and a living-dining area. I immediately called the owner who was on Hydra Island, far from Athens, and he sent a friend to write the lease. A seemingly nice guy, he agreed to bring a toilet seat with him next time. I moved into the apartment after talking to Bill and Cleo and another writer who was a friend of Cleo's, who said that it was a great buy in the heart of Athens. The friend came with the toilet seat; I knew that BJ would not like it without the seat. We've had several similar problems without the proper seat on the commode. The friend was tightening the first nut on the seat when he got annoyed with doing that maintenance work and said, "Do you know who I am?" No. "I'm the head of Olympic Air, and if I owned this apartment like Nikos does, I wouldn't rent it for … (whatever the rent was)." With that he walked out of the apartment and building. So, I tightened the screw and nut on the commode. I had paid two

NORMAN L. LOFLAND AND BETTY J. LOFLAND

months' rent — where did I get the money? I don't remember! — and subsequently in a month I paid another month's rent. That made three months' rent, all the time we were going to be in Athens, so after two months I informed the owner in Hydra that we were vacating the apartment. He sent his mother, who was not one of the gray-headed, black shawled, dowdily dressed women one sees in the doorways of Greece. She had very smartly coiffed gray hair, a fashionable summer dress, and sandals from one of the best shoppes in the Syntagma Niki Street. I had noticed them in the store window. Very fashion conscious she was as she shouted at me like a fishwife. She was in no mood for tea that afternoon, although I offered it. "Why, why won't you pay your rent this month? My son needs it (in his smart summer Greek Island home)."

"I have paid it. You have three months' rent. We are staying here three months. We are paid up." She didn't see it that way and threatened police and legal action. Now I knew why I never was able to talk with the former residents, who had had lots of trouble with the mother of this spoiled son.

Somehow we had enough money when BJ and Natasha arrived; perhaps I borrowed some again from family (as we did when we left our Iranian life). At any rate, after three months in Athens, BJ flew off to the U.S. to see her mother. Her father had died when she and Natasha were in the States visiting them, and I was stranded on the East Side of Beirut unable to contact them. I thought I had a telex number to get in touch with them, but that faded away and was not working. So, while BJ visited her mother, flying Sabena Air via Brussels, getting a free night visiting Brussels, Natasha and I packed up the things we had, including the small folding bed that BJ slept on because both Natasha and I were too long for the bed. Gregorios, my travel agent, came up with a good deal for us. Maybe I had told him of my experiences by then, and he wanted to be good to us, I don't know. Anyway, he got us all a Seaman's Fare on Tunis Air. I was the seaman and Tasha was my daughter. Bill, a real retired sea captain, looked at me a little askance and said, "How did you get this ticket?" Somehow I had the feeling that I should not be getting that ticket, but so what? We had to get to Tunis. With the Seaman's Fare the cost was less than economy and we got 44 kilos baggage for each ticket. Even so, we had to leave some of our luggage in Athens at the Cleo Hotel, to be brought later by BJ on her Tunis Air Seaman's Fare. When one flies Tunis Air out of Athens, the passenger has to point to his entire luggage as a security process. While the attendants looked on, I pointed out all 88 kilos of our bags, including the bed, and the steward asked me what ship I had served on.

"The Rotterdam," I said, "of the Holland America Lines."

He said, "Good ship!" I agreed, having sailed on it. I could have said the Queen Frederica, an awful Greek ship, but I figured it was cut into scrap metal by now since BJ and I had sailed on it years before on my first trip to Europe, when five people died on the crossing. ("Don't worry," they had said. "There were seven dead on the previous crossing.") Besides, I couldn't remember the name of the company.

When Natasha and I arrived in Tunis in 1985, I called the medical student's number and was told to tell the taxi driver directions to the apartment in the Tunis Port. We arrived and the student opened the door, and we walked through the large, mostly bare, very run-down apartment, for which I was very grateful. Tasha was cooperatively grateful, but with reservations. I did like running down the stairs to the café and getting coffee and madeleines, a delicious French pastry, eating like the port officials surrounding us, and seeing the huge ships with hulls almost protruding into our balcony. It was fun to be near our new job; well, a day's train ride from it. When we again visited Tunis in 2001, the port had been moved to La Goullette, very far out by Carthage, and all the charm had gone. Sterile and commercial ships were all that was there, plus a very big third floor departure hall housing customs, where one had to pull one's luggage up via a long ramp on one side and down a long ramp on the ship's wharf side (or, worse, come up when arriving) circling around and around to get onto the ship. Fortunately, there are still porters in Tunis to help with luggage, even when one had only one small bag apiece. No, wait, I had another small pullbag holding medicine and things picked up in Tunisia. Oh, the foibles of travel!

DIGRESSION

In Macau on January 21, 2002, as I add to thoughts written before and correct errors, I realize that one of the things that I like about my old computer is that I am used to it. It has software that automatically saves what I type because I often forget that I need to save what I write. I have lost more pages in my computer experience. They tell me that this computer is old, although I only used it one year after buying it six years ago from my student, who probably used it before me since it has so many pieces of software that I have never used, but which only frustrated me as I used the machine. I do like it, though, because I type much faster than I do on our school-provided desktop. Probably I misjudged the efficiency of the desktop since it has Chinese, Japanese, and Korean — as well as English — on the keyboard. Though I type with the touch method (left over from years on a typewriter; our son-in- law uses two fingers and is almost as fast and as accurate as BJ and I), I still like to see sometimes what keys I often hit. [Enough of these unrelated nothings.]

IN SOUSSE

In 1985, BJ, Tasha, and I took the train south from Tunis to Sousse. When I had taken this same train three months earlier, I had gone first class. I don't think I deliberately went first class, but the ticket seller just assumed that I wanted that seat. Little did I know the difference between first and second class in Tunisia. I had a lovely trip down, sometimes along the sea but usually along the desert, and the car wasn't crowded. Later we learned the difference. Second class is always totally packed, with people standing and marketable goods in the spaces between the seats. (We recently re- experienced those trips one August when we again visited our previous lives in Tunisia.) Natasha and I had previously visited Sousse and found a house to rent, one block from the sea. It was an Arab desert house, such as one can find all over Tunisia, white trimmed in blue (typical Tunisian colors), with a flat roof on which was a terrace, accessed via the stairway with a domed roof, and columns in the living-dining room. An overstuffed sofa and chair — filled with mice, we subsequently learned — a black and white television, and a twin sized daybed made up the living room. An antique dining table with a settle-style bench and old chairs established the dining area, along with a large refrigerator, which we immediately moved into the kitchen, which had enough room.

The beds were rather bad. When I took out the kilim rug from under my mattress the bed sagged so much that it became a back-breaker. I was so cold sleeping there that I put the rug on top of my blankets and, once we got our shipment from Beirut, the electric blanket. One room was charming, which we wanted for a study, and opened onto the smallish patio inside the back wall of the house with a banana palm tree growing out of the tiled Tunisian patterned floor. The patio was lovely in the summer. The wall kept back the blowing dirt from the unpaved street just over the wall, and the banana tree was luscious with its huge leaves overshadowing the whole patio. French doors trimmed in blue led from the patio into the "study" and, on the other side of the patio, into the kitchen.

The rooms also had small tiles in black and white motifs, and blue, white, and green motifs in another room. Oh, it was potentially charming. Of course, that's why Natasha and I liked it. But it was dreadfully cold in the winter, as are almost all houses in North Africa and all around the Mediterranean. We've lived around much of the Mediterranean, even in the middle of it on Cyprus. It is no colder than in Southern California, it's just that there is no heat! We all heat our houses and apartments with space heaters with little bottles of gaz that fit into little stoves with a burner about four inches by ten inches, but that only heats the immediate vicinity. In Cyprus I sat in front of the television with our heater's burner aimed toward me, wearing a heavy winter overcoat and six sweaters. In Macau the heater looked like a radiator and had hot oil inside it, being heated by electricity, but it was still the same maddening cold!

In Southern China it is very humid, but cold, and the Mediterranean is a wonderfully dry climate, but also cold in winter. Once the weather drops to 10° C, the walls go to that temperature (50° F) and stay there until spring. Often it is warmer outside than inside; certainly that is true of Cyprus, North Africa, Middle East, southern Turkey, and in

China. We wear our coats or other heavy sweaters to work in, to hold conversations — unless there are a lot of people around to heat up the space – and to dine in, although good food will help warm up the body, if only for a limited time. I even sleep in my overcoat, along with an electric blanket, two comforters, and I would add a rug, if I had one to put on top of me at the moment. I slept under a Persian Kilim, which was worth a lot of money, for six years in Macau, until we gave it to our daughter for her wedding. Wish I had it here now! Or any of the other rugs that are hanging in our condominium in Pasadena, California. Next year I may steal the rug off the little library floor.

The day we took BJ, who had been in America visiting her mother just before we moved to Sousse, Tunisia, to the campus was the last straw. I think somewhere I mentioned that the campus of the Ecole Normale Superiore was located at the edge of town, and was, when we arrived, covered with tall grass and weeds with goats eating the greens. There were walkways connecting the buildings that were two feet up in the air, I presume, to keep out of the weeds, for they were rarely cut or eaten down to the ground. I took BJ to meet the Doyen, the dean of the college, and she managed to hold a straight face and keep a cooperative attitude as she talked with him. She wanted the teaching job that had been promised to me for her. We were desperate for her income as well as mine. As it turned out, neither of us would receive any salary until Christmas. When we arrived home, all of BJ's reserve left her, and for the second time since arriving in Tunisia, she cried. Considering I had never seen her cry in our entire married life, I was most upset by her being so depressed. "The campus is so awful, and the road out to it is a muddy mess (it became worse as the winter rains began in full tumult before Thanksgiving), and the souk, while interesting, is the worst one we've had to shop at in all our twenty years in the Middle East (and that included the "garbage stores," as one of our colleagues described the grocery stores in Tehran). Oh, it is all too much!"

At that point we had not moved into our blue and white Tunisian house with the pillars in the living room but were staying with family friends of the young doctors we knew in Tunis, and in whose apartment we stayed in Tunis overlooking the port. The tiny apartment we were using in Sousse was very small, with a miniscule bedroom — Natasha slept on the Greek travel bed — and a very limited kitchen and bath.

We had enough money to pay the rent for a month. We were supposed to put down two months' rent, but the elderly gentleman who rented it to us, the grandpere of the two friends of our Greek consul friend Costas, agreed to wait for a while to get the extra month's rent. I felt it was very necessary for BJ to fly to Kansas to visit her mother. Her father had died a couple of years before while BJ was visiting them along with Natasha, who had just graduated from Scripps College in Claremont, California. Ruth Baerg was in her eighties and needed her daughter's supportive visit. It was money far better spent on an air ticket for her visit than on the extra month's rent — a rent that was very high, indeed, as we found out later.

After we moved into the house near the sea, we felt a little better. Of course, we still did not have our shipment from Beirut that BJ and Natasha had worked so hard to get to the shippers in between the shellings. BJ had spent all of her retirement money from Haigazian College to ship the boxes, trunks, paintings, books, and clothes. She gave away a beautiful pale blue suit of mine, that looked good on me, as well as lots of other things including a full length self-portrait of myself, probably because it was nude and I looked exceptionally good, the way I used to look, and still do, I believe, as I look in the mirrored bathroom in our Pasadena condo. It was painted in very warm colors, indeed fiery hot reds, yellows, browns, and blacks. Very Roualt! Too bad it's gone. I should again take up painting, but our house is full of portraits and interesting paintings by others.

We were so frustrated about our shipment from Beirut, because it was supposed to have been held in Beirut in the shipping office for three months before being shipped to Tunis. They sent it immediately, and the customs in Tunis had been charging us a horrendous storage bill while it was there. And we did not even know it was there. We were in Athens until October, the date we were to be in Sousse, and they were charging us storage. Almost $2,000! We had to keep leaving it there because we had no money to move it. It turned cold; the same kind of bitter cold described a few pages earlier, and we had no blankets! We did buy a few in the market, not very warm blankets, but nice little blankets that would be handy on a couch. (They were not warm, but our daughter Natasha used them on her beds in her too-air- conditioned apartment in Singapore.) As it got colder, I moved the huge kilim rug from under my mattress, which was there to keep it from sagging, to the top of the covers, and I crawled under it. My back hurt, but I was warm — for a while, at least. BJ and Natasha used the blankets. We had lots of beds, just no bedding! Sheets we bought, again. We have bought sheets all around the world.

Finally, I called Dr. Hedi Sioud, the Doyen in Tunis who hired us, saying he wanted us to teach at the new university he was building and heading in Kairouan, Tunisia, but the ministry insisted that we teach in Sousse. Oh, we thought, he was so nice when he said he would call his cousin who works at Tunisian customs and see what he could do. He called later and said that he could not get all the charges excused, but some of them were reduced, and we would only have to pay 750 dinars. 750 dinars was $1,000 U.S. dollars! That was a whole month's salary — a salary we had not yet been paid! It was almost Christmas and we still had not received any salary. The bureaucracy in Tunis was horrendous! We had already borrowed money to live on from the pastor of the Baptist Church, which was located in the Sousse bazaar, and was there only to serve the few ex-pat Europeans and three Americans in Sousse and all the tourists that flowed into Sousse all year around. We had to get our things out of the Tunis customs, because the storage costs kept going up.

In desperation I called my brother, Jim, who owed me a lot of favors for past favors I had done for him, and asked to borrow some money to get our things out of storage. He said, "Will they let in the money, and can you take it out again, if you want to?" He had dealt with a lot of overseas banking and business.

I said, "Yes, because we can take out one-third of our salaries — if we ever get our salaries — which they assure us we will, and get all back pay as well."

Later, when he wired it, he told me half of it came from him and half from our mother, our real mother, not our stepmother, her sister who married our father, and years before this, in 1976, while we were in Tehran, had a new will written and managed to get control of everything (an estate worth twenty-five million U.S. dollars in today's money). She and our half-brother used the worth of the oil and ranch to invest in and build the Hilton Hotel in Las Cruces, New Mexico, where they moved a year after Dad died. We four brothers received nothing. Our half-brother will receive almost all the estate, or what is left of it by the time our former aunt dies, who is now in her eighties. Our mother, her sister, lived to 93. Dad died at 69. Dad and Mother were born the same year. But, perhaps there will be nothing left of Dad's estate since they seem to have lost the investment in the hotel, until some kind of bankruptcy proceedings are cleared up with the partner of the Hilton Hotel. The partner died in an airplane crash after swindling both my stepmother and brother, or so they say.

Anyway, we received enough money to get the shipment out of customs. The school sent me and a driver to Tunis to get the shipment. It was winter, it was freezing cold, and it was about time to receive the blankets, including three electric blankets, books, and clothes — warm clothes! I met Hedi Sioud's cousin and he walked us through the process of clearing customs. It was wonderful! I was so happy! The guy driving seemed happy also to help a professor and family. We even stopped by the apartment at the port and took our suitcases that we had brought with us from Athens and had not been able to get moved to Sousse. I left the key on the dining room table with a thank you note to the young interns and returned to Sousse. Thank God He takes care of us at all times, in all places, all over the world!

TEACHING IN KAIROUAN

The experience in Kairouan was not a pleasant one, although the years in Sousse were quite pleasant and rewarding. After teaching at the Ecole Normale Superiore — encouraging students who were to teach English in Tunisian schools — we were told that we were to be transferred to another university, the new University of Tunis at Kairouan, the facility headed by Dr. Hedi Sioud. He had wanted to have us teach at the new Kairouan campus. It is a beautiful campus; very North African architecture with shutters and traditional white and blue exterior. The tiered-seating lecture halls are interesting with high ceilings and blue wooden shutters. I found them most rewarding aesthetically. It was fun lecturing in them, particularly Shakespeare; of course, it became a performance hall, since it is my belief that theatre should be taught as theatre in performance and comments as the play proceeds forward. Unfortunately, the less-able students wanted only comments that they could write down in their copybooks and write on their exams at the end of the year, without any of the ideas or theatre techniques to enhance those drama-ideas going through their minds. The bright students did well — the others did not. This became a little discouraging since our teaching techniques have been generally well received elsewhere.

The transportation from our home in Sousse on the sea to the Kairouan campus in the desert was dangerous. We rode service taxis, called "louages," old station wagons that have an extra seat placed in the back so there are five passengers plus the driver. Being so tall, I always rode in the passenger seat in the front with the driver for the hour long drive. When he became sleepy, I would speak to him in my few words of Arabic, and he would slap his knee and shout yallah, which is probably what I had just said to him. "Yallah! Shukran! Hamdallah." Since I always came back at night, this became important to keep him awake since he had probably been driving since dawn. BJ and I would go over sometimes together, but usually separately since BJ had earlier classes than I had. We would stay over in a hotel and teach the next day as well before returning home to our apartment overlooking the Mediterranean Sea. This we would do three days a week. The rest of the week we would prepare lectures and mark papers.

By the time we had strikes and the year ended, we were ready to get out of Tunisia. The experience at Kairouan was not a pleasant one, although the years in Sousse had been quite pleasant and rewarding. Our colleagues, Dr. Don Baker and Beth, suggested that we might like to teach in China, where they had taught before coming to Kairouan. We applied and were welcomed in Guangzhou, China, at the South China Normal University.

CORRESPONDANCE (1985 – 1988)

Larnaca, Cyprus
Saturday, June 1, 1985 (postcard)

Hi,

BJ and T finally got their wish, and I went out from Beirut under armed guard between rocket firing (which had stopped the night before at midnight and started after I left at 2:00 p.m.) They are still there. I'm to go back the 20th for exams; BJ finishes the 26th. I am en route to Tunis; chance of a job! Pray so; we've had it in Beirut. It is awful! Everything you see and read is true. Hope you are ok. Love to see you; can you come to Greece? We think we'll be on Paros, Greece.

Love, Norm

Tunis, Tunisia
Sunday, June 9, 1985 (postcard)

After a few days in Cyprus, on to Athens and then by train to Patras; boat to Palermo, Sicily, and same boat to Tunis, Tunisia. Interesting trip! Looks like we'll teach here for the University of Tunis at a campus in Sousse, which looks like Palm Springs/Acapulco — by the sea with bazaar and crenelated castle-like structure built in 859 AD dominating the Casbah. Should be fun! Eager for BJ and Tasha to get out of Beirut; it's hell!! Begged them to come with me; BJ is trying to get her summer salary. I won't get mine unless I get back for exams end of month. Don't want to go back for salary worth only $1,500, but …

Love, Norm

Tunisia has Roman ruins all over the place.

Athens, Greece
Tuesday, August 6, 1985 (postcard)
Dear Elma,

We've been here a month. Tasha and I flew from Beirut July 4. Norm had come nearly a month earlier. We've managed to rent a small apt. in the center of Athens. In 2 or 3 weeks we'll continue to Tunisia, where we'll be teaching next year. Tasha will go with us for a while at least. Looks like none of us will get to the U.S. this summer. Hi to Victor, Elma, and Lloyd.

With love, BJ, Norm, & Tasha

Athens, Greece
Thursday, August 15, 1985

Dear Lyla and Bill,

Norman and Tasha went to a performance by some American dance co. — part of the Athens Festival. I decided to stay home, wash my hair, and write a letter or two. Our apt. is so small it's nice to be here alone. It reminds us a little of your small house at your aunt and uncle's place. The best thing about this place is its convenient location, and it's decorated kind of cute, but there's not one comfortable place to sit. We bought a fold-up bed for Tasha—in the living room. And I must mention that the bathtub is in the kitchen, which tends to congest things at certain times of the day.

We've gone to several events of the Athens Festival: Verdi's Macbeth by Covent Garden Opera, a concert by Athens State Orchestra, and a concert by the British Bach Festival Orchestra. All of these were held in the Herod Atticus Theatre (ancient amphitheatre). It's not as much fun as the Hollywood Bowl — no food! We're getting bored with Greek food. Usually have a simple lunch at home — vegetable and fruit — sometimes pasta — and then eat dinner out.

It looks like we'll go to Tunis in about a week. We'll both teach in Sousse at a branch of Univ. of Tunis. N will teach Eng. and American literature — pretty much what he taught at Lebanese U. I'll have three sections of American history. Can you believe that English majors are required to take four courses in American history?! The last two are special topics. I may also have one composition class.

Sousse is a seaside resort town — a vacation spot, especially for French tourists. We're told that French is spoken more than Arabic. We'll be in the university's English Dept. We're trying to learn a little French; have bought a book, and Tasha's teaching us a few things. So far I know my numbers to 20, the days of the week, and a few nouns. Norman's considerably better off than I. Tasha plans to go with us to look it over, and then decide what to do. Hope your summer's going well.

Love, Betty, Norman, & T

Athens, Greece
Friday, August 16, 1985

Dear Lyla and Bill,

How are you? Well, I hope. We are tired of Athens, although it has been nice to be out of Beirut.

We've enjoyed a number of dance and orchestra concerts as part of the "Athens Cultural Capital of Europe" — the 1985 Athens Festival. It's nice to hear orchestras from London and Germany, etc., sitting in the Roman theatre at the base of the Acropolis — with the Parthenon above, lighted as a part of the sound and light show. We heard the Verdi Macbeth and Tippet's Priam from Covent Garden, London. Nice — but not Hollywood Bowl — no "hors oeuvres ala Bill."

Sorry you couldn't reach us by phone; we've moved into an apt. with no telephone. The apt. is a mix of your first LA apt/house and a set for T. Williams' Glass Menagerie, as fitted onto USC's Stop Gap Theatre. The more amusing part of the apartment is the bath facility — the tub is in the kitchen, all walls covered by mirrors — daily I look worse — no, sometimes I see elements of a better past!

We leave for Tunisia next week; a friend is lending us his apartment for a short time, while we go to Sousse to find a house. Hope it's on the beach with some heat and hot water! Did I tell you that the town looks like a cross between Palm Springs (by the sea) and Mexicali!! With mosques next to the open market. Gide's setting for The Immoralist, I understand ...

Love, Norm, BJ, T

Wichita, Kansas
Thursday, September 12, 1985

Dear Lyla and Bill,

I'm sitting in the coffee shop of the Wichita bus depot; it's 11:30 p.m. and the bus to Ft. Worth doesn't go until 2 a.m. Had a good visit with Mom. She's quite happy with her situation — still has her own apt., fixing her breakfasts and suppers. She walks with a walker, to the dining room for lunch, which is a big meal — quite good. It happens that both entertainments while I was there were music programs by Mennonite groups: the Holderman church near which I first taught, and the Adams, Ok. Church. One of the Holderman singer's father was a third grader in my class; he certainly must have been a child groom!

It was fun to be with Georgia and Dennis for a couple nites. She still has a huge, marvelous garden and lots of animals, especially cats. Kathleen will pick me up in Ft. Worth. She and I will take care of her little grandsons, James and Gregory, for a couple of days while their parents move into their new huge house.

I still plan to fly out the 18th — first to NY then to Copenhagen since I'm flying SAS, and on to Athens, where I have one nite before going on to Tunis. I sure hope Norman and Tasha have found an okay place for us to live. I also hope that Khaddafi decided not to invade Tunisia; for all the news I've heard since coming to Kansas, he may have already invaded. It's amazing how isolated these people are from what's happening in the rest of the world. My mother is convinced that we're not going to have enough food in Africa!

Marie Westervelt called me from Paris where she's studying French. She now plans to take a one-month crash course in teaching English as a second language in London during Nov. Then hopefully on to China in January. I'm enclosing the tag sticker for the Ghia.

Love, Betty

Sousse, Tunisia
Sunday, October 13, 1985

Dear Lyla and Bill, etc.,

How are you? Great I hope — we're not! This place has gotten to us. Tasha best describes it as "the pits" — I can think of other parts of the body that better give a more accurate account of it!

For tourists, it's great! 50,000 European visitors are here in Sousse daily (two-week/one-week trips) enjoying the Acapulco type 1,000-room hotels that line the glorious beaches. It's lovely! For living it's a hole! Really like Mexicali with no imported foods. Shopping is awful — although the "big supermarkets" look full — but only of Tunisian goods, which are very limited in variety and of no quality. Good wines — the exception — and old Coca Cola, and Pepsi, RC, etc. But of course, those are ok because they are made here. There are many factories of goods shipped to Europe. Some friends run a sporting clothes "factory" from Belgium. All cloth, buttons, etc., are imported and ALL must go out, even the scraps! Anything too scrappy is burned. Nothing is sold here. Only labor receives anything: money. I think the hard currency brought in is filtered through the govt. and converted into Tunisian dinars. And everything is so expensive when computed against the salary. I was led to believe all was cheap!! Our house, $300 rent, with two months in advance.

BJ and I both wish we were in Beirut!! Still the best shopping in the Middle East or North Africa!

Classes will be ok — although there are no textbooks!! Only lectures from the faculty. I teach 4½ hours for the full load (ridiculous!) because of my rank — the highest on this campus — and I earn only about $700 a month. BJ has 9 hrs. because she's among the rest of the faculty — lower rank! A guy under me teaches 6 hrs. Last year my rank taught only 3 hrs. The faculty went on strike for more pay, and the ministry raised the teaching loads. There are usually opportunities to teach additional hours at the rate of about $5 an hour, paid in three installments. But this year so many students failed (there were 45 strike days last year) there are no extra classes to teach! Certainly we aren't needed — and how we wish we were not here! Students struck over political issues (against the govt.), faculty, for higher wages. Foreign faculty have to teach during the strikes and during the make-up days!! (How I wish we were there with you to laugh at all this! We just cry!)

Our shipment from Beirut left Beirut July 4th — we still don't have it, and it's getting cold. I have only summer clothes — and no Salvation Army thrift boutiques!! Actually, a friend of ours who is a priest, White Father — youngish guy — very much a fun man-about-town, has pointed out a used clothing shop that specializes in American cast-offs for refugees: all double knits and machine-washed-out washables! From American refugee organizations.

Our shipment was to have been cleared by an Italian outfit in Tunis. We paid $1,000 (including $300 for clearing and transporting the stuff— including all my winter clothes — to Sousse) to ship this junk here. Now because the Italians did not clear it, and we couldn't find it — the airline finally found it — we have to pay another $700 (as of last Tuesday) storage costs. Everyone working on it has given up getting the govt. to "forgive us" and reduce the cost. Guess we'll have to pay it off in installments; in the meantime, we had to buy blankets because ours are in the "shipment." Everything we need is in the "shipment." We go around from room to beach talking about our "shipment." The clothes aren't worth it — except there are no replacements here. We could go to Sicily and buy a couple new things, I guess on the price of the "shipment."

In addition, the men here are awful towards Tasha. She can't walk out on the street without being attacked. The men here do "business" with the tourists. There are mother-daughter teams that come here from Germany, Scandinavia, France for sex — and it's big business. When my girls go out on the street, they are ready to join Khomeini's veiled crowds! Tasha can't wait to get out.

And almost everything is in French! Tasha does very well — has translated our negotiations for renting our house and "the shipment"— until she won't talk about it anymore. I had to go into Tunis regarding the shipment last week. Fortunately, our White Father, Thomas (he looks like a character out of Clockwork Orange film), was there and he went with me because all business (except for "the BUSINESS") is in French or Arabic. He's fluent in both.

And Lebanese University still owes me two months' salary; BJ hasn't collected one month's salary. So we are really discouraged! No, we're not on our way home — but difficult to keep cheery about all this. We hope our salary starts coming at the end of this month. A British professor who came last year said his pay was a month late, but someone said that was quick: it used to take six months. Lebanese U. took eight months to start paying me.

The irony of all this is that just before leaving Athens, the American College in Athens offered me a job — theatre. Practically begged me to stay there. How I wish we had.

Oh, and we are not allowed to cash in our air tickets (U.S. to Tunis) which we did not use. New ruling: cannot cash them in until next year's budget: April 1986. We had been told we could use the money now — to live on!!

So much for all this. How are you? We were glad to hear from you via BJ's bringing back your letter. She so wanted to come out to LA. I wish she had stayed out there and missed all this mess until she had to come. Classes still haven't started — new date: 21 Oct. Wonder how many strike days this year—there are only 25 weeks in the school year!!

Looks like Tasha will try to meet her friend in Paris in mid-Nov. They hope to find jobs! Hope they can. Anyway, she wants to get back to America before long. We'll miss her terribly. Even more so this year. Write, please.

Love, Norm, BJ, & T

Thursday, October 17, 1985

Continuing this saga. Got word last night that they are reducing the charges on the trunks — perhaps down to $120. So that's great news; nobody believed it could happen. ("A miracle," said our Wed. night prayer group — probably was!!)

We are getting most depressed over all this. Now BJ has to teach grammar with exercises to sixty students using the lecture method without books! To new kids (1st year) who probably know a dismal amount of English. That on top of three preparations of cultural history of the U.S. — in lecture, without textbooks, and little enough books in the local campus library! She's very angry. I'm the one who has the decent deal. I teach only six hours a week — two afternoons — but they are all dealing with stuff I know nothing or little about. I teach one play, that's the only thing in my field. All the rest of it I have to dig out. Fortunately, I have taught poetry before. But not History of English Literature and DH Lawrence, etc. I don't mind and would enjoy it. But, they tell me, I am teaching too much — too many hours. So I want to give BJ poetry and they take away grammar. I wonder if they will do it!

Also, I am to take a "louage"— a service taxi — to Kairouan to teach another three hours (drama lit.) for a friend who has gotten all the things done for us — he hired me and has gotten the reduction, so I feel I should do it. Kairouan is one hour or an hour and a half away. Louages are known to be dangerous — driving is chaotic. Hope I can find some place to stay overnite, so I can come back next day, because my classes go until after dark, and I don't want to be on these roads in a louage at night.

We are about ready to forget the whole thing and try to come back to the good old U.S.A. I think I might have a job in Athens in January. Wonder if People's Express has cheap tickets; we could get to Paris. Saw an ad for flights: Paris to West Coast $145; is it possible? Don't know on what airline. Probably Aeroflot via Moscow and Peking!

Forgive my asking, but if we come, could we camp out at your house for a while until we move into an apt? Tasha, I think, is later hoping for Courtney's room for temporary refuge. Your letter arrived just after I wrote the other half of this note. She was excited with your invitation.

Your letter really has made me homesick to come home, at least for a while. Could I sell clothes in Confetti? I'll take the afternoon shift — "Madam, try this silk in mauve — you look like 'peche et crème.'" Oh my error — peche means sin. Tasha says it also means what I meant — but that the customer might like the other better. Courtney's apt. sounds charming. Glad she's near home and PCC is a good school to do the basic requirements. Sorry it has been a difficult year for you in the shops. Shocking about Rita's husband. Glad Dave is back at work. Amazing fellow. Tell them hello and God's blessings on them, and on you.

Love, Norm

Friday, October 18, 1985

Just now received your letter sent June 6, 1985. We are sorry to hear that Betsy died. And yes, would love to see the 9 hr. history of civilization and Amadeus and, and, and — !!

There are some interesting things to see here. The old walled city, which now encloses the market, is fascinating. A couple days ago we took an hour's train trip to El Jem, where there's a Roman coliseum in much better condition than the one in Rome. This one's smaller — originally seated 30,000. It's right in the middle of a rather awful little town. There are other well- preserved Roman sites in Tunisia, but wonder if we'll be here long enough to visit them!? A last-minute addition has just been made to my schedule — freshman grammar — hour-long lectures to 60 students (whoever heard of grammar lectures at that level?!) plus two hours of practice — exercises, etc., and there are no books. So I'm supposed to find (possibly in Tunis) some exercises, or make them up and have them copied. Anything my American Civilization students read has to be copied also, and there's little in the library. An indication of what it's like here is the fact that all library books are arranged according to the date they were placed in the library. Take care, and write when you can.

With love,
Betty

Sousse, Tunisia
Saturday, November 30, 1985 (postcard)

Hi,

We decided that you deserved at least one card which shows how nice/interesting Sousse is. The tourists do love it. The weather's generally quite warm and sunny by day and cold at nite. We've had a week's holiday, but stayed home. We get only Christmas Day off, that is only Christians get it. The same New Year is celebrated here.

Cheerio, Betty, N, and T

Sousse, Tunisia
Saturday, January 18, 1986 (postcard)

Dear Lyla and Bill,

Marie Westervelt (friend visiting us) and I took an excursion to this place (Dougga) yesterday. Beautiful! The most complete Roman town in N. Africa. Had to think of the Getty Museum. These baths still have lovely mosaic floors intact — we walked on them! There are a number of Roman towns in Tunisia with tons of mosaics. Many have been removed to the Bardo Museum in Tunis — fantastic museum.

Sousse, Tunisia
Thursday, February 6, 1986

Dear Elma,

Forgive us, please, for not writing immediately after receiving your letter. You write such interesting accounts of life as you journalize it in your witty style. Thanks for sharing your thoughts!

Yes, by all means come to touristic Tunisia. To live here is pretty awful, but we're still here. Tasha leaves the 8th for Paris and will carry out this letter in hopes you get it sooner. Mail here is slow sometimes. Lately taking a month to arrive here.

Our house is so cold we are debating whether to move to a hotel, but it costs quite a bit over the next four months. But, for heat we are tempted. Come and share what we have. If we are here at this house, there is room; you can use Tasha's electric blanket — you'll need it! Don't know why this old house is so cold — just won't warm up with the sun and our buta gaz heater, which warms only one room — barely! If we're at a hotel, will find you a room for about $10-12 a day — and pay part of it ourselves! People seem to find packages including chartered airfare from London and hotel rooms in deluxe, four-star hotels for about 100 pounds a week, and somewhat more in the winter season. Would love to see you. Hope/

pray that your arthritis is getting better. Wonderful account of your maneuvering with the wheelchair. The kitchen here at this house would be perfect! It kills my back! Your kitchen is marvelous — this one is awful!

Love, Norm, BJ, and Tasha

Sousse, Tunisia
Monday, February 10, 1986

Dear Lyla and Bill,

Our 2½ week vacation is drawing to a close. I'd have appreciated it more at Christmas. It happens that the spring break falls at Easter. It's only one week—I think we'll try to go to France, especially if Tasha is still there. She flew to Paris Feb. 8. She'd cancelled two earlier reservations for various reasons. I think mainly because she dreaded facing the world on her own. All the bombs in Paris, plus the grim weather nearly did it again, but her Tunisian residence permit was about to run out, and she didn't want the hassle of renewing. She plans to stay with several friends while looking for work; is considering an au pair job, and wants to study French. We'll see how it goes. She left on Sat. afternoon; then Sun. morning Norman took the train to Gabes in the South where he'll spend several days with the family of one of our students. So you can imagine how quiet the house is — been kind of nice — plenty to do.

We're very tempted to move into a hotel in order to keep warm, enjoy a lovely view of the sea, with two large terraces, plus not have to clean the house and launder linens without a washer. Those are the advantages. The cost isn't too bad for Feb. and March, but after that comes the high season and prohibitive rent on our measly salaries. So we'll probably stay where we are, buy another stove and check into a nearby hotel at least once a week while the cold weather lasts. We stayed there one nite last week and enjoyed it so much.

It seems that our university is the only one in Tunisia not shut down by strikes. Why ours?! There are no private universities in Tunisia — all govt. operated. They've imposed a new plan this year in which the students take a 3-4 hour exam every two weeks, and they're given on Saturdays! But they count almost nothing toward the final grade — crazy. We don't give an exam every time. I have to do four, and Norman, two. The higher your rank, the less you have to do! All the exams here have no names on them — and there's no way to give credit to the student who contributes in class — the final exam is nearly the entire grade.

Tasha had a nice weekend in Tunis with a couple of our students. She stayed at the home of one of the girl's grandmother, who lives in a 300-year- old house filled with antiques, and located in the old town, which is mainly the bazaar now. Lots of floor-to-ceiling tiles, etc. So then Tasha and I walked through the Sousse old town — called the Medina [Ma-Dee-na] in Tunisia — looking for interesting old houses — found several. Of course everything is connected to everything else. Individual houses are only found in the newer parts of town. Tunisia certainly is exotic when it comes to architecture, dress, etc. So many men wear the heavy hooded burnoose in winter. The women (not the younger ones) generally wear a white wrap — often with blue stripes. They don't cover their faces.

It sounds like your help situation has really given both of you a workout. And what a difficult time for Martha and Dave. We think of them often and do appreciate your keeping us informed. Do give them our love. What do you hear from Rita? Are they British citizens?

We're invited to spend next weekend in Sfax (about 2 hours by train) with an American couple we knew in Beirut — very interesting people. He teaches business, I believe. Retired from teaching in Vermont, then several years in Beirut (she had grown up in Beirut) and now this is their second year here. We've not seen them here. The invitation came via a neighbor's telephone, and says something about a lecture at the Anglophone Club. Is that people who speak English? My Webster's doesn't list it — only Anglophobe! We'll probably go — haven't seen Sfax yet. Understand there are some other Americans there. So far as we know, we're the only Americans in Sousse.

Is Courtney taking classes at PCC second semester? You mentioned reading Shakespeare. I'd love to see a good Shakespeare production. This place is really a cultural desert.

Glad that Todd is enjoying his job. Tell both of them, and Tate, hi.

We've become acquainted with several Polish people who work here. One woman, Hannah, is an orthopedic surgeon, who finds working here very difficult, partly because she's a woman. Her salary is approximately the same as mine! She's learned French since coming here two years ago, and now I've started tutoring her in English. How's Bill's mother?

With love, Betty and Norman

Sousse, Tunisia
Saturday, March 1, 1986 (postcard)

Dear Lyla and Bill,

At the moment I'm giving a four-hour exam. Boring! So I'll write some cards. These students write pages and pages; quantity counts here. Summarizing or concise writing is unknown here. It's warmer now, and more vegetables are in the market, and tons of oranges. We're gradually becoming vegetarian. Would like to visit Tasha at Easter if she's still in Paris. Our spring break happens to fall at Easter. Thanks for forwarding mail. You'd love the Roman sites here. The Getty Museum has caught it!

Love, Betty and Norm

Tunis, Tunisia
Wednesday, March 5, 1986 (postcard)

Hi,

We've come to Tunis for the night to check with the ministry about getting out of paying the $100 exit tax, since we work for the govt. Tunis is fun after Sousse!! Actually like the Old French atmosphere. We stay in an old lovely French hotel with huge rooms overlooking a park; enormous bath with hot water (and the gas heater doesn't blow off the wall when used — as at our house!) Miss you. Wish you could come over!! We'll go to Paris for Easter with Tasha.

N and B

Sousse, Tunisia
Thursday, May 1, 1986

Dear Lyla and Bill,

We finally have a warm, sunny day with no sharp wind. This place is too much like Kansas in the spring. I'm presently sitting on the roof, trying to get a bit of sun. It's very public up here with all the people in adjacent bldgs. also out either hanging laundry or on their balconies watching the street activity, which there's lots of. Today is a holiday — not sure what for — someone said Independence Day, but I'm sure we celebrated that sometime ago.

Thank you, Bill, for your note and the clippings, and Lyla for your interesting letter from New York. It would be fun to visit N.Y. again — it's been such a long time. An older Lebanese friend, a lady quite French in her outlook, went to N.Y. to visit her daughter who now lives there. She was all prepared not to like it, but wrote that it was fantastic. Tasha thinks that you must visit Paris. It, too, is a marvelous city — so beautiful! For all that the French have been criticized for not resisting much the German invasion, at least Paris stands intact. We did have such an enjoyable ten days there at Easter.

Perhaps Tasha has written to you that she has decided to take an au pair job. She likes the fact that much of the day is free to pursue something better. But it does sound to me rather hopeless for non-EEC people to get jobs in France. Since she does want to stay on awhile, this job does at least provide housing (a tiny one-room apt. on ground floor; family lives above) plus tiny salary.

We're thinking of taking the train to Tunis tomorrow for an overnite — just for diversion. Sousse is so boring. At least Tunis has the American, British, and French libraries with a few cultural activities. If we're stuck here next year, we're seriously considering moving to Tunis and commuting to Sousse for our two days of teaching each week, as nearly all the professors do.

Our classes are supposed to end May 21, then the students have two weeks to "revise" before finals (written — four hours long plus orals) which sound like a real fiasco. The administration keeps impressing us with the idea that we're to give low grades. Out of 20, 14 should be the highest grade in literature, etc. That's how they keep "high standards." We want to come to California this summer if we manage to collect the owed transportation money from the university. Hope Courtney gets to do the Mexico project; it sounds interesting. Hi to her, Todd, and Tate.

With love, Betty and Norman

Sousse, Tunisia
Monday, May 19, 1986

We baked ourselves at the beach yesterday. As always, I hated it, except to look at the water. The topless quality of the Scandinavian tourists helps add a bit of sparkle to the placid blue watercolor painting stretching out in front of us. It must be very confusing to the local Moslem who is enjoying the beach—and it was loaded yesterday with locals as well as tourists. Since this is the holy month of Ramadan — when everybody abstains all bodily pleasures from dawn to dusk — those guys playing soccer on the beach (we are told, not deliberately kicking the ball — and sand — directly at the topless tourists) must concentrate deliberately on abstention. At the almost simultaneous sound of cannon and mosque at 7:20 p.m., all enjoy the pleasures of the palate — and the beaches are empty.

From about 9:30 to 1:30 a.m. the city is like "carnivale" — all coffee houses are loaded with customers — the streets are packed with shoppers who are buying. By day, everyone is asleep — except for the tourists. Because the locals must wake up and eat before dawn. I hear the cannon at 3:00 a.m. to waken people. Don't know why so early — maybe it's for the women to get into the kitchen and stir up a new long-lasting breakfast. Then all day the taxi drivers, and any other workers that wake during the day this month, and there aren't many! — go around with their tongues hanging out. Makes me feel like I should also — maybe we'll do that instead of returning to our fried squash diet!

Enough of these ramblings. Tasha is still in Paris. Has a part-time au pair job — works 4-5 hours a day, gets free room, but no food, and a small salary. Guess she's doing okay. Studies French, and of course uses it all the time, so that's good. Thank you for your offer to her; I'm sure she thinks often of coming home, although she loves Paris. She no longer is as enchanted by the French men as she used to be — wants an American. Says the French are just like the Arabs — only interested in sex.

The French fellow she liked a lot — the guy we picked up off the highway in Greece a few years ago when he crashed his motor bike — has another girlfriend and hardly shows up when he promises. Friday night on local TV I saw an old, 1936 probably, film with James Stewart and Clark Gable. Pierre, the Paris friend, looks very like young James Stewart. Pity — he would have been quite a catch — she thought — and so did I. Ah, well.

Love, N & BJ
Sousse, Tunisia

Friday, June 13, 1986

Dear Lyla and Bill,

Our classes are finished and we've given exams (written); now is the grading period (nearly two weeks) and then oral exams and meetings to decide who passes and fails. Ridiculous system! Will probably leave here the first week of July. Think we'll take a boat to Sicily, then Sardinia and on to France or Italy. Right now we're a bit undecided about it all. The university is now offering us air tickets from Calif. to Tunis, which they promised a year ago, saying we could have cash instead, by waiting 'til April. So when April came, no cash available, and they are offering the tickets. So we're trying to discover the best way to get to California and figure that it's probably best to make our way to London by boat and train, since we have time, where hopefully we can get inexpensive tickets. If it all works out, we'll probably come to L.A. in mid or late August. I want to see Mom en route and that's always so inconvenient and expensive too. And Norman gets upset at the mention of Kansas, so don't know how all that will work out.

Concerning the Chernobyl catastrophe, it sounds as though it got far more coverage in the U.S. than almost anywhere else. Our news comes from the BBC and an occasional Intnl. Herald Tribune, Time or Newsweek. Consensus is that U.S. blew the immediate story out of proportion, partly as propaganda. Alastair Cook on BBC says that possibly now U.S. and Russia are more eager to work out disarmament plan. The Tunisians appear unconcerned, but are generally misinformed anyway.

Thanks for taking care of the driver's license for me. Am enclosing check for same.

With love, Betty and Norman

PS: Since we live so near, we've been getting to the beach nearly every day—the one luxury of this place! Venice, Italy Monday, July 21, 1986 (postcard)

Come over! It's wonderful! No Americans ... almost, but lots of Germans (pushy!) Wanted coffee on St. Mark's today, but at $2 a cup will wait until Tasha joins us Wed. in Vicenza (Palladio architecture) and here. Yugoslavia a big bore! When paying hotel bill, discovered it was priced per person instead of per room. Expensive for bathless and nothing to do in Malinska, isle of Krk. Venice is always loaded with people — a few rooms available because of "terrorism!" I'm doubtful I'll come home. BJ will last of August.

Love, N and BJ

Sousse, Tunisia
Wednesday, September 10, 1986 (postcard)

Hi,

Am wondering if BJ is still there. Am frustrated as usual. Finally got the bank to send money to Kansas bank. Am trying to find apt. Would like the port, but too far to go via taxi for classes. Am looking at Madina house again—not as large as I thought, but interesting ... Today I'll see an apt. on sea over rug shop, Ave. Borguiba.

N

Sousse, Tunisia
September 1986

Dear Lyla and Bill,

I arrived in Tunis at 8:30 p.m. Fri. flights were ok and long waits in N.Y. and London not bad. Spent Fri. nite in a hotel in Tunis. Then took train to Sousse, where Norman met me at train station. We're now in a hotel, looking for apt., and I think we've found one — will know for sure tonite. Tell Tasha that Salem escaped Tunisia by the skin of his teeth and trying to get to Tasmania. It's hot here, with lots of wind from the desert. School begins Oct. 6.

Love, BJ & N

Sousse, Tunisia
Thursday, October 2, 1986 (postcard)

Dear Elma,

We're trying to get settled in for another year. Classes begin Oct. 6. Just finished re-giving exams to those who failed in June — a bore! Have found a nice apt. in the center of town with a beautiful view of the sea. You'd enjoy it! When are you coming? Lots of tourists here now, but weather's been windy and wet. Did I leave a Geo. Eliot novel at your house? If so, please bring it when you come. Trip here was ok, but exhausting: one day in JFK and the next in Heathrow. Keep in touch.

With love, Betty and Norm

Sousse, Tunisia
Wednesday, October 29, 1986 (postcard)

Dear Elma,

I came to Tunis yesterday to get some letters translated into French. They're supposed to be ready today. Then I'll take them to the Education Ministry and hope that they'll up my salary. I have to verify my experience. This place is fond of red tape! I teach only on Mon and Thurs, so that allows lots of time for red tape. Fortunately, I do rather enjoy Tunis. American Center and British Council are quite good. When are you coming? The new Education Minister has changed our holidays; our winter break now comes at Christmas. We may go to Paris. We do plan to be in Paris at Easter. Otherwise, we'll be here. Hope to see you.

Love,
BJ

Sousse, Tunisia
Sunday, November 16, 1986 (postcard)

Dear Elma,

Here's the address for Saga, an organization that brings lots of tourists to Sousse. One has to be at least 60, or accompanied by someone who is; it's supposedly cheaper than most tours. Could be cheaper even if you "threw away" the hotel and stayed with us. Saga Holidays, 120 Boylston St., Boston, MA.

They seem to bring people to London and then on to various places. If you wish to stop in Europe, mention that. The second year here is considerably easier than the first — especially since we're being paid. I'm spending two evenings each week studying French; unfortunately, mostly grammar. Hope you're getting along okay and planning to come.

Love, BJ and Norm

Sousse, Tunisia
November 1986

Dear Lyla and Bill,

It was good to hear from you. Sorry about the robbery at the shop. But the TV coverage sounds neat! You do sound busy. Upon consideration, I doubt that there's anyone in Tunisia as busy. It's amazing how little seems to get done. Most places appear to be over-staffed. In offices and shops people sit around and watch the dust collect in between customers. They're doing the customer a big favor by selling him something. I, too, have more time here than I usually have. Fortunately, I can use again some of my lectures from last year. Most of my courses are the same: American Civilization for Sophs. (two sections) Jrs. and Srs., plus Shakespeare for Jrs. Since the classes meet only once a week, I have only 6½ hrs. per week of teaching, but four different preparations. I go only on Mondays and Thursdays.

Since I do seem to have more time this year, I've signed up for a French class at the local language center, which I'm discovering is quite mediocre. It's supposed to be a beginning class, but in it are twenty or so Tunisians who speak what sounds like fluent French, but want the grammar. Then there are a German, a Belgian, and a Dutch — all young women married to Tunisians, and who know little or no French. Oh yes, also a Polish lady, Mary, the wife of our friend Paul, who teaches piano at the music conservatory. Mary has just joined him. The teacher, a spritely, glib, young Tunisian, began by asking for a volunteer to conjugate the verb etre (to be) on the board! He was quite upset to discover that several of us know no French. I'm lost most of the time in class — my knowledge of English grammar helps some. I do learn a bit each session, but not nearly enough to keep up. I figure I'll stick it out for a while at least, since it's the best available. One language school, the Borguiba Institute, has a monopoly on foreign language teaching in Tunisia. A British friend, new to our university, is about to drop his Arabic class because it's so bad.

Guess I've not written about our apt. The nicest thing about it is the lovely view of the sea. There are three main rooms, plus kitchen and bath. One enters a fairly large room which we use for dining and sitting; another large room faces the front/sea which is a bed/study/sitting room; the third room, a bit smaller, is a bedroom. The walls were freshly painted — light gray — okay, at least not bright colors. Floors are beautiful geometric patterned tiles in neutral tones. It was unfurnished, so we have had to buy things — fridge, stove, etc. — even the awful chrome/Formica stuff is expensive here. Fortunately, our landlord, a young fellow, is handy with tools. He threw together a desk/bookcase affair out of an old wooden table, which Norman painted gray to blend into the wall.

Our balcony looks down on Borguiba Avenue, and just beyond is a large open space with a few bits of vegetation, including some palm trees, then the beach. B. Avenue is lined with palm trees, so it's quite a pleasant view. The horse-drawn open carriages, which sell rides to tourists, lend a colorful touch, as does the camel which is occasionally on the beach selling rides. The port is quite near us, but because of buildings in between, we see only masts and smoke-stacks of larger ships. There are two beautiful sailing ships, which look like pirate ships, and take tourists on short cruises.

Last week I spent two days in Tunis, having some letters translated into French. These were letters from places I've taught, giving dates to prove my experience. My salary is based only on my degree — no credit for experience. When I discovered that others with same degree and less experience were being paid more than I, I began procedures to correct the situation, and understood that everything was okay, and I could expect a lump sum of back pay when I returned in Oct. So now, upon asking, (they never tell you anything) I'm told my "request" was rejected because the letters of verification were not in French. They must be translated by an official translator, with the proper stamps, etc. I discovered that only in Tunis could this be done. So I took the train last Tues a.m. to Tunis, and had Tues. afternoon and Wed. morning at my leisure while waiting for the translations. I spent much of that time at the British and American libraries, and spent the nite at the Majestic Hotel, where we enjoy staying. The Majestic is a large, old hotel, quite grand and luxurious in a now flea-bitten way. The main attraction for me was the huge bathroom with big tubs and lots of hot water. I'd thought that I'd probably have dinner in the hotel dining room since I was alone — couldn't get hold of a friend, Anne, who teaches with us and lives in Tunis. However, after a long, relaxing bath, I decided to venture out to a small French restaurant, which we discovered last year and liked a lot, Chez Nous. As it turned out, I did not feel uncomfortable — a number of people were eating alone, including a middle-aged Tunisian woman, which is unusual. [The Majestic has since become luxurious.]

The trains here have first and second classes, and a few have a luxury class. I'd taken first going to Tunis, and it was crowded with tourists, so returning, I decided to try second — there are more cars, at least. But it was crowded too, with locals — little kids, transistor radios, etc. The trains do work well, and are heavily used. They just need to add a few more cars.

We guess Tasha's doing okay. Have had a card and one rather long letter, which was mostly about her social activities. She'd had only one class at that point, and the professor hadn't shown up. Her classes are spread throughout day and week, making jobs difficult. But in France, students aren't supposed to work. She thought it impossible to change the schedule. But she didn't seem to be particularly concerned. Perhaps that will come in the next letter, when the extra-curricular activities have lessened!?

When we returned here in October, we discovered that there's a new Minister of Education, who has changed the school holidays from three: fall, winter, spring, to two: Christmas and Easter! We were shocked that people at the univ. have actually used those terms. Actually the spring one doesn't come at Easter, but before. The dates are Dec. 20 thru Jan. 4 and Mar. 21 thru Apr. 5. I wish it were after Easter instead of before. Is this too near Easter for you to leave? It will be so neat if you can come to Paris. We're trying to decide whether or not to go there also at Christmas. There is supposedly the efficiency apt. that Norman briefly stayed in last summer, available in Dec. In some ways, I'd prefer that Tasha comes here, although it would be more exciting there. It kind of depends on her situation. I don't look forward to the cold weather there.

Our church — all three regular families, plus the American family from Sfax, connected with the same mission as our pastor — is having a pot-luck luncheon tomorrow after the service. This is the first social event since we came last year, except for "dinner" on Christmas Eve. Norman is afraid they'll serve horsemeat, as the pastor's wife often cooks it for their Sunday lunch. We ate it there once, and it wasn't bad — a meatloaf. Think I'll make a pasta salad with beef-ham, which is available here.

What a shock to learn the U.S. has been making arms deals with Iran! What is it coming to?! It's against policy to even talk to the P.L.O., but not against it to provide weapons to Khomeini's crew! How do people there feel??

With love, Betty and Norman

University of Tunis, Ecole Normale Superiore
Sousse, Tunisia December 1986

Dear Friends,

Sooner or later most of us succumb to the form letter as the only way to keep in touch and share with all of you some of our recent experiences.

After the Iran debacle of 1979 (the one before the one which came with the latest Iran-Watergate-Reagan-ited error), and after fairly traumatic job- hunting months in California, we returned to the Middle East to join old friends and new in the terrible but fascinating furor of Beirut. But before relating some of the vicissitudes of life in Lebanon, we want to say that our years in Tehran were a high point in our lives; thanks to those of you responsible, especially you Damavand College people.

What marvelous (as well as tragic) memories we have of the Beirut (sometimes bullet-riddled) days. Norm loved working with the dedicated theatre students at Beirut University College for four years. After this, he accepted a full Professorship at Lebanese University in the Department of English Literature. This job was equally rewarding, but there was the problem of reaching the university by way of no-man's-land (resembling 1945 bombed Berlin), the Green

Line, and the various and sundry check- points. Often the shelling, kidnappings, etc., prevented his returning home, and he sometimes slept in rather absurd beds. During the last several months of the school term, the Baptist Seminary in Monsaria generously let him stay in one of their apartments. Then in May, 1985, after one solid month of staying in the apartment in West Beirut (the kidnap threat worsened), Norm flew from Beirut, escorted to the airport by two unknown armed men (hired by N's students), off duty from shelling the Palestinian camps. He went to Athens and on to Tunis to check into job possibilities.

During all of this, BJ was happily (most of the time) teaching at Haigazian College, a small Armenian liberal arts college in West Beirut, which is struggling to survive, as are the two larger universities in West Beirut. She loved that job, and her heart is still there, although she and Tasha were caught at Haigazian for four hours in a cross-fire battle, and she and Norm were shelled for twelve hours with thirty shells per minute. Ah well, that's life in Beirut these days. Natasha was with us during that last year in Beirut, after having graduated from Scripps College, Claremont, CA. She taught pre- university English as a second language at the American University and took several courses at Haigazian College. Natasha is now studying history of art at the Sorbonne in Paris, and plans to be with us for the Christmas holidays.

So in July when Natasha and BJ flew from Beirut airport to meet Norm in Athens, the hijacked TWA plane still stood (empty at that point) on the tarmac. Although we had earlier experienced two evacuations by the U.S. Navy, we all finally left Beirut in a more or less normal manner.

As you've already guessed, the Tunisia jobs did materialize. We're both teaching (Norm, British Literature, and BJ, cultural history and Shakespeare) at the Sousse campus of the University of Tunis. Sousse, two hours by train from Tunis, is on the Mediterranean (we've a lovely view from our balcony) and accommodates in luxury hotels up to fifty thousand tourists per day — mostly from Europe. Our apartment is rather small but will sleep at least two additional persons. Don't you want to come for a visit? Last Christmas we enjoyed so much the visits of Marie Westervelt, colleague from Damavand days, and Kay Wade from Beirut.

Although we find Tunisia interesting, with lots of Islamic and Roman sites, it's a poor country with little hard currency to import anything, so one is forced to live off the local economy. This means spending much time shopping and cooking from scratch; also, the meat is not so good here, so we eat lots of vegetables, but there aren't always many to choose from. Anyway, for us, the food is a bit difficult and dull.

The most disappointing aspect of life here is the university; there are almost no books, and students are not programmed to read. They want information to be given in lecture form so it can be memorized and fed back on final exams. Too bad. We wish our graduates were equipped with a stronger, broader concept of English literature.

Happily, Sousse has a minute Protestant group (all foreigners, mostly tourists) which meets in the British pastor's home. There is also a Catholic church (impressive building), a remnant of the French presence, and attended by only foreigners. Christianity has to keep a very low profile here. Pere Charles and Thomas, the two priests, have been good friends to us.

In spite of problems here, such as not being paid for six months and having to borrow from family and church to survive, coming from Beirut to Sousse has seemed rather like moving through a hurricane into the doldrums. But perhaps it's only the storm's eye?! Anyway, we are thankful for God's love and protection over the years, and pray that He will generously bless each of you during this Christmas season.

Sousse, Tunisia
Thursday, December 25, 1986 (postcard)

Hi,

The police finally came through with a visa for us, but the bank hasn't come through with our dollars or Italian lire for Sicily. Just as well, because the boat for yesterday was canceled, and the one for Sat. is "maybe." The sea is high with huge waves splashing up on the beach in front of us. Reminds me of Connecticut! We may forget it all and go to Tunis for a heated hotel room and huge bath tub of hot water! It's as cold as Kansas!

Bless you all,
N, BJ

Sousse, Tunisia
Saturday, January 24, 1987

Norman's British Lit class just walked out of a four-hour exam, saying it was too hard. I was supervising it since he was scheduled for two today. These long Saturday exams are too much. I wish the students would walk out of all of them; then we wouldn't have to mark them.

Mother died on Jan. 19, and her funeral was the 22nd in Garden City. She had been in the hospital most of Dec. They put her in the nursing section of the home where she'd been living, but after a few days, she was back in the hospital. She had so many things wrong with her — just seemed to be worn out in general. Fortunately Kathleen was able to be with her nearly all that time. K is now closing the apt. Her three children were at the funeral and took a few of the things from the apt. — the rest will be sold. I wonder if I'll ever return to Kansas — perhaps.

What's happening with the possibility of Paris in spring? We still plan to be there from March 20 or 21 to April 3 or 4. Actually our big problem is getting our Tunisian dinars changed to foreign currency. Tunisia is in a state of financial crisis. (Seems to be most of the time, with high officials absconding with suitcases of hard currency.) If we know by mid-Feb., we can probably get reservations at the Recamier Hotel for from about $30-$45 per nite for a double (not a king-size bed). It has a lovely view of St. Sulpice Sq.— huge fountain and next to St. Sulpice Church. It has a two-bedroom suite on the top floor which overlooks the Square. Perhaps we could share that?? Or we can get entirely separate rooms. Last year the suite was approx. $60. This includes a breakfast of croissant and coffee.

Have you read about the new Musee d'Orsay? The converted train station—now museum of 19th c. art. Sounds great. Tasha will not have a vacation at that time, so we will be somewhat on our own, but that's okay. The fairly new Picasso Museum is quite marvelous, too. Hope it works out; would be such fun to do it together. Tasha plans to come here Feb. 8 for two weeks — winter break. Hope all is well with you, and that we hear from you soon.

With love,
Betty

Tuesday, April 21, 1987

Dear Lyla and Bill,

We enjoyed so much being with you in Paris. I think that for me the high point was the Cathedral at Chartres; thank you for taking us. The Orsay was exciting, and both Notre Dame and St. Chapelle are marvelous, but somehow viewing those Chartres windows in the gloom of dusk was so neat — felt like traveling back in time.

Kathleen left yesterday and seemed to have had a good time in spite of the culture shock. She and I took a two-day excursion to the Sahara in the south of Tunisia, complete with camel ride into the dunes and carriage ride thru an oasis. Also saw some interesting Roman ruins. Then we spent two days in Tunis, sightseeing — mainly the ruins of Carthage, which are most interesting. They're just outside modern

Tunis. She took back with her three small silk carpets for her children. The two weeks here with Kathleen went surprisingly well, considering the close quarters and diverse viewpoints. Norman did take more walks than usual!

Between the student strikes and a national holiday, I've taught about half my scheduled classes since coming back. Final exams are now scheduled and it looks like we'll finish about the end of the first week of July.

Betty

PS: We are listening to Mission music; really very effective music for that film. Did I tell you that I met a filmmaker at Lina's party in Paris (the night I wanted you, Bill, to go along, as well as Kathleen and Ahmad — I knew BJ and Lyla wouldn't like it much!) who said Mission is the one film with substance made this year, that it has a soul of its own. I'm glad I saw it. Thanks.

Loved being with you two in Paris. The Ritz celebration of your anniversary was nice — thanks! And the musees! Great to enjoy the paintings again through your eyes — it adds a freshness.

This place has been on strike for 1½ weeks of the 2½ weeks we've been back. The student arrested 2½ weeks ago has died — diabetic and went into a coma. The students had come back to school last week, but now are out again. Hope they can get the rest of the material read before the exams!

Glad to know that Court is coming to Paris and Europe. It will be a good trip, and she and Tasha will have fun together.

Love, Norm

Sousse, Tunisia
Tuesday, April 28, 1987

Dear Elma,

We got your card of Vesuvius. Thanks. We had assumed that you did make it onto the boat. We're wondering how it was (the boat itself). We're thinking of going to Sicily after classes end, and the students are given two weeks to prepare for final exams. It's a stupid practice, but does give us free time. Now there are rumors that the Minister of Education is insisting on lengthening the school year a month! That would mean only six weeks holiday and no more pay. Surely teachers won't accept that! Kathleen and I spent two days in Tunis and did a fairly complete tour of Carthage by carriage. If I remember correctly, you visited the Antonine Baths; K and I agreed that those baths were the most interesting part of our tour. The Carthage museum was really a waste. I made a complaint to Sue (Peter's wife) concerning the day tour to Tunis and how everyone is dumped off a mile from the Medina — but it probably won't help. Kathleen enjoyed Dougga, but was really put off by the horrible toilet facilities!

The Tues. afternoon tea was here today. Sue brought a book with several pictures of one of the Thierstein castles she had visited. How was England? They had 75 degree weather on the weekend! K left as planned, on the 20th, but out of Monastir instead of Tunis. I believe she enjoyed Tunisia in spite of rather severe culture shock. Hope your trip worked out well and didn't leave you too exhausted. Write!

Love, BJ and Norm

Sousse, Tunisia
Sunday, May 31, 1987 (postcard)

Dear Lyla and Bill,

Classes are finished, and final exams will occupy most of June! Ridiculous! Weather's been windy and rainy —

disappointing for the tourists. Looks like we'll be here thru July, then to Paris in Aug. Since tickets are to be provided, may come home for 2-3 weeks late Aug.-early Sept. Think we can get one of those coupon tickets w/ certain no. of stops — Eastern seems to be available here. Tasha looks forward to Courtney's visit.

Love, B and N

Sousse, Tunisia
Sunday, June 14, 1987

Dear Elma,

We did get your long, newsy letter. Thank you. Sorry we're so slow answering and sorry about your being robbed in Sicily. Your whole trip sounds terribly hectic. Have you recovered? We've just finished final exams and are now marking them — then come the orals. All should be finished at end of June. We're finally having good beach weather — have swum a few times. The town is loaded with tourists. We will probably stay here thru July; then hopefully to Paris for several weeks, and maybe to the U.S. in late Aug. or early Sept. — since the tickets are supposed to be provided by the university.

With love, BJ and Norm

Sousse, Tunisia
Wednesday, July 8, 1987

Things here were pretty hectic for a while. Kathleen with us, and Elma and her friends at a nearby hotel. Elma and friends did seem a bit on the "downhill side."

Elma's at least 70, as are the others. From what E. wrote, their whole trip thru Italy to England by train was a bit traumatic — robbed in Italy — dragged along the street in the process. It was while K. was here that I began to notice my eye twitching quite a bit; then I began to have what the doctor called facial paralysis on one side of my face. This sort of spasm lasted 30-60 seconds, and increased in number until I was having up to 20 per day. After various medications including cortisone shots (very popular with French/Tunisian doctors), trips to eye and ear doctors and a dentist, etc., I finally went to a neurologist, who put me on tranquillizers which cured me in two weeks. Fortunately, classes were just ending as this problem was beginning, and I had a medical excuse (very popular here) so I didn't have to help with the written exams.

During this medical fiasco I gave up my exercise class and have decided to swim instead. I'd hoped to use the beach directly in front of our apt. — just cross the street and walk ten yards or so. But it's full of too many Tunisians, and the men are too aggressive and plain obnoxious. So now I walk a bit farther to the tourist hotel area and mingle with the Germans, who are here in big numbers. The year's terrible weather in Europe has conditioned the tourists to really appreciate the sun and beach here. The weather here isn't as good as usual either, and people are wondering if it could be after-effects of Chernobyl??

Peter (our pastor) and family have gone to England for two months, and their fill-in, Andrew, is a young British fellow who is otherwise studying French in Paris, preparing to become a missionary among Moslems in France. You're probably aware of the large numbers in France and England who are converting to Islam. The evangelical Moslems claim that by the year 2000 London will be a Moslem city! Andrew says, though, that most of the converts in England are Pakistanis, Indians, etc., rather than the non- immigrants.

Last week I spent most of three days in Tunis, mainly to get two boxes of books (shipped from Beirut) out of the airport customs. I took the train Tues. a.m. and spent a few hours in the American Library. Then went to the house of a British friend, Anne, where I spent the nite; Anne went with me to customs the next day, to translate. She'd just moved into a house for the summer months, so things were disorganized (understatement); but she's always more or less that way. And our experience at customs was horrible: red tape and more red tape — very French! Hordes of people trying to clear their shipments — all men except for us. Well, we couldn't get my boxes in one day — so I had to stay another nite, and the next day we were successful. One afternoon I went with Anne to the Palestinian Headquarters, where she works two mornings a week translating. Yasser Arafat happened to be there for a meeting — Anne says he's been there quite often recently — and as he left, he walked right past us with his bodyguards — said "bonjour," left the building surrounded by a crowd, and got into his car. Quite impressive. Then I went with Anne and another British friend who needed French Francs to Mohammad's house to get black market money. This was also interesting: his front is a tiny stall in an open air market, but his house is luxuriously furnished with opulent, ugly furniture, several TVs, video player, etc. When I finally was able to look at the books in the shipment, I was so pleased to see most of my art books. They were sent by Haigazian College where I'd left them — along with more books and other items.

Jack the Clipper sent us a review of Ben and Carol Weir's book — sounds as though they're pretty hard on the State Dept.

The sister of a friend we teach with has offered us her London apartment for the last three weeks of August, and we've decided to accept the offer. I think Tasha will join us there — perhaps we'll spend a few days in Paris en route. It looks doubtful that we'll come to the U.S. this summer. Earlier, I was encouraging Norman to visit his family — especially his mother in Liberal, but since the idea only depresses him, I've decided to say no more.

Well, the jobs at Tours [university in France] have fallen through; we're still in touch with the American fellow whom we talked with in Paris, and he says that the openings were for British Civilization courses, which we could and would have taught if offered, but a British couple who have been teaching similar subjects applied and were hired. We also wrote to the

Univ. of Maryland overseas division. They are connected with the U.S. military and have campuses all over the world. They responded very favorably, sending a huge packet of info. As well as ridiculously detailed application forms, which took hours to fill in. They also asked for transcripts and recommendations, which I had sent from McPherson. After sending it, I very quickly received a letter saying they needed no one with my qualifications, signed by a secretary for the director, who was on vacation. Norman hasn't heard anything. That's discouraging because their catalog listed so many courses that I am qualified to teach. And I'm sure there wasn't time for my stuff from McPherson to have arrived.

Tasha writes that Isabel Bentley will be in England for approx. the next three weeks. Tasha took the bus to London to spend a few days with Kathy B. who is visiting there. Hope Courtney is having a good trip and will enjoy Paris.

Love, B and N

Sousse, Tunisia
Monday, August 3, 1987

The weather is strange — chilly at times and other times hot. Haven't swum for nearly a week — was bitten on the leg by a jellyfish; it's the season for jellyfish.

The young English fellow, who is our pastor's summer replacement, is a real nerd. A young couple came from England to visit him, and he was so nasty to them that they spent most of the time with us. I don't understand him because his friends, Niki and Chris, are from his home church which provides 90% of his support. He's training to be a missionary!?

A group of eight young college students from the U.S. have been in church the last couple Sundays. They're on what they call a study tour — think it's sponsored by Operation Mobilization. It was refreshing to talk with them — perhaps a bit naïve, but so energetic. Sorry that most of them were having stomach problems. Undoubtedly because the nerd took them to some of the worst restaurants.

An Amherst student who's studying Arabic in Tunis during the summer and whom we recently met stopped by last weekend. We're amazed at how well he's adjusted — in fact, I think he's adjusted too well if that's possible. He's living with a Tunisian family — Moslem, of course, the father of which earns 130 dinars ($155) per mo. as a carpenter. Doug shares a bedroom with the two sons, who are university students. He's a Christian and trying to witness to the family and has become quite fond of them. He asked me if I knew how to get rid of bed bugs — his legs and feet were covered with bites. He doesn't want to tell the family — might spoil the relationship.

My cleaning woman (her name in English is "Mosquito"!) at times is impossibly stupid, but she does clean the floors (tile) and do the laundry — in the bathtub! And I'm told that no one I get here will be any brighter. I'm glad to give her a day's wage for two hours' work: $6. It's hard work, and I'm sure she needs the money.

Well, we're not going to make it to the States — financial reasons. Instead, we'll be in London thru Aug 27; then in Paris 'til Sept. 15. Ariane's apt. in Paris is supposed to be available; if not, we'll probably be with Tasha. She'll be with us in London. We've just discovered there's a cat in the London flat—hope it's not too bad for her allergies.

The British couple, whom we befriended when they were in Sousse, have invited us to visit them in Bournemouth. So we may go there for a few days. It sounds like an interesting area — Hardy country, Salisbury and Winchester cathedrals, etc.

I guess those tempting Mexican restaurants in L.A. will have to wait. Norman has been so stingy with the tequila and margarita mix I brought last summer, that there's still a bit left. He's discovered that a "near-enough" copy of a margarita can be made with a local fizzy lemon soda type drink and vodka, which unfortunately isn't local. But Kathleen bought a big bottle of vodka at the duty free shop when she came.

Bill, the restaurant chain that we like is Bistro de la Gare; they have the good mousse and floating island. We'll try some paté and salad at Café Francais, and will keep a lookout for Crocodile.

We have plane reservations to leave here this Friday; as usual, are having a problem changing our dinars into foreign currency. We learned today that Schiller College at Strasbourg, France, is considering us for teaching positions. They're to contact us while we're in London. Don't know much about it yet.

Did Kathleen send you a print of the two of you sitting in Tasha's apt? It's excellent; also is the one taken on the metro.

Note that we now have a mail box at our apartment.

Love, Betty and Norman

PS: I agree with you that it's definitely time for a shakedown among those religious TV programs. Would love to hear Gene Scott's comments!

Sousse, Tunisia
Wednesday, August 5, 1987

Dear Elma,

Thanks for your letter — especially the clipping on Sam Sturm. They never write — she's definitely a telephone person! Last summer he spoke of retiring, but I didn't think it would be so soon. Norm says things must be back to normal with you (after your hectic trip) if you're freezing peaches and apples. Some fairly decent apples have finally come on the market — the kind for cooking. I should make a pie, but not in the mood to bake, and we'd just gain weight.

I'm sitting on the balcony, although the morning sun is pretty hot and there's very little breeze today. It's the Eid honoring Abraham, and almost no one on this part of the beach — guess the Tunisians are at home sacrificing the sheep! Although I find it difficult to believe that many are that religious. The biting jellyfish are also discouraging swimmers. I'm sure the tourists have retreated to the hotel pools. Actually being here thru this much of the summer has been quite pleasant — almost like being on holiday. I really enjoyed my almost daily swims until the jellyfish invaded.

Have you heard about our bombs? Two in tourist hotels a couple days ago (one at Monastir and other at Hannibal Palace Hotel, Port Kantaoui) and one in Tunis a month or so ago. The fundamentalists are blamed. No one killed, but several tourists injured. Wonder how much this will affect tourism?

We were a bit surprised that Pres. Bourguiba did appear here in person for his birthday parade a week ago — looked quite good. They had put up, in view of our balcony, a huge three-story portrait of him for the occasion. Actually, we found the parade quite interesting; especially the historical floats with traditional costumes, etc.

The young English fellow who is Peter's (preacher) summer replacement has turned out to be a real nerd! He was so nasty to his friends who came to visit him — a young English couple — that they more or less took refuge at our house. We did enjoy them, and plan to visit them for a few days when we're in England.

We'll not be coming to the U.S. this summer, but thanks for the invitation—it's always fun to come to your house. We'll take a rain check.

Our plan is to fly from Monastir to Paris Fri., August 7. Then on Mon. or Tues. (11th) with Tasha, take a bus or train to London, where we'll house-sit for an acquaintance in Finsbury Park until approx. August 27; then probably to Bournemouth for four or five days (the couple we recently met) and back to France for a couple weeks before returning to Sousse about the middle of Sept. What are your plans for winter?

Love, Betty and Norm

London, England
Wednesday, September 2, 1987

Dear Elma,

We're on a fast train to London from Bournemouth, where we visited friends. Yesterday had a tour of the Dorset countryside. Corfe, with its castle (mostly ruins), was especially interesting. Wm. the Conqueror's New Forest was well worth seeing also. In London we'll take a bus and hovercraft to Paris for ten days or so before back to Sousse. Hope all is well there.

With love, Betty, Norm, and T

Paris, France
Monday, September 14, 1987 (postcard)

Paris is lovely as usual. Drizzled some this a.m., but most days sunny and pleasant. Our last four days in England were with friends in Bournemouth. Returned to Paris Sept. 2 by bus and hovercraft. Were with Tasha one week, and now in Ariane's apt., which is working out well. It's on the same metro line as Tasha's apt — nine stops away. Have gone to two organ concerts: St. Geo. Anglican and the Madeleine; a good way to see churches. Going to see A Room with a View tonite. Back to Sousse the 19th.

With love, Betty and Norman

Sousse, Tunisia
Friday, December 4, 1987

Writing lectures takes all my time. The ones for Am. History I don't mind, but dislike the ones for British Civilization mainly because of the way the course is taught — four persons teach the four groups and we give the same final exam, so have to teach the same thing. And the students are always worried that they'll not get something that the other groups get, etc. We've just had meetings to write exam questions and the hair-splitting over wording of the questions is unbelievable.

We're teaching at the university at Kairouan this year, which is an hour's drive from Sousse. The Ministry of Education transferred us there, and in some ways the school itself is better than the one in Sousse, but in more ways it's a worse deal for us. More work for the same money, plus the commute. I teach Mon., Tues., and Wed.; Norman teaches Mon., Tues., and Fri. So we spend Mon. nites in a hotel there and come back to Sousse on Tues. afternoon. I go again on Wed. and Norman on Fri. There are some other Americans teaching there; the Bakers are from Arkansas and Oklahoma — have traveled a lot and are entertaining. He looks straight out of the Ozarks—tall w/ rather bushy beard. They both wear black all the time — she, pants suits of winter and summer weight, made while they taught in China. She's short and quite heavy. Both wear lots of heavy American Indian jewelry. They like to entertain, and had one party which was fun. Now he's having a birthday party next Sat. evening and we're invited to spend the nite, which is an experience in itself. We'll perhaps go and stay at the hotel, or forget the whole thing.

Several weeks ago the American ambassador, his wife, and several others from Tunis came to Kairouan to look at the AID program there — something about cattle grazing. The Am. couple in charge of that program had a dinner party for them and included the Americans living in the area. Besides the Bakers and us, there's a young single fellow and another couple, all of whom teach at the univ. — no, the wife doesn't teach. The couple, the Hoffmans, are actually connected with a mission, which they try to keep quiet. They're nice people. Back to the dinner party — it's the one really nice social event we've been to in Tunisia. It was a sit-down dinner for

25-30 people, and everyone seemed to have such a nice time. The next day the Dean of the Univ. had a reception at the univ. for the same group plus other teachers, etc.—I didn't stay for it but heard it was awful — nobody got to speak to the ambassador — the dean gave a long, boring speech. And they served the usual Tunisian fare: soda pop and Kairouan sweets. (Pretty awful, especially without coffee to wash them down.) I do hope the ambassador enjoyed them. That was our big event so far this year.

We may be asking to move into your Quonset if a different job doesn't come up. I have pretty well decided that I'm not teaching at Kairouan another year, and I may quit before this year's finished. Not sure Norman will leave here without another job. So if bad comes to worse, I may leave without him and see what I can find. I'm not insistent on teaching — not even sure I can cope with the average secondary school job, which is probably what I'd have to take. But I'd probably earn more by staying in teaching, and I would need to support myself. Something will work out.

Norman is asking whether you're interested in going to Cairo in the spring? Our spring holiday is Mar. 19-Apr. 3. Would you please check your calendar and let us know when Easter is? I'm quite sure Egypt is pie in the sky. We'd about as soon go to Italy. How does that sound? How was your Thanksgiving? I baked two pies — an apple and a pecan made with almonds—not too bad. We had pie with our bacon and egg brunch (bacon brought from Paris in Sept.) then ate out in evening with friends who then shared our pies.

Betty and N

Sousse, Tunisia
Saturday, December 12, 1987 (postcard)

Dear Elma,

It's hard to believe it's nearly Christmas. We plan to be in Paris with Tasha for two weeks. So eager to hear some good music, to say nothing of good food! Hope it's not too cold there! Teaching at Kairouan is a bit too much — won't go into details, but we both want out! Are thinking of China; an American couple we teach with taught in China and are going back — loved it. Wonder if Bethel would need us for a year or two if not longer — probably not. We enjoyed your letter so much; we think you should write a column for a newspaper. So sorry to hear about Katie — never guessed she was that ill when here. Have a really good Christmas!

B & N

Paris, France
Friday, January 1, 1988 (postcard)

Dear Lyla and Bill,

Thanks so much for calling on Christmas Day; what a nice present! We have had such a good time here. Church services, exhibitions (one of architecture and one of sculpture), and old movies. Wanted to go to the Orsay Sunday, but line was so long, went to Louvre instead. The Champs-Élysées is like a fairyland, with trees shimmering with white lights. We'll come back down to earth Sunday when we fly back to Sousse. Happy New Year!

Love,
Betty

Sousse, Tunisia
Thursday, January 21, 1988 (postcard)

Dear Lyla and Bill,

How did we miss this? [Postcard of Printemps Department Stores in Paris] Or did you see it in your wanderings? It's gorgeous! And every Tues. a.m. a fashion show is given for tourists. One enjoys orange juice, coffee, and breakfast rolls while viewing the new collection. A "beau experience Parisien!" Our weather's as usual — mix of nice sunny and chilly, windy, dusty days. Exams begin tomorrow — anticipate bad experiences. I have 250 to mark, and Norm, 350!!

With love, Betty & Norm

Sousse, Tunisia
Wednesday, January 27, 1988

Dear Elma,

It sounds like you've been having some freakish weather in the U.S. Hope your area hasn't been hard hit. I think ours has been fairly normal: several really nice, sunny days followed by at least that many cold, windy ones — but almost no rain. It's affecting the crops so that food shortages are predicted.

We're in the middle of term exams and at the moment I'm "invigilating" in a huge amphitheatre (the Ibn Khaldun); the exam is for the Arabic Dept., and the course is Logic — I wish some would rub off! They make such a big thing of exams here, and of course it is the all-determining factor and the students are skilled in cheating. But when helping in the Arabic Dept. and observing the nonchalance of the professors, I've learned not to get too excited about what goes on! Since every paper has to be graded by two persons, I have about 250 papers to mark, and Norm has over 300! It's really awful — so boring! I've just noted that of the 76 students taking this exam, 27 are girls, three of whom wear scarves — they are supposedly the fundamentalists. Only three of the 76 are left-handed, and all three are girls. Wonder if that indicates anything?? Most of these exams are four hrs. long, so you can imagine the amount of rubbish they can think up. One of the cleaning ladies just came around with coffee, so that's a nice touch. But it's so strong I can hardly drink it. I tasted, for the first time this morning, a hot, thick soup that's made with halvah; it's quite sweet, but good — perhaps it's their oatmeal.

We did have such a good time in Paris. The day after we arrived, we helped Tasha with a party she had for about 35 of her friends. Her little apt. was crowded, but it was fun. She was taking advantage of the place before giving it up on Jan. 10. We, too, were taking advantage of having a place to stay. Paris was so beautiful. Two Christmases in Tunisia had made us extra appreciative of the sights and sounds of the season. On Christmas Eve we had an early supper and then went to the service at the American Church, which was simply but beautifully decorated. And the music, vocal and instrumental, was excellent. Then we moved on to the Church of St. Germaine des Pres, which is beautiful — interesting architecturally — and stayed for part of their service.

Christmas day we spent at home — roast pork and apple pie were the main attractions of our meal. Then we walked to the Montparnasse area for a coffee in the evening. On New Year's Eve we saw an early showing of Gigi, a musical which takes place in Paris and was enjoyable. Then we walked the Champs-Élysées, which was a fairyland of lights. White lights decorated all the trees which line the street leading up to the Arc de Triomphe, which is always lighted. It was dazzling! Nearly everything about our holiday seemed nearly perfect! That is until we arrived at Orly and checked in; then we discovered that the plane hadn't yet left Monastir (the airport near Sousse). So instead of arriving here at 10:30 p.m., it was 1 a.m. I had to be in Kairouan to teach that morning.

Tasha is presently visiting us for several weeks — partly her winter break. When she gets back to France, she hopes to have a room in one of the university dorms.

Perhaps I mentioned in an earlier letter that we want out of here. We still do! Have written a few letters of enquiry, but know it won't be easy to find something. Norm is "almost" to the point of trying it in the States. But wouldn't that be a mistake with the economy the way it is, and the seeming abundance of teachers there. We sometimes think getting another overseas job would be easier from the U.S. than from here. We're considering China—we hear that they're hiring English teachers, but not sure we really want that!

Hopefully something will work out. I don't think we'll be here another year.

We're now into the 4th hr. of this exam, and a few have turned their papers in; others are getting desperate — smoking more — even asking me to borrow cigarettes for them from their friends, which I will not do!

Take care and give our greetings to Victor.

With love, Betty and Norm

Sousse, Tunisia
Sunday, March 13, 1988

Dear Lyla and Bill,

Our "plans" seem to change from one day to the next. Things here have gone from bad to worse at the university — the very low 1st sem. exam scores incited a strike, which has now dragged on for five wks. Among other complaints, the two of us "have not given them the proper information to get them through the exams." Actually, the system has built-in failure, so one can't much blame the students for being angry, but on the other hand, most of them worked very little. We often are tempted to clear out immediately, but then we figure our finances, and decide to hang on a bit longer — especially so long as we don't have to teach and can continue to collect our salaries.

As of now, I plan to come to the U.S. around the end of March for approximately 2 mo., dividing the time between Calif., Kansas, Texas, and perhaps Miami (my niece lives there now) and Washington, DC. It's possible to buy here one of the "hop-around" tickets for non-residents of the U.S. Norman thinks he will join me in May. I'm wondering whether it's better to start in Wash. and work westward, or the opposite. Weather-wise, I should start in L.A.

We've written several letters of inquiry to schools in the L.A. area and used your address, saying that it is the address of "friends who will be in touch with us." Please open any responses that may come, and send us only those with possibilities. It's unlikely that anything will come of this, but one feels he must give it a try. We have job offers from both Univ. of Istanbul and a university in Canton, China, but want to be open to other options which might come.

It was good to have Tasha with us for a few weeks. She's now in a dormitory for graduate students, which she thinks will be "okay." So we'll be staying right here during our spring break so that we can, hopefully, clear out before long.

Love to all, Betty and Norman

Sousse, Tunisia
Sunday, March 13, 1988

Dear Lyla and Bill,

We're sitting in the sun, which today is wonderfully warm. Our house has been so cold — no windows where the sun comes in — it's made for the hot summers! We notice in the Herald Tribune that L.A. is usually warm, and we think how much we want to come "home." Perhaps we can this time.

I think we'll go to either China or Istanbul in Sept., so have to work out where to spend five months — and how to afford doing it. Such a bore! Would love to come and spend time with you in L.A. (the only place I want to go to in U.S.A.), but have to get our university-issued air tickets renewed, and it's not certain that they will do it — although they were supposed to have issued it for a year in the first place, instead of the three months they h well, will go argue with them again! It'll be the third time I've renewed it!

We want to spend a couple months in Paris. Have a couple apts., these being offered to us, a month at a time, in July and August. Could go to Zurich, Switzerland, for two months, but don't want the 32 degree temperature of that place. It's bad enough in summer. Mountains become boring after a short time. The apt. there does have lots of books I like to read! She's on a trip to China. (Hopefully she'll ask about the university where we have been invited to teach, near Hong Kong.)

I think what depresses me the most about coming home to the States is the feeling that I'm "poor relation" visiting the pseudo-rich (Kansas?! Texas? N.M.?!) relatives. You're the only ones I don't feel that way about. Guess I should have been a businessman.

Love, Norm

Sousse, Tunisia
Sunday, April 17, 1988

Dear Lyla and Bill,

BJ will come on to the States on the 7th of May. She may stay in East and Dallas before coming out. Then after the States, in July and August, will go back to Paris to be with Tasha before going on to Canton, China — unless some wonderful job appears before that!

Can you imagine our going to China? I can't!! The nearest I've wanted to be to China was near Olvera Street! But Hong Kong may be rewarding and China may be interesting. However, just read Nien Chen's Death and Life in Shanghai, and its description of life under the Cultural Revolution is so horrible I can hardly imagine those people changing. Well, guess the Germans changed! But ... ??

Tasha seems to be enjoying her life in the dormitory — sort of — meets a few interesting people. Preferred her apt.!! She'll house-sit (with us) a friend's apt. for the months of July and August.

Eager to see you all.

Love, N and BJ

Sousse, Tunisia
Saturday, May 7, 1988

Dear Lyla and Bill,

I'm flying to Paris today for a few days with Tasha, then on to Wash., where I'll see Marie W. for a few days before going to Arlington, Texas. Looks like it will be June before I reach L.A. and I trust that Norman will have caught up with me by then. Thanks for forwarding the City College letter, and the one from Northridge which, however, didn't get here. It's getting hot here, with lots of wind. Hope to see you before long.

Love, Betty

PS: Didn't know that N was also writing.

Sousse, Tunisia
Saturday, May 7, 1988 (postcard)

Dear Lyla and Bill,

I am putting BJ on a flight to Paris ... and on to Garden City with Kathleen for Memorial Day when, hopefully, I'll join her — and on to L.A. I'll stop in Las Cruces to see Alice & Liberal to see Mother. How I hate all this!

Love,
N

Washington, DC
Friday, May 13, 1988 (postcard)

Dear Lyla and Bill,

Had a good three days with Tasha before coming on to Wash. This is an exciting place. Took the Metro to the Mall today and visited three museums. I didn't know that Whistler's Peacock Room is here — fantastic! Plan to do the

Nat. Gallery and Library of Congress tomorrow. On to Texas the 17th. Look forward to seeing you.

Love, Betty

Paris, France
Friday, July 29, 1988 (postcard)

Dear Lyla and Bill,

The city is wonderful as always, sometimes hot! Really enjoyed our month with you. Thank you again and again! Repacked our six bags into four in Washington and checked them on to Paris. Tasha met us, we stored bags after shuffling stuff again, then Metroed to apt. The six floors (7 American!) are killing me. Every time I come down and Metro around and return up I am dead for two days! Tasha and BJ are ok with them.

Tasha still likes her Am. Express job. Nothing is happening at Disney; don't seem to know anything about Tasha or me. She will apply again. Tickets came for us Paris-Peking-Canton Aug. 24-25.

Love, N, BJ

CHAPTER 9

CHINA (1988 – 1990)

Summers in Paris, To Guangzhou via Beijing,
Various After-Thoughts

SUMMERS IN PARIS

In 1988 when we became disenchanted with teaching in Tunisia, North Africa, following the advice of our University of Kairouan colleagues Prof. Don and Mrs. Beth Baker, Prof. Emeritus University of Colorado, Boulder, we applied to the South China Normal University, Guangzhou, China, just north of Hong Kong. The Bakers had taught in China and strongly recommended our teaching there; we preferred to be where it was warm, rather than in cold Wuhan where the Bakers had been. South China Normal wrote back inviting us to join their English Department; BJ was to teach English writing skills, and I was to teach Graduate MA students in English Literature and History of English Literature.

But, first we went to Paris to be with our daughter, Natasha, who was a student at the Sorbonne, studying History of Art and later teaching English. Natasha found an apartment for us, the home of a teaching colleague, who was away for the summer. It was on the eighth floor near the Nation Metro stop. We took with us a folding bed we had purchased and used in Athens, which had also been so handy in Tunis and Sousse, Tunisia. Natasha was then working at the Paris American Express Office across from the Paris Opera House. We also had many suitcases of books as well as the usual clothes, etc. that go wherever we settle; most of our things which we had earlier shipped from Beirut to

Tunisia had to stay behind, stored by friends, and later becoming gifts to friends, as well as stored on the roof by our landlord Mohammad.

During our three years in Tunisia, we had enjoyed several Augusts in Paris, staying in the apartment of good friends first of Natasha and then of ours, Arianne and Jean Marie. Their huge apartment was one-half a block directly in front of the British embassy, just off the Rue Fauburg St. Honore. Our responsibility was to take care of their handsome Persian grey male cat named Mimi — a shortened version of his real name. During the almost ten years that we stayed, off and on, with Mimi, his health deteriorated. Our Paris friends used to take him along on their sailboat for the month of August, sailing around the Mediterranean. Mimi had grown too old to be a part of the sailing crew. Several years after we no longer went to Paris from China, Mimi died and was replaced by another cat, who is a good sailor and sails the Mediterranean with his human family.

But in 1988 we stayed without Mimi in another part of town: Nation. We waited for the ticket issued by Air France on behalf of the university in China. It took a long time, and when it finally arrived, very late in the summer, there was no confirmation of extra baggage. We gave our portable Mediterranean-traveled bed to a friend in the same Paris building, who was redoing her chamber de bonne (one room studio apartment) and could use the bed for guests. An excellent extra bed for a guest, purchased in the Athens Plaka market some years before.

TO GUANGZHOU VIA BEIJING

We taxied our nine bags to the Paris airport, and they issued our tickets. When the excess baggage ticket was issued, it was not for enough weight, since we were bringing a lot of books for their English library. (This was before China became very capitalistic and earned lots of money.) Finally after telexing and telephoning, the voucher arrived, and we were able to check in for the flight. We were a little surprised that it was on China National Airlines (CAAC: known by some as China Air Always Crashes; we trusted that would not be true that day — it wasn't). An early Boeing 747, which was wonderfully almost empty, provided a lot of room to stretch out for a very long flight. Fortunately the flight had a stopover in Sharjah, the Trucial Gulf States. There was no war that year in the Middle East, so it was nice to re-live for a few minutes memories of our eighteen years in the Mid-East. Then we returned to our CAAC half-way-around-the-world flight. We landed in Shanghai at the old airport, far out of the city. After a short stop we were flown to Beijing. This was to the old airport with very its old — very shabby —terminal. We deplaned and went through Chinese passport control. Our visas had been issued in Paris, I guess, although I remember meeting someone from Hong Kong when we went to the Wilshire Boulevard Chinese consulate, so maybe we went back to Los Angeles before going to Paris. (There have been so many trips it is hard to keep them straight.) We could find no luggage carts until BJ managed to get past the customs area to find two — more like miniature grocery carts than luggage carts — and bring them back again past the customs counters. I was then told to take our nine bags to a little room in the corner of the terminal to check them for the night at the overnight luggage storage. I carried them to the little room (this was before suitcases had wheels on them). An oldish lady in a grey Mao suit instructed me to lift the bags up to the vacant spaces on the shelves around the room. This, of course, was all communicated with gestures, since neither of us could speak the other's language. I pushed all but one of the suitcases into the upward shelves. My back, already in difficulty, grew steadily worse. Then she handed me a large roll of pink plastic ribbon — used all over China for tying packages — with which I was to tie the nine suitcases together. So I added more pink ribbon to the miles of it which already criss-crossed that room. She was happy. I'm sure that all of this has changed by now with Beijing's new airport.

After nearly giving up, we were finally met by two young men from the Education Department who drove us to the Friendship Hotel and dropped us off for the night. This, our first entre into the hotel world of China, was an interesting old building around a courtyard. The facilities were basic but adequate. We enjoyed a night of rest. Although I can rarely sleep at night, I was so tired I was able to sleep a few hours.

The same young men drove us back to the airport the next morning, and we checked into the flight, after I retrieved our heavy bags from the upper- shelves of the luggage storage room. (The pink ribbon did help in locating them.) We found one of the pseudo-luggage carts and pushed and carried our bags over to the check-in counter. The very nice young lady took our tickets and processed them. She then told me to take all the papers to another little room that had a tiny window that was closed with a screen-wire door that could be opened or shut from inside. Later I learned that most official offices in China have this tiny, 18-inch square window through which business is transacted. So I bent over to the four foot high window (I am 6'3") and spoke to the very disagreeable older woman behind the screen wire. She opened the door and demanded my papers. I gave them to her and watched all the transaction — all over the world we have learned to watch the papers; they may disappear. She grabbed the papers, continued sitting at her table, and started working on her abacus. She handed me a paper on which was written the amount of several hundred dollars and demanded I pay that amount in dollars and shouted "overweight." I said, "No, the overweight is paid all the way from Paris to Guangzhou." Guangzhou is ninety miles north of Hong Kong; Peking is 2,000 miles north of Guangzhou.

I said, "No!"

She shouted, "Yes!" and held up her hand. I certainly did not have the money, and Air France assured us before we left Paris that the overweight was paid for all the way. She slammed shut her screened door and went back to reading her book (a romance, I suspected), and did not give me a clearance form. I just kept praying, "What shall we do, Lord Jesus? Guide us in Jesus' name."

I walked back to the nice check-in girl, and she simply handed me our boarding passes, and pointed to the waiting area. I said to BJ, "Let's go." She wanted to know what happened. I said, "Later." We sat near the door, and I cringed every time the public address system shouted out announcements, fearing they were going to say "Dr. Lofland." The door opened, and we all rushed to the plane — a new Boeing 737. It was a mess inside, with packages and smaller bags in the aisles and no assigned seats. We found seats across from each other, with BJ one seat ahead of me on the left. As the plane took off and headed upward, the overhead storage bin above BJ opened and one of the very hard surface business bags slid out of the storage bin. I uncoupled my seat belt, jumped up, and caught the heavy bag just as it left the bin, saving BJ a headache or worse. Thank God!

We arrived in Guangzhou a few hours later after being served our box lunches and having all the lunch boxes strewn around the plane, since the boxes and rubbish were not collected. The attendants looked lost as they did (not) do their jobs. It was lovely weather as we landed in Guangzhou, the same day that another China Airlines plane overshot the Hong Kong landing runway at Kai Tak Airport. Later we heard many stories about the air travel industry in China, such as one flight that all of a sudden landed at an unscheduled stop. The people asked why? The attendant said, "The pilot needed a nap." Well, better to take a nap rather than fall asleep at the "wheel."

The next day we learned that all of China takes a nap between 1:00 p.m. and 3:00 p.m. The air service has greatly improved due, no doubt, to the hiring of Foreign Experts (our official position) who oversee the problems. Now, sixteen years later, China has pulled ahead of much of the world. The working industries, and everything else, have constant outside help, bringing them out of the nineteenth century and into the twentieth century. Maybe they will surpass most of the world in the twenty-first century, now that they have greater confidence in their working skills. But it looks as though China's agriculture may remain in the eighteenth century.

VARIOUS AFTER-THOUGHTS

It is great fun watching (sometimes joining) the ballroom dancing held nightly on this campus. Couples glide around the floor to the music of yesteryear, re-orchestrated by newer Chinese orchestras; the waltzes are lovely, as are, I suppose, foxtrots (don't really know what they are) and other vintage steps; tango and rhumba are popular, and sometimes rock and roll. BJ becomes most tired of sleeping under quilts that are terribly heavy — cotton-filled two inches thick. Fortunately, although we left many select things in Tunisia, the electric blankets did arrive here. It gets cold at night even in this climate. Bedding, in general, is strange here. The Chinese bottom sheet looks rather like a tablecloth; a British friend described it as a curtain! The top sheet looks like a huge beach towel. A graduate student went out and bought for us white cotton fabric and had two lengths sewed and hemmed into a top sheet.

Diapers are almost unheard of in this country; clothes with slits in the needed places substitute for Pampers.

There is no Rh-Negative blood in China; the locals don't seem to have it. Friends who were expecting their second child went to Hong Kong for the last month before delivery since she might need blood.

As I sit here on the balcony, two dirt moving tractors and about fifty men are spreading black dirt (coal dust, some of it) all around the ball field, especially on the running track. It's the first time I've noticed mechanical dirt movers, usually it's men and women with two-wheeled wheelbarrows. There is no use of animal power here in Guangzhou, although we noted some in Beijing. Here, all animals are eaten.

In our house we have a double bed (crowded for both of us), supportive chests (no drawers), desks, chairs, and two easy chairs with matching sofa. Sofas are back, having disappeared during the Cultural Revolution!

It is forbidden in China to have girlfriend/boyfriend relationships, but the administration on this campus is concerned that students are spending more time walking around holding hands and lying in the grass than in studying. Noting how little they study, I sympathize with the administration.

CORRESPONDANCE (1988 – 1990)

Paris, France
Thursday, August 25, 1988

Dear Elma,

Thanks for your newsy letter. Your trip to PA sounds eventful; the bit about the car crashes esp. interesting. Your trip to W. Kansas must have been a let-down after all that.

Tell Victor I can't imagine anyone wanting to see that feed lot. (Always dreaded driving past it because of the odor.) Norm is feeling better, thanks to the French doctor, although medication is nearly the same as Chinese gave. My arthritis has gone away! Just a bit of joint stiffness. The Sturms and Morses have just informed us that they submitted our applications for a job at Tabor College: teaching and advising Chinese students. We'll know tonite if they want us. If not, we'll fly to Hong Kong Sun. the 27th.

Love, Betty and Norm

Guangzhou, China
Sunday, October 23, 1988

Dear Lyla and Bill,

There's so much to write that I hardly know where to begin. Norman has intended to type up a form letter, but I'm giving up on him. This is the most unusual place we've been — as we expected. There's so much that's new — they're madly trying to modernize — but there's also so much that's ancient. They still carry loads in baskets or buckets suspended from a bamboo pole across the shoulders. So much labor is done manually. A construction site is nearby, and the heavy labor is done by women (a pregnant woman pushes a wheel barrow) and the skilled work by men. There's an electric cement mixer which runs most of the time between 7 a.m. and 6 p.m. just outside our bedroom window.

Our housing is sub-standard (by U.S. standards) but not too bad. The kitchen is definitely a disaster, and bathroom's ugly: pipes all showing and dreadful curtain strung on a string, etc. But it all works okay! A green, medium-size refrigerator graces our living room (no room in kitchen) plus a large color TV! These — esp. the color TV — are status symbols here. So we have hidden the fridge behind the TV, which stands on a cabinet. And we do have a sofa (they were outlawed during the Cultural Revolution) and two chairs covered in brown Naugahyde — comfortable, and not bad looking. The walls are painted pale green and there are plain green cotton curtains throughout the apt. Feel lucky that nothing's patterned. The floor's the worst: big square gray tile that looks dusty no matter how often it's washed.

The study has two desks and two bookcases and a hall tree [that held coats and hats]. The bedroom actually looks the best. The mosquito net, attached to a wooden frame fastened to each corner of the bed, gives the effect of a four-poster with canopy. There are a medium and small wardrobe (good looking) and two bedside tables. We came prepared with several white paper lanterns and what did we find but fluorescent lights! We bought an attractive table lamp for the living room and have placed it on one of two interesting plain green pottery pedestals we found in a storage area. We bought a jasmine plant for the second pedestal. Norman was given a painted scroll for giving a lecture, so it hangs on the wall — not bad. I received an atrocious geegaw: shrimp carved from animal horn. A Chinese friend brought us several silk tulips in an iridescent vase and insisted that we must not remove the patterned cellophane covering! But there are some very lovely things in the stores.

The kitchen has three two-ft. shelves, two sq. ft. of work space, a two- burner gas hot plate, and a small square sink that's about knee-height. (Norm thought it was a misplaced urinal!) Our building has extra rooms which operate like a hotel. The meals served in the dining room for foreign teachers and guests, which is next-door, are okay — sometimes delicious and other times not so good. But they'll have to get pretty bad before I try to cook.

The Friendship Store (mainly for foreigners) has quite a few non-perishable type imported items: Planters peanut butter, Corn Flakes, oatmeal, Tang, Nescafé, Ovaltine, good local crackers. In these stores one pays in foreign currency, or 40% extra is added to the price in local money.

Several of the big hotels have delis which sell imported food like cold cuts, Kraft cheese slices (only kind of cheese we've seen here), butter. No butter or cheese made in China. Of course, these imported items aren't cheap. Even the local things are more expensive than we were led to believe. Inflation is a real problem — don't see how the Chinese manage. There is an entrepreneur class now that's doing well — most of our students don't want to teach (we're at a teachers' college, South China Normal Univ.) but go into business. At this point, the govt. hasn't given them that option. Of course the govt. provides their education free. Teachers and other professionals such as doctors are some of the lowest paid. So in general, our students are rather discouraged about the future and use this as an excuse for their lack of interest in their studies. These students' level of English is the lowest of any place we've been. They're used to doing so little for their courses that a 15 page reading assignment puts them into a state of shock. These are seniors I'm talking about. They've read no novel or full-length play in English, (nor in Chinese I suspect — some have told us that reading is not in their culture) only summaries accompanied by Chinese translations. They do not read. All their extra time is spent in sports activities. This campus has a phenomenal amount of athletic facilities. But the students do all attend class (without any roll- checking), listen attentively, and are friendly. They're most interested to hear about the outside world — especially about life in America. All of us foreigners (6 Americans and 2 Japanese) are being asked to give talks for this-and-that student group.

I share with a Chinese teacher a course called Intensive Reading and Composition for Seniors. The book is good — used with freshmen or sophomores in the U.S. The book contains 1-3 page essays by good writers. The Chinese man gives one lecture in which he explains the essay word by word. Then I'm to give them, in a lecture, the answers to the analysis and organization questions (which the students should be answering for themselves). I then assign the composition (in which they're to apply the principles illustrated in the sample essay) and mark all of them (100 students and they're to write every two weeks). Students are required to do very little real thinking, and it shows in their compositions. Write mostly shallow trivia —unable to deal with ideas.

Norman says his grad. students are considerably better, but he teaches History of English Lit. to the seniors, and it's a real drag for they've read almost nothing — have no background to help them deal with this sort of course. Don't seem to understand concept of good vs. evil. (I must review what Buddhism entails — of course most of these kids have grown up in an atheistic climate). But how can they avoid good and evil? Of course they don't know who Satan is — and yet they're 4th year English majors! Surely it's, at least partly, a language problem. It is a challenging experience. One can quite often work in concepts of Christianity and free thought, etc. My Chinese colleague last week in his lecture repeated at least five times that Wm. I, on his death bed, "commended his soul to his Captain, Christ." I began to wonder if he were maybe a Christian.

Have now visited both an official and an underground Protestant church — interesting — will write more about that in next letter. Hope you manage to tape Jewel in the Crown. Would love to see it.

With love, Betty and Norman

Foreign Experts Building, South China Normal University Guangzhou, Guangdong, People's Republic of China Saturday, November 26, 1988 (Christmas letter)

Dear Lyla, Bill, Tate, Todd & Courtney,

In early September we left Paris for China. That was after weeks of wondering if we were ever going to get our overweight paid for so we could get through the Air France check-in to board the CAAC Chinese airlines to depart for Beijing.

Finally they approved it in Beijing and money was sent to Paris' Air France who does all the bookings for China. We left Paris on a 747 with good service, not Pan Am nor Air France, but quite okay; four meals and three movies passed the time along with stops in Sharjah, in the Emirates on the Persian Gulf, and Shanghai. Beijing Airport was colossal frustration, because all that day's flights to Guangzhou (Canton) were full, so we had to wait until the next day. The airport is most inconvenient: no redcaps (demeaning work) and the midget-sized carts are extremely scarce. So we managed to transfer our bags to a disaster area known as the left-bag room where we searched out empty spaces, usually high overhead, and Norm, climbing over piles of bags, squeezed ours in and attached them with a pink string while the woman in charge shouted what we thought was encouragement. After paying three times the official fare to get into Beijing, we paid a western price for a rather bad, though new, hotel. The next day, after a quick tour of Beijing by taxi, we flew on to Guangzhou where the airport was similar, but we telephoned our university and they sent someone to pick us up. In Paris, Air France had said it was impossible to get confirmation on any CAAC internal flight; one had to wait until he was in the country. We have learned that it's true; many persons traveling through our Foreign Residence Building have found that they are delayed because, while tickets were requested in advance, they are not available until one is on the spot. A real nuisance for busy travelers who come to China to advise the local university departments on how to better-know and teach their subject by listening to frustrated "experts" giving lectures and using slide projectors with no electricity to make them work, or no room dark enough to see the slides. These are problems mentioned frequently at the lunch and dinner times when we are all together comparing notes. There also have been references to the fact that China has bought equipment from Europe or America that it cannot use, computerized scientific equipment that would not be bought for European or American universities because it is too big or too complicated to operate. China has it, but it sits in a room which has to be entered without shoes, and dust removed to keep the equipment clean — although it is to be used for measuring tree samples or dirt samples or something necessitating getting the area dirty. Then when one is allowed to look at it, and asks to see it operate, there is no electricity to run it. And a special professor sits at the machine all day to look after it, but cannot make it work. NO ONE KNOWS HOW TO USE IT! We repeatedly hear this kind of thing. And once the machine is operating, it does not continue to do so because there is no maintenance contract with the purchase to keep it running, so the owners are always angry with the West because they sell China expensive pieces of equipment which break down and cannot be repaired.

But all this is well in advance of what I wanted to say in this letter, which has taken months to get into the typewriter. These past weeks we've had access to a word processor, but have had problems getting the information to go in correctly, and cannot correct the errors I am constantly making, so now BJ is giving it a try. Back to our arriving in China.

A dear friend in Zurich, who had just come back from six weeks in China before we came, told me on the telephone while I was standing in the rain in a phone booth in Paris, "Norman, it was a challenge from A to Zed!" How right you were, Lotti; a constant challenge! Never, in the other frustrating places we've lived, has it been more difficult to get things done. I have always felt good about remaining abroad — making what contribution we can; anyone can do our jobs in the States. But for the first time, I'm beginning to re-think the whole experience. Los Angeles and Paris this past summer were too beautiful to resist forever. We must return and enjoy our favorite cities for a while.

But, you ask, what is China like? Now I know why Lotti said, "Go and have your own experiences, Norman and BJ. I cannot describe what you will encounter." Truly it is different! We look out from our balcony over a sports field filled with students — hundreds of them — actively engaged in soccer, handball, tennis, 100-meter runs, pole-vaulting, shot putting, all going on at the same time. The Chinese are obsessed with physical exercise. This campus has an amazing number of sports facilities, and they're nearly always busy. One huge shed-like building is filled with ping pong tables! Older people do the slower-motion chee-gong exercises (Norm refers to these later). Mao was determined to change the long-robed-philosopher-with-mincing-steps image of the Chinese to one of strength and action. A popular big-character slogan is "Life Depends on Movement." If the students sat still and read for half the time that they spend in motion, our jobs would be easier and more enjoyable! Bicycles roll along en masse in front of me (I'm still on our balcony); they sometimes make walking a bit of a hazard, but one gets used to them. It is rather like Tehran traffic in that one simply stands still and lets the bicycles glide past rather than attempting to dodge them. China has few privately-owned cars; much of the often-heavy traffic consists largely of small and large trucks. Many major streets have special bicycle paths, but even so, there are many traffic accidents and fatalities.

When one goes off the campus (this one is quite large: 8,000 day-time students and another 8,000 at night, but not every night, to study in the open university and via correspondence, meeting with their professors perhaps once a month), it is another world because of the heavy motor traffic. It takes almost an hour to get to the center of town, a city of eight million.

Life in the Foreign (Residents) Building is fairly interesting in that there are eight "experts" in residence, all teaching in the Department of Foreign Languages; six are Americans teaching English, and two Japanese teaching the language that now is more popular than Russian, but not as popular as English. Russian has dropped to the bottom of the list, not quite; perhaps French and German are lower in popularity; English has jumped to the top of the heap. The English craze sprang up with China's open policy introduced ten years ago. How shall I describe that interest in English? Well, I think it is simply that they all want to get out of here and if they can learn English, it might help them to do so. English has also become the key to success in China.

The students adore practicing their English with foreign teachers, (they have on our campus complete freedom to visit foreign teachers' apts.), but this practice generally amounts to the teachers doing most of the talking. They're very curious about what it's like in the U.S. "English Corners" have sprung up mainly on university campuses — Guangzhou Public Library has one also — where people meet, always out of doors, to converse in English. If English-speaking foreigners show up, they're immediately swamped by students and questions. On our campus, 50-100 students (mainly non-English majors) meet in a garden every Friday night. So there's this kind of interest, but our fourth-year English majors aren't interested in solid academic work. They've read little in English (or in Chinese for that matter) and suffer mild panic if we assign more than ten pages of reading a week. The English level is lower here than at any place we've taught. Since they've been exposed to little literature, our students are generally unable to deal with ideas. However, Norman finds his graduate students better prepared. The Chinese teachers say, "Yes, the students are lazy; the standards are going down, especially in teachers colleges, because teachers are paid so poorly here that students have lost interest in teaching." Our students, however, are friendly and polite. They're so regular in attendance that no attendance checks are made, although it's required.

There's little interest in English Literature in this department, although it is the Department of English Language and Literature. The graduate program has more enthusiastic-than-other-times overtures. No, I go into each of the lectures believing it is the moment to enjoy Oedipus and Trojan Women and Lysistrata, as well as Hamlet; these are the offerings to the muse that we have pursued so far this semester. They seem to be getting the essence of these writers, though they often say things like, "There are so many big words!" Years ago someone said to me, "You want to act — be a teacher and you'll act all your life in the classroom." True, and the nuance of the voice seems to convey the attitude, the values, and the impact; it does help to be able to vocally interpret the material.

Besides two courses for graduate students, I teach History of English Literature to 125 fourth-year students (seniors). Most of them are majoring in translation or linguistics, so have read little literature. A few summarized things which have been translated into Chinese. I'm to lecture on subjects like Chaucer (only a bit), much of Everyman and Dr. Faustus, the Medieval Theatre and its influence upon Elizabethan writers, along with a solid introduction to Humanism and the Renaissance in English literature. It's extremely difficult when they don't understand certain basic concepts such as "good and evil." They sometimes say that they understand the words and the sentences, but don't know what they mean!

Our campus has at least three libraries which have English books; not many of them are available to the students, and thousands of volumes are falling apart because of the intense humidity. There is a sizeable collection of books sent out by Friends of China in America, many of which are being used. The Chinese use a rather obscure cataloging method with the first category, A, including only the writings of Marx, Lenin, and Mao. It was disappointing to learn that our senior students do not know how to find information in an encyclopedia. [But, now they have the internet — for research??!]

Shortly after arriving, I (Betty) went with Steve, another American teacher, to an unofficial church service. The public bus was crowded and slow, but cost only about 2 cents U.S.!

We had some difficulty finding the place — not a church building, but looked like two apartments on 2nd and 3rd floors with some of the walls removed — and were a bit late. There was no standing room: people filled the stairs and a few stood in the small street outside. A young lady suggested that at noon some would leave and we could likely get in then. So we walked about and drank a Coke (sounds so American, but it wasn't the corner drugstore); at 12 a few people did leave the church and we climbed to the third floor where people squeezed together to make room for us to sit. Both floors were crowded with rickety chairs and benches, all occupied; a closed-circuit TV screen allowed those on the lower level to see the pastor, a small, almost frail-looking man with a gentle, unassuming manner. (He'd never make it on the televangelist circuit!) He served communion to the 250-300 persons there. The place was too jammed to distribute the bread and wine in a traditional manner; trays were passed over heads and then from person to person. It was a moving experience, filled with the spirit of God's love and care. Oh yes, several songs were sung by a small traveling choir from Singapore. The pastor greeted people as they left; he spoke a little English and seemed genuinely pleased that we had come. Although the police have several times warned his church to close its doors, they are hesitant to force closure because the pastor (Rev. Samuel Lam) has become internationally known. Some time ago, Pres. Reagan sent him an autographed — by RR — Bible.

Then, several weeks ago two students took us to an official Protestant church. The attractive building has only recently been returned to the congregation, having been used since the Cultural Revolution for political purposes. We sat in the large balcony. The sanctuary, which could easily seat 700-800 people, had an airy, spacious atmosphere. We felt quite at home as the white-robed choir processed to "Holy, Holy, Holy" in Chinese, of course. Two women led the service. Our student, who has been there several times, says the regular pastors are men. The sermon, by the older lady — 70 or so — was about Joseph's experiences in Egypt. She referred to her ten-year imprisonment during the Cultural Revolution and stressed the importance of forgiveness and forgetting the past. The congregation included all ages: teenagers, young adults, family groups. (This was also true at the unofficial church.) This church has services on both Saturdays and Sundays, as well as a weekly Bible study. A Chinese American dentist, ostensibly here to set up a dental school but who is actually here to convert Chinese to Christianity, says he often attends this official church just mentioned. According to him, in spite of what is said about official churches preaching only the official line, this church really does preach the gospel of Christ. We sensed a warm, welcoming atmosphere. China does have restrictions on Bible distribution, but our univ. library has several, and the unofficial church had a stack of them.

The Friendship Store houses five floors of varied items both the local people and tourists like: imported food (such as we never had in Tunisia, but was plentiful in Beirut, and starting to have more of in Tehran before the revolution), clothes, carved furniture and screens, scrolls of art work (haven't found another collection of shrimp; perhaps it is unusual), few western-style paintings or sculpture, handicraft works: strings of jade, enamel ware in jewelry, cloisonné, boxes of various kinds, woodcarvings, rugs, fabrics, some indigo-dyed fabrics with patterns out of the Chinese tradition. On this campus students' art works are very nicely done; life drawings or now some excellent wood and linoleum-block prints with local colorful scenes: geese in a basket on the back of a bicycle with an umbrella over the head of the cyclist. Good subject matter. As I write this a boy rode past on a bicycle, holding two geese by the necks, with legs tied.

Living here has become a bit of a bore, I must say — even though you are perhaps a little excited by what you are reading, it is still dull. We are a bit far from the city and therefore limited to the campus life. Always before we have lived in the heart of the city and have had the activities of a busy city life to build upon, except for the time spent in Kairouan last year, but even so, we lived in Sousse, which was quite busy with its tourist life and hotel restaurants. Here it is only the restaurant-dining room of the Foreign Experts Building or the rather awful local establishment that some of the young Princeton graduates teaching here go to. I like the rather rustic ambience of that restaurant, but don't like the kitchen, which is unsightly in its dirt, but no more so than most other Chinese kitchens in such public eateries. The one in our restaurant seems to be cleaner. Or, one could go to the students' dining room, which has thousands coming into it, taking their rice bowls with them, filling it with rice or noodles, a little meat, some vegetables, and then off they go to their rooms to eat it in peace if not in privacy, since there will be as many as eight or more to a room. Those who eat in the dining rooms merely dump the remaining food onto the oilcloth table top and walk away after eating their fill; the last ones to use that table have difficulty in finding space to place their rice bowl while eating. A German visitor who has been traveling around was sick when he arrived here several days ago. He — an older man, a biology professor — says that our restaurant has the best food in China.

Several weeks ago I went across the boulevard in front of the campus to visit a dental clinic to have a tooth filled, which has lost a part of a filling. The professor of dentistry drilled it out and filled it, exclaiming all the time, "Where did you have this done?" I replied, "I don't know, it could have been Tehran or Beirut, or the U.S., but probably not Tunisia where I just had six teeth root-canalled and capped." The tooth seems to be okay, and it cost me $1.50. Amazing! (But, that is 10% of an average worker's monthly salary.) They apologized for its being so expensive since they had used material from Hong Kong to repair it! When I have had to go to the local clinic for help with a stomach ache, it has been free after paying the initial ten cents. And I got a lot of pills and several meetings with the doctors. The dental clinic is a part of a modern hospital, has eight dental chairs with doctors at them, with modified western-type dental chairs, with the service tray attached to the overhead crane-like extension of the small service sink. A portable drilling unit is rolled up beside the patient and the doctor drills from that unit. The service table was covered with rather old-looking bottles and cotton, stained with presumably-used-on-me-only medications. The professor who worked on me was very efficient and seemed to guide the other dentists.

Fortunately, this was not the type of dentist we heard about before we came to China: his chair sits outside the shops on the street and he pulls your tooth on the spot, without deadening medications and as a public presentation for anyone passing by. Probably costs more than I paid, incidentally, since he would be a private entrepreneur. The clinic on campus is housed in a quite run-down barracks-type building, with no equipment of any kind that I saw outside of bottles and pills and perhaps a scale, although a few days ago I noticed two trucks unloading something into the clinic, but haven't seen anything new inside. All the doctors are at small wooden desks all lined up like an old-fashioned office. The patient sits down at the chair next to the doctor's desk and hands him or her (only one male doctor here on this campus) the patient's registration booklet, which was the initial ten cents mentioned earlier. He asks for the symptoms, which have been relayed to the doctor for me by one of my graduate students in Chinese; he nods very kindly. (When I have been to the lady doctors, they just giggle because I ask for re-fills in my one word of Chinese and gestures and drawings of pills, but finally give me a refill.) All of this is written into the medical booklet, then I go off to the pharmacy or to the shot room — "with a new needle?" I asked.

Getting shots is interesting. When I had such a rash I couldn't stand it anymore, the clinic gave me a shot of something, no not with a new needle, although I did get a new one out of the sterilizer, to be sure. Before she removed the syringe, I noticed that she waved her unoccupied hand over the needle-syringe, which I later learned was part of a Chee-gong medical healing routine. I once went to a Chee-gong meeting; we were an hour late, but the Chee-gong master hadn't arrived. When she did, she was a ninety- year-old woman who had been doing the Chee-gong exercises since she was thirteen. She asked for a bit of Peking Opera music to do them by, but it was a sound of hard rock, so she said no, that was not right, so they gave her Frank Sinatra singing something about doing it all by myself; that seemed okay and to fit her experience, so she put out her hands directly in front of her as though she were going to zap you (which is a part of Chee-gong power) and she dropped her hands and touched the floor in one fell swoop, stood back up with a sweeping gesture as Frank crooned away, moved her arms into angular, then circular motions as though taking in the world and stopped "all by myself." Later I heard from our Japanese teacher friends that there was a demonstration showing the use of Chee-gong for "power." The palms were over a piece of paper, and the paper caught fire by simply aiming the palms at it. Perhaps it is true, but we've seen enough Chinese magic shows lately to suspect that it is a trick. Chee-gong is used as a self-healing treatment; seems to work.

Guangzhou, China
Tuesday, December 20, 1988

Dear Ones:

Just today received your Christmas card and letter. Wonderful to hear from you. Sorry Bill had such a time moving Mrs. Bartel, but glad she's in an apartment there. Is it in the same place where Tina Schellenberg lives? It was good to see them last year. And Todd!!?? Well, Todd can wear a different tie for each new girl; good luck to him! And to Court and to Tate.

I had wanted to go "home to L.A." for the break in February, but will go to Bangkok instead. Do you want to join us there? We fly Hong Kong to Bangkok 2 Jan. and return here 5 Feb. Then are off until Feb. 26th! Too much. May spend a few days in Hong Kong and Macau. Tasha may come in February for the rest of the year, if she has a job; otherwise probably go back to Paris after a couple months, although she is talking about going on to L.A. But, her friends who have gone back to Calif — who were doing well in Paris before — are now frustrated, looking for a job and saying, "Why did we leave Paris?" Sounds like her father. Have a Glorious Christmas!

Love,
Norm and BJ

Guangzhou, China
December 1988

Dear Elma,

We've had a long spell of sunny, pleasant days, although in Sept. and Oct. had lots of rain. The nites are quite chilly, and with no heating, the buildings are cold. Lots of people have caught the sniffles. The Chinese don't dress warmly enough. On Christmas Eve we plan to go to a choir program of Christmas music at one of the Protestant churches. Then on Christmas Day we're invited for dinner to some American friends at a nearby university. Her stove is a one-burner hot plate, so we will have a simple meal. After dinner, we'll all go to an open house given by a friend who works at the U.S. consulate where we will, no doubt, enjoy all kinds of American goodies, so that should be a pleasant change.

Norm's grad students are having a Christmas party for the foreign teachers, which is supposed to be quite Chinese. They're to entertain us with little performances of various kinds. We're having in 20-30 Americans, Chinese, and Japanese to sing carols one evening. If all come, our little place will be crowded. I've wracked my brain to plan refreshments. Have no oven, but will try my recipe for no-bake cookies without the marshmallows. Thanks to the friendship store, I managed to find tinned butter (New Zealand), Quaker Oats, peanut butter, and condensed milk. I'll also make some sandwiches of a spread from a local canned meat (an inferior version of Spam).

Yesterday we went with several others from our univ. by minibus to Foshan — only about twenty miles from Guangzhou, but it took almost two hours each way because of traffic. The outstanding attraction in Foshan is the ancient Taoist temple. Undoubtedly the most exotic architecture I've seen. Being here (in China) has made me more aware of how much Christianity and Islam have in common! Of course not the most important thing — Person, I should say. In Foshan we also visited factories for pottery — lots of figurines — for paper products — lanterns and various decorations. The city is known for its crafts.

In addition to my classes here, I'm teaching an 8-week course at the Part- time University in downtown Guangzhou; the course is British and American Cultural History as background for English study. The students are all employed at jobs requiring some English. They transport me to and from, and teaching the history is a pleasant change from my composition classes. But constantly having to make everything so simple, and s-l-o-w-l-y repeating, does wear one down.

I have two extra talks to give in the next two weeks, and Norm has one. Last week I gave a talk on Christmas customs in the U.S. — for 1½ hours. So I centered on Luke 2, and branched out to the secular activities, most of which tie into the first Christmas. I ended by having them play games like American children do at their school Christmas parties. They make small words from "Merry Christmas" and unscrambled a few seasonal words. Do American kids still do that? I don't know, but these college kids liked it! They do seem so young and naïve! Certainly different from the Arabs, who'd never want to hear about Christmas in the U.S.; instead, they'd want to hear about the CIA and who does this or that! China is a change. Many things are more difficult, but some are easier. At this time, things American are very popular here. They really don't know much that's going on in the world now or in the past. They (most of my students) like George Bush because he visited Guangzhou, I believe, when Nixon came.

Sorry we've been so slow in writing. It's been a trial putting this far-too- long form letter together. Getting copies made is not only an ordeal, but a bit expensive. So would you please share this letter with Elma and Lloyd? Also, would you please have two copies made — one for Sam Sturms and the other for my cousin, Mrs. Inez Koehn. Thanks so much. Hi to Victor. We're eager to hear about your Russian trip.

Love, Betty and Norm

Guilin, China
Tuesday, January 17, 1989 (postcard)

Dear Lyla & Bill, (Same temperature as Paris and no heat!!)
Thought you'd enjoy this card. Beautiful sight! The Chinese characters say "Fogs and rain covering mountains along the Lijiang River." The red stamp, of course, is the artist. My student friend, with whom I am visiting Guilin and Nanning, can't read it either. He's a nice young man; a good student who has taken five years off to do an MA (3 plus 2 yrs. at language school); he will get no increase in salary after getting it. Still $11 a month! Will meet his wife and daughter, age 3, tomorrow. Your big letter arrived Sat. Thanks. Loved it!!

Norm

Bangkok, Thailand
Wednesday, February 8, 1989 (postcard)

Dear Elma,
It's our spring festival holiday — 5 weeks! We came to Bangkok for 9 days and decided to extend, so are now on wait

list for Feb. 17. Tasha plans to come here from Paris on 12th and go back to China with us. She'll teach next term at our univ. It's so nice to be warm for a change. And the amount of consumer goods here is amazing — especially clothes are cheap. Copies of all the name brands. Lots of good food — not so cheap. Sounds like you're having terrible weather. Hope all is well.

With love, Betty & Norm

Guangzhou, China
Friday, February 24, 1989

We were waitlisted for 2 earlier dates, but nothing opened up. Since returning, we've had some cold days, but today is sunny and warm.

Last Saturday Tasha and I joined a bunch of foreigners who, every other Saturday, have what is called a hash — perhaps you're familiar with this activity. They go usually to the countryside and run a distance (we joined the walkers), then a lot of beer is guzzled, and they return home. This time it was a boat trip down the Pearl River to a town about 3 hrs. away. The town was quite interesting, with lovely surroundings. Saw lots of wonderful old boats and had a curry dinner on the boat.

Tonite we're going to a neighboring campus to join several other American teachers for a hot pot, which is rather like fondue bourgignon, except meat and various vegetables are cooked in a kind of broth, which at the end is drunk. Quite good, and is served during chilly weather at the little more or less outdoor restaurants

Later: The food last nite was really bad: a minuscule amount of pork, lots of tripe, boney fish, squid (tasted spoiled) and a huge mound of greens. The rice noodles saved the meal. I noticed that several persons ate little of the hot pot. Nora, the lady who arranged the affair, dashed out mid-meal with a severe stomach ache. The restaurant is attached to her apt.

bldg. We noticed that she had six bottles of Pepto-Bismol on her medicine shelf! So much of the food here is so bad!

Later: Yesterday, Saturday, the three of us did several hours of taping for the communications dept. We were shocked at some of the ridiculous material. Part of a student/teacher dialogue: "Do you think television can be used successfully in the classroom?" "Yes I do." "When were motion pictures first developed?" "Motion pictures were first developed many years ago." Our payment for the recording session was lunch at a campus restaurant, which can be quite good if the right dishes are ordered. For five of us were eight big platters of the wrong things. We asked for rice, and they brought a platter of fried rice — good. Then, as we were trying to get away from the studio, we discovered that dinner had been arranged for us at the same place. We had planned to go into town. So, after much discussion, it was decided that we would eat the dinner on Wed. I predict that there will be more awful dialogue to be recorded after dinner. Tasha swears that she'll read no more of them. So for supper we had hamburgers and hot dogs at a fast food-type place in one of the big hotels. Nice change.

South China Normal University Guangzhou, China
Friday, March 10, 1989

Dear Lyla and Bill,
We've just completed the second week of the new semester. I have one additional hour to teach, but no new preparation, so that's okay. Tasha teaches 14 hrs. of conversation and composition. She seems to be coping okay; lives with another American girl in the apt. just above ours. She brought along her roller skates — she's still learning how — and intends to skate and dance her way thru the next 4 months! We did enjoy Bangkok, but our stay became a bit long; Alitalia had only 2 flights a week, and when we decided to extend our stay, we couldn't confirm until last week.

When we arrived home last nite, Sunday, March 12, we were told that there's to be a bridal shower this afternoon for Jill, who taught here and lived in our bldg. last term. Tasha and I are invited. I really don't want to go — it's way across town at the White Swan Hotel, where she now lives with her fiancé who's with the U.S. consulate, but for several reasons I feel I should go. What for a gift? They're getting married in Hong Kong next week, and this shower must have been a quick decision.

Kathleen is arriving in Hong Kong Apr. 1, after she's toured China. T and I plan to spend a couple days in H.K. with her; then she'll be with us here for about a week.

Write when you can.

With love, Betty, N, & T

PS: Ariane Levystone, whom I think you did not meet in Paris, and husband are coming to Guangzhou Apr. 6, but won't be here more than a day or two. They plan to do a boat trip from here.

Guangzhou, China
Tuesday, June 20, 1989

Dear Lyla and Bill,

My classes have been finished for over a week now — and graduating students were a week earlier. They stuck around to get their diplomas, while many of the younger students went home early in fear after the Beijing massacre. Now the university has called them back to finish their courses, and it seems that most of them have returned. Needless to say, they're depressed. Most of them participated in the demonstrations, and especially the leaders are worried that they'll be tracked down and punished. One of the younger teachers, who's been trying to join his wife who is studying in the U.S., was foolish enough to march with the students and is now regretful. No doubt ruined his chances to go.

This whole fiasco has also ended our travel plans. It's difficult enough when things are normal. Also, the consulate has advised us to stay close to home. However, we continue to see quite a few western tourists in Guangzhou.

The doctors here have diagnosed one of Norman's problems, which he's had for at least fifteen years, as angina, a disease affecting the heart muscles. Perhaps it's deteriorated so that it's now more easily detected. He's on medication and told to rest completely for several weeks. Some days he feels pretty good, and others he has no energy and occasional chest pain. He goes back to the heart specialist (he's seen her only once so far) in a few days.

We're still hoping to go to Paris around July 15, but are somewhat concerned about all the stairs, walking, etc. Tasha and I plan to go to Hong Kong this week to pick up her plane ticket. She'll return to Paris July 7 and is supposed to have a job again with American Express. In spite of many frustrations, she seems to be enjoying herself here. She's taking guitar lessons with slow progress: sore fingers, Chinese book, too many onlookers giving advice in the dorm room where lesson is given. But she prefers to have the lesson in dorm because several interesting men live there. One of these men is helping her learn some dance steps. Another young man took her by motorcycle (sign of affluence) to a dance place called the Music Fountain. It's similar to the Dancing Waters of 1950s state fair events.

We've been to several elaborate banquets lately, but the food isn't that good. Chinese food in the U.S. is undoubtedly Americanized!

With love, Betty, N, and T

PS: Write to us c/o American Express, Paris.

Paris, France
Friday, July 14, 1989

Dear Lyla, Bill, et al:

The celebration here did not hold a candle to the Rose Bowl July 4th! Thank you. That was very nice. So was this, but not spectacular. This year we are in another of Arian's apts., 20 min. from St. Michel, and 10 min. from Tasha's cute Univ. room where she lives in winter. Although she's mentioned possibly teaching in China again next year! She starts working at American Express again tomorrow. No doubt China will look good to her then; the Chinese students are so docile — unlike the angry Americans (and French) who complain they can't get as much service out of their AMEX card as they want, i.e. Money!!! Cash!! No one complains in China. June 4th convinced them again of their position in their society. Strange and disturbing. I still can't discuss it, except to remember the hope before June 4th and the hopelessness after. We never saw the footage of Tiananmen Sq. except for before (students attacking soldiers) and after (soldiers cleaning up the Sq. — no bodies!) And the official line "nobody was killed (except for soldiers by students) by the PLA soldiers!" Isn't that amazing?! And they force it down China's throats! If we did not have the BBC and VOA and H.K. radio, we wouldn't have known about it. Some people had HKTV and saw the same footage you did — but we didn't — all controlled!! Sad!!

Oh, Bill, thanks for sending packet of early mail. They never arrived. We understand a huge amount of mail was burned last month in Beijing! Probably happens when they get a backlog! In Paris we went dancing in the streets on the 13th — night. [Night of Bastille Day celebration.] The squares around the city were set up with Firemen's balls. Great band doing oldies and newies on a great square. Loaded with restaurants. We ate at a wonderful Lebanese restaurant on a square overlooking the whole thing. Then went down and had coffees and creame de cassius with 7-Up. Joined frolickers who were shooting people with silly string. We must have injured the atmosphere with the spray cans. Then the 14th parade. We drove around on the city buses (a few worked, although most were stopped and re-routed) to see the Bastille Opera. Wild firecrackers were thrown under cars; fortunately, ours drove on!) The whole thing was fun. Wish you were here. Miss you.

Love, Norm, BJ, and T

Paris, France
Thursday, August 3, 1989 (postcard)

What lovely weather we're having — mostly warm, sunny days. The bicentennial has been interesting to watch — mainly by TV. I think we're enjoying the food here more than anything; really sick of the Chinese cuisine! But we do plan to go back for another year, but different university: Jinan University. Address otherwise the same. Norm sees a doctor here tomorrow—not been well. Chinese doctors say it's a heart problem. Hope you're in good health.

With love, BJ and Norm

PS: Back to China Aug. 25.

Paris, France
Wednesday, August 23, 1989

Dear Lyla and Bill,
We've seen two good old films: The State of the Union w/ K. Hepburn & S. Tracy and Arise My Love w/ Claudette Colbert & Ray Milland. Both excellent. Oh yes, also saw Holiday w/ K. Hepburn & Cary Grant. [It was always a thrill to go to Paris and watch wonderful earlier movies. Today, probably Netflix has competed with the tiny, charming Paris cinemas. Too bad!]

We had a good time with Kathleen, although it left me exhausted — but I'd not admit it to her. Wish you could have been here, too. She and I went to the fashion shows at both Galleries Lafayette & Printemps, but not so nice as before; they're crowding too many people in; there are so many tourists this summer. And they were still showing the summer collection, which was disappointing because we wanted to see fall things.

Yes, the chop says "Bartel" in stylized Chinese. It was Tasha's idea to add the Latin "B" ... Wish you could see the "shop" and street where it was made.

We fly to Hong Kong Sunday and hope to stay over a day or two before going on to Guangzhou by train. Right now the thought of China is a bit dismal; Norman is especially discouraged. I think the awful food and low pay are the worst things. Not to mention the political scene. With all the anti- western feeling, perhaps our jobs won't last all year. However, our university (did we tell you we'll be at a different one — just several blocks from our old one) has 60% of its students from Hong Kong, Macau, etc. — so it's generally less conservative than most.

You'll laugh at this: it seems that Lou Sturm called Tasha at work. Sturms have sent our resumes to Tabor College in Hillsboro, Kansas. They're looking for two people to run a new program for foreign students: one to teach English as a foreign language and the other to be a foreign student advisor. Lou phoned them and told them how wonderful we are! Norman did call Lou and agreed to phone Tabor in a day or two. I think nothing will come of it, but I think Norman is actually willing to go there.

Love and prayers, Betty and Norman

PS: Regarding the painting we sent you: It's by a painter whom Norman met when he went to Nanning. He uses the same technique as his teacher, one of whose works was given by the Chinese govt. to Pres. Bush on his inauguration. Hope you like it!

Jinan University Guangzhou, China
Monday, October 2, 1989

Dear Elma,

As you see, we've a different address; can't remember whom we've informed. Again it's the Foreign Experts Bldg., and they've asked us to use our apt. # on correspondence: #205. Our new university is only a mile or two from where we were last year. So far, we believe the move is for the better. I'm teaching three classes of oral English, one each of business writing, typing, and U.S. Cultural History — twelve hours a week, which seems to be a normal load for foreign teachers. Chinese teachers have only 8 hours. Norman also has 8. Public speaking for 4th year students and American Literature for graduates. Jinan is one of two universities set up mainly for overseas Chinese. Approx. ½ our students are from Hong Kong and Macau, with a couple from Thailand and one from Burma. We've had two full weeks of classes now, and things appear to be normal (whatever that means). We hear that there is unrest in places — put down immediately, of course, but no signs here.

This year we are lucky to get Hong Kong TV, and we see lots of protesting there. HKTV is restricted here. Only the tourist hotels and a few others have it. We didn't last year. We get CNN from about 3 p.m. - 8 a.m., which helps us to feel less isolated. Last week certainly was a social whirl — largely because of the PRC anniversary. No less than 7 invitations extended to foreign teachers (there are 10 of us) within seven days: an acrobatic show — excellent; small dinner party for Jinan foreign teachers given by the univ. vice-pres. — this just happened to come at this time; a women's tea given by Guangdong Women's Assoc. — called a tea but served skewered pork, fried chicken wings, ham and cheese sandwiches, French toast, and potato chips, which the Chinese at our table hadn't had before. Oh yes, the beverage was coffee. They were obviously trying hard to please the westerners; a big formal reception hosted by the Provincial Governor w/ lots of good food — carved ice and butter (wish we could buy butter!), a huge patriotic display at the sports arena, which we decided not to attend, and discovered it was on TV; lastly, dessert at the Garden Hotel's 30th floor revolving restaurant to watch fireworks — impressive. A lot of this activity was to impress the foreigners. I wonder what was done for the average Chinese. Our students did receive some extra meal tickets.

Norman is feeling better. While the French doctor prescribed the same medicine, it was in larger amounts. So now the Chinese doctors agree that he needs larger doses than their Chinese patients since he's about twice their size, and he's thin — not a fat American.

How was your garden this year? Have you ever seen green beans that grow approx. a yard long? They're great for snapping! There is quite a variety of vegetables in the big market, which is about five minutes by bicycle. Then there's a much smaller market nearby. Meat is the difficult thing — most of it tastes too fresh, or something. I've now found a place that sells western-style sausages — sort of like wieners — and sliced ham. I do find that I'm cooking more this year because we don't like the food in the dining room for foreign teachers (they do segregate)! There are a couple restaurants on campus, and we do go some, but expensive on our salaries. Our kitchen has one gas burner. The Chinese way is to cook one dish at a time, and eat everything cold!

Any trips planned? Do let us hear.

With love, Betty and Norm

PS: I'm enclosing a check for $5 to cover the expense of making those copies for us. Thanks!

Foreign Experts Bldg., #205, Jinan University Guangzhou, China

Friday, October 6, 1989

Dear Lyla and Bill,

I am watching CNN live from the Pentagon with the Defense Secretary; he's very good, it seems, as he answers difficult questions over the Panama pseudo-coup! One Hong Kong channel runs CNN all nite. But Hong Kong TV is very restricted here — only luxury hotels for foreigners have it, and we have it because our campus is mainly for overseas Chinese students. CNN's international hour is now on and showing the East Germany celebration while thousands of refugees flee to the West. Marvelous! Interesting to note Budapest — we visited that lovely city — and the communist star about to be removed from the parliament bldg.!! And all else — democracy is working there — great! Wish it had here! Don't know how Hong Kong can ever adjust to the life here. At least HKTV makes it less boring. Have never watched so much TV!

I'll add a note to N's letter. I'd hoped to have a little less to do this year, but no such luck. At least less papers to mark. I have one typing class (with Flying Fish brand typewriters!! a lot of which don't work), one business writing, one U.S. cultural history, and three oral English. And just today they've asked me to teach another two hours of extensive reading, whatever that is. This makes fourteen hours.

Last week we had lots of activities to celebrate the 40th anniversary of the PRC. Obviously backlash from the Beijing fiasco. We did have some really good food — especially at one quite elegant reception given by the provincial governor. There were huge butter carvings (wish we could buy butter in the stores) as well as ice carvings. The last affair was watching a fireworks display from the 30th floor revolving restaurant of one of the tourist hotels. Now we'll probably have no social activities until Christmas. Is Courtney majoring in studio art? Sociology? Tell her hi. Also Todd and Tate.

Love, Betty

Guangzhou, China
Wednesday, October 18, 1989

Dear Lyla and Bill:

How is Courtney? We are shocked! Just heard the news on Hong Kong TV. We are 15 hours ahead of you, so the San Francisco earthquake happened yesterday (17th Oct), is that right? 5:00 p.m. — rush hour. Unbelievable pictures of the Oakland Bridge. Why did they allow it to be built two layers? Thought such elevated highways were forbidden. New pictures (263 bodies) coming in now. "6.9 Richter scale. Shock waves felt in L.A." They recorded the shock in Hong Kong 14 minutes afterward on seismograph at Royal Observatory. That highway looks like something the Chinese would have built. (Scares me when we ride in a taxi on the one here; it's 2-layered!! No earthquakes here so far! But lots in China!)

On the 16th at noon the dept. chairman called and asked if we could go to "dinner at the Garden Hotel tonight at 6 p.m. with the vice-chairman of the standing committee of the Communist Party of Guangdong Provincial Govt.; we said "yes." We had met him briefly at the festivities of the 40th Anniversary celebration, and at that time he asked us, "Do you prefer Chinese or European style food?" BJ and I looked at each other. "Well, at the moment, we prefer European food." So off we went to probably the most elaborate French restaurant this side of Paris — marvelous food!! And because it is the Trade Fair time, they had roast beef — marvelous to us who had had lots of French food last summer! And French cognac all through the meal, which started with hors d'oeuvres of thinly sliced marinated beef, salami, ham, salmon, with half a boiled egg covered with caviar and wedges of pickles. Next, French onion soup (marvelous!); our chairman had turtle soup — I've had enough exotic food here in Asia!

Even the French variety didn't tempt me. After this a tall glass of lime sherbet served in molded ice shaped like petals of a flower to cleanse the palate.

Then came the trolley (not the Chop Stick trolley!) [a reference to a very basic but good Los Angeles Chinese restaurant] quietly pushed over the heavily carpeted restaurant arcade to our private section overlooking the city, from which we could see arch after arch "supporting" the ceiling. The waiter, whose English name was "Norman" — ah, what a night!! — served, after he sliced off handsome portions, the most succulent beef. (Except for McDonald's, we haven't had so much meat since leaving Tunisia, L.A., Paris!!) Great! After coffee and chocolate ice cream from Switzerland (the chefs are Swiss), we thanked our host and wandered out to the taxi rank to go home. Our host told us all the food is imported! The beef is from America!

He also told me that I earned three times more than he does, so I asked how he afforded to have us for this kind of a dinner. He said that he helped get this luxury hotel started, and remains on the board (I think) and they give him an allocation of a certain amount which he can use to invite people in for "goodwill." Wonder how much of his allotment we ate up! Only the main course would have been more than enough. Seeing the news on CNN over HKTV, I realized that it was the 17th (saw 16th on the screen) — and remembered our anniversary. So, we had our thirty-first wedding anniversary dinner a day early — instead of a week later, when we ordinarily would remember it; I was sorry I had not told the Chairman of the Standing Committee of the Communist Party of Guangdong and thanked him even more. So far, this year is better than last.

Love, Norm, BJ

Guangzhou, China
Monday, October 30, 1989

Dear Lyla & Bill,

Got your Oct. 19th letter today. Yes, we did see the interview of Peter Ustinov. Wonderfully fun. Not sure we saw all of it because it was recorded in Hong Kong by the carrier station and broadcast on another "wrap up" show, about ten minutes or so of it, all commercials cut.

Certainly, cut the painting in two — BJ and Natasha immediately said it should be cut into two pictures. I thought it should stay together and you could look at it and decide. Glad you like it. Chinese paintings tend to be tall and vertical, attached to a scroll, but my painter expressly said these should be framed.

We've covered our dirty walls with collages by Natasha and other visual fun, junky things, so it seems livable. People come in and, while talking, their eyes rove around. Amusing! Local homes are bare, empty, sterile, dismal.

[Sunday, November 5] Isn't it amazing that all this is happening in E. Germany and Hungary's new Republic of Hungary, dropping the "people's" part of its name. Over 100,000 mostly young people have fled E. Germany to W. Germany. Amazing! "Wonder how many will return," said a fellow Chinese professor, "because these socialist countries guarantee them jobs for life — not great salaries, but enough — and they don't have to compete with anyone as they will find in the West." Interesting!

A young graduate of last year's BA class stopped by tonight and went with us to dinner at the lakeside (Chinese of course) restaurant on campus. He's a nice fellow and trying hard to change jobs from teaching at his peasant father's village school (180 yuan a month, $30) to a factory job near Canton for 350 yuan a month. We hope he gets it — he is so depressed by his position in life. His father farms 0.6 of an acre of land, as does his mother and brother, a total of less than two acres of land growing two crops of rice a year, ploughed by a water buffalo and their hands, irrigated and insecticide-ed by ladling the liquid out of a barrel pushed between the rows of rice. All is sold and almost a living is left over: rice and vegetables and not often some meat. Sad. A graduate student from last year, 30 yrs. old, two-yr.-old son, husband, discovered she had liver cancer in June — was dead on Sept. 14. Am most depressed by it all. Thanks for writing. Love your letters.

Norm

Tuesday, November 7, 1989

Hi,

Will add to Norman's letter. We enjoyed the account of your New Mexico trip and envisioned the good food you undoubtedly had. Our food situation is about the same as last year, although there are a couple restaurants on the campus which have several pretty good dishes. Last weekend the univ. took the foreign teachers on an overnite trip to Shenzhen, which is what they call a special economic zone, where capitalism flourishes. There are quite a few joint venture businesses run by Chinese and foreign companies. We visited a bicycle factory, a Chinese/American joint venture, which was interesting. They make all kinds of beautiful high- powered bikes — all for export. Those for sale in China are all alike — black or dark green, one speed, and no accessories, not even lights. I've heard that it's illegal to have a bicycle light!? The streets here are so poorly lighted that I never ride mine after dark; it's dangerous enough in daylight! [At that time, the most popular light bulb was 40 watts. Awfully difficult to walk at night, but there is lots of moving around the grassy area, especially beside the rather charming lake next to our building; the frogs sing to the walkers and sleepers.]

Back to the trip — they took us to an amusement park that was obviously supposed to look like Disneyland — a few plaster Disney characters dejectedly stood about. But the evening was definitely a fiasco, for none of the rides were operating — only a couple gift shops were open. I understand this place is supposed to attract Hong Kong people. H.K. is very near to Shenzhen.

We also visited what they call "Splendid China" — a large park containing miniatures of many touristic spots in China. I've never really liked that sort of thing, and Splendid China reinforced my feeling. However, I did buy a pretty needlework purse there. The nicest part of the trip was dinner at the revolving restaurant in the World Trade Center — 49th floor. Good food and marvelous view of Hong Kong, South China Sea, rice paddies, etc.

We have been thinking about coming to L.A. during the Chinese New Year, which comes in late Jan. or Feb. But only if we can get courier flights. But we're afraid it won't be a good idea if you're going thru a crucial time — closing the shops, etc. We're also considering the Philippines or Malaysia. Please give us your thoughts on this. Your "shop situation" continues to be in our thoughts and prayers.

With love,
Betty

PS: Yes, there are some interesting postage stamps, but they're scarce, and we hear that whole letters sometimes disappear if they have interesting stamps!

Jinan University
Thursday, November 23, 1989

Dear Lyla and Bill,

Happy Thanksgiving! Would love to share the festivities with you. Hi to the whole family — it seems like our family!

Oh, my mother, Myrtle Schneider, may remember to send to you a small package with a ring in it for Natasha. Would you save it for her? My dad gave it to Mother when they were married (I think!?) and her second husband replaced the diamonds that were lost over the years, and now she has promised to give it to Natasha. She had asked if that was the best thing to do. I think so; get it out of her estate — if she has one. Thanks for doing all the crazy things for us.

Too bad the new 16-day-old president of Lebanon was assassinated — awful! Can only assume it was Aoun's men, even though it happened in West Beirut, unless I misunderstood CNN.

BJ is resting before we taxi downtown to the U.S. consulate for Thanksgiving Day: Turkey flown in and trained from Hong Kong, with trimmings coming from wives and guests. Last year there were about 80 partakers; some Chinese who knew nothing of the Pilgrims. Somebody played old favorites and we sang — and drank (some Chinese wine is very nice and dry) — and ate, and ate. Lovely change from the usual woked bones in pieces stir-fried with what's in season we usually get. [We were told a tasteless joke of a book entitled "Woking Your Dog."]

BJ has been cooking more this year. [BJ rides her bike a mile to the market and loads what she can carry on it and pedals back.] We just can't take the local food. Someone cooks garlic in smoking peanut oil daily just below our apt., and the smell is staggering! I cough and cough!! Open the doors to air the place. Weather is lovely here, like L.A., CNN tells us.

Love, Norm and BJ

Foreign Experts Bldg., #205, Jinan University Guangzhou, China
Christmas 1989

Dear Friends,

This second year in China seems almost like a new trip. While most things remain the same, some changes make life more pleasant; for instance, Western TV from Hong Kong gives us (as our Chinese co-teachers say) a window out of this insular land. The Chinese news service hasn't yet (we understand) reported the Eastern European call for democratic change. The June 4 tragedy is seldom mentioned — people are afraid to discuss anything political. Last year, our students and co-teachers were much more open. However, we sense no change in their attitudes toward us or foreigners in general; they continue to be friendly and helpful. They also appear to be quite happy and contented with their day-to-day lives. But so many of them are trying to get to the U.S. Australia is another popular destination. A good friend, a young medical doctor, left this week for Sydney to study English, hoping then to do an advanced degree in medicine, and then, who knows? He had just received a promotion here, which actually meant much more work for no more pay, which was 40-50 yuan ($12-20 on black market, the only way to change to dollars) per month, the same as teachers' pay.

One more bit about Hong Kong TV. (Strange how this has become a rather important change in our lives, when we've lived without television for so many years.) Perhaps that's partly the reason: it's been fun to catch up on the films and TV series of the past ten years as well as some classics of Hitchcock and others. CNN's daily news coverage is well done, although Norm must be the only person in Guangzhou that watches U.S. daytime news much of the nite, live from the States. We understand that since June 4, the government has further limited the privilege of receiving HKTV to tourist hotels and very few others. So, who knows when ours may be cut off. The only reason we have it is that Jinan is set up mainly for overseas Chinese students, and approximately half our students are from Hong Kong and Macau. They are to be kept happy, for their hard currency is needed. We have decided that working with mainland Chinese students is more interesting and rewarding.

Although the Chinese do love Christmas festivities, there is no actual holiday then; the big one comes between semesters, during the Chinese New Year. It's difficult to travel in China then since everyone is doing it; also, we felt the need for warmer temperatures and change of diet, so decided to go to Bangkok. Loved it! Natasha joined us there and came back to Guangzhou with us for the second semester. She taught

English in our department and lived in our building, sharing an apartment with another American teacher. [It was so cold I ran an electric wire from our shared electric converter out the window to her bed upstairs, above our bedroom, so we could run an electric blanket for Natasha. I used the other one; BJ found it too warm. I added a "ming toi," a very heavy quilt, on mine. I was so cold!] She had mixed feelings about living in China but says that, in retrospect, it definitely was a good experience. After the Beijing problem wrecked our travel plans, Natasha returned to Paris to her summer job at American Express. Now she is taking several classes at the Sorbonne and teaching part-time.

We followed Natasha to Paris for our summer holiday, arriving just in time for the Revolution Bicentennial. Fortunately, we were able to stay in the apartment of good friends, Ariane and Jean Marie — otherwise we couldn't have afforded Paris. BJ's sister Kathleen, who lives in Dallas, joined us for ten days in Paris; she also visited us in Guangzhou last spring. How lucky to have a sister who likes to travel! Our family has been very fortunate; although we've often been separated by great distances, we have managed to spend quite a lot of time together. God has been good to us!

We hope that each one of you will have a Very Merry Christmas and will be richly blessed in the New Year, 1990!

With love, Betty and Norman

Guangzhou, China
Friday, December 8, 1989 (back side of Christmas letter)

Dear Ones,

Our first Christmas party, which we didn't attend, was a week ago. It really got to be too much last year. Of course, there will be no day off on Christmas—classes as usual, but I doubt that any of the eight western teachers will work. We won't do much, but at least will eat out — western food. We were pleased to again be included in the consulate Thanksgiving dinner: turkey, ham, and all the trimmings including pecan pie! Wonderful food.

Have gone several times to a church group that meets in the American school (extremely small) in the Garden Hotel. The principal heads this group of approx. 30 persons, mainly teachers and consulate people. It's more of a Bible study — no preacher, and they use a Lutheran folk liturgy, which is okay, but rather strange. Reminds me of St. Mary's in Dodge City. Plan to go to the Chinese church for Christmas service and music program in the evening. Their choir is good — do selections from the Messiah, etc. Too bad there's only a bad electric organ.

We've met several interesting artists from the local art academy, and one has invited us this weekend to go to Zhu Hai (Zhu Hai is said to have a McDonald's and Kentucky Fried Chicken!) where his father owns a gallery and his mother runs a hotel where we'll stay. Zhu Hai is a special economic zone adjoining Macau that caters to H.K.-Macau tourists, who are supposedly buying quite a few paintings. Some of the professors at the academy are doing really beautiful things — some resemble Van Gogh, others Pissarro, etc.

Had a letter yesterday from Tasha. She sounds fine, but exhausted from putting in lots of hours at a language school. She's back at her old address in Paris.

Next Sat. the univ. is taking us foreign teachers to visit a "very famous" small mountain (so typically Chinese — they love mtns.) and an ancient library. They never ask us what we'd like to see or do. Actually, the library may be interesting.

With love, Betty and Norman

BJ'S ADDENDUM TO ELMA'S CHRISTMAS LETTER

It seems ages since we've heard from you; hope the winter hasn't been too severe — Kansas does sound cold. Our weather's been gorgeous all fall — the rains aren't supposed to begin until after Christmas.

At the moment I feel a bit overworked. They added two extra hours to my schedule, which makes 14, with five preparations. Here, even typewriting, which should be a snap to teach, requires preparation because the books (mostly in Chinese) are completely insufficient, and I have to copy extra material. And I've never seen so many twisted typewriter ribbons! How do they do it?? The typewriters constantly break down, and I've asked for repairs so often the Dean has told someone that I'm a complainer!

The university recently took us foreign teachers on an overnite trip to Shenzhen, a special economic zone adjacent to Hong Kong. We visited a bicycle factory which was interesting — everything was for export (a joint venture with a U.S. company) and much superior to the heavy, drab single model available here. They also took us to a theme park called Splendid China, which had miniatures of most of China's tourist spots. Rather interesting, but I don't really like that sort of thing. Next weekend we're to take a day trip to see a famous small mountain (very typical Chinese: they love mtns.) and an ancient library.

Have gone several times to a church group which meets in the American school (very small school in one of the tourist hotels). Around 30 persons attend — mainly teachers and consulate people. Headed by the school principal. They use a Lutheran "folk liturgy" which is quite strange, with really weird songs. Then there's just a Bible Study — no sermon. We plan to go to several services at the Chinese church for Christmas. They have good music. Christmas Day is no holiday here — classes as usual, but most westerners will no doubt take the day off. We look forward to getting your Christmas letter.

With love and prayers, Betty and Norman

PS: I plan to send a letter to Elma and Lloyd, so you don't have to share this time!

Guangzhou, China
Wednesday, January 10, 1990

Dear Lyla and Bill,

We had planned to eat out at one of the tourist hotels on Christmas Day, and then go to the choir concert at the Chinese church in the evening. Then the university changed the Christmas/New Year party to Christmas nite instead of Dec. 27, so fortunately the choir concert was given also on Christmas Eve, so we went then. We first had dinner at the Holiday Inn which is new — open just a few months. Wonder if they're not sorry to have come here with the drop in tourism after June 4. They're advertising rooms at half price. The food was excellent, but we couldn't be very leisurely because of getting to the concert.

The church was packed with approx. one thousand people — many college age. Lovely twenty-ft. tree. Music was good — 60-voice adult choir and 40- some little children. Fifteen minute sermon. Had also been to the morning service, which was impressive — same choirs plus an older ladies group of around twenty. After the service a young adult group presented a nativity pageant which was charming — no bathrobes! It should have been part of the service. The fellow in charge of the pageant (I think he teaches in the seminary attached to the church) spent a year or two doing something at Loma Linda. It shows. After the morning service, adults were given oranges, and children sacks of candy and nuts. One of my students, who had gone to church for the first time, thought this very strange.

At the university party, everyone was asked in advance to "do something." It was, interestingly, mainly the foreigners who came through on that "Chinese custom." Norman read from Luke (which was translated for those who didn't know

English); I had made copies of a few carols and led them in singing. Many knew the tunes and a few words for Silent Night and Jingle Bells. They enjoyed singing and many asked to keep the words. I also did carol singing in my cultural history and oral English classes.

On New Year's Eve we were invited to a Chinese teacher's house for drinks and to see their Christmas tree. His mother was German, and he's baptized a Roman Catholic. Interesting fellow — used to play violin in the Canton symphony. He doesn't seem very happy with his situation and looks forward to retirement. Says he had a hard time during the Cultural Revolution. Anyone with non-Chinese blood is suspect here — even now. A student recently told me she hides the fact that her grandmother was Russian. Can never go swimming because her hair curls when wet! After leaving Peter Tan's house, we went at midnight to a small party at one of the Portuguese teacher's apt. — in our building.

Now, after all the Christmas excitement, things are back to normal, and rather dull. Oh yes, they took away our Hong Kong TV for a week right during the Rumania crisis, the week between Christmas and New Year. We later learned the reason. Some VIPs from Beijing were here for a meeting and staying in our building, so the univ. didn't want them to know about the HKTV!

Thank you for encouraging us to come to L.A. during winter break. We'd love to, but have decided that we can't afford to travel abroad both now and in summer. The devaluation of the yuan means a 20% drop in our salaries, which are already low. So that has also influenced us. May go for a week to Hainan Island, the south of which is supposed to be warm — beaches like Hawaii!?? Then we'll probably go to Macau & H.K. for a few days.

This evening our dept. is having a dim sum tea at a nearby hotel. Norman hates dim sum here (it can be good) and I don't much like it either, but we'll go for the outing and fellowship.

Lots of love, Betty and Norman

PS: Remember those locust shells we used to pick off of trees? Lots of them plus various leaves, tree bark, etc., make up the medicine I got yesterday. Supposed to boil it in three "bowls" of water until it decreases to one bowl and then drink it.

PPS: Yes, Lyla, taxis here are cars; however, in some places in China they do carry people in bicycle-propelled taxis called pedicabs. We're told that the rickshaws pulled by men are forbidden.

Guangzhou, China
Thursday, January 11, 1990

Dear Elma,

Enjoyed your Christmas letter very much, but your weather report sounds dismal. It's not so cold here, but little heat in the buildings. Norman sleeps under four or five layers and uses an electric blanket plus a heavy Chinese comforter and two more wool blankets. Don't know how he sleeps at all under all that.

We also have a problem with cholesterol; mine is 248 and the Chinese doctor says that's not anything to worry about. I think it will be difficult to get it down. We eat few eggs and almost no butter, but too much pork and nearly everything is fried in peanut oil, which is high in c. I did find some corn oil at the friendship store. An American woman who used to teach here said that eating carp brought her's down. I ate carp once last week; it was a large fish — about 15 inches — and didn't taste very good, but will do it more often.

You asked about Guilin. The Beijing fiasco prevented our going when Tasha was here — we had planned to go in July after classes, when the U.S. consulate advised Americans not to travel. You were wise to do the Yangtze trip; we hope to do that, too.

No, we don't feel that our Hong Kong and Macau students are any better than the Mainland students. Many are worse because they're rejects of their own universities. Some do come here, though, because it's cheaper.

The Chinese church choir's Christmas Eve concert was very good. A young adults group presented a nativity pageant afterward; it should have been part of the service — excellent! They handed out oranges to the adults and sacks of candy and nuts to the children. One of my students, who was in church for the first time, thought the giving of treats very unusual and strange in China.

Beginning next week, after exams are over, we have a month's vacation and not sure how to spend it. Do plan to spend a few days in Macau and Hong Kong, but it takes too much hard currency for foreign travel. And it's too cold and crowded to travel in China.

With love, Betty and Norman

Hong Kong
Sunday, February 11, 1990 (postcard)

Dear Lyla and Bill,

We're on our spring holiday (Chinese New Year). Took the nite boat to Macau for a couple days. Macau has interesting old Portuguese-style architecture. Then by jetfoil (boat) to Hong Kong. Tonite we're having dinner at a wonderful old redone teahouse. Norman: tandoori chicken; I: ancho-chili chicken sandwich with cilantro and salsa. Good! We're at the Peak, reached by cable car. Back to the unreal world tomorrow.

Love, Betty and Norm

Guangzhou, China
Wednesday, February 28, 1990

Dear Lyla & Bill,

Vladimir Pogner (Soviet TV journalist) is on "Sonya Live in L.A." defending Soviet Russia — interesting comments!

Curious how ethnic strife exists so much now — and so much news coverage of East European change. The Chinese suggest that all of this has happened there because it earlier happened here but could not develop — wonder if it's true! At least we weren't in E. Europe when it happened; so nice to miss out on a few places of interest! Did I tell you someone at the embassy asked where we were going next, adding "I won't go there."

It was good to visit Hong Kong and Macau. H.K. has recently become the Asian New York City. Macau is a mix of wonderful old Portuguese buildings and ugly, 40 story high-rise awful towers on an island the size of the UCLA campus. It was wonderful at 4:30 a.m. to float around the island-peninsula — Macau, whose neon lights glow with birthday pinks, blues, and golds on its many casinos (round like a cake is one)! [The architect had won a contest designing a birdcage with talons at the entrance to pull gamblers into the casino.] I watched the sailors on board guide the boat into the harbor filled with sleeping junks and sampans, throwing heavy ropes to the pier — fun! BJ, of course, was sleeping; I was wandering around the gunwale.

We loved the Star Ferry in Hong Kong — watching the buildings "move toward us" — charming! Incredible architecture! Some of which I like. But, would prefer Paris architecture! Or Italian! Hope you're all okay!! It has been so cold here — but nothing like winter in U.S. Midwest and East.

Natasha wrote that she is so busy teaching all over Paris. If she had a degree in languages from a French university, she could teach full time at a high school in Paris where she teaches part time now — and wouldn't have to teach at language schools all over town.

CNN suggests that the Lebanese hostages may soon be released — hope so. A dear friend of ours [Dennis Hilgendorf], who established a center for rehabilitation of Lebanese war victims, died recently. So sad — such a wonderful guy. Fifteen years of Beirut bombings he escaped to suffer a massive heart attack when he went home for rest and recuperation in the States. Write.

Love, Norm & BJ

Guangzhou, China
Thursday, March 1, 1990

Hi,

I'll add a note before my friend arrives to have lunch with me. She goes to San Francisco tomorrow and will carry this letter. Have been quite busy starting the second term. Last nite I showed two of Alastair Cooke's America series to one history class. They're such a good series. Always enjoy seeing them again. I teach twelve hours this term instead of fourteen, but have agreed to teach a course in U.S./British cultural history at one of the part-time universities downtown. I did it last year, and it was interesting. All the students are a bit older and working in business three days a week and studying three. But their English is pretty bad, and it's exhausting to try to explain so they comprehend.

Hope this cold weather lets up soon — am tired of wearing so many layers. The Chinese describe the weather by the number of layers of clothing required. For me, it's now four or five-layer weather.

With love,
Betty

Guangzhou, China
Friday, March 23, 1990

Dear Lyla and Bill,

We just got back from having tea with a Chinese lady, a retired teacher, who now teaches for the spare-time university. She said she'd made some Chinese pudding which she wanted us — along with Peter, the young Canadian teacher — to try. The Chinese pudding turned out to be potato pancakes made with turnips instead of potatoes! They were surprisingly good, although Peter ate almost nothing. Then she served mustard greens with oyster sauce (very popular here) and noodles. She seems to be one of the lucky ones who has a passport to travel anywhere so long as she's invited, whatever that means. Has relatives in Hong Kong, Singapore, Canada, and the U.S., where she's traveled recently. If she has any money, it certainly doesn't show in her apt. — which, like all the apartments we've seen, is pretty grim: bare plastered walls with an awful calendar or two, concrete floors, unattractive furniture — mostly chairs and a color TV. She pays four yuan a month rent (80 cents). And her electricity and water bill is $4 to $5 per month.

For several weeks now we've had no Hong Kong TV. It went off the day after the evening news had several items about the harassment of foreign reporters in Beijing. We've heard that the university has been fined for having HKTV in the first place, so we've little hope of it coming back. Norman is bored enough to teach night classes on Mondays and Thursdays. We do get good news coverage from the BBC Radio, which comes all day and night. So far they've not jammed it, although they've plenty of equipment to do it, we're told. Guess they figure not so many listen to the English broadcasts. The HKTV had both English and Chinese channels.

Last weekend the university took the foreign teachers to a hot springs resort town three hours away by bus. We went, but wished we hadn't. It wasn't at all what we'd envisioned. The only baths were the tubs in our hotel (which was new and nice) where the water wasn't all that hot — no Jacuzzi, hot tubs, sauna, or massage. And the food was strange seafood and not very good. The snails were sandy (reminiscent of earlier ones in Juarez, Mexico). The major sights were a lake with waterfall, which was pretty, and a dam built by the Russians in the '50s, which was a bore. We also had the privilege ("very few see it because of security") of seeing several electric generators built underground for security —

afraid planes from Korean War would come over and bomb China. We went in a small bus with too many people. The roads were terrible, as they seem to be everywhere. However, the countryside was quite interesting. [Norm's addendum] It took three hours to go 50 miles! Drove me nuts!! To get to the hot springs. Can you believe it? Awful road, being rebuilt (for years!!) by a handful of workers!!!

[In 1993 it is now a trip of 1-1½ hrs., goes on to Macau on a new freeway. My Macau dentist (qualified in U.S.A.), who studied medicine at Jinan University, would drive the trip in one hour. The new buses do it in 1½ hours. There no longer is the 19th century riverboat that I enjoyed going overnight to and from Macau and Guangzhou. I loved the boat. Hate the bus and car. Too unsafe.]

Are going to the Chinese church in the morning with one of the young teachers who sings in the choir. Would like to go to Hong Kong for either Palm Sunday or Easter. Our plans for summer and next year are up in the air. What we'd really like to do is take the Trans-Siberian RR from Beijing to Paris, and then on to L.A. But don't think we can arrange it.

With love, Betty and Norman

Guangzhou, China
Tuesday, May 1, 1990

Dear Lyla and Bill,

Thanks for the long newsy letter and clippings. Very interesting. We too find cemeteries fascinating. In Paris, Tasha and I went to Pere Lachaise a couple years ago; it's a marvelous place that requires miles of walking. A terrible thunderstorm forced us to take shelter in the doorway of one of the small house-tombs. We finally had to find our bus stop in pouring rain and arrived home thoroughly soaked. I hope to get back sometime. Sousse, Tunisia, had a most interesting Christian cemetery, with mainly French and Italian graves, but in a terribly run-down state. A caretaker lived there, but only to discourage looters. Most of the little house-tombs had been broken into — tombstones toppling and chickens running about. Rather like something out of a horror movie! When in Macau, we visited the Old Protestant (European) Cemetery, which is beautifully taken care of and a tourist attraction. [In future years this tourist attraction was very important to us, especially when BJ wrote with our priest, Rev. Dr. Michael Poon, a book on the nineteenth century missionaries, all of whom went into China via Macau. The most famous missionary, Robert Morrison — who first translated the Bible into Chinese — is buried in the cemetery, along with the famous painter Chinnery — who visually documented Asia.]

We're curious about Chinese burials. Have seen lots of individual tombs (perhaps family) in the countryside — usually a kind of semi-circular concrete façade set into a hillside — they're caves. Also we've seen rather large pottery jars, sealed, with Chinese characters painted on them; we're told they're "graves." I've read that in cities cremation is required, but students say not so.

Bill, have you been to the small cemetery near French Creek, Hillsboro [Kansas]? Not a "proper" cemetery — just a small area of graves set apart in the middle of the wheat fields, graced by several ancient-looking pine trees—impressive for its simplicity. My Schroeder great-grandparents are buried there: Peter and Elizabeth Schroeder.

The Nineveh tomb find is especially interesting to us because we knew the archaeologist quoted, when he headed a British cultural organization in Tehran. It does make one want to visit Baghdad. When we drove thru Baghdad, the museum was being redone, and most of our concentration was on car repairs, which took all our money. We borrowed money from the YMCA director for the last lap of the journey: Baghdad-Beirut. That was in the spring of 1965. We miss that part of the world. We also recognized the author of one of the Beirut articles; surprised that she's still there.

No, they don't wear so much black here, but they don't wear many bright or interesting colors. Last nite we went to see the Shanghai circus, and at least nine out of ten persons wore white shirts or blouses. In general, the clothes here are quite blah — not dynamic. And 90% of the women wear slacks — partly because of riding bicycles, I think. During the Cultural Revolution everybody wore blue, and skirts were forbidden. The circus wasn't that good—only one ring — but the panda was cute as he climbed the ladder to slide down the slippery slide. A tour is really the best way to see China; traveling around independently is extremely difficult for many reasons. No round-trip tickets are sold, and one can literally spend days trying to get a ticket to the next place. "Stop- overs" as we know them are non-existent. Also, if you're a foreigner, you're charged higher prices for transportation, and must stay in the luxury hotels, except for some hostel-type places for backpackers.

I'm trying to remember which cut-outs we sent — if they look costumed or are masks, they're characters from Chinese opera. And here again, we've not been able to discover what the Chinese do with them. One lady did say that they're sometimes glued onto windows. I glued some of the opera masks on a black background and mounted that on a scroll. The glue stained the cutouts—otherwise it looked quite nice until it began to fade, which happened fast. We did visit a factory where they're made — cut by hand, with something like an exacto-stylus — approximately fifty at a time. They also make larger ones which are less interesting. We're enclosing some opera character cutouts, and some butterflies, which are numerous here; especially common are small, white butterflies, which travel in pairs. There's a Chinese folk-tale, similar to Romeo and Juliet, in which the lovers turn into butterflies.

What are the ultra-fundamentalists saying about the fall of communism, etc.? The political unification of Europe? It is rather scary how rapidly things are happening. The Chinese govt. is working hard to prevent changes here. I had the TV on most of today, thinking there'd be a big May Day military parade in Beijing, but not so. Did, however, see repeated several times some propaganda to show how the people love the army: women serving tea to soldiers, and men hugging the soldiers and placing white chiffon-like scarves around their necks. These scarves signify respect. And all the while the soldiers give too-big smiles and exhibit much appreciation. We hear that the army is now spending at least 50% of its time on propaganda/indoctrination. They gave a three hour lecture/film on our campus; according to the students, the main theme was that the PLA (People's Liberation Army) soldiers are busily and happily rushing around helping people, and all of us should also help each other.

We have heard that Samuel Lam's house church has been shut down. That's the one of R. Reagan/Bible renown; and several senators and B. Graham visited it. So far as we know, Rev. Lam's not in prison this time, but being interrogated. The clamps have definitely been put on here. It will be interesting to see what happens when the Goddess of Democracy arrives and begins broadcasting. [When we visited Rev. Samuel Lam's church, he told us that Reagan's Bible and Billy Graham's words kept him out of prison a few times. He has spent years in prison for preaching the Gospel to crowds that fill the three floors of his narrow house in Guangzhou. One time when we tried to attend his service, we could not get in; too full.]

Sometimes we do want to return to the U.S., but not sure we are willing to cope with being without, or with low-paying, jobs over a long period — which is a real possibility. Medical costs alone could be prohibitive without insurance, which we wouldn't have unless it came with a job. Norman is now on a medication for his heart, which costs ten times in France what it costs here, and it's reimbursed here because medical care is free here. By the way, the Chinese alternative to the "balloon treatment" has helped Norman. This doesn't mean we want to stay in China. We'll leave if a decent job comes along. There are several possibilities: in Amman, Jordan, and Damascus, and a couple other places in Turkey, etc. We've tried again for France, but the British get those jobs. I bet lots of English teachers will now be going to Eastern European countries.

[A word about the "alternative" to the angioplasty heart treatment: I was strapped inside a suit very much like astronauts wear from the waist down to the ankles which have balloon pockets inside and they are attached to an air pump, which is activated by an EKG attached to the chest. As the heart beats the air very rapidly bursts into the pockets and squeezes the blood throughout the body. It is very loud and rather scary, and when the heart gets frightened it bursts and swishes faster. I calmed down, and it was okay. I was treated with this machine probably once a week during the academic year. The circulation was improved. Perhaps that is why the echocardiograms taken now seem to be "normal," although one did indicate that the aorta is enlarged. Chinese doctors indicated the machine was invented in Germany — East, I would suppose.] If we can wrangle a place to stay for two or three weeks in Paris, we will probably go there in Aug. with a short stop or two in Italy if we can arrange the tickets that way. Can you believe that school here doesn't stop 'til mid- July? Twenty weeks per semester! But the students complain that they've nothing to do during the holiday.

Would love to hear Malcolm Miller's lecture on Chartres Cathedral. Bethel does have a lot going. Chinese universities have no concept of inspiring students with lectures, symposiums, etc. — the students might start to think about something other than Marxist-Leninist thought. Here the campuses are boring, boring! They show third-rate movies occasionally. This letter has gotten out of hand — must stop.

Love, Betty and Norman

Guangzhou, China
Sunday, May 6, 1990

Dear Elma,

What fun it always is to get your letters! Thank you. You do seem busy — and loving it all! We are rather bored, and having to add more work to keep from becoming comatose … ?! The first of the school year seemed ok; it went fast — the Hong Kong TV helped. We had not been around TV for twenty years, so it was sort of fun to find out what shows people had spoken of in the past, what they really were. And Christmas programs and symphonies and plays were wonderful! Then came Romania and others, and our TV was cut off shortly thereafter. Second semester has been almost like incarceration, although we can go and come as we like … but, to what? It is not easy to get to and from H.K. Guess we'll go next weekend. So, we rather envy you!!

Bartels sent us a copy of the Bethel Alumni Bulletin. We do have fond memories of those years. Fonder memories of the years after when we were in Beirut with you. Thank you for all those wonderful experiences, which you started!! We applied to Damascus for next year — just can't get the place out of our blood!! BJ says we want to go back to Palmyra to see all those pillars and capitals standing!! Wonderful memories. I keep thinking you'll show up here this year; but, once is enough! If nothing exciting comes for next year, guess we'll be back here. We told them we would come back … but … ?! The best thing about teaching here is the video library — a few excellent films from HKTV and Alistair Cooke's America films: excellent for background for Am. Literature.

Natasha is still in Paris. She teaches at a language school, where they send her all over the city — sometimes to an armaments factory to teach Arabs English. She hates the bomb factory! On Fridays she teaches at a Paris high school, which she likes. If she would get a French degree — or a certificate — from the Sorbonne she could teach full time at the high school — and earn enough to live on decently. Now she teaches 60-80 hours a week! Horrid!! 12-14 hrs. is a full load at colleges and 20-25 in high school in the States. In France, the high schools arrange the schedules so that teachers have quite a lot of time off — don't have to go every day! More like colleges in U.S. Tasha still loves Paris, but finds it terribly difficult to survive without these heavy hours, and we can't send her anything. We'd like to get back to the Mediterranean to be nearer her — miss her terribly! Guess it's good we left Beirut; we loved the place so much we might have stayed too long, and I would be hoping to get out — like Dr. Polhill, Teri Waite, and others!!

Love you, Norm and BJ

Hong Kong
Sunday, June 3, 1990 (postcard)

Dear Lyla and Bill,

Am enjoying H. K. in spite of lots of rain. Came with Karen, another American teacher, who's meeting me in a few minutes for lunch at the Sheraton — our big splurge! Then we're off to some evangelical/charismatic church that meets in the cultural center. Back to Guangzhou tomorrow.

With love,
Betty

PS: Later: My friend and the preacher had a big argument over Mary Baker Eddy, whom Karen defends.

Guangzhou, China
Tuesday, July 10, 1990

Dear Lyla and Bill,

I gave my last two exams yesterday. Can't believe how they drag them out, and it's really hot and humid now. Everything should finally finish July 14, although the Jrs. and Srs. have been gone for some time.

We will be teaching in Macau next year, which is 2-3 hrs. from here by bus, or 8 hrs. by boat — and an hr. by boat from Hong Kong. No airport. Governed by the Portuguese, and to revert back to China in 1999. We preferred to get closer to the U.S./Europe, but feel this should be good. Macau is interesting — Oriental with lots of western influence such as western food. The university is quite new — six years old, and expanding rapidly. We expect our jobs (I don't have a contract yet) to be less pleasant, more demanding than in China, but the pay compensates. This change of jobs has caused problems with travel arrangements for summer, and moving personal goods between China and Macau is complicated. Haven't yet figured out how to do it. Guess things will eventually work out. [Finally a tour bus from China Travel moved our goods, after the customs police asked if the videotapes I was moving contained any pictures of China. They were movies made in Hollywood and London of classic novels and the America series by Alistair Cooke for BBC. Nothing Chinese. The customs guy smiled and let us go. The driver of the bus was my former student at Jinan University, just joining the China Travel in Macau.

[Now, in 2017, the Macau International Airport has flights to everywhere in Asia and, via Taiwan and Bangkok, flights to anywhere. A new freeway to Guangzhou, Canton, now takes 1½ hours instead of the six it did when we taught in Guangzhou. And the longest bridge in Asia (I was told) connects Macau with Hong Kong (where do they put all those cars?) in addition to the jetfoil boats, which run every fifteen minutes, to and from Macau and Hong Kong. In the last several years, 27 million visitors have poured into Macau every year. With high-rise casinos and hotels, it is no longer the sleepy, charming Portuguese enclave of the past four hundred years. We still love it.] Since it took so long for Norman's contract to arrive, and since the mail's not reliable, we decided to carry the contract back. We took the nite boat Mon. nite, spent Tues. nite at the Pousada Mong Ha, the guest house for govt. officials — thanks to our Portuguese friends, and returned to Guangzhou on the Wed. nite boat. Were able to make some arrangements for housing — will be on the campus — check on my job, etc. The university administration (Portuguese) doesn't seem to operate very efficiently — everything takes lots of time. The British dept. chairman, who's leaving, says her office isn't responsible for the delays! She's quite nice, but an administrator stereotype.

We're scheduled to fly from Hong Kong to Paris July 24. At Univ. of East Asia we'll get two weeks at Christmas plus three weeks at Chinese New Year (Feb.) plus forty-some days in summer. Am enclosing a brochure on Macau to tempt you to visit!

Lots of love, Betty and Norman

PS: I've enjoyed wearing the brown 2-piece dress you sent last summer. Thanks!

Guangzhou, China
Wednesday, July 18, 1990

Dear Elma,

I'm watching Chinese Opera on TV (sound off) and listening to the BBC. So the asylum-in-embassy situation in Cuba was possibly staged by U.S. elements to give Czech. an excuse to stop representing Havana in Washington, since Bush doesn't want Czech. representing Cuba!?? (Now the BBC is discussing the Savings and Loan fiasco in U.S. and the problem of greed.)

Classes and exams finally ended. I think China's school year is the world's longest. Now we're again packing up our stuff for another move! We're really sick of this aspect of our lives. We've been quite happy here at Jinan and had indicated that we'd be back next year. At the same time we'd written a few letters of enquiry about jobs elsewhere — wanting to be closer to Europe and U.S., and needing to earn some money. The Univ. of East Asia (note map in brochure) offered us jobs — actually I've not yet signed a contract although Norm has. There seems to be lots of red tape — the univ. is run by the Macau govt. (Portuguese). I do hope we'll like it there and stay several years. We've visited Macau several times; it's 2½ hrs. by bus from Guangzhou, but we find the best way to go is the overnite boat. Boat is the only way to travel between Macau and Hong Kong — takes an hour by jetfoil. Macau has no airport, so one flies into H.K. Don't you want to come for a visit?

Now the BBC is interviewing several Poles about how they feel about German unification. Have the Germans really changed? These Poles weren't convinced. But it seems to be quite unpopular to have such doubts!

Have you read Michener's Poland? Do, if you haven't. I'm nearly half finished and think it's excellent. We plan to fly from Hong Kong to Paris July 24, and from Paris to Macau Aug. 31. Address in Paris is c/o American Express. In Macau in c/o the University of East Asia.

Paris, France
Sunday, August 26, 1990

Dear Lyla and Bill,

It's nearly time to leave Paris, and it seems like we've just arrived. Perhaps part of the reason there seems to be so little time is that Tasha decided not to do the Am. Express job, so we tend to talk late into the nite, sleep late, and the day's gone before we know it. Also, we've been eating more at home, which consumes time. Things here do seem more expensive, partly because the $ keeps dropping in value.

Norman was in Tunisia for a week, to get some things we had left, including a rug. Now for sure we'll be overweight flying to Macau, and unfortunately the university got our tickets on British Air, which is so strict on weight. We're sending several boxes of books by mail. He also sent one box of things to your address from Tunisia. Will you please put it in the attic with our things. It's filled with art books, and please do look at them if you like. I think the trip was good psychologically for Norman — kind of finished things off.

Tasha says to tell you that she won't be coming in September. Now that she's taking her vacation earlier, she plans to begin teaching again at the language school in Sept. She's been seeing quite a bit of an American fellow who works at the U.S. embassy in London. He came for a weekend right after we arrived in July, so we met him. He'll be transferred to Brazil in December, so perhaps that will be a turning point.

Kathy Bentley was here for a few days. She came over from London where she was looking for a teaching job — she seemed almost ready to give up on a job; it's very difficult, although England's very short of teachers. It was fun to have her here; Norman was in Sousse then, conveniently making room for her.

We did try to go to one of the small museums described in the clipping you sent, but it was closed during Aug., as are many shops and restaurants. Many Parisians leave town during August. We've had lots of good food here — Italian, Greek, Lebanese; we bought taco shells and sauce and made our own Mexican. Going to a Mexican restaurant here is like eating at a French restaurant in the U.S.: expensive — plus the servings are small. We plan to go back to the Lebanese place for Norman's birthday dinner.

We fly back to Macau on Aug. 29 via London (just a 2 hr. stopover) and Hong Kong.

Hope you enjoy these art nouveau cards; we're also mailing separately a Chinese painting on silk and a small gift for Courtney's graduation.

Lots of love,
BJ, N, and T

CHAPTER 10

MACAU (1990 – 1996)

University of East Asia, Trans-Siberian Railroad,
Musings About Macau

UNIVERSITY OF EAST ASIA

In 1990, BJ and I joined the University of East Asia, Macau, China, less than 50 miles from Hong Kong on the South China coast. Oh, what fun and interesting things were available there. Macau had not yet been returned to China by Portugal, who had possessed it for four hundred years.

The first Sunday in Macau, BJ went to Morrison Chapel with another faculty member or two. When she came home she told me that they rode home in a bakery truck with a baker who played the organ at church and was so interesting to talk with, as she dusted the flour off her dark clothes. Andrew Stow was such an interesting fellow to know; he would help persons who needed help, gave work to a large staff of bakery personnel, most of whom he trained himself. As the years went by and his bakery establishment enlarged several times over, Andrew became even more of a contributor to Macau, particularly to the expat population, but also to the Chinese and Portuguese living here in Macau.

So many events happened that included Andrew and later his sister Eileen, who joined his bakery firm, which expanded into several small restaurants in Macau all serving similar fare.

Our six years at University of East Asia — which name was later changed to University of Macau — were good ones. Norman taught literature, film, and public speaking, and BJ had mainly English language classes, along with Intro to English Literature and Western Civilization, which has always been her favorite. We lived on campus in faculty housing in one of the penthouses, which had a huge terrace where we did much entertaining.

Unfortunately, the English department was the black sheep, with Portuguese and Chinese departments enjoying the blessing of the administration. Following our first dean, Tom Rendall, was a series of unqualified and inept deans, who at times made life difficult, plus a majority of the English teachers were British, who are heavy on a linguistic approach to teaching English. But the students were generally receptive and made our work rewarding. Also, we were finally able to put aside money for retirement, and in 1994 we purchased our Pasadena condo, which was paid for within a year.

TRANS-SIBERIAN RAILROAD

During the summer of 1994 we traveled by Trans-Siberian Railroad to Russia. Making preparations for this journey — tickets, visas, etc. — meant that BJ had to stay several days in Hong Kong where an excellent travel office organized the trip. We started by boat from Hong Kong to Shanghai, where we stayed at the Peace Hotel, formerly the Cathay Hotel. (We'd done this part of the trip before, one Christmas.) Then on by train to Beijing, where we did some sight-seeing — the Great Wall, Forbidden City, Summer Palace—before boarding the Chinese train — a confusing hassle — not the Russian one, which we'd been told was inferior.

Our train was quite comfortable. We had a compartment with a wc/shower shared with an adjacent compartment, two bunks, and an "easy" chair. This was supposed to be a five-day journey, but ours was two days longer because of a wash-out of the tracks in Outer Mongolia; two hundred workers repaired the tracks while we passengers were entertained by Mongolian horsemen. The "dining car" ran out of food, but managed to secure eggs from a nearby farm, which they fried and sold for $2 each — one egg alone — no bread, etc. We'd been told to bring food, since trains usually ran out, so we didn't suffer. Also, at every stop along the way, local people sold whatever food they had: bread, strawberries, a bunch of carrots, etc. We bought some delicious blini from an old woman, and nearly everyone in our car bought $2 bottles of pretty bad champagne.

An interesting feature of this trip is the changing of the wheels, which takes place at the China-Russian border. We got off the train (could have stayed on) and checked the station for snacks. It seems that some countries have varying gauge rails for defense purposes — to prevent invasions.

Also interesting was the fact that quite a few Chinese passengers were traveling salesmen of a sort, with all kinds of merchandise: leather jackets, watches, socks — goods not readily available in Russia. When we pulled into a station, these merchants either jumped onto the platform or simply displayed their goods through the lowered windows. The Russian locals appeared eager to bargain and buy. Two of the passengers were Chinese doctors who said they were going to Moscow to set up a clinic.

When the train was stranded in Mongolia, they busily gathered plants growing along the tracks to use in their herbal medicine. One of them earned a few dollars by giving Norman a back treatment with those heated suction cups — which left his back slightly burned!

After seven days of Siberian landscape, we were ready for Moscow, where we were met by our guide, who took us to our hotel and immediately to the Kremlin, where we had a shortened tour, because of our losing two days on the train. After another day of museums and churches in Moscow, we trained overnite to St. Petersburg, where we again had a guide. Unfortunately, he was determined to spend time at a huge cemetery for the thousands who died during the terrible WWII siege of Leningrad by the Germans. But we did get to the fabulous Hermitage and Catherine the Great's Winter Palace. Our hotels in Russia had huge, gloomy, run-down rooms that were expensive!

From St. Petersburg the train took us to Warsaw, Poland, where our planned tour ended. After much difficulty finding a hotel near the station, we took a room at the French Sofitel, which was also expensive, but lovely, and a welcome change from Russian gloom. We were impressed by Warsaw's beautiful main town square which, after being bombed, was rebuilt exactly as it had been. The blueprints of the original buildings had been preserved!

We were now quite exhausted and ready to head for our final destination: Paris. So after paying almost $1,000 in cash for tickets, we again boarded a train. By the time we reached Paris, Norman had developed a back problem, which finally took him to a French chiropractor, after having consulted a medical doctor. From the train station we taxied directly to Natasha's apartment, where we spent several weeks before returning to Macau.

MUSINGS ABOUT MACAU

Oh, how Macau has changed. As of 2017, it has hundreds of high-rise buildings, including the almost fifty-story MGM Casino. The island where the University of Macau grew up is filled with perhaps a hundred high-rises, plus an airport, which makes it easier to fly everywhere via Taipei, Bangkok, Kuala Lumpur, Shanghai, and other cities rather than taking a jetfoil hydrofoil to Hong Kong, which we did until 1997. The area between Taipa Island and Coloane is filled up with land recovery and houses many new casinos from Las Vegas and Asia, including the Macau Venetian, which has three canals instead of the one canal in Vegas. When they were building the Venetian I asked a friend of ours, who was the architect in charge of how everything looked at the finish, "How many persons work on the Venetian each day?"

"Well, usually it's 20,000, but today I just learned there are 22,000." Another friend, a British nurse, worked in the infirmary of a new (2016) casino/hotel (perhaps the new Sands, the second one in Macau; the first is a lovely one in Macau City), which employed a similar work force — all from China. Macau seems to think this boon will continue since 28 million visitors came to Macau in 2014, but in 2015 it was 27 million (mostly from China) coming to "throw away their money" say some wags. In 2016, Beijing ceased to allow Chinese to carry out large amounts of money, stopping the "high rollers" from gambling away the Chinese economy. There are rooms especially for them. BJ saw one when the door was left open and she was with other persons meeting in the MGM Casino, but when we went there subsequently to see the tapestries hanging in the room, we were turned away, "No, No not for you!" I wonder how she knew!? Instead we had tea and delicious cakes at the MGM tea house, where I frequently joined our sometimes boss and 26-year-long friend, Dr. Eric Chan, principal of the Anglican Choi Koh Schools, Chinese campus, where BJ and I worked as volunteers for sixteen years and loved helping out in the English program after we retired from the University of Macau.

Our University of Macau has moved to a new campus to house and teach 20,000 students located on a tiny island in the Pearl River a few feet from Taipa Island. Architecturally a dull design made up of square boxes, some fairly high-rises, and not nearly as exquisite as the original University of East Asia campus which became the University of Macau, and had splendid views from the top of a hill overlooking the Pearl River and Macau City. We loved it when we lived in one of the penthouses above the view. At night the city glowed with the hundreds of lights from the city's high-rise buildings and harbor lights reflected on the heavy waters of the Pearl River. Great for parties, therefore many of the department soirees were held on our huge terrace on the Penthouse floor, which was number thirteen, but somebody put a "P" on the wall next to the elevator rather than "13".

I understand the students and faculty who do not live on the new campus will enter and leave the campus via a tunnel so they will not have to clear passport control into and out of China (Macau). There will be, I assume, a stop near the tunnel entrance on the new train that circles Macau, Taipa, and "Cotai," the new casino area. Macau has lost its innocence and filled up with people pushing their way to another casino. Someone said years ago that in Hong Kong and Macau walking was like leaving a rock concert; they should walk it now! But the youth always offer BJ and me a seat on the bus. BJ thanks them and shakes her head. I thank them and sit down! Very gratefully! Oh, the complications of "One Country, Two Systems."

CORRESPONDANCE (1990 – 1992)

Paris, France
Tuesday, July 24, 1990 (postcard)

Dear Lyla and Bill,

It is so good to get out of China! We'll be here until Aug 31. Macau will be great fun, we think; so tired of the frequent misunderstandings or always kowtowing to the authorities! Good for Eastern Europe! I wish China could do the same. Eager to talk with you. Hope to come to L.A. next Feb. Tonite we plan to see the film Anna Karenina. Weather here is lovely.

Love, B & N

Macau
Sunday, October 7, 1990

Dear Elma,

How are things in Kansas? Think I'm a bit homesick for the U.S. This is the longest I've been away. We did have a good visit with Tasha in Paris. Norm even made it to Sousse to get a few things — including a gilim — we had left behind. We've now been in Macau for one month and think we'll like it. Our jobs aren't perfect. I have all basic English courses — rather boring; Norm also has two 1st year classes in addition to Shakespeare and Modern Drama. But when one is paid a decent salary, he doesn't mind. Our apt. — on campus — is comfortable and is the penthouse (13th floor) of one of the apt. buildings for faculty. I have a stove with an oven! And a large terrace with a lovely view of the Pearl River and Macau, to which our island, Taipa, is connected by a long bridge. It's dazzling at nite when lighted. Nearly everything is available in the stores, and most things are quite inexpensive, including restaurants, which are plentiful and of various kinds: Portuguese, Chinese, Italian, Thai, etc. — even a McDonald's.

Have become somewhat involved with the very small Anglican English service group which meets in a small chapel built by Protestant missionaries over 100 years ago. The nearby Protestant cemetery is most interesting. I've now learned that there's also a Baptist English service, which I shall check out. Why do the British sing such strange hymns? And pitched so high??

Since we had several holidays last week, we took the nite boat to Guangzhou, where we stayed on the Jinan campus. Saw friends, etc., and Norm had some treatment for his circulation. It's also quite easy to go to Hong Kong — 1½ hrs. by jetfoil and no visa required. Of course China does require a visa each trip. There are quite a few Americans teaching here — one couple about our age grew up in Pittsburg, Ks., and went to K-State. Have I sent you the tourist pamphlet on Macau? If not, let me know and I'll send one. Hope all is well with you. Please share this with Elma and Lloyd.

Love and prayers, Betty and Norman

Macau
Tuesday, October 23, 1990

Dear Lyla and Bill,

We have finally gotten another house into shape; I'm sick of "doing" houses — I feel like a professional decorator who never gets paid!! Forgive us for not writing. Saturday we had a party — like the ones we used to do in Palm Desert and Connecticut, etc. — I say 50-80 were here — BJ says 60; we're exhausted and want no more parties for a long time! We're both teaching more than sometimes in the past — they expect us to earn our money here! It now seems that I am to teach a full load, direct a play (small now, maybe more later!) and do educational TV on teaching English for Macau TV as extras!! At the moment I feel like I think Bill feels: I never want to direct another show. (I assume Bill feels that way about houses?!)

By the way, you'd like this apt. It is the penthouse — 13th floor (labeled in the elevator with a P for penthouse; the number 13 is avoided here) — with an enormous terrace overlooking the sea, river, mountains of China, and city of Macau with its awful high-rise hotels and Bank of China structures, which look wonderful at nite, lighted up like Vegas, two and a half miles across a long bridge. We are on the island of Taipa, one of the two islands connected by bridges to Macau, which is connected to the mainland by a tiny peninsular causeway.

We could have gone to a concert here on campus tonight. A German orchestra doing Mozart, but we would have had to get into Macau to get tickets; they are not sold at the door!! And it was all too much — BJ had classes straight through from 9:30-5:30 today, and I had them all afternoon, so we went out to dinner here on the island instead, and came home to watch Art World on TV afterward. Radio Days is on Thursday; I liked that in Paris.

Natasha is thinking of getting married to an American guy who works at the Am. Embassy, London. She finds him "cute and amusing — not at all what I always go for!! But I like him … He's due to rotate at Christmastime to Washington for six months' of language training, Portuguese, then he is to go to Brazil for two years, then decide whether or not he wants to stay in it. He's a graduate of Georgetown in Political Science, I think. Guess he's quite a brain. Oh, did I tell you, he's Jack Brown's (the clipper) nephew!! Isn't that wild?? Jack wrote Paul Natasha's address in Paris. (I did the same to Tasha thinking she might need a free place to sleep in London. She said, "Oh hum" and ignored it.) Paul wrote her and invited her to stay if she's in London. She likes London, went — and maybe the rest is to be history!? Or maybe not. She keeps writing that she doesn't want to go to

Brazil for two years — may come here instead and do her MA in Chinese Art!!

Love, Norm

Wednesday, October 24, 1990 Hi,

I'll add to N's letter. I'm on a jetfoil boat to Hong Kong. They go every 15- 20 min. day and nite. All foreigners have to leave Macau every 20 days until given a residence permit, which some never get. Last time we went to Guangzhou on the nite boat. Stayed at the guest house of Jinan, where we were last year. Was fun — saw lots of friends, etc.

Yes, we are back in the real world. We work a full schedule, but we also get a real salary, so it's good. Actually, I teach the same no. of hrs. as last year, but they do expect the extra bits here — committees, research, etc. I have all first year English so it's quite boring — and if I taught it like the coordinator (a Brit straight out of language school) does, it would be more boring: all oral drill from a tape — his students do no reading, no writing — no homework. And they give university credit for that! Some of the Chinese teachers disagree with his method, and I think there will be a showdown eventually. I've never met such rascally (actually anti-American) British. The two in our dept. wouldn't come to our party. It really irks them that at least in this part of the world — at least in education — the Americans have taken over. Four of the seven foreigners in the English dept. are from Calif., and one from Canada.

We do like Macau — it's small, but most interesting. Almost everything is available in the stores. Food may be a bit more expensive than in Calif. (according to others from Calif.) but eating out is generally cheaper. And there are lots of good restaurants — even on Taipa, our little island. Also, there's a McDonald's and a Pizza Hut.

We've been going to the Anglican church, which meets in a small, interesting chapel built by early missionaries. It's a small group, mostly Americans from the university. But the pastor is Chinese, who also has a Chinese congregation and is principal of a sizeable school. Now we've discovered that there's a Baptist English service. I've gone to that one once. More people and livelier. The Anglican music is strange and pitched too high. Since they meet the 1st and 3rd Sundays a.m. and 2nd and 4th Thurs. evenings, one can do some of both, I suppose. Oh yes, the Assembly of God has an English service every Sun. nite, and some other Baptist group also does. This group runs a language school that teaches English with the Bible as the text book. Interesting.

Hong Kong is coming into view, so must stop. Am going to check on air tickets to Paris for Christmas. Want to come to L.A. in Jan/Feb — Chinese New Year.

Love,
BJ

Macau
Wednesday, November 28, 1990

Dear Lyla and Bill,

We do really enjoy your descriptions of your wanderings through the back country. Thanks for sharing. Glad things there seem to be okay for you. We keep hearing about recession … Todd's romantic life certainly isn't dull, is it? Think of what those parents miss, whose kids marry their childhood sweethearts right out of high school.

Well, Natasha now has an engagement ring; perhaps she's written you. No date set for wedding. His name is Paul, and we did meet him in Paris last summer — briefly. Would like to have spent more time with him. He seems rather shy, but nice enough.

We have air tickets from Hong Kong to L.A. on Jan. 31, arriving there I believe on Feb. 1 and to return Feb. 18. I hope this will not be a bad time for you. It's the Chinese New Year holiday here. We're eager to see you and catch up on what's happening there. What happens if Kathleen comes to L.A. while we're there? Will there be a sofa for her to sleep on? I just wrote her that we're coming — not sure I'll be able to go to visit her.

The Anglican Bishop of Macau and Hong Kong is coming to Macau Saturday, and the reception for him is to be at our house — probably 40-50 people from both Chinese and English congregations. Work for me! But others will help.

Love, Betty

Macau
Pearl Harbor Day 1990

Dear Elma:

Greetings from Macau. Did you ever get over here? Very interesting — so many wonderful old churches and old, tiny, winding streets wandering around this tiny island hooked by a small causeway to China. Over 600,000 people live in 1½ x 2 mile space. Our campus is on another island hooked by bridge to Macau city. It's empty except for the university and a couple hotels and a lovely old village (like a Greek village) filled with good restaurants. There is a third island hooked by a half-mile causeway that is bare woods and hills, soon to be changed to high-rise buildings!! Too bad. Wonderful village facing China about fifty yards away that has a church housing 17th century (I think) bones from Christian martyrs in Japan, and the elbow bone of St. Francis Xavier, who was here in Macau, and then died somewhere — another relic! The shops are delightful. A new airport is to be here in 1993. H.K. is also to build a new airport. Seems stupid to me; the cost is amazing! Why do it? Shenzhen in China, near H.K., has a new airport opening now. Three of them within 60 miles of each other — all serving the same area, with three different passport controls: China, Hong Kong, and Macau.

Hope you all have a good Christmas and New Year! We'll go to Paris to be with Natasha — amazing that we can go this year — at least we have two weeks off!!

Love, Norm, BJ

Hong Kong
Wednesday, May 15, 1991

Dear Elma,

Natasha and I are sitting in the boat terminal, hoping to get back to Macau before midnight. For some reason, the boat's delayed. We came over this morning to shop. We were quite successful. Also checked on some airline tickets. It looks like we'll be coming to the U.S. in July — unless Natasha and Paul change the place of their wedding. They've had a terrible time working it out. She really wanted to be married in Paris but his schedule is so tight — almost no time off. Since he's now intensively studying Portuguese in Wash. DC, they've pretty much decided to be married there. You'll probably get an invitation before too long.

We still enjoy living in Macau, but the university leaves so much to be desired. For instance, the exam procedure is complicated and blown up into a big affair. In our dept. they even bring in an "expert" from Australia as an external examiner for our advanced students — to make sure all is done properly and the correct grades are given. I think this is British. My estimation of British education continues to go down. We're now on the boat—the "High Speed Ferry" — which usually takes 1½ hours and 10 min. Well, I don't have a class until 11 a.m. tomorrow.

Are you moved into your new place? Or are you doing it slowly, in stages? What has Victor decided to do? I wish the weather weren't so bad in Kansas. Except for that, I like the idea of retiring there — not sure that Norm would agree. We used to think it would be Calif.; now not sure. Isn't the aftermath of the war awful? I wonder if Bush has any regrets

— we've not heard of any. It sounds like things may be better in Lebanon now, but will the hostages ever be released?

So, is it correct that Lou Ann Sturm Ritchie is Mrs. U.S.A.? We never do hear from Sturms. And Miss America contest was in Wichita! We saw the very end of it on Hong Kong TV. Maybe we'll see you this summer.

With love, Betty and Norm

Macau
Saturday, September 21, 1991

Dear Elma,

Now that classes have begun, things are really chaotic — always so confusing at the beginning — students dropping and adding courses — changing our schedules around, etc. We had a good time in the U.S. during the summer. Appreciated getting to see your new apartment — very nice; you should be comfortable there. One of the best things, it seems to us, is that you have so many interesting people around you.

The Bartel wedding near Santa Rosa was interesting, but a bit hectic. Afterward, Bartels and we (Natasha was with us — she flew out for that wedding) toured the wine country one day (beautiful) and spent a day in San Francisco. Had forgotten how beautiful that city is. Had tea with Frances Gray, former president of BCW. Must be in her early eighties, but hasn't changed much. Still teaches religious art classes.

Love and prayers, Betty & Norm

Macau
Saturday, October 24, 1992

Dear Elma,

All of you friends at Newton have been in our thoughts the past several days. We received a fax from Norma Morse, which included the obituary of Tina Schellenberg. I'd forgotten that she did her bachelor's degree after a long career — like you! Two remarkable ladies! We're enjoying lovely autumn weather, and hope you are, too. Did we tell you that this year we're joined by two couples, friends of earlier days: Dawn and David Nottingham (Beirut) and Beth and Don Baker (Tunisia) — all over sixty. Think some of the younger teachers aren't sure about this geriatric take-over. It's a pleasure to chat without culture/generation gaps. Our new dean is younger, but also American, with many of the same values and similar education philosophy that we have. He has decreed that we don't all have to give the same final exam in the English language classes, and what an upheaval that has caused! Hope he can stand firm against some of the troublemakers.

I just finished reading The Small Woman by Gladys Aylward, the English missionary to China — well-written and interesting. Now we're going to rent the videotape of Inn of the Sixth Happiness, which is based on the book. Must have been made in the late 50s or 60s with Ingrid Bergman.

I've finally decided to do something about my need for exercise and have joined the "swimming club" at one of the hotels with an indoor pool. It simply means that I can swim any day between 9 a.m. and 9 p.m. So far, I've gone probably five times a week, but I suspect it will drop off drastically when the weather turns cold and wet. I do need shorter, easier-to-manage hair.

We're trying to decide what to do during our holidays this year. Wish it weren't so expensive to fly to Brazil. Tasha and Paul seem to be coping better, but suffering a lot from the pollution — respiratory problems.

We're eating with the Nottinghams tonite at an Italian restaurant, and I must change clothes. We hope all is well with you. We enjoyed so much the lunch with you in your very nice dining room. You're lucky to have such good food — unlike most institutional kitchens.

With love, Betty and Norman

Guangzhou, China
Friday, May 17, 1991

Dear Mr. and Mrs. Lofland,

It is already three weeks since I left you and Macau. But the happy days with you and the quiet city are still lingering in my mind. Indeed the experience in Macau is the most exciting and beautiful one in my life, although I have been to quite a lot of places in China.

Since the early days when I got in touch with English culture through studying the language, I have been dreaming of seeing for myself the baroque buildings of western style, the serene church with its high-pointed spire, the brilliant neon in the busy streets . . . Today my dream has come true, for which I am indebted to you. It is most kind of you to have brought me a chance of coming to such a fascinating land.

In spite of Macau's dense population, the city shows no sign of the disgusting hues and cries when I was wandering in the downtown. I did not have to worry about bumping into other people, whereas in Guangzhou I usually have to elbow my way in Beijing Rd. During my stay in Macau, I took French leave from the conference and went out sightseeing, as you have kindly advised me, "Make full use of the time and see the place." I had expected the church was out of use, when I found the door half open. I pushed it carefully. An old man, the door-keeper, welcomed me in. "May I have a look inside?" I asked. "Yes, please. You can take photos as you please," the old man replied smiling, seeing me carrying a camera. To my surprise I found a clean and tidy auditorium before me. The chairs were painted creamy yellow. On the front wall was a niche where stood a statue of the sad-looking Madonna, with roses and chrysanthemums as sacrifice at her feet. On the right-hand wall stood a statue of Jesus Christ, and on the left was the platform of sermon. The other walls were decorated with fine wood-carving pictures of Bible story. The old man was so kind as to switch on the lights. Suddenly the front niche turned into a beautiful sight. The Blessed Virgin Mary was set off by the azure sky dotted with some light clouds. Around it were sparkling colorful electric lights -- red, yellow, blue, green, white . . . So beautiful! So charming! I was so fascinated that I seemed to have arrived in the mysterious heaven where I can communicate with the goddess. I had forgot all my frustrations and anxiety. I wish I were a believer or a disciple who can regularly wash away his secular troubles and can seek consolation from the God.

The most unforgettable experience, however, is the dinner together with you at a Portuguese restaurant in the downtown. It was so generous of you to treat me to a rich dinner. And it was considerate of you to see through my interest in Portuguese food in a Portuguese colony. I was indeed carried away by the Western European domestic atmosphere the moment I entered the restaurant. Never before had I had such an opportunity to taste the genuine dish. From now on I can boast to others about my experience of Portuguese food.

Besides the food, the reception evening at your sweet home, the interesting bus ride you took me around Taipa, the visit of porcelain exhibition and so on, have also deeply impressed in my mind. Macau, together with your friendship, will be the best memory in my life!

Thank you again for your precious friendship, the food, Norman's midnight film, and BJ's chocolates. Also please give my regards to Michael Poon. Please tell him that I am always ready to go and work in Macau!

With love and best wishes, Yours,

Zheng Danmian

Beirut, Lebanon
Spring 1987

Dear Norm and BJ,

I received your letter written after the deaths of Leigh, Philip, and Peter. I and most everyone else here have been in shock for the past three weeks, and it seems like it happened just yesterday one minute, and that it's been forever another minute.

I don't know whether to write to you at the Ecole or at the Kairouan so I chose the Ecole. I am glad to hear that you have decided to stay there another year. It seemed to me to be such a lovely place, but of course the fact that we were all together was part of it. I just loved Marie and I wish I had an address for her so I could keep in touch. Anyway, stay there if you can. I did see that there was some sort of trouble in Tunis last week -- maybe when Amine Gemayel [president of Lebanon from 1982 to 1988] was there.

The day of the murders I had gotten a ride with Wanis Seman because after the Tripoli bombing it wasn't safe to go on the street. (Ingrid is in E. Beirut.) I haven't seen or heard from him since as I ended up staying four nights at the President's house at AUB (Marquand House) as I wasn't allowed to leave campus. When Brian Johnston and 16 Hariri people left on that Sunday (4-21) I was alone there, so I moved to Brian's flat.

I have been having so much difficulty getting around because I tore some ligaments in my right knee. Brian and I were joking that between us we had one good pair of legs because he now has a metal plate in his left leg and walks with a cane. I guess he fell off a second story balcony while he was in Pittsburgh. Anyway, Brian had joined the AJME [Americans for Justice in the Middle East] Editorial Board when he returned to Beirut and, of course, Leigh was also on it -- along with me, Fawzi, Peter Yff, and Elaine Larwood; Marilyn Rasihka having gone to Jordan. So we all had gotten to be close due to our mutual involvement in AJME. Now we are back to our basic staff -- minus the Brits. I promise to send you the past four issues of the AJME News. Sorry if you haven't been getting it.

Jeremy Carter left when Brian did. I guess he went to Hull, England. I'm not sure. Barbara Sayers says he has accepted a job in Columbia, S.A., but I hope he reconsiders. Penny and Fawzi are still at the Manara, but now that Nabil Matar has been kidnapped, Fawzi is at great risk and is pretty much trapped in his flat, as you were Norm, when you were here. Nabil is a Palestinian Christian with Lebanese citizenship and a Lebanese wife, but he is very Westernized (no mustache). He lived right across from AUB and when he stepped out of his building at 7:15 a.m. last Wednesday, some men were waiting for him and took him away. There has been no word at all about him.

Now AUB Faculty Association has voted to "abstain from teaching until satisfactory word is heard that Nabil is safe" (released, I hope). So I had made the decision to stay until the end of the semester and so had Barbara, but now there are no classes so we will just sit here waiting to see what happens.

To continue the saga of housing, I couldn't stay at the little place where Brian was because there was a man hanging around watching me. I don't know what his intentions were -- maybe to rob me, but I decided not to stay there to find out, because he had both a gun and a knife. Now I am camping out in David Jacobsen's apartment until the end of the semester. He was kidnapped a year ago, and we think he's being held in the Bekaa with Tom Sutherland and Terry Anderson and Father Jenco. Who really knows?

Janie Miller is here this semester, and I am still teaching at BUC. Nabila, Janet Hyde-Clark, Leila Debbs are all still there. Janie will be leaving at the end of the semester, but I don't know what Janet will do.

I got one letter from Tasha, but since all my stuff is still at the Manara, I don't have her address. I am going off campus to BUC three days a week, but only by private car. I did go to the Manara two weeks ago, but Hassan is staying there now, watching all my things. Leigh's friend Zaki is in his flat, so there are no "ajanib" left at the Manara except Penny and Fawzi.

All of Leigh's friends have left -- Peter Kemp, Diane Sevill, Liz Sly, Alistair. There are essentially no foreigners left except about ten at AUB and 3 or 4 at BUC. I will talk with Huda at BUC about mail and also call Haigazian when I can.

Barbara and I will be leaving Beirut about the first of July. You can reach me at my daughter's after that, but I don't have any idea where I'll go.

Fondly,
Kay

CHAPTER 11

TRAVEL (1996 – 1998)

Macau, Athens, Istanbul, Cairo

MACAU

After our students at the University of Macau helped us celebrate our retirement from UMac with a dinner at the Macau Club located in the Teatre Dom Pedro on the hill above the Leal Senado, we flew to Paris for a celebration and a renewal of our happy days in Paris. Walking around the interesting streets past the Louvre, Notre Dame, and all around the town renewed our love for the City of Lights; the cuisine also helped.

ATHENS

From Paris we flew on to Athens, a city we have loved from the many flights of escape from the sites of Beirut when the war was too much even for our stubborn selves; as well as when we left the city of Tehran when the U.S. embassy was saying that "nothing was happening" during the run-up to the revolution, when I daily telephoned them to ask about the shooting not far from our front door. Well, the world soon knew what went on.

So, we again visited Athens, with its sunny squares filled with coffee houses with their umbrella-covered tables, and the Plaka with its tourist shops filled with mementos and memories. For years we had stayed at our favorite small hotel just off Syntagma Square, the Hotel Cleo, a potentially charming, well-run hotel with reasonable prices. We had stayed there for almost eight weeks during the Iranian Revolution, through the winter months, which are very cold in Athens with little or no heat — and we were very fond of the owners, Bill and Cleo. Cleo ran an inexpensive guest house called Cleo's House, where many traveling students stayed.

With all these memories we were "shocked" to learn that the Hotel Cleo was no longer there; the building had been renovated into a charming, five star boutique hotel, at ten times the price. So, we walked around and found an old, primitive house near the Cathedral that was cheap enough, but rather depressing. We looked around again; most of the cheap accommodations were gone. There was more money floating around, it would seem. I spoke to a man sitting on the steps of another small hotel and asked if the hotel would give us a monthly rate. "I don't know mate, but you can ask Bill when he comes on duty later." We came back later and saw Bill. "Bill," I shouted, "It's you!" And, it was the same Bill from the Cleo, where we'd once stayed for two months and at every trip for ten years after. We learned that the new owners of the Cleo had sold it, and the new owner had thrown out all the beds, ironing boards, sheets, towels, etc., onto the street. Bill had to deal with that and received no income from the deal. We received a small discount on the room — very nice, overlooking the Greek Orthodox Cathedral — and we stayed there several weeks again enjoying the loveliness of Athens.

ISTANBUL

We decided to take a train to Istanbul. Bill was most alarmed by that since he, a retired Greek naval captain, still had bad feelings toward the Turks. We stored our bags at the hotel and boarded a train to Thessaloniki. It was a sleeper, with three layers (as I recall) of students stacked up in the car. I remember being in the middle — but perhaps I am mixing it up with being in the U.S. Army — or maybe it seemed like the train in Dr. Zhivago. I only recall it was a very tight fit. It was interesting talking to a couple of the students. (We have spent our lives talking to students!) In Thessaloniki we visited a memorable Aegean-Seaside castle-museum, wonderfully ancient churches, and the quite new museum which houses the fabulous artifacts —much magnificent gold jewelry — from the tomb of Philip of Macedon, father of Alexander the Great.

After a brief but rewarding stay in Thessaloniki, we embarked on the overnite journey to Istanbul on the most dilapidated train one could ever imagine. Everything in sight was in bad repair — even the door to the loo hung on one hinge. Unbelievable! We understood why there were so few of us on this train — only a handful of foreigners, one of whom had his wallet stolen during the trip.

Between a very chilly one and two o'clock in the morning, our spectre train derailed in the town of Drama, Greece. Perfect! It was not a big drama; the whole train merely stopped with a loud noise. We got off and looked at the wheels. (We had suspected a flat wheel for the many hours we had already been on this local train.) We were never told so, but it occurred to us that bad blood between the two countries may have contributed to the choice of train that ran between the two cities. Then a Turkish train took us on to Istanbul, where we pulled into the train station with feelings of excitement and relief. As we carried our bags into the station, the colorful stained-glass windows glowed, breathing a kind of life into our very tired bodies.

The station's hotel placement office guided us to a lovely old house, converted into a hotel in the old section of Istanbul, very near the Santa Sophia Church and the Blue Mosque, glorious structures reflecting the depth of the religious ideals of both Christian and Moslem faiths, even though the Santa Sophia had been turned into a mosque and then into a museum.

Though Istanbul with its rugs, Grand Souk-Bazaar, and many monuments whetted our appetites, the weather was getting cold, and we had seen many of the sites on previous trips, so, seeking warmer weather, we flew south to Cairo.

CAIRO

We had fond memories of our previous visits to Egypt: in 1963 when BJ chaperoned a group of BCW students, and in 1972 when we were en route to Iran. Neither hotel we'd stayed at on those trips existed now, and after guiding a taxi to several that were full, we found a very satisfactory room at the Carolina which, however, wasn't as central as we liked.

We headed first for the National Museum with its magnificent holdings, so inadequately displayed, and were again amazed by the dazzling King Tut artifacts.

A pleasant afternoon was spent on the lovely campus of the American University of Cairo, where we'd long wanted to teach. I had been offered a job there in 1972 but was already committed to teach in Tehran. One unique discovery in the neighborhood of our hotel was a Kentucky Fried Chicken restaurant that was almost completely staffed by deaf employees! Amazing how well it appeared to operate.

After a week of museums and enjoying lots of tea in the Hilton and other luxury hotels, we flew back to Athens only to find the small hotel where we'd left our bags closed for the winter. I phoned Bill, and he got the owner to reopen the hotel and allow us to stay, but the room was so cold that we had to move. We were hoping to fly out of Athens, but the flight was always full — that is why we took advantage of the time by going to Istanbul — so we finally flew back to Paris and took the EVA Air flight to Taipei and on to Macau.

CORRESPONDANCE (1996)

Thessaloniki, Greece
Monday, October 7, 1996 (postcard to Bartels)

We have finally seen the wonderful artifacts from Philip of Macedon, Alexander's father's tomb. It is a bit out of the way to come here — had an exhausting train trip last night coming here; tomorrow we have a worse one going on to Istanbul. Last night we had couchette-sleepers; tomorrow, chairs (no sleepers)! 16 hours! May fly back to Athens. Wanted to take a boat, but none available. We are getting very tired of travel; it's exhausting (even flying) going to hotels, etc. Ready for Mexico or a tiny apt. in Glendale. Had dinner in very interesting part of town by the sea; reminded us of Pasadena

Old Town; now sipping hot chocolate in old ruin-turned-into-glass house; tons of glass, but too much metal around; but nice! Jazz playing very un- Greek!! BJ says that's the Turkish influence, but I don't think so.

Love, Norm and BJ

CHAPTER 12

NORTH CYPRUS (1997 – 1998)

We made a hurried departure from Glendale in early October. Norman had agreed by telephone to be the Dean of Arts and Sciences and to establish a graduate program in English at the International American University in Girne (Kyrenia), North Cyprus. BJ would also be teaching "whatever was needed." Although the university was a disaster, North Cyprus was most interesting with its ancient relics: castles, monasteries, abandoned Greek churches, and lovely scenery. Its location also allowed us to visit places in the Middle East.

CORRESPONDANCE (1997 – 1998)

Girne (Kyrenia), North Cyprus
Sunday, October 19, 1997 (postcard)

Dear Lyla and Bill:

Thank you for taking us to the airport. It was a long trip — 40 hrs., mostly flying! We arrived at 11 p.m., met and were taken to a beautiful resort on a mountainside overlooking the sea; really lovely! Villages are like all M.E. — rather like Mexico. Bought a Persian needlework saddle bag 3' x 2½' and an interesting basket. Haven't seen school or where we'll live. They drive on the left, and all over the road. A crusader castle is on the mountain above us. Write.

Love, N, BJ

Girne (Kyrenia), North Cyprus
Saturday, October 25, 1997

Dear Lyla and Bill,

We've now been here a week and are in permanent housing, so that's some progress at least. Have been to the university five days, but still lots of confusion there. The asst. pres. who hired us is out of the country indefinitely. (He never returned!) The methodology courses which I was to teach (he said) are for upper level students, of which we have none. They needed someone for Intro to Education and Educ. Sociology, which I agreed to do. Then Norman, as dean, and with permission of the Registrar (a young man who appears to run the school), has created two new courses (actually from the catalog but not offered now) in American Culture and World History. But what students will take these courses? There aren't many in the English program, and most are already signed up for 5 or 6 courses. There seem to be other classes with one or two students. Norman's classes aren't really set yet, either. They say the MA program, which ended when the teachers left a year ago, will be revived in Nov. It's in English lit. and six students are in it. Well, so much for our jobs. Oh yes, the library, which is one room seating approx. 20 persons, has mainly English lit. books — 3,600 of them — lots of fiction, which we will enjoy. World Book is the only encyclopedia. No periodicals or card catalog. (No internet or e-mail here.) All the lit. books were donated by the former univ. president, who was gung-ho about this place until he became disillusioned. He's American and did many good things for the university.

We enjoyed our week at the mountain resort; the univ. driver came for us each day. Very nearby is a bronze-age cemetery, which isn't very interesting to the uninformed: us. The resort has a lovely setting, and the restaurant was charming and served good food. The setting of our present house is less stunning, but does have a small view of the Mediterranean, and from our kitchen table can see the 11th century crusader castle perched on a precipitous mountain. We wonder how people got up and down. Supposedly Richard the Lionheart spent time there. Our house — quite new and very clean although sparsely furnished in pale colors — belongs to Turkish people who spend most of the year in London. There's a huge kitchen, quite well furnished, two bedrooms and bathrooms, plus three balconies.

It was nearly time for the stores to close when we discovered there were no bed sheets, so dashed out and bought some rather awful ones — no choice.

There's a pretty good restaurant nearby called the Chicken Bar. In addition to several chicken dishes, they serve a few lamb and beef dishes along with salad and French fries. So far we've enjoyed our lunches at the school cafeteria. They serve a soup, several hot dishes, and rice in addition to sandwiches — hotdogs, hamburgers, etc. [Lots of garlic and peppers in excellent Turkish food — which drove N mad.]

Norman has signed his contract in which they cheated him $11,000; he complained, and they said $6,000 of it was a clerical mistake, and explained away the rest. Then they said we must pay for our work permits (we've never had to pay for these in other places) which are approx. $165 each, as well as medical tests at $80 each — to make sure we don't have AIDS. Our house is a good deal — about $100 less than the Glendale rent. If they give me the housing allowance too, which they probably won't, our combined allowances will cover 2/3 of the rent. There is an Anglican church in Kyrenia, so I must find out where it is. Quite a few British live here; many run restaurants.

Love, Betty

Girne (Kyrenia), North Cyprus
Tuesday, November 4, 1997

Dear Lyla and Bill,

We've been eating a lot of chicken. About two blocks from our house is a restaurant called the Chicken Bar, which serves chicken prepared in various ways as well as beef dishes; but side dishes are limited to French fries and salad. Near this place is the Milano Patisserie, which sells quite good pastries on a pleasant terrace, which would be even more pleasant if the traffic were less noisy, the several dogs in residence disappeared, and the glass table tops were cleaner. Nevertheless, we enjoy sitting in the sun — sort of takes the place of Burger King. The clothes washer, a new Turkish one, has already stopped working; repairman is to come. A cleaning lady is to start next week, coming every other week.

The Anglican church, of course, was totally British — okay sermon and small, pretty-bad choir. Building is interesting and approx. 100 yrs. old. It's forbidden to ring church bells here. The mosque call-to-prayer blasted off just as our service ended. It's very near the church, as is the huge crusader castle, which is right on the harbor and still used as a police headquarters.

We've now seen The English Patient for the third time and enjoyed it. Our friend, Ugur, drove us to the town's one theatre, which seats sixty. There were two intermissions — to change reels. It was in English with Turkish subtitles.

Ugur has offered to drive us to Nicosia on Sunday; it's approx. 15 miles from here, and is the town thru the middle of which runs the boundary dividing Turkish and Greek Cyprus.

In North Cyprus are six universities, all with varying degrees of incompetency; however, they're all efficient in awarding diplomas for tuition paid. One has been set up specifically to keep guys out of the army — here they're exempt when in school. We're told those guys never attend class — they save on teachers' salaries that way. Our students are pretty bad about not attending, and so far we've received no class lists from the registrar.

Betty

P.S: The enclosed card doesn't show the 11th c. crusader castle located on the harbor. Above the town, on the highest peak, is Richard the Lionheart's 11th c. castle, which is now a monastery. Many of the Gk. Orthodox churches have been turned into mosques by the Turks; we often hear the minaret call to prayer; however, someone said, "no one here prays!"

N

Postcard encl: This picture is of Bellapais Monastery, one of many on Cyprus. Bellapais was founded by French rulers for Augustine monks who were forced by the Saracens to flee Jerusalem.

Girne (Kyrenia), North Cyprus
December 1997 (Christmas letter)

When we were last in touch with most of you (July 1996), we were preparing to leave Macau, with plans to travel for a few months. So we began with our usual month-of-August-in-Paris, taking care of a friend's cat. We shall always cherish those Augusts of drinking in the beauties of that lovely city. Once again, Natasha joined us for several weeks, but husband Paul was unable to come.

From Paris we journeyed to Greece for more than a month's stay. In Athens we lived at the small Hotel Imperial, just across the street from the National Cathedral, and our room looked onto the Acropolis, with a stunning view of the Parthenon. Leaving our heavy bags behind in Athens, we took a train to Thessaloniki, which we found very interesting historically: ancient churches; the charming esplanade along the sea, with the old tower housing a priceless exhibit of icons; the fabulous artifacts from the tomb of King Philip of Macedon (father of Alexander), which are displayed in a modern museum. The modern city offered good restaurants and several unusually nice coffee shops, which made our stay very pleasant. From Thessaloniki we continued on to Istanbul by train — a train which we definitely do NOT recommend for reasons I shall not enumerate. However, in the middle of the cold night, the train derailed, appropriately at the small Greek town of Drama!

We were very happy to pull into the wonderful old Istanbul station where we located a helpful tourist office. This office sent us to a small hotel, which was a converted old Ottoman house. Lovely! And it was within walking distance of Santa Sophia and the Blue Mosque. We found Istanbul as fascinating as ever; the grand bazaar is still extremely exotic and mysterious. When the weather turned chilly, we made plans to fly to Egypt, where we spent the next several weeks. Cairo was a bit disappointing because of so many changes. Tahir, the main square was all torn up with subway construction. The city has expanded all the way out to the pyramids. But the museums are still marvelous, and Kan El Khalili bazaar is still fun. Also, the American University remains an oasis in the heart of the city. (However, we understand that a new campus is being built in the suburbs.) When the Cairo days became cool, we returned to Athens to collect our bags before continuing on to Macau by way of Paris, where we enjoyed three idyllic, although chilly, wet days.

In Macau we jumped at the opportunity to rent one of the church apartments. It was good to be with friends after being on our own for several months, and celebrating Christmas once more in Macau was a real joy — the holiday season is always festive. And through the years we have become very fond of our Morrison Chapel friends.

Visa problems finally obliged us to depart for California in late January. It was good, in some ways, to be back home; but in others, we had difficulties adjusting. In June we visited Natasha and Paul in Washington, DC. Shortly after, they moved to the Philippines. From Washington we flew to Dallas, Texas, to visit my sister Kathleen and her family; then on to Kansas to see Norman's mother and brother as well as many friends. In Newton we participated in a cousins' reunion, which was both entertaining and rewarding (they were my cousins). Norman continues.

At 1:30 a.m. the phone in Los Angeles rang; it was the Vice President for Administration of International American University, Cyprus. He asked if I wanted to come to Cyprus and serve as Dean of Arts and Sciences and Chairman of the Dept. of English as well as Prof. of English. I said that BJ and I would consider it. The next night at 4:30 a.m. I said yes, wondering how I could possibly be awake in the mornings, considering my sleeping insomnia habits/problems. The V.P. said that BJ could also teach. So, we flew to Zurich and on to Istanbul, then to Ercan, Northern Cyprus. After a week in a lovely holiday resort, we moved into a spacious furnished house (which, as it has gotten cold, has reduced our living area to only the large kitchen which has a heater. We had forgotten how cold it gets in these unheated houses!) In spite of there being past problems of salary payments, the university is interesting, has some good students, an adequate library in English literature (and nothing else including no card catalogue and no periodicals). They had paid us for the forty days here as of December first. Tomorrow we institute the newly revived MA degree in English and TEFL. The Ph.D. is being worked out with another Turkish university; we have one and possibly three Ph.D. students. We wish we had brought our laptop computer; this typewriter's ribbon is hardly adequate for our needs.

We have enjoyed the area as we travel around to Salamis (ancient Mycenaean culture as well as home of Saint Barnabas), the Saint Barnabas Monastery and Church, now a stunning icon museum. The Girne (Kyrenia in English and Greek) crusader castle guards the entrance to the old harbor. Saint Hilarion Castle on the highest peak of the mountains behind our house (and viewed from our kitchen table where I am writing this) is one of a number of crusader castles dotting the map of Cyprus and goes back to Richard the Lionheart and to the Bronze Age. The ruin of a 3rd century church has Christian mosaic floors, but structure (mainly gone) that reminds one of an ancient (pre-Christian) temple. Girne/ Kyrenia is a lovely seaside tourist center which reminds us of Sousse, Tunisia — with overtones of the mud village element of Kairouan, Tunisia.

We are enjoying much of North Cyprus, in spite of its being one of the more difficult places to get things done that we have lived in. BJ misses swimming almost daily, and I miss my Chinese tea house: both assets of Macau. So far we've kept warm (as usual I've carried my electric blanket around the world), and I have been able to wake up in the mornings for classes. If we could write like Lawrence Durrell — who wrote Justine in his mountain home in Bellapais, just above Kyrenia, where we celebrated Thanksgiving with American, British, and Cypriot friends — we could feel fulfilled.

May Christ's Spirit of Joy and Goodwill be with each of you at Christmas and during 1998.

Girne (Kyrenia), North Cyprus
Monday, December 29, 1997

Dear Lyla and Bill,

This card shows where we went yesterday. But the picture is inadequate. The castle is scattered over two high peaks, with large portions of the crenelated walls still standing. Many gothic arches and some vaulted ceilings still intact — undoubtedly restored many times. The guide book says "the castle of St. Hilarion was first fortified by the Byzantines and named for a hermit who fled from the Arab invasion of the Holy Land."

It was surrendered to Richard I (Lionheart) by Isaac Comnenos in 1191. There are three major crusader castles in

Northern Cyprus. Haven't seen the other two yet. This one is only a 20 min. drive from our house — can see it from our kitchen window.

Our friend Ugur drove us there, and on the way back we stopped at one of the two online cafés in Girne. Ugur's addicted to the internet. So we drank tea and read while he chatted online for about an hour. This café is managed by a young Canadian couple (Mennonite background) who originally came here to teach.

On leaving the café, we discovered a small museum next door with a lovely collection of Bronze Age artifacts — mainly pottery and tools — belonging to the building owner who is a collector. There's also an interesting museum in the Girne castle, which contains a wrecked ship from the time of Alexander the Gt. — 2,300 years ago. It contained nearly 400 pottery jars of probably wine or oil, and lots of almonds, which they believe was the main food of the four-man crew.

We had an okay Christmas. On C. Eve we ate out with an American friend—from California — who teaches in Nicosia. Went to the oldest restaurant in Girne — a kebab place, and had what they call the full kebab dinner. It includes 4 or 5 kinds of meat delivered to the table on skewers, one at a time—haloumi cheese is also broiled, and the best thing served. With the meat is served a large selection of appetizer-type dishes including salad, French fries, and rolled grape leaves. The ambience is nice — a large grill is built into the center of the dining room, and the chef does all the broiling there. We think you'd like it. Afterward, Loren, our friend, took us to his apt. — lovely carpets, paintings, etc. — for tea. From there we went to St. Andrew's (Anglican) for the midnite mass, as they call it. On Christmas day we, of course, took the day off — many of the students had gone to Turkey anyway —and I cooked dinner: chicken with sage dressing, boiled potatoes (no potato masher), cranberry sauce, avocado salad and artichokes. Strange vegetables for Christmas, but that's what looked best in the market. We did have a few

Christmas sweets: baked two kinds of cookies and spiced nuts — walnuts and almonds.

Lyla, you should be very pleased to have been so successful with your diet. Norman thinks he's lost weight; I'm sure I've not — for one thing, we eat too much bread and rice. Several kinds of bread are available, and they're delicious toasted, with the local honey. Packaged sliced bread is available, but we don't buy it.

Norman complained to the landlord's brother (he lives next door and looks after this place while the landlord's in London) about how freezing cold this house is, and the next day a bottle-gas heater was brought, with the offer to deliver the bottles as needed. And a carpet has been installed everywhere except kitchen and baths. So we now sit near the heater in many layers of clothes to watch the TV, which once-in-a-while has a good English movie.

With love to all, Betty and Norman

Girne (Kyrenia), North Cyprus
Saturday, January 10, 1998

Dear Lyla and Bill,

The sun is sparkling on Kansas-like clouds over the mountains with the castle on top. Quite lovely, I must admit. There have been several sunny days this year — yesterday, for example, as we sat on the terrace beside the swimming pool outside the university canteen overlooking the sea. Lovely! But most days are cloudy, with often rain for part of the day. It is supposed to have 360 days of sunshine here, but I don't believe it — lots more than 5 days of rain just since Christmas. It goes from 40/50F to 32F at nite. How we would welcome your furnace now! Sorry about your lemon tree. We'd love to share the lemons on ours; it's loaded with clusters of lemons, like yours was.

The new carpeting (blue, with most of the furniture white) does make the place a little warmer. Now the landlord wants to put it in the kitchen, which is 15 x 18 feet in size. BJ doesn't want it, thinking it will be too hard to clean. But I think he wants it done — says the cleaning lady can take it onto the balcony and clean it. It's true that we spend most of our time in the kitchen. They also hung a curtain to separate the living room from the 15 x 12 foot entrance hall, and this keeps out some of the cold air. Anyway, they've tried, and have spent a lot of money trying to make it warm for us. So, guess we can't move out.

Do wish we were closer to the sea and to the center of town! There are huge houses around us, so guess we're in the Bev. Hills area of this dumpy town, which, if the sea and mountains were removed, would make me think of Kansas — think Dodge City was more interesting! Well, no, we have 50 times more interesting restaurants. The mountains here are like in Palm Springs: right next to the town, with the sea in front of it. Same kind of mountains, with wonderful sunsets like now.

Oh, do pay the rent on the Pioneer apt. by Feb. 3rd or they charge $50 extra. Thanks for doing so much, sending the medicine, coat, etc. It helped! It started raining the day the coat arrived!! It was just in time!

N

Hi,

It's a cold, windy day. I'd planned to go to church, but changed my mind. We both stayed in all day. I cooked dinner New Year's Eve (pretty much a repeat of Christmas dinner) and invited our Turkish friend, Ugur, to join us. Then on New Year's Day we three went to Nicosia, realizing most things would be closed. But seeing the town was interesting. The main museum was headquarters for a sect of whirling dervishes until Ataturk shut them down in 1925 — unusual architecture. A couple of ancient caravansaries are being redone. A huge church appears to be straight out of France, except for the removal of stained glass and interior decoration when turned into a mosque. They also have added two minarets. It was built in the early 13th c. with the help of King Louis IX of France (St. Louis) who came thru on crusade, bringing along architects and engineers. The Green Line, which separates Turkish and Greek Cyprus, runs right thru Nicosia; we could see right into the Greek side, only a stone's throw away.

Is El Nino bringing lots of rain to California? The BBC mentioned heavy rains there.

Love, Betty

PS: We will have approx. three weeks' break between semesters. We plan to go to Macau for one week and to Manila for the rest. We'll leave here Jan. 28 and return Feb. 21. We should warm up in Manila! We eat out here about as much as we did in Glendale. Actually, maybe a bit more since we eat most lunches at the university canteen. We're beginning to be a bit tired of the canteen food. So far there have been lots of avocados and artichokes in the market, and quite cheap. Generally good fresh produce. It's a problem to get good meat; they don't age it — something about Islamic law —and tend to put lamb into lots of things, including hot dogs. Sometimes labels are in Turkish only. Some pork is imported for the English population.

As ever, Betty and Norman

Girne (Kyrenia), North Cyprus
Thursday, January 22, 1998

Norman is really fed up with the university. We're both kind of off and on. He's there today giving exams. Tomorrow I give one of my own and invigilate two others, which makes a full day, starting at 9 and ending at 7, when it's dark, and then one has to find his way home. Often the university buses have disappeared by that time, although they're supposed to be there. The campus is several miles out of town. Miss going with you to Souplantation or Bob's.

B

Hello,

I am about to give the president my resignation — others feel the same. We've been paid only 1½ months' salary: Dec. and Jan. are not paid. Some teachers are really hurting! And all the staff also. I am getting half of what they faxed us my salary would be: they take out over half of it in taxes and deductions — it is really a scam!! And the chairman of the board, who owns this joke of a university, is in Europe "trying" to find someone who will lend him 1½ million $ to keep going. So far no one will, although last week the president said they had it! He has done this for four years now, we understand! We are eager to get away from this mess for a while. We depart on Jan. 28 for Macau via Istanbul and Malaysian airlines to Kuala Lumpur (with a free overnite in a hotel) and on to Macau for a week. Then on to Manila for 2 wks with Natasha and Paul. Back here the 21st Feb. We'll check to see if we've been paid before returning.

They want BJ to teach Western Civilization next term; the fellow who had been teaching it has left for Prague — along with another teacher. In one semester, the former teacher went from the Greeks through "American Imperialism." Amusing how one's prejudices come through. He's a Brit! And a journalist, not historian.

If we come back, I refuse to come here every day! Most of the semester I sat in this office wondering what to do — I have lots of ideas, but no students or teachers to do them! And I die every morning. I'm almost ready to go back to Burger King! Ugh!! Excuse me; I'm going down to get a cup of tea to wash down my pills. Received a letter from Dr. Reyes at Kaiser. I think I'm doing the right regime (is that the word?) of food and medication. He was encouraging!

I'm now into the second 3-hr. exam. Poor guys! I'm actually making them think and write about ideas — first time really!

Anouilh's Antigone, Hemingway's A Farewell to Arms and For Whom the Bell Tolls, Pygmalion, Waiting for Godot, Tartuffe, School for Scandal. Two classes, not one. Although one student who goes to Paris next year did both, but gets credit for one. Anyway, they are exposed to new ideas, and actually writing about them. So maybe it was not a wasted four months here.

Love, Norm and BJ

Istanbul, Turkey
Saturday, February 21, 1998

Dear Lyla and Bill:

Just got off a 28 hr. series of flights on Airbuses — I hate Airbuses! — from Manila to Kuala Lumpur to Dubai to Istanbul, and now waiting for a flight to Cyprus. Sick of it. Burger King's restful terrace sounds good just now.

Yesterday I called Cyprus to see if the teachers and workers had been paid—our colleague said yes, for December and one-half of last month. So we struggle on. Then she said that the government came to the campus last week and took away all the furniture and computers and sold them at auction the following Monday. So our men went to the auction and bought it all back. So it's all back in place. Isn't that a Kill! We'd heard that they hadn't paid their taxes for a long time. But we also heard that if the owner didn't come up with money (they now — again — say he has!?) that the govt. would take over the university. I wonder! I can see the Registrar trying to get the computers that have all the grades, transcripts, curriculum, class registration lists, etc. Isn't it all a mess?! Everything is printed out of those master computers!

In case we are here for another month (at least that, so we can travel to Beirut) or so, would you please send me a California tax form. I mainly need the 1040 or 540 or whatever the main cover form is.

Love,
N

Girne (Kyrenia), North Cyprus
Monday, March 2, 1998

Dear Lyla and Bill

We've just arrived home from having lunch on The Terrace, a seafront restaurant, where it was cold, so we moved to the leeward side of the bldg. still in the sun. Then went to the Dome Hotel — the old, luxurious, seafront establishment with several lounges, where we sat for three hours enjoying our tea, reading, and watching the sea. Then went for pizza and chicken, and arrived home in time to watch a western film set in Mexico — shot in Borrego Springs. Last nite we watched Schwarzenegger's Twins followed by Al Pacino in Scent of a Woman, a very fine film, very on the theme of The Dead Poet's Society. Great job by Pacino.

We hear nothing on local TV about Clinton; the only news here is about Cyprus and Greece and Turkey. CNN Int'l now comes all night and day until 6 p.m. to 11 p.m. (when the last movie ends). CNN has very little about Clinton except for int'l affairs (just now about Iraq and Saddam). The local weekly English newspaper has a story sometimes. The Istanbul and Ankara papers had a lot on him in Turkish earlier when Monica first spilled the beans—or flies. Nothing now — at least no pictures of Monica and Bill ... what keeps Clinton's rating so high? Yes, I agree that there does seem to be a conspiracy. Larry King Live had the lady on a couple days ago who is in prison because she refused to testify against Clinton. Her statements were very revealing. The BBC has coverage quite often when anything happens. In fact, we learn more about the U.S.A. from BBC than from CNN.

N

Girne (Kyrenia), North Cyprus
Monday, March 23, 1998

Hi,

We complain about the cold here, but realize that we've missed some miserable weather in California. What's irritating is how so many people talk about the wonderful weather here — 300+ days of sunshine, etc. — pure fable. I just finished reading Laurence Durrell's Bitter Lemons, his account of living in Cyprus for several years in the '50s. It's highly romanticized, which one would expect, but interesting in spots. [Durrell wrote about Girne/Kyrenia. Durrell lived just above Kyrenia, near our friend's house.]

Yes, the students (most of them) are back from their semester break, but some have already left for the next holiday, which is supposed to begin April 7 and last a week, although we're told they'll take 2-3 weeks. Some of my students said they'd be back on April 30 and hoped I'd not give the midterm exam earlier!

One of my classes this term, however, should be rewarding. It's the second part of the graduate course, World Cultural History for Literature, offered mainly for teachers in the pre-university program who need MAs. One is a Canadian woman who lives here. Several of the students are very bright and will no doubt keep me hopping! Wish we had more library resources; I do enjoy the preparation. In my worst class — freshmen — they're reading a simplified version of Tom Sawyer and most know nothing when given a simple quiz. But it's not that they're incapable, but that they don't try. Many of the students here plan to get a degree without learning anything, and some are obviously succeeding. This whole university ought to be shut down and turned back into a resort — have I said that before??

I'd like to go someplace during the "Easter" holiday (actually it's the Abraham/Isaac Islamic one), but may just take several day trips to places I'm eager to see. Norman says he's seen enough!

Love to all, Betty and Norman

Famagusta, Cyprus
Friday, June 12, 1998 (postcard)

Dear Elma,

As the mosque call blasts forth in the St. Nicholas Cathedral [picture on postcard] (changed in 16th c. to a mosque after heavy bombardment!), we think of you, Elma. We received your welcome letters. They are great! Yes, we are still here. Leave end of June; try to go to Beirut, but have to go to Istanbul to go there. No boats to Syria or Lebanon. Can't go to Larnaca to take boat to Beirut, so have to go to Ist[anbul]. Ugh! May try to go from Izmir to Venice by boat.

Love to you, Norm and BJ

Kyrenia, Cyprus
Tuesday, June 16, 1998

Dear Elma,

The man who painted this card is the father of a friend of ours who teaches here, but not at our university. It's a bit too perfect/precise, isn't it? He's a psychiatrist. The old harbor and castle area is wonderfully charming; this painting doesn't do it justice. One day we explored some ancient caves, not far from the harbor, where Christians lived during the 3rd century. We saw signs of habitation — niches carved into the stone for cupboards, etc., but couldn't get to the most interesting ones, which have small chapels with some wall paintings still visible. They're behind barbed wire in a military zone.

Last weekend we went by dolmus (mini-bus packed with people) to Famagusta, which is a most unusual place. The new city is ugly and boring, but the old town is completely walled with massive ramparts. In the 14th/15th centuries,

Famagusta was one of the richest cities in the world, controlled by the Italian Lusignans and later the Venetians. This was after the fall of Acre, and the Holy Land refugees came here. The old city is full of ancient churches in different stages of ruin. When the British came, they reported that the city contained 300 churches! The population of the city now is 20-25,000. Most of the damage seems to have occurred when it fell to the Turks in the 16th c. If one likes church architecture, it's an explorer's paradise.

We stayed at the only hotel within the walls, which was adequate. Reminds us of some of our earlier travel experiences in the Middle East.

The Turkish side of Nicosia is also quite interesting to explore — two caravansaries, the architecturally magnificent French Gothic Cathedral, which St. Louis helped build, and the former headquarters of the whirling dervishes — now a museum. In both cities things are close together, so one can explore on foot.

Thanks for sharing with us the information about the Mennonites who were exiled to the Valley of Carrots. Hopefully, you'll hear more from Mrs. Wiens. Yes, it is unbelievable that Germany is accepting all these people. Good luck on getting those letters translated this summer.

Your trip to see the Platte River cranes sounds interesting. I understand what you mean about every building being mentioned in her novels — that is, in Willa Cather's Red Cloud. I'm especially fond of My Antonia and taught it to my students in Macau. Natasha sent me a magazine article which was kind of a tour of Red Cloud, with tons of places mentioned.

Yes, I've heard about that Garden of Eden — it does sound weird! Thanks for sending the articles about Joanna Andres; she must have been an interesting lady — her brother, my Uncle George, certainly was an unusual person. I understand him better now, thanks to you for sending the two batches of information about the Sudermann/Enss family. The first packet arrived just before we left Calif. In Oct., but I managed to read it and left it there. The second came here, and I found both articles enlightening. The second, I sent on to Kathleen who was so appreciative — she's saving it for me. It's strange and sad that that aunt and uncle became so estranged from our family, so that the rest of us hardly knew those cousins. My cousin Lucille Saunders, who lived in Newton, died last month, and Kathleen, who went to the funeral, wrote that Frederick Sudermann, who teaches history at Wichita State, was at the funeral. He did not come to our cousin's reunion last year. Beirut and Damascus — also would like to make it to Aleppo since we've not been there. Still trying to decide where to go after that. We're determined to hang around here until we collect our pay. The university is again behind — haven't yet paid us for all of April.

Yes, we did go to Macau and Manila during the big Moslem holiday at end of Ramadan. Especially enjoyed Manila, which was nice and warm. Arrived in Macau during the height of the Chinese New Year, which is always a frenzy. When living there, we always managed to be away at that time.

Tell Elma Wiebe hello. We didn't hear from them at Christmas this year, although usually do. But mail is chancy here.

Love and prayers, BJ and Norm

Istanbul, Turkey
Monday, July 20, 1998 (postcard)

Dear Elma,
Istanbul is like a breath of fresh air after N. Cyprus. We're staying at a wonderful, old hotel filled with Victoriana. Yesterday I went to an Armenian Orthodox service in a huge church hidden away in a covered shopping street. Ritual was entirely sung, and almost no one there. Also visited the whirling dervish museum. They still perform once a month. Spent one day getting visas for Syria. Supposed to

be able to get Lebanese visas at Beirut airport. Hope we're lucky in finding our friends there, and hope you're having a good summer.

Love and prayers,
Betty & N

Istanbul, Turkey
Monday, July 20, 1998 (postcard)

Dear Lyla and Bill,

We're staying in a wonderful, one-hundred-and-six-year-old hotel filled with antiques, high ceilings, painted ceilings in lobby-bar. Wonderful ambience (although the baths need to be redone) with parrots in the lobby windows, plus a collection of old radios and heating stoves. Either you or Tasha sent us the clipping about the Buyuk Londra Oteli, the Grand Hotel de Londres. Great fun. Thanks!! Hope the shipment wasn't too much hassle. Thank you for taking care of it. We go to Beirut Wed. 22nd. Hi to all.

Love, N, BJ

Beirut, Lebanon
Saturday, July 25, 1998 (postcard)

Dear Elma,

You've been in our thoughts lots since we've arrived in Beirut. I walked past your building this morning, and it appears much the same. But so many changes and lots of renovation. Haigazian is simply completely renovated and much building on BUC & AUB campuses. The Presbyterian (community) church in Bab Idriss is completely rebuilt and in use. Hariri has built a huge "palace" next to BUC. We plan to go to Aleppo the 27th, then to Damas and back here to catch our flight back to Istanbul.

With love, Betty and Norm

Aleppo, Syria
Tuesday, July 28, 1998 (postcard)

Dear Lyla & Bill,

We came yesterday to Aleppo from Beirut by taxi; supposed to be a shared car, but after much bickering, ended up with a private one. Wild driver, but arrived safely. Staying at Baron's Hotel — old and famous; many prominent persons have stayed here; interesting although rather down-at-the-heels. The old covered bazaar is huge and wonderful. We bought a small gilim and a striped Bedouin runner. Beirut is, we feel, pseudo-western compared to Aleppo. Tomorrow will go to the National Museum and the Citadel. Plan to take midnite train (sleeper) to Damascus the 30th; hope it's a good experience. Then, a day or two later, to Beirut by taxi to catch our flight to Istanbul where we may stay for several weeks. Hope all's well there. It's hot here. [Great train ride; very like U.S. trains in '50s when I first went to college.]

Love,
Betty and Norm

[How sad that the civil war has destroyed what was a beautiful, historic city/nation, killing so many warm, kind, loving people whom we had the pleasure of knowing. We felt the same way about Beirut and their civil war! "Please, Dear God, forgive our foolish ways …"]

CHAPTER 13

GLENDALE (1998 – 1999)

Christmas Letter 1998

This Christmas finds us back in the United States for the first time in more than twenty years. Being back, not surprisingly, is a mixed blessing; adjusting is not easy, but there are one or two signs of progress: we are coping quite well with our HMO that provides such extensive care that one could wonder how we managed so well with so little for so many years.

As most of you know, we both taught in North (Turkish) Cyprus last year. Although the jobs were the least rewarding we've had, the island is beautiful, with a wealth of ancient historic sites. We enjoyed a wonderful trip during the semester break when we visited friends in Macau, which was during the Chinese New Year, a festive and congested time. Then we went on to Manila to be with Natasha and Paul, who are now in their second year there. We pray there are no more embassy bombings. After a great time together we returned to Cyprus for the second semester.

The thing that probably kept us from chucking our jobs was the fact that the university consistently owed us 2-3 months' salary. Also, as spring brought warmer weather, the beauties of the island seemed adequate compensation.

In early July, after fulfilling our obligations to the university, we managed to collect back pay and leave the island. After spending a week in Istanbul, in a fascinating turn-of-the-century, one-hundred-year-old hotel overlooking the Golden Horn, we flew to Beirut, where we had lived from 1963-65 and six years in the 1980s. We had never returned because of the travel ban. Although much rebuilding is taking place, many bombed-out areas remain. The university campuses look good, with considerable improvements. It was a real joy to see so many of our friends, some of whom had returned after fleeing the war.

From Beirut we went by taxi to Aleppo, Syria, a city we had long wanted to visit, and we had such a good time there. The people were friendly and a bit surprised to learn that we were Americans — evidently few visit there now. We stayed at Baron's Hotel, a famous old hotel built to accommodate passengers traveling the Berlin-to-Baghdad Railroad in the early 20th century, as did Agatha Christie and T.E. Lawrence. Staying at Baron's is a good experience because it attracts many interesting people. Aleppo is full of lovely old architecture; the souk is endless and mysterious, with exotic merchandise as well as plastic stuff. A highlight was a day trip to the environs of St. Simeon the Stylite, who lived on a pillar for forty years, and several of the abandoned desert cities as well as the archaeological site of Ebla. [In 2013-14 we watched Aleppo and all of Syria destroy itself. How sad! Now in 2017 Aleppo is destroyed, and hopeful Syrians are trying to return to Aleppo. Please, Dear God, bless and keep them safe.]

We reluctantly left Aleppo for Damascus by overnite train (our cheapest ever travel experience: $6 each for air-cond. sleeper), then on to Beirut by taxi, and eventually back to Istanbul where my sister Kathleen joined us.

In late August we returned to California and on to Kansas to visit friends and Norman's 92-year-old mother. No travel plans at the moment.

CHAPTER 14

MACAU 2 (1999 –)

CHOI KOU SCHOOL – REFLECTIONS FROM BJ

Early in 1999, we wrote to Michael Poon, friend and head of the Anglican program in Macau, asking whether one of the church apartments would be available for us to rent for several weeks in December and January. The Handover of Macau back to China was scheduled to take place in December, and we thought it would be interesting to be on the spot to observe the occasion. Michael responded by suggesting that we do something constructive by coming for a whole year as volunteers at Choi Kou School, the Chinese curriculum Anglican primary and secondary school. A new building was being dedicated in September, and our job would be to help establish an English library and offer teacher training. The school would provide air tickets, housing, and a small monthly stipend. We immediately accepted the offer.

The year's work went quite well although book-buying was limited to books available locally and across the border in Zhuhai, and most of the teachers didn't really want to be trained. Our contract with the school ended, but we quite enjoyed life in Macau and asked the school if they would continue to sponsor us, which meant signing for our residence permit from the Immigration Department. In return, we would continue to help part-time in the English program and cover our own expenses. The school agreed to this, and the arrangement continued for fourteen years until 2014.

We spent approximately six months in Macau (September or October through March) and six months in Pasadena, California. Over the years, our work has been more with students; Chinese teachers tend to see teacher training as a put-down — it suggests that they aren't properly trained. Norm has worked mainly with sixth form (year 12) students; and although primary students are not my specialty, I've enjoyed working with Ms. Tarrosa, Filipina in charge of the elementary school English program.

We once helped with an English language weekend retreat, which was held at a convent on Coloane Island — an interesting experience. Possibly the most successful project was an English-teaching workshop for approximately forty teachers from various Macau schools, many of whom had been our students at the university. This was held at our school but sponsored by the Macau Education Department. This was during the summer holiday and covered five days. For some reason, these teachers were very responsive and appreciative of our help, unlike our experience at Choi Kou.

Another cultural difference I experienced was revealed when I suggested to the school principal that we have a mini-conference for all Macau English teachers at which we shared ideas and teaching methods. His response was shocking to me. "I don't think that would work here. Chinese teachers don't like to give away their secrets."

For me, a highlight of our time in Macau came in 2007, which was the 200th anniversary of Robert Morrison's arrival in China. Morrison was the first Protestant missionary to China, residing most of the time in Macau. He translated the Bible into Chinese and wrote a Chinese-English Dictionary as well as many other books and articles. Just behind Morrison Chapel, where we attended services, is the Old Protestant Cemetery where Morrison and several family members are buried. Also resting in this little cemetery are a number of notables, including a great uncle of Winston Churchill; Joseph Adams, grandson of John Adams and nephew of John Quincy; a godson of George Washington; and three infant great-grandchildren of Thomas Jefferson.

I headed a committee, along with Christine Duggan and Samiya Allan, to plan the celebration of Morrison's arrival. We had many good ideas, but Vicar Judy, who had to approve each suggestion, felt we were far too enthusiastic. She said that "people will think we're worshipping Robert Morrison instead of Jesus!"

Well, we succeeded in bringing several of our ideas to fruition. I put together a series of monologues and readings, which were presented in an evening performance of "Voices from the Past: Contemporaries of Robert Morrison Speak of Life in Macau during the 1820s and 1830s." We held a Sunday morning Thanksgiving service with the archbishop from Hong Kong as well as Rev. Dr. Michael Poon, former vicar, now from Singapore, giving the sermon. St. Joseph University invited me to give a lecture on Morrison, along with a partial repeat of the "Voices" program. And our most exciting accomplishment was convincing the Macau Post Office to issue a commemorative stamp, actually two, for Robert Morrison. This was no easy achievement, but I will not go into detail. The stamps came out in September, with a different version of Morrison's portrait on each stamp. More than one person asked us, "Who from Morrison Chapel works at the post office?"

In October 2008 we celebrated our 50th wedding anniversary with a buffet supper for twenty friends at Lord Stow's Library Café on the University of Macau campus. We earlier had a celebration supper at Charlie's in Newton, Kansas, with a dozen friends, most of whom had participated in our wedding. One advantage of these last years in Macau has been its proximity to Manila, Singapore, and Kuala Lumpur, where Natasha and her family have lived. We have visited them in these cities a number of times.

For the last several years, our work at Choi Kou was minimal, and we appreciated Principal Eric Chan's willingness to continue sponsoring us. Macau continued to offer us a pleasant lifestyle: no necessity to drive due to efficient and cheap public transport; many excellent concerts by the Macau Orchestra and by numerous international groups that are inexpensive and easily accessible; worship at Morrison Chapel, where we enjoy longtime friendships. Indeed, discounting the fact that our medical help presented a problem, our quality of life in Macau surpassed that which we enjoyed in Pasadena.

CORRESPONDANCE (2000 – 2010)

Manila, Philippines
Sunday, January 2, 2000

Dear Elma,

Happy New Year! We're in Manila with Natasha and family and are grateful for no Y2K problems so far; Manila was/is on the high risk list. We're to fly back to Macau on Tuesday (the 4th) having been here for two weeks. Kind of dread returning to the cold weather in Macau — it's quite warm here, and the rainy season has just ended. We've not done much here, but the time goes fast. Helena is now 4½ mo. and "talking" a lot. She'd keep us all busy if she had her way. She recently had a bad stomach upset, but is okay now.

We're enjoying being back in Macau, although our work at the schools seems to me to progress slowly. The woman in charge of the English program at the primary school is eager to try new methods, etc., but the elderly woman in charge at the high school is traditional in the extreme and sees anything different as a threat. All the English teachers are over-worked and have approx. 40 students per class — students who, unlike the students in China, are not motivated to learn English. I'm supposed to be giving a series of seminars/workshops for the teachers during the second semester, in which I hope to offer a few ideas concerning methods and mostly encouragement. Norman is supposed to direct a play and is wondering how that will be when their spoken English is so bad. Our friend, the principal and head of the Anglican mission in Macau, is determined to improve the school's academic standards. I'm glad not to have his job.

It was quite interesting to be in Macau for its handover to China. Unlike many Hong Kong people, those of Macau appeared happy about it all, cheering the Red Army into town with a huge parade. Of course the schools were all expected to participate.

Please share this letter with Elma Wiebe; we've sent no Christmas letters and are behind in correspondence.

With love, Betty and N

Macau
Christmas 2000

Dear Friends,

In spite of dire predictions, we all survived the turn of the millennium (not to mention the handover of Macau to China)! Even Manila, where we were for that event, and which was high on the list of likely catastrophe spots, made a smooth transition into the new century.

Once again predictions bring anxiety and discord as our government grapples with the vote-counting fiasco of the Presidential election. Hopefully, that confusion will be sorted out before this letter reaches you. Life is never dull for long. As most of you know, we returned to Macau last October for a year as volunteers, helping with the Anglican schools' English programs. Our work was challenging and rewarding; we enjoyed renewing old friendships and attending Morrison Chapel. We look forward to returning to Macau in January for approximately another year.

Macau hasn't experienced big changes since the handover to China. Life appears to continue as usual. However, quite a number of Mainland Chinese are moving in, and schools are noticing the increased student numbers. Also, workers have demonstrated discontent with the influx of cheap "foreign" labor since many blue-collar workers are unemployed. Mainlanders cross the border daily to work for lower pay than the locals will accept.

From Macau it was only a two-hour flight to visit Natasha, Paul, and Helena in Manila. They have now moved to Singapore where we visited in August to help celebrate Helena's first birthday. Our family is indeed fortunate to be able to spend considerable time together despite distances.

Shortly after returning to California from Macau in September, we visited friends and relatives in Kansas and Texas. A highlight of this journey was attending Norman's high school class reunion. Neither of us had been to one before, and it was rewarding and full of surprises for both of us.

We cherish fond memories from our years of teaching in the Middle East and are deeply concerned about the recent escalation of the Israeli-Palestinian crisis. Please join us in praying for peace and justice for that troubled land, a land which was rebelling against Roman oppression two thousand years ago when Jesus came to teach his message of peace and salvation. As we again celebrate Jesus' birth, may our lives be filled with His peace and joy.

Have a blessed Christmas and a New Year filled with good health and good cheer!

PS: [Elma] Well, we're stuck with Geo. W. Bush whether he deserves it or not! As one of our friends says, "If we survived Reagan, we'll survive Bush!" [Little did we know just how disastrous the Bush years would be.]

Palermo, Sicily
Sunday, August 26, 2001 (postcard)

Dear Elma,

We're finally experiencing Sicily, and are wondering if you had as many difficulties as we do, just getting around. English isn't widespread here, and everything seems to be set up for group tours. Monreale Cathedral is marvelous. We'll see the Palermo cathedral this afternoon and Royal Palace tomorrow. Back to Tunis August 30; then to Singapore via Paris.

Love,
BJ and Norm

[9/11 in New York City happened a few hours after we returned from Paris to Singapore.]

Macau
December 2001

MERRY CHRISTMAS MERRY CHRISTMAS
MERRY CHRISTMAS
"O LOVE, HOW DEEP, HOW BROAD, HOW HIGH!
HOW PASSING THOUGHT AND FANTASY THAT GOD,
THE SON OF GOD, SHOULD TAKE OUR MORTAL FORM
FOR MORTALS' SAKE."

Dear Friends,

As some of you know, we returned to Macau in February to continue to help with the English program at the Anglican Choi Kou schools. We've been doing mostly teacher training; however, BJ is also helping this year at the primary school, teaching conversational English — which is more challenging than you can imagine! She also is working on another book, this time on the influence of non-Portuguese Westerners upon Macau's history. Norm is again encouraging our teachers to better express themselves in spoken English. Today he watched these teachers do a dress-rehearsal presentation of "The Macau Town Musicians," which was potentially delightful, and he wishes they would present it to the students next week at the English Corner's Christmas Party but, of course, they are too shy. Norm also is following his tradition of encouraging the building of theatres: this time at the third Choi Kou School, where they made the mistake of asking him to help make their Hall function as a theatre. This same thing happened in Tehran when they asked him to join the Frank Lloyd Wright design team turning the lecture hall into a theatre: Wes Peters and Norm and Taliesin West in Tehran turned it into a magnificent theatre, which was finished after the revolution. We trust this one will not have the same delays. It is certainly simplified, as compared to Damavand College's.

We again will join Natasha, Paul, and Helena in Singapore for Christmas, returning here in January and on to Pasadena sometime later. We loved visiting North Africa in summer. In Tunis we visited old friends with whom we had taught; then sailed over to Sicily to view Monreale Cathedral, Cappella Palatina (Royal Chapel), and other medieval sites before returning across the Tyrrhenian Sea to Tunis and down to Sousse to visit good friends there, where we taught 1985-88. Fortunately, we returned to Singapore the day before the horror of September 11th; it was good to be with our family when the BBC news hit the world. Macau seems strangely isolated from these tragic world events; here, life goes on as usual. We wish for each of you a Glorious Christmas and a Blessed New Year.

HAPPY NEW YEAR HAPPY NEW YEAR HAPPY NEW YEAR

PS: [Elma] We're wondering if we'd not be smart to stay here longer instead of returning to the U.S. in February. Norman needs to get a supply of medicine from our HMO plus a medical check-up. What a world situation! The Middle East does sound hopeless! And airport security in the U.S. sounds like it's not improved much. I remember your last year's Christmas letter and envision medieval monks sitting at their work tables (probably stiff from cold) peacefully copying manuscripts. What a different world that was, although it wasn't peaceful outside the monastery then, either. I wonder if the new hand-copied Bible is on schedule? We leave for Singapore via Bangkok, where we'll have three nites at the Christian Guest House, one of our favorite places to stay. They have an excellent library/lounge, where one can relax when tired of running about. Have a good Christmas and keep in touch!

Blessings, Betty and Norman

El Rancho Hotel, Gallup, New Mexico
Wednesday, July 31, 2002 (postcard)

Hi Elma,

We think you'd like this hotel — it's architecturally
interesting; built in 1937. Our train was an hour late arriving
in Newton, and the same arriving here. The truck (driven by
Jeff Sturm) with our stuff from storage will (hopefully) leave
Newton Aug. 5, giving us a little time to figure out where to
put it all. Good luck with your Russian letters project.

Love, B & N

Macau
Monday, November 24, 2003

Dear Elma,

How are things in Kansas? We did have an email a while
back from the Morses, who are still busily remodeling their
huge house. They just installed a metal circular staircase from
the second floor to the attic. They do this in their spare time!
We're much less ambitious. Norman teaches two classes a
week, and I do three. And we manage to keep busy enough,
although N does complain occasionally of being bored. I
swim nearly every day, and still do a few bits on the book
which is finally with the publisher, the Cultural Institute of
Macau, and it's supposed to be completed by July.

Our pastor, Michael Poon, decided that Morrison
Chapel should have a Thanksgiving dinner, and wanted
it as traditional as possible. The only Americans attending
the Chapel besides us are a couple with a little girl, and a
single, middle-aged man who's been away from the U.S. so
long he doesn't know what's traditional. Well, the dinner
took place this past Saturday evening, Nov. 22, and was held
at a restaurant/bakery (actually more of a sandwich/salad
place) run by a British church member. Their bakery ovens
aren't tall enough to bake turkeys, so we had chicken and
ham instead, and no dressing or mashed potatoes and gravy.

Had potato salad and lots of other salads, a bit of cranberry sauce, and several desserts, including pumpkin pie, which was quite good. Seventy-four people came, which was excellent, considering that our Chapel attendance is around 30-35. [The food was excellent!]

In order to save us from balloons, I volunteered to do flowers for the tables. So I went to the flower market near our house in the morning and bought some lovely baby mums in autumn colors — enough for ten bouquets. Flowers are very cheap here — they're brought from just across the border in China.

Michael wanted a program and asked a Scottish missionary in his eighties to tell of his experiences working in several Asian countries. We added a couple numbers: brief history of American Thanksgiving by the other American woman; her daughter read the poem "Over the river and through the woods ..." And I led them in two traditional songs, which of course most people didn't know, but I had made copies from the Baptist Hymnal. Can you believe that the Anglican church here still does not have hymnals with music notes! And the singing is awful.

Do you remember meeting George and Tobia Veith in Newton, who were on their way to Macau to start a church? That was a few years back. We've seen them now and then; were at their church dedication a couple years ago. We had George and the three children for supper a couple weeks ago; Tobia couldn't come because she had to make an emergency trip to her family in Canada. It looks like they'll be taking a year off to be with her family starting in summer. I've been intending to get to their church sometime; it's all in Chinese, of course. At the dedication George's sermon in Chinese sounded good to us. And Tobia is good at the piano. The kids are a handful! But basically good. [In 2011-2014 George stayed in our Pasadena apt. each January while doing his Ph.D. at Fuller Seminary. Since 2015 George and Tobia are working in Harbin, China. I hope to give George my Ph.D. academic robe, but he hasn't been by to pick it up.]

Norman says hello, and says to tell you that we now have a library in our Pasadena apartment. The carpenter who built the shelves (floor to ceiling) finished them barely before we left, so we didn't have time to fill them, although put some books in place. Will do the rest next trip.

Norman still has lots of trouble with his feet; he feels best lying down, reading a book, although our sofa is too short for him.

We think that your book should be put on the internet — in order to make the information available. But don't ask us how to go about it. Guess it has to be scanned first. It's quite easy if one knows how to do it. A paper I wrote several years ago for a conference was subsequently put into a book by Univ. of Macau. Now that article is on the internet, although I'm not sure how it got there. Is your history professor still around? Was his name Springer? He might be knowledgeable about such things. Not sure there'd be anything in it for you, except the satisfaction that the information is accessible.

We plan to spend Christmas in Singapore with Natasha and family.

With love and prayers, Betty and Norman

PS: We read with great interest the Mennonite Weekly Review article (Sept. 8) about the recognition of Ida Stoltzfus. I remember so vividly the visit to their Hebron school. Thank you, Elma, for taking us there. Has she retired in the West Bank/Israel?? Or can there possibly be a retirement center in Pennsylvania called Tel Hai??

B

Macau
November 2004

Dear Elma,

How are things in post-election North Newton? It's good to be far away. People here are happy with the economic boom. There's always some festive event — International Music Festival (excellent!), Arts Festival, and now a Food Festival from mainland China — all cooked in booths in the main square. Most of that's not very tempting to us. Our church, Morrison Chapel, has a new pastor, a woman from Australia. She's good — very energetic with lots of ideas for more events/services for all of us to attend. We plan to go to Bangkok for two weeks over Christmas and New Year — mainly for warmer weather, but the weather here has been very nice so far. Last nite we heard a lovely concert in a 16th c. baroque church. The Macau chamber orchestra did some Handel and Schubert. Natasha and family are not enjoying being back in Washington. We'd like to travel the Silk Route, but are concerned about those parts where there is no railroad. How is your reading machine working out?

Much love, Norm and Betty

Bangkok, Thailand
Thursday, February 10, 2005 (postcard)

Dear Elma,

We're back in Thailand for the Chinese New Year. Got your letter from the Wichita hospital and tried to phone you, but don't have your access extension no. Hope you're okay. We go back to Macau in a week.

Love, Betty and Norm

Macau
Thursday, December 8, 2005 (Christmas card)

Dear Elma,

Norman's classes at the nite school finally begin tonite. I've agreed to help a few hours a week with the English program of the nursing college at the Chinese hospital. The retired American who's come to upgrade the place is a real pusher. She's having the nurses give a Christmas program, which was reluctantly agreed to by the non-Christian administration. I'm to teach the nurses Christmas carols.

Tomorrow nite we have a concert — Macau orchestra playing Brahms and Weber with a Russian violinist. Heard some good lectures on American literature by Fulbrighters at the university. God bless and keep you!

Much love, Betty and Norm

Macau
Monday, April 3, 2006

Dear Elma,

We're doing quite well, but having lots of dental work done before coming home. It's cheaper here. Our preacher, an Australian deaconess, has many services lined up for Easter. Palm Sunday, instead of a sermon, we'll have a dramatized version of Mark chaps. 14 and 15, with a procession of palms starting in the cemetery. Maundy Thursday is evening communion with one of the Chinese congregations. Good Friday liturgy at 10 a.m. Easter Saturday, 8 p.m. communion, lighting of Pascal candle and renewing of baptismal vows (have you heard of this??), and Easter morning, communion again.

On April 7 the Macau orchestra performs Brahms' A German Requiem with the Hong Kong Oratorio Chorus and Shanghai Opera Chorus in a 16th century baroque church.

You mentioned having one of your books rebound. Do you know of a place where one can have one or two books bound with hard covers?

We plan to return to Pasadena shortly after Easter, so don't send any more mail here.

God bless, Betty and Norman

Macau
December 2006

How proper it is that Christmas should follow Advent. For him who looks toward the future, the Manger is situated on Golgotha, and the Cross has already been raised in Bethlehem. Dag Hammarskjold
Dear Friends,

MERRY CHRISTMAS from Macau! We returned here from Pasadena, California, in early October and are continuing to volunteer at Macau's Anglican schools. Our actual time working is minimal: Norman teaches a class in the night school, and I'm to help prepare students for an oral English exam which comes out of London and of which I strongly doubt the value! But the students (especially their parents) want it, so I'm happy to help. I've also been working one day a week at the Chinese hospital's nursing school. The hospital is adding a new building which will cater to westerners — the intention is to compete with places like Thailand, etc. So there's a big push to improve the nurses' English. It seems to me they've a long way to go.

We continue to enjoy excellent concerts, mainly by the Macau Orchestra, although the Italian State Orchestra performed during the International Festival, and the Johann Strauss Capelle de Viena comes next month. One feels a bit extravagant, indulging in approximately one concert a week, but the tickets are so cheap! It's all heavily subsidized by the government. West Side Story and Guys and Dolls from New York, and operas from Europe fill out the Macau Music Festival.

Norman always suffers from the cold in the winter here, and feels rather like Harriett Low, a young lady from Salem, Massachusetts, who lived in Macau from 1829-1833. She wrote in her diary: "December 27, 1832. Terrible cold. I do not like cold weather in this country — great barns of rooms, great cracks under the doors and the floors you can see through. The carpet does not seem to do much good. And it is so rainy now we cannot get a walk, and one's limbs are almost stiff with the cold. It makes me shudder at the thought of encountering our winter, though I know you have more comforts at home, that nice warm basement room; I wish I was in it. The Chinamen all look as thick as they are long now. So many clothes on. The Portuguese, many of them go to bed and there lay." Well, thanks to improved construction technology and smaller rooms, not to mention global warming, we've not been very cold so far this autumn. [I was cold, and like Harriett Low I stayed in bed under many blankets; one electric, unlike Harriet.]

Although there's still much to be said for life here, many changes are bringing problems and rapidly making Macau a less pleasant place. Norman is going to write something about those changes.

This is a city of three islands: the one attached to China is one and one-half miles long by one-half mile wide, the second and third are half that size, all connected by long bridges and a causeway over a mile long. Fortunately, we don't need a car here; taxis and busses are cheap and efficient. While many here are buying cars — the traffic becomes horrendous — we're happy not to have to drive! The new casinos coming in from Las Vegas and elsewhere not only increase the traffic, but have increased to nearly twenty million tourist visitors annually coming in from the Chinese mainland and from Hong Kong and all Asia. Every fifteen minutes a three-hundred-seat hydrofoil goes between Macau and Hong Kong; there are many daily flights between Macau and China, Singapore, Bangkok, Taiwan, Japan, Korea, Vietnam. [In 2013 and '14, 28 million visitors came to Macau, mostly from Mainland China.]

The Sands Casino-Hotel opened over a year ago, and the forty-story Wynn, by far the most luxurious, opened recently. The new Macau Venetian Casino- Hotel will have three canals (the Vegas Venetian has one canal) and the first hotel of the complex has four thousand rooms; the next two will make a total of thirteen thousand rooms. [MGM's 50 story casino-hotel is lovely.] The income per casino table greatly exceeded that of Vegas even before Vegas moved into Macau. I hear that the Macau casinos will need sixty thousand workers to operate them. Where will these workers live? The China border crossing is now congested with the daily arrival of construction workers. And the immigration offices are an overworked, confused madness! Everyone seems happy with the booming economy, but there's a gradual awakening to the social evils inherent in the gambling industry.

For our family, the high point of 2006 occurred in July, when we were at home in Pasadena. While Natasha and daughters, Portia* and Nina, were with us, my sister Kathleen came from Texas for a short visit. Kathleen's daughters, Georgia from Kansas and Kathy from Colorado, also joined us, and we had a wonderful time together! Some of us hadn't seen each other for a very long time, and Natasha especially enjoyed reacquainting with her cousins.

It was great to have the three girls from Washington, DC, for much of the summer, and Paul was able to join us all for a week or so between his trips to Paris. In the autumn Natasha finally got to return to Paris to see her friends from the years she lived there before marrying Paul.

We have been blessed in many ways during 2006 and are thankful. And we wish for all of you God's richest blessings during a very MERRY CHRISTMAS and a HAPPY NEW YEAR!

Betty and Norm

PS: Our church had a lovely Lessons and Carols Service Sunday evening. The Macau Orchestra and Taipei Oratorio Chorus are doing "Bach's

Christmas Oratorio" Dec. 23. Then we'll go to Bangkok for a week so Norman can "thaw out."

B & N

Macau
Saturday, December 30, 2006
(postcard: Bangkok Christian Guest House)

Dear Elma,

This is where we always stay in Bangkok. It has a friendly ambience, with interesting people passing through. Also excellent restaurants, etc., nearby. And Anglican Christ Church is in walking distance. We had Christmas dinner at a restaurant with Canadian friends who teach here.

With love and best wishes for 2007,
Betty & Norm

Macau
December 2007 (Chinese Christmas card)

Hi, Elma,

This is the kind of card that lets you imagine any message you like! We've moved to a different apartment, but mailing address and tel. # remain the same. As you know, moving is not fun.

I recently went across the border into China to do a little shopping. There's an interesting, huge market right under the border gate. But too many people! One thing I noticed is that there's more affluence, and things are more expensive than a year ago.

We continue to have lovely, warm weather here. We plan to again be in Thailand for the Christmas holidays.

We wish for you God's blessings at this happy season and throughout 2008!

Love always, Norm and BJ

Macau
December 2008

MERRY CHRISTMAS FROM MACAU! How quickly the old year draws to a close! The events of 2008 leave the world in worse shape than ever, and could leave one discouraged, even in despair for the future. But thankfully, the arrival of Advent brings hope and expectations for the joys of Christmas and a better 2009.

However, for our family, it's been a good year, for which we're thankful. Health-wise, we're doing okay. Norm's coping with the usual problems plus a new one: vertigo. And I've recovered from a hysterectomy, for which surgery we returned to the U.S. earlier this year.

2008 held for us two big events. One was the visit of Natasha, Portia, and Nina for the months of June and July. Portia and Nina were kept busy with swimming and gymnastics lessons, and two Bible schools, Methodist and Congregational!

The second big event was our 50th wedding anniversary, which we celebrated with two dinner parties. First an early one in August when we were in Newton, Ks. Ten of our friends from the old days (several from our wedding party) joined us for dinner at Charlie's, a "down-home" type favorite place of ours. Then in Macau we celebrated late, with twenty friends, one of them owning the restaurant — Lord Stow's, where the food and service are excellent! The top photo is from that party.

Another event which occupied much of our time was the presidential campaign — far too long, but nonetheless fascinating. Fortunately, the election's outcome has brought hope to many people. Let's pray that they are not disappointed... .We have made plans to again spend the Christmas holiday in Thailand, where it's warm, but now we're waiting to see whether the problems there are sorted out by then.

We wish for each of you a joyous Christmas and God's blessings during 2009!

[*Helena chose to use her second name, Portia. Her school friends kept calling her "Heleena," which she didn't like, so she's now Portia, as in Merchant of Venice.]

Macau
October 21, 2010

Dear Jack [Francis Brown],

In your last letter you asked about the production of Die Fledermaus with Lily Pons. Yes, that was at Christmastime in 1971, and the sets were designed by Jane Rowe, now Putnam.

When we were living and teaching in Palm Springs/Palm Desert, Ca., I was asked to direct Die Fledermaus by Richard Strauss for the Palm Springs Opera Company, founded by the renowned Metropolitan Opera diva Lily Pons. I took one look at the tired sets they were going to use and decided they had to be redone. I contacted Jane in New York and asked her to come out to Palm Springs to help redo the sets. She was quite ill at the time, but another friend and I shared the cost of the airfare to bring her to California. The mutual friend, Elaine Kleeman, a New York executive in advertising, called awhile before Christmastime and told me Jane was ill and asked if I could bring her out to Palm Springs to recover.

I was worried about the shabby sets they planned to use in Die Fledermaus, and it was an inspiration to involve Jane in redoing them with me. The set Jane created for the Vienna Grande House was splendid, with a chandelier and a scrim-walled entrance so the soprano could be seen in the front door hallway as the cue came for her grand entrance. Tom Aitchison and I did the beribboned ballroom and flowered gazebo-jail. Tom's cockatoo bird, in his three-foot-high cage atop the Turkish ottoman, had a microphone above him, and he competed singing with the outstanding soprano during the ballroom scene, sensationally bringing the show to an unexpected high point. The conductor was angry with the bird's competition. Jane was exhausted by it all. While in New York, she had been depressed due to the flu and from an artist's lack of wealth, and we pulled her into the Palm Springs mess by putting her to work designing and executing the sets. She brilliantly succeeded! Just as she had with Finnegans Wake for the Holland Festival in 1969. Besides, I hated the crappy sets they were using, and if I had to do the show, it was going to look great!

The whole town thought the opera would fail, but Tianne, my choreographer, told them, "Oh, no, it won't fail. They have Lofland to direct and do the sets." The fact that they were not going to pay Jane caused me to withhold the sets until they paid her. Tom, a musician himself, hammered the stage braces in place to the beat of the kettle drums, highlighting the glorious overture. What a bitchy place and situation this all was.

Jane stayed on in the Springs for Christmas. Fortunately, her luck turned when John Putnam, Art Director of Mad Magazine, proposed.

It did my heart good to encourage theatre in the Springs with such productions as Pantagleize, J.B., and The Boyfriend, Edwin Booth, as well as a number of small shows. But one really rewarding moment was when Judith Anderson played Hamlet, staged by Bill Ball, creator of the American Conservatory Theatre in San Francisco, which was started at Carnegie Institute of Technology when I was there. Judith Anderson, after touring much of America, was doing her last performance in Palm Springs and as she did her curtain call, I stood up in my tuxedo and forced that audience into giving her a standing ovation. They did! My boss — who was a scholar of repute but who was made timid by driving lots of wealthy, prominent ladies around the desert, including Lily Pons and Elizabeth Taylor's mother, Sara Sothern —

was horrified that my standing up encouraged the audience to reverse their unfavorable early comments and show respect for one of their hometown actresses who dared to follow Sarah Bernhardt in performing Hamlet.

Fascinating.

Well, Jack, this has given you far more than you asked for. BJ joins me in sending love, and we hope you can again visit us, as you have in the forty years we've been friends.

Bless you,

Norm

CHAPTER 15

NATASHA (1962 –)

Natasha was born at Bethel Deaconess Hospital at Newton, Kansas. I was then teaching at Bethel College, and BJ was director of the Girls' Dormitory and assistant to the Dean of Women. Her office was across the hall from our one-bedroom apartment in the dorm, making it convenient for her to look after baby Natasha while on the job. Another advantage was that the dorm provided an abundant supply of babysitters.

When we set out on our first overseas teaching jobs, Natasha was nine months old, so she had no input in our decision to move to Beirut. And in later years she didn't often complain about places we lived. She did sometimes say she wished we had a home to go to in the U.S. She wanted more stability.

When we left Newton to teach in Beirut, Natasha was wearing a removable plastic brace, which was supposed to correct a problem from birth: she was born with no right hip socket. Upon arriving in Beirut, we realized the brace wasn't working, and Dr. Suheil Bulos, trained at London's Orthopedic Hospital and highly recommended, replaced the brace with a plaster cast from just under her arms to the ankle on one leg and just above the knee on the other. With two adjustments, Natasha wore this cast for a year.

Since both BJ and I were teaching, we hired a young Druze woman, Yaffa, to care for Natasha while we were at the college. Yaffa was a kind, gentle person who was recommended by our neighbors, the Dr. Abu Chars. In addition to caring for Natasha, she cleaned, infrequently cooked, and occasionally shopped for groceries. She'd worked for

Americans before, and said they'd had her cook steak and salad every day. I usually prepared

Natasha's food. The main one was ground beef mixed with potatoes and carrots; one could buy much imported food in Beirut, but baby food was expensive. The markets were full of lovely, inexpensive local fruit and vegetables.

During her second year with us, Yaffa had her own baby girl, Sausan (Susan), whom she brought with her to work. We bought her a stroller to transport the baby, and friends lent us a second baby bed for Natasha's room. The baby added entertainment for Natasha, who, not being able to walk, spent lots of time in her playpen; they didn't really play together but observed and "talked" to each other. Natasha was well over two years old when she first walked.

Day trips to the various mountain villages occupied many weekends, and a few times on weekdays, when we'd finish classes early and the weather was warm, we'd pack a picnic lunch, pile into the convertible along with Yaffa and the two babies, lower the top, and head for Beit Mary. It's too bad that Natasha was too young to remember anything from that first time in Lebanon, for it was a happy time with many wonderful trips in our Karmann Ghia convertible. Besides the day trips to the mountains, we took her with us to Damascus several times, as well as to Jerusalem, Petra, Palmyra, and all the way to London and back.

Natasha stayed with Kermit and Sharon Yoder (managers of Beirut Menno Travel) and Baby Carmen during our car trip to Iran; and with Neil and Joyce Houck, fellow teachers, and their two children, when we chaperoned students on a trip to Egypt. May, a student from the college, and Mary Abou Char from next door, babysat on several occasions, but we didn't go out often; I occasionally went to a movie, and often attended college functions alone while BJ stayed home with Natasha.

After two years in Lebanon, we moved to Pittsburgh, Pennsylvania, where I studied for and completed my Ph.D. at Carnegie Institute of Technology, now Carnegie Mellon University. Although I had a sizeable grant from the Heinz Food Company, BJ needed to teach to help support us, and I also taught full time at Duquesne University.

We felt very lucky to find the Hill House, an excellent daycare center. It was operated by the city, with all Black children, but they were trying hard to integrate, so were very happy to register Natasha, their first white child.

She loved her time at Hill House and always cried when I came to pick her up. The director said, "Since most of the children are still here when Natasha leaves, she probably thinks that this goes on all night and that she's missing it. Why don't you come to pick her up very late sometime, so she sees that the others go home, too?" I did, and that was the end of her crying.

After finishing my doctorate, I took a job at University of Bridgeport in Connecticut, and we lived in nearby Milford. Natasha had kindergarten through second grade at Milford's Calf Pen Meadow School. We lived right on the beach of Long Island Sound, first on Sea View Beach in a large, old, rented house with seven entrances. Then we bought a newer three-bedroom house on Bay View Beach. Natasha spent many hours playing on the beach, sometimes with neighborhood friends and sometimes alone, gathering seashells and glass shards. She took ballet lessons during one school year, and made her closest friends at Westminster Presbyterian Church in Bridgeport. Her Sunday school teacher was Miss Lucy, an older lady who was kind but quite strict about the kids memorizing their Bible verses. In addition to kids from the neighborhood, Natasha's best friends were from the church: Olivia Fleming, her younger sisters, and Donna Gibbs.

We pulled Natasha out of the second grade several weeks early to go to the Holland Festival in Amsterdam, with my Bridgeport University cast of Finnegans Wake. This was a good experience. While I was busy with the production, Natasha and BJ visited interesting places in and around Amsterdam.

Before we found two reliable babysitters, a neighbor girl turned out to be a disaster of a sitter. We returned one night to find the house rather a mess, with cigarette ashes, etc. Natasha reported that lots of kids had been there, yelling and running up and down the stairs. "Weren't you afraid?"

"Yes, but I stayed in my room with the door shut." The next day we heard from one of the neighbors that someone had called the police, who came and sent the kids home.

In Palm Desert, California, where I'd taken a job at College of the Desert, Natasha completed the third and fourth grades. She joined Brownies (Girl Scouts) and she and BJ (who volunteered to help) suffered through a week of daily bus trips to the nearby mountains for a day camp. We had a swimming pool, and when her cousin Georgia visited for several weeks, she taught Natasha how to swim. Then she took lessons at the public pool and became a good swimmer. She also had lots of fun learning to twirl a baton. The highlight of that experience was participating in a two-hour parade in Indio, in intense heat, which left all the kids exhausted and dehydrated.

In 1972 we moved to Iran, and Natasha entered fifth grade at Tehran American Community School. Her teacher was a young, scatterbrained American who wore her skirts far too short for where she was, and who had some rather insane ideas, like telling the kids that the Shah would probably attend their class performance of The Prince and the Pauper. Thank goodness he didn't! It was with her approval that one day Natasha got off the school bus with a large dog, which had wandered into the school yard, and which went back to school with her the next day.

Community's teachers of the elementary classes were generally good, preparing the students for their middle and high school years. But in the junior high and high school, many of the assignments didn't make sense. All students were expected to fit the same mold; there was little or no concern for the average or struggling student. Natasha did well for the most part and liked the school because of her many friends, but she, like many of the students, didn't learn to really enjoy the work because it was too much of a burden for children of their age.

Although she wasn't always eager to do so, Natasha frequently accompanied us to social functions, because it was nearly impossible to get babysitters in Iran. She'd always take along a book and could usually find a secluded spot to read. She liked going to the performances at Rudaki Hall — excellent operas, ballets, and symphonies. One of our younger colleagues, Carol Fisher, who gave Natasha piano lessons, stayed with her once, but had a bad experience on her way home. It was very dark in her "kuchie" (alley) and a man chased her to her door. So that was the end of her babysitting.

An important family event that occurred while we lived in Tehran was Natasha's baptism. This took place at the lovely old Presbyterian mission compound in the southern part of the city. Our pastor, Rev. Bob Pryor, baptized her by immersion in the water storage reservoir, much like a large swimming pool. This followed the Sunday worship service, which was in the late afternoon. Afterwards we celebrated the occasion with refreshments, and later, a concert at Rudaki Hall, which was only a few blocks away.

After the Damavand campus moved to the north part of town, transportation to Community School, in the center of Tehran, became too difficult; not only was it far away, taking an hour of bus or taxi commuting, but during the year of the revolution the female students were frequently threatened with acid thrown in their faces if they didn't wear a head covering. I begged Natasha to tie a scarf over her hair as she and a couple other Community School girls rode down the mountain to school. The scarf was on, under protest, when she left the house, but I wondered how long it stayed on. Oh, there were worries.

Finally, since we were living in the northern part of the city to be near the Damavand campus, we decided that Natasha should switch to Tehran American School, which was much closer. She was pleased to discover that TAS offered an excellent choice of courses, with good teachers. And a few of her friends from Community had also moved there. One class that she especially enjoyed was an advanced course combining American history and literature. It was a real disappointment when the revolution forced the schools to close abruptly in December, and all Americans were told to leave. She'd been at TAS for less than one semester of her junior year.

Damavand College had been closed for more than a week, so BJ had been substitute teaching at Iran Zamin and TAS, the international schools. Things were pretty chaotic, with some foreign teachers already having left the country, so the international schools were desperate for substitutes. BJ happened to be teaching at TAS in early December of 1978, on the day an announcement came over the intercom: "Listen carefully. Today will be the last day of classes before Christmas. Report cards are being distributed to teachers, who will fill in your semester final grade. Semester exams have been canceled. Be sure to take your report cards, as well as all your books and belongings, with you when you leave school today." The message was repeated, and what chaos followed!

BJ was teaching English classes, to students she'd never seen before that day, and they were asking her to assign their semester grades. She went to the office, where one of the secretaries agreed to assign the grades. I've wondered why she didn't simply give everyone a "C" … or perhaps an "A"?

So we had to leave Iran, shortly before the Shah left, and before Khomeini returned from exile to establish the new Iran. Our college had advised all foreign teachers to leave the country for a while, until things calmed down. What a mess the airport was. Everyone was desperate to depart the country, and it looked doubtful at the time as to whether we'd make it onto a plane. Marie Westervelt and her mother Jeffie were with us, also with tickets on Royal Jordanian Airlines. They had to wait for a later flight, but met us that night at the Amman, Jordan, hotel where the airline put us all up for the night. The next day we flew on to Athens where we met many Americans in the same situation.

After waiting in Athens for six weeks, and finally realizing that returning to Iran was impossible, we went to Los Angeles, California, and Natasha enrolled at Hoover High School in Glendale. Interestingly, she graduated one semester early because Community School had required so many courses that she easily met graduation requirements. She really wanted to stay at Hoover for another semester because she enjoyed the school and her new friends, but since Daddy now had a job in Beirut — I'd gone on ahead of BJ and Natasha, while she was finishing her last year — she and BJ joined me in January of 1979.

It was wonderful having them back with me in Beirut, although I was in the middle of dress rehearsals of a production of Jean Anouilh's Eurydice, being performed in dance and drama. With two theatre majors who were excellent dancers, we turned Anouilh's dreamy, romantic drama into a pas de deux when the lovers were together, which enhanced the whole impact of the production, but more of that elsewhere.

Natasha attended one semester and summer school at Beirut University College and seemed to enjoy it very much. So much so that when she was notified of her acceptance with a large scholarship at Scripps College, Claremont, California — just outside Los Angeles — I secretly wished she could stay at BUC instead of going nine thousand miles away, across the Mediterranean, the Atlantic, and the United States. But what would happen in Beirut with all the bombs and shooting? She wouldn't be safe — no one was safe in Beirut, and many wanted out. But we loved teaching there — for many years Beirut's been our favorite city.

Natasha flew home to Beirut for Christmas and for the summer holiday, when she took a course at BUC, drew, and painted. It was all rather difficult for her, but she liked Scripps College, finding the courses challenging, becoming especially interested in art and theatre, and graduating early with a major in History of Art and minors in Theatre and Literature. After graduating with her BA she returned to Beirut and taught English for a year at the American University of Beirut.

When the kidnappings became very bad in Beirut, Natasha moved with us to Tunisia, North Africa. Since she was fluent in French, and Tunisians spoke almost no English, she did a lot of translating for us, helping me set up a bank account, rent an architecturally-interesting (and sometimes frustratingly awful) Arab house, get utilities working, and become acclimated in the Sousse, Tunisia, lifestyle. After Christmas, and after helping us entertain guests from Tehran and Beirut days, Natasha moved to Paris, enrolled in the Sorbonne University — studying History of Art. She lived in Paris for the next seven years, supporting herself first by working as an au pair and then teaching at an English language institute.

We loved having her in Paris, for we could often visit her there during the school breaks in Tunisia and before, during, and after two years in China. Natasha joined us for one semester to teach English at South China Normal University at Guangzhou, Canton. She also visited us in Macau when we lived there. Oh, that girl has spent much of her life living and traveling around the world.

Natasha and Paul were married in Washington, DC, where she was completely on her own to plan their lovely wedding, which was held in the beautiful and historic Church of the Epiphany.

CHAPTER 16

LETTERS FROM FRIENDS

ALICE E. LOFLAND
Norman's Stepmother and Aunt

Liberal, Kansas
April 1964

Dear Ones,

Don't hardly know where to start, so many things have happened and still really not a whole lot has come to head. Jim finally got out of jail yesterday afternoon. He called his Daddie and sounded like he had a terrible cold, and at 2:30 this morning his lawyer called and said they had taken him to the hospital. And they called again today and said they were keeping him in the hospital until Monday; then they are putting him on a plane and sending him home, as he is tired mentally and needs rest. After 5 weeks in jail I am sure it has done something to Jim. They aren't allowing him to have company, however Marj called at noon and said she was going up to see him and would call us after she got back home. I don't know what to think or do. This ordeal has sure not been a picnic on Daddie and I, that is for sure. I am sure Daddie has lost 15 or 20 pounds and looks so old. The lawyers have just worried him to death for money, bonds, and so forth, and have stripped us of our working capital for seed and so forth to work this summer with. I am so discouraged and so is Daddie. Sometimes I think we should sell out and buy a little trailer house and move so far away it would take .50 cents to get a letter like you have done. I can't for the life of me see where we have failed, to where our kids aren't self-supporting when they reach the age of maturity. My Daddie gave me $5.00 after I was 14 years old, and that was all. Bless his heart, he taught me something that I am sure my kids don't know. Daily Marj or someone was going to put up bail and so forth and daily they didn't do it. Marj didn't put up a cent; neither did Anky. I honestly believe the people in

N.Y. don't know what truth means, or anyway the people who Jim deals with.

I started this Saturday, when I was very low; now that it is Tuesday I will try to finish it.

Jim is out of the hospital, however no one has secured the bond for 10,000.00 yet and he isn't able to leave N.Y. until it is secured. I don't understand it, but that is what he says anyway. Saturday night Jim's lawyer called Anky and tried to scare her into blackmail, telling her that he was a lawyer from Reno, Nevada (where Gloria is), and that Gloria was going to name her in a divorce case and so forth and so forth. We were called three times during the night about it. Marj called Gloria; she told Marj she loved Jim and had no idea of divorcing him and hung up. Gloria was all upset, Marge was upset, Anky was upset. Then Sunday Jim found out that it was his lawyer that did it, and you can imagine what it did for him. Daddie is terribly upset about it, and says he is going to prosecute this lawyer for pulling a stunt like that. So I don't know whether he will be able to talk Anky into putting up security for the bond or not. I never saw such lying, blackmailing, and so forth in all my life. Rex says he has seen such on T.V. but didn't really think this existed. I still think Jim is going to have to get a good, honest lawyer from the central states, like Rex or Howard Phillips, that he can trust to whip out these shysters, or will never get it all straightened out. One of the fellows who filed the Civil Action against

Jim called Daddie yesterday, and Daddie pointed out that he had not only delayed Jim being able to get this through so his holdings would be worth something, but had broke Jim completely and now if something was done to make it all worth anything, the ones who had bought interests would have to furnish money to get it all done, as Jim was broke, because of filing the Civil Action against him. They wanted to form a Trust and have Daddie to be one of the trustees. Daddie told him that he didn't know anything about it, and felt it was up to the ones who bought interest in it to get ahold of it and get it straightened up.

Gurney and I went to Amarillo yesterday, and Gurney got his new saddle that he had made; sure is nice. We visited with Nell and I got two new pairs of shoes. Left in a dirt storm and was beautiful down there all day; just south of Perryton ran into the dirt again. If we don't get some rain pretty soon, I don't know what we are going to do. Is really the dirty 30's again. Saturday is May 2nd, Pioneer Day at Guymon, and the boys are to ride with the Trail Riders. I do hope it is a pretty day and not windy and dirty. They are looking forward to riding, and they enjoy it so much, especially with Gurney with a new saddle. Nell is fine. Upset about Jim; she is such a wonderful person. We are so fond of her.

Your trip to Jordan sounded wonderful and I think it is wonderful that you can do those things. Miss Fulton (draft lady) said to tell you "Hello for her" and how pleased she is that you are doing all these things while you are young and can enjoy them. She is always asking about you, as are many other people.

I would of liked to have seen parts of BJ's letter concerning the Jordan published, but I doubt that her folks will have it published unless she writes and suggests it. I know there are so many people who would be so interested in it. I am sorry I can't write a more encouraging letter, and more happy letter, but things are pretty heavy here in a lot of ways; surely things will ease off pretty soon. If this is a wilderness surely it will be a promised land when we get through it, providing we do make it. Write often, and enjoy life. Give our love to Tasha and BJ. I will make some more of the dishes as soon as they get some more poured. They also have a coffee warmer that I think will be nice. The next time Nell comes up she wants me to have some here at home and she wants to paint some of them for you. Write real often. Love U All.

Mother

COMMENTS BY NORMAN ON THE LETTER FROM HIS MOTHER

I have just run across a letter from my mother sent to BJ and me in Beirut, dated April 1964. It is interesting in that it fills me with nostalgia of the years that my brother was indicted by the state of New York and convicted of fraud by the Securities and Exchange Commission. It is so complicated that I can only use a general statement about the whole situation. But, to indicate what was happening and how it influenced us, I must recall that BJ, Natasha, and I were in Beirut at that time. How curious! No wonder I don't recall the trauma of the experience. We were overseas, not at the ranch where much of the emotion was happening.

Apparently Dad had put up the bond for brother Jim. $10,000 — a huge amount of money in 1964, for it must have secured a $100,000 bail. Mother wrote that it had taken most of the working capital for the summer's ranch expenses. She wrote that the New York people did not come up with the money they promised for the security of the bond. Jim's friends in New York including Mrs. Anky Revson (Revlon cosmetics), who was a very close friend at that time, was one of several persons who had indicated that they would support Jim during the trial. They didn't, and so Dad had to commit the money in cash.

We missed all the trial scenes for we were that summer in London. We had driven from Beirut, Lebanon, through Turkey, Yugoslavia, Europe to London since I was attending a three month course in Modern British Literature at the University of London. A great course, with excellent lecturers, including lectures on art and music as well as written literature. How I wish I had had that sort of introduction to literature when I was an undergraduate. I would not have been so bewildered by James Joyce — on whom I wrote an MA thesis after my confusing undergraduate days. How surprised that young teacher would have been to learn that I produced a dramatized production of Joyce's Finnegans Wake as well as a many paged interpretation of the novel's dramatized scenes. Anyway, that's why I cannot remember the court case in 1964, which ended with Jim's sixteen years in prison — more than any of the ENRON or subsequent Wall Street crooks will receive.

Las Cruces, New Mexico
Tuesday, July 4, 1989 [after Tiananmen Square protests]

Dear Norman, BJ, and Tasha,

Was so pleased to get your letter and the picture is lovely. You both look really good. All the trials and tribulations you all have gone through don't seem to have hurt you much. Is wonderful how God has sustained you all through it all ... I felt sure you would survive since you all have proved to me that you are survivors. I told the family you have been through more dangerous places than this was, since you all were several hundred miles away from the hot spot; however, it could and may move over the entire continent ... America isn't such a bad place to live; you might want to try it for a change. There are unpleasant places here also, only not nationally ... I am sure you will figure it all out, without any help from me.

Gurney and some friends and I went out to the university to see the fireworks display, which was really nice. The kids didn't have fireworks this year; they are growing up so fast. Gurney Lee is pretty much as he should be for 16, but Leanna is 13 going on 18. She has always been older for her age and is not old enough to do such and so. They are both really good kids, so they are fine. Von is in Washington taking his bar exam; he will put it on hold for the time being, but wants it valid if and when he finds an opportunity to go there. Kathi is living in Hobbs, N. Mex., which is a far cry from Tulsa, but so far she is coping O.K. Her husband works for an oil company, but plans to go into the ministry. She works at the church, and they have a Christian school in conjunction with it, and she's going to teach next year also??

Gurney's wife had an "Emotional Crisis" and has been over to her mother's for 100 days. Has been a really hard thing on everyone. Gurney is trying to find something to do; he doesn't know just what he does want to do. He kept her store open for a long time, but finally had to close it. [I understand Alice poured $200,000 into those stores.] Gurney hasn't had it all good by any means. We are still fighting the lawsuit on the Hilton Hotel. Only God knows how that will come out.

Myrtle [Norm's mother and Alice's sister] wants to come down since she has never been here, and wants Annie Fransen [a wonderful lady who took care of the house and cooked all weekday noon meals at the ranch from1951 to 1977; a great friend of the whole family] to bring her; so will see what happens there. She spent last winter with Teddie and Vuleen, and seemed to enjoy that, but is very lonely since being home this summer. I would love to have them for a few days … will see. She plans to stay with Ted again this winter. I miss working every day; would love to find a job that paid some money for a change. I hate staying home all the time … I miss being with people. There don't seem to be many jobs for my age but I could handle it just fine … will see.

My neighbor is coming by and we will run into town for a bit, so must hurry. Write when you can and hope you all have a lovely summer. Tell BJ Happy Birthday!!

Love, Mother (Alice)

Las Cruces, New Mexico
Thursday, November 9, 1995

Dear Norman and BJ,

Hope and pray that you are all doing really well and happy. Must be terribly busy as you don't seem to have the time to write, and I am sorry about that. I am enclosing a clipping I found in a paper some time ago and laid it aside and never got it to you, but again this morning I came across it and thought I must send this to Norm and BJ. Honestly how is school and how are you both?? We love you all so much and have admired you all so much. Give it some thought ... You are still one of our family and we love you dearly. If you are hurting let us know, if you are happy let us know.

Your Aunt Lois passed away the other day, she had a stroke. Lois was your Daddie's youngest sister and the last of the brothers and sisters. Myrtle called and told me. I haven't heard from any of the Lofland family for years. Guess when I moved to N. Mex. everyone thought I was out of the U.S. Ha ha ... Annie and Eliz are in the Good Samaritan Center. Annie can't drive anymore as one eye is about gone, and on and on ... Myrtle is 89 years old now and doesn't think Ted is going to ask her to come down there again this winter as Terry is home now ... So I am in hopes Jim will take her for the winter. Gene is still in California doing the same thing. I am 80 and don't feel that I can take her and feel I have my hands full as it is ... Anyway that is life.

Vora Lee has been very ill and had surgery; has cancer and they put in a colostomy. She went to California for a month and thought she was doing really well again; then she got to doing too much and ended up in the hospital again but is back with Von again. Kathi lives at Okla City and has 3 children now and finances aren't very good with her. Her mother (Ivis) is still living; 92 and is now in a home ... My, oh my.

Gurney Lee [grandson] and family will be in Las Cruces for Thanksgiving; Devin will be a year old on the 24th of

November and they are having a birthday party for him. Gurney Lee will be 23 on the 25th. Leanna was 20 on the 5th of November. She is still in college, she is such a pleasure, is such a happy and beautiful young girl. Having fun dating. She doesn't run around a great deal as she is studying hard and wanting to be a dentist, so she is very conscious about her time. She also works part time; we honestly don't see her very often anymore. She lives at the sorority house.

Gurney is now making barn siding clocks; they are beautiful; he has a lot of them made and is going to get them on the market before Christmas, so he is really busy and seems to be really happy doing it. He has gotten so discouraged working with people in trying to raise money for projects. [Promoting oil and hotel development?] Is really hard. [His Miss New Mexico cousin and he were divorced sometime while we were in Beirut.] He has a lady friend that is a real encouragement to him; she lives about 10 minutes from me. I don't know what I would do if I didn't have Gurney, he is so good to me, and we enjoy each other so much. [They should with all of Dad's assets-turned-into-investments they took.] I would sure be a lonely person if I didn't have him … God knew what was in the future, I am sure.

Jim [Norm's brother] and Pat [enjoying her condo in one of the newer high-rises in London's East End Wharf] just got back from a month's tour to Italy and Europe; they enjoyed it so very much, only was real tiring they said. I am sure you know all about that as you have traveled more than all of us put together.

Take care of yourselves and please let us hear from you. We all love you dearly and want the best for you.

Love, Mom (Alice)

KATHLEEN SHRAUNER
Betty's Sister

Arlington, Texas
Saturday, January 6, 1996

Dear Norm and Betty,

It's cloudy out and cold! We've had a lot of cold weather in the past couple of weeks — and I don't like it, causes aches and pains, plus I don't have that many heavy clothes to wear since I've moved down here — do have the coats and hats, though. Finally got all my Christmas stuff down and put away yesterday — took me two days to do it.

Thought I'd told you about our family taking a cruise – anyway, we left for Miami on the 16th — took the Carnival ship "Inspiration" and returned the 23rd. We really enjoyed it, although the kids had griped because they had to dress for dinner a couple times. Regardless, they brought suits and everyone looked really nice. Deanne even bought a new dress. Dennis said he thought it was the best trip our family's taken. We stopped at Cozumel — rented a couple of VW convertibles and toured the place. Kids snorkeled, did some shopping; supposed to land on Grand Cayman, but they had such big swells we couldn't land. The kids had planned to scuba and were disappointed about that. We landed at Ocho Rio — ate Jamaican food, shopped, and went to the beach. I even had a few braids put in my hair. All in all, we had a good time—lots of food.

On Christmas I went to Roger's and had a big dinner: turkey, dressing, and the works, and then I went to Kath's and had a big dinner, roast beef and all the rest. I hope you got the package I sent early in December: peppernuts and a little candy.

I've been really busy since coming back, going out every evening. Tonite I'm playing cards with my church group. Last night our other singles group met; we were asked to bring our baby pictures, and to guess who they were. There were only 16 pictures — really hard. I guessed 6 people and won the prize.

Georgia and Dennis will go to Jamaica in a week for two weeks in the sun. Had a nice letter from Tasha with their Christmas card; sounds like they're getting along fine, although she's got a cold. Roger is still busy with his ostriches; Deanne's got a new job at a hospital, starting Monday.

Just about forgot the recipe [Texas Soup]: 1 can corn, 1 can potatoes, 1 can carrots, 1 can tomatoes, 1 can ranch style beans, 1 can black eyed peas, 1 can chili, may add ½-1 lb. fried ground beef.

Love, Kathleen

HUGH AND ANNA FLEMING
Friends from Connecticut Days

Bangor, Northern Ireland
December 2001

Dear Norm and BJ,

Found your letter with your address — so here goes. We as a family are all keeping well. Olivia is married, and just lives a few minutes' walk away from us. They have no children, except Matthew, Olivia's stepson. Olivia is keeping very well, and still working in Belfast City Hospital, with greatly reduced hours. Hope still lives in Hollywood, in the same area. Hope and Anto now have 4 children. The latest are twins, now 17 months old — called Orla & Conor. Maureen and Steven are now living in Bangalore, India. They have been in India just over 1 year. Hugh and I were visiting them for four weeks, Oct./Nov.; are back in N.I. just 2 weeks today. India is a wonderful place, the smells, the people, the color. We loved it. Their three older children attend an international school, and Sara goes to an Indian school in their neighborhood. She is the only white child and loves being the center of attention. Kirstie and Peter live in the heart of the County

Down countryside, in a lovely area, with gently rolling hills (called drumlins). Andrea works for Youth for Christ N.I. as a school worker and also manages a creative arts team; she loves it — she is now engaged to Damien, an English chap and will be moving to England after her wedding in May.

Hugh is keeping really well, and we both love being retired. You would think that we would be bored and have lots of time on our hands, but we always seem to be busy. Although we are "in peace" here in N.I., and there are not the bombings and shootings we had some years ago, yet there is still much unrest. People are being "pipe bombed" and "petrol bombed" in their homes. In certain areas, both sides of the community seem unable to live at peace with each other. Of course when our politicians are always fighting (verbally) about flags, decommissioning, etc., etc., etc., it sends a message out. Don't get me wrong; we are a lot better off than we were before the Good Friday agreement.

The building trade here is booming, and it seems as if planning has gone mad. Planning permission has been given for old Victorian houses, with large gardens, to be demolished, and apartments to be built on the site. Some are well planned and lovely, and others are like boxes crammed in together. The River Lagan in Belfast has been redeveloped, and it is lovely, with walkways and apartments. A new concert hall has been built beside the Lagan.

BJ, your daughter looks exactly like you. Take care of yourselves and keep in touch. Have a wonderful Christmas, wherever you are.

Lots of love,
Hugh and Anna

EVELYNE ACCAD
Professor Emeritus, University of Illinois and
Lebanese American University

Beirut, Lebanon
Thursday, March 15, 2018 (e-mail)

What memories! Thanks for sharing!

Jay and I were also married in the Church of God, but it didn't work as well as for all of you! No regrets!

I don't know if you realize what a tremendous influence and role model you and BJ have been in my life; you specially, Norm, had a great impact in giving me confidence in myself and helped me develop many sides of my personality, not the least being the creative one!

You should definitely publish this important work of memories and so many historical details that need to be preserved.

Thank you for writing it, sharing it, and keeping in touch!

All my love,
Evelyne

JACQUELINE HAJJAR
Colleague in Beirut

Beirut, Lebanon
Monday, March 12, 2018 (e-mail)

Dear Norm and BJ,

Yes, your book is wonderful, but I have not finished reading it. I am very busy with the shelter. We are taking care of dealing with beaten and raped women.

I want to thank you very much for sharing your experiences with us. It is fascinating.

With love,
Jacqueline

[Jacqueline and Evelyne, sisters, established a shelter for battered and raped women in Beirut, Lebanon. The kindness and humanity they have shown is highlighted by their Christian beliefs and treatment and love for those harmed ladies.]

SAM CHUNG
Chinese Teacher

Guangzhou, China
Saturday, November 7, 1992

Dear Norman,

It's great to learn that you have a doctoral program in drama. I'm very interested in it and would like very much to study under your guidance.

I've been teaching in South China Normal University for three years, and I think I could hardly go on here. You know the school very well; it is really different from Jinan, and it's a pity that I can see the difference only now. I have an impression that SCNU is the most politics-oriented school I have ever been to. I don't even have the freedom to teach what is not in the curriculum. What they enjoy teaching here are the works of the proletarian writers — works that lay bare the evils of capitalism. It gives me an impression that people here don't know that it's already the 20th century.

Sincerely yours,

Sam Chung [Sam taught at the first university where BJ and Norman taught in China.]

DAVID NOTTINGHAM
Colleague at Beirut University College and University of Macau

Westminster, Maryland
Friday, March 8, 1996

Dear Norm and BJ — !

No question that this passing winter and the two torridly hot months of July and August last year (infra-red spots literally burned into the grass) have to do with global warming and the greenhouse trap that international governments are beginning to pay attention. Of course, all of the new consumer nations' (China, India, Russia, Africa, Latin America, Indonesia, etc.) pursuit of a car, a color satellite linked TV, and a 6-pack of Coke in every family refrigerator makes much progress very dim. These blossoming markets are the focus of international exploitation on a grand scale and will add billions of tons of carbon dioxide, methane, and other gasses for at least another century. A Beacon Press PB titled The Greenhouse Trap, by Francesca Lyman, et. al., is a good short reader on the greenhouse phenomenon. But how are we to control rising expectation and mass consumer markets in these new nations?

Man, [our student, now with a Ph.D. and teaching at University of Macau] in a recent letter here, commented on how cold this passing winter was in

H.K. and Macau. It's the same changing weather variables of Mother Nature letting us to close the ozone hole above Antarctica, which now is the size of the United States!!! Man also wrote, by the way, that he wants to be a TZ and eventually a professor. He's bright, very bright, but this is a bad idea. He should get out of there before the Chinese take it all over, including Casino Tech with its Portuguese illusions. He should be a journalist in TV. That's a future without all the pettiness in higher education. Gave me more news about the Portuguese rumble to take over everything, to downgrade English Studies, etc., which was no surprise. I could smell it wafting off of Dines [academic dean] before I left ... POWAH! Which the Portuguese, of all people, have never known how to use — hence the worst of the colonialists and the poorest of European countries. Maybe the recent elections will change their incipient elitism but not in time to save that so-called university. Besides, the Chinese have their own ideas for H.K., Macau, and Taiwan. It is the way of history and with our China trade deficit, no amount of hypocritical Amarikan rhetoric will change the course.

Business in Amarikan small towns is essentially dead, except for tattoo parlors and small beaneries and hideous modern crafts stores where even the dolls gleam in the dark. Wal-Mart, Lowes, etc., have taken over — they just build more and more of these huge, glutted ware emporiums, which become consumer social meeting places like large churches with stained-glass everywhere. In place of a cross, fountains shooting up. Many elders exercise by walking at top speed around and around in the early mornings in these malls. So much changing so fast. Anyhow, you will get a taste of it all soon enough ...

I have conflicting info regarding your recontracting: one side says no! another side says yes! Whichever, good luck and for Pete's sake stay in touch. Give our best to Don and Beth who are apparently leaving? It appears that Ramos shifted his favoritism or respect or whatever, according to Don, without much explanation. I would rather see all expats outa there! Our best to everyone surviving in Portuguese Putsch!

Cheers,
Dave

[David worked so hard developing a Communications major and creating a TV Studio on campus in the existing auditorium building, using the stage and greenroom as production space. This letter indicated how it was not fully supported by the then Dean, although the studio was created in a modified version and the excellent teacher,

L.L. Alexandria — who typed the first manuscript of this book — used the studio successfully the following years.]

Monday, October 21, 1996 Winter entereth …

Dear Norm and BJ,

Almost everyone I knew once is gone or going. What a weird fact to face. Also, our kids have their own lives and heavy schedules now. We hear from them infrequently as their kiddies sprout like weeds. We are not fond of Denver or its environs — we are accustomed to trees, grass, and birds — and the people are young, materialistic, and brash, if not vulgar — more like consumer products or commodities than people, thanx to TV and the secular religion of "buy, buy, buy, and run-up the plastic." Popular Culture and its tastelessness have "dumbed-down" intelligence, which was once a virtue. Most of the Denver ilk all look and live alike in their middle class supermarket worlds. Even the housing developments all look alike except for color variations in dimmed-down pastel variations. And heavy pollution from too many cars. National Geographic says 60,000 acres a year "around" Denver are lost to houses and asphalt. But aside from this, kids today grow up in a technological whirl of gadgets and things with too much outside stuff to choose from for fun. Grandparents visit occasionally but are not part of their real experience. So, grandparents become "now and then strangers" often ignored except for the gifts they bear or buy! (A Dutch couple we met flew from Holland to New Zealand to see a grandson … after the initial "hello there," the kid ignored them; did not really know or understand who they were, nor did he care!) All that distance … the same sense of not belonging in Denver. So, we do not go out there nor do they visit here often. The men now have highly technical jobs and very competitive co-workers, all working 50-60 hours on salary. A world changes in the midst of families growing up. Elders do not fit into such a scenario. There is no time to stop; no time to live!

David

Tuesday, January 7, 1997 At the farm …

Hey ho, Norm and BJ,

Great to get your card. Man said that you had retired, which makes McArthur's claim solid. We believe that Beirut and Macau have a strange attraction, even when disintegrating most surely. George Gibb wrote from

H.K. at Xmas about visas there and mass migrations outa there. New H.K. leader Tung strikes us as a Mandarin not to be fooled with and a quisling firmly in Beijing's pocket. Yet, me thinks that China has a right to do as it pleases to tighten things up a bit. It was, after all, the English who traded the opium first and who destroyed things following the Boxer Rebellion. It is also true that Patton was a bit late with the "new democracy" push. Things being what they truly are in our major cities (Baltimore and DC still murder- high urban chaos), we have no real stones to cast. Wait and see, I say. So that goes …

David

Innesfree Farm, Westminster, Maryland
Thursday, December 28, 2000

Hey ho, Norm and BJ,

Macau bound and ready for the S.A.R.!

Yes, waal, the world turns wearily — or warily? Israel on fire from Palestinian intifada, oil prices (and gas) soaring as a South American OPEC is born to join the ME OPEC … Venezuela, Bolivia, Ecuador, Peru, and Mexico on its edge. "Payback time" for the West. Storyline: Man gets a haircut and it costs $35. Tells a friend as he is badly shaken that a haircut costs $35! Friend consoles him. Says that the barber wants to live in a nice house like the friend has, too. (Raucous, evil laughter …) So, we live with it for now. With a new

Florida-elected Bush in the Oval Office — Bantam Rooster Bush (him or he with the crooked smile) — has everything scripted on 3 x 5 cards when at a mic in the public TV eye. He is not overly bright (Clinton a mountain being scaled by a mouse) and a happy delegator for others to do the real work. A kind of Clintonesque "poetic justice" in human form that also breathes and smiles. When Congress gets at him, it will be fun. But costly for the American adventure. Frankly, I have totally disengaged from this society of driven consumers and power-mad politicians. It's not just the testiness and the stress, but the blatant hypocrisy and its underlying corruption (soft monies, lobbying, corporate welfare, etc.) that turns voters off. That so-called statewide election brouhaha in Florida was an absurdity beyond comprehension, as the GOP dominated Supreme Court teamed up with the Florida courts to anchor Bush into an office without complete vote tallies, hence without a mandate!

So, it went … and the jokes fly about still. And a possible recession looms as well. Well, Bush and his father's mafia earned it. However, the next four years go — for better, the status quo, or worse — nobody will forget. "W" is a marked man before he is inaugurated. And with a divided House, o'boy look out!

L.L. and I still exchange letters. She is very bright and an excellent writer, friend to George Gibb in H.K., and travels daredevil on horseback or biped or rickshaw. She has also done much and has created small miracles at Macau Tech. She should move on soon using that experience to the full somewhere whence she is more appreciated. Hopefully.

Dawn sent a card to Tasha (a book earlier that disappeared never showed up). Whether the last letters got to them we don't know. Yet, we rest assured that all is well as you visit them now in Singapore. (Get their Singapore address to us, please.)

Everything OK with us. Aches and pains only! We are having an extremely COLD winter (Dawn asked me to embolden that word) with one bad ice storm and snow so far and all kinds of media weather predictions ahead. So, it comes or not, whichever, and it goes away. We renovated our front screened-in porch, doubling its size. We added a patio (accessed from the porch) on the house far side. And we built a terraced rock garden with another stone wall above the patio, adding a trickling rock fountain for summers. Our last projects ... other than maintenance, painting, mowing, and repairs. 44 years of renovation and historic rescue — DONE!

Dawn and I wish you the best of luck in your endeavors with Reverend Poon (his school and Morrison Chapel in Macau). Someday, if possible, find me a photo or postcard of Chinnery's tomb or resting place behind the Chapel. L.L. sent me a book, and I have gathered several of Chinnery's paintings and his interesting life. Where have his kind gone? Into the maw of political correctness? His life, all told, was a wowzer! His paintings and drawings unique. (Museums now search for his works.) Anyhow, have fun too, as we know you most certainly will. (Whatever happened to Peter the Great Glassman, eh?)

You may "hate to travel," Norm, but you ain't happy in the U.S. of A. Happily, you are immersed in a past of experience that only you and BJ know. Keep your health above all, as you well know. BJ is your rock of the ages, as we know. So, live life well. Adventure — ah, yes; but frankly we enjoy Innisfree so much now, realizing how intelligent was our decision to purchase this old home place so many years ago. Surrounded by large hills, we are most removed from it all, hidden in peace and quiet, just three miles from the stores. It will last while we are here. Our son Paul and his wife may return in two years from Denver to build a house on a lovely view-sodden hill. That will help with the heavier chores and give some deeper meaning to our knowledge of the fairies in the garden (Voltaire). It has been a wonderful retirement life so far, close to nature, the animals, the birds, the trees, and the green hills. What else is there to say? (Sandra may be gone on your return ...) Students: the whole face of the earth is gradually being "dumbed-down" as an egalitarian world emerges, pushed on by global media and capitalism in its many free market forms. People in the Third World have seen, have heard, have listened to the sights and sounds of the "new economy" and they want it for themselves. It can not be stopped short of a nuclear disaster. The new technology is everywhere, racing far ahead of our ability to understand it or control it, for this new global economy is of things and stuff in vast markets galore. This push to technically co-optate and control men and women, to commodify the earth, reaches now into space. (One can book ahead some $10K for three days there!) Everything (and soon everybody or every body) will be standardized, sanitized, and virtualized into a new kind of existence worldwide. And a few corporations will control the masses entoto. No, thank you; we had the best years at the end of history as we know it. For most people, history is now bunk ... progress is moving forward with everything, removing all obstacles for a new age of (WHATEVER) ... (?)*** I love the past, the archeology of past times and places. And frankly, we don't fit no more! (I sold my computers.) As "a world of sameness" emerges, humankind becomes mechanical clones — people acting on the orders of others and the programs of others. No, thank you!

    *** VIRTUAL REALITY (?) ANARCHY (?) SPACE LIFE (?)

Cheers, David (and Dawn)

Westminster, Maryland
Wednesday – Thursday, January 30 – 31, 2002

Dear BJ and Norm,

    Westminster changes, but slowly. The real population increase has been in the southern part of the country, which now has water and traffic problems. Ironic, for most are people escaping Baltimore and its crime-drug-race problems, which are quite serious for families who want security and normalcy in community living. These are indeed shocking times in urban America, no matter where. We will rebuild Afghanistan after bombing the living hell out of it (those "evil ones") whilst our own big cities are near ruins for the most part. Anyhow, Westminster in the north of the county still has some of the old county flavor. The notion of "progress" never pauses to see what it has done. And the developers never stop. So, too, population that just grows and grows. Out there on that huge prairie where Denver sits with the mountains in the background of it all (Pike's Peak and the Rockies). 66,000 acres go into housing yearly. Everything is roads and cars and bland houses and malls. There are no old people there. It's the good life for younger, eager professionals. Well we've been there, done that, so … The kids like it and other than the usual "job" worries, so, too, parents. Schools are good. Families live well and appear close. But the pace of life is scary. Everybody of any age just goes and goes, mostly in cars. Everything is standardized down to the size of toothbrushes. Everything is like everything else. Everybody is like everybody else. Sameness is dullness. But Denverites don't see it that way. Frankly, the whole country is becoming of a sameness, thanks to media and corporate games to dumb down everything, especially difference and quality, in order to control what people buy, eat, or drive … a kind of social correctness. Most people go about in a daze, blind of reality. [Marijuana easily becomes legalized.]

Westminster still has its little stores (or malls, if you choose) and lots of real characters that make life interesting, alive. This great putsch to cleanse the doubters, the questioners, has not arrived yet in this neck of the woods. But it's coming as it has come already in much of the country. Business and money rule. You can't escape the fact. Life is being commodified totally. And an anti-intellectual fundamentalism broods everywhere in a subtle guise of the new morality of political correctness and an intolerance of new ideas. University and college campuses in the U.S. are closed to faculty who do not accept a certain philosophy of research and teaching. I am happy to be out of it; happy to be free of the world.

The world is a dreadful mess thanks to the madness of power for its own sake. Which brings me to our Cowboy President from Texas who, if he could, would like to rule the world. Nothing is worse or more dangerous to a nation than leadership by the self-righteous. "We will prevail," he sayeth, in his State of the Union address. Apparently, Bushy Baby knows no limits to what he (and us) can do militarily, economically, politically, or socially anywhere in the world. 9-11 may have changed our world (meaning the U.S. of A.), but it has not changed human nature and our propensity for hero worship and our hopes of controlling (or owning) the earth by any means to remove evil. It's apocalyptic prayer voiced aloud. Watch the Middle East and the Israeli-Palestinian Civil War anew. It could bring down the world economic house along with those dreams of rebuilding Afghanistan. (There was never anything permanent built there in the first place … !) Dear Me! And billions for this and billions for that. Something will indeed backfire to temper or end this wildest of national dreams.

I believe this barely literate President and his very protective Gang of Five (Cabinet) have hood-winked the American populace so far. That was not a war in Afghanistan. It was a preemptive military strike of vengeance and retribution on a primitive people living ancient lives of tribal lore and warlord actions buried from time deep in history. We had all of the technology of modern warfare at our disposal; the people of Afghanistan had none of it to speak of. As in the so-called Gulf War ten years earlier, the "enemy" (or evil ones) had no defenses, no air force, no chance. Yet, everybody connected to both "wars" were heroes! Yes, old bin Laden, we assumed, was the big chief evil one and the person we were really after (he could be on the beach in Fiji as I write) and for whom we still search. The politics of the "war" in Afghanistan had to do with much more than bin Laden ... it was an image creator for Georgie Bush. This "war has not only complicated life in the U.S., but it has also made life for the future very expensive. We could have sent in a hit squad to remove bin Laden. And the awful Taliban have shrunk to isolated pockets. Yet, we have angered millions of Moslems and Arabs throughout the world who now suffer a loss of face and honor. It will haunt us; it will create an insufferable paranoia among Americans; and it will assure a future pay-off or backlash beyond our dreams ... when the ends justify the means to regain face and honor once again. Arabs never forget an insult." So endeth my sermon for today.

Hey, guy, our regard to Rev. Poon. We are glad you both are enjoying such a positive mission.

Best regards,
D & D

[Dr. David Nottingham suffered cancer, complications, a massive heart attack, and passed away before the Middle East "Arab Spring" which, along with subsequent wars, indicated David's analysis to be substantial. Some would say "right on!"]

DON BAKER
Colleague at Kairouan, Tunisia, and University of Macau

University of Colorado at Boulder Saturday,
February 14, 1998

Dear Norm and BJ:

We received your two hilarious letters and laughed ourselves sick. The life of the ex-pat teacher encapsulated! It is a bit worse than we had anticipated, but not that much worse. Received an e-mail from Man, and one from L.L., reporting your flying trip through Macau and appreciating seeing you again. We presume that you poked around a bit in the Philippines. Any luck? We are getting a bit tired of painting and organizing repair of children's houses—we leave here March 15 to undertake the same at our place in Friday Harbor — and I, at any rate, am anxious to get back to teaching again — well, not really teaching again, but living outside the U.S., and at the moment the only way to do this is to resume teaching. I have even thought of setting up a small, evening language school, and would be happy to do this in Macau if in some way the legal and Portuguese barriers would be removed. We would be happy to come to Cyprus if the situation seems to improve, and there should be room for us. To this end, or other ends, I enclose my CV.

The year 1997-98 will have been a profitable year in a family sense — we bought for cash a house for our son Geoff in Maine, having paid off the mortgage for a house for son Keith. We are busy paying away at the mortgages for our daughter Alison and son Craig. I know that you, BJ, have no great sympathy with this project, but we have set ourselves the task, and now, of course, our money is gone, most of it. Speaking of "BJ," the latest scandal to break surface in Colorado is that our sainted governor Roy Boy Romer has been conducting a sixteen-year affair with his administrative assistant, one "BJ" Thornberry. The governor gave an extremely Clintonesque press conference in which he acknowledged the relationship — very "affectionate and supportive"— but not SEXUAL. (I didn't inhale!)

Speaking of Clinton, by the time that you receive this, we may be bombing Iraq again in what will be an annual "touch up," but the combination of Russia's strong opposition and the reluctance of Congress to endorse an action which seemingly has no real end or purpose may bring him to his senses. Speaking of Congress, our Secretary of State made a tactical error of the first magnitude in her appearance before the Senate. She became a bit miffed at the stream of questions and remarked testily to Trent Lott that "WE didn't leave Saddam Hussein in power!" Considering that the Republicans are/were the strongest supporters of Clinton's projected action, such snideness was extremely silly. The whole mood of Congress was changed in the course of a single afternoon by her foolish partisan remark — the Democrats were not keen to begin with.

We hope that you found Natasha and her husband well and content, and that you are both well and continue to enjoy Cyprus and to laugh at the world.

Love, Don

PS from Beth: You've got to write up your experiences as a novel! Your letters sounded like a third Olivia Manning trilogy, but updated to this year's world. I've just reread the Abbe's Around the World in 11 Years; you could make it 20+.

It sounds pretty grim in Macau now — Sandra as usual snapping at everybody (but still with her sainted Jaime) — Ray and Catherine such proud parents, but seeing few because baby takes their full attention. Max of course gone — but you know more about all that than we do having just been there. We're eager to see your "Memoirs." Like you, we would go almost anywhere just to be away. Too soon we'll have to hang up our running shoes, anyway. We think of hanging them up somewhere warm and away. (I hate snow, and even Don has learned to hate it this winter in Colorado.) How did the Philippines strike you as a "retirement" spot?

Keep writing us — we LOVE hearing from you.

Love always,
B.

PS: Max is the computer man at the University of Western England in Bristol—the English city that he likes best. We're so glad for him.

Don

University of Colorado at Boulder
Monday, June 8, 1998

Dear Norm and BJ:

Well! We gather that you have resigned as threatened and promised, for we received a midnight fax from IAU offering us, essentially, your jobs. What are you planning on doing now?

Please fill us in. We appreciated your earlier, newsy, and informative letters, but now need some nitty gritty stuff from you. We are faxing IAU saying that we are indeed very interested but need more information. Specifically, I am asking that they fax us a copy of the program of "arts and sciences." What are the "sciences"? In case they demur, we would like you to send us one post-haste. I have asked about taxes, the "provident fund," (and would like to know if you are successful in getting your money out of the fund)! I am asking about housing CLOSE TO THE CAMPUS.

But what I need from Norm most especially is a brief description of the teachers presently on the job, who are competent and who are not, who are leaving, etc. Are you staying on this summer?

If the initial information is forthcoming from IAU, and is reasonably satisfactory, we may accept quite soon. The salaries, taken together, are roughly equivalent to a Fulbright stipend, and that would, if the salaries are paid, allow us to retire most of the mortgage on our elder daughter Alison's house, which is a powerful incentive for going. As well as pay off our credit cards. Another is that I have never been to Turkey, not even Istanbul.

We seem to recall that you had said earlier that they required a medical examination in northern Cyprus?

We have been working like mad on our house and grounds this summer. I have finally got our old (much older than your Karmann Ghia) MGTD running, and have yet to deal with Dolly Parton (our 1955 Cadillac camper), which needs a thorough face-lift. We think that, if we do go to Cyprus, we will have a friend simply caretake our house for us, so that we do not have to go through the torment of coming back once again and having to find everything and put everything back in order. Our greatest concern is for our marvelous cat, whom we have come to love all over again. We may also drive to Alaska in August with our son Geoff and his daughter. Another advantage of having the IAU job. Start in October, if we go.

All the best, ever, Don and Beth

PS: Are there two campuses?

[In the end, Prof. Baker and Beth did not go!]
Friday Harbor, Washington
Thursday, April 26, 2018 (e-mail)

Dear Norm and BJ:

Beth was brought up listening to her father's accounts of Oxford and wandering through Europe as a young man, whereas my father's stories were few and very different — he had had no desire to travel the world, for in 18 months he had seen enough as a machine-gunner on the western front, and as a part of the occupying forces in the Rhine Valley. Remarque's Im Westen Nichts Neues [All Quiet on the Western Front] pretty well summed up his view of the world.

In short, when Beth and I married, I was very content to have a career in some little teachers' college in Iowa. Beth, however, was not. She stayed with me through Texas A&M, University of South Dakota, and the University of Mississippi, always urging me to explore the world.

Finally, by 1961, I had published enough stuff so that I was awarded a Fulbright to Finland. I was a bit scared, but excited. That year in Finland changed me utterly. The world was exciting and dangerous. That was the year that

Khrushchev exploded his 100-megaton hydrogen bomb in the peninsula just above us.

Beth and I hitched a ride on a Scandinavian student propaganda tour organized by the KGB and traveled from Leningrad to Moscow making friends all the way — Rita, a 30-year-old teacher of English in Leningrad, and Kari, a 60-year-old Finnish translator, who for two weeks became our bosom buddies. They traveled with us apart from the students — the Kirov in Leningrad, the great Moscow traveling circus with Popov the greatest of clowns, then on to Moscow. Intourist, with usual socialist inefficiency and stupidity, had assigned two guides in Moscow, but sent Kari and Rita with us anyway. It was great — the Intourist guides were East German models of everything that East Germany was, whereas Kari and Rita delighted in showing us around and calling in favors ... Dostoyevsky's house, Tolstoy's dacha, getting me official library cards in the Lenin Library (marked "Kap" for kapitalist), and finally a box seat at the first night of Khachaturian's "Spartacus" conducted by Himself. In a box seat across from us was Marshal Rokossovsky, commander of the Soviet army.

On the train back to Leningrad, the four of us shared a sleeping compartment and laughed all the way. We were invited to have another Fulbright year in Finland, but had to return home to find a job because Mississippi had in effect fired me (the legislature had passed a law forbidding the use of state funds to pay anyone who was a member of the ACLU) — but, fortunately, I had secured an offer from Colorado (Ole Miss was by no means a bad experience, meeting Faulkner and Eudora Welty).

From Colorado I secured a faculty fellowship, which enabled us to spend two years in Oxford, then back to Colorado, and in 1970 we moved the whole family to Dublin. (I would go back and teach a term while the family remained put.) It was wonderfully cheap in those days — the two older boys graduated from one of the great universities, Trinity

College Dublin, and the girls got a splendid education at Alexandra College — a year's professorship at the University of Kent — back and forth to Colorado.

Then in 1985 we applied for a job with the Chinese government. Beth had grown up in DC next to a family who had been missionaries in pre-war China. Immediately (with a letter beginning "Hi!") we were offered jobs at Wuhan University — 800 miles up the Yangtze from Shanghai. Wuhan (8,000,000 pop.) was a city unknown outside China — actually three cities: Hankow, Hanyang, and Wuchang. The university had a beautiful campus designed by French imperialists with little Chinese gable touches.

We were there for a year, asked to stay, but again hit the Fulbright trail — to Kairouan for two years. In the interim, I had again been awarded a Fulbright — to the University of Tehran — but in January of 1967 our son with Down syndrome, Nick, was born. Beth, for a change, didn't think she could cope in a strange environment, so we returned briefly to Colorado, but as I noted, then set off again, to Ireland, partly to get Nick into the wonderful Steiner system, which we were able to do.

In 1990, shortly after the Gulf War, we were given another Fulbright, this time to Jordan — a tiny town called Mo'tah (or "Place of Death" — so called because one of Mohammad's first attempts to tackle the Byzantine Empire ended in defeat for the Moslems, but what a wonderful piece of stationery, from the University of Death!?). Its military university was modeled on The Citadel. Beth was given a job as an honorary man, because the students couldn't be taught by a woman. But we did meet the King! Then, at your suggestion, the application to Macau, talking with Francis Dzau, dealing with Peter Glassblower, and you know the rest.

On leaving Macau I did apply for yet another Fulbright, to Uzbekistan, but for the first time did not get it … I think that they had grown weary of me. At your suggestion I applied for the northern Cyprus job, but withdrew upon learning that they had not paid the previous incumbent.

As I look back upon my Fulbright-riddled career, I realize that I was their utility man — I never got a plum posting — Oxford, Helsinki, Tunis, Beijing—oh, no. The State Department man at Tunis told me openly that I had been selected because there was no one else, it was a new posting in the desert, and the fact that I had taught in a Chinese university so far up the Yangtze made them confident that Beth and I would manage to survive. We almost didn't.

But friends! Friends everywhere — after twenty, thirty, forty, fifty years — you and BJ foremost among them. And the incredible conclusion — here on our little island — with three of our six children: Alison, the school nurse; Leslie, the County Librarian; and Keith, with whom we share his house.

All best, ever,

Don

Friday Harbor,
Washington Friday, April 27, 2018 (e-mail)

Dear Norm and BJ:

Vaguely connected to my family history is the fact that, like yours, Beth's parents were Kansans. Her father was a farm boy in the Sedan area. He was an agricultural laborer who followed the crops up to Montana and back, and got a frequently-broken high school education in a two-three room schoolhouse. (He was inspired to read because a farmer who was too poor to pay him gave him a partial set of Dickens books instead — it was in his library when he died.) He attended the University of Kansas, and while at Lawrence, the Rhodes Scholarships began. He applied for one, but didn't get it. Thinking he would have a better chance from the territorial university in Arizona, he WALKED from Lawrence to Tucson, following the Union Pacific. At Arizona, he applied again for the Rhodes, and got it. Foreign applicants in those days had to pass the same leaving exams as British students, which were heavy on Latin and Greek. His crabby high school teacher (an old maid come west to spread culture in the spirit of Chautauqua) had crammed Horace and Homer into the heads of farm boys and girls, and fortunately for Dad Disney, he had been required to memorize in school most of an Horatian ode, which he was required to translate on the Rhodes exam!

Having no money, he worked his way to England on a cattle boat from Vera Cruz, Mexico. Among his contemporaries at Exeter College, Oxford, was Hubble, the telescope guy, and J.R.R. Tolkien. Dad Disney read law, worked as a lawyer in Oklahoma, was appointed chief justice of the U.S. Tax Court of Appeals, and was short-listed for a nomination to the Supreme Court by F.D.R., but the post went to Felix Frankfurter instead.

All this, by way of explaining Beth's passion for travel and love of England.

You and BJ lived everywhere in hotels, of a sort. In our case, with 3-6 children, it was impossible. We, in true 60s and 70s style, had a VW camper which every summer plied the back roads of France, Spain, Italy, then- Yugoslavia, Greece (camping on the Med under Mt. Olympus)! I would drive all day, and Beth and the kids would make the camp. As a commemoration of those nights under the stars and lulled to sleep by nightingales, our daughter, Leslie, had a cake made for our sixtieth anniversary in the shape of a VW bus, with me lying beside it! We didn't see much of Paris, but we saw a helluva lot of France.

All best, ever,
Don

Friday Harbor, Washington
Monday, April 30, 2018 (e-mail)

Dear Norm:

You and BJ and Beth and I were Olivia Manningish, though a bit short of Anna and the King of Siam. If I had been granted yet another Fulbright, I am sure that Beth and I would have proceeded to Uzbekistan. Our granddaughter, Heather (she of Nigeria), did two years in Kazakhstan teaching science in Russian. As she is a near-fluent Russian speaker, we hoped that our state department might make something of this find, but in state department tradition sent her to a largely English-speaking country. This seems traditional (a former teacher, who was fluent in Icelandic and patriotically offered his services when the U.S. was building its great airfields in Iceland just before we were Pearl Harbored, was gratefully accepted and, naturally, sent to India — good for him, for he learned Sanskrit).

With no intent to insult your son-in-law (or my granddaughter), I must say that my observation of the state department is that it has been the home of intellectual misfits who are confident of their knowledge of nothing. A dear friend (Bill Eagleton) was ambassador to Syria and Algeria, and three others were CIA disguised as "cultural attaché," "labor attaché," etc. One of them, a CIA "labor attaché," remarked upon leaving our front porch in 1974, "Well, I'm off to lose another small Asian country," and succeeded. (He was the man appointed to lead our POWs out of the Hanoi Hilton.)

They all had the same general opinion of State — well-educated, insufferably opinionated, and ineluctably ignorant. In short, I don't think that Trump has hurt State much — I think that they remain the same. We continue to observe.

All best,
Don

Friday Harbor, Washington
Tuesday, May 8, 2018 (e-mail)

Dear Norm:

If I were summarizing my overseas teaching, I would proudly proclaim that I was probably the only English professor to be the center of TWO university student protests on a single day on separate campuses!

In 1992 I returned from Macau to be on the doctoral committee for our old friend Mohsen Hamli. His oral examination was at the granting institution, Tunis. While we were there, "students" confronted the gendarmes, throwing Molotov cocktails against the shields of the police. The struggle blocked our pathway to the lot where our car was parked. We were isolated for some two hours before we were able to seize a moment, when the two sides were exhausted, and dash across to our car. We drove as fast as we could to Kairouan, arriving just in time to see the dean's house burn down! Quite exciting, but perhaps not so exciting as your story of you and BJ in Beirut patiently waiting in your building's doorway until the stream of tracer bullets subsided before dashing across the street to a party! Sic transit gloria.

All best, ever,
Don

PS. About Mohsen's degree — the committee was loaded, with a nasty Palestinian determined to sink Hamli, and he failed his exam. I refused to sign the report, and, I am pleased to say, my action caused the Education Department to void the committee's report and grant Mohsen his degree anyway. I thought then, and think now, that any Arab Moslem (whose father was an imam) who did a dissertation on the gynocriticism of the novelist Margaret Drabble deserved a doctorate!

Friday Harbor, Washington
Wednesday, May 30, 2018 (e-mail)

Dear Norm:

Perhaps we have told you before, but our Manningish career had other amusing aspects. Until about twenty years ago, our younger daughter Leslie had been convinced that her parents were CIA. There was a little pearl of fact—when she graduated from college in 1949, with nothing to do in DC, Beth got a job as a file clerk in the first CIA, just spinning off from OSS [Office of Strategic Services] before it went to Langley. After a few months she quit, went to her home state of Oklahoma, to its university, where we met.

End of that story, but I could see where Leslie was coming from.

My later career was a series of government fellowships, first to Finland in 1961-62 at the height of the Cold War, with Khrushchev exploding his 100- megaton bomb about three hundred miles above where we living. I had asked for Helsinki, but, no, they wanted to place us near the Soviet border. Oh, well. I should have been in Tehran, but begged off.

Then we volunteered to teach in China just as the Cultural Revolution ended. Then, the Fulbrights in Tunisia, a hundred miles below the PLO headquarters. Then a Fulbright to Jordan immediately after Operation Desert Storm. Then years in Macau, a notorious den of spies.

We certainly knew CIA people, as I am sure you and BJ did, and were interviewed a number of times — various "cultural attachés" and "labor attachés" came down from Tunis or Amman to quiz us and buy our lunch. "Your taxpayer dollars at work," they happily said.

It is true that we were frequently parallel to Manning's British Council people. We were close to one in particular, a young woman just graduated from Oxford, who went out as British Council to Finland, subsequently to Poland and Israel, then quit, went straight, married, had children, and became a lawyer specializing in children's law. She had been with us in our Soviet escapade, helping us to sneak aboard a Soviet-sponsored tour for Scandinavian students. We had always thought that there was something suspicious about that!

At any rate, I am sure that there is actually something about us in the CIA files, perhaps under the category of "informants." Perhaps we might be eligible for a small government pension!

All best,

Don

L.L. ALEXANDRIA
Colleague at University of Macau

Fruitport, Michigan
Monday, January 22, 2018 (e-mail)

Dear Norm and BJ,

How wonderful to hear that you are working with an agent to get your memoirs published! You have such amazing, unique, insightful experiences to share of your life and your years spent teaching overseas.

As I reflect on our years together in Macau, and on my time spent overseas, I am filled with fond memories, frustrating professional moments, and excitement beyond the wildest dreams of a girl born in a small town in the Midwest.

When I accepted the teaching position at the Universidade de Macau, I knew almost immediately that I was in for an adventure, with all of its ups and downs. My plane landed in Hong Kong on a Friday night, and no one from the university met me. In fact, they told me that I couldn't come to Macau that weekend because the university would be closed. Really? Thankfully, I still had friends in Hong Kong — from my days of living in Japan as a missionary — who allowed me to stay with them for the weekend.

I took the jetfoil to Macau on Monday morning, and no one met me at the ferry, either. It was raining heavily, and I was struggling with all of my water-logged luggage; after all, I had packed enough for a two-year stay in a foreign country. As I stood outside of the ferry dock, drenched, I fished in my pocket and found a slip of paper with the address of the university on it. I showed this to the taxi driver, and he promptly drove me to the university, unloaded my bags, and left me at the bottom of a hill. It felt like a much higher climb, up the hill to the university's administration building, than it actually was.

Soaked, tired, and alone … I started my first of seven years teaching at the university.

Thankfully I met wonderful friends like you, who helped me laugh through the adversity. I was also blessed, as we all were, with enough time off to discover the mysterious Orient and historical Europe.

What I loved most about my travels through Asia was the entrepreneurial spirit of the people. On a two week vacation to the Philippines, I wandered the back streets of Cebu City until I found a bicycle shop. As men stood around fixing their high-end bikes, I asked the owner if I could rent a bike for a week to travel around the island. He initially looked scared, not trusting I would return with his merchandise. He turned to a friend, who was working on his bike, and asked if he thought I could make the journey on my own. The cyclist looked me up and down, frowned, and then shook his head "no." The owner rented me a bike anyway, and I later discovered that he had charged me almost enough to purchase the bike. His insurance policy, I am sure.

Twice I went to Cebu and solo cycled around the islands of Cebu, Leyte, and Negros. What an amazing experience. The people were kind, helpful, and I am still in touch with a sweet family from Argao. Writing letters and sending packages, however, have turned into composing e-mail messages and posting on Facebook!

It almost broke my heart to leave Italy after five weeks there. The architecture, the museums, the cathedrals, and the countryside are all etched in my mind forever. To save money, I often stayed in monasteries and abbeys. I had purchased a book that gave advice on how to stay in monasteries. It included a sample letter in Italian that you were to send to the monastery in advance of your arrival. Rarely did I get confirmation that I could stay, but I trekked to these holy institutions nonetheless and was always greeted with a welcoming smile by a nun, who invariably was holding a copy of my letter in her hand. They could never speak a word of English, and my Italian was no better, but I stayed in these sparse but clean rooms, often on the edge of town, and had quite the experience.

I rented a car and toured the island of Sicily for four days. I was often lost, but keeping the sea on the same side meant that I was completing a circle, so eventually I would wind up back at the car rental place, right?

Breakfast every day consisted of a loaf of bread, a jar of marmalade, and a pot of coffee with cream. On my tight budget, dinner every evening was either pizza or pasta. And yet, I still lost 11 pounds on this trip because of how much walking I did.

In Thailand, my traveling companions deserted me in Bangkok to go to Phuket. Alone again, I took a train north to Chiang Mai and rented a scooter for the day. I guess that I forgot to confirm how long I could keep the vehicle, because when I returned the scooter I was aghast to see that the shop was closed! Since I had given them my passport as collateral, and since the only train that could get me back to Bangkok in time to catch my flight home was leaving at five o'clock in the morning, I was understandably concerned, if not outright panicked. Neighbors loaded me into their truck and drove me to the shop owner's home. It was late at night, very dark, and we pounded on his door until we woke him up. He begrudgingly returned my passport ... much to my delight!

I also took the Trans-Siberian Railway and enjoyed China, was fascinated with Mongolia, and fell in love with Russia. Traveling alone, I was often in a cabin on the train with unknown companions. Once I shared a berth with three Russian men. They mostly ignored me, but sleeping was difficult as they removed their shoes and the odor was, shall we say, asphyxiating.

Three weeks in Tibet, volunteering with Mother Teresa's Missionaries of Charity in Singapore and in Calcutta, and getting an audience with the Dalai Lama in Dharamsala, India, were all part of the wonderful experience that was living and teaching in a foreign land.

Teaching in the English Communications department at the Universidade de Macau was a time of personal and professional development. I learned how to teach without textbooks, how to communicate to eager students who struggled with the language, and how to establish a video production department with a small budget but a supportive staff. Thankfully, David Nottingham had laid all of the foundational work for this project. But, oh how I wish I had been able to work with him. Sadly, he left Macau before my contract began.

Best of all are the friends who have kept in touch over the years. Traveling before the era of Facebook, Instagram, and blogs, friends remained close because the experience was personally shared, not merely communicated via social media. We learned to write and treasure letters. We sent and received picturesque postcards. We even met again, overseas or in the United States, when our paths crossed.

And I am blessed to include in that small circle of friends … both of you.

Fondly,
L.L.

LAUREN FRIESEN
Student from Bethel College

David M. French Professor Emeritus of Theatre, University of Michigan - Flint and Docent at the Oriental Institute - Chicago

Chicago, Illinois
Thursday, October 4, 2018 (e-mail)

Hello Norm,

When I look at Bethel and all the accomplishments by this small group and the alumni, it is remarkable. Maybe alumni of all colleges think that way about their alma mater, but I have my doubts about that.

Life in Chicago has been wonderful — museums, theatre, parks, lakefront, and all that.

Working [at the University of Michigan-Flint] and chairing the theatre and dance program for many years was a dream come true, and sometimes even I find it hard to believe that I did all that. Great alums also! While I was there I started an M.A. in American Theatre Studies and an M.A. in Art Administration. Both programs are flourishing with graduates now from around the world (sort of).

Janet and I have been married 48 years and have 2 children and 4 grandchildren. Our son and his family live in Berkeley and they are doing well. Our daughter lives in Chicago and is the costume coordinator for Court Theatre. She has been at this job now 15 years and probably will continue for some time in the future.

I published a series of essays on my life entitled Prairie Lands, Private Landscapes: Reframing a Mennonite Childhood. I did not give adequate credit to many and I regret that. But I highlight how important Waiting for Godot was and my Bethel theatre experience — the only place I felt "free" at that time.

Our travel plans are somewhat limited these days. We were in Italy a year ago, and it was splendid. Saw many historic sites, of course. I will go to Germany again for research in March or April of next year. My main area is 1890-1915 and the works by Hermann Sudermann (1854-1928), playwright, novelist, and Mennonite father. He was a friend of Ibsen and highly praised in his day although forgotten now. He was a strong advocate for women's rights, against the rise of German antisemitism, and critical of the centralization of power in Germany. He thought Germany as a militarized nation would blunder into unending wars (this was in the early 1900s), and so he advocated that Germany was really a language and a culture. National boundaries were immaterial to him. If you have the leisure, read his The Mad Professor. It's about a brilliant scholar who aims to get tenure and when he doesn't, goes mad. Sudermann's Menno ancestry makes him a unique character in many ways. I did translate one of his plays, The Storm Komrade Sokrates (University Press of America), but that was for a promotion and not exactly for publicity.

Hermann's father was a Mennonite and his uncle was the pastor of the large Mennonite church in Elbing, Prussia. Hermann attended that church for a number of years and later wrote in his autobiography that "it warmed his heart to know he was related to all of those people and yet at the same time he felt like a bird in a cage."

Sudermann and Ibsen were often seen together and their mutual rival was Hauptmann, who ended up as a Hitler advocate. Sudermann was arrested on his way to the opening of his play The Storm Komrade Sokrates. The order to arrest came from the emperor's censor since the play is a comic farce on politics. This is what happened next. After the first act on opening night, the police let Sudermann go since the order had been to arrest and there was no order to hold him in jail! So Sudermann went to the theatre during the intermission and received a 20 minute standing ovation! Then act II began.

Lauren

[Lauren and other former Bethel College students toured the country, including the Frank Lloyd Wright Taliesin West, performing a production of Waiting for Godot. At Taliesin West, the architect William Wesley Peters showed them the drawings of a gigantic theatre designed for the city of Tehran. It was never built. This illustration was, however, the basis for the theatre he designed for Damavand College. Peters also designed the entirely new Damavand College campus, which was finally built. And then the Iranian Revolution closed the college.

Regarding his rise to achievement, Lauren Friesen said several times to me, "… and it all started with Waiting for Godot." My production!

Lauren shared a story with me of when, as a young man, he walked past the San Francisco Opera theatre and saw a "help wanted" sign in the window. He went in. They wanted someone to do the backstage support work. He aced the test of distinguishing between the "straw, steel blue, chocolate, surprise pink, lavender, etc.," lighting gels, tossing them all into the right bins. With his enthusiasm, they hired him on the spot. And, he added, he learned it all at Bethel College.

At one point, we each considered going to Union Theological Seminary to study in their Drama in the Church program headed by Tom Driver. That's when I turned around in the middle of the snow driven highway and went instead to sunny California to the University of Southern California and learned great theatre design techniques from John Blankenchip, who was trained at Carnegie Tech and Yale. His recent obituary said that "John always made us feel we could do it!" I'd like that for mine!]

KATHRYN KASPER
Student from Bethel College

Asunción, Paraguay
Monday, December 3, 2018 (e-mail)

Hello,

I continue to have a career at the age of 78!

I have been working in Asunción for 12 years now after retiring from Bethel College in 2006. At that point I had I received a six-month Fulbright Grant to teach with the opera company at Uni-Norte in Asunción, Paraguay, after which we fully expected to retire in North Newton, Kansas. But, it soon became evident that voice teachers with any technical know-how are not in Paraguay.

Before we left Paraguay, I had offers of employment for the following year so we returned after Christmas to teach at the Mennonite Seminary, Paraguay, which has two degrees — theology and music. After three years, the National University — UNA — began the second Bachelors of Music in the country, and I began work there, developing the voice program. Currently I am teaching at UNA, another U., and in my house. There are not enough hours in the day.

Another very important connection now is with the choir for the National Catholic Cathedral. I have been working with the director as voice coach for three years. Arlo and I also sing with the group. The choir just returned from a trip to Italy where we participated in a Liturgical Conference at the Vatican following with a tour of the major cities of Northern Italy.

Familywise, this is possible because we always return to the States for Christmas for 6-8 weeks. New York City is easy to get to and that is where our daughter, a Broadway singer, Rachel and her family live, so we plan a visit there at least one other time a year. We see all our grandkids at least once a year and probably would not see them more if we lived in North Newton.

My best to you both.

Kathryn [Kathryn's husband, Arlo Kasper, was my Professor Higgens in Pygmalion by G.B. Shaw, my first production at my first job at Bethel College in North Newton, Kansas. Arlo was also brilliant as Hamlet in my last production at Bethel College, performed on the outdoor steps of the marvelous castle-like Administration Building in the Summer Theatre. He earned a Master's Degree in theatre and took my job at Bethel a couple years after we left to go to Beirut for the first time. After he and Kathryn, who taught voice in the Bethel Music Department, retired, they worked in the Asunción, Paraguay, Opera and taught at the University of Asunción, Paraguay.]

ZIAD ABUABSI
Student from Beirut University College

On stage, Ziad Abuabsi was powerful, yet subtle, in his handling of Hamlet or of less complicated characters such as General St. Pe in The Waltz of the Toreadors by Jean Anouilh. He portrayed the general remarkably; remembering past glories on the battlefield, conquering the enemy on horseback, and writing his memoirs while Madame St. Pe lies helpless on her bed behind the scrim. On the backdrop was painted a glorious, young Gen. St. Pe atop a horse standing on hind legs rearing. I was very happy that another student, an art major, was willing to have her work exhibited on stage ten feet high on thirty feet of scrim.

The play begins as Madame St. Pe calls out, "Leon, what are you doing?" "Writing." "Liar, you are thinking of our neighbor's breasts." Madam St. Pe, played brilliantly by Dawn Nottingham, wife of Dr. David Nottingham, professor of Communications, chastises the general. Although claiming to be paralyzed, she exercises gingerly as the lights gently brighten and reveal her presence on her bed behind the scrim, which is directly upstage behind a large period desk at which General St. Pe sits writing. It is a very comedic scene.

Ziad worked in several local, popular theatres as an actor and director, often writing the scripts in either Arabic or English. He left BUC, going to the University of Texas for a Master's Degree and pursuing a doctorate in Philosophy and Classical Literature. After driving a cab for several years to make a living while studying, he returned to Beirut, taking a teaching post at one of the local colleges. He also wrote, directed, and acted in radio dramas, usually serials, recorded in Beirut, and sometimes networked throughout the Arab world, particularly the Gulf and North Africa and Egypt. He taught at the American University of Beirut and other colleges, locally, teaching Humanities Cultural Studies, a series of required courses involving history, literature, philosophy, drama; the same course BJ taught at Haigazian College.

He recently proposed to the Swedish Embassy to establish an Ibsen Colloquium Festival to be held locally. Sweden showed great interest. Other proposals have met with success, or slightly less, in the Emirates, usually with the same success ratio of theatre and art programs in the rest of the world. Macau is the exception with its huge support of the arts, made possible by money gleaned from the casinos.

Ziad is a very ambitious guy; I pray his health allows him to achieve all the conquests he is due.

NADINE CAMEL-TOUEG
Student from Beirut Days

Monday, April 10, 2017 (e-mail)

My dear Norman,

How nice to hear from you.

Yes, what a sad and terrible news. Actually, Alfred was about to go [to cover the Palm Sunday bombing of our Coptic Church in Alexandria near Cairo], but he already had a plane ticket to go cover the holy week and Easter in Kurdistan in two villages just recently freed from ISIS. He is following, since a while, Christians in this part of the world, which has been the cradle of Christianity.

I am so happy that you are doing well with BJ.

Raphael is doing very well. He chose Ukraine as his terrain. He has a lovely girlfriend, which I already embraced as my own daughter. Not having one I am blessed with Elsa, who is a sweet, beautiful girl from Bourgogne!!

Ivan is 21 and is giving us a bit of trouble as he starts projects but then drops them!! He has this brilliant idea. He printed Alfred's picture on a piece of linen, and then sewed them on a sweatshirt. He had articles and participated in show rooms, but he needs to be more pushy.

Sebastien, 19 years old, is following a very good gourmet school for chefs!! We are now studying. (Yes, "we," as I still have to push them and help them in their study projects!)

I just came back from a yoga teacher refresher course. I work with the disabled and give classes to brain damage survivors and women that had cancer. I also teach in a university in Paris. So I have a wide range of active university students to people with special needs. It is very rewarding, indeed.

I am doing quite well. At such a point where this year I decided to give up seven classes as it was too much work.

My dear Norm, I miss you so much. I often think so fondly of you and BJ.

Lina is doing extremely well in her work. [Lina Abeyad, the dancer in my production of Eurydice.] She works in two different directions. Her scripts are all original, written by her. One method is that she picks up a theme and interviews the person for over three months, and then creates a character and a monologue out of all what was said. Specially anecdotes that seemed insignificant to the person, Lina picks them up, and points them out, to give a lighter, more intimate touch to the script.

She did a remarkable work on the true story of a "martyred" terrorist who hijacked a Boeing of Sabena in 1972 and was killed by an Israeli Commando. The play was a one woman show by the daughter of the commando. The play had hilarious moments as the actress is a real bomb on stage … she keeps her audience without one minute of dropping the energy. The play toured in several countries.

Lina managed to tell the story of this absent father who is a hero for some, a terrorist for others, in a universal story full of emotion and hysterical funny moments. She then can work on written texts, but completely re-writes and adapts them to the Lebanese situation. All is acted in Arabic with amazing actors and non-actors. Her other masterpiece, which you would have loved and gone hysterical, is an again written play by Lina on a text that has only one character that speaks about sexual problems of women. She broke the one character into five. The text had no particular setting. She placed the five women in the waiting room of a gynecologist!

She made Marcel Abou Chakra, a man (huge), play the role of a woman. He was out of a Fellini film. The five characters: a prostitute (the man playing as a woman); a totally veiled woman; a mother totally desperate; a single woman, a lesbian; I can't remember the other one. Anyway, it was incredible with the bed of the gynecologist and the two bars to hang the legs. She does not even know how all this passed the censorship with a scene where at one point one of the woman masturbates. Of course, all of this brilliantly staged by Lina.

I have seen none of the plays, but I follow so closely her plays that it is as if I was in the audience. This is love and true friendship.

So here are the news.

I can hear your laughter.

Such a blessing to have known you. We learnt so much on the essence of space in theatre. Space is so important. You gave us precious tools.

Love you and miss you. Happy Easter,
Nadine and all her boys

[A former theatre-communications student in Beirut, Nadine acted in a number of my productions, including Anouilh's Eurydice and J.B. by Richard Wilbur. Nadine was a newscaster for French Radio in Beirut during the civil war while we were there. She moved to France soon after our daughter Natasha lived in Paris. Nadine married Alfred Yaghobzadeh, a photo journalist, who covered the Middle East mainly. In addition to photographing wars and runways, he also took photos for several articles on Christians around the world, in particular in Iran and Syria. Their son, Raphael, follows in his father's footsteps. In a recent interview, Raphael confirmed that his heritage was Armenian, Assyrian, Persian, Coptic, and Lebanese.

Lina, married to an architect, was an actress in my theatre productions. She moved to Paris about the time we left Beirut, feeling the impossibility of living in Beirut with the thirteen year war. After the war finished, she packed up family and they returned to Beirut where she taught at my old theatre job. Her husband joined in the creation of the new Beirut with the sponsorship of the new Prime Minister Hauriri, who funded most of the repairs and new buildings until he was assassinated. She's a brilliant producer of theatre.]

AGNES WAKIM DAGHER
Student from Beirut College for Women

Pasadena, California
Monday, November 19, 2018 (e-mail to Agnes)

Dear Agnes,
BJ and I were looking for an address in the U.S.A. to send a small contribution to CRC [Contact and Resources Center] and can't find the one we used to use. Could you please send it to us via e-mail?

We have retired in Pasadena, California, for health reasons. When you were in the States we were in Macau, China. How are you and your family? Well, we pray. Your Christmas letters have been such an inspiration to us. The last one we have on file is from 2011. In an earlier letter you were kind to have remembered me/us and those powerful moments. Thank you.

I also believe in Angels to guide us, as did my father. I think they watched over us during all 44 years teaching in wonderful places like Beirut and traveling everywhere God lead us. Thank you for the thoughts. How warm are our memories of those days in Beirut! Particularly well remembered are the ones during the BCW days. We loved them!

In between the BCW days and BUC years, we were in Pittsburgh, at Carnegie Mellon doing a Ph.D., then Connecticut and Teheran, Iran, again with Dr. Frances Gray at Damavand College, where we oversaw the building of a new theatre on the campus newly designed by the Frank Lloyd Wright Taliesin West architects. Beautifully conceived based on the caravansaries that housed travelers. After that we were challenged in Beirut like everyone during the eighties when we were there until 1985. At BUC (now LAU) we were constantly in theatre productions with students doing plays that spoke of significant events, ideas, values.

How great it was when I started teaching at Leb U., on the East side campus, and you let me stay at the CRC House of Learning for hopefully recovering injured persons learning to live in a changed world! That was all such a good program. The night that Dennis was kidnapped and God opened the door and led him home safely was inspirational! That was an Angel story! I was sleeping on the inner balcony as Dennis prayed all night. I wanted to join him but felt that he wanted only to talk with God, so I prayed with him in the Holy Spirit on the other side of the balcony. Dennis was a wonderful guiding spirit for all of us in Beirut then. Thank you for the years of your dedication, Agnes, along with the support of your husband.

Does CRC work with Evelyne Accad and Jacqueline Hajjar on the women with physical challenges, i.e. battered, abandoned, etc.?

How is my former student – I've forgotten his first name — Wakim? Tell him hi. I sometimes hear from Ziad Abuabsi, my former student, who brought me to see you at your home the last time BJ and I were in Beirut, the year we were teaching in North Cyprus in 1997-98 after retiring from the University of Macau, China, near Hong Kong.

After leaving Beirut in 1985 we taught in Tunisia, thanks to Dr. Evelyne Accad, and then on to China for the next 30 years, including 20 volunteering with an Anglican Chinese school, Choi Koh in Macau, helping English teachers improve their skills. Some teachers had been our students at the University of Macau. We enjoyed living in Macau. Great 17th century churches and architecture from the 400 years the Portuguese controlled Macau. BJ, along with our Anglican Vicar, wrote a book on the 19th C. missionaries that entered China only through Macau.

Sorry for boring you with these thoughts. E-mail us, please.

God bless you and your family.

Norm and BJ

Beirut, Lebanon
Thursday, December 13, 2018 (e-mail)

Dear Dr. Norman ...

What a beautiful surprise and a loving message ... made my day.

Yes. Those were good days and good years ... AND ... thanks for sharing all those memories and loving thoughts.

Now it is time for me to share a beautiful memory of you that I will never forget. It was the first time I saw you and met you at BCW.

It was a few nights before Christmas Eve. Our church choir was practicing the Anthem by Handel: How Beautiful are the Feet of Him that Bringeth Good Tidings. We were in the basement of the music building. In walks a very handsome, bearded, tall gentleman. He stood there watching with a smile on his face 'til the last note resounded in the hall. I think he had tears in his eyes. He remained quiet for a while then clapped with joy and approached Else Farr, our choir director, and said, "That is the most beautiful time I have heard this anthem!!!" The choir director hugged him back and said, "Choir, I would like you to meet Dr. Norman Lofland." That was the first time I met you.

Dr. Lofland, you are a beautiful man, and that is a beautiful memory that I cherish very much. Later, many memories followed of your kindness and care to us and many, many Lebanese. Thank you. You will never be forgotten.

Much love to you and your good family. They all have been so supportive.

Agnes

[Rev. Dennis Hilgendorf started the Contact and Resources Center (CRC) in Beirut, Lebanon. He came to Beirut to establish a Lutheran Church. He observed life in Beirut and decided it did not need another church, as there are many churches in Beirut, but that what it needed was an organization doing Christ's work. The Lebanese Civil War broke out, with families fighting their neighbors, sometimes even their own family members, and permanently injuring many civilians as well as political fighters. Dennis felt that God wanted someone to care for and guide the maimed persons to become self-sufficient. This decision came after establishing a counseling center in West Beirut, near AUB and the Near East School of Theology, just off Ave. Hamra, Ras Beirut. Before many months he realized counseling was not enough; the maimed had to have guidance. So he, with support from some believers, acquired a large house in East Beirut, where he spent much of his time, although his large family lived — as we did — in West/Ras Beirut. They added a long ramp at the front entrance for wheelchair access, removed walls, and added a lengthy balcony surrounding a center living complex. It opened with a substantial number of wheelchaired persons, without all their limbs or legs, and taught them to take care of themselves so they were no longer a burden on their family or friends. It worked. All of this went on while the various factions were shelling each other from different locations in the mountains overlooking Beirut. The Lebanese Civil War lasted fifteen years, from 1975 until 1990. During this time, CRC morphed into an organization for disabled people and was recognized by the Lebanese government. My wife, BJ, and daughter, Natasha, left Beirut after I did in 1985, going to Tunisia. Agnes Wakim Dagher was the director of CRC for many years.]

CATHERINE (WAI IENG) WONG
Student from University of Macau

Macau
Wednesday, May 26, 1993

Dear Professor Lofland,

Thanks a lot for your encouraging comment in my journal. It's really touching — so touching that I really can't express my gratitude in person, but put it in words on a card. To me, you are really a wonderful professor who can create an atmosphere of sense of belonging in class and stimulate students' sense of participation. This is something vital in teaching. Down in my heart, it's an honor to be your student, and I hope I can be your student again one day! To tell the truth, I really hope one day that my students can enjoy my teaching as much as I enjoy yours.

With best wishes, Catherine (Wai Ieng) Wong

Macau
Tuesday, December 3, 1996

Dearest Professor Lofland and Mrs. Lofland,

How are you getting on all these days? I miss you two!

It's nice to receive your postcard, learning that you two had a wonderful holiday! Whenever I have English play and radio play activities with my students, I made use of all the techniques I've learned from your lectures. Also, thanks to Mrs. Lofland for her Myth (booklet) from which I could rewrite short plays or radio plays for my students. It's a good reference book, practical, and interesting. In fact, during these past years, I was lucky enough to have such dedicated tutors at university.

Now I'm having more time for my rest, but sometimes I still miss the lessons I had!! Finally, may I wish you a Merry Xmas and a Happy New Year.

Best Wishes, Catherine (Wai Ieng Wong)

[Catherine's principal won't let her retire, although she is now 67 and wants to. She was an excellent student!]

CHAPTER 17

AFTER-THOUGHTS (2017 –)

China and the world have changed since those days of "coming out of the bamboo curtain." China has become number two economically, surpassing Japan, and developing on many fronts, which appears daily in news headlines. But still, there is severe poverty in their countryside, as workers leave the farm to join the manufacturing assembly line, supplying the world with tons of goods — everything from plastic gee-gaws to iPhones and cars. Great wealth is achieved by a few, with millions of workers and farmers suffering severe hardship.

As Dr. Nottingham has written, television has increased the demand for western goods and services, resulting in resentment and disillusion when these desires cannot be satisfied. Especially in the Middle East, there are often no jobs for the educated young, making impossible the fulfillment of the dreams stimulated by their education. I have observed unemployed Tunisian university graduates, sitting at tea houses, hopelessly fearing they will never be any better off than their parents and grandparents. Hence, the massive migration of many of these youth to Europe in 2016.

The Lebanese have been less susceptible to this syndrome of hopelessness; they seem to have instinctive abilities to make deals and turn missed opportunities into future rewards. They must have inherited the spirit of entrepreneurship from their Phoenician ancestors. Also, Lebanon was exposed to western education and culture generations earlier than most of the Middle East. The American University of Beirut and Beirut College for Women, now Lebanese American University, were established over 150 years ago by the Presbyterian

Church Mission Board from Riverside Drive, New York City. There is also the French educational influence.

But Lebanese resilience and resolution continue to be severely tested: the inpouring in 1948 of Palestinian refugees when Israel was established, a devastating civil war of sixteen years with the intrusion of the Iranian Hezbollah, and now the flood of Syrian refugees escaping their own horrific civil war. In the midst of overwhelming disruption, the Lebanese struggle to turn the chaos into some form of order for a better future. Because of Hezbollah, Lebanon is threatened with destruction of its infrastructure.

And what about Iran, where we believed that educating women was the key to improving society? At Damavand College we taught women from September 1972 until it closed in December 1978. This educational institution was also established by the Presbyterian Mission Board and was closed by the revolution. Now post-revolution Iran, with its harsh form of Islam, has gone backward, dragging the status of women with it. One might wonder whether western education was wasted there. But Iranian women are strong and, hopefully, they are finding some of what we brought them helpful in coping with their lives.

When thoughtfully evaluating the results of our life-investment — that of educating the young people of various countries, some of which countries are now unfriendly to the United States — we realize that all the results are not positive. I'm reminded of a comment by the Shah of Iran when still in power: "Concerning our learning from the West, Iran will accept only those things/ideas which are positive and will improve our society; all others we will reject." Perhaps that's the prevalent attitude of the present Iranian government with their nuclear program!

Unfortunately, it doesn't work that way, for Iran, or anyone else. We have aided China with its acquisition and domination, but it is struggling to keep out the undesirable, such as the Internet. China, so eager for the English language and western technology, is, along with Iran, a good example of "turning and biting the hand that fed it."

For us personally, the results have been overwhelmingly positive. Living abroad for 46 years and working with students and faculty from different cultures has been exciting and rewarding. It has broadened our views as only travel can do. Our work has brought travel opportunities otherwise unavailable to us.

But nothing in this world is without its downside. Forty-five years ago in Tehran, Iran, I contracted meningitis for the second time, after being ill with it in Beirut in 1965 following an overland motor-trip in our Karmann Ghia to and from Tehran, which was the beginning of health problems, and I have not enjoyed good health since.

Living abroad, one misses out on much that is going on with family and country, and upon retirement, it's been difficult to settle back in. We've just given our 1972 classic refurbished beautiful red Karmann Ghia to Mennonite Central Committee to be auctioned off for funds for relief for the refugees from Syria. This was our fourth and last Karmann Ghia. Previously two of the same cars in the MCC auction sold for $15,000 each. God will use these funds to help the hopeless.

All in all, we've had wonderful lives and continue to be thankful for God's guidance and protection, which made it all possible.

May God Bless Us Everyone, Norman and Betty Jean (BJ) Lofland

An "After Thought" from a former student, now directing an opera house in Asuncion, Paraquay. The letters between Arlo Kasper and Norm Lofland are interesting, and offer comment. Arlo's wife, Kathryn, teaches voice in the Department of Music, University of Asuncion, Paraquay, South America. Her comments are elsewhere in this book.

***

Dear Arlo,

Congratulations on an adventure very well done!

Please write a book expanding what you've done, filled with details. Those crazy moments that later filled you with wonder.

Where are you?

I'll get your letter into the second edition of HOW NOT TO TRAVEL. Perhaps I should insert a section on how to travel in these unusual situations that come up. But, each of us has our own opportunity! I can only advise each of us to prepare for such opportunities, and do it. Both you and I could have stayed on the farm, but we prepared ourselves, taught at colleges and universities, learning our craft, and when the opportunity came, we could say "Yes, thank you dear Father in Heaven, we will go!" And we did! It's the same with Lauren Friesen, our Bethel College student who became Professor and Chairman of the Department of Theatre and Dance, University of Michigan, Flint campus. And so did Rosalind Enns, another Bethel College student, our theatre acting colleague, who became a Dean at the University of Vermont.

So many opportunities. . . ! If we weren't 89 and 91 we would again "Go for it!"

Best,
Norm

***

August 10, 2022
Dear Family and Friends,

Today we have been bombarded by reports of local, national and global unrests. But would you consider making a phone call in behalf of Gazans and other Palestinians who are literally being bombed out of existence by overwhelming Israeli air and land power. In 2002, I was in one of the camps distributing food to the poverty stricken population created by Israel's ethnic cleansing of the Palestine area in that region in 1948. Attacks against citizens have gone on since that date but nothing quite like the strength of what is taking place right now. That follows a pattern that the nation of Israel follows when the world, especially the US is not paying any attention to what is going on in the Middle East. I was a guest of the Baptist church in Gaza and the food came from a number of charities. Please call this number, 202 224 3121 in Washington DC representing Congressional officers who are most likely in their home districts but saying little about the Middle East and less about Gaza and Palestinians living and dying in their homes inside and outside of Israel. Thanks for your call even to talk to an answering service.

David

***

August 11, 2022

G'morning Norm,

The Palestinians have always been the "forgotten" people - your friend's note says it well, though sadly, for what's happening: ethnic cleansing. I know there are folks in Israel who object, but the government, mostly rightwing in recent years, has been intent on getting rid of the problem by getting rid of the people as a people. Western governments seem satisfied to keep their eyes closed, and if and when questions are raised, accusations of anti-Semitism are hurled.

Came across this today from Louise Bogan, poet and critic: "I cannot believe that the inscrutable universe turns on an axis of suffering; surely the strange beauty of the world must somewhere rest on pure joy!"

Take care … see you soon.

Tom

Epilogue

Three Years Later

So much has changed in the Middle East. The dictators, who were so firmly heading the strongest countries in the Middle East have been tossed off their thrones. Some like Saddam Hussein heading Iraq, were brutally treated in the end, perhaps echoing what he and his troopers did to the people of Iraq. So too for Khaddafi. I met dictator Khaddafi, after attending his four day seminar on his Green Book based on Greek and other philosophies. He was removed. I've wondered why his bodyguard of beautiful young ladies did not protect him, but maybe they were more for show than for expediency. So, following this, the whole of the previous Middle East has become a continuous war among their leadership. It makes one remember the quiet enforcement of the previous dictators.

Tunisia. The Arab Spring brought new hopes started by the young man's burning body. President Bourguiba's leadership paved the way for democracy, but unfortunately, has now slipped back to one-man rule. We hoped during our three years of teaching there we helped the country, but with so many university graduates sitting in tea houses, wanting a job where there are no jobs. . . . Sad!

Lebanon, where we lived for eight years, two in the 60s and six years of civil war in the 80s, managed to continue its progressive way of life, even with difficulty in the value of their currency; then the port blew up, like a bomb, when the stored chemicals for fertilizer exploded near the stored grain in the grain elevator. [It's interesting how in Kansas and other grain growing states there are enormous "grain elevators" that hold many tons of wheat (remember the film PICNIC?) and by rotating the grain there are no explosions.] This trauma has again destroyed the economy of Lebanon. It would seem the change from Service ("Siirrveeeece) Taxis to private ownership of cars has over run the gas stations. When it goes to only electric cars with 100% import tax, pedestrians trying to shop in the old markets might wish for the Service Taxis as a real service of the old fashioned costing-less kind.

We left Iran in the midst of an Islamic Revolution which has brought intermittent unrest and violence. Presently women are leading the protest, demanding more freedom of dress.

The women protesting now are likely the daughters of our students at Damavand College, Teheran, where we established and taught English Literature and Liberal Arts, under the Shah. The students, all girls at first, were encouraged to look at the facts of the literature they read and come up with ideas and concepts that would affect the characters in the story, sometimes applying such ideas outside the story. We've recently learned from BJ's nurse in her hospital that our Damavand College has become a very large coed university. "I graduated from that university," said her nurse.

China continues to vie for first place in the world while horrendous human rights violations have been exposed.

Our thoughts on China cover thirty years of soft contact with China. In 1988 BJ and I began teaching at South China Normal University, Guangzhou, China. The next year we were at Jinan University, the same city. It was challenging and most interesting teaching graduate courses in English Literature. In the senior undergraduate class seminar on literature, one student did not hesitate to tell me, "I cannntshundgerstand your EngkishP!" I am a speech teacher and a theatre director, so in my best pronounced English, I retorted kindly, "I can't understand your English either!" These students, like Tunisian and other students, wanted their lectures to be given to them on a handout sheet so they could memorize them and feed it back in tests, without ever analyzing and using the content. So, I decided that since they were to be teachers, they could begin lecturing, via panel discussions using the textbooks provided by the government, lecturing to the whole fifty student class. It became a public speaking class. After each panel discussion, I would analyze their presentation and content and inform them of the West's view of the same material. The brighter students seemed to enjoy the experience and excelled. After thousands of Chinese students studied in the West, an explosion of "architecturally advanced" cities came forth. Shanghai is the primary example with its new city across from the historically famous "Bund." I prefer the Bund because it is the Shanghai of literary interest. Thirty years ago I would say, when someone would mention how many companies were shifting their factories to China because of the financial advantage in spite of human rights violations, "but, has the government told you what I heard in China, that every non-Chinese company has to have a Chinese partner, the People's Liberation Army, the military government, who owns 51% of the company." It is the greed of factory owners and buyers of their products that is causing China to become the biggest military embodiment on the earth, dwarfing Russia, and trying to do so to the US. An amusing happening by China was when China bought an unfinished aircraft carrier from Russia, brought it across the Black Sea, through the Bosporus, through the Suez Canal, finally into the China Sea. I heard the BBC announce that China said that she bought the aircraft carrier to be a casino in Macau. We were living in Macau, and this was before the big Las Vegas casinos moved into Macau. An aircraft carrier brought to Macau would get stuck in the bottom of the Pearl River which surrounds the very large casinos of Asia, where sampans with flat bottoms ply the river. A few years later China announced that "it had built their first aircraft carrier." The great copier had begun. The military had taken off. It would grow! So, too, has the rest of China grown! Their economy seems steady for they are building a currency-economic evaluation center in Macau, just in front of a friend's apartment.

Now that our traveling days are over, we often reminisce, and try to evaluate our life's work. Little did we know, when we went to Lebanon to teach at Beirut College for Women, that it was the beginning of a forty-four year span of teaching jobs, mainly in the Middle East. Both coming from farming and ranching communities in Kansas, we had plenty to learn about living and working with people of other cultures; and the people we met are the best thing about the entire experience. We didn't become millionaires, but we gained a wealth of friends and experiences: some experiences were pleasant and memorable; some were sad or frustrating and forgettable; and many were challenging. The biggest challenges were not always in the classroom, but in the kitchen or plumbing in the bathroom. Just keeping edible food on the table was sometimes a challenge. [That's when Norman learned to make pumpkin soup from a fresh pumpkin with a side order of sautéed squash and onions with cheese, "the only things I could find to eat in the market." Delicious, and it was a good thing, for BJ brought home with her another teacher, male British, who had run out of money. "Come along home with me, Norm will have something to eat, I don't know what. . ."] We realize how fortunate we've been with the twists and turns (sometimes unplanned) our lives have taken, and would happily do a re-run . . . (Well, maybe with a few reservations).

We received so much in so many ways and hope those we lived and worked with have been as richly blessed by our work.

Providence watched over us all those years, so too now that we are retired. But the nostalgia that comes with remembering those four and a half decades of adventures makes us again realize how God protected us. We are so grateful.

Norman and Betty (BJ) Lofland
Pasadena, L.A., October 2022

Lightning Source UK Ltd.
Milton Keynes UK
UKHW022028191222
414191UK00005B/91